More praise for *Our Dreaming Mind*

"This long awaited book by one of the founding fathers of the dreamwork movement pulls together all the diverse work and thought on dreaming. It is a superb compilation and a must-read for us all."

—Jayne Gackenbach, Ph.D.
Author of *Control Your Dreams*

"I would urge all dreamers to join Dr. Van de Castle on his journey through the world of dreams; it is to be enriched by a guide who is both knowledgeable and humane."
—Milton Kramer, M.D.
Director, Sleep Disorders Center of Greater Cincinnati

"For those eager to explore the land of dreams this is an amiable guide, with lots of leads on how to get more deeply involved."

—*Kirkus Reviews*

"This book unifies the field of dream studies like no other has done before. The range of its scope is dazzling. Not since *The Interpretation of Dreams* by Sigmund Freud has a book been published that should be read by everyone who wishes to research the dreaming soul. I'm grateful to Dr. Van de Castle that he has combined the thoroughness and patience to give us this elegant work. Anyone who picks up this book and doesn't find value in it can not pretend to be truly interested in dreams."

—Robert Bosnak, J.D.
Author of *A Little Course in Dreams*

"The author's solid knowledge, encompassing such diverse subjects as ancient omens and modern statistics, and enthusiastic lucidity beckon a huge readership."

—*Booklist*

"Wonderfully thorough and scholarly, yet easy to read, *Our Dreaming Mind* surveys just about everything we know about dreams and makes daring forays into what we do not know."
—Ernest Hartmann, M.D.
Author of *Boundaries in the Mind*
and editor-in-chief of "Dreaming"

"When a book appears that is timely, scholarly, comprehensive, and well-written, it stands as a landmark. . . . Such a book is *Our Dreaming Mind*."

—Montague Ullman, M.D.
Author of *Working with Dreams*

OUR DREAMING MIND

ROBERT L. VAN DE CASTLE, PH.D.

BALLANTINE BOOKS · NEW YORK

Grateful acknowledgment is made to the following for permission to
reprint previously published material:

BASIC BOOKS AND MARK PATERSON AND ASSOCIATES:
Excerpt from *The Interpretation of Dreams* by Sigmund Freud,
translated from the German and edited by James Strachey. Published in
the United States by Basic Books, Inc., 1956 by arrangement with George Allen &
Unwin, Ltd. and the Hogarth Press, Ltd. Reprinted by permission
of Basic Books, a division of HarperCollins Publishers, Inc. and Mark Paterson and Associates
on behalf of Sigmund Freud Copyrights.

CHIRON PUBLICATIONS:
Excerpt from *Let Your Body Interpret Your Dreams* by Eugene Gendlin.

HARPERCOLLINS PUBLISHERS, INC.:
Excerpts from *Dreams and Nightmares: A Book of Gestalt
Therapy Sessions* by Jack Downing, M.D. and Robert Marmorstein. Copyright
© 1973 by Jack Downing, M.D., and Robert Marmorstein. Reprinted
by permission of HarperCollins Publishers, Inc.

ORIGINAL BOOKS:
Excerpts from *The Interpretation of Dreams: The Oneirocritiea
of Artemidorus*, Books I-IV, by Robert White.

Illustration credits appear on page 517.

Library of Congress Catalog Card Number: 95-94192

ISBN: 0-345-39666-9

Cover design by Barbara Leff
Cover painting: Leonora Carrington, *The House Opposite*, 1947.
Reproduced by kind permission of The Trustees of the Edward James Foundation,
West Dean Estate, West Dean, Chichester, England

Manufactured in the United States of America
First Ballantine Books Trade Paperback Edition: November 1995
10 9 8 7 6 5 4 3 2

This book is dedicated to the memory of

My father
Omar George Van de Castle
whose own dream was put on hold in service to his family

My son
Brett Omar Van de Castle
who didn't have the opportunity to complete his dream

My mentor
Calvin Springer Hall
who taught me to appreciate and honor dreams

Contents

Contents

Acknowledgments

This book has come into existence because many individuals have supported its development throughout a very long gestation.

The person who bore the brunt of the responsibility for transcription and typing was Tomoko Curry. During the years of seemingly endless revision, she managed to come up with a smile whenever I handed her another cassette or newly corrected copy. Kristen Weiss and my wife, Susanna, also contributed typing assistance. Will Martin converted all our floppy disks from WordStar to WordPerfect format. Carol Fungaroli transferred the manuscript from floppy disks to compact disks and tied up several loose ends. Paige Rohmann brought the final edited manuscript, references, and concluding chapter into polished form.

I am deeply indebted to Beth Rashbaum for her valuable critiques and helpful suggestions regarding rearrangement of the order and emphasis of the original text. Upton B. Brady also made useful editorial revisions as the text reached its final stages. Phebe Kirkham played an important role in the selection of illustrations. I am also extremely appreciative of the emotional support and understanding that was continuously extended by Joelle Delbourgo in her role as editor in chief of Ballantine Books.

My friend and colleague Henry Reed offered constant encouragement and perspective whenever my spirits momentarily sagged.

Wide-ranging assistance was provided by the department of psychiatric medicine at the University of Virginia Health Sciences Center.

I am also deeply grateful to my family for valiantly carrying on, when I was sequestered in the backyard cabin, trying to breathe life into what sometimes seemed like a lump of clay, rather than an emergent book. I regret that I was unavailable for so long.

My Personal Odyssey in the Land of Dreams

I taught my first graduate seminar on dreams over thirty years ago at the University of Denver. My subsequent career has included many years working in research labs with shiny equipment, talking with natives of tropical forests and islands about their dream beliefs, tabulating tens of thousands of scores from written dream reports, standing in front of blackboards illustrating differences in dream theories, struggling to comprehend provocative but puzzling dreams from clients in my office, and listening appreciatively as members of a dream group in my living room offered thoughtful comments on each other's dreams.

I have been the white-coated scientist attaching EEG electrodes to a subject's head and face to study his or her sleep and dream patterns, and I have been the pajama-wearing research subject to whom other scientists have attached EEG electrodes. This book will chronicle some of my personal experiences during that thirty-year odyssey in the land of dreams. It will also present my views on studies carried out by others and what we have collectively discovered about the remarkable potential of "our dreaming mind."

When people ask how I got started in dream work, I often wish I could explain my belief in the power of dreams by recounting some dramatic anecdote—being blinded by a brilliant light, as Saul was on the road to Damascus, and having my vision restored when I opened myself to the inner light shed by dreams. In fact, my appreciation of dreams came very gradually and subtly and didn't begin until after I had received my Ph.D. in clinical psychology in 1959. There was a brief mention of dreams in one of my undergraduate courses at Syracuse University, but none that I can recall during my master's program at the University of Missouri. It's not surprising that dreams went unmentioned during my studies, since they were not yet considered academically respectable. It was only in 1953, the year I received my M.A., that the breakthrough paper, by Eugene Aserinsky and Nathaniel Kleitman of the University of Chicago, described the objective EEG indicators of dreaming associated with rapid eye movement (REM) sleep.[1] In my doctoral work at the University of North Carolina, I was fleetingly exposed to some Freudian references to dreams.

A year after receiving my Ph.D., I began to teach graduate courses in personality theory and measurement at the University of Denver. I occasionally came across a mention of dreams and wondered whether they might reflect personality attributes in any way similar to what was revealed by the various personality tests I was discussing in class. I had some doubt that they would, because my limited exposure to Freud had led me to believe that dreams represented primarily sexual instincts and that they always portrayed these instincts in some deviously disguised manner. But I decided to investigate by giving students in some of my courses the assignment of keeping dream journals during the semester. Those same students completed several projective personality tests, such as interpreting inkblots or drawing human figures. By the time ten dreams had been reported, the personal leitmotif of each dreamer began to emerge fairly clearly.

As I examined this material, it seemed that each person had a psychic thumbprint that they impressed upon each test they took. Individuals who gave predominantly aggressive inkblot responses generally also reported overtly aggressive themes in their dreams. Individuals whose human figure drawings were characterized by faint lines and small figure representations usually described dreams reflecting timidity and minimal social interactions.

In my previous academic training, I had learned to assign scores—percentage figures or ratios—to certain personality patterns, such as hostility, measured using a standard battery of psychological tests. I knew how to score responses to inkblots but was very uncertain how to proceed with the dream reports. Could they also be evaluated in some objective fashion to yield numerical scores? If there was no way to represent dreams in an objective manner that others could agree upon, it would be impossible to compare or contrast the information dreams contained with that available from other standardized psychological tests. It would also be impossible to objectively compare the dreams of one person with those of another or to examine how the dreams of a given person changed over time or in response to intervening events.

While at Denver, I came across references to some exciting work that Calvin Hall was carrying out to measure the content of dreams. His approach, from what I had read, seemed to be exactly what I had hoped to find: a way of quantifying what people dreamed. I also hoped someday to learn more about how the presence of a dreaming state could be quantitatively measured with physiological monitoring equipment in a laboratory setting. It was at this time that Morpheus, the god of dreams, apparently became aware of my desires, because both of my wishes were granted simultaneously. I received an invitation from Calvin Hall, after a brief exchange of letters, to join him in a new project he was starting at the Institute of Dream Research in Miami, Florida.

At that time, Dr. Hall was the leading researcher on dreams in the world. During his tenure as chairman of the psychology department at Western Reserve University, he had supervised a large number of dissertations dealing with dream issues and had written a popular book on dream interpretation called *The Meaning of Dreams.*[2] When I joined him in 1963, Calvin had just received a grant from the National Institute of Mental Health to investigate whether dreams reported in a laboratory setting differed from dreams reported in a home environment and whether dream content varied from one REM period to another in a single night.

My first assignment, after I became the project director on this NIMH grant, was to learn how to operate the EEG machine. I can still recall the excitement of that first night as we sat in front of the EEG machine and watched with fascination as the recording pens zigzagged rapidly across the slowly moving paper. It seemed almost magical to be observing shifts in depth of sleep by means of those ink squiggles. When the configuration of the tracings signaled the presence of stage 1 sleep with accompanying rapid eye movements, and we woke the sleeping subject and heard him report a detailed dream, we felt more like Merlin the magician than dispassionate researchers. Watching those REM periods appear, again and again, night after night, gave me an appreciation of how many dreams we have available to us that we never salvage from our slumbering state.

A personal bonus arose from the availability of the lab. I had the rare chance to become an experimental subject myself and undergo the startling experience of hearing my name called and awaking with vivid imagery from a dream adventure. I became accustomed to being awakened every ninety minutes or so for a REM report, and I gradually became aware of the subtle subjective state accompanying a REM period. After a while, I found that these experiences enabled me to "program" myself to spontaneously awake from most REM periods. When I placed a small tape recorder by my pillow at home and applied my newly discovered "psychofeedback" skills, I found I could usually awake and remember a detailed dream about three times a night. In a month's time, I had recorded over ninety home dreams to compare with my laboratory dreams.

Calvin and I also examined large numbers of written dream reports from college students, which he had available in his voluminous files. We used these dreams to establish "normative" tables containing information about the frequency of appearance of a wide variety of dream elements and categories. We developed explicit guidelines for identifying dream elements, so that two different people independently reading the same dream would both recognize the presence of a given element. Once the elements were identified and their frequencies tabulated, we had a scientific basis for stating, for instance, that most dreams contain element X or that men dream about element X more than women do.

To provide our normative data, we randomly selected five average-length dreams (fifty to three hundred words) from each of one hundred male and one hundred female students' folders. The resulting one thousand dreams were then scored for the presence or absence of the various elements and categories we included in our scales. These scales were not developed to represent or illuminate any particular theoretical viewpoint, but were simply a cataloging of the types of elements that often occurred in dreams. To illustrate how theoretical scales could be developed if one wished to do so, we also provided several scales for scoring such Freudian constructs as the castration complex, orality, and regression. Our final results were published in *The Content Analysis of Dreams*.[3] Chapter 11 of this book discusses the topic of content analysis at some length.

Familiarity with our normative material has aided me immensely in some of my subsequent work with dreams. Because the percentage figures for various elements are almost "hard-wired" in my memory, I can hear a dream and quickly process it in terms of which items are typical and which should be considered atypical. By paying attention to the less common imagery, one is able to recognize each dreamer's unique perspective and to infer characteristic ways in which he or she may react to problems.

In one project, I carried out a large-scale analysis of the significance of animal figures in dreams.[4] I examined 4,000 dreams from American college students, 741 dreams from American children ages four to sixteen, and 1,002 dreams from persons from other cultural groups, such as Australian aborigines and Hopi Indians. I found a striking relationship between age and the frequency of animal characters in American dreams; there were over five times as many animals in the dreams of children ages four to five as there were in those of American college students, and the percentage frequency of animal dreams decreased in a fairly linear fashion as chronological age increased. This finding suggested that the percentage of animal figures might serve as a rough index of cognitive maturity in the American dreamers. In most American dreams, the animal character usually frightened and attacked the dreamer and seemed to represent fear of the dreamer's instinctual drives. Among native populations, the dreamer was usually engaged in some hunting or fishing pursuit of the animal who more often represented a potential dinner. Other findings regarding animal figures in dreams are taken up in chapter 11.

This indication of the role that cultural factors could play in dreams whetted my curiosity. I wished I could interact more directly with members of a culture that had not been completely "whitewashed" by Western influences to discover how they viewed their dream life. Once again, Morpheus seemed to know of my wish and I was granted the opportunity to spend a few weeks on some remote islands in the Caribbean. A friend of Calvin's had done some genetic research on these islands and told us about their interesting dream lore. Intrigued by his comments, Calvin and I applied for and received a small grant to study the Cuna Indians on the San Blas Islands off the Atlantic coast of Panama. The Cunas were still living in a fairly traditional manner; the women wore gold rings in their noses, dressed in colorful *mola* blouses and saronglike skirts and decorated their arms and legs with bands of intricately patterned beadwork. The primary deity in this matriarchal society is the Earth Mother and their version of how the earth's first inhabitants arrived is quite different from the account in Genesis. According to the Cunas, on each day of the world's creation the Earth Mother menstruated a different color blood, and various animals and creatures flowed from her womb. Eating turtles was taboo because humans and turtles had been delivered at the same time.

During that first visit, in 1964, I established a strong relationship with the Cunas. For some reason, I felt impelled to bring along a black felt cowboy hat, although I ordinarily dislike wearing hats and I always resented cowboys' adversarial stance against Indians in the movies. I also experienced an inner prompting to bring along some onyx eggs for gifts. After arriving, I was surprised to discover that *neles*, the Cuna medicine men who are dream interpreters and curers of bad dreams, all wore black felt hats almost identical to mine, and that *aqua nusas*, or river stones with a layered or ringed appearance, were considered to possess powerful healing properties. Eggs, it turned out, were used for special friendship ceremonies, so when I presented one of my onyx-layered stone eggs to a *nele*, a strong bond quickly formed between us because he felt my gift had enhanced the power of his "medicine basket." I found it very easy to speak to chiefs and other officials in the council houses if I submerged my professorial persona and responded to my *nele* inner voice.

I made seven subsequent trips to visit and live briefly among the Cunas. During six of these trips, I collected dream reports written in Spanish from adolescents who were attending the only existing government junior high school. These reports were translated by Mac Chapin, a member of the Peace Corps who had lived there for three years and was very familiar with local customs and idiomatic expressions. Mac, who had trained in anthropology, was collecting material on Cuna mythology and recording tribal chants, and I sometimes accompanied him when he was engaged in this fieldwork. I obtained dream reports from over six hundred Cuna teenagers during my visits and also carried out group tests of ESP ability with these same students. Students showing reduced repression in their dreams obtained higher ESP scores. Reports of long dreams, the presence of animal characters, direct sexuality, and aggressive interactions were considered signs of reduced "repression." My testing

A Cuna nele with his wooden nuchu figures, the spirits of which accompany him when he travels to one of the underground or aerial levels in his dreams.

procedures and preliminary results were presented in my 1970 presidential address to the Parapsychological Association in New York City,[5] and my overall findings were reported at an international conference in London.[6]

My experiences with the Cuna Indians had a strong emotional impact upon me. The realm of archetypes and the construct of the "collective unconscious" became far more meaningful to me, more immediate than when I had read about them in Jung's writings. After witnessing and participating in some Cuna ceremonies, I could appreci-

ate better Jung's account of how he felt almost possessed when observing native dancing by firelight in Africa. Jung's views about dreams and the collective unconscious will be discussed in chapter 7.

I was also impressed by the Cunas' high regard for dreams. If someone had what was considered an important dream, there would be no hesitation to report it at a town council meeting. A man who dreamed about a fish hook, for example, would be excused from a community labor project in the jungle because he would be considered at high risk for receiving a snake bite. Ordinarily, failure to report for a community labor project would result in social censure and a large fine, but the responsibility would be readily waived in the case of an ominous dream. The Cuna word for dream translates as "to see in the hammock." I feel that my many nights in Cuna hammocks helped me to see dreams from a very different cultural perspective.

The middle-class American culture in which I was raised laughed at or dismissed dreams as silly and meaningless. My experience with the Cunas taught me that dreams could play a central role in societal functioning: their messages were heard and shared collectively and the warnings they contained were heeded. The Cunas had developed procedures to help alleviate troubling dreams; one technique was to bathe the dreamer's eyes with special potions to wash away the disturbing visual imagery. Someone who dreamed four times of sexual relations with the same person, when that person was not the dreamer's spouse, was obligated to confess it to the *nele* so that medicinal baths and chants could be undertaken to abort its fulfillment. The person dreamed about would also be informed so that he or she could be sure to be circumspect in future behavior with the dreamer. Insanity was the feared outcome if these procedures were not followed. Since the Cunas place great emphasis upon morality and their culture accepts the prophetic power of dreams, their efforts to achieve a closer congruence between dreaming morality and waking morality is understandable.

The Cunas' strong beliefs about the importance of respecting dreams and correcting in waking life any undesirable im-

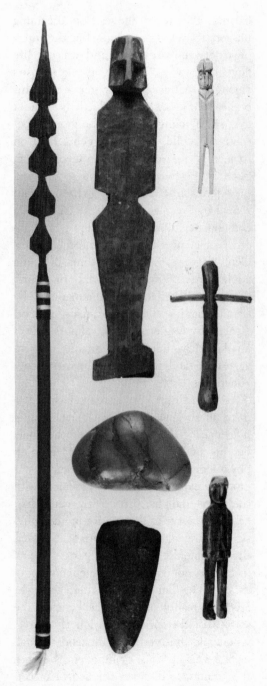

Objects used by Cuna neles to help eliminate bad dreams.

balances they reveal moves from dreaming imagery to waking behavior. But the interplay between dreaming and waking life flows both ways. During my eight visits among the Cunas, I never saw a child hit or heard one severely scolded. Nor did I ever see a young child on the ground, because the child was always being held on someone's hip or sitting in someone's lap. Such indulgence produced a secure and confident child who felt extremely accepted by every member of the tribe. As a consequence, there was an almost total absence of competition, rivalry, or Cuna-to-Cuna aggression in the dreams of Cuna adolescents. The aggressors in Cuna dreams consisted of the Panamanian National Guard, evil spirits, animals, and foreigners. By way of contrast, almost half of all American adolescent dreams involve aggression and it is generally with other Americans.

As I think over my career development in dreams, I'm aware of subliminal influences. I didn't realize it at the time, but my understanding of dreams as both physiological and spiritual phenomena was probably expanded by my experiences with the Cuna Indians, particularly with their *neles*, who serve as dream interpreters, physicians, and also oral historians. In fact, their cosmology presents a perfect set of metaphors for the multilayered nature of dreams. The Cunas believe there are eight levels of reality or existence beneath the surface of the land on which they live. One could thus vertically descend through eight levels of *kalus*, or kingdoms beneath the ground, to discover the source of certain dreams. I have observed *neles* inhaling

cocoa bean smoke in their attempts to descend to these deeper *kalus*, with the aid of their wooden *nuchu* dolls, which acted as assistants on their underground journeys. Corresponding to the eight underground regions are eight aerial levels to which the *nele* may ascend for progressively higher levels of understanding and transpersonal functioning. It seems, in retrospect, that my activities with dreams after the first San Blas expedition could be looked at as explorations into the deeper underground, or biological, levels of expression, which can be reflected in dreams, and the higher psychic, or transpersonal, dimensions, which can be attained in dreams.

The biological emphasis came about after I returned to Miami and began some research on the effect of the menstrual cycle upon dreaming.[7] For me as a male, menstruation hadn't carried much in the way of personal implications. However, after my experiences in the San Blas Islands, the topic began to take on new significance. Menstruation is of central importance to the Cunas. All forms of life were created through the menstruation of the Earth Mother, and the arrival of a girl's first menstrual period is the occasion for a joyous public announcement and a subsequent four-day feast and celebration. In our culture, the arrival of a girl's first period is *not* an event proudly proclaimed to the community.

I was teaching some psychology courses for nursing students in Miami and used this opportunity to collect dreams, dated with regard to their menstrual cycles, from approximately fifty young women. Two things became apparent when

I examined the dream reports they turned in. One was that the phases of the menstrual cycle had a noticeable effect upon the types of dreams reported, and the other was that individual differences were prominent. Dreams experienced shortly before ovulation, for example, were quite different from those experienced after ovulation. The types of social interactions shifted markedly between these two phases. Before ovulation, more male characters were present, and they were viewed as very interesting and appealing, while other women receded into the background or were cast in somewhat competitive roles in relation to the dreamer. After ovulation, women seemed to feel an affiliative connection with other women, but an attitude of hostility toward men was detectable. Interactions between personal history, attitudes toward menstruation, and dream scores during the menstrual cycle are discussed in chapter 13.

I next spent two years at the University of North Carolina Medical School, where I was the chief psychologist for psychiatric inpatient services. While there I also taught some psychology classes, and my students received credit for turning in dreams obtained from special populations. Several class members collected dreams from pregnant women recorded over a period of several months. The changes occurring in the pregnant women's bodies were sometimes symbolically reflected by means of architectural imagery, references to tilting skyscrapers or newly appearing front porches, for example. Imagery involving the unborn child increased dramatically during the third trimester of pregnancy.

The baby typically had some unusual physical attributes, such as a small baby's body but the head of the dreamer's husband, or the baby could walk and talk at birth.

After I arrived at the University of Virginia Medical Center, my pregnancy findings[8] were described in some popular women's magazines and I was able to recruit readers to send in more dreams. Thus I eventually obtained dream collections from over two hundred pregnant women. My analysis of the significance of pregnancy dreams during the various trimesters was discussed throughout Eileen Stukane's book *The Dream Worlds of Pregnancy*.[9]

My work with menstrual and pregnancy dreams made me aware that dreams can be sensitive indicators of biochemical or physiological changes. When dreams serve as diagnostic indicators of impending physical problems, they are referred to as "prodromal" dreams. Chapter 13 examines the neglected topic of prodromal dreams at some length, because I feel this class of dreams should be given more serious consideration by contemporary dream workers.

I saw a metaphorical connection between the Cuna *neles*, who sent their spirits to various underground levels of existence to discover the source of a tribal member's somatic disturbance, and my own body-related studies, dealing with menstruation, pregnancy, and the relationship between male adolescent body build (somatotype) and dream activities.[10] In our different ways, we were exploring how dream imagery could be strongly influenced by the status of the somatic substrata of the dreamer's current physical condition.

Were there any parallels between the

aerial levels to which the Cuna *neles* ascended and experiences recognized in my research activities or taking place in my personal dream life? It was difficult to determine exactly what these upper levels signified for the *neles*. I wasn't sure whether the problem resided in the ambiguities of translation from one language to another or whether achieving definitional clarity was unlikely in the cloudy realm of metaphysics, even if the only language involved was English.

I once cotaught a course on altered states of consciousness and parapsychology in the anthropology department at the University of Virginia. The students were always trying to pin me down as to exactly how the rungs were arranged on the stepladder of consciousness. Was meditation higher than daydreaming? Was hypnotic trance higher than lucid dreaming? Was a mystical state higher than a drug-induced high? I found myself increasingly frustrated by my inability to answer my students satisfactorily. Then I had a dream which supplied the answer.

I dreamed I was in a huge torchlit cave high on the side of a mountain among a large group of young Buddhist monks with shaven heads and saffron robes. They were seated in a semicircle around a wizened man with a flowing white beard, who was seated on a tall but simple throne. One of the young men slowly approached the old man, bowed, and earnestly asked, "Oh, master, you who know all things and are the keeper of the keys of wisdom, what should we do to learn the secrets of the universe?" The old man pondered for a moment, his eyes began to twinkle, then he smiled and said in a tone both solemn and mischievous, "You must make it a practice to drink *sage* tea regularly."

I began to chuckle in my dream and awoke smiling and aware that I was still laughing softly. The old man's response made me realize that no simple answers could be given to my students' inquiries; they would have to seek them out on their own. Besides the obviousness of that advice, they needed to be mindful of the importance of humor while searching; too much solemnity could cause them to overlook treasures that would only be revealed to someone with a smiling countenance. I savored my sage tea dream, not only for the wise advice dispensed by this ancient mentor, but also because it was another testimonial to the incredibly creative aspects of our dreaming mind. I am a very poor joke teller in my waking life and had never heard or thought about the wonderful pun that could be brewed with the concept of *sage* tea, yet when I needed a great punch line to deliver in my classroom, an inner dream comedian found his voice and coached me supportively from the sidelines.

The message from that dream also seems apt in attempting to describe my own dream journeys to the upper levels referred to by my *nele* consultants. Which of these dreams are closer to an earthly plane and which might be categorized as at the seventh level or the sixth level?

After the sudden death of my oldest son Brett in a motorcycle accident one week after his twentieth birthday, I was deeply distraught and inconsolable for a long period of time. I eventually experienced a dream in which he was sitting among his four brothers and his body was giving off a faint golden illumination, as if he were a neon light with a human form. As I embraced him, tears of joy ran down my cheeks, and I found my pillow wet with these tears when I awoke. This dream gave me great comfort, as it enabled me to conceptualize him as if he were currently existing on another plane of reality. In another dream, I was able to step effortlessly through solid walls and to rise through ceilings and the top of a pagodalike building. This latter dream suggested that apparent physical barriers are actually an illusion and that matter does not actually possess the properties of solidness we impute to it in our waking life.

If our spirit journeys to the "other side," does it ever return? Does it accompany us through other lifetimes? Perhaps if dreams serve as a portal through which recently deceased spiritual entities can "enter," they may allow us to "exit"—to journey "outward" on this same mysterious plane to catch glimpses of our own past lives in earlier times. Shirley MacLaine has focused popular attention on the possibility of reincarnation and Dr. Ian Stevenson, a psychiatrist in our department at the University of Virginia, has presented the results of his careful scientific investigations on this topic in several scholarly books.[11]

I have had a few dreams that had a reincarnation feel to them. In one, I was with a group of several dozen spear-bearing Aztec warriors going through a sort of close order drill. In another, I was in a hut with several other people, including a shaman or priest. The shaman engaged in various magical activities by a small fire and I found myself frustrated because I could only communicate through various grunts and guttural sounds. In another dream, I was an Indian brave in battle, with a beaded quiver on my back. I was busily shooting arrows at a group of enemy warriors. At one point a spear that had been thrown at me deflected off my belt and broke, but later in the dream I experienced some pain as two arrows struck me in the back.

As a sentient human being, I was pleased that my dreams intimated other planes of reality or existence, but as a scientist, I felt they left something to be desired. There was no trace, no tangible remnant of their appearance: you could receive a precious gem in a dream and awake empty-handed. For me, psychic or paranormal dreaming represents the experience of awaking with a gem in your hand, because you have a report or record of your private internal dreaming scenario that can be compared objectively with some external "real world" scenario. If an impressive correspondence between a dream and some highly unlikely incident exists, it offers evidence that your dreaming mind didn't just *imagine* but actually perceived the incident, even though that information lay outside the apparent sensory boundaries within which we operate during our waking hours.

I had read a little about parapsychology as an undergraduate student and found the subject intriguing. My serious interest in parapsychology began after Dr. J. B. Rhine invited me to discuss some of my informal ESP work with him at the Duke Parapsychology Laboratory in 1951. Rhine encouraged me to continue my developing interest in ESP, and I wrote my M.A. thesis on a parapsychological topic. I later spent a year as a research associate at the

Duke Parapsychology Lab and became familiar with the experimental studies of individuals with apparent psychic abilities. Although I achieved some low level success at guessing ESP cards, I would not have considered myself as possessing any unusual ESP talents. Certain experiences at the Institute of Dream Research, however, began to convince me that it took the state of dreaming to facilitate whatever ESP ability I might have.

Calvin Hall and I had had several discussions regarding the credibility of paranormal dreams. Although he claimed to have a fairly open mind on the subject, his attitude seemed to me a rather skeptical one. On March 12, 1964, I was spending a night in our lab as a dreamer, and Calvin got a very strange look on his face after he heard me report a dream. Here are a few excerpts from that dream:

> There was a boxing match going on. There were two young lightweight boxers who were fighting and one of them was doing much better than the other. It seems his opponent became vanquished and then another lightweight contender got into the ring with him. This new contender now started to give a pretty savage beating to the other boxer. . . . I remember standing up and throwing a few punches in the air myself because I was so involved with the action in the ring.

After I recounted my dream, Calvin told me that while he was monitoring the EEG machine in the next room, he had been concentrating on the Sonny Liston-Cassius Clay (Muhammad Ali) fight during the REM period from which he had just awakened me. He had decided to find out firsthand whether it was possible to influence a dream telepathically, but had not informed me about his intention. Calvin had wanted to add a little live action to his imagined activities, so he had thrown a few punches in the air himself as he was thinking about the boxing imagery.

Five nights later, when I was again sleeping in the lab, one of my REM reports involved specific and detailed skiing imagery. The imagery that Calvin had been concentrating on during that REM period was a skiing scene! Could coincidence explain these striking correspondences between my dream imagery and Calvin's waking imagery when he was trying to influence my dreams? Maybe boxing and skiing were themes that I often dreamed about. A frequency count of these elements in my home dreams ruled out that explanation. I had recorded a total of ninety-seven dreams at home, and punching activity in any form appeared in only four of those dreams. The only time I reported a boxing match was during the REM period when Calvin had concentrated upon boxing imagery. Similarly, there were no occurrences of skiing imagery in any of my home dreams; the only time I had dreamed about skiing was when Calvin concentrated on skiing imagery during that REM period. Calvin's skepticism soon eroded and he was so impressed by his successes with me and five other male subjects that he published a paper describing his results.[12]

I later participated as a telepathic dream subject for Montague Ullman, a psychoanalyst, and Stanley Krippner, a psychologist, at their Maimonides Laboratory in Brooklyn. I participated a total of eight nights during a forty-four-week period and was successful enough with three different agents or senders to be dubbed "Prince of the Percipients" (telepathic receivers). A chapter bearing that title and recounting my results appears in their book *Dream Telepathy*.[13] My experiences as a percipient at Maimonides, at the University of Wyoming,[14] and in my own laboratory at the University of Virginia are described in chapter 14. My experiences as a telepathic dreamer in four different laboratory settings have firmly convinced me that telepathic dreams, by which I mean dreams in which messages are received from another person, are possible and that they occur with much greater frequency than is generally recognized. There are more ways of communicating with each other than those acknowledged by current science.

After Brett's death, I participated in some monthlong dream workshops sponsored by the Association for Research and Enlightenment (A.R.E.), where personal and spiritual growth were emphasized. The A.R.E. is an educational organization located in Virginia Beach that disseminates information about the trance-based "readings" of Edgar Cayce, the psychic known as the "sleeping prophet." Through my activities with A.R.E., I met Dr. Henry Reed, a former psychology faculty member at Princeton University, and we became involved in some A.R.E. research projects. One of the guiding principles of A.R.E. was that everyone participating in a research project should have an opportunity to experience personal growth as a result of his or her participation. This was a new twist for me. I had been accustomed to carrying out studies similar to those at Denver or Chapel Hill, where I collected data from subjects about something that I was interested in, but the subjects, who were obliged to participate, received only class credit. I wasn't used to thinking about how to enhance the personal growth of a research subject.

Henry had been aware of my participation in the Maimonides studies and approached me to ask how some happy fusion might be found between the experimental protocol developed at Maimonides and the humanistic service-oriented protocol that was typical for A.R.E. projects. I wasn't sure that such a rapprochement could ever be accomplished, but as Henry and I traded thoughts on the topic, we eventually developed a protocol that we called the "dream helper ceremony."[15]

We decided to utilize telepathic dreaming in a group context as a way to be of service to others. Rather than focusing upon a target picture, the "dream helpers" focus telepathically upon a target person. This target person acknowledges that he or she has some troubling emotional problem but does not discuss it or give even the slightest hint what it is. The dream helpers dedicate all of their dreaming activity for that night to helping the target person better understand the problem and place it in a new perspective.

On the following morning, the dream helpers gather and each describes in detail all the dreams they remember from the preceding night. As the dreams are recounted, a pattern of consistencies may be detected that seems to be related to the problem, which the target person reveals after the dreams have been processed. Henry and I have participated in the dream helper ceremony on many occasions, and each time we have been impressed with the collective accuracy of the dream helpers in identifying the problem for which the target person sought help and sometimes coming up with a possible solution for it. Serving as a dream helper allowed each participant an opportunity to experience a journey similar to that undertaken by a Cuna *nele* when he ascended to one of the higher aerial levels. Some examples of dreams from dream helper workshops will be presented in chapter 14.

In addition to offering workshops on dreams, Henry and I tried to raise public awareness of the value of dreams by serving as coeditors of the *Dream Network Bulletin*, a popular grass-roots newsletter, for about eighteen months. (Information about this and other resources on dreams is presented in the appendix.) This book has also been written to raise public awareness of the value of dreams.

WHAT DISCOVERIES AWAIT YOU IN THIS BOOK?

Many, I hope. There are fifteen chapters organized into six parts. In part 1 you'll be introduced to the puzzling dilemma of whether "reality" is better glimpsed with open eyes during daylight hours or with closed eyes while dreaming. A plethora of examples are provided to document the significant changes that have occurred in the worlds of art, music, drama, literature, films, architecture, politics, military conquest, athletic performance, scientific discovery, and religion because somebody acted upon inspirational imagery revealed in a vivid dream. If you haven't previously appreciated dreams, I hope that reading this first section will encourage you to consider becoming an aficionado of the exciting nocturnal dramas that await you every night. You were issued a lifetime pass to free dreams at birth. Why not take advantage of it?

In part 2, you'll become acquainted with your ancestors' experiences with dreams. Dreams have been revered, feared, and puzzled over since the dawn of history. You'll learn about how dreams were viewed by the ancient Mesopotamians, Egyptians, and Greeks; how dreams fared under the Christian church fathers and the followers of Muhammad and other faiths; and the prominent place dreams held in the nineteenth century before Freud "discovered" them.

Part 3 explains the main features of the leading twentieth-century dream theories. In my view, the contributions of Freud have been exaggerated, while those of Jung have been underappreciated. I have made an effort to rebalance the scales to reflect their respective contributions. The valuable interpretive approaches presented by more recent workers, such as Boss, Perls,

Gendlin, Hall, and Ullman, are also presented.

The second half of the book describes efforts to approach dreams experimentally. Part 4 presents the results of early scientific investigations into factors that influence dreams, both physiologically and psychologically, and describes how dreams are currently evaluated by means of EEG (brain-wave monitoring) technology. The advantages and possible disadvantages of studying dreams in the imposing setting of a modern sleep laboratory are examined.

In part 5 you will learn about how scientists tabulate the elements found in dreams to discover the patterns of dream content that exist for an individual or a particular class of dreamers. Data are presented to show how dreams change as we age, how the dreams of men and women are different, and how stress can influence the outcome of our dreams.

In the final part of the book, I will introduce you to the exciting frontiers of knowledge concerning dreams—what I have referred to as the "twilight zone" of dreams. In chapter 12, examples are given and discussed of how dream imagery has the potential to serve as a "mental X ray," allowing diagnosis of an impending physical problem before it shows up with full-blown, obvious symptoms in waking life. The effect of the menstrual cycle on women's dreams is followed through its various phases to reveal how attitudes toward men and women wax and wane in response to hormonal fluctuations. Dream imagery changes dramatically during pregnancy, and examples of dreams associated with subsequent miscarriage or birth complications will be presented to substantiate the

proposition that dreams can sometimes be prodromal in nature.

Dreams can also sometimes be prophetic or predictive of the future in situations where somatic factors are not involved. Chapter 14 deals with the topic of paranormal dreams. I share various dreams that I have experienced while serving as a telepathic dreamer in four different laboratories. Dreams that emerged during the dream helper ceremony are also described and their connection to the target persons' previously undisclosed problems are traced out.

The last chapter explores the exciting realm of lucid dreams—dreams in which the dreamer is consciously aware of participating in a dream. Repetition of these experiences can often lead to enhanced feelings of freedom, self-confidence, and rapture and cause dreamers to examine metaphysical questions with a seriousness and urgency that, for many people, may be surprising and without personal precedent.

My own tour, or personal odyssey, in the land of dreams has been enchanting, challenging, immensely rewarding, and deeply satisfying. I would be extremely honored if you would allow me to be your guide, by means of this book, to the dark continent of dreams, which rotates on its axis every night and reveals exotic dreamscapes that surpass those found in *National Geographic*. My hope is that I can help you to discover and explore more thoroughly the fascinating dreamscapes that will appear to you as you develop your ability to see in the dark. My wish for you is that your night vision will improve to 20/20 for all the exciting nights that lie ahead for you.

PART 1

THE TREASURE CHEST OF DREAMS

CHAPTER 1

DREAMS:

PORTALS BETWEEN OUR INNER

AND OUTER WORLDS

Dreams have always fascinated humankind. Many speculations have been advanced to account for their presence. They might be visits from an external god, the wanderings of the dreamer's soul, a shift in dimensional planes enabling the dreamer to peer into the future, the reworking of unresolved emotional tensions from the preceding day, or fallout from some temporary disturbance of the brain or digestive system. The various theories offered to explain dreams will be dealt with in later chapters, but for now I'd like to offer some challenging comments from individuals who have struggled with the perplexing problem of deciding whether dreams are "real."

The ancient Greeks wrestled early on with the question of which was most real, waking reality or dreaming reality. The philosopher Socrates, who lived in the fourth century B.C., is described in Plato's *Theaetetus* as engaging in a lively intellectual discussion with Theaetetus. Socrates puts forth the question "What proof could you give if anyone should ask us now, at the present moment, whether we are asleep and our thoughts are a dream, or whether we are awake and talking to each other in a waking condition?" Theaetetus was not able to come up with any satisfactory proof that they were awake and acknowledged that they could both be dreaming. The issue was addressed more personally a century later by the Chinese philosopher Chuang-tzu. He dreamed that he was a very happy butterfly who was quite pleased about himself. He suddenly awoke and pondered the question of whether he was a man dreaming he was a butterfly or a butterfly dreaming that he was a man.[1]

Thousands of years later, such questions are no nearer to being answered. The distinction between reality and illusion is questioned continuously in Lewis Carroll's famous book *Through the Looking-Glass*. In one memorable passage, Tweedledee comments to Alice that the Red King is dreaming about her and were he to awaken Alice would be "No where" because she is only a sort of thing in his dream. Tweedledum confirms that Alice would go out "like a candle" if the king were to awaken. When Alice complains that their loud talking may wake the king, Tweedledum counters, "Well, it's no use *your* talking about waking him when you are only one of the things in his dream. You know very well you're not real." Her frustration mounting, Alice insists, "I *am* real!" and begins to cry.

Not everyone reacts with consternation when confronted with the enigma of the waking/sleeping distinction. Gerald Bullett, an English novelist, seemed to enjoy the enrichment provided by being a resident of both the waking and dreaming worlds:

In my childhood I conceived the notion that we live, each one of us, a double life.... Sleeping and waking I supposed to be not two processes but two aspects of the same process. To fall asleep "here" is to wake "there." My head sinks gratefully into the pillow, and the world dissolves; and at that very moment, on another plane or planet, I rub my waking eyes and begin a new day, resuming, without thought or sense of strangeness, the life in which my sleep—my waking life here—has been a quiescent interval.[2]

In Bullett's delightful essay he provides other interesting metaphors for these two domains of existence. He refers to "two self-contained rooms with the swing door called sleeping-and-waking, waking-and-sleeping, pivoted between them."[3] Bullett seems equally content with each self-contained room and life: "And in which of these lives am I more truly myself? In neither, says Logic; for both are equally mine notwithstanding that I here am a stranger to me there, and I there a stranger to me here."[4]

The philosopher Schopenhauer also emphasized the equivalence of our dreaming and waking states. He wrote that "life and dreams are leaves of the same book" and contended that there was no clear distinction between their natures. Do the leaves of this book turn forward or backward? The direction confused the English author D. H. Lawrence, who confessed: "I can never decide whether my dreams are the result of my thoughts or my thoughts the result of my dreams."[5]

Helen Keller had a childhood illness at nineteen months that left her deaf and blind. She reported that, before she was taught by her remarkable teacher, Anne Sullivan, to read, write, and talk, she "lived in a sort of perpetual dream." When she was able to make a distinction between her waking and dreaming conditions, she acknowledged that some similarities existed between them. But she seemed to relish what took place after passing through "the portals of sleep." She explained: "Once across the border, we feel at home, as if we had always lived there and had never made any excursions into this rational daylight world."[6]

She published a fascinating account of her dream life in her book *The World I Live In*. She described visiting foreign lands in her dreams where she had never been in reality and conversing with peoples whose languages she had never heard: "I do not remember ever to have met persons with whom I could not at once communicate."[7] She very rarely used her fingers to spell in her dreams; she was self-sufficient and enjoyed "an independence quite foreign to my physical life," with no one guiding her. "Wherever I turn my steps, my mind is my faithful guide and interpreter."[8]

Keller offered eloquent testimony to the ability of our dreaming mind to display "clear-seeing at night." She described a wonderful light which sometimes visited her at night and the delight she derived from the sunsets she experienced. She movingly recounted the range of potential awareness awaiting us in our dreams:

I am moved to pleasure by visions of ineffable beauty which I have never beheld in the physical world. Once in a dream I held in my hand a pearl.... In dreams we catch glimpses of a life larger than our own.... Thoughts are imparted to us far above our ordinary thinking.[9]

Another exponent of "clear-seeing at night" was Samuel Clemens, a.k.a. Mark Twain. In his *Notebook*, he described the unusual visual acuity possessed by his dream self:

My other self, my dream self, is merely my ordinary body and mind freed from clogging flesh and become a spiritualized body and mind and with the ordinary powers of both enlarged in all particulars a little, and in some particulars prodigiously....

Waking, I cannot form in my mind the minutely detailed and living features of a face and a form and a costume which I have never seen, but my dream self can do all this with the accuracy and vividness of a camera....

My dream self meets friends, strangers, the dead, the living ... and holds both rational and irrational conversations with them upon subjects which often have not been in my waking mind and which, in some cases could never have been in it.[10]

With such rich visual rewards in the offing, it's not surprising that Luis Bũnuel, the famous film director, would choose to immerse himself in the sensory extravaganza which can be encountered in dreams. His first film, *An Andalusian Dog*, which came out in 1928, originated from his dreams. His 1985 autobiography, *My Last Breath*,[11] had a chapter entitled "Dreams and Reveries." He wrote, "If someone were to tell me I had twenty years left, and ask me how I'd like to spend them, I'd reply 'Give me two hours a day of activity, and I'll take the other twenty-two in dreams.'" Buñuel added the provision that he would want to remember his dreams during that time.

Why is our capacity for sensuality so much greater in dreaming than in our waking life? What might account for the ease with which we can become a frolicking, exuberant member of a midnight Mardi Gras spectacle or a participant in raucous carnival activities? The answer, according to Nobel Prize winner Henri Bergson, the French philosopher of vitalism, is that waking life requires intense concentration and choices among sensations and memories so that "common sense" can prevail. Because of this constant vigilance, he felt we were more limited in our waking life. In one of his papers he remarked:

The dream state ... is the substratum of our normal state. Nothing

is added in waking life; on the contrary, waking life is obtained by the limitation ... of that diffuse psychological life which is the life of dreaming. The perception and the memory which we find in dreaming are, in a sense, more natural than those of waking life.[12]

Are there any limitations to the inventiveness available to us when dreaming? The answer would be a resounding No! for Frederick Greenwood, the London editor of the *Pall Mall Gazette*. In his 1894 book, *Imagination in Dreams and Their Study*, he recognized that while dreaming, "we draw on a power of invention which it would puzzle us to equal with our eyes open."[13] He posited that "no conception of the sweep and force of imagination is too wide to be brought to the study of dreaming, and that its possibilities include what is now called miraculous power."[14]

Another enthusiastic proponent of the superiority of our dreaming mind was Havelock Ellis, the English physician who achieved international recognition for his *Studies in the Psychology of Sex*, published in 1898. He maintained that all the restraints and qualifications of waking life were removed during sleep. A new sense of freedom was then possible, because "in our dreams the fetters of civilization are loosened."[15] In the following exuberant passage, Ellis suggested that there actually were no limits to how far our dreaming mind could travel:

Dreaming is thus one of our roads into the infinite. ... It is only by emphasizing our finiteness that we ever become conscious of the infinite. The infinite can only be that which stretches far beyond the boundaries of our own personality. It is the charm of dreams that they introduce us into a new infinity. Time and space are annihilated, gravity is suspended, and we are joyfully borne up in the air, as it were in the arms of angels; we are brought into a deeper communion with Nature.[16]

A consensus seems to exist among the authors quoted so far: crossing the threshold from the waking state to the dreaming state enriches our sensory imagery and empowers our creative capacity. Travelers who pass through the "portals of sleep" arrive in a wondrous land where crystal palaces gleam, enchanting music plays, and they are endowed with wizardlike power to solve the vexatious riddles that were unsolvable in their limited waking world. Havelock Ellis proposed that the opaque curtain between the present and future can also be drawn aside when we take a seat as a spectator in the nocturnal theater of dreams.

Ellis also speculated that "we are

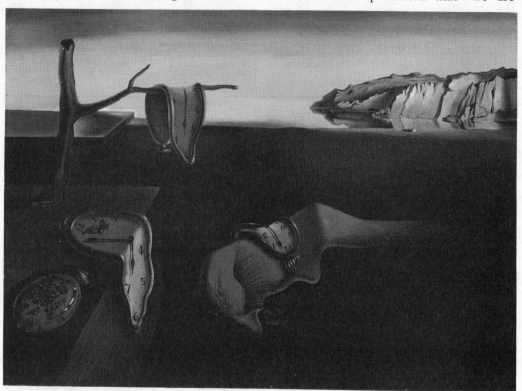

Dreams unlock our imaginations: anything becomes possible within them. Even time can become fluid.
The Persistence of Memory *by Salvador Dali ([*Persistence de la mémoire]
1931. Oil on canvas, 9½ x 13"). The Museum of Modern Art, New York.)

brought into a deeper communion with Nature" when dreaming. What might be expected from people whose fetters to civilization had never been fastened and who already participated in a deeper communion with Nature? Would the boundary they drew between waking and dreaming reality be less distinct, and would their conception of time be affected? An answer has been provided by anthropologist Geoffrey Gorer after conducting fieldwork with West African natives. In his book, *Africa Dances*, he concluded:

> Their idea of time is extremely peculiar. The present, the past, and the future are inextricably mingled.... Most dream experiences are believed as implicitly as physical ones.... It is my belief that natives, without the inhibitions which our view of time and a causal universe impose upon us, regularly dream the future as much as the past, and as vividly, with the result that the ideas 'present', 'past', and 'future' have no meaning to them as they have to us.[17]

What is time? It is the eternal riddle; it possesses no solidity, no substance, no tangible properties. A character in one of Graham Greene's novels, *Ways of Escape*, nicely summarizes the difficulty of finding a temporal anchorage point: "The present has no duration, and it comes between the past, which has ceased to exist, and the future, which has not yet started to exist." We chop time into bits and pieces that we label seconds, years, weeks, minutes, months, and days and order them into a line, so that time proceeds predictably: yesterday, today, tomorrow. Such predictability gives us an illusory feeling of control; we can then print calendars, construct watches, and anticipate meetings in our appointment books.

But who is to say whether our conception of time is correct? It is, after all, only a current conception, and even the most universally agreed upon conceptions have been shown to be fallacious—a former conception of a flat earth evolves into the current conception of a round earth. Yesterday's impossibilities become today's possibilities and tomorrow's facts.

J. W. Dunne, a pioneering aeronautic engineer, experienced numerous dreams which corresponded to events that later transpired. In his book, *An Experiment with Time*,[18] he developed an elaborate theory of time, which he called "serialism." Greatly simplified, Dunne's hypothesis was that time is not a single dimension but a series of dimensions. We remain on one dimension of time simply because of conditioning, but if we are able to rise to another dimension we will have the ability to scrutinize the past, present, and future of the previous dimension as if it were a single landscape. He suggested that our usual approach toward time can be likened to that of a man rowing a boat up a river. Because of the position taken for rowing, he can easily see where he has come from but not where he is going. However, through the transforming quality of dreams, it is possible to enter a new dimension of time and gain an aerial perspective that enables us to view the entire river of time laid out below.

It's reassuring to know that I'm not

alone, and am in very good company, when it comes to offering testimonials about the treasures awaiting us in the land of dreams. The enthusiastic quotes in this chapter speak encouragingly about the benefits available to travelers who are willing to journey at night. These authors promise dreaming will enable us to see resplendent sights inaccessible to daytime travelers. Traveling at high speeds, under cover of darkness, we will arrive at destinations days or weeks ahead of the usually expected arrival date.

These advertisements sound impressive. Are they to be believed or are they just slick promotional claims put out by a tourist agency consisting of an assortment of famous but woolly-headed eccentrics? Has anyone returned from the land of dreams with souvenirs or bargains that would make the trip worthwhile? Are there any photos or tape recordings to document that there was something special about nighttime journeys?

Except for Buñuel's *An Andalusian Dog*, no specific object or document has been designated as evidence to back up the rather lavish claims made in this chapter for the imaginative capacity of our dreaming mind and the rewards to be found by paying closer attention to our internal dreamscapes. The intent of this chapter has been to suggest that there is something unique about our dreaming mind that deserves greater recognition. The next chapter will survey some of the jewels that have been found by those willing to open the lid of the treasure chest of dreams.

CHAPTER 2

DREAMS THAT HAVE CHANGED THE WORLD

E very modern history student is routinely exposed to the innovations that have had a significant impact upon the development of our civilization: the discoveries of fire, plant cultivation, animal husbandry, the wheel, writing, gunpowder, the printing press, electricity, airplanes, and atomic energy. Each of these sources of radical cultural shifts is cited in the sixty-two-page index of *The Columbia History of the World*,[1] an authoritative reference source written by a panel of forty eminent historians. But no entry appears for dreams. Historians have generally ignored achievements originating from nocturnal inspiration, perhaps because the sleeping third of our lives is spent in a passive posture, not actively manipulating the external environment. Nevertheless, dreams have had a dramatic influence on almost every important aspect of our culture and history. Dream images have expanded our artistic, musical, and literary horizons, spurred generals to conquer empires, and led to inventions and industrial products that have revolutionized science and society. Dreams have also given us a basis for believing that there is a nonmaterial component to our existence, as well as a continuity of existence which is not interrupted by physical death.

DREAMS AS PATRONS OF THE ARTS

Many areas of the arts have been enriched by imagery experienced in the dream studio of artists and performers.

We are captivated by Henri Rousseau's painting *The Dream*. The reclining nude woman, Rousseau said, in dreaming was "transported into the forest." And what a magical forest it is: two large-eyed lions peer through the lush foliage with its giant pastel flowers and ripe fruit, a full white moon bathes the enchanted forest, and a mysterious black snake charmer plays a haunting melody on his flute. The rich sensual imagery seductively captures the erotic quality present in many of our dreams.

In his earlier *Sleeping Gypsy* Rousseau also skillfully communicated a sense of mood. This painting, too, used the full white moon, a large-eyed lion, a reclining figure, and a musical instrument, but their placement in a bleak, barren desert with faint, sandy mountains in the distance gives the eerie, empty feeling of a moment fixed in endless time. Timelessness, eternity, and the flexibility of time are characteristically associated with the special state of dreaming.

Who can forget the soft watches draped limply over a barren branch and a wide wall in Salvador Dali's *Persistence of Memory*? Dali's fascination with dreams was stimulated after reading Freud's *Interpretation of Dreams*, which he considered "as one of the discoveries in my life." Like some other surrealists, Dali attempted to preserve his dream imagery on canvas and to enhance the mood that permeated his nocturnal visions. The surrealists' goal, according to French poet André Breton, was "the future resolution of these two states, so contradictory in appearance—dream and reality—into a kind of absolute reality, or surreality."[2] Dali referred to his work as "hand-painted dream photographs," and to heighten the visual intensity of his dreams, he liked to sleep with an intense light on.

The famous visionary artist William Blake's waking life and dreaming life were closely intermingled. How highly he valued dreams is suggested by the titles of some of his works, such as *Queen Katherine's Dream* and *Oh, How I Dreamt of Things Impossible*. His most specific acknowledgment of the inspiration he received from his dreams is found in a pencil portrait showing the facial details of *The Man Who Taught Blake Painting in His Dreams*.

Jasper Johns was supporting himself as a window dresser in New York City in the mid-1950s when he had a dream about painting an American flag. He acted upon his dream inspiration and that flag painting became part of a revolution in American art.

Dreams and films share many common features: moving visual images, changes in settings and characters, spoken conversations, perceptual distortions, temporal discontinuities, flashbacks. They even share a similar physical aspect: both are observed in the dark. The Spanish film director José Luis Borau felt that the cinema was able to enlarge and expand the richness of our dreaming life, which could in turn enrich our waking life:

> We use the cinema in order to dream "better" and more easily (which does not mean more frequently). Our dreams and their images have been enriched by the movies. This enrichment occurs both in the theme or content and also in the form or visual terms. . . . In movies we witness events that would be difficult to live out in daily life. . . . Such indirect experiences, which were once impossible, now offer the subconscious suitable vehicles for expressing our eternal yearnings and preoccupations. On the purely formal level, they provide new ways of visualizing our dreams—camera angles, slow motion shots, combinations of colors and of black and white—techniques we have learned only in movie theaters.[3]

In The Man Who Taught Blake Painting in His Dreams, *Blake acknowledged that dreams were an important source of creative inspiration for him.*

The director best known for his incorporation of dream imagery into his films is the Swedish filmmaker Ingmar Bergman, who reproduced episodes from his dreams as accurately as possible in such films as *Naked Night* (the American title; in Britain, *Sawdust and Tinsel*) and *Wild Strawberries*. In an interview Bergman said, "I discovered that all my pictures were dreams. Of course I understood that some of my films were dreams, that part of them were dreams . . . but that *all* my pictures were dreams was a new discovery to me."[4] Bergman recognized that dreams have the ability to draw people together. He was also very much interested in getting people "close to their dreams."

Carlos Saura, a Spanish director known for films focusing on the crippling effects of social and political forces on individual development, was asked if his films drew directly from his own dreams. His answer was, "Yes, of course I use dreams. Not complete dreams, but fragments and images—especially certain atmospheres. I try to reconstruct the images that are clear in my mind."[5] Robert Altman's *Three Women* was likewise based upon one of his dreams.[6]

When Orson Welles, the American actor and director, was asked about the dreamlike, but seemingly connected rooms in his film *The Trial*, he responded, "I attempted to make a picture like a dream I have had. . . . I move from architecture to architecture in my dreams." Asked whether the film was intended to be a certain character's dream—the film began with this character opening his eyes— Welles insisted, "No, it's *my* dream. I dreamed about *him*."[7] Italian director Federico Fellini also drew heavily upon dreams to generate the grotesque and surreal characteristics typical of the classic 8½, and his other films.

Theater curtains have also risen on many plays which premiered in the playwright's dreaming mind. Jean Cocteau produced an unusual version of the legend of King Arthur based on a dream: "I woke with a start and witnessed, as from a seat in the theatre, three acts which brought to life an epoch and characters about which I had no documentary information." The provocative dream challenged Cocteau to do some research about the characters and events, which culminated in his production *Knights of the Round Table*.[8]

William Archer was a journalist and theater critic in London. His posthumous book, *On Dreams*, contains sixty-four dream experiences selected from a dream journal that he kept for ten years. One of these dreams, from September 1919, occurred on "a night of rather romantic dreams vaguely connected with India." In it, Archer was with some friends, and "the population and authorities were very hostile, but on the surface polite." Archer and his friends heard muskets firing, which they interpreted as Europeans being shot. It turned out that some Europeans had been captured by Indians, who appeared as "cultured barbarians applying a sort of torture by courtesy to Europeans. . . . The leading spirit on the barbarian side was a woman, whom I conceived as a singularly able personality."[9] Expanding upon these dream elements, he began sketching out a play. Archer's play, *The Green Goddess*, became the success of the season in New York, and he was barely able to obtain a seat in the sold-out theater. Three years later, it was a great success in London.

A 1902 play by William Butler Yeats, who later won the Nobel Prize for literature, carried potent political significance. Yeats told Dublin producers that *Cathleen ni Houlihan* had come to him in a dream.[10] Its title was the traditional name for Ireland as a woman who requires young men to sacrifice themselves for her. An early success for the new national theater company, *Cathleen ni Houlihan* seemed to nourish Irish nationalism, and many felt that the inflammatory play influenced events which culminated in the Easter uprising in 1916.

Sculpture, too, has benefited from perceptions of shape and form that emerged in artists' dreams. The striking arrangement of the figures of Christ and the apostles in French sculptor Jean Depre's *Pieta* came in a dream, but despite the beauty of his composition, the artist lamented his failure to reproduce the grandeur of the image he had dreamed.[11]

An article in the April 1979 issue of *Arizona Highways* contained interviews with several prominent Native American craftsmen. The interviewer noted that whenever he asked, "Where did this idea come from?" the artist began by replying, "I had this dream." One artist, White Buffalo, explained how he had created a large silver Indian bust after a dream in which a man with silver hair, a silver face, and feathers confronted him. Jesse Monongye began his career in inlaid jewelry after a dream in which his deceased mother gave him files and jewelry tools and told him that if he took the tools he would become a famous Indian. Jesse won honors at the prestigious Gallup Ceremonial for an inlaid bear piece inspired by that dream.

Dreams are not limited to visual images. They incorporate screams, animal sounds, bells ringing, rifles firing, and other noises. But for musicians, whose livelihood and principle aesthetic satisfaction derives from patterns and arrangements of rhythmic sounds, dreams have also provided the stimulus for compositions of varying complexity and length.

Sullivan composed the *Lost Chord* in a dream but was only able to remember the first few bars.[12] In contrast, George Frederic Handel heard the last movements of his oratorio *The Messiah* during a dream.[13] Richard Wagner wrote to a friend, regarding his opera *Tristan und Isolde*, "For once

you are going to hear a dream, I dreamed all this: never could my poor head have invented such a thing purposely."[14] Schumann claimed he recorded a song that he heard in a dream, and in 1954, Steve Allen recalled from a dream portions of what has become his most popular song, *This Could Be the Start of Something Big*.[15] At the age of twenty-one, Guiseppe Tartini had a dream in which he handed his violin to the devil:

> But how great was my astonishment when I heard him play with consummate skill a sonata of such exquisite beauty as surpassed the boldest flights of my imagination. . . . I awoke. Seizing my violin I tried to retain the sounds I had heard. But it was in vain. The piece I then composed, the "Devil's Sonata," was the best I ever wrote, but how far below the one I had heard in my dream.[16]

The August 10, 1987, issue of *Time* magazine reported a recent account of dream-inspired music. Joseph Shabalala, a black South African minister, founded and, until his death, served as the lead singer of Ladysmith Black Mambazo. He recorded twenty-five albums and created two tracks on Paul Simon's album *Graceland*. Shabalala was quoted as saying:

> Every time when I am sleeping, I have music in my mind. All the time, like when you sleep, like a dream. There is a stage, but there are children not on stage. They

are between the stage and the sky, floating and always singing. They are like my teachers who teach me exactly this sound.

Dreams are often noteworthy for the marked sense of movement we experience in them. We run, jump, dance, swim, or climb over obstacles. It seems as if this vigorous kinesthetic activity compensates for the stationary, inert posture we maintain while sleeping. For those professional performers who must exhibit agility and coordination on the playing field or in front of a crowd, dreams have revealed ways to improve their waking athletic or sporting activity.

The famous acrobat, Tito Gaona, stated in the April 8, 1974, issue of *Sports Illustrated*:

I have sometimes dreamed my tricks at night . . . and then tried to master them from the dream. . . . I also do what I call a double-double. . . . It is a double forward somersault with a double full twist at the same time. It has never been done before. No one else does it. It is a trick I dreamed one night.

In the June 27, 1964, edition of the *San Francisco Chronicle*, golfer Jack Nicklaus described how he had fallen into a bad slump. Despite intensive analysis of what could be wrong, he continued to do poorly. He then experienced a dream in which he was holding his golf club differently and swinging perfectly. He told the newspaper reporter, "When I came to the course yesterday morning, I tried it the way I did in my dream and it worked. . . . I feel kind of foolish admitting it, but it really happened in a dream." After the dream, his scores improved rapidly.

Dana Cushing, an acquaintance of mine from Boston, has made a hobby of riding old-fashioned, high-wheeled bicycles. After he bought his first one, he spent about three months repairing it. During this interval, Dana had several dreams in which he joyously rode this velocipede. He was surprised by this because he had never actually ridden one in his waking life. When the repairs were finished, Dana discovered that he was able to successfully ride his velocipede on his very first attempt. It seemed as if the "practice" sessions in his dreams had enabled him to achieve waking mastery of the complicated balancing skills necessary for such a performance.

The visual imagery of dreams, particularly of nightmares, has also been captured in word pictures. Many authors have tried to describe the haunting visages that peered at them during their terrifying nocturnal experiences.

Let me begin by citing a former student of my own University of Virginia: Edgar Allan Poe. We may each have our own favorite story by this master of the macabre, but Poe's own favorite was *The Lady Ligeia*. He was particularly captivated by her eyes, which had met his in a dream. Her eyes were "far larger than the ordinary eyes of our race. They were even fuller than the fullest of the gazelle eyes of the tribe of the valley of the Nourjahad."[17]

Many people would agree that the

most compellingly frightening imagery in a literary creation is the story of Frankenstein. One night in June 1816, Percy and Mary Shelley, Lord Byron and his mistress, and a local doctor were telling ghost stories at Byron's villa. After hearing several of these stories Byron encouraged everyone there to write a horror story. Mary Shelley emerged as the most successful among this accomplished group. Here is a partial account of the nightmare she experienced in response to Byron's challenge:

> My imagination, unbidden, possessed and guided me, gifting the successive images that arose in my mind with a vividness far beyond the usual bounds of reveries. . . . I saw the pale student of unhallowed arts kneeling beside the thing he had put together—I saw the hideous phantasm of a man stretched out, and then, on the working of some powerful engine, show signs of life, and stir with an uneasy, half-vital motion. Frightful must it be; for supremely frightful would be the effect of any human endeavor to mock the stupendous mechanism of the Creator of the world. . . . He would hope that, left to itself, the slight spark of life which he had communicated would fade; that this thing which had received such imperfect animation would subside into dead matter, and he might sleep in the belief that the silence of the grave would quench forever the transient existence of the hideous

corpse which he had looked upon as the cradle of life. He sleeps; but he is awakened; he opens his eyes; behold, the horrid thing stands at his bed side, opening his curtain and looking on him with yellow, watery, but speculative eyes. . . .

> Swift as light and cheering was the idea that broke in upon me. "I have found it! What terrified me will terrify others; and I need only describe the spectre which had haunted my midnight pillow." On the morrow I announced that I had thought of the story.[18]

Her novel *Frankenstein; or, The Modern Prometheus* was published in 1818. The word "Frankenstein" has now come to represent anyone who is threatened or destroyed by his own creation. Mary's husband, Percy Bysshe Shelley, attempted to preserve some of his own haunting dreams in his *Catalogue of the Phenomenon of Dreams, as Connecting Sleeping and Waking*.

Another British author who acknowledged his heavy indebtedness to dreams is Robert Louis Stevenson. His most famous nightmare story is *The Strange Case of Dr. Jekyll and Mr. Hyde*. Stevenson was in dire financial straits and had been "racking my brains for a plot of any sort" for two days. On the second night, he dreamed "the scene at the window, and a scene afterwards split in two, in which Hyde, pursued for some crime, took the powder and underwent the change in the presence of his pursuers."[19]

Most of Stevenson's experiences with nightmares occurred earlier in his life. As a child, he was "an ardent and uncomfortable dreamer." He would fight off sleep but eventually find "his struggles were in vain; sooner or later the night-hag would have him by the throat, and pluck him, strangling and screaming, from his sleep." In his later years, Stevenson came to rely heavily upon his dreams for his literary productivity. His book *Across the Plains* included "A Chapter on Dreams," which described how he came to depend upon "the Little People" who worked in the nocturnal theater of his mind whenever it was necessary for him to conceive a new story. "And for the Little People, what shall I say they are but just my Brownies, God bless them! who do one-half my work for me while I am fast asleep." Stevenson guiltily considered that perhaps he was not a storyteller at all and that "the whole of my published fiction should be the single-handed product of some Brownie, some Familiar, some unseen collaborator, whom I keep locked in a back garret."[20] In one of his passages, Stevenson raised a question which we might all ponder:

> The more I think of it, the more I am moved to press upon the world my question: Who are the Little People? They are near connections of the dreamer's beyond doubt; . . . they have plainly learned like him to build the scheme of a considerable story in progressive order; only I think they have more talent; and one thing is beyond doubt, they can tell him a story piece by piece, like a serial, and keep him all the while in ignorance of where they aim. Who are they, then? and who is the dreamer?[21]

In a fifth century account, Synesuis of Cyrene indicated that his writing style was improved through the editorial revision provided by another "unseen collaborator":

> How often dreams have come to my assistance in the composition of my writings! Often have they aided me to put my ideas in order and my style in harmony with my ideas; they have made me expunge certain expressions, and choose others. When I allowed myself to use images and pompous expressions, in imitation of the new Attic style . . . a god warned me in my sleep, censured my writings, and making the affected phrases to disappear, brought me back to a natural style.[22]

Individuals who spend a great deal of their waking life in written pursuits sometimes report dreams in which printed words appear on pages. Herbert de Hamel, a dramatist, reported a recurring dream in which a large history book with olive wood covers opened each night at the beginning of a new chapter. Each chapter was headed with the actual day, month, and year of its opening event, and each chapter revealed information about the customs and habits of the period. According to de Hamel's account, "the words are large and clear. As I read, the book speaks the lines out loud."[23] If the dreamer fails to keep up with reading the lines word for word with the voice of the book, the covers close and the voice ceases.

Novelist and poet Maude Meagher gave an example of one of her "word dreams" and claimed, "I dream the words as printed on a page before me, and create them as I read. The text is never anything that I can remember having read."[24] William Burroughs, the author of *Naked Lunch*, stated, "A good part of my material comes from dreams. A lot of it is just straight transcription of dreams with some amplification, of course."[25] Robert Penn Warren, the novelist noted for such works as *All the King's Men*, wrote:

> I've dreamed many nights the next scene of a novel I've been working on, in great detail, even dialogue and details. One time just in a couple of dreams (which solved a novel) and in my last one, almost every night for months.[26]

Jack Kerouac so closely entwined his dream world with his writing that it is almost impossible to separate the two. His *Book of Dreams*, published in 1961, contains nearly 250 dream reports, ranging from very brief accounts to lengthy descriptions "scribbled after I woke from my sleep . . . sometimes written before I was even wide awake."[27] Aware that many of his dream events were similar to events in his novels, he actually provided a key in his preface, indicating which characters in his dreams had appeared, with different

names, in such books as *On the Road* and *The Dharma Bums*.

Franz Kafka crafted many of his novels to give them a "dream narrative" quality. In his *Diaries*, he observed: "My talent for portraying my dreamlike inner life has thrust all other matters into the background." He found it difficult to sleep because he was plagued by dreams, "as if they were being scratched on me."[28] His story "In the Penal Colony" refers to a machine that "scratched" the condemned man's crime on his body. In another passage, he describes a sort of parallel existence, in which "I sleep alongside myself, so to speak, while I myself must struggle with dreams."[29] Kafka left behind a record of thirty-seven dreams in his diaries and letters. A content analysis study found some similarities in the themes of his dreams and his novels.[30]

In some dreams, an author seems to become completely identified with one of the characters. Katherine Mansfield, a well-known author, wrote in her journal, "I *dreamed* a short story last night even down to its name, which was *Sun and Moon*." Mansfield said the story was all about children and that she was actually in part of it. She indicated that the hero was about five years old and "In my dream I saw a supper table with the eyes of 5. It was awfully queer—especially a plate of half-melted ice-cream."[31]

When British novelist Graham Greene was confronting financial despair, he had a dream that he had been sentenced to prison for five years and separated from his wife. This anxious dream was the source for his novel *It's a Battlefield*. He said *Hon-*

orary Consul also began with a dream. Greene, in fact, became so immersed in his dreams that the boundary line between himself and his characters became blurred. Here is how he described it in *Ways of Escape*:

> Sometimes identification with a character goes so far that one may dream his dream and not one's own. That happened to me when I was writing *A Burnt-Out Case*. The symbols, the memories, the associations of that dream belonged so clearly to my character Querry that next morning I could put the dream without change into the novel, where it bridged a gap in the narrative which for days I had been unable to cross. . . . When an obstacle seems insurmountable, I read the day's work before sleep. . . . When I wake the obstacle has nearly always been removed: the solution is there and obvious—perhaps it came in a dream which I have forgotten.[32]

Other authors have also reported breaking through writer's block while asleep. Charlotte Brontë, best known for her novel, *Jane Eyre*, told a friend that she used dreams to help her describe sensations she had no way of understanding in reality. If she needed to know what it would feel like to take opium, she would fall asleep "wondering what it was like, or how it would be. . . . She wakened up in the morning with all clear before her, and then could describe it, word for word as if it had happened."[33] She incorporated these descriptions into her novels.

Dreams and poetry share some common characteristics. In both, a plethora of meaning can be communicated through a paucity of images. Coleridge's *Kubla Khan* is the most heralded and quoted example of dream-induced poetic creativity. Coleridge, who was an opium abuser, alleged that during a three-hour sleep he composed two to three hundred lines of his poem. Upon waking he immediately wrote down the fifty-four lines we know today, but he was interrupted, he said, by a businessman for more than an hour and by the time he returned to finish the poem, the remaining lines had faded away. Coleridge had a reputation for irresponsibly boasting about sudden creativity and scholars have discovered earlier drafts of his famous poem which belied his claim of its instantaneous dream origin.[34]

John Masefield's poem "*The Woman Speaks*" appeared in a dream "engraved in high relief on an oblong metal plate, from which I wrote it down."[35] Voltaire acknowledged that he knew of many poets who in their dreams "have composed verses. I have made some myself which are very passable. It is therefore incontestable that constructive ideas occur in sleep."[36] Among his "passable" verses was a whole canto of *La Henriade*. Goethe also claimed that many of his poems came to him in dreams.[37] Christina Rosetti was often impressed by the imagery of her dreams and attempted to capture the scenes in poetry. An outstanding example of this is her poem entitled "The Crocodiles," in which the narrator stands beside the Euphrates and sees young crocodiles covered with gold and polished stones.[38]

Aware that many authors have acknowledged a debt to dreams for some of their literary products, Richard Jones, a psychologist and educator at Evergreen State College in Olympia, Washington, decided to sensitize his students in creative writing to their dreams and observe whether it had any effect upon their writing skills. He was very gratified with the outcome of this classroom project. Many examples of the creative writing and creative dreaming from his dream reflection seminar are provided in his book *The Dream Poet.*

During one class period, the students would read a work of great literature and engage in a detailed discussion of its possible meanings, as well as their personal reactions. On a subsequent morning, someone would relate a dream and distribute copies of it to the seminar for discussion. Class members would attempt their own visualizations of the dream's imagery and would report whatever feelings it aroused in them. They would also comment upon "how the dream's various images might have functioned as metaphors for personal conflicts in their lives if the dream had been their own." The dreamer would then reflect upon the other students' dream "projections" and identify what daytime events preceded the dream. The class would discuss what the dream might be saying to them and what they might wish to say back to the dream:

> In this latter venture we learn
> to respond to the dream's play
> on words and images; its sound

symbolisms and flourishes of synesthesia; its visually alliterative sequences; its deployments of the figurative and literal; its double entendres, stagings, artifices, puns, and jokes.[39]

Following these lengthy discussions, the students would go off individually to write for two hours. This writing might consist of a poem, an essay, a letter, a story, or a dialogue that linked the student's reflections on the dream to the previous reading assignment. When the seminar reconvened, each person would read to the others what they wrote.

The benefits of participation in Jones's dream reflection seminar included such personal rewards as "lots of hearty laughter" and becoming "more sensitive to everyone, more civil, more thoughtful, more human." One student commented that "the quality of uncertainty characteristic of the dream reflection seminar seems to act as a catalyst freeing our thoughts from their usual musty pathways." The literary gains from this catalytic process were also impressive. Here are a few responses given by the students when they were asked to describe the effects of the dream reflection seminar on their writing.[40]

> I guess one of the main causes for everybody's amazing creative output is tied in with the tremendous energy flow and excitement of the seminars. Bantering with key words from the dream; playing with phrases and images; reversing cliches.
>
> I attribute my success in writ-

ing this year to the dream poet. I was so amused by the metaphors utilized in the dreams that I was inspired to let go and give him a little competition.

Having to force a connection between a dream and an essay seems so impossible, but it turns out to be so excitingly easy.

It helps me write from the heart. Not just the mind.

A. E. Van Vogt also attempted to use his dreams to increase his literary fertility, but he did it alone in a sort of home study arrangement. To tap into his dreaming activities, he set his alarm clock to rouse him every ninety minutes, the normal time interval between periods of rapid eye movement. After waking, Van Vogt would momentarily turn on the light and glance at his bedside table, where he had earlier placed a card containing the title of his current story and the basic idea of the story as far as it had gone:

> Thus began an organized dreaming approach to writing which, so far as I have been able to discover, has never been duplicated by another "square" anywhere in the world. During the next seven years, the alarm went off every 1½ hours 4 times a night about 300 nights a year.[41]

Apparently his efforts were successful, since Van Vogt has authored over fifty books, mostly science fiction novels, including *The Voyage of the Space Beagle*.

DREAMS AS STIMULI FOR ACTION

There are also many cultural events that have been set in motion because a dreamer decided to undertake a project or pursue a goal according to directions originating in a dream. The end result may be the construction of a building or the destruction of a city, the beginning or ending of a war, or the development of a different form of social organization. In these cases, we can only discuss the consequences of an individual's interpretations of a dream.

The following classic account should probably be considered something of a folktale, because it has come down to us from the fifteenth century with many variations. It was described in a history of Nor-folk County in the eighteenth century, and the author had transcribed it from earlier written accounts.[42] It involves the dream of the Swaffham tinker, John Chapman.

Chapman had a dream indicating that if he journeyed to London and placed himself at a certain spot on London Bridge, he would meet someone who would tell him something of great importance regarding his future affairs. He thought about making the trip but was at first dissuaded from doing so by his wife, who laughed at him for being so foolish. However, when the dream recurred the next two nights, he decided to go to London, regardless of how much his wife belittled him. Upon arriving in London, he stood for three consecutive days at the bridge. Toward night on the third day, when his confidence in the dream was beginning to wane, a stranger came up to him and asked why he had been at that spot for so long. The tinker told him but did not let him know where he came from. The stranger smiled tolerantly and suggested that he return home and pay no more attention to dreams. To emphasize how silly dreams were, the stranger told him that he had recently dreamed that if he went to a place called Swaffham and dug under an apple tree in a certain garden on the north side of town, he would find a box of money.

Astonished, the tinker returned home and began to dig on the spot he thought had been indicated by the stranger. After he had dug down a few feet, his spade struck something hard, which turned out to be an iron chest. He carried it home and found it to be full of money. Engraved on the lid of the box was a Latin inscription, which some schoolchildren read for him: "Under me doth lye another much richer than I." Digging deeper in the original hole, the tinker found an even larger treasure chest, full of gold and silver coins.

The tinker's story sounds fanciful and probably has become more impressive with each successive telling. Whatever actually happened, Chapman's dream achieved fame because he showed his gratitude for it by donating a sizable sum of money to the construction of a church in his hometown in 1454. Pew carvings and stained-glass windows depicting the tinker can still be seen today in the Church of St. Peter and St. Paul at Swaffham in Norfolk County.

Sir Thomas White, Alderman of London in the sixteenth century, was a very rich and public-spirited man. He dreamed that he founded a college at a place where three elms grew out of one root. On a trip to Oxford, he discovered a single elm tree near Gloucester Hall and, thinking that perhaps this was the elm of his dream, acquired the building, repaired it, and opened it as a hall for one hundred scholars. When he later walked by the convent where the Bernardines formerly lived, he was amazed to discover an elm with three trunks growing from the same root. He purchased the land around it and founded St. John's College at this Oxford location.[43]

Before the American Civil War, Harriet Tubman, an escaped slave, led hundreds of other slaves to freedom by means of the "Underground Railroad," a system of meeting spots maintained by antislavery advocates. Tubman made nineteen rescue trips to the south to lead her people on their dangerous journey to the north, with slave-hunting patrols vigorously pursuing her. She claimed that dreams helped her to find the safe pathways and she never lost a single "passenger."[44]

A dream also expedited political freedom in India. By imposing the harsh Rowlett Act, England attempted to suppress any agitation which might lead to the liberation of India. Mohandas Gandhi had been eagerly seeking ways to free his people from colonial subjugation. After weeks of meditation, he had a dream which suggested that the people of India suspend their usual business activities for twenty-four hours and devote that time to fasting and prayer. The resulting nonviolent mass strikes, or *hartals*, of 1919 marked a turning point in India's efforts to achieve self-determination.[45]

It's interesting to note that an American admirer of Gandhi, Martin Luther King, Jr., emphasized the words "I have a dream" in his compelling and inspirational message in 1963 at the Lincoln Memorial. In his speech, he urged his country to work toward liberation of its oppressed minorities. Although his "dream" wasn't identified as having a nocturnal origin, if King had sought to convey the idea that only a waking wish were involved, he could have said, "I have a vision" or a "fantasy" or a "day-dream." But as a minister aware of the power attributed to biblical dreams to foresee vast political change, he instinctively linked his clarion call for political reform with the more potent nocturnally-associated word—"dream."

Freedom of a different sort was entailed in releasing the United States from the cancerous influence that the Vietnam War was having upon the American people. A dream experienced by President Lyndon Johnson made a little-known contribution to the cessation of the Vietnam War. In a biography entitled *Lyndon Johnson and the American Dream*, Doris Kearns, who worked in the White House Fellows program during Johnson's tenure, discussed several of the former President's dreams.[46] Her revealing psychohistory described Johnson, in his robe and pajamas, knocking on her door about 5:30 every morning. As Kearns sat in a chair by the window, Johnson would climb into her bed, pull the sheets up to his neck, and begin to reminisce about his life.

In those dawn talks, he described a vivid recurrent childhood nightmare of sitting paralyzed in a chair facing a cattle stampede. After he became vice-president, in 1961, the setting for the nightmare became the Executive Office Building. As he sat at his desk, he finished signing a stack of letters and decided to go home but discovered he couldn't leave because his legs were manacled to the chair with a heavy chain. With a sigh, he would reach for another stack of mail and begin to work again. The paralysis dream intensified after the 1968 Tet offensive in Vietnam. He now dreamed that he was lying immobile in a bed in the Red Room unable to speak; his head was his own, but his body was the thin, paralyzed body of Woodrow Wilson. To diminish the panic associated with this dream, Johnson took to walking through the darkened halls of the White House with a flashlight until he came to where Wilson's portrait hung. He would then touch Wilson's picture to reassure himself that Wilson was dead and that he, Lyndon Johnson, was alive and still capable of movement.

As the Vietnam conflict dragged on and casualties mounted, Johnson faced a dilemma. His Texas image of manhood would not let him quit, but continuing in office was jeopardizing support for his social programs. Johnson then had a dream which clarified his situation. In the dream, he was struggling to swim from the center of a river toward one of the shores, but he could not reach it. When he tried to swim toward the other shore, he was equally unsuccessful. Instead he wound up going around in circles. This dream dramatized the impossibility of the situation Johnson found himself in and he realized he must extricate himself. Shortly thereafter, Johnson announced his decision not to seek another term. His withdrawal from office seemed to catalyze a national demand that the government actively seek some way to disengage from this demoralizing debacle.

Throughout history more wars or invasions have been initiated than have been terminated on the basis of dream imagery. In 1863, Otto von Bismarck told his family about a dream in which he was riding on a narrow alpine path with a precipice on one side and rocks on the other. When the path became so narrow that his horse refused to proceed, Bismarck struck at the rock with his whip. The whip grew very long, the rocky wall dropped away, and a broad path appeared in which Prussian troops with banners were moving forward.[47] In a letter to Emperor William I in 1881, Bismarck acknowledged that this dream gave him the confirmation he sought to proceed with his plans to invade Austria.

American general George S. Patton, Jr., firmly believed that he had served as a warrior in several incarnations. Patton also felt he possessed unusual psychic faculties which enabled him to intuit the intentions of the enemy better than his G-2 intelligence staff.[48] He frequently called his personal secretary, Joe Rosevich, in the middle of the night, to dictate battle plans that had appeared in his dreams. According to his biographer, Ladislas Farago, "His secretary had so often responded to calls in the night that he knew very well how close the general was to his dreams, and how ready to act when inspiration came in them."[49] One of these involved a successful surprise attack on German troops just as they were getting ready to mount an offensive on Christmas Day during the Battle of the Bulge.

Before the liberation of Rome in 312 A.D., Emperor Constantine experienced a waking vision of a cross of light which bore the inscription Conquer by This. Christ appeared in Constantine's dream that night and told him to have the insignia represented on the shields of his soldiers to serve as a safeguard against his enemies. Constantine passed this command on to his soldiers before his attack. After defeating Maxentius "in a remarkable manner" at the Milvian Bridge, Constantine ended the widespread persecution of Christians, converted to Christianity, and endorsed it as the official religion of his far-flung Roman empire.[50]

In another example, the angel Gabriel appeared to Muhammad in a dream and encouraged him to leave the city of Medina, where he had been in exile, and lead an army to Mecca.[51] After his triumphant conquest of Mecca, Islam quickly spread. A little more than one hundred years after Muhammad's death in 632 A.D., Muslim dominance stretched from the Atlantic beaches of Portugal to the western fringes of China. The Moorish invasion of Spain in the eighth century was precipitated by a dream in which Tariq bin-Zayyad saw Muhammad and his companions armed with swords and lances entering Andalusia. After hearing the Prophet say he should advance, Tariq began to make his battle plans.[52]

Genghis Khan reported having two important dreams which inspired and sustained him through his impressive military career.[53] In the first he was told that he was destined to reign over the Mongols. After subduing all the Mongolian tribes in 1206, he changed his name from Temujin to Genghis Khan, or "universal ruler." In a subsequent dream, he was told that heaven wanted him to conquer other kingdoms and countries. His empire eventually came to include Persia, Afghanistan, southern Russia, and northern India.

There are at least three possible explanations for reports of dreams in which some supernatural figure exhorts an already ambitious leader to overrun neighboring peoples. One is that the dream is a deliberate fabrication, intended to justify the conquest and rally support from credulous followers. Or the zeal for power may have been so strong and pervasive in the leader's waking life that it seeped through to the unconscious and led to a dream congruent with the dreamer's agressive drives, a rationalization of those desires disguised as a divine endorsement. The remote third possibility is that the dream did originate from a supernatural source. I reject this possibility not on the basis of patent absurdity, for I have come to accept that some dreams may owe their existence to the influence of a transpersonal energy or spiritual source, but on the basis that a "genuine" spiritual dream would not have as its intent the slaughter of thousands of victims.

This raises the question as to whether there are any examples of dreams in which a message delivered by a supernatural figure led to a positive outcome. The same caveats apply, of course, to constructive dreams as to destructive dreams.

In the eighth century, Aubert, the bishop of the small French town of Avranches, claimed that the archangel Michael visited him in a dream and ordered him to build a chapel. The abbey he founded, Mont-Saint-Michel, was constructed a mile off Normandy's southern coast and has been a pilgrim's sanctuary for more than a thousand years.[54]

When Giovanni Bosco was a nine-year-old boy in 1825, he had a dream in which a luminous man in a white cloak appeared and told him he must win boys over with kindness, not the violent punching behavior he displayed in the first part of his dream. Then a woman in a brilliant, sparkling garment showed him some wild animals, which turned into lambs as he watched. She told him, "That is your field of activity. That is where you must work. What you see happening to these animals, you must make happen for my children." He had several more dreams as a teenager in which the Madonna appeared and encouraged him to look after abandoned youth. In a dream in 1844, he was again in the middle of a group of animals when a shepherdess appeared and signaled him to follow her and to accompany this strange flock. As they journeyed along, many of the animals turned into lambs and eventually some of the lambs turned into shepherds. Don Bosco became a priest and founded the Salesian order, which consists of monks who care for homeless children. When Pope Pius IX heard of Father Bosco's dream at age nine, he ordered him to record it for the benefit of his Salesian order. Father Bosco was recognized by the Catholic church as a saint in 1934.[55]

A different form of supernatural figure clothed in white made an appearance in the dream of another Italian, Jacobo Dante, the son of the famous poet. The last thirteen cantos of Dante's *Paradiso* were missing and it was assumed that his work had been left unfinished, because a protracted search had been unable to discover the cantos. Eight months after Dante's death, Jacobo dreamed that his father appeared, clothed in white with a radiant face, and answered his son's questions about Dante's continued existence. When his son asked about the missing work, Dante indicated he had finished it and led Jacobo by the hand to a room where Dante had frequently slept. He touched one of the walls, saying, "What you have sought for so much is here," and vanished. After waking from his dream Jacobo aroused Piero Giardino, one of Dante's disciples, and they sought out the house where Dante died. In his bedroom they found a mat on the wall and lifted it; there, in a small window, lay the missing thirteen cantos, covered with mold.[56]

In the dreams just reviewed, the issue of credibility resides with the dreamer. Was the dreamer telling the truth? Did a radiant figure really offer advice or commands to the dreamer? In the next group of dreams, the issue of credibility concerns the correctness of an interpretation of dream imagery given by someone other than the dreamer. The reader is again warned to be wary. Sometimes the interpreter's apparent accuracy might be attributed to the fact that the interpretation followed the event.

Alexander the Great had a dream during his siege of Tyre whose interpretation is considered a classic example of wordplay in dreams. A satyr appeared at a distance in Alexander's dream and mocked him. At first, the satyr eluded Alexander's grasp when he tried to catch him, but after much chasing finally fell into his hands. The dream was interpreted, by dividing the Greek word for satyr (*satyros*) into two words (*sa*, "yours," and *tyros*, "Tyre"), to mean that "Tyre will be yours." Encouraged by the dream, Alexander intensified his efforts and captured the city. On Alexander's campaign through the Persian Empire, he took along Aristander of Telmessos, who had written a book on dreams, as his dream interpreter.[57] Alexander conquered most of the known world before he died in 323 B.C., at the age of thirty-three.

One of Julius Caesar's oedipal dreams received an interesting interpretation. Caesar, after his victories in Gaul, reported a dream in which he was sleeping with his mother. His mother, according to an interpreter, represented the mother city of Rome, which he would soon possess. Bolstered by this prediction, Caesar crossed the Rubicon, led his army southward, and entered Rome without a struggle.

Hannibal, the Carthaginian general, sabotaged his own cause when he accepted a dream interpretation offered by a figure within the dream itself. In the dream a huge black serpent moved along, destroying everything in its path. The sky was filled with smoking clouds and illuminated by piercing flashes of lightning. A young man, as beautiful as an angel, appeared and assured Hannibal that he had been sent from the council of the gods. He explained to Hannibal that the dream was showing him the ruin of the Roman Empire and exhorted him, "Go! The fates are going to be accomplished." Acting upon this dream, Hannibal began his invasion of Italy in 218 B.C., with twenty-six thousand men and a parade of elephants.[58] He smashed three Roman armies in succession at Trevia, Trasimene, and Cannae, but his invasion stalled because various allies remained loyal to Rome. Hannibal's personal ambitions and hatred of the Roman Empire may have led to the convenient creation of the young man who appeared within his dream to offer such a welcome favorable interpretation.

Of course, dream interpretation can become a very slippery operation whenever personal ambitions enter the process. Shakespeare shows great insight when he provides an excellent example of how dream interpretation can have a self-serving function for the interpreter in his play *Julius Caesar*. Caesar's wife, Calpurnia, experienced a disturbing dream in which she saw her husband's statue stabbed by several knife-wielding Roman senators. She was sure her dream was prophetic and that Caesar would be assassinated the next day at the Forum. Caesar was uncertain as to whether he should accede to his wife's pleas to stay home. When Decius, one of the senators, arrived the next morning to escort Caesar to the Forum, Caesar described his wife's dream to Decius in the following lines:

She dream'd tonight she saw my statue,
Which, like a fountain with a hundred spouts,
Did run pure blood; and many lusty Romans came smiling,
and did bathe their hands in it:

And these does she apply for warnings, and portents,
And evils imminent; and on her knee
Hath begg'd that I will stay at home today.

Decius, himself a conspirator, countered with the following interpretation:

This dream is all amiss interpreted:
It was a vision fair and fortunate:
Your statue spouting blood in many pipes,
In which so many smiling Romans bath'd,
Signifies that from you great Rome shall suck
Reviving blood; and that great men shall press
For tinctures, stains, relics, and cognizance.
This by Calpurnia's dream is signified.

Perhaps in response to the tragic event acted out at the Roman Forum on that fatal March day, Emperor Augustus, who eventually succeeded Caesar several years later, issued the proclamation that anyone who dreamed about the commonwealth must announce the dream in the marketplace.

Examples of dreams with far-reaching implications are not limited to questionable accounts with B.C. datelines. The March 24, 1974, *New York Times Magazine* contained a report about a dream that Lieutenant Colonel H. R. P. Dickson, a British political official in Kuwait, experienced in 1937. One day, a violent sandstorm carved a hole by a palm tree in his compound. That night, he dreamed he approached the hole and saw a sarcophagus at the bottom. Inside he discovered a shroud, and when he touched the shroud a beautiful maiden rose to life. As the dream continued, shouting strangers arrived and wanted to bury the girl alive in the desert, but the colonel chased them away.

Perplexed by his dream, Dickson consulted a local Bedouin woman who had a reputation as a dream interpreter. She explained that the girl symbolized wealth beneath the sands of Kuwait and the men trying to bury her were strangers from across the sea who wished to prevent its discovery. At that time, a British oil company crew had been drilling nothing but dry wells for two years at Bahrah on Kuwait Bay. The Bedouin interpreter told Dickson he should move the team to the desert of Burgan and concentrate drilling activities by a lonely palm tree, where they would find great treasure. When the drillers laughed at Dickson's urgings to move the team, he sailed to London and told his dream and its interpretation to the company executives. One of them, who believed in dreams, felt the dream interpreter's instructions deserved a try. He cabled Kuwait and the team was moved about thirty miles south to Burgan. In May 1938, the drillers discovered huge oil deposits there in the desert by a lonely palm tree.

PROPHETIC DREAMS

Unheeded dreams foretelling events—especially dreadful events—raise interesting questions. How might the world have been different if people had paid attention to these prophetic dreams, many of which concerned assassinations? The symbolism in the dream of Henry III of France, who ruled during a time of great religious warfare, was fairly straightforward. Three days before his assassination in 1589 by Jacques Clement, a monk, he dreamed that all the royal vestments, the royal tunics, and the orb and scepter were bloodied and trampled underfoot by monks.[59] His successor was also assassinated, an end foreshadowed by less direct dream imagery. Henry IV dreamed, on the night before his assassination by François Ravaillac, of a rainbow over his head.[60] This was interpreted as a portent of a violent death. Similarly, his wife, Marie de' Medici, dreamed just before the assassination that the brilliant gems of her crown changed into pearls, which were recognized as a symbol of mourning.[61]

In some other assassination dreams, the attempts were pictured quite clearly. One of the most dramatic examples was a dream recorded on the morning of June 28, 1914, by Bishop Joseph Lanyi of Grosswardein in Hungary. He had once been a tutor for Archduke Franz Ferdinand of Austria. The bishop arose early in the morning from a disturbing dream in which he had gone to his desk to look through some letters. On the top was a black-bordered letter bearing a black seal with the coat of arms of the archduke. The bishop recognized the handwriting as that of the archduke and opened the letter. On the upper part was a light blue picture, somewhat like a postcard, which showed a street and narrow passage. The archduke and his wife were sitting in a motorcar with a general facing them. Another officer was sitting next to the chauffeur. A crowd was assembled on both sides of the street. Suddenly, two young men jumped out from the crowd and fired at the archduke and his wife. Accompanying this picture was the following text:

Dear Dr. Lanyi,

I hearwith inform you that today, my wife and I will fall victims to an assassination. We commend ourselves to your pious prayers.

Kindest regards from your
Archduke Franz,
Sarajevo, the 28th of June,
3:45 A.M.

The bishop jumped out of bed and, with tears streaming from his eyes, noted that the clock read a quarter to four. The bishop went to his desk immediately and wrote down everything that he had seen and read in the dream. About two hours later a servant entered and noticed the bishop saying his rosary. The bishop requested that the servant call the bishop's mother and a houseguest because he wished to offer mass for their highnesses. The three of them went to the chapel and the mass was held. The bishop drew a sketch of the assassination scene because he felt there was something peculiar about its imagery. He had his drawing certified by two witnesses, then sent an account of the dream to his brother Edward, a Jesuit priest. Appended to the letter was a sketch of the narrow passage, the motorcar, the crowd, and the murderers jumping toward the car and firing the shots. The drawings were in close agreement with the photographs published in the press several days later, except that there had been only one assassin rather than the two in the bishop's dream.[62]

Questions have been raised as to whether the bishop was really so thorough in recording all of these events on June 28. A reporter from the *Wiener Reichspost* investigated the matter; he apparently examined the drawing and talked to the two witnesses, who confirmed the story. The bishop's brother, Edward, had been questioned immediately by the editor and writer Bruno Grabinsky, who stated that the priest confirmed receiving the letter and sketch. This dream is of considerable historical significance since the assassination of Franz Ferdinand set off World War I.

A less well known, but also vividly detailed, assassination dream was reported by John Williams on May 3, 1812. In his dream, he was in the lobby of the House of Commons and saw a small man enter dressed in a blue coat and white waistcoat. He then observed a man in a snuff-colored coat with metal buttons fire a pistol, and a large bloodstain appeared on the left breast of the small man's white waistcoat before he fell to the ground. As the assassin was grabbed by several men nearby, the dreamer asked about the victim's identity, and was informed that it was Mr. Perceval, the Chancellor of the Exchequer.

Williams awoke and told the dream to his wife, who told him to disregard it. He had the dream a second time and again told it to his wife, who again told him it was just a dream and to forget it. After experiencing the same dream a third time that night, Williams became very agitated. He consulted with several friends as to whether he should try to alert someone in authority, but was strongly advised not to, lest he be ridiculed and considered a fanatic. Perceval was assassinated about a week later, on May 11, 1812. The details of the assassination, including the colors of the clothing, the buttons on the assassin's jacket, and the location of the bloodstain on Perceval's white waistcoat, were identical to those Williams said had appeared in his dream.[63]

A much better known American assassination dream was one in which the victim himself dreamed of his assassination. About two weeks before John Booth's bullet struck Abraham Lincoln in Ford's Theater, Lincoln dreamed that he heard subdued sobs, as if a number of people were weeping. Curious about the origin of these sobs, he left his bed and wandered downstairs from room to room, continuing to hear the same mournful sounds along the way. When he arrived at the East Room, he saw a coffin lying on a platform. The corpse was wrapped in funeral vestments. Soldiers, acting as guards, were stationed around it and there was a throng of people. Some gazed mournfully upon the corpse, whose face was covered. When Lincoln demanded of one of the soldiers, "Who is dead in the White House?" the soldier replied, "The President. He was killed by an assassin!" The loud burst of grief from the crowd, when they heard this, woke Lincoln from his dream. After Lincoln's assassination, his casket was placed on a platform in the East Room of the White House where it was guarded by soldiers.[64]

A more recent assassination dream was reported by George Wallace, Jr. He stated, in the October 11, 1982, issue of *Time* magazine, that he had had a dream, a few nights before his father, then a Democratic presidential candidate, was wounded while campaigning in Maryland in 1972, in which just such a shooting occurred, except that in the dream, his father died.

Dreams which are prophetic or come true are called precognitive. One of the problems with precognitive dreams is that they often do not provide a perfect reproduction of the tragic events; some of the details are blurred or inaccurate. An English housewife, Barbara Garwell of Hull, dreamed in early March 1981 that she was riding in a car with two Germans wearing uniforms resembling those of the Nazi SS. A large limousine approached and stopped, and a man stepped out whom Garwell uncertainly identified as a well-known actor. The two SS men got out of their car; one drew a pistol and fired several shots at the actor, who fell to the ground. Three weeks later, on March 30, 1981, the former actor and then-president, Ronald Reagan, stepped out of his limousine and was shot and severely wounded by John Hinckley, Jr. As in Bishop Layni's dream, two assassins were seen, whereas in actuality there was only one. The SS uniform may have been relevant; Hinckley had once been a member of a neo-Nazi group, but was expelled in 1978 because of his violent ideas.[65]

This same Mrs. Garwell, later that same year, in September 1981, had a vivid dream in which she saw a single row of men seated in a stadium. The men were wearing dark suits and had "coffee-colored skins." The dreamer knew the locale was somewhere in the Middle East and there was "sand nearby." She saw two soldiers, also with "coffee-colored skin," rush up to the row of men and spray them with automatic-rifle fire. A three-week interval between the dream and later event was again involved. On October 6, 1981, President Anwar Sadat of Egypt was assassinated when four Egyptian soldiers jumped from a vehicle in a military parade and sprayed helpless dignitaries on a curved reviewing stand, somewhat resembling a stadium, with automatic-rifle fire. Sadat, who was wearing a dark uniform, was killed. Once again, the number of the assassins was wrong; Garwell saw two soldiers but there were four attackers. Both of these dreams had been told to others before the fateful events occurred, and witnesses signed statements confirming the priority of Garwell's dreams.[66]

In 1881, a pamphlet entitled *A Word of Warning* was published anonymously by Hile Wechsler, an Orthodox Jewish rabbi from western Europe. It related a series of Wechsler's dreams, which he felt foretold a genocidal fate for the Jewish people in western Europe. Rabbi Wechsler's dreams are reprinted in *The Reluctant Prophet* by James Kirsch, a Jungian analyst.

Wechsler foresaw that anti-Semitism would become extremely harsh. "One wants to destroy the Semitic element lock, stock and barrel . . . one wants to rack and ruin the Jews so radically that their atoms will never be connected and resynthesized."[67] The dreams that led to such dire predictions were more symbolic than literal, but their content impressed itself very powerfully on Wechsler. Here are two of

the twelve dreams described in Wechsler's pamphlet (labeled dreams six and seven by Kirsch):[68]

About five years ago I saw myself in a dream standing on a high mountain in Rumania, persuading the Jews there that they should not nourish any false hopes that by the aid of the Alliance Israelite, or by the aid of big European powers, they would achieve equality. They should rather go to Palestine, settle there and take up agriculture. A large number of my hearers wanted to act on my proposals.

Another time I saw, in the East—in the proximity of Rumania—a terrible thunderstorm, and from there a mass of threatening dark clouds move all around to most of the European states. But it came to Germany earlier than to Austria-Hungary. This struck me very much. Continuing dreaming, I thought: the meaning of this is that the Rumanian spirit of hostility against the Jews will make its rounds in other states, but it will strike roots first in Germany before it grips other countries.

Rabbi Wechsler's ominous forecast tragically came true a half century later when Adolf Hitler rose to power and began his persecution of the Jews.

Hitler himself was said to be influenced by dreams. According to one story, Hitler felt he had been selected to carry out some divine missions because his life was saved during World War I through a dream.[69] He is alleged to have dreamed of being buried under an avalanche of earth and molten iron, with blood flowing down his chest. After waking from this dream, he decided to leave the trench where he was, and soon after a shell exploded where he had been sleeping and killed all his companions in the trench. In another version, Hitler had been eating dinner in a trench when a voice urged him to vacate his position before the shell landed.[70] Neither the dreaming or waking version is mentioned in Hitler's autobiography, *Mein Kampf.*

Dreams may also have prompted some actions during World War II. Rudolf Hess, the deputy leader of the Nazi Party, felt he was losing favor with Hitler, but he was encouraged by an astrologer who told him in late 1940 that peace would come and Hess would be the person to bring it about. How this would happen was not specified. But then Professor Karl Haushofer, a geopolitician who was very popular with Hitler, had a dream which he shared with Hess. In the dream, Haushofer saw Hess "striding through the tapestried halls of English castles, bringing peace between the two great 'Nordic' nations."[71] Bolstered by this dream, Hess flew to Scotland in 1941, allegedly to conduct personal peace talks with the Duke of Hamilton, an acquaintance from the 1936 Berlin Olympic games. Haushofer's dream became a nightmare for Hess, because he was detained as a prisoner of war and sentenced to life imprisonment at the Nuremberg trials.

The dreams of some of the German people under Hitler's dictatorship indicated that they felt mentally imprisoned by his totalitarian regime. Journalist Charlotte Beradt collected dreams from over three hundred Germans between 1933 and 1939, when she was forced to flee from the country. Many of these dreams are recorded in her book *The Third Reich of Dreams.* They make for chilling reading. It is possible to follow how the population gradually succumbed to the totalitarian pressure for conformity. Propaganda devices were prominent in the dreams: one dreamer heard a radio blaring over and over, "In the name of the Fuhrer, in the name of the Fuhrer"; another dreamed of posters on the corner listing the twenty words people were not allowed to say. Another dreamer observed the loss of privacy: "As far as the eye could see no apartment had walls any more." One dreamer reflected the developing sense of paranoia, describing her fear as a storm trooper invaded her kitchen to open her oven door, so that the oven could repeat every word that her family had said against the government. Dreamed telephone conversations were interrupted by a voice announcing, "This is the monitoring office."

Some individuals could discern the unhealthy path the nation was taking but felt helpless to alter it. One housewife dreamed that she tried to rip the swastika off the Nazi flag each night but it was always sewn on tightly again in the morning. Another dreamer wept with anger and guilt as he realized he was slowly, "inch by inch, raising my arm in the Nazi salute." An office worker described a dream where he sat at his desk and decided to submit a formal complaint about prevailing conditions, but put a perfectly blank piece of paper in the envelope.

It seems that government brainwashing became increasingly effective. The dreams of the German people showed greater resignation; protest within dreams was reduced to a blank sheet of paper. However, as long as dream awareness survives, the state has not totally abolished the spark of freedom. The liberating inner light of hope burning in an individual's dreams may serve to ignite a chain reaction when shared with others. In George Orwell's *1984*, disobedience to Big Brother starts in a dream.

The organization leader of the Nazi Party, Robert Ley, said in 1938: "In Germany there are no private matters anymore. If you sleep, that's your private matter, but the moment you wake up and come into contact with another person, you must remember that you are a soldier of Adolf Hitler." People gradually began to fear that not even sleep was private, that their sleeping or dreaming behavior might be used against them. A woman milliner dreamed:

> I was talking in my sleep and to be on the safe side was speaking Russian (which I don't know) so I'd not even understand myself and so no one else could understand me in case I said anything about the government, for that, of course, is not permitted and must be reported.[72]

A forty-five-year-old doctor dreamed he was being accused of writing down dreams. A young man reported a dream in which the corrosive effects of censorship had leached down to the level of his personal dream symbols: "I dreamt that I no longer dream about anything but rectangles, triangles, and octagons, all of which somehow look like Christmas cookies—you see, it was forbidden to dream."[73] Once a people accept the idea that it is forbidden to dream, perpetual darkness and subjugation are certain to follow.

DREAMS AND THE WORLD OF IDEAS, INNOVATIONS AND INVENTIONS

We're all familiar with the concept of brainstorming, letting ideas, thoughts, and images roam freely with the hope that they may lead to some new solution to a vexing problem. How many of us have ever considered the possibilities of "dreamstorming"? Not only does our dreaming mind have an uncanny ability to sort through a large number of details, but it also processes material in a way that's not limited by the usual rules of logic and can thereby sometimes suggest very novel and innovative solutions. When frustrated by a problem in our waking lives, we may find ourselves in a rut, going back and forth across the same familiar but unproductive ground. In dreams, it seems we can almost hover, like a hummingbird, or fly back and forth, up and down, or sideways, in order to see the problem that is stalemating us from a new angle or perspective.

On the night of November 10, 1619, when he was twenty-three years old, Rene Descartes had some dreams in which he achieved new perspectives that had a profound effect upon the worlds of philosophy and mathematics.

In one of his dreams, Descartes started out terrified, walking along on a tilt because his right side was too weak. He was spun around several times on his left foot by a powerful wind and tried to seek refuge in a college chapel, where he hoped to pray, but the wind forced him back. Then someone told him a man in the college courtyard had brought him a gift of a melon from a foreign country. The dreamer, still bent and unsteady in his gait, was surprised to observe that those gathered around the man were upright and steady on their feet, and he was simultaneously aware that the force of the wind had now greatly diminished. Descartes's interpreted the foreign melon as a sexual symbol. The dream thus suggested that he had been proceeding in an unbalanced manner but that the strong unseen forces causing him to lose his footing would diminish if he could learn to accept and become more familiar with the "foreign" physical side of his life. Religious concerns were also involved; the chapel entrance where spiritual communication (prayer) takes place was located away from where the melon was.

To reformulate his dream in an oversimplified manner, it seems the task posed for Descartes by this dream was to reconcile the domains of the body and the spirit and to understand their interrelations in a scholarly setting (the college courtyard). His eventual solution was to develop the philosophical theory of dualism; man's physical body functioned in a manner similar to that of other animals, but his mind operated on a nonphysical basis, under the influence of a soul. Descartes's description of how the body and the soul act upon each other are described in his *Passions of the Soul*.

In another dream, Descartes found an unfamiliar book on a table and, when he opened it, found that it was a dictionary, which he hoped would be useful to him. At the same time, he found another unfamiliar book, a complete anthology of ancient Latin poets. Opening the latter book, he chanced upon the line *Quad vitae sectabar iter?* ("What path of life shall I pursue?"). Then a stranger appeared and recommended a piece of verse beginning with *Est et non* ("To be and not to be"), which Descartes considered to be related to an important concept of Pythagoras. Descartes concluded that the dictionary meant that all the sciences should be combined and the stranger's quoting a Pythagoreanlike text meant that mathematics would provide the means of accomplishing this goal. He felt the dream was encouraging him to pursue a career as a mathematician as well as a philosopher.

Before Descartes's time Euclidian geometry and algebra had been two separate descriptive systems for apprehending mathematical reality. In his *Analytical Geometry*, Descartes was able to combine the two by showing that any geometrical proposition has an algebraic expression and that any algebraic expression can be represented in terms of plane geometry. By means of his "Cartesian coordinates" it became possible to geometrically represent any system of quantitative relationships and thereby to integrate them into a unified system of measurements.

Other mathematicians have also worked out unexpected solutions on the blackboard of their dreaming mind. At the beginning of the twentieth century, Edmond Maillet distributed a questionnaire about the value of dreams to a group of mathematicians who had been in their profession for at least ten years. Four of his respondents described mathematical dreams in which a solution was actually found in the dream; three of these solutions referred to problems of elementary geometry. Eight respondents acknowledged finding the beginnings of a solution or useful idea in a dreaming state, and another fifteen indicated that as soon as they awoke they had achieved complete or partial solutions to questions posed the previous night.[74]

According to a 1948 *Scientific American* article on "Mathematics and the Imagination," one mathematician was particularly favored with help from a mathematical mentor in his dreams. A Hindu goddess named Namakkal would appear to the Indian mathematician Srinivasa Ramanujan in his dreams and present him mathematical formulae which he would verify after waking. This pattern of receiving mathematical formulae "repeated itself throughout his life," and his accomplishments were so substantial that one commentator stated, "It was doubtful so prodigious a feat had ever be-

fore been accomplished in the history of thought."

In 1869, Dmitri Mendeleyev, a professor of chemistry at Saint Petersburg, went to bed after trying unsuccessfully to conceptualize a way to categorize the chemical elements based upon their atomic weights. He later reported, "I saw in a dream a table where all the elements fell into place as required. Awakening, I immediately wrote it down on a piece of paper. Only in one place did a correction later seem necessary." As a result of this dream, the periodic table of the elements was created.[75] It enabled Mendeleyev to predict the existence, as well as the properties, of three new elements; those elements were discovered within fifteen years.

The most famous account of creative scientific dreaming is associated with Friedrich A. von Kekule, a professor of chemistry at Ghent, Belgium. Kekule had been attempting for some time to solve the structural riddle of the benzene molecule. He fell asleep in a chair and began to dream of atoms flitting before his eyes, forming various structures and patterns. Eventually some long rows of atoms formed and began to twist in a snakelike fashion. Suddenly one of the snakes seized hold of its own tail and began to whirl in a circle. Kekule awoke "as if by a flash of lightning" and began to work out the implications of his dream imagery. He constructed a model of a closed ring with an atom of carbon and hydrogen at each point of a hexagon. This discovery revolutionized organic chemistry.[76] It is not surprising that when Kekule was describing his dream-discovered insight to a scientific convention in 1890, he concluded his presentation by urging the audience, "Let us learn to dream, gentlemen, and then we may perhaps find the truth."

One Nobel Prize winner in physiology and medicine, Albert von Szent-Gyorgyi, acknowledged in regard to research problems, "My brain must continue to think about them when I sleep because I wake up, sometimes in the middle of the night, with answers to questions that have been puzzling me."[77]

Frederick Banting, a Canadian physician, was carrying out research on the causes of diabetes. He awakened from his sleep one night and wrote down these sentences: "Tie up the duct of the pancreas of a dog. Wait for a few weeks until the glands shrivel up. Then cut it out, wash it out and filter the precipitation." This new approach resulted in his successfully isolating the hormone now known as insulin, which is secreted in insufficient amounts, or not at all, in diabetics. The discovery, by Banting and his colleagues, of a means of extracting this substance from nonhuman pancreases has since saved the lives of untold millions of diabetics.[78] The humanitarian benefits of Banting's nighttime accomplishment led to his being knighted.

Given the recognition these scientists have received for discoveries incubated in their dreams, one might think that other scientists would rush to emulate their efforts. Not so! When some scientists were asked to comment on Kekule's famous discovery, they were quick to point out that his story presented "a damaging picture of scientists" because scientists "get hard facts" and "don't dream things up."[79] Apparently these scientists are only comfort-able with results derived from daytime perspiration. They seem threatened by the notion that nocturnal inspiration could lead to recognition of relations between elements that might otherwise be overlooked because of waking biases. The myopic view of these hardheaded scientists seems to be that if our eyes are closed in sleep, we can't see anything original.

Many books on dreams have reported that Danish physicist Niels Bohr conceived the model of an atom as a nucleus with electrons revolving about it from a dream in 1913. But when William Dement, a leading contemporary sleep researcher, wrote to Bohr over fifty years later to obtain further information, Bohr denied having had this dream and said that he had never received any usable idea from a dream in his life.[80]

Industry has profited from new or improved products derived through dream mentation. James Watt, the inventor, dreamed of walking through a storm in which he was showered with tiny lead pellets instead of rain. The dream imagery stimulated a hypothesis that if molten lead fell through the air like rain, it would harden into spherical shapes. To test this idea Watt dropped several pounds of molten lead from a church tower into a water-filled ditch and produced the desired rounded lead pellets. To make shot prior to then, bars of lead were pounded into sheets, the sheets cut into cubes, and the cubes rotated in a barrel until their corners were rolled off. Watt's discovery simplified production, and from that time on towers were built for the purpose.[81]

A more recent improvement in firing power was triggered by a dream from D.

Parkinson, a Bell Laboratory engineer, in 1940. He was attempting to develop an automatic level recorder to improve the accuracy of measurements in telephone transmission. In his dream, he was with an antiaircraft crew in a gun pit. One of the guns brought down an airplane with every shot. One of the crew members beckoned Parkinson to come closer to the gun and pointed to the exposed end. To Parkinson's surprise, he saw that the control potentiometer of his level recorder was mounted there. From research based upon Parkinson's dream, the first all-electric gun director evolved and became known as the M-9 electrical analog computer. The M-9 was the precursor of guidance systems for later antiaircraft and antiballistic missiles.[82]

Elias Howe had been working unsuccessfully for years to perfect a lock-stitch sewing machine but was using a needle threaded through the middle of the shank. He experienced a nightmare in which he was going to be boiled in a pot by a group of cannibals when he became fascinated by their spears, which had eye-shaped holes near their tips. After waking from this "potboiler," Howe whittled a model of the dream spear with a hole located at the tip and thereby discovered the detail he required for his sewing machine to work satisfactorily. In another version of the story, the spears were held by guards who were going to execute him because he couldn't finish his machine.[83]

Ernst Chladni had been wishing for a musical instrument which would have a special sound. He awoke from a dream in 1789 with the detailed image of how such an instrument should look. A few preliminary experiments convinced him that his

dream blueprint was correct, and he proceeded to develop the euphonium, a brass instrument like the tuba but having a more mellow tone.[84]

In 1879, a new synthetic language, Volapuk, was created in a dream by J. Schleyer, the German linguist. In thirty years of study, he had mastered more than fifty languages and was seeking a way to express the common patterns that existed between their grammatical structures. None of his working organizational schemes were successful, but in a dream the necessary letters, forms, and processes appeared "in an orderly array"[85] and he created his new language for auxiliary use in international communication.

Dr. Herman V. Hilprecht, professor of Assyrian at the University of Pennsylvania, offers a final example of the creative problem solving dream. He was working late one evening in 1893, attempting to decipher the inscription on two fragments of agate thought to be from Babylonian finger rings. Dozens of similar fragments had been found in the ruins of the temple of Bel at Nippur. The few discernible cuneiform characters and lines allowed Hilprecht to tentatively assign one fragment to the Cassite period while the other he placed with a large number of unclassifiable fragments. Feeling uncertain about his classifications, he fell asleep shortly after midnight and had the following dream:

A tall, thin priest of the old preChristian Nippur, about forty years of age and clad in a simple abba, led me to the treasure chamber of the temple, on its southeast side. He went with me into a small, low-ceiled room without windows, in which there was a large wooden chest, while scraps of agate and lapis lazuli lay scattered on the floor. Here he addressed me as follows: "The two fragments which you have published separately on pages 22 and 26 belong together, are not finger rings and their history is as follows: King Kurigalzu (Ca. 1300 B.C.) once sent to the temple of Bel, among other articles of agate and lapis lazuli, an inscribed votive cylinder of agate. Then we priests suddenly received the command to make for the statue of the god of Ninib a pair of earrings of agate. We were in great dismay, since there was no agate as raw material at hand. In order to execute the command there was nothing for us to do but cut the votive cylinder into three parts, thus making three rings, each of which contained a portion of the original inscription. The first two rings served as earrings for the statue of the god; the two fragments which have given you so much trouble are portions of them. If you will put the two together you will have confirmation of my word. But the third ring you have not found in the course of your excavations and you never will find it." With this the priest disappeared.

In commenting upon his dream, Professor Hilprecht wrote:

I woke at once and immediately told my wife the dream that I might not forget it. Next morning—Sunday—I examined the fragments once more in the light of these disclosures, and to my astonishment found all the details of the dream precisely verified in so far as the means of verification were in my hands. The original inscription on the votive cylinder reads: "To the god Ninib, son of Bel, his lord, has Kurigalzu, pontifex of Bel, presented this."[86]

This remarkable dream, published in the *Proceedings of the Society for Psychical Research*, raises fascinating questions. How did Hilprecht come to know that the fragments had been part of a single votive cylinder presented by King Kurigalzu, dedicated to Ninib, and subsequently made into a pair of earrings? What could account for the presence of these extraordinarily accurate details in the dream? Perhaps there was a psychic, or "extrasensory," element involved. Perhaps logical, associative reasoning, assembling bits and pieces of subliminal information, is the explanation. If so, such superb deductive skill would put Sherlock Holmes to shame. Whatever its origin, Professor Hilprecht's dream offers a dramatic example of how "dream-storming" can lead to a creative rearrangement of existing information.

I think sufficient evidence has been brought forth to demonstrate our dreaming mind's heightened capacity for creative problem solving, operational thinking, and imagination. Many people who have devoted serious attention to dreams have come to similar conclusions. For example, Marie de Manaceine, a Russian physician from Saint Petersburg, drew up a list in 1897 of many creative people who had found inspiration in their dreams. She also voiced the opinion that our cultural heritage has been enriched by these dreams; I strongly concur with her opinion:

> A great many men of science, poets, philosophers, musicians and others have declared that they received important ideas and suggestions in dreams (Burdach, Lotze, Voltaire, Condillac, Condorcet, Coleridge, Tartini, Mac-

ario, and many others). Some of these facts, which have been recorded too often to be repeated here, are undoubtedly reliable, though others rest on vague and more uncertain evidence. And certain authors (N. Lange, Helmholtz, Griesinger, Brodie, Maudsley, Beneke, Herbart, Fechner, etc.) have in this way found ground for believing that much that we honor in literature, science, and art is the direct result of mental work during sleep, and due to unconscious cerebral activity.[87]

DREAMS AND SPIRITUAL DIMENSIONS

Dreams have not only led to scientific and artistic developments, but have also served as channels for spiritual inspiration. Some form of dream imagery is embedded in the beginnings of most of the world's major religions.

Most of the events surrounding the birth and early years of Christ were announced in dreams. Joseph was told the source of Mary's pregnancy in a dream and instructed to name the child Jesus (Matthew 1). In later dreams, Joseph was warned that he should flee to Egypt with Mary and the child to avoid Herod's soldiers and was informed when the time was safe to return to Israel (Matthew 2). A dream was also associated with events surrounding Christ's death. Troubled by her disturbing dream about that "just man," Pilate's wife unsuccessfully urged him to release Christ (Matthew 27).

In 544 B.C., the Buddha's mother, Queen Maya, dreamed her bed was transported by four kings to a high Himalayan peak, where four queens adorned her with jewels and brought her to a golden palace. A white elephant with six shining ivory tusks appeared and painlessly pierced her side with a thrust of its tusk. She awoke to the song of a blue bird and realized that she had immaculately conceived.[88] Her dream was interpreted as signifying that her child would become a universal monarch. Five of the Buddha's dreams, along with dreams of his father, King Cudhodana, and his wife, Gopa, appear in the Pali scriptures and describe his future vocation as a wandering monk.[89]

Muhammad received his divine mission in a dream. In his famous *Nocturnal Journey*, the original version of which contained fourteen chapters and sixty-five pages, he

Buddha was conceived when his mother, Queen Maya, dreamed that a white elephant descended from heaven and pierced her side with one of his six tusks. From a tenth-century Chinese painting.

traveled on a white mare called Elborak and was guided by the angel Gabriel through seven celestial spheres. Along the way he met biblical figures, such as Abraham, Joseph, and Jesus, who declared him to be the greatest of all the prophets. After leaving the seventh celestial sphere, he arrived in the Garden of Delights, where four rivers sprang from the base of the gigantic Tree of Life. He next went to the House of Adoration, built of red hyacinth and surrounded by continually burning lamps, where seventy thousand angels paid daily homage to the Eternal. After saying his prayers, Muhammad was handed three full cups: one of wine, one of milk, and one of honey. When he chose the cup of milk, Gabriel congratulated him and they then traversed vast stretches of heavens and oceans of light and approached the throne of God. God ordered Muhammad to pray daily. After some additional dialogue about the appropriate number of prayers, Muhammad resumed his flight back to earth.[90]

Much of the Koran, the sacred book of the Muslims, was revealed to Muhammad in his dreams over a period of several years. Each morning Muhammad would ask his disciples about their dreams, offer them interpretations, and then share his own dreams with them. After hearing the dream of one of his followers, Muhammad instituted the practice of *adhan*, the daily ritual call to prayers from the minarets, the towers of the mosque. Dream interpretation was greatly revered among the Muslims. They considered it a noble science, taught to Adam by God himself and passed by Adam to Seth, by Seth to Noah, and so on down to Muhammad.

The establishment of the Church of Latter Day Saints has been attributed to dream revelations received by Joseph Smith in upstate New York. In 1820, he dreamed that God bid him to establish a church, and in 1823 the angel Moroni appeared in a dream and revealed to him the existence of the Book of Mormon.

Aside from their role in the development of specific religions, dreams have suggested answers to many pervasive and eternal questions: Who are we? Where did we come from? Why are we here? Of what are we made? Where are we going? What is death? Is there an existence after death? If there is an existence, of what does it consist? People of all times have pondered these tenacious and troubling questions. What is seldom recognized is that dreams have helped to provide some answers.

Long before the advent of sacred texts, our ancestors' dreams gave them inklings of a realm beyond the physical and inspired their first spiritual strivings. Sir Edward Tylor, occupant of the first chair of anthropology at Oxford University, stated that "the religious beliefs of the lower races are in no small measure based on the evidence of visions and dreams." Tylor proposed that prehistoric peoples were greatly perplexed by two enigmas: (1) the ability of a motionless, sleeping individual on waking to describe physical adventures and social interactions in distant places, and (2) the difference between a living body and a dead one. By developing the concept of a nonphysical soul, they resolved both puzzles. Dream experiences could be explained as brief journeys or wanderings of the soul, and death as the permanent departure of the soul from the body.[91]

Belief in the existence of an afterlife also probably arose from dreams, since dreamers often encounter deceased individuals who exhibit the same behaviors characteristic of them when they were alive. Havelock Ellis observed:

There is a special mechanism in the typical dream of a dead friend, due to mental dissociation during sleep, which powerfully suggests to us that death sets up no fatal barrier to the return of the dead. In dreams the dead are thus rendered indestructible; they cannot be finally killed, but rather tend to reappear in ever more clearly affirmed vitality.[92]

If our beliefs about the existence of a soul originated in dreams, then dreams should be recognized as having contributed a fundamental premise about the nature of human existence that has been a subject of debate and reflection in all civilizations and all ages.

Based on the material presented in this section, the conclusion that dreams have had a profound effect upon our history seems inescapable. Dreams have enriched our culture through the arts, sounded the call to battle or to territorial expansion, laid the cornerstone for the construction of new buildings, stoked the fires of freedom, changed philosophical premises, led to the invention of labor-saving devices, and served as a source of spiritual illumination and an expanded vision of our very nature and essence. Even if some events alleged to be dream-inspired are dismissed as fabrications, exaggerations, or literary devices invented to dramatize or persuade, enough well-documented cases remain to sustain the judgment that dreams have had a powerful cumulative influence on the course of our history.

Most citizens of our increasingly technological society are not aware of these dream-inspired achievements. They can easily recite the names of famous authors, artists, generals, politicians, singers, movie stars, and athletes, but draw a blank if asked to list famous dreamers or important cultural developments based on dreams. We have become an unbalanced society, in which technology is viewed as the ultimate accomplishment. Our fascination with machines—machines that can clear hundreds of acres of rainforest in a single day, machines that can unleash instant destruction on those with whom we politically disagree, and machines that, in speeding communication, also tend to homogenize our opinions into a common ideological cast—threatens our continued existence on this planet. Dreams may help us to balance our relations with nature and with each other. In dreams, the human spirit and creativity reign supreme, yet we have been taught to scorn or ridicule the messages they contain. Has this always been the lot of dreams or have there been times when people looked to dreams for guidance and accorded them the respect they now lack?

There were ancient civilizations whose cultural paths were lit, not by electricity, but by the internal illumination provided by dreams. Perhaps a look back to these civilizations will help us put our own accomplishments into perspective and sensitize us to our lopsided favoring of machines over the wisdom of the heart and the higher imaginative faculties. Ancient wisdom shouldn't be ignored simply because it's ancient; the geological strata of the Grand Canyon are not less awesome because they are old.

Let's return to those earlier times, trace out the meandering development of beliefs about dream imagery, and consider whether some nostalgia for the "good old nights" might not be beneficial to our current dream-denying, planetary-eroding society.

CHAPTER 3

DREAMS FROM THE DAWN OF HISTORY THROUGH ARTEMIDORIS

I hope the preceding section has given some credibility to my claim that dreams have been underappreciated as an agent of historical changes and that dream residues have enriched many areas of our current culture. I'd like to broaden our historical perspective now by taking a look at how dreams have been viewed in other times and in other cultures.

THE FIRST DREAM

When did the first dream occur? It was many millions of years ago—perhaps, on some dark night when a hairy creature reexperienced briefly during sleep a strong smell that had caused its nostrils to twitch during the preceding day, or the taste of some earlier feast.

Much of our speculation about the evolution of dreaming is based upon comparative studies of animals that display different levels of central nervous system differentiation. By means of brain wave recordings and behavioral observations, scientists have concluded that amphibians such as bullfrogs do not sleep, reptiles may or may not sleep, and birds and higher mammals display two different stages of sleep. The stage of sleep usually associated with dreaming may have evolved in mammals about 130 million years ago.[1]

The waking ability of anthropoids to think and conceptualize has been studied quite extensively. For example, the famous chimpanzee, Washoe, was taught a large number of elements in sign language, among them the signs for "water" and for "bird." He then combined these two signs to create his own sign for "duck." Monkeys have been trained in their waking state to press a lever when patterned stimuli flash on a screen. Later during sleep, they have been observed to gesture as if to press the lever, implying that they were responding to similar visual stimuli. Based on such evidence scientists have inferred that some experience analogous to dreaming takes place in these monkeys. As evolution progressed and protohumans developed increased cortical differentiation, it seems plausible to assume that their dreaming imagery also gradually became more complex.

Lewis Mumford expressed the following thoughts about the significance of dreaming for our ancestors:

> We shall not go too far astray, I submit, if we picture this protohuman as a creature pestered and tantalized by dreams, too easily confusing the images of darkness and sleep with those of waking life.... From the beginning, we must infer, man was a dreaming animal; and possibly the richness of his dreams was what enabled him to depart from the restrictions of a purely animal career.... Did this breach between the inner and outer world not merely cause wonderment but invite further comparison and demand interpretation? If so, it would lead to a greater paradox: that it was the dream that opened man's eyes to new possibilities in his waking life.[2]

THE NATURE OF EARLY DREAM IMAGERY

What imagery was likely to appear in these dreams of long ago? Since much of our early ancestors' waking lives was spent chasing or being chased by various animals, it is probable that interactions with animals were a prominent theme in their dreamlife. Perhaps some of the crude drawings of animals etched and painted on cave walls ten to twenty thousand years ago were intended to preserve the nocturnal images that appeared in the dreams of the cave dwellers who resided there. Sometimes these paintings portrayed animal-human combinations.

Because man's preagricultural destiny was so dependent on animals, their influence was pervasive and they sometimes achieved the status of deities. An example of this is found in ancient Egypt, where dozens of deities were represented as having animal heads. Some of these were Bast (cat), Sebek (crocodile), Horus (falcon), Heket (frog), and Amon (ram). These animal-headed deities may have first emerged in dreams. Since dreams often are associated with fear or awe for the dreamer, there would have been a strong urge to communicate their intriguing imagery to others. The cave paintings may have been one vehicle for this, and dance and dramatic reenactment may have been another.

As human cultures developed, there was a corresponding increase in the ability to tell stories. In his book *The Roots of Civilization*, Alexander Marshack contends that the ability of humans to process "storied thinking" is responsible for all cultural evolution:

What then is "story?" The simplest definition is that it is the communication of an event or process—that *is* happening, *has* happened, or *will* happen. . . . It is in the nature of the "story equation" that it must always be told in terms of someone or something. . . . This holds whether one uses words, mime, dance, ritual, or refers to the symbolism of dream and trance. . . .

. . . every story is an event which includes characters (whether spirit, god, hero, person . . .) who change or do things in time.[3]

Marshak contends that our knowledge base expanded as people became more frequently involved in stories in which characters changed and the role of time became more complex. Dreams, of course, represent "storied thinking" par excellence, and as dreams are shared new outcomes can be imagined. A considerable contribution to the "storied thinking" of ancient peoples came from characters who were spirits, gods, or heroes and their presence was frequently described in dreams. The attributes and activities of these characters varied from culture to culture, but spiritual or mythological figures have been omnipresent in the dreams of all ages.

ANCIENT MESOPOTAMIAN BELIEFS

Our earliest clues about the content of ancient dreams are derived from materials dating back approximately five thousand years. The dreamers were inhabitants of the first urban centers in Mesopotamia, "the cradle of civilization," a region roughly corresponding to the central region of modern Iraq. With the development of irrigation canals, agriculture flourished in the previously arid land, and substantial cities, some containing over a hundred thousand inhabitants, gradually developed. The Sumerians were the first cultural group residing in Mesopotamia and were followed by the Akkadians, the Babylonians, and the Assyrians, as well as several invading tribes from the north and east.

Kings ruled from impressive palaces such as the one at Mari, which covered roughly seven acres and contained nearly three hundred rooms. An elaborate pantheon of deities evolved. In the city of Babylon there were fifty-five shrines to Marduk, one of the principal gods, fifty-three temples to other great gods, three hundred to earth gods, and six hundred to heavenly gods. Hundreds of altars to receive gifts and sacrifices were scattered about the city. The waking and dreaming Mesopotamian mind gave prominent attention to kings and deities.

Our knowledge of Mesopotamian dream lore is based upon the fragmentary written material unearthed by various archaeological expeditions. The Sumerians' earliest records, which date to approximately 3100 B.C., involved pictographs, but by around 2700 B.C. they had developed cuneiform, a form of writing utilizing wedge-shaped indentations pressed into clay tablets or cylinders. As the cuneiform system expanded to more than seven hundred different signs, the Sumerians were able to record not only business transactions and accounts of royal battles and other deeds, but also the mythology and religious beliefs of the time. Later Mesopotamian languages also used variations of cuneiform script. The most extensive and authoritative source on Mesopotamian

dreams is *The Interpretation of Dreams in the Ancient Near East with a Translation of an Assyrian Dream-Book* by A. Leo Oppenheim, a professor of Assyriology at the University of Chicago's Oriental Institute.[4]

Most of the clay tablets containing information relevant to dreams were excavated from Assurbanipal's royal library in Nineveh, his capital city. Assurbanipal, an Assyrian king who ruled in the seventh century B.C., was a dedicated scholar. Nearly twenty-five thousand clay tablets collected from many historical eras were found in his archives, including twelve broken tablets recounting the epic adventures of the legendary hero-king, Gilgamesh. Oral versions of this earliest of all classic stories probably existed for hundreds of years before a scribe first recorded it in cuneiform writing, and variations of the epic poem also appeared in later accounts.

The Gilgamesh epic represents a remarkable chronicle of dream events, among them the first known references to sequential dreams from the same dreamers. The role of dreams in heralding impending tragic outcomes is also important. When the dream imagery involves such cataclysmic events as heaven roaring, the earth trembling, and lightning flashing, we are put on notice that tragedy will soon befall an important character. A similar awareness of the correlation between outer and inner turmoil characterizes many great works of literature, including Shakespeare's tragedies.

In the Gilgamesh saga, dream interpretations which turn out to be correct bring good fortune, while incorrect interpretations bring misfortune to the dreamer. Indications are given that dreamers could utilize various techniques to induce dreams or to increase the possibility that a deity will manifest itself in a dream to provide some form of guidance. However, the most salient aspect of the Gilgamesh epic, with regard to dreams, is the sophistication it demonstrates concerning the symbolic and metaphorical nature of dream imagery.

Gudea, a Sumerian king who reigned in the city of Lagash around 2200 B.C., was the first known historical figure associated with a dream. His dream experiences were preserved on two clay cylinders that were not part of Assurbanipal's library. Gudea wished to build a temple for his god, Nin-Girsu. The god sent him an enigmatic dream in which a gigantic human-shaped figure, wearing the headgear of a deity but winged like a divine "cloud-bird," appeared flanked by two lions. Gudea seemed perplexed, so the god continued, showing him the sun rising and introducing two additional figures. One was a woman pondering a tablet listing the "favorable stars," the other a warrior drawing the outline of a temple on a lapis lazuli tablet. A basket to carry earth and a brick mold with a brick in it were placed before Gudea. The dream closed with an image of an impatient donkey pawing the ground before the giant figure.

Puzzled by his dream, Gudea approached the goddess Gatumdug for assistance in understanding its meaning by engaging in extensive rituals and prayers. She explained that the giant figure was Nin-Girsu, identified the other figures as deities, discussed the significance of the tools, and concluded that the impatient donkey represented Gudea in his zeal to build the temple. Gudea seemed to be im-

perfectly satisfied by the goddess's interpretation and prayed for a clearer message from his god. Nin-Girsu then appeared in a dream, standing at the head of Gudea, and promised him a sign which would indicate the day on which the work should start.

These dreams are presented in some detail, so the reader can develop an appreciation of the close affinity that existed between the Mesopotamian dream and the realm of the divine: Gudea wished to honor his god with a temple; his god sent a symbolic dream with a cast of divine characters; a goddess explained the meaning of the dream; and Nin-Girsu appeared himself in a later dream and spoke directly to Gudea.

Sometimes a deity might send a dream message to a priest or to a large number of dreamers simultaneously. On the eve of an important battle against Elamite invaders, Assurbanipal apparently felt some reluctance to attack. One of his priests reported a dream in which the goddess Ishtar appeared with a quiver on either shoulder and a bow in her hand. She indicated that Assurbanipal should "eat food, drink wine, enjoy music, and exalt her divinity" because she would insure victory for him the next day. A magnificently preserved series of large engraved panels in the British Museum graphically details the defeat of the Elamites which followed. In another account of this incident, Ishtar also appeared in the dreams of members of Assurbanipal's army and promised them victory.

It is difficult to catalog or classify ancient dream reports because very limited datable source-material is available. In the case of Mesopotamian dreams, we have the Sumerian description of King Gudea's dreams (2200 B.C.), a Hittite text describing the dreams of King Hattushili and his wife (twelfth century B.C.), and texts from the Akkadian kings Assurbanipal (seventh century B.C.) and Nabonidus (sixth century B.C.). Although no specific historical person or era was involved in the epic of Gilgamesh, this literary text in Sumerian and Akkadian does provide valuable information about ancient dream beliefs and practices. The typical dream report in the above sources contains what Oppenheim refers to as a "frame": information is provided about the dreamer, the locality and circumstances of the dream, the content of the dream, the ending of the dream, the dreamer's reaction, and the eventual outcome of the promise or prediction contained in the dream.

Based upon Mesopotamian, Egyptian, and Old Testament sources, Oppenheim proposed classifying dreams from the ancient Near East as message dreams, mantic dreams, and symbolic dreams. Most *message dreams* were experienced by kings: a deity or its representative would appear at the ruler's head and deliver a message about an event of personal significance to the dreamer. The dreamer generally woke suddenly after the deity disappeared.

Oppenheim proposed that message dreams are most easily explained as literary embellishments of dreams experienced at an incubation site. Although descriptions of incubation procedures are rare in the cuneiform texts, there are enough brief references to suggest that the practice of incubation or dream-seeking was familiar to the Mesopotamians. An incubant would sleep in a special temple and offer a prayer such as the following to the deity associated with that site:

> Reveal thyself to me and let me behold a favorable dream. May the dream that I dream be favorable; may the dream that I dream be true. May Makhir, the goddess of dreams, stand at my head, let me enter the temple of the gods and the house of life.

A ruler who sought a message dream would go to a temple or sanctuary of the deity, engage in various preparatory rituals, and stay there overnight. The setting would be strongly suggestive, so the dreamer might well experience imagery of the type expected to be associated with that deity's appearance or attributes. If the dreamer were less than completely successful in securing the desired dream, subsequent accounts of the ruler's incubation experience would probably be modified and edited to correspond with the particular theological traditions of that time and region.

Mantic dreams were those consulted for indications of what the future would bring.[5] Citizens of the ancient Near East frequently tried to discern their personal destiny by scrutinizing various signs, called *omina*, which could range from patterns of stars in the sky to the movements of birds in flight to the shape of a puddle in front of one's door. *Omina* associated with the patterns found on sheeps' livers held as much interest for diviners as did dreams, but a few omen-texts involving dreams have survived.

Omen-texts consisted of lists specifying the outcomes associated with a number of signs in short, cause-and-effect statements. Generally, categorically related signs were listed together. With regard to dreams, various outcomes were listed for a man who dreams of turning into various kinds of animals, wearing various types of clothing, or visiting various locations. The text might say, for example, "If a dead person kisses a man, one near to him will die," or, if a man dreams he "spatters himself with his own urine, he will forget what he has said." These interpretations sound plausible if certain assumptions are made; in the latter case one might take the deterioration of personal hygiene to be symptomatic of intoxication or senility, both of which are accompanied by memory loss. Many of the *omina*, however, seem to us to have no rational relation to the events they were thought to foretell, perhaps in part because it is impossible to uncover the puns and verbal associations buried in a dead language.

The third class of dreams was called *symbolic* by Oppenheim.[6] These complex dreams involved unusual interactions with gods, stars, people, animals, or innumerable objects; in short, they expressed the dreamer's personality dynamics. These dreams were considered dangerous and indicative of disease or encounters with evil and demonic powers. To mention them increased their potency, and they were hardly ever recorded unless their interpretation somehow served to diminish the threatening quality.

The Mesopotamians not only attempted to understand dreams and their future implications, but also to forestall any negative events that they predicted. The root word used in various ancient Near East languages for dealing with dreams had two associated meanings: one that implied comprehension and the other that suggested removal. In English, there is a similar linkage in the word "solve" and its derivative "dissolve." The Mesopotamian dreamer wished both to "solve" a dream, by determining its meaning, and to "dissolve" its potential evil consequences.

We might sometimes share our dreams with a family member or a friend in an attempt to understand them and thereby destroy the emotional power they have over us. The Mesopotamians had a ritual in which they told their dreams to a lump of clay for just that reason. The dreamer would take the lump of clay and rub it over his entire body, saying, "Lump! In your substance my substance has been fused, and in my substance your substance has been fused!" The dreamer then told the clay all the dreams and said to it, "As I shall throw you into the water, you will crumble and disintegrate, and may the evil consequences of all the dreams seen be gone, be melted away, and be many miles removed from my body." Another variation was to tell the dream to a reed and then burn it, blowing on the fire to insure its complete destruction. Amulets or charms to protect against bad dreams were also used. These rituals were particularly common when the dream was a nightmare or involved forbidden activities or sexual practices. The disturbing content of such dreams could not be mentioned to others and had to be dispelled magically to ward off possible evil consequences.

Just as pleasant dreams were viewed as

a sign of divine favor and good health, evil dreams were considered to arise from the presence of demonic forces. They occurred because protective spirits, who would guard the person's happiness and well-being, were absent. If these protective spirits abandoned a person, then ill health and other misfortunes could occur. Various demonic figures were always ready to swarm up from the underworld to attack people in their dreams, and evil dreams could also be sent by enemies if the dreamer were unprotected. The evil dream was not really in a separate category but rather fit into the general Mesopotamian demonology, in which magic and countermagic beliefs and practices were heavily emphasized. There were apparently very few dream interpreters in Sumer and Akkad; such individuals were held in low regard and were often women who also practiced necromancy, or communication with the dead. Dream interpreters were also conspicuously absent at the later court of Assyria, although there were numerous diviners, soothsayers, and exorcists present.

HEBREW BELIEFS

Dreams, and the gifts God bestows in dreams, figure prominently in the Old Testament. Psalm 127 says that the Lord "giveth unto his beloved in their sleep." God granted Solomon's gift of wisdom in a dream.[7] Elsewhere, God announced: "If anyone among you is a prophet, I will make myself known to him in a vision, I will speak to him in a dream."[8] The story of Jacob offers a striking example of God's speaking in a dream. Jacob dreamed of a ladder extending from earth to heaven with a procession of angels ascending and descending the ladder. God stood above the ladder and told Jacob that his offspring would spread throughout the world.[9] The ladder can be viewed as a powerful visual metaphor for the dream as a connecting link between God and his selected prophets.

In addition to giving guidance to the Hebrew prophets for the benefit of their own people, God also appeared in their dreams to provide interpretations for dreams which were troubling their Gentile rulers. Daniel gained political power in Babylon by interpreting Nebuchadnezzar's dreams, as did Joseph in Egypt when he explained Pharaoh's.[10] In both cases, this power eventually led to the freeing of the Jews from bondage.

Dreams are viewed in a broader context in the sixty-three volumes of the Talmud, the collection of rabbinical literature that connects the Old Testament with contemporary Judaism. Representing the contributions of over two thousand scholars from various countries, the Talmud is divided into a Palestinian Talmud, dating from around 500 B.C., and a larger Babylonian Talmud, compiled during the Greco-Roman period from 200 B.C. to about 300 A.D.

There are 217 references to dreams in the Talmud, attributed to many different sages and scholars, so it's not surprising that many different viewpoints toward dreams are expressed.[11] Mesopotamian influences may account for the belief that supernatural entities such as evil spirits, demons, and the returning dead could instigate dreams. One demon, thought to cause erotic dreams, was described as hairy and resembling a goat. Another demon associated with sexual dreams was Lilith, who preyed upon those who sleep alone in a house. She appeared in a female form when approaching men and in a male form when approaching women. Lilith's sister, Naamah, and another female spirit called Igrath also caused sexual and emission (wet) dreams.

A fifteenth-century representation of Jacob's ladder.

The Jews also believed that good supernatural entities could be sources of dreams. Angels, who resided in a special department in heaven, were sent in dreams as messengers from God. The chief angel, Gabriel, was known as the prince of dreams. Soul travel was yet another explanation for dreams. The Jews believed that it was possible for a part of the soul to depart during sleep and travel all over the world. What it saw would constitute the dream.

Some dreams were thought to have a physical cause, such as when bad dreams originat from an overindulgence in food. Temperature could also influence dreams; heat and moisture produced pleasurable dreams, while coldness and dryness yielded unpleasant dreams. Events from the previous day could also contribute to the creation of dreams. Many factors, including the dreamer's occupation, economic circumstances, and state of unhappiness, had to be taken into account when making an interpretation and interpretations could vary. Rabbi Binza reported that he once consulted twenty-four dream interpreters who were in Jerusalem at one time and received different interpretations of his dream from each, all of which were subsequently realized. This is a very cogent observation. Too often, we view dreams as having only a single possible meaning. The Mesopotamian omen-texts exemplify this type of reductive thinking. Our most significant dreams typically have multilayered meanings; they simultaneously address the status of our physical, emotional, and spiritual functioning. Recall the classic story of the blind men describing an elephant. Each perceived a different attribute, but although the statements differed from each other, all were accurate statements, which could be validated by a sighted observer.

Probably the most quoted Talmudic statement about dreams is that of Rabbi Hisda, who said, "An uninterpreted dream is like an unread letter." Rabbi Jonathan displayed a profound insight into the psychological nature of dreams when he said, "A man is shown in his dreams what he thinks in his heart."[12] Dreams express the constant antagonistic struggle between the good and higher inclinations in personality (*Yetzer Tob*) and the immoral and impure impulses (*Yetzer Hara*).

On the high holy days, when the *cohen* blesses the community during service, the community prays for the elimination and changing of bad thoughts and dreams. Rabbi Jehuda said that one should wish for three things, which were of great importance: a good king, a good year, and a good dream. It was recognized that a king's dream was particularly important because the actions he took as the result of the dream could influence the larger movements of history.

Egyptian Beliefs

The Egyptians were less concerned than the Mesopotamians or Jews with demonology. But like the Mesopotamians, they interpreted dreams as messages from a pantheon of gods. The dreams of royalty were given special attention because the gods were more likely to appear in them. One such royal dream was that of Thutmose IV (1400 B.C.). The god Hormakhu came to Thutmose in a dream and promised to grant him riches and a united kingdom, but in return he had to agree to remove the sand covering the Sphinx, which represented this god. Upon ascending the throne, Thutmose kept his promise to remove the sand and recorded the events of his dream on a stone column, or stela, in front of the giant figure.[13] The stela, which can be seen today, is considered to be a reconstruction of the original.

Serapis was the Egyptian god of dreams, and several temples were devoted to his worship. The one at Memphis, contructed about 3000 B.C., was one of the most important. Oracles or professional dream interpreters, known as "the learned men of the magic library," resided in these temples. A professional "shingle" found at the office door of one of them read, "I interpret dreams, having the gods' mandate to do so; good luck; the interpreter present here is Cretan."

Incubation was widely practiced; sometimes a surrogate dreamer was sent to a temple to have a dream on behalf of someone else who could not make the journey. Dreams could be sent to another by writing down a dream incantation and request and placing this message on a mummy's mouth or in the mouth of a dead cat (cats were considered sacred animals). A dreamer would fast and employ various magic prayers, drawings, and rites to procure a personal dream. In one of these techniques, the person desiring information in a dream would take a clean linen bag and write upon it the names of five different deities. The bag was then folded, saturated with oil, placed in a lamp as a wick, and set afire. Before retiring, the individual approached the lamp, repeated a certain formula seven times, put out the lamp, and then went to sleep to receive the sought-for answer.[14] The dwarf god Bes was a merry god who protected the household against bad dreams. His likeness was frequently carved on a commoner's wooden headrest or on the headboard of a wealthy individual's bed.

Two collections of dream *omina* have survived from Egypt. In Mesopotamia there were many types of divination by omens, but in Egypt, dreams were the only type collected. The earliest collection dates from the twelfth dynasty (2050–1790 B.C.) and is known as Chester Beatty Papyrus III, in honor of Chester Beatty who donated it to the British Museum.[15] The papyrus is incomplete at both ends, presumably part of a larger text. The name of the priest who compiled it is unknown.

The core of the work consists of a table listing 143 good and 91 bad dreams, along with their interpretations. A vertical column of large hieratic signs runs along the edge of the page and can be read as "If a man see himself in a dream . . .", a clause which has to be read before each horizontal line. The word for good is always written in black and the word for bad in red. The *omina* appear to be randomly scattered within the group of good and bad dreams, and no apparent pattern or schema can be detected.

Many of the interpretations involve a

correspondence of ideas and words; for example, removal of the dreamer's fingernails indicates the removal of the dreamer's works from his hands. Others have symbolic aspects; absolution may be represented by plunging in the river. Familiarity with Egyptian religious beliefs is necessary to understand others, while knowledge of the Egyptian language reveals some word plays or puns that are lost in the English translation. For example, the interpretation that one will become an orphan if one uncovers his own backside does not seem so strange when we realize that the Egyptian word for buttocks and orphan is the same.

The *omina* are followed by a short paragraph providing ritual protections against the evils foretold in bad dreams. It prescribes that the dreamer rub his face with fresh herbs, moistened with beer and myrrh, to remove the contagion of the dream. An incantation is recited to the goddess Isis. After being petitioned by a "follower of Horus," the text indicates Isis commanded: "Come out with what thou hast seen, in order that thy afflictions throughout thy dreams may vanish."

This papyrus is classified as *hieratic* because it was recorded in a style of cursive hieroglyphic writing used by priests. Due to its early date, this material may represent indigenous Egyptian dream lore that was not influenced by later Mesopotamian concepts. The other remaining Egyptian collection of dream *omina* is found on a *demotic* papyrus dating from the second century A.D. Demotic refers to a writing style used by public scribes. These *omina* appear on the Carlsburg Papyrus. Since Mesopotamian astrology and astronomy

had been partially absorbed in Egypt during this period, it's possible that Egyptian dream knowledge had also incorporated some Mesopotamian material.

There were originally more than 250 *omina* in this text but nearly one hundred were seriously damaged. They seem to have been arranged under section headings, of which six remain in rather incomplete fashion. Some of these sections concerned the outcomes to be expected if one dreamed of drinking various kinds of beer, engaging in different kinds of swimming, or performing particular types of sexual intercourse. Another dealt with women's dreams. No other Near Eastern dream book had a category for women's dreams. The dreams of women seem to have been ignored in these ancient cultures. No female dreamer is mentioned in the Old Testament, for example. There were also other small groups of *omina*, ranging from dreams of receiving wreaths of various flowers to the eating of feces from various animals. The scatological content of the latter group may seem surprising, but we may be dealing with lost idiomatic expressions peculiar to the Egyptian language.

Some scholars state that the Egyptians believed dreams were caused by a temporary traveling of the *Ba*, or soul, during sleep.[16] The *Ba* was sometimes depicted in paintings as a jabiru bird and sometimes as a human-headed bird, and when it departed at death, it retained the ability to be conscious, autonomous, and lucid in the afterworld. Another psychologist claimed that dreaming was not regarded animistically as a journey of souls, but was associated with the hypersensitiveness of the sleeping condition. That is, the sleeping state allowed dreamers to see and hear things that are always in existence.[17]

CHINESE BELIEFS

The Chinese have had a long and sophisticated tradition of appreciating subtle energy fields. Their knowledge of how energy fields work at a physical level led to the practice of acupuncture, a technique now gaining wider acceptance by Western medicine. The Chinese also developed interesting theories regarding how mental and psychic functioning depends upon different energy forms. They considered the dreamer's soul to be one of the principal agencies of dream production but made a distinction between the material soul, or *p'o*, which regulated body functioning and ceased with its death, and the spiritual soul, or *hun*, which left the body at death and carried the appearance of the body with it.[18] It was the *hun* that was involved in dreams, because it could separate temporarily from the body for nighttime excursions to the land of the dead. There it would communicate with spirits or souls of the dead and return to the body with impressions from these visits. Since dreadful consequences would follow if the soul failed to return quickly enough to reunite with the body, the dreamer was thought to be in a very vulnerable state; great care was taken not to suddenly arouse a sleeper. Traces of this belief persist to the present: alarm clocks are viewed with apprehension in many areas of China.

The *T'ung Shu* is an ancient Chinese almanac of life that has a nearly four-thousand-year history.[19] It contains a section on dreams called "Chou Kung's Book of Auspicious and Inauspicious Dreams" that dates back to 1020 B.C. and was written by Chou Kung, a mathematician reputed to have assisted in the compilation of the *I Ching*. The term "Mr. Chou" has ever since been associated with dreaming, and even today, a student dozing in class is likely to be awakened by his teacher with the question, "Have you been visiting Mr. Chou?"

Seven categories of dreams are discussed in the *T'ung Shu*. One deals with "Heaven and the Weather," indicating, for example, that if one dreams about the sun or moon rising, one's family will be healthy, prosperous, and well educated. Another category is "Houses, Gardens, Forests, Etc.": To dream of an orchard bowed down with ripe fruit portends that one will have numerous children and grandchildren. The category "Human Body" states that dreaming about having teeth fall out signifies one's parents are in danger. The "Animals and Birds" category notes, "A parrot calling you signifies a major quarrel, and a swallow flying to you means that a friend will come to visit you from far away." Under the category "Clothing and Jewelry" is the statement that to dream of a clear mirror indicates good fortune, but to dream of a cloudy mirror is a bad sign. It's recognized that puns contribute to understanding dreams. In order to comprehend some of the initially strange interpretations, one has to be aware, for example, that the words for "coffin" and "financial windfall" sound alike.

Chuang-tzu (350 B.C.), or Master Chuang, was associated with the development of Taoism. Taoists believe that everything in the material world is relative; concepts exist only as contrasts, but behind duality and illusion is a unifying, primary principle called the Tao. The emphasis upon duality and illusion is beautifully captured in the classic dream of Chuang-tzu, mentioned in my first chapter, in which he tried to decide whether he was a man or a butterfly dreaming.

The *Lie-tseu* is a Taoist work that defines several classes of dreams, such as ordinary dreams (without previous emotion), dreams of terror, dreams of thought (what one thought about during the day), dreams of waking (what one said during the day), and dreams of joy. The work discusses how everything is in union, the correspondence between the microcosm and the macrocosm, and the concept of Yin and Yang energy. If Yin is strong, for example, one might dream about crossing water; if Yang is strong, one might dream of walking through a great fire. The powerful need for harmony and reciprocity leads to what we would currently call "compensation" in dream function: a sated man might dream of giving or a hungry man of taking. If one dreams of singing and dancing, one will weep. The role of physical factors was also considered; it is mentioned that if one sleeps lying on a belt, one dreams of a snake. In order to interpret a dream, one must also take into account the year and season when it occurred, as well as the positions of the sun, moon, and stars.

Incubation of dreams in temples was widely practiced. Various preparatory rituals, including burning incense, were carried out before the image of the temple god. If the supplicant had a dream, he or she would go through a further step of divination to determine whether the dream was really sent by a god. If it was thought to come from a god, the dreamer would carefully study the dream or consult a dream interpreter to decide on a course of action. In the province of Fu-Kien, it was customary for people to sleep on a grave to induce a dream revelation. The Buddhist monk, Kwan Hiu (832–912 A.D.), recited a prayer so that his dreams would reveal the likeness of a saintly figure known as an Arhat. He eventually painted the sixteen Arhats with bushy eyebrows, drooping cheeks, and high noses. In honor of this artist, a temple was erected called the "Hall of the Arhats Corresponding to Dreams."[20]

Incubation temples also served a political function among the Chinese up to around the sixteenth century. Before any high official visiting a city was accepted, he had to spend his first night in a temple of the city's god to receive dream guidance for his mission. Judges and other government officials were also required periodically to seek dreams in these temples to obtain the insight and wisdom necessary for balanced political judgment. It's fascinating to speculate what would happen if our government encouraged its officials to spend some nights in a dream temple, seeking and sharing guiding dreams.

INDIAN BELIEFS

The sacred books of wisdom in India, called the Vedas, were written sometime between 1500 and 1000 B.C. Various favorable and unfavorable dreams are recounted there; for example, to ride an elephant is a lucky dream, while to ride a donkey is an unlucky one. The goddess Usas is described as being able to drive away the effects of evil dreams, and several verses or hymns are available which could be sung to dispel evil dreams. The effects of bad dreams could also be counteracted by rites of purification or various types of baths.

The Atharva Veda indicates that images of violence and aggression were considered to lead to success and happiness if the dreamer were actively and assertively engaged in carrying out these activities. The positive outcome held even if the dreamer became mutilated as a result. Should the dreamer, however, passively experience an injury or amputation, or any other bodily defect, such as loss of hair or teeth, it was considered an ill omen. These dreams might be thought to express character structure rather than prophecy per se, since it would make intuitive sense to believe that those who take an active role in their dreams are likely to be more active, and therefore more successful, in their daily lives.

The Atharva Veda also contains some provocative speculations concerning the relation between dreams from different periods of the night and the time of their expected realization. It suggests that dreams from the first period of sleep will not come true for a year and those of the second period for eight months, while those arising from the last part of the night are already half realized. Along somewhat similar lines, it proposed that if several dreams succeed each other only the last should be interpreted. This sophisticated notion implies that the temporal unfolding of dreams reflects a hierarchical arrangement of psychological motivation. In this schema, the issues underlying our first dreams of the night have not yet been fully processed psychologically and will therefore take longer to be assimilated into waking life, while the last dreams deal with material whose mental gestation has almost been completed and which will soon be expressed in daytime activities. The last of a succession of dreams can be understood to represent our most up to date reaction to the material being digested by our dreaming mind.

The Upanishads, written between 900 and 500 B.C., are primarily philosophical treatises dealing with personal salvation and deliverance from the material world. In the Brhadaranyaka Upanishad, there are two theories about dreams. One is psychological and proposes that particular objects appear in dreams as expressions of the dreamer's inner desires: "There are no (real) chariots in that state, no horses, no roads but he himself (creates) chariots, horses, and roads. . . . He indeed is the maker."[21] In the other theory, a metaphysical one resembling that described by the Chinese, the soul leaves the body during sleep and wanders to distant locations where it encounters the horses and roads, which exist externally. If a sleeping person were to be suddenly awakened, the soul might not have adequate time to return to the body and the person could die.

In this same Upanishad is an outline of the different states of the soul:

> There are two views with regard to the different states of the soul. One of them makes a distinction between the waking and dreaming states while the other regards them as having no real distinction. Another state of the soul, *viz*, the state of dreamless sleep or deep sleep, is the state in which the individual soul becomes identical with the Absolute.[22]

The concept of reincarnation seems apparent in a proposal put forth by Dvivedagana concerning the existence of another world: "In early childhood, our dreams consist of the impressions of a former world, later on they are filled with the impressions of our senses, and in old age they contain visions of a world to come."[23]

The Sushruta Samhita, a collection of medical and surgical lore, was compiled about 600 B.C. by the surgeon Sushruta.[24] It contains several comments about the interpretation of dreams, particularly those dealing with illness. Prophetic dreams play an important part in the great Indian epics, the *Ramayana*, composed around 200 B.C., and the *Mahabharata*, composed between that time and 200 A.D.

GREEK BELIEFS

The earliest references to dreams among the Greeks are found in Homer's epic poems. Dreams are associated with important turning points in the lives of his heroes. Homeric dreams usually have a divine origin and are sent to the dreamer. In the *Iliad*, Zeus is the god who sends dreams to chosen people, and the recipient is always a male; in the *Odyssey*, it is Athene who sends dreams, and the recipients are female. The messages sent are generally straightforward and direct, and their meaning is readily understood.

There are several important exceptions to these general patterns, however. In the *Iliad* it is the spirit of the deceased Patro-

clus, rather than a deity, that appears to Achilles in a dream and demands a burial. The *Iliad* also describes a dream experience still encountered frequently in modern times, the dream of being unable to run successfully in a chase; Achilles' efforts to overtake Hector under the walls of Troy are likened to the sensations of paralysis common in dreams.

An example of an allegorical dream, in which neither a deity nor deceased spirit is involved, is Penelope's dream of the geese and the eagle in the *Odyssey*. In her dream, she has twenty geese that she joyously feeds in her house; a great eagle comes from the mountain, breaks the necks of the geese with his crooked beak, and throws them in a heap. Penelope is later told in her dream that the eagle represents her husband who will deal harshly with his wife's suitors on his return.

In the Greek tragedies, dreams seldom come from divinities. Most are instead allegorical in nature, and therefore require interpretation. In *Prometheus Bound* by Aeschylus, dream interpretation, or oneiromancy (based on the Greek word for dream, *oneiros*), was regarded as one of the important signs of civilization. Prometheus declared himself to be the pioneer teacher of the art.

The allegorical dreams in the tragedies are prophetic and experienced by women. I will discuss one to give a flavor of their content. In *Choephoroe* by Aeschylus, a dream of Clytemnestra is described. Queen Clytemnestra has murdered Choëphori, her husband, with the help of her lover, because he had sacrificed their daughter to the gods. In her dream, she gives birth to a snake which draws blood as well as milk from her breasts. The queen interprets her dream as representing the anger of her dead husband and therefore sends gifts to pacify his spirit. Her son Orestes instead interprets the serpent to be himself and concludes that he must kill his own mother. He eventually kills her and her lover and is later punished, because of another dream experienced by the Furies, the feminine deities of revenge.

Of course, I cannot refer to the Greek tragedies without drawing attention to the most famous tragedy of all, the one immortalized by Sigmund Freud—*Oedipus Rex*. In this drama by Sophocles, when Oedipus finally becomes aware that he has been

sleeping with his own mother, he attempts to shun her bed. His mother, Jocasta, tells him that he should "have no fear of the bridal alliance with thy mother," because "many among mankind" have "done incest with a mother" in their dreams.

The dramatists' conception of dreams can be seen to have moved from a more fixed locus in the epics, where direct messages were sent from deities to a sleeping person, to a view in which psychological factors predominated. Dreams had come to be seen as rooted in the important events and emotional experiences of the dreamer's waking life.

The earliest Greek view of dreams was that a real god made a tangible visit in a recognizable physical form. Since Greek rooms had no point of entry except for the door, it was thought that the deities entered through the keyhole, delivered their message while standing at the head of the bed, and then exited by the same keyhole. This view is similar to that encountered in Mesopotamian message dreams. Dreams were a passive experience for the Greeks. They 'saw' dreams but did not 'have' dreams. During the fifth century B.C., the idea was introduced through contact with other cultures, probably Indian, that the soul was able to leave the body, take trips, or visit with the gods. The fifth century B.C. is also when the first recorded dream book in Greek came into existence. It apparently was written by Antiphon, an Athenian statesman.

Aesculapius is thought to have been a healer who lived during the eleventh century B.C. and later became deified. In his deified form, he was the son of Apollo and received his medical training from the centaur Chiron. He was eventually able to affect miraculous cures, including restoring the dead to life, but aroused the anger of Hades by transcending the destiny of a mortal and Zeus struck him dead with a thunderbolt. The first shrine to Aesculapius in Athens was established in the fifth century B.C. by Sophocles. Other shrines dedicated to Aesculapius were quickly constructed, and over three hundred active temples were still functioning throughout Greece and the Roman Empire in the second century A.D. These shrines were dedicated to healing, and dreams became the principle vehicle for securing relief or a cure of physical symptoms.

Mesopotamians and Egyptians practiced dream incubation, but under the Greeks, the practice became a highly developed art. The person seeking a healing dream went through rather elaborate preparatory procedures, which varied from temple to temple. Generally the person had to refrain from sexual intercourse, follow a special diet, and engage in frequent cold water bathing. Animal sacrifices were made and the dreamer would sleep upon the skin of the animal sacrificed, which was often a ram. Evening prayers or hymns were held during the "hour of the sacred lamps," at which time the supplicants would beseech Aesculapius to provide them with their desired dream. Within the temples were statues of the god and testimonial plaques from previous visitors regarding their healings. In some temples, snakes, the emblem of Aesculapius, crawled about on the floor (we preserve the association of snakes with healing in the caduceus, the modern symbol of the medical profession). After the torches were

extinguished, priests would move about among the expectant devotees with words of encouragement. It's obvious that the preparations involved—the purification rites, the sacrifices, the prayers—as well as the atmosphere created by the god's statue, the testimonials, and the priests' exhortations, created a situation in which the role of suggestion would be greatly enhanced.

When Aesculapius appeared to the dreamer, he would indicate what type of medicine should be administered or what course of action the person should follow. Sometimes female members of the god's family, such as his daughters Hygeia or Panacea, served as the healing figures.[25] At a later date, the role of the interpreters became more pronounced and they indicated the appropriate treatment on the basis of the dream recounted to them. For example, one person suffering from pleurisy was told by a priest to take some ashes from the temple altar, mix them with wine, and apply the mixture to his side.

Aristides, who lived from around 530 to 468 B.C., contributed the earliest continuous dream diary known to western civilization.[26] It has been estimated that his dream diary originally ran to some three hundred thousand lines.[27] Portions have been lost, but the bulk appears in his five books entitled *Sacred Teachings*. Many of these dreams include descriptions of the manner in which Aesculapius appeared, spoke, and acted in Aristides' dreams. The medical solutions proffered by Aesculapius often involved such harsh treatments as bathing in frigid streams, undergoing mud baths in freezing weather, running barefoot in winter, or taking hot baths for more than five years. These prescriptions seem almost penitential in nature. If they originated from Aesculapius, he sounds like a somewhat sadistic god; if they originated from Aristides, he apparently had a rather masochistic nature.

Many accounts of cures associated with Aesculapius have been published in translation.[28] Some come from literary sources and rely primarily on the comic poets Aristophanes and Plautus. Many of the temple inscriptions were written or supervised by priests, and some were clearly fictional: supplicants with missing eyeballs were able to see from the sockets; a woman who had been pregnant for five years delivered a child that washed its face and walked immediately after being born; a broken goblet placed in a bag was withdrawn in perfect condition. It seems probable that some actual nocturnal surgery may have been performed on the supplicants. Several accounts describe embedded spearpoints or arrowheads being withdrawn and placed in the supplicant's hands; Aesculapius is described as cutting the body open, withdrawing leeches or lancing internal abscesses, and sewing the wound closed. Blood was sometimes present on the floor of the *abaton*, the chamber where the supplicants slept, the following morning. Barren women reported having intercourse with a snake in their dreams or dreaming that a handsome youth lifted up their tunic and fondled them.

The most famous shrine to Aesculapius was established at Epidaurus around the fifth century B.C. Its beautiful pastoral setting was about five miles inland from the sea, and visitors can still enjoy its beauty today. This center was gradually built over a period of 100 or 150 years.

The limestone temple honoring Aesculapius was built in 370 B.C. and took four years and eight months to complete. It measured seventy-six by thirty-nine feet. A nearby hotel (*katagogion*) contained 160 rooms and several *abatons*. There was also a temple to Hygeia, an altar, a place for votive offerings, a sacred well, and a library. A stadium that held fourteen thousand spectators was added later. Other sites, such as those at Pergamos and Cos, were also set in magnificent landscapes, and the exquisite beauty of these natural environments helped to establish a harmony between the external and internal worlds of the supplicant. In order for a new site to be affiliated with the central one at Epidaurus, a holy snake from Epidaurus was ritualistically transported to the center.

HIPPOCRATES

Hippocrates (469–399 B.C.), a contemporary of Socrates, has been called the father of Greek medicine. The "Hippocratic Collection," includes nearly one hundred medical works circulating from the Alexandrian medical school. How many he actually authored is a matter of dispute, but at least one essay in the collection, "On Dreams," is considered to have been written by Hippocrates himself. His theory was that the sense organs were predominant during the day while the soul was passive, but that during sleep the emphasis shifted, and the soul then produced images and impressions instead of receiving them. This cycle of sleeping and waking was mediated by changes in blood temperature: "When we feel the desire to sleep, our blood cools down." He placed emphasis upon the four humors (blood, phlegm, yellow bile, and black bile), as well as the corresponding principal organs (heart, brain, liver, and spleen).

Hippocrates believed in prophetic dreams, diagnostic dreams, and psychologically revealing dreams. With regard to diagnostic dreams, he maintained that a humoral imbalance could be detected by noting whether dreaming events repeated the events of waking life in a concordant fashion or whether irregular and discordant patterns were present. Atypical astrological configurations, for example, could indicate that bodily tension or disturbance was present. The body was judged to be optimally functioning if a dream depicted the heavenly bodies shining brightly and in their usual places. If a star appeared dim and placed above its usual position, difficulties in the region of the head were indicated, while a downward placement signified a disease of the bowels. Dreaming of overflowing rivers meant an excess of blood, dreams of springs indicated bladder trouble, and dreams of barren trees were associated with insufficient seminal fluid. Hippocrates was interested in discerning how disharmonious dreams could detect somatic malfunctioning, but he also displayed great astuteness regarding their psychological source. His comment on this aspect of dreams sounds amazingly modern: "All the objects we believe to see indicate a wish of the soul."[29]

PLATO

Plato (427–347 B.C.) was interested in the emotional implications of dreams and proposed a very psychodynamic formulation of dreaming. In the ninth book of the *Republic*, he asserted: "In all of us, even in good men, there is a lawless wild beast nature which peers out in sleep." Plato pointed out that since reasoning ability was suspended during sleep, the passions of desire and anger could reveal themselves with full force. Incest, murder, and sacrilege might thus be the activities pursued in dreams, although the dreamer would also be capable of experiencing morally superior dreams if reason were stimulated.[30]

ARISTOTLE

Plato's student, Aristotle (384–322 B.C.) argued against an astrological interpretation of dreams and rejected the notion of their divine origin. Animals were also observed to dream, he argued, and the gods would never send dreams to such lowly creatures. His theories were outlined in three brief books: *On Dreams*, *On Sleep and Waking*, and *On Prophecy in Sleep*. Aristotle proposed that dreams could be sensitive indicators of bodily conditions. Since the perception of external stimuli is reduced or absent during sleep, greater attention would be focused upon minimal internal sensations; awareness of somatic disturbances would therefore be more pronounced than during the waking state and could be represented in dream imagery. (Dreams portending *future* somatic dysfunction are known as "prodromal" dreams and will be discussed in chapter 13.)

Another of Aristotle's contributions was to point out that dream images may serve as the starting point for waking thoughts and thus may stimulate waking behavior similar to that in the dream. Such dreams might then erroneously be viewed as prophetic, when in fact their link to events was causal. Since many different dreams are dreamed, he said, coincidence was the most reasonable explanation for other apparently prophetic dreams. Aristotle made an extremely insightful deduction when he wrote, "The most skillful interpreter of dreams is he who has the faculty of observing resemblances." Such resemblances may involve similar shapes, colors, textures, actions, or the sounds of words (puns).

GALEN

Galen was a Greek physician, born around 130 A.D., who began his training at a medical school attached to the shrine of Aesculapius in Pergamum. His works had a great impact upon European medicine; a translation of his book *Parts of the Body*

runs to 802 pages in English.[31] A dream at age seventeen caused him to shift his program of study from philosophy to medicine. He felt dreams had diagnostic utility and indicated imbalances of bodily substances. Dreaming about fire indicated yellow bile problems, for example, while dreaming of smoke or fog signaled black bile problems. Disturbing dreams could also alter the pulse rate.

Evaluation of dream imagery was complicated, he noted, because dreams sometimes reflect memory of waking actions and at other times are prophetic. Galen trusted dreams sufficiently to be willing to carry out operations on the basis of dream-received guidance and claimed he had saved many lives as a consequence. His positive views are conveniently summarized in this statement: "It is necessary to observe dreams accurately both as to what is seen and what is done in sleep in order that you may prognosticate and heal satisfactorily."[32]

ROMAN BELIEFS

The Romans were influenced by the Greeks and established several shrines for dream incubation. A novel proposal about dreaming was advanced by Lucretius, a Latin poet who lived from 98 to 55 B.C. He suggested that dreams actually consisted of separate stationary images but an illusion of motion was created because the images replaced one another so rapidly. This statement could be easily embraced by some current neurophysiological theorists if the images were considered to arise from neu-

ronal discharges in the brain, but Lucretius attributed their source to outside sensations. In light of his proposal, Lucretius struggled with the problem of accounting for the close parallelism between dream images and the dreamer's character. He gave an extremely clear description of the predisposing role of "day residue" when he wrote:

Generally to whatever pursuit a
man is closely tied down and

strongly attached, on whatever subject we have much previously dwelt, the mind having been put to more than usual strain in it, during sleep we, for the most part, fancy that we are engaged in the same.[33]

One of the great cynics about dreams was the Roman orator Cicero (104–8 B.C.). As an indication of the inconclusiveness of dreams, he gave several examples of contrasting interpretations offered for the same dream. In one, a runner who intended to run in the Olympic games dreamed that he was being driven in a chariot drawn by four horses. One interpreter told him he would win his race because the qualities of strength and swiftness, suggested by the horses, would be with him; another said he would lose because the horses reached the goal before he did.

Some measure of the disdain in which Cicero held dream interpreters is apparent in this remark: "Even if true interpretations of dreams could exist, it is certainly not in the possession of those who profess it, for these people are the lowest and most ignorant of the people."[34] He concluded that because dreams had such infinite variety, and the same dreams could be followed by different results for different people, it would be impossible to ever discover any "order or regularity" in them or to make them a topic of research or experiment. As a consequence of his conclusion, he proposed:

> Let us reject, therefore, this divination of dreams, as well as all other kinds. For, to speak truly, that superstition has extended itself through all nations, and has oppressed the intellectual energies of all men, and has betrayed them into endless imbecilities.[35]

ARTEMIDORUS OF DALDIS

Artemidorus, a contemporary of Galen, was born in Ephesus, an ancient Greek city that was the birthplace of many famous men, but he chose to inscribe his book *Oneirocritica* ("The Interpretation of Dreams"), with the name Artemidorus of Daldis so that the small, obscure town in Lydia that was the birthplace of his mother would be memorialized. Little else is known of his life except that he authored earlier works dealing with such topics as augury (divination). Most of what is known about Artemidorus comes from autobiographical comments within his dream book.

The first complete English translation of *Oneirocritica* from the Greek was carried out by Robert White, a member of the classics department at Hunter College, as part of his doctoral dissertation at Yale University. White published his translation as a book in 1975.[36]

The *Oneirocritica* is an extraordinary encyclopedia of dreams and contains five books. The first three, containing a unified and structured treatise on dream interpretation, were intended for the general public; the last two were intended for the private use of Artemidorus's son, a novice dream interpreter. White provides extensive scholarly notes for each of the five books and includes an index of all the dream topics and people mentioned in the text. Perhaps the easiest way for the reader to grasp the breadth of the *Oneirocritica* is to survey the topics contained in some of the books, and to sample the comments given by Artemidorus.

BOOK 1

In book 1, Artemidorus covers eighty-two numbered units, dealing primarily with dreams about the human body and its activities. (A unit in these books may be as brief as two sentences or as long as four pages.) The classification of topics is very thorough and extremely orderly. In dealing with the human body, Artemidorus literally covers it from head to toe. He starts with variations in the size of heads and in the kind of hair on the head, then continues downward, mentioning in order the forehead, ears, eyebrows, eyes, nose, cheeks, jaws, beard, teeth, tongue, vomit, neck, shoulders, chest, arms, body wounds, penis, thighs, knees, shin bones, ankles, and toes. Dreams of being beheaded fall, appropriately, between discussions of the neck and of the shoulders. The subsequent categories concern bodily transformations; physical or craft activities, such as pruning vines, forging metal, and writing; the consumption of food and beverages; and forms of sexual activity.

As an example of an interpretation associated with a specific group of objects, Artemidorus says in unit 52: "All tools that cut and divide things in half signify disagreements, factions, and injuries. . . . Tools that smooth out surfaces predict an end to enmities."

BOOK 2

Book 2 contains seventy units dealing primarily with dreams about objects and events that occur in the natural world. Categories include clothing, weather, fire, animals, bodies of water, the gods, deceased individuals, flying, and numbers in dreams. Concerning the weather, Artemidorus indicates in unit 8: "A sky that is clear and bright is a good sign for everyone. . . . But a sky that is gray, gloomy or full of clouds, signifies failures and afflictions." In unit 68, dealing with flying, Artemidorus proposes: "But it is best of all to fly at will [wishing to soar above] and to stop at will. For it foretells great ease and skill in one's business affairs."

The same exhaustive approach employed in book 1 appears in book 2. Under animals, for example, his listing displays an orderly subgrouping of related animals: domestic mammals (dogs to oxen), wild mammals (lions to wild boars), reptiles (snakes and chameleons), sea creatures (fish and frogs), and creatures of the air (birds and insects). In unit 12, he observes: "There is an affinity between all wild animals and our enemies. A wolf signifies a violent enemy. . . . A fox indicates that the enemy will not attack openly but will plot underhandedly."

BOOKS 3, 4, AND 5

Book 3 has sixty-six units covering topics which are "somewhat loose and disconnected" but included for the sake of completeness. In unit 8, Artemidorus indicates: "Bugs are symbols of cares and anxieties. For bugs, like anxieties, also keep people awake at night." Thorns and prickles are dealt with in unit 33; they "signify griefs because they are sharp, hinderances because they are capable of holding onto objects, and anxieties and sorrows because they are rough."

Book 4 has eighty-four units and deals primarily with suggestions to his son with regard to his role as a dream interpreter. It also serves as sort of a "how to" manual on techniques of interpretation. The dream interpreter needs to know "the dreamer's identity, occupation, birth, financial status, state of health and age"[37] and to "examine closely the habits" of the dreamer.[38] The interpreter "should learn local customs and the peculiarities of every place," so that interpretations can be in accordance with them.[39] Every detail of the dream, and how the dreamer felt about each detail, should be ascertained. The internal structure of the dream also must be evaluated to determine if the events were plausible or bizarre, appropriately interconnected, and customary for the dreamer. Before offering any interpretation, Artemidorus advised his son: "You must consider the systematized totality of the dream images."[40]

Book 5 is a collection of ninety-five dreams that Artemidorus had collected, the outcomes of which he had personally verified. These examples were intended as practice materials for his son and as generic models to illustrate how individual variations arose from general principles.

AN APPRAISAL OF ARTEMIDORUS

Artemidorus indicates that he took special pains to procure every book written on dreams and consulted with interpreters in the marketplace for years. "Field research" took him to many cities in Greece, Asia Minor, Italy, and the larger islands. Near the end of book 2, he emphasizes the empirical basis for his statements:

> I have always called upon experience as the witness and guiding principle of my statements. Everything has been the result of personal experience, since I have not done anything else, and have always devoted myself, day and night, to the study of dream interpretation.[41]

In book 4, he again describes his pragmatic approach and indicates the original nature of his contributions:

> I did not rely upon any simple theory of probabilities but rather on experience and the testimony of actual dream-fulfillments. Furthermore, wherever early writers

planted only the seeds of an interpretation without working it out completely, I elaborated upon their ideas by making subtle but irrefutable distinctions. In addition to this, I included all those things that either pointed to a new outcome or which were themselves entirely new.[42]

The *Oneirocritica* can be considered the great-grandfather of all dream books and stands as an impressive monument to the dedication and diligence of its author. It is a model of thorough and detailed taxonomy, but at the same time it urges flexibility in attempts to derive the meaning of a particular dream for an individual dreamer. Artemidorus showed a sophisticated appreciation of symbolism and was very aware of the dreaming mind's capacity to employ metaphors and puns in communicating its messages.

I have given a few examples of his mastery of metaphors. Some of his metaphors are as relevant today as they were over eighteen hundred years ago when Artemidorus first offered them. Others can only be understood by knowing the customs, beliefs, and superstitions of his time.

The *Oneirocritica* is unique in several ways. It is the only surviving complete text from the twenty-seven books mentioned in antiquity. Its scope is enormous and covers practically every domain of dreaming as a psychological experience. Since we don't have the other books of that era to compare with the *Oneirocritica*, we have only Artemidorus's comments to go by, but it appears that these other books were very limited in their coverage of topics. The many examples given by Artemidorus concerning the actual procedures he followed in working with dreams did not seem to be covered in other dream books. Considering the eighteen hundred years since its introduction, the methods he proposed to understand a dream's meaning bear striking parallels to those followed by contemporary dream workers. His impressive contributions warrant Artemidorus a prominent place in the annals of dream history.

White, in his preface, offers some statements about dream history that I enthusiastically endorse:

> Although modern research has increased our knowledge of what goes on in the sleeping state, it seems in no way to have robbed dreams of their mystery or stripped them of their allure. Their study and interpretation continues to be a field with a future.
>
> It is also a field with a past: a heritage of considerable richness and complexity. In a sense, Freud, Jung, and others were not so much innovators as restorers, since they were reassigning to dreams and dream-readings the importance that they had held in antiquity, and which they had lost in more recent centuries. Assyrians, Egyptians, Hebrews, Greeks and Romans (to mention only the Mediterranean world) were all profoundly convinced of the significance of man's dreams. Indeed, the gravest personal, political, and economic decisions often rested upon their interpretation.[43]

CHAPTER 4

DREAMS AND DEMONS:

THE SECOND TO THE

EIGHTEENTH CENTURIES

I f every generation's task is to reexamine its past to see which concepts or ideas should be retained and which discarded as irrelevant to current cultural concerns, then it is important that we not discard our ancestors' views toward dreams. Instead, this history should alert us to possible ways to extend our range of dream experiences, which might assist us in regaining a more balanced view of our latent human potential.

Cicero's comments remind us that even in ancient times there were individuals dedicated to dream-slaying and nay-saying when it came to appreciating the promise of dreams. We can expect to encounter recycled Cicero comments in every century, our own included. Cicero's observations about the ambiguity which can arise when interpreting dreams should be kept in mind regardless of which historical period is under consideration.

To present briefly how the pattern of views toward dreams evolved since the time of Artemidorus, it will be necessary to consider the treatment different religious denominations and, to a limited degree, different cultures have accorded dreams. To organize a discussion of dream history on the basis of theological doctrines may seem surprising to the reader, but if one remembers that there has always been a close affinity between dreams and divine revelations, the decision will not seem so arbitrary. Knowledge of how supernatural figures were conceptualized enables one to comprehend better how dreams were viewed.

Since more information is available in English about dreams in the western world, my review will focus primarily upon that region. However, material from other regions will be given to contrast the more positive regard given to dreams by non-Europeans with the progressively greater disdain given to dreams by Europeans.

DREAMS IN THE NON-CHRISTIAN WORLD

As mentioned in chapter 2, dreams were an important source of inspiration for Muhammad, not only in his military conquests, but also in the establishment and development of his religion. Influenced by the personal example Muhammad set by discussing his disciples' dreams with them and by the statement in the Koran (12:6) that the science of dreams was "the prime science since the beginning of the world," Muhammad's followers have always given dreams a prominent place in their lives. G. E. von Grunebaum, a Near East historian, noted: "There is hardly any phase in the life of the community and the individual where dreams will not play a part."[1]

After the death of the Prophet of Islam in 632, a rich oral tradition of dream interpretation developed, and scattered references to specific dreams and the interpretations given to them have been preserved in chronicles dating from around 700 A.D. The most famous of the early Muslim interpreters was Ibn Sirin, who died in 728.

Many of his rules were taken down in writing by others and eventually collected and published in manuscripts bearing his name after the tenth century. Ibn Sirin became a sort of legendary figure, "a kind of abstract personage, the very incarnation as it were, of Arab oneiromancy."[2]

Toufy Fahd, Director of the Institute of Islamic Studies at the University of Strasburg, offers the opinion that "enriched by a Greek element working within like ferment, Arab-Muslim oneirocriticism reached heights no other civilization seems to have known."[3] It was claimed that seventy-five hundred dream interpreters existed in the tenth century. One line of enrichment came from Artemidorus, whose book was translated from the Greek into Arabic in 873 and helped to stimulate efforts to classify dreams. Another important Greek source was provided by *The Oneirocriticon of Achmet*. "Achmet" was the honorific pseudonym of a highly educated and well-traveled Christian

Greek who lived in the tenth century. This book provides the most erudite work on dreams from the Byzantine era of Greece, a period stretching from the fourth to the fifteenth century. An English translation of this medieval Greek and Arabic treatise on the interpretation of dreams became available in 1991. The book bears many similarities to the one provided by Artemidorus except that Achmet had access to the works of Arabic scholars and Byzantine Christians. Like Artemidorus, Achmet was insistent that the individual characteristics of the dreamer be taken into account when offering an interpretation:

> Dreams, as already stated, are judged in different ways for various people. For, given the same dream, there is one interpretation for a king, another for his subjects; one for a warrior, another for a farmer; one for a noble, another for a poor man; one for a man, another for a woman.[4]

The most important Arab-Muslim treatise was written by ad-Dinawari and appeared in 1006. In describing ad-Dinawari's book Fahd stated:

> It is an immense compilation bringing together the oneiric material as a whole, material reflecting all man's activities, his preoccupations, his social milieux, his religious concepts, his hopes and anxieties. The dream is like a screen on which is projected the daily life of every class in the society of tenth century Baghdad.

> Obviously influenced by Artemidorus, the thematic classifications developed in this rich compilation came to dominate all later tradition, which introduced only minor variations.[5]

Another important Muslim dream book was compiled by an-Nabulusi, who died in 1731. This two-volume work, comprising six hundred pages, contains an alphabetical listing of dream objects and their associated interpretations. Dream books, or *Tabir Namehs*, are found in all the principal languages of Islam-Arabic—Persian, Turkish, and Hindustani. Many of these books attempt to justify their interpretations by linking them to statements made by the Prophet or passages in the Koran.

Since dreams were so closely interwoven with Muslim life, the autobiographies of many prominent Muslim figures contain extensive dream diaries and accounts of decisions based upon dream revelations. Even in the twentieth century, important political actions were often ostensibly based on the dreams of Muslim leaders. One example concerned the Shah of Persia, Muzaffar ad-Din, when he was trying to decide whether to seek a loan from Russia in 1902. He dreamed that a famous theological figure dressed in primitive Muslim garb approached the Shah and threw at his feet a sack containing gold and silver. The fairly obvious interpretation of this dream was that the Shah shouldn't make any new loans with unbelievers but should trust that his subjects and fellow servants of the faith would restore his finances.[6]

Unlike the Greeks, Muslims did not generally associate dreams with medical cures, and nocturnal incubation of dreams wasn't practiced. Instead, the practice of *istikhara*, or seeking a dream by reciting a special daytime prayer, was developed.

The Hebrews' interest in dreams was clear in the Old Testament and was reflected in the Babylonian Talmud, written between 200 and 500 A.D. Four chapters on dreams appear in the opening tract of that book. The Jews' interest in dreams continued in the later centuries. As an article in the *Jewish Encyclopedia* recognized, "that the most famous teachers frequently discuss dreams and enunciate doctrines regarding them, shows the strong hold dreams had even on the intellectual leaders of Judaism."[7] Dreams were discussed in a favorable light by the eminent twelfth-century physician, rabbi, and philosopher, Maimonides, who believed that dreams were a kind of prophecy. He wrote, "The action of the imaginative faculty during sleep is the same as at the time when it receives a prophecy."[8]

The Chinese compiled some dream books (the *Meng Shu* around 640 and the *Meng Chan I Chih* in 1562), practiced incubation, and developed an appreciation of paintings containing dream figures. Chinese judges and other officials frequently went to temples to incubate dreams for guidance in civil affairs during the Middle Ages. In Japan, a tenth-century dream book has been lost, but many of its features are assumed to be present in the *Shomu Kikkyo Wago Sho*, published in 1712. An official class of Japanese dream interpreters called *om myoshi* developed, and the sick slept in temple sanctuaries where they hoped to see the boddhisattva Yakushi as a monk in their dreams. Dreams remained a topic of great interest in India, and around 810, the theologian Sankara wrote detailed and authoritative commentaries on the Vedic texts, in which dream beliefs have a prominent place.

This cursory review shows that the high regard for dreams, discussed in chapter 2 for the ancient cultures, remained fairly constant in later centuries for non-Europeans; succeeding generations made no efforts to divorce their dream life from their waking life or to deny dreams regular visitation rights.

EASTERN CHRISTIAN VIEWS

Within the branch of Christianity referred to as the eastern, or Greek, branch, there were several prominent bishops or officials, trained in Greek philosophy, who were associated with the Egyptian city of Alexandria around the third century. (In the fourth century the center of the Eastern church moved to Constantinople.) These early Greek Christian theologians espoused certain common views about dreams. One was that it was possible to experience God in dreams and another was that our irrational emotional experiences could erupt in dreams. Both of these concepts, strongly influenced by Plato's views of dreams, continued to be characteristic of the eastern church during the centuries under review in this chapter.

Some brief statements from early Greek Christians will be given to set their views in perspective. In the third century, Origen wrote that God provided dreams "for the benefit of the one who had the dream and for those who hear the account of it from him."[9] He declared that many pagans had been converted to Christianity by means of dreams. In the fourth century, Gregory of Nyssa wrote, "While the imagination of sleep naturally occurs in a like and equivalent manner for all, some, not all, share by means of their dreams in some more Divine manifestation."[10] Gregory apparently considered the prophetic dreams of the Bible to be closer to miraculous occurrences than to the realm of dreams. He was very aware that levels below the divine could be expressed in dreams:

> Most men's dreams are conformed to the state of their character . . . these fancies are nowhere framed by the intellect, but by the less rational disposition of the soul, which forms even in dreams the semblances of those things to which each is accustomed by the practice of his waking hours.[11]

For Gregory "the echoes of daily occupations" are often "framed with regard to the condition of the body," and he indicated, "the young man in the heat of youthful vigor is beset by fancies corresponding to his passions."[12] Gregory felt emotions arose from our animal heritage:

> For those qualities with which brute life was armed for self-preservation, when transferred to human life, became passions; for the carnivorous animals are preserved by their anger, and those which breed largely by their love of pleasure.[13]

Our animal tendencies, through "the alliance of thought," become "the parent of many varieties of sin."

Another Alexandrian bishop of this same period, Basil the Great, acknowledged that his dreams sometimes became a source of embarrassment to him, and he warned a friend that it was better not to sleep too hard, because this opened the mind to wild fancies. A century later, Saint John Chrysostom from Constantinople pointed out that the dreamer was not responsible for acts committed in dreams and should not feel disgraced by what he saw or guilty for what he did while dreaming. The cumulative weight of these opinions suggests that the early Greek church maintained a very balanced and comprehensive outlook toward dreams as both connecting us to a recognition of the divine and acting as conduits for the expression of baser human motives. The most eloquent spokesperson for the eastern Christian stance toward dreams was Synesius of Cyrene, in whose writings the pinnacle of praise for dreams was reached.

SYNESIUS OF CYRENE

Synesius of Cyrene was a married Greek convert in the fifth century who eventually became the bishop of Ptolemais. He wrote a short book, *On Dreams*,[14] which has been characterized by Morton Kelsey, an Episcopal minister, as "the most thoughtful and sophisticated consideration of dreams to be found until we come to the modern studies of Freud and Jung."[15] Synesius was the author referred to in chapter 2 who received editorial assistance for his writings while he was dreaming.

Synesius found dreams to be an almost inexhaustible source of riches. "I am not surprised that some have owed to sleep the discovery of a treasure; and that one may have gone to sleep very ignorant, and after having had in a dream a conversation with the Muses, awakened an able poet." For Synesius, dreams enable the soul to ascend "to a superior region" which allows it "the perfect inspections of true things." Some hint as to just how far the human spirit can soar in dreams is given in this lofty, almost astronautical passage:

> There is no law . . . in the way of the sleeper, to forbid him from rising from earth more happily than Icarus, from soaring above the eagles, or reaching a point above the loftiest spheres themselves. So one looks steadily upon the earth from afar, and discovers a land not visible even to the moon. It is also in

his power to hold converse with the stars and to meet the unseen gods of the universe.

Synesius recognized the extraordinary ability of the dreaming mind to engage in actions on multiple levels: "In dreams one conquers, walks, or flies simultaneously, and the imagination has room for it all; but how shall mere speech find room for it?" He repeatedly recognized the infinite flexibility of the imagination in dreams: "Nothing is so characteristic of dreams as to steal space and to create time. Then the sleeper converses with sheep and fancies their bleating to be speech, and he understands their talk. . . . I even think that myths take their authority from dreams, as those in which peacock, fox, and sea hold converse." He recognized that dreams are not "heedless of the animal in us" and said that we could have "a steady and much more distinct view of things below" in the dreaming state than when "mingled with the inferior elements" or emotions in our waking life.

With regard to divination through dreams, Synesius enthusiastically urges that:

> men should not despise it, but rather cultivate it, seeing that it fulfills a service to life. . . .
>
> This art of divination I resolve to possess for myself and to be-

queath to my children. In order to enter upon this no man need pack up for a long journey or voyage beyond the frontiers. . . . It is enough to wash one's hands, to keep a holy silence, and to sleep.

Of divination by dreams, each one of us is perforce his own instrument, so much so that it is not possible to desert our oracle there even if we so desired. . . . She repudiates neither race, nor age, nor condition, nor calling. She is present to every one, everywhere, this zealous prophetess, this wise counselor . . . to announce to us good tidings; in such wise as to prolong our pleasure by seeking joy beforehand; to inform against the worst so as to guard against and to repel it beforehand.

Dreams can also provide helpful assistance with intellectual tasks and problem solving. No other thing is so well calculated to join in man's pursuit of wisdom; and of many of those things which present difficulties to us awake, some of these it makes completely clear while we are asleep, and others it helps us to explain. . . . At one moment one seems like a man asking questions, and at another the same man discovering and in process of thought. It has frequently helped me to write books.

Synesius warns against resorting to dream books for help in understanding the dreams of a given individual, because each person has such a diversity of "imaginative spirit." One would not, he says, expect the same image from a plane mirror, a concave mirror, and a distorted one. To help a person discover the relation between waking life events and subsequent dream imagery, he encouraged that a dream journal be kept.

It would be a wise proceeding even to publish our waking and sleeping visions and their attendant circumstances. . . . We shall therefore see fit to add to what are called "day books" what we have termed "night books," so as to have records to remind us of the character of each of the two lives concerned.

Synesius advanced many more astute suggestions and observations about dreams. He was a fervent proponent of the many practical applications to be derived from cultivating dreams, as well as of the uplifting joy that can be experienced from the sense of communion with a higher spiritual source.

Synesius was a torchbearer, but there seemed to be no one willing to carry his torch in the western Christian church in the subsequent centuries. In fact, his views on dreams were completely omitted from the thirty-eight thick volumes contained in *A Select Library of the Nicene and Post-Nicene Fathers of the Christian Church*.[16] In the early part of the fourteenth century Nicephorus Gregoras, of Constantinople, had been very impressed by Synesius's "most remarkable work on Dreams," and had worked diligently to elucidate it by means of a lengthy commentary. An acceptable English translation of Synesius's work was not, however, available until 1930.

WESTERN CHRISTIAN VIEWS

Morton Kelsey has provided an extensive and scholarly review of how the dream has fared during various periods of Christianity. When Kelsey began to review what the early western Church leaders had written about dreams, he was surprised to discover that a great deal of material regarding dream views had been deleted in the English texts. The example of Synesius's complete omission from the contributions of the Church fathers has already been cited. In order to uncover what these early authors had said, he had to have a large number of volumes translated from Latin, a project that took approximately ten years to complete. Much of the material presented in the following pages is based upon Kelsey's research.

TERTULLIAN

Tertullian was a lawyer from Carthage who became a priest in Rome. Called the "creator of Christian Latin literature," he was influential in the third century. References to dreams were scattered throughout his many books. Tertullian summarized his theory of dreams and their relation to the Christian doctrine of revelation in his major work, *A Treatise on the Soul*. Eight chapters of this work were devoted to his study of sleep and dreams. His views remained prevalent in western Christianity for well over a thousand years, until the thinking of Thomas Aquinas came to dominate western Europe.

Tertullian was very knowledgeable about contemporary dream views and cited a large number of authors to refute the claims of the Epicureans that dreams had no validity. He believed that everyone, including sleeping infants, dreamed, and asked the question: "Now who is such a stranger to human experience as not sometimes to have perceived some truth in dreams?"[17]

Tertullian ridiculed the idea that the soul leaves the body in sleep, as if taking a vacation, and claimed that dreaming showed the soul was perpetually active and thereby gave proof of its immortality. The soul operated through the power of *ekstasis* (literally, "standing outside"), which enabled it to experience feelings such as joy, sorrow, and alarm, but since we were not masters of this power, we were not accountable for our feelings and actions. "We shall no more be condemned for visionary acts of sin, than we shall be crowned for imaginary martyrdom."[18] The ability of the soul to remember its dreams was "an especial gift of the ecstatic condition."

There were four sources of dreams, according to Tertullian. One was demons: "Dreams are afflicted on us mainly by demons, although they sometimes turn out to be true and favorable to us."[19] God was another source of dreams: "Almost the greater part of mankind get their knowledge of God from dreams."[20] Another category of dreams were those "which the soul itself apparently creates for itself from an intense application to special circumstances."[21] These were associated with "the action of nature" and might refer to weather or astronomical conditions. The final class involved dreams due "to what is purely and simply the ecstatic state and its peculiar conditions." Because the vigor of the soul emerges toward the end of the night, dreams are "more sure and clear" at that time. This last class seemed to invoke intense or bizarre imagery from the unconscious, because these dreams went "beyond the reach of ordinary expectation, usual interpretation, or the possibility of being intelligibly related."[22] After considering the factors of food, fasting, and sleeping positions, Tertullian dismissed as "ingenious conjecture" the possibility of somatic factors creating dreams.

Among the books widely circulated during the third century was the *Martyrdom of Saints Perpetua and Felicitas*. In his introduction to this book, Tertullian asserted that dreams were one of the gifts from God, a *charisma*, and this gift was not restricted to "the ancients" in the Bible but was "equally promised to us." Perpetua was a North African who described four of her dreams while she was imprisoned before her martyrdom. When she asked God for a dream that would reveal her fate, she saw a golden ladder reaching to the heavens with a dragon at its foot. Attached to the ladder were daggers and hooks to slash the careless who did not keep looking up. She saw herself and her fellow prisoners mount the ladder and awoke knowing that they must die. From the imagery in another dream, she recognized that the forthcoming agony and suffering were not caused by men, but by the power of Satan. Martyrdom was obviously a matter of concern to early Christians and there were other accounts of how the devout were prepared for this outcome in their dreams. Cyprian, who was bishop of Carthage in 250 A.D., when a new wave of Christian persecution began, was beheaded. In a dream beforehand, he saw a "young man of unusual stature" who revealed to him what was to happen and thereby prepared him to go on.

SAINT JEROME

Jerome was born into a wealthy Christian family in the fourth century. He read widely in Greek and Latin literature and collected a library of pagan classics which he treasured. He was also a student of the Bible and found himself conflicted over how to reconcile its teachings with those of the pagan writers he admired. He had an astonishing dream in which his dilemma became resolved. In his dream, he was dragged before the judgment seat, which was bathed in light, and asked about his identity. When he replied that he was a Christian, he was told that he was a liar because he followed Cicero instead of Christ. He was ordered to be scourged and he received numerous lashes. Jerome called out for mercy to the Lord and some bystanders fell to their knees and pleaded with the Judge to give Jerome a chance to repent. Jerome swore an oath and called out, "Lord, if ever again I possess worldly books, or if ever again I read such, I have denied you." After taking this oath, Jerome was dismissed in his dream. When he awakened, his eyes were drenched with tears and his shoulders were black and blue. He reported that he subsequently "read the books of God with a greater zeal than I had been giving to the books of men." Soon after this transforming dream, he went into the desert as a hermit.

Jerome later became a great Bible scholar and consultant, well versed in Greek and Hebrew. Pope Damasus I called him to Rome in 382 to translate the entire Bible into Latin, the official language of the Roman Empire. His translation, later known as the Vulgate, served as the authoritative Latin version of the Bible until the twentieth century. This literary event had a cataclysmic effect upon how dreams were viewed by western Christians for the next fifteen centuries. Jerome apparently deliberately mistranslated the Hebrew word for witchcraft, *anan*, which was considered a pagan superstitious practice, as (*observo somnia*), "observing dreams." The word *anan* appeared ten times in the Old Testament; seven times Jerome correctly interpreted it, as witchcraft or a closely related practice, such as divining; but in the other three cases, where the Hebrew text is specifically condemning witchcraft (*anan*), he redirected the condemnation against dreams.[23] Thus, the prohibition "you shall not practice augury or witchcraft" became "you shall not practice augury nor observe dreams." Since he had correctly inter-

preted *anan* seven times, Jerome was clearly aware of the word's accepted meaning, but somehow when it came to the statement of the law in Leviticus 19:26 and Deuteronomy 18:10, the meaning of *anan* was switched.

It's possible that the change was ordered by church officials, but Jerome may also have had personal reasons for his mistranslation. He obviously wished, after his conversion dream, to dissociate himself from pagan influences and practices. He considered it an "abomination" that idolaters "are accustomed to stretch out on the skins of sacrificial animals in order to know the future by dreams."[24] Jerome may have sought to shore up his defenses against his pagan impulses by insuring that prohibitions were erected against seeking dreams in the wrong places.

Kelsey also refers to some acrimonious exchanges between Jerome and his former friend Rufinus in which heresy charges were hurled at Jerome for not keeping the oath he made in his conversion dream. Other dreams were cited in their papers and Jerome mentioned personal dreams involving his own death and dreams in which he flew over lands, mountains, and seas. If he were able to negate the validity of dreams, Jerome could relax more about his death dreams and feel less embarrassed by his high-flying dreams, which may have seemed too pretentious for someone in the human role he played as head of a monastic community in Bethlehem.

Jerome's mistranslations changed the course of Christian belief and practice regarding dreams. Within two centuries, Gregory the Great, a Roman known as the "teacher of the Middle Ages," would cite the mistranslated passages in discouraging the faithful from giving too much attention to dreams. This link between dreams and forbidden practices had its main effect in the Latin-speaking western Christian church; the favorable view toward dreams in the eastern Christian church, which followed the Greek Bible, was not significantly altered.

MACROBIUS

Little is known of Macrobius except that he was a contemporary of Jerome known for his book, *Commentary on the Dream of Scipio*.[25] In the first part of his book, Macrobius reviewed the popular dream theory of his day and presented a classification system for dreams which had many similarities to that of Artemidorus. He included two types of dreams, however, not really considered by Artemidorus: the nightmare (*insomnium*) and a category of apparitions (*phantasma*), during which "in the moment between wakefulness and slumber . . . [one] imagines he sees specters rushing at him or wandering vaguely about." Included in the latter category were the *incubus*, a male demon who produced a sensation of weight while sexually possessing a woman, and the *succubus*, a female demon who seduced male dreamers. References to seductive demons, such as Lilith, had appeared in the Talmud but had not previously appeared in Christian writings.

The *Commentary* became an extremely influential book and thirty-seven printed editions appeared before 1700. It was the most important and well-known dream book in medieval Europe. Its inclusion of

the fear-inspiring sexual demons was to play a role in supporting the paranoia about evil spirits that developed during the later centuries.

SAINT THOMAS AQUINAS

Somewhere around the eleventh century, the Greek language was rediscovered in Europe and emphasized in French and Italian universities. The principal Greek influence on early Christianity had been Plato, but the emphasis now shifted to Aristotle. He claimed that the only way humans could know or comprehend reality was by sense experience and rational thought. Man was a "rational" animal and was most human when acting rationally and logically. Dreams, according to Aristotle, could not provide any information about the divine or the nonphysical world. Instead, they were natural phenomena arising primarily from somatic sources.

Saint Thomas Aquinas, in the thirteenth century, attempted to write all of Christian theology in Aristotelian language and categories. By following Aristotle's premises, Aquinas thought he would modernize Christianity. His *Summa Theologica* became the authoritative text in Catholic theological studies until after the second Vatican Council in the mid-1960s.

In considering the question of divination in dreams, Aquinas refers to the passage in Deuteronomy 18:10, "Let there not be found among you him who observes dreams," which had been mistranslated by Jerome. Aquinas concluded that divination would not be unlawful if dreams proceeded from divine revelation or natural causes:

But if divination of this kind arises from a revelation by demons with whom there is an agreement either openly because they have been invoked to this end, or implicitly because a divination of this kind is extended beyond what it can possibly reach, the divination will be unlawful and superstitious.[26]

Aquinas went on to describe four causes of dreams: two inward ones, arising from daytime preoccupations and from physical humors, and two outward ones, arising from physical sources (temperature or astrological forces) and from God or demons.

Aquinas's efforts to diminish the value of dreams must have created some conflict for him when he experienced a very non-Aristotelian dream. In his waking life, he had been struggling to complete a certain theological passage in the *Summa*, but every attempt to dictate it to his scribes had been unsuccessful. One morning he began to dictate the difficult passage as effortlessly as if he had been reading a manuscript aloud. When questioned about his new-found fluency by a surprised scribe, Aquinas explained that he had experienced a dream the night before in which he participated in a dialogue with the apostles Peter and Paul, who instructed him on how to deal with this difficult theological passage.

THE DARK AGES

The stage had now been set by the western Church fathers to relegate dreams to the nether regions. Jerome had altered the Bible to prohibit Christians from "observing dreams"; Macrobius's *Commentary*, containing the most widely acclaimed classification of dreams, warned of the dreaded incubus and succubus; and Aquinas, the Church's most authoritative theologian, had issued warnings about the possible direct or indirect invocation of demons in dreams.

Demons and devils became an obsessive concern for western Christians. The paranoid fear of their constant presence and their potential for evil is vividly portrayed in this statement by Martin Luther: "Yea, we are day and night beset with mil-

lions of devils; when we walk abroad, sit at our board, lie in our bed, legions of devils are round about, ready to fling whole hell into our hearts."[27]

Gaspar Peucer, writing on divination from a Calvinistic viewpoint in the 1500s, slightly elaborated the theories of Macrobius. After discussing divine dreams, he considered demons as possible sources of dreams. Peucer admonished that they could produce deceiving dreams such as those received during incubations at ancient pagan temples and in the visions of the Anabaptists. He felt that the investigation of dreams was dangerous, unless the dreamer were a man of God. Dreams from God were not sent "to everyone promiscuously, nor to those who strive after and ex-

This sixteenth-century engraving, Man Tormented by Demons, *illustrates that epoch's belief in devils, and the influence they had over sleep.*

pect revelations of their own opinion." Dreams from God were sent instead to "Holy Patriarchs and Prophets" to deal with "the governance of the church, with empires and their well ordering, and other remarkable events."[28]

The opening section of *De Magia*, written in 1598 by a Jesuit priest, Benedict Pererius, states that "most [dreams] should be entirely discredited." In another passage, he notes that "whenever the Scrip-

tures wish to point out something vain, tenuous, elusive and fallacious, they express it most frequently through comparison and similarity to dreams."[29] In a section entitled "Is a Christian permitted to examine dreams?" Father Pererius responds, "The answer to this is easy and immediate, for they are permitted to examine certain dreams but not others."[30]

Father Pererius indicates that some dreams are given by "divine inspiration" and others "are thrust upon mortals by the cunning and malice of the devil." Pererius reminds the reader that "the devil is most always implicated in dreams, filling the minds of men with poisonous superstition and not only uselessly deluding but perniciously deceiving them."[31] Father Pererius gives two main criteria for distinguishing dreams originating from the devil from other dreams. First, "If dreams take place frequently which are significant of future events or occult matters . . . it will be considered, and not rashly, that the initiator of the dream is the devil."[32] Second,

> If dreams that are obscene, repulsive and full of cruelty and impiety come so very often to sober, upright and religious men, it is not unjustly held that these dreams proceed from the devil. For the devil tries to pollute the bodies of sleeping men with impure dreams and defile them so that he may make their minds, when they awaken, somehow partners in his foulness.[33]

Similar concerns about the linkage between Lucifer and sexual perversity in dreams were expressed by Father Gracian, the confessor of Saint Theresa:

> Other dreams are evil, sent by the devil, and often show obscene images, and some stir up the humors of the body and provoke sensual movement, against which the Church sings: "Remove dreams and nocturnal phantasies from me,

and restrain our enemy so that our bodies will not be sullied."[34]

Moral Christians were gravely concerned with threats of "sullying." In a treatise published in 1657, Philip Goodwin referred to other statements (apparently by Luther) about "our foes, sin and Satan, [who were] the friends and fathers of filthy dreams." The language used to describe an erotic dream was often quite lyrical. Goodwin referred to a condition in which "a man's Delilah-lust . . . leaneth upon his lap in his sleep." He also provided a graphic account of the outcome of a pollution dream: "In the midst of man's sleep, may this sin arise and run out in his dreams."[35] The appearance of sexual dreams was dreaded because "it is certain men's sinful lusts have no allowance from God's law in time of sleep."[36]

Father Gracian had warned that "it is a sin to believe in dreams." Aside from a belief in them, dreaming itself had now become a hazardous nocturnal activity. The church was always diligently looking for sinners who might be in collusion with or possessed by satanic forces. Since in dreams "much of Satan, in his subtle designs, may hereby come to be discovered," dreams provided a bountiful hunting ground for inquisitors seeking evidence of Lucifer's cloven hoofprints. Based on the pronouncements quoted above, one might assume that a suspect was in grave trouble if it was determined that he or she had dreams "significant of future events," containing "obscene" imagery, "full of cruelty," or displaying "impiety." Since sexual and aggressive imagery have apparently always been prominent in dreams, and since precognitive dreams are not that rare, there was a strong probability that any individual reporting a dream would be found guilty under these "devil-detecting" guidelines. Such an unfavorable verdict could lead either to severe torture, so that the devil would leave the dreamer alone, or to burning at the stake, for those whose dreaming minds had become the permanent abode of the devil.

It is understandable that people would not want to risk such disastrous consequences by talking about their dreams and would fervently hope they would not recall even the slightest trace of a dream. Martin Luther prayed to God for lack of dream recall, so that he would not have to face the difficult task of deciphering whether a dream had come from God or Satan. Dreaming became something people tried actively to suppress.

Why did demonology come to play such a prominent role in later western Christian concerns about dreams? Was celibacy a factor? (An Eastern Orthodox priest may keep his wife if marriage occurs before ordination; Roman Catholic priests take a vow of perpetual chastity.) Judging from autobiographical accounts, the Catholic saints were constantly tempted and struggled to remain vigilant against carnal desires. It would not be surprising if celibate priests frequently experienced seminal emission or "pollution" dreams. Since Aristotle made no provision for unconscious libidinal drives to be expressed in dreams, the source of these foul and polluting dreams had to be attributed to an external source: the Devil. If Plato's internal "wild beast" was denied by Aristotelians, then an external wild beast had to replace it through projection. If Christians couldn't acknowledge the devil within, they had to fight an ever more intensive crusade against the Devil without. Dreams were not viewed as allies, which could help discharge libidinal energy in harmless, tension-reducing imagery, but as enemies to be avoided or vigorously combated.

Dreams, in effect, had been banished, and we see here, as later in the case of Nazi Germany, what happens to a culture when the authorities limit people's autonomy and prevent creativity from flourishing by discouraging them from "observing their dreams." Dreams reflect our wholeness, our possession of interrelated somatic, emotional, and spiritual components of existence. Our stature as human beings seems to shrivel whenever dreams are banished, or whenever an effort is made to restrict the range within which they operate. We need dreams to enlarge our individual and collective aspirations. Acceptance of the personal freedom experienced in dreams may stimulate efforts to seek political freedom in waking life. In George Orwell's *1984*, disobedience to Big Brother starts in a dream.

The Dark Ages took a terrible toll, not only on thousands of innocent victims tortured or slowly burned alive, but on an entire population, whose collective creative pursuits in the arts, literature, and sciences were squelched for centuries. Some have characterized it as an age of "cultural squalor." The lesson to be learned from these tragic dream-dismissing periods of history seems inescapable. When we fail to honor that which is illuminated in our dreams in dark bedrooms, we will spend more of our daylight hours dwelling in the dark cells of self-imposed solitary confinement.

The mistrust of dreams has remained fairly persistent in many western Christian denominations, particularly Catholicism. Father Meseguer, a Jesuit priest, presented the modern Catholic viewpoint toward dreams in his 1960 book, *The Secret of Dreams*. He displayed a strong Aristotelian emphasis on rationality and consciousness in a section entitled "Limitations on the Part of the Nature of Dreams":

> The first and most fundamental limitation is that the normal means of directing human life to its proper ends is the conscious mind, understanding and will, which occupies the responsible centre of our being and makes us persons. The invasion of the conscious by the unconscious eventually leads to madness, through intermediate states which become more morbid with the progressive invasion by the unconscious. . . . From which it follows that dreams, the typical product of this unconscious state, are not the function best qualified to regulate conscious conduct. . . .
>
> Many authorities agree that in dealing with children, one should not use dreams. Generally speaking, I think that this should be extended to include young people. . . .
>
> The special dangers that this "descent to the depths," giving as it does official recognition to dreams—though controlled by faith and reason—represents for the individual in question should not be forgotten. They are, for example, that attributing too much importance to dreams can produce a tendency to live in a world of fantasy; that violent temptations may be unleashed; or that he may become aware of instincts which, if he lacks the maturity to understand and direct them, were better kept from his knowledge.[37]

SECULAR DREAM BELIEFS IN THE SEVENTEENTH AND EIGHTEENTH CENTURIES

After the Dark Ages, dreams come under increasing review by philosophers. The remarkable dreams of Descartes, and their wide-ranging impact, were discussed in chapter 2. His dualistic system gave strong emphasis to the independent role of the mind, but others increasingly began to emphasize the role of physical or somatic factors in creating our mental states. Thomas Hobbes was a seventeenth-century representative of this latter "mechanical" or "empirical" approach. He proposed that:

> Dreams are caused by the distemper of some of the inward parts of the Body; divers distempers must

needs cause different Dreams . . . lying cold breedeth Dreams of Fear . . . overheating of the same parts causeth Anger, and raiseth up in the brain the Imagination of an Enemy.[38]

These two contrasting points of views about dreams have continued up to the present. There are those who consider dreams as expressions of some relatively independent mental faculty, and those who look upon dreams as responses to internal humoral or neural events or external stimulation. In the seventeenth century, there was some reawakened recognition that the content of dreams bore a marked similarity to the concerns and character structure of the dreamer's personality. Sir Thomas Browne, a British physician, wrote:

Many dreames are made out by sagacious exposition and from the signature of their subjects. . . . Men act in sleepe with some conformity unto their awakened senses, and consolations and discouragements may be drawne from dreames, which intimately tell us ourselves.[39]

Even clearer on this point is Browne's contemporary, Owen Feltham, in his essay *On Dreams*:

Dreams are notable means of discovering our own inclinations. The wise man learns to know himself as well by the night's black mantle, as the searching beams of the day. In sleep we have the na-ked and natural thoughts of our souls. . . . Surely, how we fall to vice, or rise to virtue, we may by observation find in our dreams. The best use we can make of dreams, is observation and by that, our own correction or encouragement. For 'tis not doubtable, but that the mind is working in the dullest depth of sleep.[40]

Minor variations on these themes also appeared in eighteenth-century works. David Hartley, an English neurologist, for example, wrote:

A person may form a judgment of the state of his bodily health, and of his temperance, by the general pleasantness or unpleasantness, of his dreams. There are also many hints relating to the strength of our passions deducible from them.[41]

In addition to recognizing that character development was mirrored in dreams, there was also the awareness that dreams could have a powerful impact upon waking behavior. David Simpson, an English clergyman, wrote these comments in 1791:

Dreams are of great consequence in the government of the world, of equal authority with the Bible. . . . And has not the experience that many men have of significant dreams and night visions a more powerful effect on their minds than the most pure and refined concepts?[42]

Finally liberated from the centuries of shackles imposed on them by the black-frocked inquisitors, dreams were now dissociated from the devil and associated with scientific inquiry. Dreams were available again to be studied by philosophers, physicians, and psychologists. As indicated by these quotations from the seventeenth and eighteenth centuries, light was beginning to stream through the partially opened door which had been closed during the Dark Ages. The door would swing further open in the nineteenth century and the potential of dreams would be rediscovered.

CHAPTER 5

A ROMANTIC ERA:

THE NINETEENTH CENTURY

Though Freud and others who have followed in his footsteps have often dismissed the value of nineteenth-century writings on dreams, this was a fertile time for dream theory. Many of the ideas presented during the nineteenth century prefigured Freud's, as well as those of other important dream theorists.

The following observations made by William Hazlitt, a British essayist, early in the nineteenth century expand on earlier notions:

There is a sort of profundity in sleep; and it may be usefully consulted as an oracle in this way. It may be said that the voluntary power is suspended, and things come upon us as unexpected revelation, which we keep out of our thoughts at other times. We may be aware of a danger that yet we do not choose, while we have the full command of our faculties, to acknowledge to ourselves; the impending event will then appear to us as a dream, and we shall most likely find it verified afterwards.

Another thing of no small consequence is, that we may sometimes discover our tacit, and almost *unconscious* sentiments, with respect to persons or things in the same way. We are not hypocrites in our sleep. The curb is taken off from our passions and our imagination wanders at will. When awake, we check these rising thoughts, and fancy we have them not. In dreams, when we are off our guard, they return securely and unbidden. We may make this use of the infirmity of our sleeping metamorphoses, that we may *repress* any feelings of this sort that we disapprove in their incipient state, and detect ere it be too late, an unwarrantable antipathy or fatal passions.[1] (Italics mine)

THE ROMANTIC SCHOOL

Hazlitt makes an explicit reference to *unconscious* sentiments in his essay. Several other British writers around this time also refer to the unconscious and in Germany the concept was elaborated during the Romantic movement. In the eighteenth century, Enlightenment philosophy accorded great respect to the intellect, and as the Industrial Revolution developed in the late 1700s there was an increasing emphasis on material goods and productivity. The Romantic School developed in opposition to these movements; Romanticists encouraged emotional expression and reverence for nature, the soul, and the unconscious. Mysticism was in vogue among Romanticists and they focused upon individual flowerings and metamorphoses rather than societal roles. Dreams were a topic of intense interest to members of the Romantic School. These Romantic writings were an antecedent to most of the concepts later developed by Freud or Jung.

In 1814, Gotthilf von Schubert published *The Symbolism of Dreams*. He described the special "picture language" existing in dreams, which could combine many images or concepts into one picture. He likened the picture language of dreams to hieroglyphics such as those used by the ancient Egyptians and Chinese. A universal language of symbols which existed in dreams applied to both ancient and modern dreamers. Unlike speech and writing patterns, which must be learned, the language of symbols occurred spontaneously. The symbol of the snake, he suggested, represents the sensuous nature of the body. Dreams can be a source of revelation and tell the individual in an instant things for which the dreamer has been searching for years. Sometimes dreams can be prophetic, but they more frequently express an amoral quality because the neglected or repressed aspects of personality are activated in them.

Carl Carus was a physician and painter whose book *Psyche* was published in 1846. It was the first attempt to give an inclusive and objective theory of the unconscious. The book opens with this sentence: "The key to the knowledge of the nature of the soul's conscious life lies in the realm of the unconscious."[2] For Carus consciousness arose gradually in life and was always under the influence of the unconscious. He distinguished three layers of the unconscious and described seven of its features. The unconscious was indefatigable, had its own inborn wisdom and healing power, and enabled us to remain in connection with our fellow beings, he wrote. The individual unconscious is related to the unconscious of all humans, an idea that was a precursor of Jung's "collective unconscious." Carus described three kinds of dreams, which he associated with the three "life circles": mineral, vegetal, and animal. He attempted to interpret dreams according to their form rather than their content.

The social philosopher Eduard Von Hartmann, who published *Philosophy of the Unconscious* in 1869, was another Romantic. He also described three layers of the unconscious and documented his theories by citing facts concerning perception, the association of ideas, wit, emotional life, and the role of the unconscious in language, religion, and social life. He wrote:

> As for dreams, all the troubles of the waking state are prolonged into the dormant condition . . . a joy cannot well be otherwise expressed in dreams than as a pleasant, cheerful *mood*, *e.g.*, the feeling of being disembodied, of floating, flying, and the like, whilst displeasure is expressed not only as a mental mood, but also in all sorts of definite inconveniences, vexation, chagrin, quarreling, and conflict, inability to accomplish one's desires, or other cross purposes and disappointments.[3]

As is evident from these comments, the Romantic School very much appreciated the significance of the unconscious; it was viewed as a powerful source of creativity, wisdom, and healing and as an agency for transpersonal connectedness. Carl Jung would later attribute many of these same properties to the unconscious. Romanticism held sway mainly during the first half of the nineteenth century.

FRANK SEAFIELD: A NEGLECTED HISTORY OF DREAMS

An important, but extremely neglected, book about dreams was published in 1865 by Alexander Grant under the pseudonym Frank Seafield. A second edition, published in 1869, bore the grandiloquent title: *The Literature and Curiosities of Dreams: A Commonplace Book of Speculations Concerning the Mystery of Dreams and Visions, Records of Curious and Well-Authenticated Dreams, and Notes on the Various Modes of*

Interpretation.[4] No reference to this book appears in Freud's bibliography, which has been referred to as the most comprehensive summary of studies before 1900. Apparently nothing is known about this author except that he indicated he had an M.A. degree. In his preface to the first edition, Seafield explained his purpose in writing the book:

> The great object of this volume has been to select, from all sources, whatever is most characteristic of the opinions which have been held on the subject of Dreams, and of the examples upon which these opinions have been founded.

Seafield's review was quite extensive. His book was 518 pages in length and his "list of the principal authors, treatises, and opinions cited or quoted in this work" contained 210 references, ranging from Abercrombie to Zeno. Part 1, "On Dreams," written by Seafield, skillfully wove together various observations and speculations by others and offered some original comments of his own. Part 2, "Opinions on Dreams," was primarily an anthology of articles from such sources as the *Journal of Psychological Medicine*. Part 3 provided a collection of dreams, arranged chronologically, and the twenty-one-page appendix represented a dictionary of interpretations.

Seafield clearly recognized the following properties and possibilities in dreams:

1. Dreams have intelligible meaning.
2. Dream content is primarily traceable to the dreamer's personality structure and to the intensity of the dreamer's thoughts and emotions during the preceding day.
3. Dream imagery can reflect incorporation of external physical stimuli or internal symptoms of physical illness.
4. The dreaming mind is capable of problem-solving.
5. Dreams can compensate for satisfactions lacking in waking life and thereby serve as safety valves.
6. The vividness and credibility of the imaginative faculty in dreams raises important questions about mind-body relationships that should be investigated by psychologists.
7. Introspection about one's dreams can give the dreamer valuable insights about the elements of his or her character which might need modification to produce a better-balanced personality.

This list is not all-inclusive but should serve to indicate that there was an extremely active interest in dreams in the nineteenth century and that a reasonable base of knowledge existed concerning their special properties and potential value. Seafield concluded: *"In somnio veritas,"*[5] "Truth is in sleep."

We tend to think of sexuality as having been locked away in Victorian closets in Great Britain [but it seemed to be 'out of the closet' in Germany]. The philosopher Arthur Schopenhauer had described in 1819 the presence of two irrational forces in the will or unconscious. One was the instinct for self-preservation, and the other, more important one, was the sexual instinct. "Man is incarnate sexual instinct, since he owes his origin to copulation and the wish of his wishes is to copulate." In conflict with the sexual instinct, "no motivation, however strong, would be sure of victory."[6] Schopenhauer wrote that "life and dreams are leaves of the same book," and indicated that "we need not be ashamed to confess ... the intimate relationship between life and dreams."[7] Given that he was convinced of the overpowering supremacy of the sexual instinct in life, he presumably would have been very open to the presence of sexual imagery in dreams. The relationship between sexuality and dream images was developed in considerable detail by Karl Scherner about forty years later.

KARL SCHERNER: SEXUAL SYMBOLS

Karl Scherner's book, *Das Leben des Traumes* ("The Life of Dreams"), appeared in 1861. He strongly emphasized the importance of symbolism in the following passage:

> The images [of the dream] throw off all the shackles of the ego so that the activity of the soul which we call phantasy is free from all the rules of reason and is also free from all restrictive factors, and thus rises to unlimited heights. ... It is extremely sensitive to the most delicate emotional stimuli and it immediately changes the inner life into pictures of the outer world. The dream phantasy lacks a conceptual language—what it wants to say it must paint perceptually ... [and] it paints in all the fullness, power and splendor of the perceptual form. The clearness of its language, however, is impaired by the fact that it does not represent an object by its proper image. Rather it chooses a strange image, provided that it can express that aspect of the object which the dream chooses to represent. This is the symbolizing activity of phantasy.[8]

Religious symbols for Scherner could involve the appearance of a respected master providing guidance or revelations; intellectual concerns might be portrayed in the form of a discussion between equals; and diminished vitality represented by encountering a sick person. Clear thinking was revealed by light in dreams while imprecise feelings were signalled by the presence of chiaroscuro.

Scherner was particularly interested in somatic symbols. A house, he proposed, symbolized the human body; various parts of the house represented various parts of the body. He mentioned a woman who went to bed with a violent headache and subsequently dreamed the ceiling of her room was covered with cobwebs swarming with large spiders. After studying the relationship between physical functioning and corresponding dream imagery, Scherner suggested that increased functioning of the lungs was associated with flying dreams and circulatory conditions were represented by such images as heavy traffic moving through streets. Muddy streets could be traced to an intestinal stimulus and a foaming stream to a urinary stimulus. Of particular interest, in light of Freud's later emphasis, was Scherner's twelve-page discussion of sexual symbols. The penis, he claimed, could be represented as a high tower, a knife, or a clarinet, while the vagina could be symbolized by a soft, slippery, narrow path across a courtyard or by a staircase up which one could climb. Freud discusses Scherner at several points in *The Interpretation of Dreams*, and although he is frequently quite critical of him, does credit him with being "the true discoverer of symbolism."[9]

HERVEY DE SAINT-DENYS: MASTER OF LUCID DREAMING

The Marquis Hervey de Saint-Denys was a French professor of ethnography who taught Chinese and Tartar-Manchu. His anonymously published book *Les reves et les moyens de les diriger*, which appeared in 1867, contained a lengthy description of his personal explorations of dreaming. Freud indicated he had attempted to obtain a copy of this book but was unsuccessful. An English translation entitled *Dreams and How to Guide Them* was published in 1982.

Beginning at age thirteen, Saint-Denys began to record his dreams and within a year was also including drawings of his dreams in an album. His preoccupation with dreams enabled him to achieve an exceptionally high level of dream recall and he eventually filled twenty-two notebooks with dreams recorded from 1,946 nights. Many verbatim reports of his lavishly detailed dreams, including frequent encounters with exotic women, appear in his book.

Throughout the book, Saint-Denys argued strongly that "the fabric of dreams" and their seemingly "bizarre complications" could eventually be understood as "perfectly simple and logical phenomena." From his own explorations, he proposed several principles to account for the nature and patterning of dream images. Ideas were represented in dreams by pictorial images which emerged in the same succession as the sequence of ideas. "The moving panorama of our visions corresponds exactly with the train of ideas arising in our mind."[10]

For Saint-Denys, "*abstractions* are the most common form of link between ideas."[11] Abstraction refers to the process whereby "the mind transfers the qualities or mode of being of one subject on to another."[12] He mentioned the various sensory qualities that could be associated with an orange and explained, "I can consider the idea of its shape, its colour, its consistency or its smell *separately* from the others, and considered in this way these ideas become so many *abstractions*."[13] Abstraction could also "refer to some detail such as a key ring, a doorknob . . . and so on, which the mind separated from a complex whole to which the detail belongs."[14] In discussing "abstractions of qualities on the sensory level," Saint-Denys said, "The vast majority of our memories have entered our mind through the eyes. Therefore the mind makes abstractions frequently from external appearances."[15] A statue, for example, could become a living person, "a closely packed crowd with heads turned toward some spectacle" could become transformed "into a field full of daisies, and then into a huge mosaic scattered with regularly spaced medallions."[16]

"Abstractions founded on resemblances between words" were also discussed and he gave several examples, among which was the following:

I admire a manuscript done in a superb script. I say to myself that it is in *a beautiful hand* and however unlikely this may seem I dream that the characters are written on *a beautiful hand* cut out and bound together.[17] (Italics mine)

Another category of abstractions discussed by Saint-Denys was "abstractions of a purely abstract order." He observed:

Besides moral ideas such as generosity, pity . . . and those which become moral abstractions . . . such as greatness, smallness, inequality, etc., the mind of a cultured man conceives many more or less complex ideas resulting from the existence of a social state: beliefs, traditions, symbols and so on.[18]

As an example, Saint-Denys noted that a portrait of Saint Peter might lead to the abstract idea of religion, which might then be transferred on to some familiar pious person known to the dreamer. The following is another example:

I see myself in the courtyard of an inn, where horses of quality and draught horses are crowded together round the same drinking trough. I think think of the inequality of the care that is given to different horses and the work that is imposed on them, and without realizing it I immediately transfer this abstract idea of inequality on to the pipes through which the water flows. Previously I had seen a trough with four lead pipes of identical proportions, and now these pipes appear to me to be all of unequal length.[19]

Frontispiece from Les Reves

Another variation of abstractions which Saint-Denys included in his "abstract order" class, was one in which "we include ourselves within a situation which we have first of all imagined outside ourselves," for example: "I dream I am the spectator at some terrible accident; the sight of a wounded man fills me with pity; I imagine what he must be suffering; and it is then I who am the wounded man."[20]

Saint-Denys was aware of how central his notion of abstraction was for the understanding of dreams. He wrote, "Abstractions are such a frequent operation that I think it would be difficult to analyse in detail of any length without discovering several of them."[21] Saint-Denys's concept of abstraction became Freud's concept of displacement over thirty years later.

The dreamer's mind could also engage in internal debate and then externalize these discussions:

Another observation which has often struck me is the way the mind constantly proceeds by means of a dialogue with itself as soon as it starts to reason or contemplate. Hardly has a dream begun when we seem to be engaged in conversation with some imaginary person. . . .

This class of dream includes a remarkable variant.

It often happens that, without becoming the interpreters of any personality alien to ourselves, we suffer a kind of moral dichotomy in which we find all the elements of a violent controversy within ourselves. We plead with ourselves for and against the contrary opinions that preoccupy us; at times we are the pleaders, at others more or less impartial judges, watching a discussion among the imaginary beings who are talking on our behalf. I can think of few subjects more fertile . . . than the analysis of these internal debates in which our conscience, our instincts and all the interior voices of our feelings are heard through the mouths of characters which our imagination has thought fit to choose for their expression.[22]

Over a century later those employing a Gestalt approach to working with dreams emphasized the recognition that different characters could be created by our dreaming imagination to portray internalized aspects of ourselves.

In addition to formulating the concept of abstraction to account for how "the course of our dreams is guided by psychological affinities," Saint-Denys also observed that there was another factor which "could have linked a series of entirely heterogeneous ideas."[23] This factor or category involved "transitions in the association of ideas due to the chronological order in which recollections are stored in the memory."[24] As an example of this, he described one of his earliest dreams, in which he was dining with his family but had the bishop of his diocese and two mythological divinities as guests at their table. In tracing back the elements of his dream, Saint-Denys recalled that while he was translating a passage from Ovid's *Metamorphoses* involving divinities, he was told to change his soiled schoolboy's jacket for a more respectable one because the bishop of the diocese had just arrived and was going to join the family for lunch.

Saint-Denys was aware that dreams could appear ridiculous or incoherent at first glance, but he insisted there was always a rational explanation for the association of ideas present or for the succession of images that appeared before the mind's eye. One of the chief sources of incoherence was that "two conflicting ideas frequently unfold together."[25] To illustrate this principle, he described another early dream in which he picked an enormous peach from a tree. The peach looked exactly like a neighbor's daughter. Earlier that day, Saint-Denys had heard someone remark that the cheeks of this little girl were like a velvety peach.

When two ideas competed for recognition, there could be an accompanying conflict of images. Saint-Denys observed this phenomenon on a number of occasions and referred to the process as the *superimposition of images*. This same process was later called *condensation* by Freud. When explaining the superimposition of images, Saint-Denys likened the process to what would occur if a second slide were placed in a magic lantern (slide projector) before the first one was removed.

> Either the figures on the two slides appear side by side, forming an incongruous ensemble in which Bluebeard, let us say, faces Tom Thumb; or they are superimposed to a greater or lesser degree, so that Blue-

beard appears with two different heads, four legs or an arm emerging threateningly from his ear.[26]

Saint-Denys carried out several interesting experiments to "show how the application of the psychological laws I have expounded" would reveal "the close connection that exists in the memory between particular sensations and particular ideas."[27] These experiments will be described in chapter 9 where research studies on dreams carried out before 1950 are presented.

As the result of his own observations, his extensive review of the published studies by others, and hearing the dreaming experiences of his friends, one of whom solved a difficult chess problem in a dream, Saint-Denys concluded that creativity was possible in dreams.

> The imagination therefore can *create* in a dream, in the sense of producing visions not seen before. Admittedly, these visions are formed by materials already contained in the dreamer's memory, but they are formed like the fortuitous combinations of pieces of glass in a kaleidoscope, or as a rational neologism is formed from already known word-roots.[28]

Saint-Denys's career was translating French words into Chinese ideograms and vice versa, so it is not surprising that he was motivated to find out how waking ideas became translated into nocturnal pictorial images. The combination of his "picture-writing" translation skills, his training in painting, and his highly developed dream recall faculties enabled him to make significant strides in describing the rules of syntax which governed the structure of dreams.

Saint-Denys has become most noted for his amazing ability to master *lucid dreaming*. A lucid dreamer is consciously aware of being in a dreaming state and is able to direct the course of an ongoing dream. Saint-Denys did not encounter such a dream until his 207th night, but then became so fascinated by its possibilities that he undertook a program of mental "gymnastics" to develop his skills in this area. He was quickly rewarded with Olympian success. Six months later, he was achieving lucidity "on average two nights out of five, and after a year three nights out of four. Finally, after fifteen months, it was present almost every night."[29] He felt that anyone interested in doing so could develop the "faculties of attention and will during sleep" and thereby gain great benefits.

> The incoherent dreams become less disrupted under the influence of the will; and in the emotional dreams, full of tumultuous desires or unpleasant thoughts, the new consciousness and freedom of mind that we have acquired enable us to banish painful images and favour happier ones. The fear of disagreeable visions weakens as we perceive how foolish it is, and the desire to see agreeable ones becomes more active as we develop a growing power to induce them of our own accord.[30]

Saint-Denys provided many examples of lucid dreams with favorable outcomes.

These ranged from conjuring up some beautiful harem slaves to fixing his eyes on a frightening, pursuing monster, causing its movements to slow down and the menacing figure to change into a floating bundle of rags. Saint-Denys discovered that placing his hands over his eyes in a dream could blot out the existing setting and enable him to fix his attention on whatever new objects or events he wished to evoke.

Saint-Denys proposed that the imaginary events of dreams followed logic which was borrowed from memories of real life. If this were so, he reasoned, he should be unable to have a dream image or sensation for a situation he had never experienced in waking reality. He decided to test his theory by attempting to induce a previously unexperienced event, a suicide jump, into a lucid dream over which he had control. In his next lucid dream, Saint-Denys leaped from the top story of a house which seemed very high. He described his immediate feeling as "full of anxious curiosity" as to what would happen next. The dream scene suddenly shifted and he found himself in a crowd gathered around a dead man. When the body was being carried away on a stretcher, someone informed the dreamer that the man had thrown himself from the cathedral tower. As he predicted, Saint-Denys failed to experience the unfamiliar sensation of fatally landing on the ground below.

Saint-Denys noticed that it was much easier to maintain prolonged attention to some small material object, such as a flower or a leaf, than to an animate form, particularly a face. He reported that if he tried "to hang on to a particular idea or image which was tending to slip away," he would experience a fairly acute pain which pressed against his temples and then "spread to the back of the brain."[31]

Many fertile ideas for research are scattered throughout Saint-Denys's provocative book. One of the techniques he advocated to diminish the effects of a disturbing dream would be called desensitization by modern behavior therapists. Saint-Denys had a horrifying, recurrent nightmare in which he realized that he had a serpent around his neck instead of a cravat. With his usual investigative zeal, Saint-Denys saw this as an opportunity for an experiment. He took a leather belt filled with lead-shot that rattled and vibrated at the slightest movement and wore this device around his neck for several days. He frequently removed and replaced some of the pieces of shot. The next time his nightmare recurred he "remembered the false serpent and what it contained. . . . I imagined that I removed the inoffensive 'cravat' and calmly loaded a gun with the shot."[32] The dream moved on to an agreeable conclusion. Saint-Denys reported that this disturbing dream "returned once more, with similar results, and then did not appear again." His conditioning procedure had desensitized him; his horrifying serpent no longer appeared or had the power to terrify him.

It is unfortunate that this classic work was unavailable and remained a collector's item for nearly a century. One wonders if it would have had any impact upon Freud had he been able to obtain a copy of it. Relying upon some brief references to this book by other French authors, Freud acknowledged that Saint-Denys would have been "the most energetic opponent of those who seek to depreciate psychical functioning in dreams."[33]

YVES DELAGE: DREAMS AS INCOMPLETED ACTS

The French biologist, Yves Delage, first sketched out his dream theories in 1891. Delage asserted that the great majority of nocturnal dream images come from incompleted acts or inhibited and suppressed perceptions of the preceding day. Impressions that have a very strong charge of energy and are complete can break through to awareness, as in the case of nightmares. Old memories, he noted, can be dreamed about because of associations with recent memories and the chains of association existing in dreams can sometimes be reconstructed. He also mentioned that there could be fusions of representations into one image (condensation) and attribution of a neutral act to another subject (displacement). Delage, like his countryman Saint-Denys, also experienced lucid dreams. He observed:

> I realize that I am dreaming and I say to myself: Since I have nothing to fear I am going to meet my enemies, I will defy them. . . . Several times, I have in this way thrown myself on purpose into some danger in order to see what would come of it.[34]

F. W. HILDEBRANT: DREAMS AS SELF-DISCLOSURES

F. W. Hildebrant published a short book in German on dreams in 1875 which contained many important insights later incorporated by Freud. Hildebrant claimed it would be possible to explain every dream image if enough time were available to trace it to its origin in "the chambers of one's memory": "It is impossible to think of any action in a dream for which the original motive has not in some way or other—whether as a wish, or desire or impulse—passed through the waking mind."[35] Hildebrant's awareness of the potential for self-disclosure in dreams is cogently expressed in this quotation:

The dream sometimes allows us to look into the depths and folds of our very being—mainly a closed book in states of consciousness. It gives us such valuable insight into ourselves, such instructive revelations of our half-hidden emotional tendencies and powers that, were

we awake, we should have good reason to stand in awe of the demon who is apparently peering at our cards with the eyes of a falcon. . . .

The dream warns from within with the voice of a watchman guarding the very center of our psychic life. It warns us against continuing on the paths which we are treading.[36]

Freud chastised Hildebrant for offering too much of an "enthusiastic eulogy" for dreams, but also acknowledged "of all the contributors to the study of dreams which I have come across, it [his book] is the most perfect in form and the richest in ideas.[37] As we will discover in the next chapter on Freud, two authors of a popular psychoanalytic book on dreams attempted to pass off an inspirational passage written by Hildebrant as actually originating from Freud.

W. ROBERT: DREAMS AS AN ELIMINATION PROCESS

W. Robert (1886) speculated about the function of dreaming and proposed that man *must* dream in order to eliminate the excess images that burden his mind. This excess imagery could occur because of an overflow of outside perceptions, internal fantasies, or incompletely thought-out

ideas. "Dream-work" (*traumarbeit*) is the term he introduced to describe the elimination process which led to perceptions either being incorporated into memory or forgotten. Eliminated images were perceived as dream images; they were "chips from the workshop of the mind." Robert advanced the idea that "a person from whom one would take the capacity for dreaming would sooner or later become mentally deranged." The type of mental derangement would be related to the preoccupying ideas that had not been eliminated in dreams. Robert's views about dreams acting as an elimination conduit for excess and unnecessary perceptions antedated the "Draino" theory of "dreaming to forget" by almost a century.

MARIE DE MANACEINE: A RUSSIAN PERSPECTIVE

Marie de Manaceine was a Russian physician from Saint Petersburg whose book *Sleep: Its Physiology, Pathology, Hygiene and Psychology* appeared in 1897. Her chapter on "The Psychology of Sleep" contained ninety-eight pages, plus a bibliography of 166 references, but was not mentioned by Freud in his review of the nineteenth-century dream literature.

De Manaceine reviewed several studies of dream content. She cited Ernest-Charles Lasegue's observations that the disturbing imagery of *delirium tremens* appeared initially in dreams before progressing onward to waking manifestations. Sante De Sanctis reported that alcoholics had *microzooscopic* dreams, in which small animals such as insects predominated, while *macrozooscopic* dreams involving large animals appeared in 62 percent of the dreams of severe hysterics and 35 percent of those with slight hysteria. He also studied the relationship between daytime and dreaming emotions for several groups of subjects, such as normals, criminals, psychiatric patients, mentally retarded individuals, and prostitutes, and with some specified exceptions, concluded it was "waking emotions of medium intensity which most readily reappear in sleep." William James investigated the "phantom limb" phenomenon in 185 persons who had undergone amputations. These individuals did not use crutches in their dreams but continued to walk on their feet, although in time the dreamed limb might become shorter.

In a five-year study of her own involving thirty-seven persons of varying age and intelligence, de Manaceine found that the more intelligent subjects had better recall and reported a much greater variety and originality of dream content. She also found that "in the majority of cases dreams decrease in number as old age comes on."[38] The author strongly agreed with Novalis that dreams serve as a shield against the monotony of life, as friendly companions on our pilgrimage to the grave. Without them we would grow older much more rapidly and find life more wearisome. She gave an example:

> I have myself known an old woman of sixty who preserved the memory of a dream as the happiest recollection of her whole long life. She would become radiant with animation as she narrated that sacred dream which had thrown up its single ray of splendor on an existence made up of petty miseries and petty satisfactions. In that memorable

dream she had been to the palace of the Tsar himself, and she never tired of telling the dream.[39]

Examples of "collective" dreams, in which a large number of people sleeping in the same location all experienced a similar dream were mentioned by Manaceine. One of these involved a group of several hundred soldiers who slept in a "haunted" abbey because quarters were scarce. They awoke screaming and fled the building in terror, complaining that a large dog with long black hair had jumped upon their chests and disappeared through an opening. They refused to sleep there the following night unless the officers stood watch in the building. Although the officers obliged, "about one o'clock, in all the rooms at the same time, the cries of the previous nightmare repeated, and again the soldiers rushed out to escape the suffocating embrace of the big black dog." These dreams vanished after they left that location.

The significance of dreaming for de Manaceine bears a strong resemblance to Carl Jung's view of archetypes and the collective unconscious:

But not only are the bounds of personal consciousness extended vaguely in sleep so as to cover all the past life of the sleeper. It is even possible to hold that the consciousness of the species, and even its predecessors, may be represented in the psychic organism and reappear in sleep. . . . All that our ancestors lived, felt, and suffered during countless ages of time, all that they condensed into images and faculties and definite movements has been passed on to us, not indeed, as such, but in the shape of latent capacities and possibilities inherent in our neuro-cerebral system. And thus it may well be during sleep, when the immediate personal consciousness is inactive, that these latent characters of the psychic organism inherited from our remotest ancestors stir within us, and fill with strange images and unforeseen desires our inner world.[40]

JAMES SULLY: AN ENGLISH PERSPECTIVE

James Sully studied psychology under Hermann Helmholtz, published the two volumes of *Human Mind* in 1892, and became Professor of Mind and Logic at the University of London. His book *Illusions*, initially published in 1881, came out in a fourth edition in 1897.[41]

The following summary of Sully's view toward dreams appeared in an article in 1893. It contains many of the concepts that Freud utilized in his own theory of dreams, but Sully was not acknowledged by Freud until the fourth edition of *The Interpretation of Dreams*, in 1914. This is what Sully advanced:

The perception or imagination of a thing may rouse a momentary *desire which we repress* as foolish or wrong. The next night these half-formed psychical tendencies, relieved of all restraint, work themselves out.... We may assume, perhaps, that in each case *the dream was the expansion* and complete development *of a vague fugitive wish* of the waking mind ... the dream becomes a revelation. It strips the *ego* of its artificial wrappings and exposes it in its native nudity. *It brings up from the dim depths of our subconscious life the primal, instinctive impulses,* and discloses to us a side of ourselves which connects us with the great sentient world.... Some writers would regard dreaming in general as a kind of *pictorial symbolism....* Like some letter in cipher, the dream inscription when scrutinized closely loses its first look of balderdash and takes on the aspect of a serious, intelligible message.[42] (Italics mine)

FREDERIC W. H. MYERS: DREAMS AND THE SUBLIMINAL WORLD

Frederic Myers was a classical lecturer at Cambridge who later carried out investigations in psychical research. He coined the term "telepathy" and was one of the founders of the Society for Psychical Research in 1882. Myers died in 1901 and his book, *Human Personality and Its Survival of Bodily Death,* was published posthumously in 1903.

Myers defined his scientific posture as follows: "I felt if anything were knowable it must be discovered by simple experiment and observation, using exactly the same methods of deliberate, dispassionate, exact inquiry which have built up our actual knowledge about the world which we can touch and see."[43] Myers used the term "supraliminal" to refer to the "current of consciousness which we habitually identify with *ourselves.*" The term "subliminal" referred to events taking place "beneath that threshold." Myers wrote, "I propose to extend the meaning of the term, so as to make it cover *all* that takes place beneath the ordinary threshold, or outside the ordinary margin of consciousness."[44] He asserted that this "life beneath the threshold or beyond the margin seems to be no discontinuous or intermittent thing" and that "there also is a continuous subliminal chain of memory (or more chains than one) involving ... [what] we commonly call a Self.... What was once below the surface may for a time, or permanently, rise above it," he noted, and when reaching consciousness:

the subliminal uprushes ... are often characteristically different in quality from any element known to our ordinary supraliminal life. They are different in a way which implies faculty of which we have had no previous knowledge, operating in an environment of which hitherto we have been totally unaware.[45]

Myers systematically set out to include all the following phenomena under his subliminal classification: personality disintegrations, genius, sleep and dreams, hypnotism, sensory automatism (the products of inner vision or inner audition), motor automatism (automatic writing or speech), phantasms of the dead, trance, possession, and ecstasy. He presented hundreds of independently witnessed or corroborated accounts to support his theory. In his chapter on sleep, he stated:

We cannot treat sleep—as it has generally been treated—in its purely *negative* aspect. We cannot be content merely to dwell, with the common text-books, on the mere *absence* of waking faculties. . . . We must treat sleep *positively* . . . as a definite phase of our personality, coordinate with the waking phase.[46]

His positive approach was exemplified in the following statement:

The permanent result of a dream is sometimes such as to show that the dream has not been a mere superficial confusion of past waking experiences, but has had an unexplained potency of its own—

drawn, like the power of hypnotic suggestion, from some depth in our being which the waking self cannot reach.[47]

Myers proceeded to give the details of twenty-nine dreams, and the circumstances existing before or after they were dreamed, to illustrate a progressively greater range of dreaming potential. He began by citing dreams which left either negative or positive "traces quite as persistent as any hypnotic suggestion could implant from without." Next he examined several dreams which revealed the location of "lost" objects. Following that, some dreams were described in which a novel solution to a perplexing intellectual problem was discovered. Included here was the dream of Professor Hilprecht, described in chapter 2 of this book, involving the Babylonian agate earrings. Myers also discussed precognitive dreams, dreams containing information about a distant relative's unexpected death, examples of two people sharing a similar dream, and clairvoyant dreams in which the dreamer was provided information about an event happening in a distant location. At the end of the chapter, Myers offered the following summary:

In reviewing the phenomena of sleep we were bound to ask whether the self of sleep showed any faculty of a quite different order from that by which waking consciousness maintains the activity of man. We found that this was so indeed; that there was evidence that the sleeping spirit was susceptible of relations unfettered by special bonds; of clairvoyant perception of distant scenes; of telepathic communication from distant persons, or even the spirits of whom we can predicate neither distance nor nearness.[48]

Myers's classic work has been largely ignored by historians but has received high praise from those familiar with its contents. Aldous Huxley said, "His account of the unconscious is superior to Freud's in at least one respect; it is more comprehensive and truer to the data of experience."[49] In summarizing Myers's contribution, William James, the greatest American psychologist of his day, wrote in 1901:

> For half a century now, psychologists have fully admitted the existence of a subliminal mental region, under the name either of unconscious cerebration or of the involuntary life; but they have never definitely taken up the question of the extent of this region, never sought explicitly to map it out. Myers definitely attacks this problem, which, after him, it will be impossible to ignore.[50]

Freud's only reference to Myers was that he understood Myers had published a collection of hypermnesic dreams. Myers's 1892 hypermnesic dream article and a 1903 review of Myers's book by William James were published by the Society for Psychical Research. Since Freud became a member of that society in 1911 and published in the society's *Proceedings* in 1912, it seems puzzling that he would have remained unfamiliar with Myers's book.

Myers attempted to examine the age-old beliefs about dreams possessing paranormal qualities and to consider these beliefs in an empirical context. (Modern empirical studies of paranormal dreams will be reviewed in chapter 14.) He displayed great originality and breadth of scholarly knowledge in his efforts to include such a wide range of phenomena under his subliminal umbrella. Anyone reading his work cannot fail to be impressed with his erudition and skill in coping with the challenge he posed for himself to integrate these puzzling pieces of behavior into a unified picture of "human personality." The historian of psychiatry, Henri Ellenberger, is one of the few modern writers to give Myers the recognition he deserves. He refers to him as "one of the great systematizers of the notion of the unconscious mind."[51]

DREAMS IN PERIODICAL LITERATURE

Another way to evaluate the nineteenth-century climate is to examine how dreams were presented and viewed in popular periodicals. A superb review of this material was carried out by Hendrika Vande Kemp in her 1977 dissertation and a subsequent journal article.[52] She surveyed eighty-four periodicals published in English between 1860 and 1910 and found nearly two hundred articles that had appeared in eighty-one periodicals and journals (forty-seven American, thirty-two British, two Canadian). There were 154 authors represented, about one-half being Americans. None of these American authors had written a book on dreams, and she concluded that discussions of dreams were almost nonexistent in the pages of the leading American psychology texts of the period (at least until the last decade).

Vande Kemp made the following comments on how dreams fared in the hands of psychologists:

> The scientific community was *not* united in its pursuits of the mysteries of dreaming, and a unity of tradition and awareness of other work became possible (if not mandatory) only after Freud published his summary and (scientific) bibliography in the *Interpretation of Dreams.* . . .
>
> Of all the approaches to dreams prevalent in the twentieth century, mainstream psychology, in its emphasis on dream investigation, has chosen the approach which is, in the strict sense of the word, least, "psychological," and most blatantly ignores the psychological needs expressed by the popular interest in dreams.[53]

Dreams in the hands of nonpsychologists were petted and praised much more lavishly. "Those whom we regard as famous shared their dreams as willingly and unabashedly as the man and woman on the street."[54] Public awareness of the theory of the unconscious, and its relationship

to dreams, could be inferred from the existence of an 1871 article by Frances Cobbe in *MacMillan's* magazine entitled "Dreams as Illustrations of Unconscious Cerebration."[55] This article was reprinted the same year in two other popular periodicals. Cobbe was an activist for women's rights and various social causes. Many others from all walks of life and fields of inquiry joined in the dream "cause."

A good feel for the kinds of dreams presented in these periodicals can be gained by thumbing through the 263 illustrative dreams Vande Kemp included in her dissertation under such headings as: experimental dreams (Maury, Lewis, Stanley); kinaesthetic dreams (falling, flying, etc.); nightmare/incubus; prophetic/premonitory; telepathic dreams; dreams of death; dreams in the law-courts; hypermnesic dreams; the moral sense; reasoning; dream-consciousness; dreams illustrating the Freudian mechanisms; and dreams as clinical material. In view of this diversity, it's not surprising that she concluded, "Theories and speculations about dreaming during the half century in question were much more comprehensive and diverse than one would suspect from reading Freud's review of the scientific literature."[56]

I would heartily agree with Vande Kemp's proposal that we must broaden our psychological horizons to include the full range of dreaming experience:

> Any adequate psychology of dreaming must transcend both Freud and his followers, reinstating into the realm of acceptable data those dreams earlier classified as "parapsychological," dreams which

their predecessors at least acknowledged, even though they
were never adequately explained.[57]

Many individuals writing in the nineteenth century urged that more active consideration be given to the creative
problem-solving potential of dreams. Writing in 1879, Henry Maudsley, the British
physician after whom the prestigious hospital and school of psychiatry in London are
named, argued that dreams are not the result of a simple association of ideas. "We
are dealing with . . . an actual constructive
agency, whereby ideas are not merely
brought together only, but new products
are formed out of them."[58] Impressed by
"the extraordinary creations of dreams," he
predicted that a study of dreams would be
"full of promise of abundant fruit."

Several examples have been provided
in this chapter to illustrate how widespread
the acceptance of dreams was among all
levels of society. The rewards to be attained by holding dreams in higher regard
are nicely summarized by Ralph Waldo
Emerson in an 1883 essay:

Dreams have a poetic integrity
and truth. . . . They seem to us to
suggest a certain abundance and
fluency of thought not familiar to
the waking experience. . . . They
have a double consciousness, at
once sub- and ob-jective. Wise
and sometimes terrible hints shall
in them be thrown to the man
out of a quite unknown intelligence. . . . A skillful man reads his
dreams for his self-knowledge; yet
not the details but the quality.
These whimsical pictures, in as
much as they originate from us,
may well have an analogy with our
whole life and fate.[59]

PART 3

DREAM THEORIES IN THE TWENTIETH CENTURY

CHAPTER 6

SIGMUND FREUD:

DREAMS AS DISGUISED

SEXUAL WISHES

FREUD AND PSYCHOANALYSIS

Since the word unconscious first appeared in English in 1751 and in German in 1776,[1] many writers have obviously been familiar with the construct of an unconscious region that influenced our waking motives and our dreaming imagery. Freud followed up on these conceptualizations and made the unconscious the bedrock of his psychoanalytic theory. Sexuality was a very important component in Freud's analysis of the unconscious.

Freud was born in 1856 and began his career as a neurologist specializing in the treatment of nervous disorders. He studied hypnosis for a year with the famous French psychiatrist Jean Charcot, who used hypnosis to treat hysteria, a condition in which no neurological basis can be found for a patient's physical complaints. Freud's next mentor was Joseph Breuer, a Viennese physician, who had discovered

Sigmund Freud sent this 1906 photograph of himself to Carl Jung.

that neurotic patients often were cured of their symptoms when they talked about them. Breuer and Freud published a book called *Studies in Hysteria* in 1895, but Breuer later severed their relationship because of Freud's heavy emphasis upon sexual conflicts as being at the root of hysteria. The role of sexual frustration as a factor in the development of hysteria was fairly widely accepted at the time, but Freud took the idea to such an extreme that he alienated himself from his medical contemporaries.

When Freud encouraged his patients to talk freely about their symptoms and memories, he became aware that they often included references to their dreams. A link was forged between neurotic symptoms and dream formation in Freud's mind and he considered that they both originated from early sexual conflicts and developed in a parallel fashion in the patient's life. Freud extended his psychoanalytic speculations to account for the "psychopathology of everyday life," which included slips of the tongue and temporary memory blocks.

Freud founded a psychoanalytic school, which included a professional organization, conventions, journals, and a method of training that included both several years of intensive exposure to the doctrines of psychoanalysis and a personal analysis under the watchful eye of an approved training analyst. Freud exercised a strong hand in the shaping and directing of this movement and decided who was loyal and who should be banished because their views deviated too far from orthodoxy. Among the latter "Oedipal ingrates" (Freud's words) were Carl Jung, Alfred Adler, Otto Rank, and Wilhelm Stekel, all of whom developed alternative theoretical approaches which gave far less emphasis to sexuality. In describing Freud's stance, the psychiatric historian Henri Ellenberger commented: "His conviction of the truth of his theories was so complete that he did not admit contradiction. This was called intolerance by his opponents and passion for truth by his followers."[2]

Freud received intense criticism during the earlier years of psychoanalysis and he continually complained about the resistance he encountered to his theories. In a paper entitled "The Resistances to Psycho-Analysis," Freud pointed out what he felt was relevant about the discipline: "Psychoanalysis disposed once and for all the fairy tale of an asexual childhood. It demonstrated the fact that sexual interests and activities occur in small children from the beginning of their lives."[3] He concluded: "The strongest resistances to psychoanalysis were not of an intellectual kind but arose from emotional sources. This explained their passionate character as well as their poverty in logic."[4]

Freud also referred to some "external difficulties" that contributed to the resistance to psychoanalysis. One of these was that "it is not easy to arrive at an independent judgment to do with analysis without having experienced it oneself."[5] Critics have argued the reverse: no independent judgment is possible after the analytic candidate has been systematically exposed to a narrow theoretical viewpoint for several years by an analyst already committed to the Freudian position.

FREUD'S ASSESSMENT OF DREAM HISTORY

The highlights of the history of dreams have been presented in the preceding chapters of this book. Around 400 B.C., Plato recognized that our irrational wild beast nature could peer out in dreams. Plato's observation about the expression of irrational impulses in dreams was finally anchored to the concept of the unconscious by the beginning of the nineteenth century. As the nineteenth century progressed, various authors commented upon the pictorial language of dreams, the presence of sexual symbols, the dream work mechanisms of condensation (superimposition) and displacement (abstraction) and the role of wish fulfillment in dreams. In addition to these theoretical contributions, a technique for working with dreams involving associations had been proposed by the German writer Christian Friedrich Hebbel in 1850:

If a man would collect his dreams and examine them, and would add to the dreams which he is now having all the thoughts he has in association with them, all the remembrances, all the pictures he can grasp from them, and if he would combine these with the dreams he has had in the past, he would be able to understand himself much better by this than by means of any other kind of psychology.[6]

Ask the average person on the street, Who first discovered the unconscious? Who first discovered dreams? Who first suggested using the dreamer's associations to understand dreams? The answer will be the same to all three questions: Sigmund Freud! Yet it is clear that this is not historically accurate. How has this erroneous image of Freud's primacy been created? The answer is simple: Freud and his followers minimized the contributions of their predecessors and magnified the claimed originality of Freud's ideas.

Although Freud's book *The Interpretation of Dreams* actually appeared in print in 1899, at his request the publication date was given as 1900 in order to give the impression that his views were not linked to those of the nineteenth century but were the harbingers of new twentieth-century thinking. The first draft of *The Interpretation of Dreams* was actually completed by June 1898 but its publication was delayed because Freud dreaded the required chore of reviewing what others had written about dreams. After nearly a year, Freud overcame his resistance to this task and spent a few weeks compiling his literature review. The first chapter of *The Interpretation of Dreams* opens with a review of that pre-existing literature, but a succinct summary of Freud's evaluation of his predecessor's contributions is presented in the second paragraph of page one: "In spite of many thousands of years of effort, the scientific understanding of dreams has made very little advance . . . little or nothing that touches upon the essential nature of dreams." Such a sweeping statement seems to dismiss or downplay the existence of any meaningful predecessors in the realm of dreams. In a 1909 letter to Oskar Pfister, a minister who had pointed out some information about earlier writers, Freud confessed: "I am really very ignorant about my predecessors. If we ever meet up above they will certainly greet me ill as a plagiarist."[7]

Freud also had a difficult time appreciating the contributions of his contemporaries to understanding dreams. In his 1933 *New Introductory Lectures on Psychoanalysis*, Freud raised the question of whether there had been any "new discoveries" in dreams since his own, but stated, "I am afraid you will find that it amounts to very little"[8]— this despite the enormous contributions by Jung, Stekel, Adler, and many others. If earlier writers had made comments about dreams similar to his own, Freud had a peculiar habit of minimizing their value or appropriating such comments as his own. Referring to remarks made by Havelock Ellis in 1899, Freud commented that they "strike us as happy anticipations of our own assertions." Thus Freud is clearly the referent point or standard against which other contributions are viewed. Freud didn't happily confirm the earlier observations of Ellis; Ellis's significance was in happily anticipating Freud. As pointed out in the last chapter, James Sully in 1893 eloquently described many of the concepts later claimed by Freud, so Sully was magically incorporated by Freud in the following fashion: "We have been able to *accept entirely as our own* what Sully has written"[9] (Italics mine). It is interesting to note that Sully was completely overlooked until the fourth edition of *The Interpretation of Dreams* in 1914. It's probable that Sully's contribution came to belated recognition only because Otto Rank had assumed chief responsibility for reviewing the dream literature for Freud for the third to sixth editions of *The Interpretation of Dreams.*

Another example of Freud's distortion of what the dream scene was like before he arrived is contained in the first paragraph of chapter 2, which deals with dream interpretation. He declared:

> My presumption that dreams can be interpreted at once puts me in opposition to the ruling theory of dreams and in fact to every theory of dreams with the single exception of Scherner's . . . [but] the scientific theories of dreams leave no room for any problem of interpreting them, since in their view a dream is not a mental act at all, but a somative process signalizing its occurrence by indications registered in the mental apparatus.[10]

Freud's claim to primacy was echoed by his disciples. Frank Sulloway, a science historian, contends "that Freud's devoted followers carefully nurtured the image of his pioneering originality to establish a cultlike orthodoxy around his theories."[11] An example of this can be found in a 1972 book by William Stewart and Lucy Freeman entitled *The Secret of Dreams: A Key to Freudian Dream Analysis.* Stewart is a prominent psychoanalyst and Freeman is a popular writer on psychoanalytic therapy. These authors propose that Freud's "discoveries have many conceptual parallels to Einstein's theory of relativity."[12] They also inform us that "only Freud was equipped to observe what he had reported."[13] We are told that, before Freud, there were "four thousand years of history in which man was frightened, puzzled or contemptuous of dreams and their interpretation."[14] Apparently no one had ever enjoyed, appreciated, or received inspiration from a dream during those four dreary millennia. Stewart and Freeman indicate that "Freud's major work, *The Interpretation of Dreams,* was one of the few books to change the thinking of the Western world."[15] The authors go on to reveal, "The book marked the birth of a totally new science. There were no coworkers. *Freud was the first to walk the path of dreams.*"[16] (Italics mine)

Stewart and Freeman, in describing the many values of Freudian dream analysis, proclaim, "We can literally free creative and constructive aspects of our personalities from which we have been alienated. Our dreams give evidence of this creativity." A quote follows, which they attribute to Freud:

> There emerges from time to time in the creations and fabrics of the genius of dreams a depth and intimacy of emotion, a tenderness of

feeling, a clarity of vision, a subtlety of observations, and a brilliance of wit such as we should never claim to have at our permanent command in our waking lives. There lies in dreams a marvelous poetry, an apt allegory, an incomparable humor, a rare irony. A dream looks upon the world in a light of strange idealism and often enhances the effects of what it sees by its deep understanding of their essential nature. It pictures earthly beauty to our eyes in a truly heavenly splendor and clothes dignity with the highest majesty, it shows us our everyday fears in the ghastliest shape and turns our amusement into jokes of indescribable pungency. And sometimes, when we are awake and still under the full impact of an experience like one of these, we cannot but feel that never in our life has the real world offered us its equal.[17]

This inspirational passage would certainly incline one to think that Freud had banished those dreary days of contempt for dreams forever, but no footnote or page reference was given for this stirring quotation. I became curious because the appreciation of dreams presented in that passage did *not* sound, even remotely, like anything I had ever read in Freud's writings.

Intrigued, I began some lengthy detective work to trace down the source of that quotation. I finally found it, on pages 62 and 63 of *The Interpretation of Dreams*. Ironically, the "Freudian" passage quoted by Stewart and Freeman was written by F. W. Hildebrandt in his 1875 book on dreams, and Freud cited this "enthusiastic eulogy" critically to indicate how misdirected its author was. Freud indicated that such views belonged to "the intellectual period which has now been left behind, when the human mind was dominated by philosophy and not by the exact natural sciences."[18] Freud dismissed Hildebrandt and others who wrote in a similar way about the "psychical achievements of dreams,"[19] by declaring that those who "represent dreams as an elevation of mental life to a higher level, seem to us now to be scarcely intelligible; to-day they are repeated only by mystics and pietists."[20]

Despite its many shortcomings, Freud's literature review did serve to alert a professional audience to the existence of much previous work on dreams, even if almost all of it was distorted when seen through Freud's eyes. It is useful as an index to earlier sources on dreams, particularly with regard to German works, which are very inaccessible to current scholars.

HISTORY OF THE INTERPRETATION OF DREAMS

Freud was a very prolific writer; his collected publications run to twenty-four thick volumes. He discussed dreams extensively in twenty-six different articles or books, but his major exposition on the topic was *The Interpretation of Dreams*. The frontispiece to the first edition bears a Latin motto: *Flectere si nequeo superos, Acheronta movebo* ("If I cannot bend Heaven, I shall move Hell"). One speculation as to why Freud chose this theme as the leitmotif for his book was that he identified with Goethe's *Faust,* who was unsuccessful in conquering the secrets of Heaven through his studies and consequently made a pact with the Devil for understanding.[21]

Only 600 copies of this first edition were published and after six years only 351 copies had been sold. The second edition was published in 1909, and the first English translation by Brill appeared in 1913. Eight editions of the book eventually appeared, and it was translated into most of the world's major languages.

The prefaces and postscripts to some of these editions provide an interesting commentary on Freud's views about his dream theory, its reception, and the theoretical contributions of others. In the preface to the first edition, he said his volume will not have

> trespassed beyond the sphere of interest covered by neuropathology ... [because] *the dream is the first member of a class of abnormal psychical phenomena* of which further members, such as hysterical phobias, obsessions and delusions, are bound to be a matter of concern to physicians. As will be seen in the sequel, *dreams can make no such claim to practical importance.*[22] (Italics mine)

Freud's prefatory remarks are noteworthy for the negative emphasis he gave to

dreams: they are in the sphere of neuropathology, they are abnormal psychical phenomena, and they are of no practical importance. The quote above and all subsequent quotations are from the revised 1953 edition of *The Interpretation of Dreams* unless otherwise specified.

In the preface to the second edition (1909), Freud was peeved because

> my psychiatric colleagues seem to have taken no trouble to overcome the initial bewilderment created by my new approach to dreams. The professional philosophers ... have evidently failed to notice that we have something here from which a number of inferences can be drawn that are bound to transform our psychological theories. The attitude adopted by reviewers in the scientific periodicals could only lead one to suppose that my work was doomed to be sunk into complete silence. ... I am glad to say that I have found little to change in it ... it has stood the test of time.[23]

In a postscript to the 1909 edition, Freud explained that he had not extended his literature review to cover developments since the first edition, because: "The intervening nine years have produced nothing new or valuable either in factual material or in opinions that might throw light on the subject."[24] He also said that since his work had remained unmentioned, he would "certainly be justified in my turn in disregarding the literature that has been issued since the publication of this book."[25]

According to Ellenberger, the book actually was extensively reviewed during this period.[26] Freud also declared in this postscript: "A large number of dreams have been published and analyzed in accordance with my directions in papers by physicians," and "these publications have merely confirmed my views and not added anything to them."[27]

In the preface to the third edition (1911), Freud acknowledged:

The theory of dream-interpretation has itself developed further in a direction on which insufficient stress had been laid in the first edition of this book. My own experience, as well as the works of Wilhelm Stekel and others, have since taught me to form a truer estimate of the extent and importance of symbolism in dreams (or rather in unconscious thinking). Thus in the course of these years much has accumulated which demands attention. . . . Herr Otto Rank has given me valuable assistance in selecting the additional matter.[28]

The preface to the fourth edition (1914) was extremely brief and acknowledged that Otto Rank had again corrected the proofs. In the preface to the fifth edition (1919), Freud reported that he had not been able to bring himself to embark upon any fundamental revision of the book. In the preface of the sixth edition (1921), Rank's contribution to completing and bringing the bibliography up to date was acknowledged and Freud complained about the "obstinate misunderstandings"

that still existed about dreams. The eighth edition (1930) noted that several foreign translations of the book had been published. Freud also dropped the section which included dream work by others, probably because Rank was no longer reviewing the literature for him.

The remarks Freud made in the preface for the final (1932) English edition have frequently been quoted:

This book, with the new contribution to psychology which surprised the world when it was published, remains essentially unaltered. It contains, even according to my present-day judgment, the most valuable of all the discoveries it has been my good fortune to make. Insight such as this falls to one's lot but once in a lifetime.[29]

This quote stresses how important this book had always been for Freud; as early as 1907, in a letter to Carl Jung, Freud said he "clung to *The Interpretation of Dreams* as to a rock in the breakers."[30] In a letter to Wilhelm Fliess in 1900, Freud described a later visit to Belle Vue, the house where he first analyzed his "specimen" dream. "Do you suppose," he wrote, "that some day a marble tablet will be placed on the house, inscribed with these words":

IN THIS HOUSE, ON JULY 24TH, 1895.
THE SECRET OF DREAMS WAS
REVEALED TO DR. SIGM. FREUD

What was the secret of dreams revealed to Freud? Let's look at some of his theoretical constructs and his procedures for unlocking the secret of dreams.

MANIFEST AND LATENT CONTENT

The cornerstone of Freud's theory of dreams deals with a distinction he made between two levels of the dream. The content of a dream which one is able to consciously remember is referred to as the *manifest content*. If you were to tell some friends the dream you had last night you would be reporting the manifest content. Manifest content, in Freud's view, possessed no meaning or significance because it was the disguised representation of the true thoughts underlying the dream. These thoughts make up the *latent content* and consist of unconscious wishes and fantasies which have been denied gratification. They find an outlet through being expressed in a transformed way and eventually appear in an unrecognizable form in the manifest content. It is as if two different languages were involved, with one representing a cleaned-up version of something much more raw and crude. We sometimes engage in such transformed speech in everyday life, as when one excuses oneself to go to the "powder room" or "rest room" to "freshen up." This manifest speech is understood to express the latent meaning "I feel a strong urge to urinate or defecate and will now leave to do so."

The unconscious is composed of innate, instinctive material which has never been conscious, as well as additions which have been banished to the unconscious because they were consciously unacceptable. Responsible for maintaining the boundary between the conscious and the unconscious is the *censor*. The censor acts as a sentinel, or border guard, preventing the instinctual material from gaining access to the domain of consciousness, while at the same time forcing any threatening thoughts that develop in consciousness into the region of the unconscious. The censor carries out these monitoring duties using the force of *repression*. During the special conditions of sleep, however, the censor is not quite as alert and can be duped into allowing unconscious material to pass the border. The nighttime censor is willing to accept a forged passport and, with a knowing wink of the eye, to wave the anxious tourist through the sentry station.

DREAM WORK

The process whereby the unacceptable, unconscious latent content is transformed into acceptable manifest content is called the *dream work*. Several modes of operation are available for the dream work to carry out its disguising function. One of

Figure 1

Figure 2

these is referred to as *condensation*. The material of the latent content is always far more extensive than that of the manifest content. An example is shown in the cartoon in which composite figure has resulted from the fusion of several disparate elements (fig. 1). The resulting manifest dream element is said to be overdetermined, since it has not been derived from a single element in the latent thoughts but from a number of them.

After a dream has been analyzed, it can often be shown that what appeared to stand out most conspicuously in the manifest content was derived from an extremely minor dream thought, or that what appeared to be an inconsequential detail in the manifest content was, in fact, derived from a latent element of major importance. This transformation of emphasis from the important to the unimportant and vice versa is referred to as *displacement*. An example of displacement is provided in the other cartoon, where we observe the artist

118

apparently painting a nude woman holding flowers (fig. 2). We later see, however, that he has focused all his attention upon the details of the flowers and overlooked the nude woman holding them. This cartoon illustrates how displacement shifts the emphasis from important to unimportant elements, selecting ideas that are sufficiently remote from the objectionable idea to allow them to pass censorship.

Freud considered dreams to be a special form of thinking because the thinking used sensory images as units of communication, without reference to abstract verbal concepts. Although other sensory modalities can be involved, dreams most commonly consist of visual metaphors and the dream can be considered as a kind of pictographic script. "Of the various subsidiary thoughts attached to the essential dream-thoughts, those will be preferred which admit of visual representation."[31] Freud was fond of using the analogy of a rebus, or picture puzzle, to describe the method whereby latent thoughts came to be represented in concrete visual images. Such a transformation is necessitated by "considerations of representability," and the dream work must find a means of achieving this through pictorial representation.

An attempt has been made to convey this process in figure 3, where objects have been selected to convey the abstract verbal concept of "pictorial representation." The first object shown is a "pick," the next is something "tore," and the third object in the top line is a fishing "reel." Each object visually portrays a syllable of the word "pictorial": pick-tore-reel. Combining them enables us to arrive at the concept of pictorial. To convey the idea of "representation," an image of congressmen was used because they provide "representation" to their voters.

The final mode of transformation to be considered is that of *secondary revision*. Secondary revision occurs because of "considerations of intelligibility," which means there is a natural tendency to organize any disconnected or jumbled elements into a unified, coherent whole. This composition of the dream into a connected whole results in the *dream facade*. Freud seemed uncertain when, in the dream-process, secondary revision occurred. In one passage, Freud described secondary revision as an integral part of dream work and said it occurred "before the manifest dream is arrived at." In another passage about secondary revision he said, "Strictly speaking, this last process does not form part of the dream work." In still another passage, Freud described secondary revision as a variable factor, because it "is not to be

Figure 3

found in operation in *every* dream." All the quotes in this paragraph can be found in the section on secondary revision in the officially approved *Basic Psychoanalytic Concepts on the Theory of Dreams* by H. Nagera.[32] Although to an outsider it might seem that Freud was inconsistent, Nagera explained, "His basic point of view and conception of the process and functioning of secondary revision remained unaltered."[33]

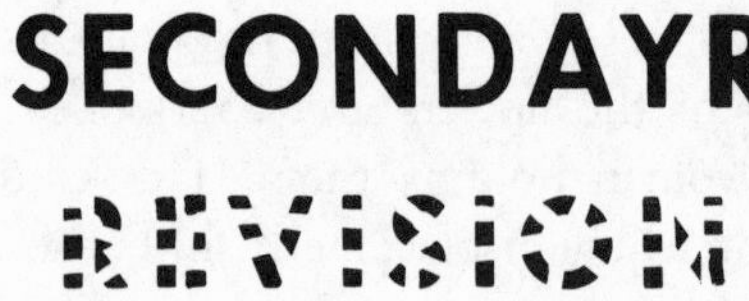

An attempt has been made in figure 4 to illustrate two of the principles operating to create the dream facade. Our inclination is to read these words as "secondary revision." In actuality, the first word is misspelled, but we tend to rearrange the posi-

SECONDAYR REVISION

Figure 4

tions of the letters *r* and *y* into the order that we expect. Similarly, although no actual letters are present in the second line, we perceptually fill in the gaps between the black spaces to create letters which will spell the word "revision."

Coherent Dreams

Freud's efforts to cope with coherent or "well-constructed" dreams called forth a great deal of ingenuity. There were two classes of dreams that didn't fit Freud's procrustean dream bed. One was telepathic dreams: if dreams originated from *outside* the dreamer, then they could conceivably appear as well-constructed, since the latent dream thoughts wouldn't have to be disguised if they didn't belong to the dreamer. Freud's ambivalent attitude toward telepathic dreams will be discussed later in this chapter.

The other troublesome dreams were those in which some intellectual or reasoning faculty appeared to be present. Freud proposed, "When a dream deals with a problem of actual life, it solves it in the manner of an irrational wish and not in the manner of a reasonable reflection."[34] One solution was to demote reports of coherent, well-constructed nocturnal imagery to the class of "dream-fantasies," reserving "true dream" status for only those productions in which the disguising efforts of dream work could be detected. Thus, paradoxically, disguised dreams are true dreams, while organized and clear dreams are "dream-fantasies." Freud's other solution was to assume that anything which sounded reasonable was never part of the dream at all, but instead an afterthought quickly appended by secondary revision to present a dream facade which gave a deceptive, superficial appearance of higher mental faculties being present.

Freud's rejection of the possibility that dreams could possess any reasoning or reflecting capacity was bluntly stated:

> I do not know why the dream should not be as varied as thought during the waking state in which we have so many different acts of judging, inferring, refuting, expecting, deciding, etc. I should have nothing against it. For my part it could be so. There is only a trifling obstacle in the way of this more convenient conception of the dream; it does not happen to reflect reality.[35]

SYMBOLS IN DREAMS

The topic of symbolism was largely ignored in the first edition of *The Interpretation of Dreams*. Freud first discussed symbolism as a separate topic in the fourth edition, and indicated that his principal influence in achieving a full appreciation of symbolism was the contribution made by Wilhelm Stekel. Freud defensively pointed out, however, "that I recognized the presence of symbolism in dreams from the very beginning."[36] Freud's official biographer, Ernest Jones, conceded:

> Stekel was a naturally gifted psychologist with an unusual flair for detecting repressed material, and his contributions to our knowledge of symbolism, a field in which he had more intuitive genius than Freud, were in the earlier stages of psychoanalysis of very considerable value. Freud freely admitted this. He said he had often contradicted Stekel's interpretation for a given symbol only to find on further study that Stekel had been right the first time.[37]

Freud considered a *symbol* as being something standing as a substitute for something else—a perceptual replacement for something hidden—which had some characteristics in common with the unseen thing. Since dreams make use of symbols in the disguised pictorial representation of latent thoughts, symbols are related to the dream work, but they are not formally considered one of the processes associated with dream work. Freud wrote, "Symbolism is a second and independent factor in the distortion of dreams, alongside of the dream-censorship."[38] Dream work was regarded as effecting some change upon the latent thoughts, while a symbol existed more or less as a fixed object "which could be deployed by dream work in representing latent elements but would not itself be transformed." A symbol was considered as a preexisting entity having a "genetic character" that extended back to prehistoric times. A common symbol often transcends the use of a common language. Freud noted that dream symbolism was a smaller part of the overall province of symbolism, which also included myths, fairy tales, poetic fantasy, songs, and colloquial speech. He acknowledged that there were numerous unsolved problems attached to their significance.

Freud's theoretical interest in finding similarities between the formation of neurotic symptoms and dream images forced him toward a rather narrow interpretation of symbols. He summarized his position as follows:

Though the number of symbols is

large, the number of subjects symbolized is not large. In dreams those pertaining to sexual life are the overwhelming majority. Mostly they deal with the human body as a whole, with children, brothers and sisters, birth, death and nakedness. They represent the most primitive ideas and interests imaginable.[39]

The following quotations show how fully Freud committed himself to the posi-

For Freud, objects in dreams were really symbols. A pipe was not really a pipe. Instead, it might be a penis. La Trahison des Images by Rene Magritte

tion that most symbols had a sexual referent:

All elongated objects, such as sticks, tree-trunks and umbrellas (the opening of these last being comparable to an erection) may stand for the male organ. . . .

Boxes, cases, chests, cupboards and ovens represent the uterus, and also hollow objects, ships, and vessels of all kinds. Rooms in dreams are usually women; if the various ways in and out of them are represented, *this interpretation is scarcely open to doubt.* . . . A dream of going through a suite of rooms is a brothel or harem dream. . . .

Steps, ladders or staircases, or, as the case may be, walking up or down them, are representations of the sexual act. . . .

A woman's hat can very *often be interpreted with certainty* as a genital organ, and, moreover, as a man's. The same is true of an overcoat. . . . In men's dreams a neck-tie often appears as a symbol for the penis. . . .

It is *highly probable* that all complicated machinery and apparatus occurring in dreams stand for the genitals (and as a rule the male ones). . . . *Nor is there any doubt* that all weapons and tools are used as symbols for the male organ: e.g. ploughs, hammers, rifles, revolvers, daggers, sabres, etc. In the same way many landscapes in dreams, especially any contain-

ing bridges or wooded hills, *may clearly be recognized* as descriptions of the genitals. . . .

Children in dreams often stand for the genitals. . . . Playing with a little child, beating it, etc., often represent masturbation in dreams. To represent castration symbolically, the dream-work makes use of baldness, hair-cutting, falling out of teeth and decapitation. If one of the ordinary symbols for a penis occurs in a dream doubled or multiplied, *it is to be regarded* as a warding-off of castration. . . .

The genitals can also be represented in dreams in other parts of the body: the male organ by a hand or a foot and the female genital orifice by the mouth or an ear or even an eye.[40] (Italics mine)

In his chapter on symbolism, Freud referred to Stekel's 1911 book as containing the fullest collection of interpretations of symbols, but Freud then disparagingly commented that Stekel's "lack of a critical faculty" rendered his interpretations unusable. Some of Stekel's interpretations were listed along with comments from Freud as to whether or not he had found them to be accurate. He disagreed with Stekel's interpretation that the luggage one travels with could represent a load of sin that weighs one down. Freud explained: "But precisely luggage often turns out to be an unmistakable symbol of the dreamer's own genitals."[41]

Typical Dreams

Typical dreams are those which a high percentage of people acknowledge having experienced at some time in their life. Freud proposed probable meanings for several typical dreams "which almost everyone has dreamt alike and which we are accustomed to assume must have the same meaning for everyone."[42] It should come as no surprise that most of Freud's suggested meanings involve issues of sexuality or childhood conflicts. My own views about typical dreams will be presented in chapter 12, but an illustration of how I would differ from Freud will be given after his first example.

The first typical dream Freud discussed was being naked or insufficiently dressed in the presence of strangers and feeling shame and embarrassment; "dreams of being naked are dreams of exhibiting,"[43] although "the people upon whom our sexual interest was directed are omitted."[44] The familiar individual before whom the dreamer actually exposed himself or herself, by means of a "wishful contrary," is replaced in the dream by a collection of strangers who ignore the dreamer.

In my experience such dreams have little to do with exhibiting or sexuality. Since clothing is used to indicate whether one is a nurse, policeman, astronaut, factory worker, business executive, or waiter, appearing naked in public deprives the person of his or her occupational status and social position or rank. Clothing is used to "make a statement" about who the person is, and people are often judged by the type and condition of the clothing they wear. The underlying question posed by these dreams is, "What would people think or feel about me if they could see or know the way I *really* am underneath?" The underneath can refer to clothing or to behavioral facades.

The answer to this question is contained in the typical response of the other dream characters—they either ignore the dreamer, or are not put off by the dreamer's appearance and indicate through their interactions that they continue to find the dreamer personally and socially acceptable. Such dreams are therefore likely to surface whenever the dreamer is experiencing doubts about self-worth or social image and wondering how he or she would be received if the world knew the real person under the "front" we all put up.

In another typical dream, someone the dreamer is fond of dies. Such a dream is considered typical by Freud only if the dreamer is "painfully affected." "The meaning of such dreams . . . is a wish that the person in question may die."[45] Freud subsequently clarified his statement to indicate that the dreamer may not wish for that person's death at the present time, but that it had been wished for at some time or other during the dreamer's childhood.

When Freud initially turned his attention to flying and falling dreams, he speculated that they were related to a reproduction of movement sensations experienced in childhood. A flying dream was originally related to an uncle holding a child in outstretched arms and rushing across a room, and a falling dream to his pretending to drop the child while bouncing him on his knee. In the 1911 edition, Freud mentioned the "attractive" theory of Federn that "a good number of flying dreams are dreams of erection . . . involving as it does an apparent suspension of the laws of gravity."[46] Interpretation of dreams of falling "offers no difficulty in the case of women, who almost always accept the symbolic use of falling as a way of describing a surrender to an erotic temptation."[47]

People who have frequent dreams of swimming "have as a rule been bedwetters."[48] In dreams of fire, there is also "an underlying recollection of the enuresis of childhood."[49]

Freud said that the meaning of dreams "with a dental stimulus" escaped him for a long time because of strong resistances against their interpretation. However, "overwhelming evidence left me at last in no doubt that in males the motive force of those dreams was derived from nothing other than the masturbatory desires of the pubertal period."[50] If the tooth was pulled out by someone else, it signified castration. A footnote indicated that Jung claimed such dreams in women are birth dreams.[51] This footnote is one of the two very fleeting references to Jung's dream theories in any of the editions of *The Interpretation of Dreams*. After presenting these interpreta-tions of typical dreams, Freud summarized his viewpoint:

> The more one is concerned with the solution of dreams, the more one is driven to recognize that the majority of the dreams of adults deal with sexual material and give expression to erotic wishes. A judgment on this point can be formed only by those who really analyze dreams, that is to say, who make their way through the manifest content to the latent dream-thoughts, and never by those who are satisfied with making a note of the manifest content alone.[52]

In the final paragraph of his section on typical dreams, Freud offered the following observations about the origin of dreams involving robbers and ghosts:

> Robbers, burglars and ghosts . . . all originate from one and the same class of infantile reminiscence. They are the nocturnal visitors who rouse children and take them up to prevent their wetting their beds, or who lift the bedclothes to make sure where they have put their hands in their sleep. Analyses of some of these anxiety-dreams have made it possible for me to identify the nocturnal visitors more precisely. In every case the robbers stood for the sleeper's father, whereas the ghosts corresponded to female figures in white night-gowns.[53]

Method of Dream Interpretation

Freud began his chapter on dream interpretation by mentioning two techniques that had been employed for this purpose in earlier times. One involved *symbolic* interpretation of the dream as a whole, as in the example of Joseph interpreting the seven fat cows in the Pharaoh's dream as representing seven years of plenty. The other was a *decoding* method in which dreams are considered as a form of cryptography in which each sign can be treated as another sign in accordance with a fixed key. Artemidorus was given as an example of this approach.

Freud then asserted: "It cannot be doubted for a moment that neither of the two popular procedures for interpreting dreams can be employed for a scientific treatment of the subject."[54] Freud's "original" scientific approach involved using the method of "free association," a technique which he discovered while therapeutically engaged "in unravelling certain psychopathological structures." This is how his thinking evolved:

> My patients were pledged to communicate to me every idea or thought that occurred to them in connection with some particular subject; amongst other things they told me their dreams and so taught me that a dream can be inserted into the psychical chain that has to be traced backwards in memory

from a pathological idea. It was then only a short step to treating the dream itself as a symptom and to applying to dreams the method of interpretation that had been worked out for symptoms.[55]

In discussing his technique, Freud mentioned that if the dream as a whole were presented to the dreamer for comments, the dreamer's mind generally became a blank.

> If, however, I put the dream before him cut up into pieces, he will give me a series of associations to each piece . . . thus the method of dream interpretation which I practice already differs in this first important respect from the popular, historic and legendary method of interpretation by means of symbolism and approximates to the . . . "decoding" method.[56]

Since transformation of the latent content via the dream work resulted in the final product of the manifest dream, to interpret a dream the process had to be reversed; that is, the analyst used the manifest content as the starting point and attempted to retrace the various distortions back to their sources in the latent dream-thoughts. The intent of dream interpretation was thus to unscramble the dream message that had been scrambled initially by the dream work. So important was the technique of free association that Freud called it the fundamental rule of psychoanalysis and even referred to it as the "sacred rule."

In the "original classical" method, associations were brought up to the elements of the dream in the same order in which they occurred in the account of the dream. In a 1923 paper, Freud said that other techniques were also acceptable and no one of them was especially preferable in working with others' dreams, although the classical technique was better for analyzing one's own dreams. The other techniques involved picking out a particular element from the middle, starting off with some spoken words in the dream, letting the dreamer decide which associations to begin with, or disregarding the manifest content and asking the dreamer what events from the preceding day were associated with the dream. The most important factor was not the technique chosen, but the degree of resistance to association that the dreamer displayed. If resistance was too high, associations might broaden instead of deepening, or they might be very sparse. In the latter case, "one is content to put before him (the dreamer) a few translations of symbols that seem probable."[57]

The question naturally arises as to how much influence the analyst can exert on the patient's dreams. Freud was willing to concede that this influence could be quite considerable:

The fact that the manifest content of dreams is influenced by the an-

alytic treatment stands in no need of proof. . . . So it is not to be wondered at that patients should dream of things which the analyst has discussed with them and of which he has aroused expectations in them.[58]

Freud not only conceded that the manifest content could be influenced, but also said that the latent dream-thoughts obviously could be influenced or suggested by the analyst.

One technique which Freud said "never failed" him, was to have the patient report the same dream twice. By paying attention to those parts of the dream in which different terms were used, he could detect where the "weak spots" of the dream's disguise were located. If two dreams were spontaneously reported from a single night, one of them would frequently have as its central point what is on the periphery of the other, and vice versa, so such dreams should be considered as complementary.

Despite the early optimism that Freud displayed with regard to having discovered the technique for revealing the secret of dreams, he eventually acknowledged there were limitations to his approach. In the 1923 paper, he said: "A number of dreams which occur during analyses are untranslatable even though they do not actually make much show of the resistance that is there."[59] He made a similar comment in a 1925 paper: "Only a certain portion of a patient's dream-products can be translated and made use of, and even at that not completely."[60]

DREAMS AS THE GUARDIANS OF SLEEP

For Freud, dreams had a quite limited function—that of insuring sleep:

> It is misleading to say that dreams are concerned with the tasks of life before us or seek to find a solution for the problems of our daily work. That is the business of preconscious thought. . . . There is only one useful task, only one function, that can be ascribed to a dream, and that is the guarding of sleep from interruption. A dream may be described as a piece of phantasy working on behalf of the maintenance of sleep.[61]

In this statement, Freud was reiterating his stance that dreams didn't function in a problem-solving capacity. But even if the function of dreams is to insure the continuation of sleep, that doesn't mean it wouldn't be of value to examine the by-products of dreaming for clues to repressed emotional problems.

Censorship helps to insure that the disturbing latent dream-thoughts will be sufficiently disguised that the superego, or conscience, will not be offended and wake the dreamer. Sometimes censorship fails. In discussing the issue of "moral responsibility" for dreams, Freud observed that sometimes dreams "really mean what they say and have undergone no distortion from the censorship. They are an expression of immoral, incestuous and perverse impulses or of murderous and sadistic lusts."[62] The reason for the appearance of such dreams is that "the censorship has neglected its task, this has been noticed too late, and the development of anxiety is a substitute for the distortion that has been omitted."[63] Another function of the dream was to allow repressed instinctual impulses to be gratified in a hallucinated fashion. In this way, dreams served as a safety valve to drain off accumulated psychological tensions that might have been stirred up during the preceding day.

THE ROLE OF WISH FULFILLMENT

The motivating force for a dream, Freud insisted, was that of wish fulfillment. A dream cannot be formed without the energy being provided by some wish from the unconscious. Four possible origins for wishes can exist: (1) consciously remembered wishes that were aroused during the day but left unfulfilled; (2) wishes that arose during the day but, because of their unacceptability, were repressed into the unconscious; (3) wishes arising during the night stimulated by such bodily needs as hunger or urination; and (4) wishes originating in the unconscious that are incapable of ever passing beyond the censorship into conscious awareness. Although the first three types of wishes could represent a starting point for some wish that might be expressed in the dream, this expression cannot occur unless such a wish is able to link up with an unconscious wish, since only the latter have sufficient energy available to them to initiate the dream work. This point was clearly made by Freud:

> My supposition is that a conscious wish can only become a dream-instigator if it succeeds in awakening an unconscious wish with the same tenor and in obtaining reinforcement from it . . . [because] a wish which is represented in a dream must be an infantile one.[64]

Although Freud emphasized that the wish represented in a dream must have been joined to an infantile desire, he was not always completely consistent in this regard. Richard Jones, who has reviewed several dream theories in depth,[65] has pointed out that there is not a single example in *The Interpretation of Dreams* where Freud analyzed a dream back to an infantile source. One possible explanation for this would be that Freud used many of his own dreams in this book, and he indicated, for reasons of discretion, he would not reveal certain personal details that he knew, from his own self-analysis, lay at the root of the dream. It is surprising, never-

theless, since this was to be the book in which he illustrated his viewpoints and techniques in clearest detail, that such an analysis was not carried out upon any of the numerous other dreams presented. Infantile sources, however, were brought to light in some of Freud's clinical papers when he discussed the dreams used in the analyses of some neurotic patients. Freud wrote a very short popularized account of his dream theory, *On Dreams*, which was first published in 1901. Infantile wishes were not referred to in that book as the necessary instigators of dreams and, in fact, Freud said: "I should like to lay it down that no dream is prompted by motives other than egoistic ones."[66]

Although Freud hesitated to accept as "genuine" any dream in which the evidence of the dream work could not be ascertained, he allowed some exceptions. He believed, for example, that in children's dreams the wish fulfillment was expressed without any distortion. He gave several examples of children dreaming about food they had desired during the day or about continuing pleasurable events, such as a boat ride. Freud cited related examples that could be found on occasion with adults, such as when hungry explorers would dream of lavish banquets not available to them in their waking life. Such dreams were sometimes called *infantile dreams*, because they represented the open fulfillment of a permitted wish.

There were several classes of dreams that Freud dealt with at some length because they seemed to oppose his notion that all dreams were wish fulfillments. One class was called *counter-wish dreams*, since the dream account portrayed the frustration of a wish. For these dreams, Freud pointed out that the frustration occurred *only* in the manifest content and that interpretation would reveal an underlying wish of a masochistic nature. Since some people find pleasure in being humiliated or mentally tortured, these people, through experiencing unpleasant dreams, actually obtain a wish fulfillment for their masochistic inclination. He also observed that when his patients were resisting him, or when they had been first introduced to his theory, they produced dreams that appeared to go against his theory. The wish that was involved in these situations, Freud explained, was to prove his theory wrong and such dreams therefore represented a fulfillment of their negativistic tendencies.

Freud did eventually come to acknowledge that anxiety and punishment dreams were not derived from repressed wishes that existed in the unconscious id, but belonged to the unconscious region of the ego. This marked an important distinction, because it gave greater emphasis to the more rational and reality-oriented component of personality described by the term ego.

The other dreams which seemed to run counter to the wish fulfillment notion were those associated with the traumatic neuroses. These repetitive dreams resulting from some traumatic experience, such as might occur on the battlefield or in some civilian catastrophe, presented a definite problem for Freud:

> So far as I can at present see, dreams that occur in a traumatic neurosis are the only *genuine* exceptions and punishment dreams are the only *apparent* exceptions, to the rule that dreams are directed towards wish-fulfillment.[67]

Freud, however, seemed to reverse his view ten years later. In his later position he considered that these dreams did have wish fulfillment as their goal, but that the attempt to fulfill the wish had failed. Thus, in order to stretch his theory to include *every* type of dream, he was forced to say that these dreams represented the *attempted fulfillment* of a wish. By resorting to this elastic concept, Freud attempted to fulfill his own deepest wish—that no exceptions be found to cast doubt upon his theory of dreams.

TELEPATHIC DREAMS

A reader of *The Interpretation of Dreams* would not suspect that Freud was intrigued by *telepathic dreams*, since only one brief footnote about them appeared in this book. But Freud discussed telepathic dreams at some length in several papers, and since chapter 14 of this book will be devoted to paranormal dreams, a review of his position will be given here. These papers by Freud, as well as a collection of several papers on this topic by other analysts, appeared in the book *Psychoanalysis and the Occult*, edited by George Devereux, an anthropologist.[68]

Freud read a paper entitled "Psychoanalysis and Telepathy" at a psychoanalytic conference in 1921, but it was not published until 1941, after his death. He began by claiming that occultists are not motivated by a thirst for knowledge, but by "an old religious belief, which, in the course of human evolution, has been pushed into the background by science, or else it represents still another faith, which is even closer to the obsolete convictions of primitives."[69] Freud discussed how psychoanalysts aspired to "kinship with the representatives of science," and stated, "Psychoanalysts are fundamentally unreconstructed mechanists and materialists."[70] Freud went on to indicate the consequences of accepting occult phenomena: people would no longer have the "obligation of thinking rationally," and there would be "a dreadful collapse of critical thoughts and of mechanistic science."[71] We see, in this paper, two of the reasons why acceptance of psychic phenomena was so threatening for Freud. First it would be tantamount to accepting religion, and Freud insisted throughout his life that he was an atheist, an "infidel Jew." His other fear was that various hard-earned scientific accomplishments, including those of psychoanalysis, would collapse.

Freud's next paper on "Dreams and Telepathy" was published in 1922. In it, he said he had never personally experienced a telepathic dream. Freud wrestled with the issue of whether telepathic dreams might prove to be an exception to the way

dreams generally are constructed. He proposed that a telepathic message, like any other external or internal stimulus, "with the help of a lurking repressed wish, becomes remodeled into a wish fulfillment."[72] The telepathic message "can thus make no alteration in the structure of the dream."[73] Freud progressed to the thorny issue of how to explain "telepathic dreams in which there is no difference between the event and the dream, and in which there is nothing else to be found but the undisguised reproduction of the event."[74] He came up with a simple solution:

> Supposing, then, that we are brought face to face with a pure telepathic "dream," let us call it instead a telepathic experience in a state of sleep. A dream without condensation, distortion, dramatization, above all, without wish fulfillment hardly deserves the name.[75]

Later in this paper, Freud concluded that it was an "incontestable fact that sleep creates favorable conditions for telepathy."[76] If this were so, and if a "dream" had to demonstrate all the hallmarks of dream work, it is understandable why Freud would say, "I think it would be in the interests of scientific accuracy to keep 'dream' and 'state of sleep' more distinctly separate."[77]

Toward the conclusion of this paper, Freud stressed that the possibility of telepathic occurrences shouldn't be dismissed because the event and message "do not exactly coincide in astronomical time."[78] He pointed out that it was perfectly conceivable that a telepathic message could arrive at the same time as the event, but might not penetrate to consciousness until the following night during sleep. He noted that a similar phenomena was true for many dreams, because the latent thoughts existing during the day had to wait until night for the contact with the unconscious wish that shaped them into a dream.

Freud's next related paper, "The Occult Significance of Dreams," was published in 1925. In it, he spoke much more positively about telepathic dreams and said that if they were examined critically, "a kernel of truth" would be found. He then provided some personal endorsement of telepathy: "I have often had an impression, in the course of experiments in my private circle, that strongly colored recollections can be successfully transferred without much difficulty."[79] He claimed that many of the transferred thoughts, however, would have remained undiscovered if the associations of the person receiving them had not been exposed to analytical examination.

"Dreams and the Occult," published in 1933, started out with a very open-minded approach:

> Occultism assumes that there are in fact more things in heaven and earth than are dreamed of in our philosophy. Well, we need not be tied down by the narrow-mindedness of the Schools; we are ready to believe whatever is made plausible to us.
>
> We intend to treat these things in just the same way as we treat any other material for scientific investigation.[80]

Freud indicated that an investigator had to be flexible in seeking out situations where such phenomena might appear, and be careful to utilize appropriate methods of control for detecting fraud. "The study of the occult has become a specialized and difficult pursuit, a form of activity which one cannot carry on side by side with one's other interests."[81]

In the final pages, Freud suggested that analysts should "think more kindly of the objective possibility of thought-transference."[82] He confided that when his own thoughts turned toward this topic more than ten years earlier, he felt afraid that "our scientific outlook might be endangered," but his current posture was, "One is displaying no great trust in science if one cannot rely on it to accept and deal with any occult hypothesis that may turn out to be correct."[83] He went on to indicate that "if one gets used to the idea of telepathy one can account for a great deal by means of it."[84]

Since Freud was so enmeshed in his speculations about the possible existence of telepathic dreams, Ernest Jones devoted a thirty-two-page section to "Occultism" in his biography of Freud. In the opening paragraph of this section, Jones, in discussing Freud's attitude toward occultism, said:

> In it we find throughout an exquisite oscillation between skepticism and credulity so striking that it is possible to quote just as many pieces of evidence in support of

his doubt concerning occult beliefs as of his adherence to them.[85]

Jones was a definite skeptic, who was clearly embarrassed by Freud's occult interests and made strenuous efforts to limit Freud's public statements in support of his positive beliefs. Jones was concerned that the credibility of psychoanalysis would be endangered if Freud became a proponent for psychical research. Freud recognized that Jones's concern had to be considered, but he made many strongly worded statements to the effect that facts were facts and could not be ignored for mere political expediency. In a letter to Jones, he asserted: "My own experiences through tests I made with Ferenczi and my daughter won such a convincing force for me that the diplomatic considerations on the other side had to give way."[86] Freud emphasized that he had to "proclaim a conviction without taking into account any echo from the outer world."[87]

Freud's enthusiasm waxed so strong that in a 1921 letter to Hereward Carrington, a prominent psychic researcher, he wrote, "If I were at the beginning rather than the end of a scientific career, as I am today, I might possibly choose just this field of research, in spite of all its difficulties." Freud asked, however, that Carrington refrain from mentioning his name in connection with Carrington's ventures. The letter from which I took the above quotes was number 192 in the collected letters published by Freud's son, Ernst Freud.[88] When an analyst, who had heard about the letter from Carrington, questioned Freud in 1929 about whether he had made such a positive statement, Freud

replied: "I deplore the fact that you yourself did not read my letter to Carrington. You would have easily convinced yourself that I said nothing to justify his assertion."[89] This response seems to reflect Freud's ambivalence with regard to this emotionally charged topic.

A ploy that Freud used to make himself comfortable with psychical phenomena was to assume that an underlying physiological or neural level of reality produced these phenomena. After Freud and Sandor Ferenczi, another psychoanalyst, had visited a "soothsayer" in Berlin, Freud wrote to Ferenczi that he considered the woman to have clearly demonstrated thought transference. The explanation he offered was that the woman possessed a "physiological gift." He ventured what, to me at least, seemed a remarkable conclusion:

It's only a question of thought transference. If this is demonstrated one has to believe in it. *It is not a psychical phenomenon, but a purely somatic one*—one, it is true of the first rank in importance.[90] (Italics mine)

Occultism was a topic that Freud confessed "always perplexed him to distraction."[91] At one point, Freud said he was "prepared to lend the support of psychoanalysis to the matter of telepathy."[92] If Freud were willing to consider such a giant step on the basis of what sounded like rather trivial anecdotes in his papers, one can't help but wonder what his response would have been to the substantive laboratory evidence available today for the reality of telepathic dreams. Perhaps he would have actively joined the ranks of parapsychologists and investigated telepathic dreams with the zeal and tenacity characteristic of his other explorations of the human mind. But, then again, given his ambivalence, perhaps he would not have.

FREUD'S SPECIMEN DREAM OF IRMA'S INJECTION

Perhaps the best way to evaluate Freud's approach toward dreams would be to examine the dream that provided the foundation for his new insights—his famous "specimen" dream. It was through his study of this dream that the "secret" of dreams was revealed to Freud. Freud was thirty-nine when he had this dream, on the night of July 23–24, 1895:

A large hall—numerous guests, whom we were receiving—Among them was Irma. I at once took her on one side, as though to answer her letter and to reproach her for not having accepted my "solution" yet. I said to her: "If you still get pains it's really only your fault." She replied: "If you only knew what pains I've got now in my throat and stomach and abdomen—it's choking me"—I was alarmed and looked at her. She looked pale and puffy. I thought to myself that after all I must be missing some organic trouble. I took her to the window and looked down her throat, and she showed signs of recalcitrance, like women with artificial dentures. I thought to myself that there really was no need for her to do that.—She then opened her mouth properly and on the right I found a big white patch; at another place I saw extensive whitish gray scabs upon some remarkable curly structures which were evidently modelled on the turbinal bones of the nose.—I at once called in Dr. M., and he repeated the examination and confirmed it.... Dr. M. looked quite different from usual; he was very pale, he walked with a limp and his chin was clean-shaven.... My friend Otto was now standing beside her as well, and my friend Leopold was percussing her through her bodice and saying: "She has a dull area low down on the left." He also indicated that a portion of the skin on the left shoulder was infiltrated. (I noticed this, just as he did, in spite of her dress.) ... M. said: "There's no doubt it's an infection, but no matter; dysentery will supervene and the toxin will be eliminated." ... We were directly aware, too, of the origin of the infection. Not long before, when she was feeling unwell, my friend Otto had given her an injection.... And probably the syringe had not been clean.

Freud supplied a preamble for this dream in which he informed the reader that he "had been giving psychoanalytic treatment to Irma, a young lady who was on very friendly terms" with Freud and his family. He indicated that such "a mixed relationship" could cause disturbed feelings in a psychotherapist and that he had proposed a solution to her which she "seemed unwilling to accept" and treatment had been suspended during this period of disagreement. Otto was a junior colleague and one of Freud's "oldest friends," who had recently visited him and also stayed with Irma and her family. When Freud asked Otto about Irma, he responded, "She's better, but not quite well." Freud found himself annoyed by Otto's answer because it seemed to be some form of "reproof." To justify himself, Freud wrote a summary of Irma's history the night before his dream to share with Dr. M., "a common friend and leading figure" in their circle. (Subsequent research by others has revealed that Dr. M. was Josef Breuer, Freud's previous mentor and coauthor with Freud of a book on hysteria.)

Before going on to analyze this dream within the framework of his new approach, Freud steadfastly asserted his rejection of the significance of manifest content, declaring, "No one who had only read the preamble and the content of the dream itself could have the slightest notion of what the dream meant."[93] "After the patient has told us a dream," Freud stated in 1933, "we decide to concern ourselves as little as possible with what we have heard, with the manifest dream,"[94] because "dreams are not in themselves social utterances, not a means of giving information."[95]

I believe, however that it is worth examining the manifest content of this dream as a social utterance. The dream opens in a large hall in which numerous guests are being received. This social setting is, however, set aside as soon as attention is directed toward Irma, the patient, and it never reappears. This suggests that the dreamer's life is dominated by professional concerns, with little time allotted to social activities. (Freud's biographer, Ernest Jones, wrote, "In Vienna, there was little besides work.")[96] Freud initially treats Irma rather badly. He "took her" aside, "reproached her" for not accepting his solution, and blamed her for any pain she might be experiencing. Only when Irma indicates that she is in considerable pain does Freud let up and become more compassionate. Still, he remarks upon the "recalcitrance" she demonstrates before "open[ing] her mouth properly" for examination. These exchanges seem to typify Freud's self-acknowledged difficulty in understanding women. (He once said to Marie Bonaparte, a female analyst, "The great question that has never been answered and which I have not yet been able to answer, despite my thirty years of research into the feminine soul, is 'What does a woman want?' ")[97] Ernest Jones noted that "it might perhaps be fair to describe [Freud's] view of the female sex as having as their main function to be ministering angels to the needs and comforts of men."[98]

Freud then describes in detail what he saw when he looked in Irma's mouth. Why would the dreamer provide such an exacting description of Irma's symptoms? A plausible reason might be that these symptoms had special importance for the dreamer himself. In fact, Freud suffered from sinus infections, had already undergone surgery for his condition once, and underwent a second surgery a few weeks after this dream. Freud also was "making frequent use of cocaine at that time to reduce some troublesome nasal swellings, and I had heard earlier that one of my women patients who had followed my example had developed extensive necrosis of the nasal mucous membrane."[99] Thus this nasal dream imagery could have represented Freud's preoccupation with the status of his own health.

After Freud discovered these disturbing symptoms in Irma, he sought confirmation from Dr. M. (Breuer), but Freud described his former mentor as both handicapped and lowered in status, since Viennese professionals of that time were expected to have beards. Freud did in fact consult with Breuer when confronted with a medical challenge; he had written up Irma's case history for Breuer just that evening, seeking to have his evaluation and proposed treatment affirmed. But Jones's biography provides ample evidence of the ambivalence Freud held toward Breuer as an authority figure and chronicles how their relationship deteriorated and left Freud with feelings of bitterness and betrayal.

Following the consultation with Dr. M., two younger males specifically described as friends appear. (Freud's appreciation of the support of younger colleagues is very evident in a letter he wrote to another analyst: "The affection of a group of courageous and understanding young men is the most precious gift that psychoanalysis has brought me.")[100] At least one bit of

wordplay may be diminished in the English translation of this dream account. The German word *Spritze* is translated as "syringe," which is technically correct, but it also carries a colloquial meaning of "squirter," which has possible sexual connotations. There are many other hints of sexual intimacy in the manifest content (Freud examines one of Irma's orifices, Leopold feels her body, and Otto injects her with his unclean "squirter"). Since Freud, understandably, did not disclose any information regarding these matters, this theme cannot be developed. Nonetheless, it seems significant that the dream concludes with Freud's evaluation being confirmed and the blame for Irma's condition shifted to Otto. Given that Freud was writing up Irma's case before falling to sleep, because he thought Otto had expressed doubts about his handling of it, the manifest dream represents a continuation and expansion of Freud's waking thoughts and concerns.

Once Freud had the "secret" of dreams revealed to him through this dream, he stated, "Our procedure for interpreting dreams enables us to disclose a *latent* content in them which is of far greater significance than their *manifest* one."[101] Freud's fourteen-page analysis of this dream came to the following conclusions about its significance:

When I came to consider all of these [possible themes], they could all be collected into a single group of ideas and labelled, as it were, "concern about my own and other people's health—professional conscientiousness." . . . [because] when

Otto brought me the news of Irma's condition ... [i]t was as though he had said to me: "You don't take your medical duties seriously enough. You're not conscientious; you don't carry out what you've undertaken." Thereupon, this group of thoughts seemed to have put itself at my disposal, so that I could produce evidence of how highly conscientious I was, of how deeply I was concerned about the health of my relations, my friends and my patients. It was a noteworthy fact that this material also included some disagreeable memories, which supported my friend Otto's accusation rather than my own vindication. ...

If we adopt the method of interpreting dreams which I have indicated here, we shall find that dreams really have a meaning and are far from being the expression of a fragmentary activity of the brain, as the authorities have claimed. *When the work of interpretation has been completed, we perceive that a dream is the fulfillment of a wish.*[102] (Italics in original)

I will leave it to the reader to decide how much more significant and deep this latent-content analysis by Freud is than the one I put forth from a consideration of the manifest content alone. Which approach gave you more clues about the dreamer's character, preoccupations, and interpersonal style of relating to women and men?

I wish to make it clear that I am *not* opposed to the use of associations to help make obscure details of the manifest content more comprehensible. Associations can often be extremely useful in that regard, but they can also be distorted in being told to an authority figure with strong a priori convictions about what they will reveal. Freud's proclivity for attributing sexual meanings to a large number of symbols and typical dreams has already been documented; that his patients, after their initial "resistance" was overcome, eventually produced sexual associations to their dreams, becomes a self-fulfilling prophecy. Associations can also be employed in a defensive manner to obfuscate understanding; Stekel cited the example of a patient who brought in over one hundred pages of written associations to a single dream. The dream simply becomes washed away in such a flood of associations.

Why are associations assumed by Freud to be so sturdy as to be immune to the all-powerful effects of the censorship that sends the fragile latent dream thoughts twisting and tumbling into meaningless disarray? Why aren't waking associations subjected to this same powerful censorship?

It should be apparent by now that I think it would be a tragic mistake to follow Freud's dictum that we should "concern ourselves as little as possible with ... the manifest dream." For Freudians, the dream's manifest content is like an envelope that conceals the letter's latent content; we must tear open (and generally discard) the envelope if we wish to learn about the hidden message. I would like to propose a different analogy. Imagine that we carefully pressed large sheets of tinfoil to fit tightly over Rodin's statue *The*

Thinker. We could claim that the tinfoil prevented us from *seeing* a single detail of the original statue. It could be argued that a very good likeness of the statue's size, the position of its head relative to its arm, its posture, and many other details could be discerned by a careful examination of the manifest appearance of the tinfoil.

An Assessment of Freud's Contribution

How does one put Freud into perspective? Was he, as his disciples claim, an incredible genius who singlehandedly advanced our understanding of dreams with his prodigious and original discoveries? Or was he a self-aggrandizing user of other people's ideas, whose only originality lay in his ability to combine already existing concepts of dream formation? The truth obviously lies somewhere between these two extremes. My own evaluation puts him quite some distance from the image of genius.

I think everyone would agree that Freud focused attention upon dreams in a way that had not been equaled in modern times before *The Interpretation of Dreams* was published. His literature review, although incomplete and selective, made people aware that there had been a long tradition of interest in dreams. His insistence that dreams could be meaningful and could be studied scientifically created a desire for more knowledge about them by the public and by professionals. As psychoanalysis achieved greater recognition and acceptance, so too did dreams, and so too did Freud. Freud, psychoanalysis, and dreams are now irrevocably associated with each other. Viewed this way, Freud can be considered to have significantly advanced the cause of dreams.

It could also be argued that it is precisely Freud's legacy that has prevented wider acceptance of the full meaning of dreams. Freud forged a strong link between neurotic symptoms and dream formation. No one wants to voluntarily court neurosis. Dreams and sex also become synonymous, and to openly share one's dreams has been considered equivalent to publicly confessing one's private sins and secret sordid desires.

Freud did not insist that *every* dream had a sexual origin, and he made this point in the following paragraph, which appeared in the 1919 edition:

> The assertion that all dreams require a sexual interpretation against which critics rage so incessantly, occurs nowhere in my *Interpretation of Dreams.* It is not to be found in any of the numerous editions of this book and is in obvious contradiction to other views expressed in it.[103]

On the same page, however, Freud went on to say that "strikingly innocent dreams may embody crudely erotic wishes,"[104] and this was "also true for many dreams which appear to be *indifferent.*" In the next paragraph, Freud described the initial denial that he encountered "when I *insist* to one of my patients on the frequency of Oepidus dreams, in which the dreamer has sexual intercourse with his own mother"[105] (italics mine). Thus, it *is* possible that not every dream has a sexual wish behind it, but this motive seems to be assumed unless additional evidence specifically contradicts it. Through his intense focus upon the neurotic, infantile, and sexual aspects of dreams, Freud gave dreams a bad name.

One gets the impression, however, that as Freud's experience with dreams broadened, he began to appreciate the wideranging diversity of motives from which they might spring. One has to scrutinize footnotes closely, however, to detect this belated and subtle shift. This footnote in the 1925 edition may illustrate his late-blooming awareness: "Since anything whatever that occurs in preconscious thought can pass into a dream (whether into its actual content or into the latent dream-thoughts) that possibility is equally open to altruistic impulses."[106]

Although Freud constantly referred to his studies as "scientific," he certainly did not follow the methods of quantification generally accepted as necessary to merit that label. He provided no ratings, rankings, percentage figures, tables, graphs, or statistics to document his claims. It was his clinical judgment which represented the ultimate criterion as to whether something was true or not. Freud acknowledged that a great deal of suggestion and influence by the analyst on a patient was possible; it is therefore not surprising that his clinical observations seemed to continually confirm the correctness of his views. If you know beforehand what you're looking for in an ambiguous situation, you're very likely to find it.

Freud possessed extraordinary literary talents. The psychiatric historian, Henri Ellenberger, noted that the mark of a great writer was the ability to make the most implausible story seem true. The last book Freud wrote was *Moses and Monotheism*, in 1939. A Hebrew historian, commenting on the book, compiled a long list of its inaccuracies and impossibilities, but added that by his great talent, Freud had woven a plausible story of this network of impossibilities.[107] It's a further tribute to Freud's talents that he managed to persuade so many people that he was really the first to discover the secret of dreams and that the secret he discovered was an accurate accounting of how the realm of dreams works. A great deal of work still needed to be done by others before the full power of dreams could be appreciated and understood.

CHAPTER 7

CARL JUNG:

DREAMS AS MANY-

SPLENDORED THINGS

C arl Gustav Jung was born in Switzerland in 1875 and died there at the age of eighty-five. He traveled widely within Europe, visited North Africa, went on safari in East Africa, spent some time with the Pueblo Indians in New Mexico, and journeyed to India. In addition to his native Swiss German, he was fluent in French, Italian, and English, read Greek and Latin, and had some knowledge of Swahili.

His father and maternal grandfather were Protestant ministers with special interests in the Hebrew language, and eight uncles were also parsons. His paternal grandfather, Carl Gustav Jung, a physician who became a rector of the University of Basel and Grand Master of the Swiss Freemasons, was alleged to have been the illegitimate son of Goethe. Jung's mother and maternal grandmother were described as possessing psychic abilities. These family influences highlighted and shaped the contours of Jung's subsequent professional development.

THE RELATIONSHIP BETWEEN FREUD AND JUNG

Jung began his psychiatric training in 1900 at the Burgholzli Psychiatric Hospital in Zurich, where he worked with many psychotic patients. After spending a year studying with Pierrer Janet in Paris, he returned to the Burgholzli and eventually became the clinical director. In addition to teaching courses on hysteria and psychotherapy, he began in 1903 to carry out experimental studies on the word association test. His results were so impressive that this test became widely used in Swiss mental hospitals, and served to stimulate other projective tests like the Rorschach Inkblot Test. Jung frequently encountered repression in the form of blocked or delayed responses to emotionally significant stimulus words. Jung was impressed with *The Interpretation of Dreams* and admired the way Freud had applied the concept of the repression mechanism to dreams. But although the two men agreed about the mechanism or process of repression, they disagreed upon what was being repressed. For Freud, it was sexual content; for Jung, the content was much more varied.

Jung's interest in Freud's ideas led him to visit Freud in 1907. During their first meeting in Vienna, they talked "virtually without a pause for thirteen hours."[1] Jung subsequently became very active in the psychoanalytic movement and served as the first president of the International Psychoanalytic Association, from 1910 until 1914. Regular correspondence between Freud and Jung began in 1906, and after 330 letters the exchange was terminated in 1913. The two men never met again after 1912.

In a 1909 letter, Freud wrote to Jung that he had "formally adopted you as an eldest son, anointing you as my successor and crown prince." Other excerpts from that same letter reinforce Freud's insistence in attempting to establish his authority with regard to Jung:

> I must fall back again into the role of father toward you in giving you my views. . . . I therefore don once more my horn-rimmed paternal spectacles and warn my dear son to keep a cool head. . . . I also shake my wise gray locks . . . and think: Well, that is how the young folks are.[2]

Since Jung had experienced a very unsatisfying and ambivalent relationship with his own father, such patronizing attitudes on Freud's part were bound to create a schism. In one of his last letters to Freud, Jung angrily wrote:

> Your technique of treating your pupils like patients is a *blunder*. In that way you produce either slavish sons or impudent puppies. . . . You go around sniffing out all the symptomatic actions in your vicinity, thus reducing everyone to the level of sons and daughters who

Carl Jung

blushingly admit the existence of their faults. Meanwhile you remain on top as the father sitting pretty.[3]

The letter in which Freud shook his "wise gray locks" had been written to chide Jung for attaching any paranormal significance to some loud reports they both heard spontaneously emitted from a bookcase in Freud's home. In Jung's account of the incident, Freud "stared aghast" after Jung correctly predicted that a second detonation would occur a few moments after the first. In his letter, Freud acknowledged

that the event initially "made a powerful impression" upon him but that he subsequently managed to persuade himself that it was "wholly implausible that anything of the sort should occur." He sarcastically commented that the furniture now stood before him "spiritless and dead." In concluding the letter, Freud said he was looking forward "to hearing more about your investigations of the spook-complex" and Jung's "lovely delusion."[4]

Thus, in addition to whatever rankling Freud produced by his paternal posturing, he also alienated Jung by denigrating a subject that Jung took very seriously. Jung had carried out experiments with his cousin, Helene Preiswerk, a young woman who was involved as a medium in spiritualist circles. These studies provided the material for Jung's medical dissertation. Freud's marked ambivalence toward psychic phenomena has been documented in the previous chapter; Jung was unwavering in accepting the legitimacy of parapsychological investigations. Their different views on such an emotional topic were bound to create tension between these strong-willed men.

The two men also had many other theoretical disagreements. Freud insisted on the centrality of the Oedipus complex and the role of sexual libido as the driving force of all motivation. Jung did not accept the Oedipus complex and felt libido was better viewed as generalized psychic energy.

As might be expected, their conceptualizations of dreams diverged markedly, and it was during a discussion of dreams that Jung realized he could never work in a genuinely collegial way with Freud. During their seven-week trip to the United States in 1909, they exchanged comments daily on each other's dreams. One day, however, when Jung asked Freud for additional personal details so that his dream could be better understood, Freud refused to provide them. When asked why, Freud explained, "I cannot risk my authority."[5] Jung realized that this foreshadowed the end of their relationship, because Freud put his personal authority above truth.

One of the dreams Jung presented to Freud for interpretation during this trip began with Jung in a comfortable sitting room on an upstairs floor of what appeared to be his home. The room was furnished in the style of the eighteenth century, with old oil paintings on the walls. It occurred to him that he had never really noticed this room before and he began to wonder what the ground floor might look like. He went downstairs and found a rather dark area containing medieval furnishings dating from the sixteenth century or earlier. The floors were of red brick. His curiosity was now aroused; he decided to explore the whole house and made a trip down to the cellar. In the cellar, he found a door that opened onto a flight of stone steps. He descended this stairway into a large vaulted room with large slabs of stone on the floor. The walls looked very ancient, and as Jung examined their composition, he realized they were of Roman origin. In a corner of the room, he discovered an iron ring on a stone slab. When he pulled the ring, another flight of narrow stone stairs was revealed. At the bottom, Jung found a prehistoric cavelike tomb containing two half-disintegrating skulls thick with dust on the floor, some other bones, and a few shards of pottery.

Freud experienced great difficulty in analyzing this dream and kept focusing on the two skulls. He urged Jung to find some wish in connection with them and pressed him to identify whose skulls they might be. Realizing that Freud wanted him to develop some secret death wish, and that a disagreeable quarrel would erupt if he contradicted or failed to placate Freud, Jung reluctantly proposed that the skulls might belong to his wife and sister-in-law. Freud readily accepted this suggestion and seemed relieved at this "confirmation" of his wish-fulfillment theory.

After the dissolution of their relationship, Freud minimized Jung's contributions to dream theory and psychoanalysis and criticized Jung as unable to tolerate authority and being "relentlessly devoted to the furtherance of his own interests."[6] Jung, however, in his autobiography and other subsequent writings, readily acknowledged and praised Freud's achievements, even while expressing his disagreements with his former mentor.

Jung's Waking Life and Dream Life

A key to understanding Jung's life is his autobiography, *Memories, Dreams, Reflections*.[7] He wrote the first chapters when he was eighty-two years old and dictated the subsequent chapters to his secretary, Aniela Jaffe, who later edited and published this insightful view of Jung's inner world. As might be expected in the subjective realm of autobiography, there are discrepancies between Jung's descriptions of the external events of his life and those supplied by other informants. The book was not intended as a careful chronology but rather, as the title suggests, as a collection of reflections that appeared to Jung when he peered into the reservoir of his own accumulated memories.

In the opening sentence of the book's prologue, Jung claimed: "My life is a story of the self-realization of the unconscious." "Recollection of the outward events of my life has largely faded or disappeared,"[8] he admitted, but he was nevertheless able to describe in amazing detail certain subjective experiences from the second and third years of his life. He recalled, for example, lying in a baby carriage on a beautiful sunlit day and the pleasant smell and taste of warm milk and bread while sitting in his high chair.

Jung's recall of his dream life was equally vivid. He reported that his earliest remembered dream, dating back to when he was three or four years old, preoccupied him all his life. The dream began in a meadow, where Jung discovered an opening leading to a stone stairway. On descending, he encountered a doorway with a rounded arch closed off by a richly brocaded green curtain. When the curtain was pushed aside, a long, rectangular, arched chamber of hewn stone was revealed. A red carpet in the center led to a low platform on which sat a magnificent golden throne, and on the throne was a huge object, nearly fifteen feet tall and two feet thick, reaching almost to the ceiling. It was made of skin and had a rounded head with a single eye on top. Above the head was a bright aura. The terrified young dreamer heard his mother's voice announce in the dream that the object was a man-eater. Jung realized, years later, that the object was a phallus and understood, decades later, that it was a ritual phallus.

With such an awe-inspiring introduction to the world of dreams at such an early and impressionable age, it is not surprising that Jung took on the challenge of trying to better understand the significance and meaning of dreams as a primary goal of his life. By following the messages appearing in dreams, Jung believed that the path leading to self-realization and personal wholeness could be discovered. His belief was affirmed in a dream he experienced just before his death. In it he saw, "high up in a high place," a boulder lit by the full sun. Carved into the illuminated boulder were the words "Take this as a sign of the wholeness you have achieved and the singleness you have become."[9] Anchored by dreams at both ends, his life had come full circle. In his childhood dream, he discovered a mysterious illuminated object in a stone-hewn underground chamber; at age eighty-five, the hewn stone was now external and visible, high above the ground, the illumination was much brighter, and the meaning of what he had seen was unambiguous.

Not only were the first and final phases of Jung's life marked by impressive dreams, he was ever alert to the inspiration they could unexpectedly provide: "You know, with dreams, there is always a chance of the Eucharist every night."[10] Jung described forty-two of his dreams in *Memories, Dreams, Reflections* and several were also discussed in his letters.

Dreams served as signposts for making important decisions throughout Jung's personal life and professional career. As ma-triculation from school approached, he was uncertain which areas of study he should pursue; two dreams resolved his uncertainties and led him to choose science. In the first, he was in a dark forest along the Rhine River when he came to a burial mound, began to dig, and discovered the bones of prehistoric animals. In the second, he was also in a woods, but this time the ground was threaded with watercourses. In a dark place, surrounded by dense undergrowth, was a clear circular pool, and in the pool was a wonderful round animal, a radiolarian, shimmering in opalescent hues and made up of innumerable little cells or tentacle-shaped organs. These dreams, which stirred Jung at a deep emotional level, made him aware of how much he wished to expand his knowledge of evolution and to explore the mysteries of nature.

Jung wrote extensively. His published works cover eighteen volumes in the Bollingen Series of Princeton University Press. His correspondence and several additional volumes of letters and interviews are also included in that series. Two of his books, the *Black Book* and the *Red Book*, remain unpublished. The latter contains many stunning paintings that Jung made to capture his dream images.

PERSONALITY DIMENSIONS RELEVANT TO DREAMS

THE COLLECTIVE UNCONSCIOUS

It is difficult to trace the source for all of Jung's concepts. Vincent Brome, who has written biographies of several prominent individuals, also completed one on Jung. In a chapter entitled "Jung's Sources" he observed:

Any attempt to summarize the sources of Jung's thought and work must do serious violence to its encyclopedic complexity in many languages. Philosophers, theologians, psychologists, psychiatrists, novelists, poets, mystics, orientalists, ethnologists all figured multitudinously in his erudition.[11]

One can easily sense from Jung's dreams his profound interest in the past and in relics to be found buried deep beneath the surface. In his childhood dream, he descended into an underground chamber where he encountered a giant ritual phallus on a throne; when seeking direction for his future studies, he dreamed of discovering the bones of prehistoric animals by digging in a burial mound. He intuitively recognized that the significance of the dream he shared with Freud extended far beyond any supposed death wish or infantile sexual desire. He eventually realized that the house represented himself and portrayed a summary of his mental life and its historical antecedents. The upper story stood for his current state of consciousness; the main floor represented the first, or personal, level of his unconscious; and the subterranean regions signified a much earlier stratum of evolutionary mental awareness. The "collective unconscious" was the term Jung proposed to designate those prehistorical mental aspects of personality which functioned far below the level of the individual unconscious.

In his autobiography, Jung described how he came to understand the significance of his house dream:

It obviously pointed to the foundations of cultural history—a history of successive layers of consciousness. My dream thus constituted a kind of structural diagram of the human psyche; it postulated something of an altogether *impersonal* nature underlying that psyche. It "clicked," as the English have it—and the dream became for me a guiding image which in the days to come was to be corroborated to an extent I could not at first suspect. It was my first inkling of a collective a priori beneath the personal psyche. This I first took to be the traces of earlier modes of functioning. Later, with increasing experience and on the basis of more reliable knowledge, I recognized them . . . as archetypes.[12]

Late in 1913, Jung began an intensive exploration of his own unconscious that lasted for over five years. He wrote down and drew his dreams every morning and attempted to stimulate his daydreaming activity by imagining that he was digging into underground galleries and caves within the earth. Jung soon encountered many fantastic figures, among whom was Philemon, a winged figure with the horns of a bull. Philemon was a very wise and learned old man holding a bunch of four keys, one of which he clutched as if he were about to open a lock. He told Jung that one could be taught things about which one is ordinarily unaware. Philemon became extremely real to Jung and they engaged in long "conversations." A portrait of him appears in Jung's retreat home, and his name was inscribed over the entrance. After a few years of intense exploration of his subterranean regions, there was a brief outburst of paranormal phenomena: family members saw ghosts or had blankets snatched off their beds; one afternoon the front porch bell rang repeatedly though two maids watching the bell saw no one there.

Jung's "creative illness" finally began to draw to a close when he discovered he was drawing progressively more complex circles. Jung associated these circular shapes, or mandalas, with healing energy. (Mandalas will be discussed shortly.) It was from this odyssey to the depths of his being that Jung extracted the principle concepts of his view of the human mind, such as the collective unconscious and archetypes.

Jung proposed that the collective unconscious contained information that predated any individual's personal existence but was rather a mental remnant of the species's ancient past. There is unquestionable evidence that human beings have acquired their particular anatomy as a result of an evolutionary process. Traces of gills appearing during embryonic development attest to our aquatic ancestry, and vestiges of a tailbone in the human fetus reflect our mammalian heritage. Jung theorized,

Just as the human body represents a whole museum of organs, each with a long evolutionary history behind it, so we should expect to find that the mind is organized in a similar way. It can no more be a product without history than is the body in which it exists.[13]

ARCHETYPES

Archetypes are the psychic structural components of the collective unconscious that parallel the physical components of our common human bodily structure. They create predispositions to certain forms of images and contain a large element of emotion. Their presence can be detected not only in dreams, but in the content of myths, fairy tales, psychotic delusions, and religious rituals. An archetype is not a specific image. In volume 18 of his *Collected Works*, Jung explained: "The archetype is . . . an inherited *tendency* of the human mind to form representations of mythological motifs—representations that vary a great deal without losing their basic pattern."

Jung said that one of the experiences that first led him to the idea of archetypes was the case of an old schizophrenic patient of his who was constantly hallucinating. The patient reported that he saw the sun with a phallus the movements of which produced the wind. Jung later came across a recent book containing the text of an ancient papyrus which described how the wind originated in a tube hanging from the sun. Such a specific and unlikely coincidence of images suggested the existence of universal symbols which can appear in either religious myths or psychotic delusions.

Another example cited by Jung involved a dream told by an uneducated black man from the American South. In his dream he saw the image of a man crucified on a wheel. To see a figure crucified in any manner would certainly not be usual, but Jung considered the image of crucifixion on a wheel to be archetypal because of its mythological motif. Jung related it to the ancient sun-wheel and the sacrifices made on it to propitiate the sun god, and he traced it through Rhodesian sculptures to paleolithic ages. Jung also pointed out that the man on a wheel is repeated in the Greek myth of Ixion, who was punished by Zeus by being fastened upon an incessantly turning wheel.

The term "archetype," which comes from Saint Augustine, is sometimes given a biological cast, as if it referred to a genetic encoding or imprinting of brain tissue, but its more frequent usage is to refer to the imagined representation of archetypal energy. One way to illustrate the properties of archetypes is to contrast them with instincts; instincts, Jung said, are "typical modes of action" based on physiological urges, whereas archetypes are "typical modes of apprehension" or perceiving.

Jung's theory of personality development and his ideas about dream expression are teleological in nature: the human psyche inexorably moves toward an ultimate goal—that of maturity, completion, and fulfillment. Life is a series of metamorphoses, and archetypal imagery is generally more prevalent around the time of crises. These crises lead to progressive maturation as they are confronted, overcome, and assimilated.

There is no exact order in which the archetypes will emerge. Archetypal dreams stir up strong emotions and involve situations not encountered in everyday life: encounters with hidden treasure, temples, bright light; intense awareness of configurations of the sun, moon, and stars; experi-ences of temporal or spatial infinity; fusion with the earth, fire, or water; feelings of disorientation or euphoria; or, in general, dreams that seem to be cosmic in nature and command the dreamer's attention. Besides architectural objects or situations, there are also archetypal figures. The hero archetype, for example, can be recognized in the story of David and Goliath and that of Saint George and the dragon. The basic pattern or motif can be detected even though its representations may vary greatly in detail.

The *persona archetype* represents the energy we expend in social roles. The term derives from the Greek word for the mask that actors wore in dramatic productions. We all enact various roles—student, employee, spouse, parent, club member. Some investment in these social roles is necessary for successful interactions with others in family and professional settings, but we can sometimes become so involved in carrying them out that we neglect the person behind the mask. Criticism of our performance in a particular role can then lead to feelings of rejection or inadequacy and a sense of being empty inside. We confuse "what we do" with "who we are." Dreams offer some indications of how extensively we have invested in these public roles; consider how much concern we show in dreams with clothing or other external signs of recognition, and how often the setting is a stage or other public arena.

The *shadow archetype* deals with the dark, primitive, animal-like instincts that man has inherited from his evolutionary ancestors. Animals express their aggressive and sexual urges freely, but we may feel threatened by the thought that such strong impulses might also reside within us. As children, we learn to disown and split off these impulses, because they lead to condemnation and retribution by parents or other family members responsible for our "socialization." Feelings of reprehension and guilt usually arise when our shadow side begins to move into conscious awareness. The energies it represents need to be confronted eventually, however, in order to utilize them in appropriate assertiveness and creativity as adults. If we try to deny this lurking atavistic presence within us, we will pay a very high price.

The shadow is literally the "dark side" of our personality, expressed as a human form. Dreams can serve to sensitize us to this "atavistic" feature in our nature and help us gradually assimilate or integrate it, rather than being overwhelmed by it. The shadow is expressed in dreams as a character of the same sex as the dreamer. Acceptance of these disowned, instinctual layers of our personality provides a source of additional energy for continued maturation in our later years.

In one of Jung's first dreams during his self-analysis, he was with an "unknown, brown-skinned man, a savage" in a lonely, rocky mountain landscape. They lay in wait for Siegfried, who appeared in a chariot made of the bones of the dead, high on the crest of a mountain in the first ray of the rising sun. Siegfried drove at furious speed down the precipitous slope, and Jung and his companion shot and killed him. A tremendous rain then began to fall. Jung commented on this dream: "The small, brown-skinned savage who accompanied me and had actually taken the initiative in the killing was an embodiment of the primitive shadow. The rain showed that the tension between the conscious and the unconscious was being resolved."[14]

The shadow may appear as a drug addict, pervert, thief, criminal, or Nazi, as physically deformed, or as a sinister presence lurking in the darkness. Jung's *Red Book* contains a later portrait of his shadow. In this impressive painting, a cloak-and-dagger figure cowers in a far corner of a basement room covered with black and white tiles. The posture of the potentially menacing, but now subdued form suggests that Jung had gained some degree of control over this furtive figure, which resided in the subterranean region of his psyche.

Jung also described the archetypes of the soul, the *animus* and the *anima*. The animus archetype represents the masculine side of a woman's personality and the anima archetype, the feminine side of a man's personality. Relationships with the opposite sex are always difficult. Volatile interactions may occur as we confront our internal representations of the opposite sex—enigmatic creatures who seem so defiantly different from ourselves. Professor Higgins's plea in *My Fair Lady*—"Why can't a woman be more like a man?"—is echoed by frustrated women who decry the lack of emotional communication from their silent male partners.

By getting in touch with the archetypal portrayal of the opposite sex within oneself, one is better able to apprehend the nature of the other sex. If we project an excessively idealized image of the opposite sex without a careful consideration for reality, we may fall deeply in love at first sight with someone completely inappropriate. Conversely, if we project a negative animus or anima archetype onto a partner and remain blind to their actual behavior, considerable tension and discord can result.

When we encounter strong emotional responses to a character of the opposite sex in our dreams, it is very likely that information about our animus or anima is being imparted to us. By paying careful attention to our dreams over a period of time, we can learn to recognize dreaming interactions with the opposite sex which consistently clash with our conscious intentions to develop more harmonious and rational exchanges. Comparisons between our dreaming and waking images may eventually enable us to see our partners as they really are, unencumbered by these deep, archetypal forces.

Jung proposed that during the first half of life a man projects his anima onto external women. This pushes him toward more intense emotional relationships with them and thereby helps establish his masculine identity. During the second half of life, a man's task is no longer to project the anima, but to come to terms with and incorporate it as an agency of his own unconscious. If successful, he will soften his character and feel more comfortable in nourishing, empathic roles, somewhat like a kindly, old grandfather.

There are many ways in which the anima can be experienced and projected. A man can respond to a woman ambivalently, relating to her as either a madonna or a whore, an angel or a witch. Fear of his own anima often inhibits a man from becoming more openly intimate with a woman. Generalizations cannot predict the ways in which the anima will manifest at different junctures of a given man's life, but in the preadult years a maternal anima is common, while as an adult one's anima may take the form of an attractive woman. In a man's advancing years, the anima may appear as a young girl or child.

Women also experience a variety of animus figures. The animus can appear in dreams as a known figure—a father, teacher, or judge—or in the role of a priest, artist, or tour guide. In his negative aspect, he may be imagined as a robber, murderer, or rapist. Jung considered cases in which a woman's competitive tendencies caused her to value material success more highly than comfortable involvement with family to represent possession by the animus, rather than a balanced relationship with it. When a woman becomes aware of her strongly-rooted, internal animus force, she can begin to integrate and utilize its energy in a more blended and harmonious way. In the classic fairy tale, it was only *after* Sleeping Beauty accepted the kiss from Prince Charming that she was able to awaken and realize her full potential.

An example of how animus figures gradually changed in a dream series was reported by my friend, Carol D. Warner,[15] when she undertook a systematic analysis of her dreams over a period of seventeen months. Her dream series began with a large, burly black man in Africa who offered to help get the dreamer back to her camp when she became lost. Her animus thus began as a potentially helpful guide to a more secure place. In a dream six months later, she found herself in the "mail room" she regularly visited but was aware that "a new modern development had taken place" there. This pun on mail (male) room reveals that the dreamer was aware that her attitude toward her masculine side was changing and new developments were occurring. In later dreams, male characters who were competent, assertive, and amiable began to appear more frequently in Carol's dreams. In one encounter, she and an appealing blond man walked hand in hand along a canal before she asked him to go with her to buy a dream book. In a later dream, she and a male coworker were working on a secret scientific experiment involving a powerful substance called "energy" which was stored in a freezer. Carol noted a dream in which a powerful positive animus appeared was frequently followed by one containing a negative animus figure that threatened the gains the dreamer felt she was making. This process of the "return to the opposite" was called *enantiodromia* by Jung, a term from Heraclitus, the ancient Greek philosopher. It refers to a sort of push-pull, self-regulating quality which occurs whenever change takes place in the journey through the unconscious.

In a dream which occurred in the Arizona desert, she and a male friend sat on an overlook and the dreamer was surprised to observe, in this presumably arid setting, a series of waterfalls with lush vegetation on either side. Then a broken-off piece of an iceberg came floating down the widening stream. This last dream nicely illustrates several patterns of change: the dreamer's horizons have expanded from being involved in a secret project to sitting on an overlook with a wide-ranging view; the energy stored in a freezer has now

thawed, and a piece of iceberg has broken off from its larger unseen source; and the previous canal has now become a wide, flowing stream with lush vegetation on either side.

Following dreams in which a woman friend married a black man, an evil king was killed and dismembered. The dreamer realized: "After the marriage with the dark side, the reign of the evil king is over ... the raging, destructive side has lost its powerful ability to devalue and undermine the feminine side." In the final dream of the series, a huge boat was stranded on the sand near a sea. A male figure, representing a composite of several of the dreamer's positive animus figures, poured water under the ship's prow from a vase with a never-ending supply of water. Eventually the water became deep enough for the ship to float free and glide into the sea.

At the time of this last dream, Carol felt her life had changed in several positive ways: the number and quality of supportive relationships with male friends had increased; a "stalemate" in a primary love relationship had been amicably resolved; her career had changed for the better; and she had acquired a home and become more skillful in financial management. Carol now has a very successful psychotherapy practice and is chairperson of the board of directors of an international dream organization. The changes within Carol's dreams seemed to precede the external changes in her life. This is often the case, which raises the question: Do our dreams know where we're headed or do they provide the stimulus to change?

Another pair of dream archetypes, the old wise man and the *magna mater* (great mother), is concerned with the spirit. These archetypes usually confront the dreamer when a difficult situation must be faced. Jung's discovery of Philemon during his own self-analysis has already been mentioned. The old wise man can appear as a monk or shaman or, with an evil aspect, as a wizard. The *magna meter* may be represented by the Holy Virgin or a female ancestor or its negative aspects may be reflected in the figure of a witch.

Vincent Brome presented a previously unpublished case in which Jung worked with Anna Maria, an eighteen-year-old English woman suffering from anorexia nervosa (self-imposed semistarvation), insomnia, impaired concentration, and an inability to make decisions.[16] It took hours for her to choose which dress to wear each day, and her mother would eventually make the decision for her. As Jung worked with this woman, he realized that her mother was at the center of her problems. She began to experience a recurrent dream in which a female spider sat in the center of a web directing traffic on the silken threads by means of signals flashing on and off. This was Anna Maria's response to working with Jung on this dream:

> When he made me see that I was really in the power of my mother it came as a great shock because I thought I loved her more than anything else in the world. . . . But it released something. I felt as if a barrier had broken and my emotional life began to flow again. But my mother didn't like it because as I recovered a little I became that much more independent.[17]

The patient began to make progress with her eating behavior, and Jung urged her to get a separate room for herself in the hotel where she and her mother now shared a room. When her mother heard this, she threatened to remove Anna Maria from therapy but had to relent because she couldn't deny the improvement in her daughter's eating behavior. A period of regression followed as the conflict of wills between mother and daughter escalated. This is another example of enantiodromia, the "return to the opposite" described in Carol Warner's dreams.

During Anna Maria's slow recovery, she had the feeling that some powerful but frightening energy was welling up within her. In one dream a monstrous mountain shaped like two giant breasts slowly opened and engulfed her. She awoke with such terrifying screams that several other hotel guests heard her and reported the incident. Jung felt the dream reflected the myth of the Earth Mother, with which Anna Maria was completely unfamiliar. She now began to experience a deep sense of emptiness, longing, and a craving for something which she couldn't readily identify. At first she thought it related to food, but she was now eating well. When the "Earth Mother" dream recurred, Jung encouraged her to pursue the imagery further, and within a week, three variations of the dream theme emerged. In the first dream, she was engulfed by "those beautiful, soft, huge breasts"; in the second, she was embraced by them; and in the third, she was reborn between them.

Following therapy, Anna Maria gained weight, felt more comfortable regarding her relationship with her mother, resumed her study of English literature, and moved into an apartment in London with a room-mate. In an interview when she was seventy years old, Anna Maria reflected upon the factors which she thought contributed to her positive therapeutic outcome: "It was really due to a kind of alchemy Jung exerted which activated something in me from a long dead past—a past to which I belonged, but wasn't really mine."[18]

Earth Mother imagery was prevalent throughout all ancient cultures. In Mesopotamia she was known as Ga-Tum-Dug; in Greece as Gaea, the deep-breasted earth; and in Rome as Tellus Mater, who protected the fruitfulness of the soil and watched over marriage and procreation. She was depicted in one Roman bas-relief sitting with children by her breasts, fruit and flowers on her lap, and corn growing beside her.

An archetype acts somewhat like a magnet, attracting relevant experiences. Once sufficient experiences have clustered around an organizing archetype, it can become energized and break through into consciousness. After reaching consciousness, an archetype can continue to develop and become increasingly refined. Energy from each of the individual archetypes gradually fuses with that of the others and ultimately the archetype of the Self can be perceived.

The central and most fundamental archetype is the Self, whose meaning is better conveyed by the German word *Selbst*, or "the itself." The Self expresses the unity of the personality as a whole and is based upon a merging of the many levels of the unconscious and conscious mind. Some-

times the term Self is used to reflect a larger transpersonal totality—God.

Many Jungians capitalize the word Self to reflect the term's unique and broad meaning in Jungian theory, which is quite different from its meaning in other personality theories. The Self is the final product or energy constellation resulting from the process of individuation. An acorn goes through the process of individuation and eventually expresses the Self archetype when it becomes a large, sturdy oak tree with many branches and luxuriant green foliage. When one gets in touch with the archetype of the Self, one senses that some larger creative force is leading the way, as though a hidden plan were being followed. Each new discovery of things intricately "coming together" brings forth fresh feelings of surprise and appreciation.

If a lengthy dream series is considered overall, one sees a pattern of movement toward wholeness and completion. After the elements of personality have been differentiated, the various systems can then be integrated by what Jung described as *transcendent function*. This function has the capacity to unite opposing trends and to energize the archetype of the Self.

Some images of the Self which might appear in dreams are the divine child, the quaternity, and the mandala. *Quaternity images* represent the concept of "fourness"; they may involve a geometric square or the placement of four objects, such as four stones or the four directions. For example, in Cuna culture Four was a sacred number; the *neles* would place either four, eight, or twelve cacao beans on the embers of an incense pot, then inhale the smoke to develop the power of "clear-seeing." The

Jung painted this mandala image after a powerful dream in which he found himself in a dirty city. All of the streets led to a center. This dream pointed Jung to what he called the center: the Self.

concept of balance is suggested by fourness; ahead and behind are equally distant, as are left and right.

The *mandala image* is more frequently associated with the Self archetype. Mandala is a Sanskrit word meaning circle or magic circle. A mandala is a concentrically arranged and balanced figure, frequently divided into four sections. Monks in Tibet and India focused upon drawings of mandalas during meditation to facilitate entry into deeper states of inner awareness. The famous Aztec sun calendar could be considered a form of mandala.

Mandala symbolism figured very prominently in a dream series that Jung discussed in his book *Psychology and Alchemy* (*Collected Works*, Volume 12). The dreamer was a young man with an excellent scientific education who reported a series of over one thousand dreams and visions. Jung worked on the first four hundred, reported during a ten-month period. This man was not a regular patient of his, although the last forty-five dreams were reported directly to Jung. Jung uncovered strong parallels between the symbols employed by the dreamer to portray his problems, and the symbols developed by medieval alchemists to represent their efforts to transform base materials into gold. The dreamer, however, was totally unfamiliar with alchemy. According to Jung, these commonalities provided evidence for the existence of the collective unconscious. Just as the alchemists aspired toward the chemical creation of gold, the human psyche aspires toward the psychological creation of a fully developed Self. Transformation of less desirable materials into improved and enriched ones was thus

the goal of both the alchemical and the individuation processes. To illustrate the marked similarity with his dream imagery, over one hundred alchemical drawings were reproduced in Jung's book.

In one of the young man's dreams, his mother was pouring water from one basin into another, very solemnly, as if the act possessed great significance for the outside world. In this dream, the young man was then rejected by his father. Jung pointed out that the anima had become a life-giving factor in this dream, much like the life-giving substance alchemists referred to as *aqua vitae* ("water of life") or *aqua permanens* ("permanent water"). This imagery seems reminiscent of the final dream reported by Carol Warner, in which a supportive male figure poured water from a continuously flowing vessel and thereby set a ship free from the sand. One of the alchemical drawings, from a fifteenth-century codex entitled "Fountain of Youth," showed bathers in a very large basin into which water was continually flowing from vessels held by statues. Another, a fourteenth-century manuscript, depicted an "Imperial Bath with the Miraculous Spring of Water."

Various forms of mandala imagery were also portrayed in this young man's dreams. One of the earliest dreams (dream 8) involved fairly simple imagery. The dreamer found himself aboard a ship occupied with a new method of taking his bearings. The dreamer saw a chart on which was drawn a circle with a center point. Sometimes his focus was directed too far away and sometimes too near; to accurately take his bearings, he needed to focus on the center. As the dreamer gained self-awareness and internal balance, the number of mandala symbols progressively increased. There were ten mandalas in the first hundred dreams, eleven in the second hundred, twenty-two in the third hundred, and twenty-eight in the last hundred.

The mandalas increased not only in frequency, but also in complexity as the dream series unfolded. In one dream, there was a circular table with four chairs around it, but both the table and chairs were empty. Jung commented that this indicated the mandala was not yet "in use." Five mandala dreams later, a yellow light like the sun loomed through the fog, but was murky; eight rays shone from the center. Because the light was murky, Jung speculated that the dreamer was still showing insufficient understanding. Six mandala dreams later, the dreamer saw a starry figure rotating, and at the cardinal points of the circle were pictures representing the four seasons. In discussing this dream, Jung observed that elements of time are necessary to define reality and the rotation motif "indicates that the symbol of the circle is to be thought of not as static but as dynamic." It would require too much space to trace all the progressively evolving differentiation of the mandala imagery, but these examples will give the reader a glimpse of how the mandala dream symbolism reflects the individuation process.

COMPENSATION

Compensation is the process whereby the psyche attempts to gain balance by developing an awareness of neglected aspects of the personality and striving for their ex-

pression. Just as the body attempts to maintain a steady temperature, perspiring when the temperature rises and shivering when the temperature drops, the psychic goal of achieving individuation or selfhood can only be realized when all of the components of one's personality are balanced. Dreams can help to sensitize us to the neglected aspects of our personality by zeroing in on blind spots in our awareness.

Jung once sat across from an older general and his middle-aged adjutant on a train journey. The general spontaneously shared a dream in which he was on parade with a number of young officers who were being inspected by the commander in chief. When the commander in chief reached the dreamer, he surprised him by not asking a technical question but instead demanding a definition of the "beautiful." The dreamer found himself embarrassed that he was not able to supply a satisfactory answer. The commander in chief moved on to a very young major and asked him the same question. The major gave an excellent answer, and the dreamer felt that he would have liked to have given the same answer. The general experienced great distress at this point and awoke from his dream.

The general asked Jung if he thought dreams had any meaning and wondered what such a dream could possibly mean. After affirming that he did consider dreams to have meaning, Jung asked whether the general had noted anything peculiar about the young major's appearance. The general replied that the major looked just like the general had when he was a young major. Jung suggested that perhaps the dream was calling attention to something that he had possessed when he was a major but had since forgotten or lost. After a few minutes of reflection, the general burst out with the explanation that when he was younger he was very much interested in art, but that this interest had been overwhelmed by the rigidity of military routine. The dream thus prompted the dreamer to consider whether he might wish to reincorporate this previously stimulating, now neglected, interest into his current life situation.

Jung experienced a dream which pointed to an imbalance he needed to correct. Jung had been seeing a woman in her early twenties whose promiscuous lifestyle had earned her the nickname "the great whore of Babylon." Although Jung attempted to conceal his discomfort, her makeup and flamboyant clothing embarrassed him when she showed up for her appointments. No progress was being made in their therapeutic work.

In the corrective dream Jung subsequently experienced, he was on a highway at the foot of a hill upon which stood a magnificent castle. A high tower with a beautiful marble balcony rose from the castle. Looking up, Jung noticed the elegant figure of a regal woman sitting on the balcony. As he tilted his head upward to obtain a clearer view of this radiant woman, he suddenly realized that she was his patient. After waking, Jung wondered why his unconscious mind had placed this young woman in such a high position. Jung came to the uncomfortable realization that he had been behaving very badly toward this young woman, looking down on her in his waking life. He decided to share this dream and his reaction to it with the young woman. Following a mutual discussion of the dream and its implications, Jung reported that "it worked miracles" in terms of subsequent therapeutic progress.

JUNG'S APPROACH TO DREAM INTERPRETATION

When he was seventy-nine years old, Jung wrote a letter to Calvin Hall in which he stated, "For many years I have carefully analyzed about 2,000 dreams per annum, thus I have acquired a certain experience in this matter." Although Jung did not write any systematic book on dreams, a useful collection of his papers on the topic has been compiled and translated by R. F. C. Hull.[19] A book edited by William McGuire, entitled *Dream Analysis*, contains fifty-one lectures by Jung between 1928 and 1930 on a series of thirty dreams he obtained from a wealthy retired businessman in his forties.[20]

THE PROSPECTIVE ASPECT OF DREAMS

Jung claimed that he had no theory about dreams and insisted that each dream had to be considered on its own without regard to theoretical presuppositions. He felt, however, that if we paid serious attention to dreams, they would reveal practical and important hints about where the unconscious was leading the dreamer. The dream could be considered as a meeting point between all that the individual had been in the past and all that the individual might be in the future. Jung once wrote, "I want to know for what a man is preparing himself. That is what I read out of his dreams."

A provocative example of how a dream can both reflect on a person's past and provide hope for the future is described in John Sanford's book *Dreams: God's Forgotten Language*.[21] Sanford's father was an Episcopal priest who had been ordained while serving briefly in China. During the last five years of his life, he experienced mounting physical illness and became increasingly anxious and depressed as he contemplated his own approaching death. He had never expressed any interest in dreams, but the week before his death, he reported a dream to his wife, who recorded it as follows:

> In the dream he awakened in his living room. But then the room changed and he was back in his room in the old house in Vermont as a child. Again the room changed: to Connecticut (where he had his first job), to China, to Pennsylvania (where he often visited), to New Jersey, and then back to the living room. In each scene after China, I was present, and in each instance being of a different age in accordance with the time represented. Finally he sees himself lying on the couch back in the living room. I am descending the stairs and the doctor

is in the room. The doctor says, "Oh, he's gone." Then, as the others fade in the dream, he sees the clock on the mantlepiece; the hands have been moving, but now they stop; as they stop, a window opens behind the mantlepiece clock and a bright light shines through. The opening widens into a door and the light becomes a brilliant path. He walks out on the path of light and disappears.[22]

This dream led to a state of deep contentment for the dreamer. His family also found solace in the dream and felt reassured by the image of his departing spirit walking out on the brilliant path of light. To permanently honor this comforting image, they incorporated the phrase "the path of light" on his tombstone.

SYMBOLS

For Freud, the term "symbol" had a very concrete meaning. A snake was a symbol for a penis, and a purse was a symbol for a vagina. It would be more correct to consider such equations as involving signs rather than symbols. Jung used the term in a much more dynamic fashion: in his theory a symbol not only represents an attempt to satisfy a frustrated instinctual impulse, but it also embodies archetypal material. Dream symbols can serve to carry messages from the instinctive to the rational parts of the mind, and can also represent lines of development which are striving for future completion and wholeness. Symbols thus have both a retrospective and a prospective side: retrospective because of their instinctual origin, and prospective because they are process-oriented and move in the direction of further development and growth. The content of a symbol cannot be fully expressed in verbal concepts or rational terms.

The essence—and dynamism—of Jung's theory of symbolism is captured in this quotation: "The significance of a symbol is not that it is a disguised indication of something that is generally known, but that it is an endeavor to elucidate by analogy what is as yet completely unknown and only in the process of formation."[23] Some extremely compelling examples of how symbols can do this were furnished in several dreams shared with me by Jeanette Fusco. I will describe and discuss one of these dreams at some length and also give excerpts from two of her other dreams that are fairly self-explanatory. These dreams, if approached from a Jungian viewpoint, can offer illumination, comfort, and consolation to the dreamer.

The main dream that I will discuss covered four and a half typewritten pages in Jeanette's dream journal and is densely packed with intriguing symbols. The connecting theme of the dream is a series of interactions with her husband, Ray. The dream is marked by many changes in setting and activities and by the physical appearance of her husband.

The dream opened with Jeanette and Ray in Florida, where they had lived twenty years before. They were traveling together in a car. After they passed under a bridge, the scene shifted to Pennsylvania, where they were living at the time of the dream. They came upon a vacant house and decided to explore the lot on which it

was located. What follows are excerpts from Jeanette's dream journal:

> This seemed very important to me; where the house sat in relationship to the overpass. . . . We went into the front yard and then walked around to look at the back. There was a large stream running through the backyard which opened into a smaller stream up a ways and to the right. The larger stream was shallow and very dirty, with logs and bits of stuff and floating debris. . . . In the backyard was a small pier. It stood at the junction where the larger stream and the smaller stream joined. Ray and I stood on this main pier, and at that moment as I looked at him, Ray was a young man. Suddenly, without saying a word or giving any kind of warning, Ray decided to cross the stream to look for something. I couldn't imagine why he went down the small ladder hooked onto the pier that went into the water, but it was shallow, about knee high, and I wasn't worried. It did bother me though, not knowing what he was doing.
>
> He was near the pier after just entering the water, when I saw something moving swiftly into the larger channel. It was gliding just under the surface and pushing the water above it into large swells, shooting ripples off to the side banks. I looked with horror at a gigantic snake moving towards us.

I had never seen anything so monstrous, and I screamed at Ray to hurry back out of the water onto the pier. The huge serpent swam closer and now I could see its large triangular-shaped head and shiny black eyes. It came right up to the dock, and raising its gross head, looked directly at me. The shiny black shoe-button eyes held mine and I was amazed to see an intelligence coming out, rather than the flat, black eyes of a reptile. The snake's gaze locked into mine and held me frozen where I stood, unable to break free of its almost mesmerizing force. The powerful creature looked like a giant anaconda. Incredibly, I realized that I was not frightened by the snake. Of course I did not intend to go into the water with it, but I was not afraid of the snake itself, only what it would do to Ray. I screamed repeatedly to him to hurry onto the pier, but he deliberately took his time. Terror overwhelmed me. . . .

At last, he was climbing up the ladder onto the dock. One leg, from the knee down, was still in the water when suddenly the snake reared straight up from the water and grabbed him around the knees and feet. I could see the snake's eyes clearly and its long brownish body. Terrified, I watched from my perch on the pier, as this huge snake turned into a gigantic octopus right before me. It transformed itself into a gargantuan octopus with a giant hump and many short powerful legs. The monstrous creature from the dark underwater murk grabbed Ray and wrapped its legs around him and covered him with its huge hump body and dragged him under the water. Ray's face was void of expression and he uttered no cry, nor attempted any struggle. Screaming and shouting, hoping the octopus would be distracted by the noise didn't work. Watching with horror, this awful thing dragged him under and I saw bubbles coming up to the surface.

Jeanette had this dream in August 1985. Her husband Ray was in good health and "had never been sick a day in his life." In the first week of January 1986, without any warning symptoms, Ray was diagnosed as having cancer of the colon. He underwent major surgery, including a colostomy, received chemotherapy, and died seven months later. The cancer had perforated through the colon into the abdomen.

The snake in this dream captures our attention in the same mesmerizing fashion as it did that of the dreamer. To insist that this snake symbolizes a penis, as mandated by Freud ("above all those most important symbols of the male organ—snakes"[24]), seems irrelevant and is demeaning with regard to its significance in this dream. In a dream analysis seminar involving a wealthy businessman, Jung said, "A snake in one case may mean something favourable, 'the wisdom of the depths,' in another something unfavourable, such as a physical illness. . . . A snake may have seven thousand meanings."[25] In the same seminar he proposed: "When the unconscious is full of the future, or is an activated form of the past which has not been realized, then it prevails over man. Therefore the snake can mean the past or the future."[26] In another passage, Jung remarked that "the serpent is the cold-blooded animal . . . it means darkness . . . it symbolizes death, fear. It is poisonous."[27]

The symbol of the snake in Jeanette's dream seems to incorporate many of these attributes: physical illness, being poisonous, the future, death, darkness, and fear. Although the dreamer experienced terror in the dream, she indicated she was not afraid of the snake itself but of what it would do to Ray. He became the victim of the snake, which pulled him down into "the dark underwater murk."

In this dream, the unconscious did seem to be "full of the future" and to indicate precognitively that Ray would be struck with a sudden illness that would lead to his death. But there is simultaneously another component, one that Jung suggested could have a "favorable" meaning, having to do with "the wisdom of the depths." Jeanette "was amazed to see an intelligence" in the shiny black eyes of the snake. What can we make of this?

In her letter to me, Jeanette indicated that during her husband's seven-month battle with his cancer they both "had very unusual spiritual occurrences" and that she was writing a book to share those happenings. Ray's growing spiritual awareness helped him both physically and emotionally in dealing with his illness, and Jeanette also had many remarkable dreams during this time which gave her an en-

hanced philosophical and spiritual perspective on this sudden and dramatic change in both their lives. Below are a few brief excerpts from one of Jeanette's dreams approximately a month after Ray's cancer was diagnosed:

I was in a very expansive place and . . . everyone was there— thousands of entities like myself who belonged there and were also in spirit . . . we were all one, yet each of us was separate. We were in a paradise of complete warmth, happiness, and comfort. . . .

I was shown that the physical is actually almost like what we consider the dream state.

I also realized how time-oriented, primitive, encumbered, and tiny the Earth is compared to the place from which I was observing it. There was no time—past, present, or future. It just *is*. Even though I experienced this, I can't explain it in words. . . . Looking at the Earth and the physical realm from there made it seem insignificant. I could not imagine why I had worried and was so concerned about what went on down on Earth. . . .

From out there the Earth seemed but a speck of sand. I realized that the concept of time went hand in hand with the physical dimension, one reason being that there has to be a time limit on our Earth lives for the assignments we are trying to fulfill. It is hard to explain the insignificance of an

Earth life from this other perspective. While I felt detached from the Earth, I was also still strongly me while on Earth. The most amazing thing, however, was the realization that I had gotten the whole thing reversed and that the dream is actually the physical.

The snake thus seemed to have a definite dual symbolism: the dark, sinister association with future illness and death, and a healing association with the acquisition of spiritual intelligence, which enabled the dreamer to develop a sense of cosmic consciousness concerning the significance of earthly life.

The snake's transformation, in the dream, "into a gargantuan octopus with a giant hump and many short powerful legs," foreshadowed the metastatic spread of the cancer within the body of the dreamer's husband; the "tentacles" of the cancer spread from the colon to the stomach. The colon may have been depicted by the large stream running through the backyard, "very dirty, with logs [feces] and bits of stuff and floating debris," and the stomach by the "smaller stream up a ways." The "junction where the larger stream and the smaller stream joined" could be the perforated area through which the cancer spread from colon to stomach.

As Jeanette's dream continued, she "knew time had run out," and since she "couldn't see any more thrashing" in the water, she "jumped in to pull him out, praying the octopus was gone." It was. After much anxious searching, she finally found her husband and "thought that surely Ray had to be dead." Jeanette man-

aged to "get him out and onto the pier." At that point the scene became dramatically brighter, suggesting that some form of regeneration had taken place:

> The sun was shining brilliantly, and I saw green trees and brightness all around me. We were in the middle of a beautiful clear, large lake, surrounded by tall green fir trees along the shore. I had the impression of being in the far north, high up in the mountains. The water was a deep blue and the sun reflected brightly off the ripples making the lake one shimmering body.

In the next section of Jeanette's dream, Ray's appearance changed:

> Staring down at Ray, I was surprised to see that he now looked like a wind-up toy, much like a child's metal roly-poly man. . . . His metal body was encased in a hard, plasticlike covering . . . [and] he reminded me of the fairy-tale characters, Tweedledum and Tweedledee. It confused me when I saw him, but I knew it had to be him.

The physical alterations of Ray's body can be looked at from several points of view. After the spiritual regeneration symbolized by the beautiful lakeside scene, any physical functioning could be considered as taking place on a rather mechanical level, "like a wind-up toy." What can be made of the references to a "roly-poly man," and "Tweedledum and Tweedledee"? Since the spread of the cancer to the stomach led to marked abdominal distension, these images of rotund figures accurately predicted another way in which Ray's body would eventually change. The reference to a "metal body" also becomes clear when we learn that Ray underwent two treatments with cis-Platinol, an anticancer compound containing the metallic element platinum.

The final element of prefiguration regarding Ray's body occurred in the last section of Jeanette's dream, when she discovered that his body was filled with water that needed to be drained because he was having trouble breathing. She took a long reed from some nearby rushes and "stuck the tube down his throat using the pipelike reed to serve as a breathing tube. To my further amazement it also pumped the water out." In the second month after the cancer was discovered, Ray suffered from double pneumonia and pleurisy and had to be placed on an inhalator which served as a "breathing tube." In the following month an abdominal catheter tube was placed to drain off fluids. In the final sentence of Jeanette's dream, she had written: "I knew he was all right in one way, but really not a human being anymore."

Jeanette's dream also has many examples of wordplay and puns. Near the beginning of the dream, she focused upon the importance to her of the "relationship to the *overpass*." If this word were turned around, it would become "pass over"; the whole dream seems intended to help the dreamer achieve some understanding and acceptance of Ray's "passing over" and how her "relationship" with him will be affected by the process. There is also an interesting use of the word "body." Around

the middle of the dream, Jeanette recovered Ray's presumedly dead physical body from the dark water; immediately afterward she described a magnificent scene with clear blue water and green pine trees surrounded by mountains. She reported that the sun reflecting off the lake made it "one large shimmering body." The word usage here suggests a transformation of Ray's physical body into a spiritual body that reflects brilliant, shimmering light.

Jeanette had another interesting dream involving light imagery. The dream began with Ray and Jeanette running down a rocky road because they were afraid they were being chased. With Jeanette's help, Ray had just escaped from a prison. The prison had been a large sandstone structure that resembled "a large sand castle." At the end of the road was a river, with

papyruslike reeds growing near the shore, and I knew without doubt that it was the river Styx. Anchored in the reeds was a wooden boat, almost like a dugout, but with a bow, rising both in the front and the back. We quickly got into the boat and started paddling out onto the river. It wasn't quite twilight and the sun was starting to set. . . . The sun was a bright orangy red ball now . . . leaving a rippled path of color like a road, wide and shiny at its point under the earth's rim, and then narrowing down to a small path by our boat. We were in the middle of the river, coming into safety, when I turned to see Ray lean out over the side of the boat and then swiftly and silently slip into and under the water. I was stunned.

This dream occurred in late June 1986. Ray died approximately one month later. Many symbols in this dream presaged his death: the sand castle (a very temporary structure); the approach of twilight, the setting sun; and the mythological river of death, the Styx. Jeanette was aware that when Ray slipped overboard from the boat into the river Styx, a very bright light was visible that extended from a narrow path by the boat to a wider one at the horizon. This "path of light" symbolism parallels, in a remarkable way, the path of light upon which Sanford's father departed in his dream. Jeanette was unfamiliar with the latter dream and felt a sense of bonding when I pointed out the striking correspondence.

I recently encountered a dream reported by Kenneth Kelzer, a psychiatric social worker, that shared many similarities with Jeanette's dream of the gigantic snake whose "gaze locked into mine and held me frozen where I stood." Kelzer published a book, *The Sun and the Shadow*,[28] discussing a series of lucid dreams he experienced over a period of several years.

His dream, which also contained a strong emotional response to a snake's gaze, was entitled, "The Arrival of the Serpent Power." In the third scene of this long dream, Kelzer was lying facedown on the earth when a huge snake about thirty feet long encircled his body. He described the snake's eyes as follows:

Its eyes are a strange yellow-green in color, and they gaze at me

calmly and steadily, continuously emitting their soft, yellow-green luminescence from within . . . it watches me through its glowing eyes with a calm and amazingly neutral objectivity. . . . I look upward. Our eyes meet and the impact is extremely powerful—absolutely unforgettable.[29]

The dreamer attempted to wrestle with the snake but eventually yielded to its overwhelming strength. The snake then gently rotated the dreamer's body into various positions. The scene changed and another slightly smaller, but equally powerful, snake arrived and again encircled the dreamer's prone body. This snake also gazed down intently upon the dreamer, who described the experience as follows:

Again I stare upward for a time into the amazing powerful eyes of the serpent, trying to fathom its intent. I am entranced with the soft, yellow-green luminescence that steadily flows from somewhere deep, deep within the serpent's eyes and even from beyond its eyes, as if from the untold reaches of another world.[30]

The dreamer's sense that the serpent's entrancing gaze was somehow connected with "another world," is interesting when we remember that Jeanette experienced her dream of viewing the Earth from another world after also encountering the mesmerizing gaze of a snake in her dream.

Kelzer reported two distinct changes after his serpent dream. One was "an increased sensitivity to my own feelings," and the other was "an 'energy awareness' in which I saw the entire physical world as a huge mass and sea of energies, all vibrating at different frequencies and moving in different directions."[31] When pondering these changes, he wondered whether they might have something to do with kundalini energy. Hindu yogis have used the metaphor of a coiled serpent to represent the potential psychic power residing at the base of the spine, which when awakened can rise up through various layers of consciousness in the spine, referred to as chakras.[32]

The appearance of a snake in someone's dream or deep meditative trance is considered a portent that kundalini energy is rising in that person's consciousness. This movement of energy may lead to certain consequences:

> The recipient would, supposedly, experience more and more shifts in his thinking and ways of seeing the world. Among the benefits received would be an increase in his psychic powers of perception and in his intuitive abilities. In everyday life this often fostered an increased ability to see clearly through the maze and complexity of the world, and to discern the truly essential issues and concerns of any given situation.[33]

It would take us too far afield to discuss the possible existence of kundalini energy, but both Jeanette and Kelzer experienced noticeable shifts in their perceptions of the world and its attendant reality following their dream encounters with giant serpents.

These two snake dreams have been presented at some length to give the reader an appreciation of the multilayered complexity which can be involved in dream symbolism and the power of the Jungian approach as an interpretive tool. The simplistic Freudian axiom, that a snake almost invariably represents a penis, fails to take into account the richness of meaning that may be embedded in a dream symbol. Jung was able to grasp the far-flung meanings which could be evoked by snake imagery because of his wide-ranging inquiries into myths and ancient religions and his immersion in non-Western cultures in Africa, India, and the Native American pueblos of the southwestern United States. Jung's emphasis upon dream symbols as revealing what "is as yet completely unknown and only in the process of formation" seems particularly appropriate in considering the prospective imagery present in Jeanette's three dreams and in Ken Kelzer's dream.

DRAMATIC STRUCTURE OF DREAMS

In one of his letters, Jung characterized the dream as a "drama taking place on one's interior stage." A drama is presented by means of a structure similar to that found in most dreams. A drama or dream usually has four components, according to Jung: (1) an opening scene which introduces the setting, characters, and initial situation of the main character; (2) the development of a plot; (3) the emergence of a major conflict; and (4) the response to the conflict by the main character. This outcome is called the *lysis*.

Let's return to the dream of the general Jung encountered on his train trip. The opening scene involved a parade setting in which young officers were being inspected by the commander in chief. The plot unfolded as the commander in chief demanded that the dreamer supply a definition of "beautiful." A conflict emerged when the dreamer was unable to answer satisfactorily. The commander in chief put the same question to the next man, a young officer who resembled the dreamer when he was younger. The younger man responded with an articulate answer that the dreamer admired and wished he had been resourceful enough to give.

Some dreams are too short or fragmentary to be explicated by this structural approach, but it can offer an excellent entry point into understanding a dream. The sequence in which the dream unfolds often corresponds to the stages of problem solving unconsciously selected by the dreamer in waking life. The dream opens with a statement, expressed metaphorically, to the effect of "Here's the problem or issue I'm currently struggling with," then proceeds to indicate how the dreamer has been dealing with the problem. The lysis or ending of the dream portrays possible strategies that the dreamer might employ to cope with the issue presented in the opening scene.

TECHNIQUE OF AMPLIFICATION

After clarifying the various components of the dream, the interpretation next explores amplifications of the dream images. *Amplification* is a very different process from the free association technique advocated by Freud. In the latter, the dreamer gives a series of continuing, sequential associations to an isolated element of the dream. Viewed graphically, the process might resemble climbing down a tree, limb to limb, from an element of the manifest content at the top to the buried roots of the latent infantile sexual wish. Knowing how the top of the tree looks does not provide any useful information about the underlying root structure. Perhaps a ball of string will serve as a suitable visual metaphor for amplification. Imagine that each element of manifest content is wrapped in many layers of string. Amplification involves systematically unwinding the skein of connected meanings coiled about the core dream image. Each ball of string is tied together with every other ball of string, each of which is wrapped around its own separate dream element. The overall dream would thus be portrayed as a large sphere of collected balls of string, each wrapped around an individual dream image.

If one dreamed of a bull, Jung would ask the dreamer to describe what a bull could possibly represent, or how it looked or behaved in the dream. A favorite question of Jung's was: "Suppose I had no idea what the word bull meant, describe this object to me in such a way that I can not fail to understand what sort of thing it is." The dreamer would be required to keep circling about the central concept of a bull, indicating that a bull is big, a bull is strong, a bull is masculine, a bull has horns, a bull is dangerous, a bull is used for breeding, a bull provides beef, a bull provides bullshit, and so forth.

If the dreamer instead free associated starting with the idea of bull, the sequences might be bull—cow, milk, bottle, baby; or bull—bull pen, baseball, diamond, engagement ring; or perhaps, bull—bull market, stock market, crash, 1929. Such continued, sequential associations only increase the distance between the dreamer and the dream element, rather than closing the cognitive and emotional gap between the dream element and its embedded meaning for the dreamer. Jung proposed that free association revealed something about thought process, but not about the rich meaning of the dream element. If one wished to scrutinize the associational thinking process, Jung suggested that a postage stamp would be as useful a starting point as a dream.

The first phase of amplification, which has just been discussed, involves an exploration of the personal meanings attached to the dream image by the dreamer and an inquiry about the feelings which are evoked in response to it. During the second phase, attention focuses upon the cultural meanings that the dreamer's societal group might link with that image. A Latin American or Spaniard accustomed to bloody bullfights would react quite differently to the image of a bull than would someone from India where Brahman bulls are revered and wander unharmed in the village streets. A still deeper level of amplification involves attempting to find archetypal connections to the image. The analyst may help during this third phase to provide a context by referring to a particular fairy tale, myth, or religious practice.

The analyst might recall that in ancient Egypt the sacred bull, Apis, was worshipped as the reincarnation of the god Ptah. The bulls who succeeded him were mummified and received elaborate funeral services before being buried in immense granite tombs. Jung, in his dream analysis seminar, referred to the role of the bull in the Persian cult of Mithras and the fact that aspects of Mithraism were adopted by the Roman legions.

A full exposition of Jung's amplification process can be found in the published notes from his dream analysis seminar.[34] These notes demonstrate the impressive level of erudition Jung displayed in pursuing the possible contributions of archetypal material to the dreams under discussion. After the various levels of amplification have been examined, an effort would be made to discover whether any "vertical" themes *within* a particular dream connected them. Jung would also consider previous dreams in the series to determine whether "horizontal" trends or patterns *between* dreams were apparent.

One "vertical" dream analysis involved the dream of a young man who had had a rendezvous with a housemaid the night before but had not yet consummated the affair. His dream was: "I was standing in a strange garden and picked an apple from a tree. I looked about cautiously, to make sure no one saw me."[35] His amplifications included a memory of having secretly plucked some pears from a neighbor's garden when he was a boy. He also recalled being severely punished as a boy when his father caught him secretly watching girls bathing. He could not understand his punishment. In amplifying the apple image, the dreamer remembered the Garden of Eden, and said he could not understand why eating the forbidden fruit there should have led to such dire consequences.

The themes uncovered by amplification were thus secrecy, sexuality, and guilt. Consciously, he felt justified in furthering the current relationship in an erotic way: all of his friends were doing the same thing. The dream, however, suggested that moral issues were involved. The dream imagery related to the Fall in the Garden of Eden helped to sensitize him to the fact that he needed to observe a moral standard and be mindful of the consequences which could develop from his actions. Jung noted that "the theft of the apple is a typical dream-motif ... [and] also a well-known mythological motif."[36]

Thus all the strata or levels of the secret apple-plucking dream converged toward a similar statement: if he lived his life in an unbalanced way without taking into account issues of morality, harsh negative consequences might be in store for him. The dreamer's personal and collective unconscious collaborated to produce a short but powerful dream message sufficiently intense to catch his attention. Examples of dreams with "horizontal" themes that gradually evolve between dreams over time include those of Anna Maria, with the Earth Mother imagery, and of the dreamer with the alchemical and mandala imagery.

OBJECTIVE AND SUBJECTIVE INTERPRETATION

The dreamer's conscious or waking situation then has to be surveyed to determine whether the dream images should be regarded in an objective or a subjective fashion. An interpretation is referred to as *objective* when a character in the dream is considered to reflect an external person with whom the dreamer has an actual waking relationship. Interpretation is characterized as *subjective* when the dream character is considered to portray some part of the dreamer's personality in an archetypal fashion. If we, for example, experience an angry confrontation with a taxi driver during the day and later dream about him at night, does the dream tell us something about that interaction (objective), or is it pointing to an animus or shadow figure within who is in the driver's seat (subjective)? These are the kinds of questions Jungian dream interpreters consider.

There is a striking theoretical similarity between Jung's conceptualization of the subjective style of interpretation and Fritz Perls's Gestalt approach, which was developed several decades later and will be discussed in the next chapter. Below are Jung's words about the subjective level:

The whole dream work is essentially subjective and a dream is a theatre in which the dreamer is himself the scene, the player, the prompter, the producer, the author, the public and the critic. This simple truth forms the basis for a conception of the dream's meaning which I have called *interpretation on the subjective level*. Such an interpretation, as the term implies, conceives all the figures in the dream as personified features of the dreamer's own personality.[37]

OTHER ASPECTS OF INTERPRETATION

Many factors need to be weighed when a dream is to be interpreted. The age of the dreamer may be pertinent. Jung gave an example of a dream in which a group of young men were riding horses across a wide field. The dreamer, who was in front of the group, jumped a ditch full of water and barely cleared the hazard. The riders following him fell into the ditch. When this dream was reported by a very cautious and introverted young man, Jung felt it indicated what he *should be doing*. He needed to take the lead more often, to be active, to take risks, to stretch himself more, in other words, to charge at life rather than withdrawing. Jung heard a very similar dream from an old man who had led a very active and adventuresome life, but who was now creating a great deal of trouble for himself, his doctor, and his nurse, having injured himself when he defiantly ignored medical instructions. In this case, the dream was telling the old man what he *was doing but shouldn't*. He needed to stop continually engaging in such risky behavior and work more closely with the members of his medical team. Thus similar dreams carried two dissimilar messages; the young man should accelerate the pace of his life and take greater risks, the older man should slow down and take fewer risks.

The dreamer's social position may also affect the meaning of a dream. Jung cited an example of a very snobbish matron noted for her prejudices and stubborn arguments. She had a dream in which she was invited to a great social affair. The hostess received her with the words "How nice that you have come, all your friends are already here and are expecting you." The hostess led her to a door, opened it, and the dreamer stepped into a cow shed.[38] This dream nicely illustrates a tenet of Jung's about the manifest content: "A dream is quite capable . . . of naming the most painful and disagreeable things without the least regard for the feelings of the dreamer."[39] It is clear in this dream that this woman would have to examine her behavior if she wished to improve her social standing, because she was viewed by others as standing ankle deep in the by-products found on the ground in a cow shed.

Dream interpretation should not be a constricted intellectual exercise to be approached as if it were a crossword puzzle. Simply recalling past events or recognizing archetypal images is not sufficient; one must fully assimilate and integrate in the conscious mind previously unavailable contents. For assimilation to occur, the various emotional responses attached to these contents must be dealt with and processed. Jung stressed that "emotional value must be kept in mind and allowed for throughout the whole intellectual process of dream interpretation."[40]

ACTIVE IMAGINATION

In addition to processing the emotional components of the symbols that appear in dreams, Jung encouraged the dreamer to explore the potential significance of a dream symbol by engaging in the technique of *active imagination*. When utilizing this method, the dreamer enters into a quiet meditative state, focuses attention upon the dream image, and observes how the form or appearance of the image gradually changes. The person does not make any conscious effort to direct the evolving imagery, but allows unconscious sources to modify the original dream image. The resultant product may yield important clues about the message behind the image.

A process similar to active imagination was employed by Norma Churchill in developing and expanding the imagery of a snake. Churchill is a California artist and poet who kept a journal describing her dreaming and visualization experiences for several years. She entitled this particular visualization experience, "The Serpent as Wounded Healer." The initial image involved a beach where she was searching for the footprint of a god in the damp sand. When she found it, she felt compelled to place her foot in this footprint and experienced instant pain and agony. Below are some subsequent excerpts from her journal:

A golden serpent comes up out of the sea and surf and wraps itself around me and drags me into the sea. We go under the waters.

Still, I suffer. We come to a tranquil beautiful island where the serpent lays me on a bed of cool green grass. He plucks some moss and packs it around my foot. . . .

Suddenly the serpent lurches back and becomes numinous.

With unhinged jaws it holds a huge faceted diamond ball which lights up the world. I am astonished, wonder-struck!

He slithers forward and presses the brilliant stone into my forehead . . . like a miner's light.

My light now shines brilliantly out into the void (the world). I also suffer with this weight of light.

I ask, "Why am I so wounded?" nodding toward my crippled foot.

The serpent answers, "You must not step into another's path."

My head lights up with brilliance. Still, I am in great agony. I realize I will remain crippled in life if I take a path other than my own.

"Help me," I beg the serpent.

He rears back, giving me a steely look with his mysterious sky-blue eyes. Then, he swiftly strikes my crippled foot and bites it with his powerful jaws. I nearly faint at the pain of it, and both my feet and legs turn black and rotten. I look at the serpent in astonishment.

One half of me glows with light, the other half is putrid and black with rot. Then in a flash, my legs and feet turn to diamond and light up like my forehead.

"Who are you? I demand. His image fades in and out—this serpent does not like to speak.

I stay with bringing the image back, again and again and again

. . . until it is once again strong before me.

The serpent looks me in the eye and says, "I am the wounder and the healer. We will meet again."[41]

Churchill provided several stunning paintings of her snake imagery in her article. She reported that "my life took a 180-degree turn" after she experienced this and subsequent visualizations of serpents "in many guises." She became attracted to bodywork and described how "energy actually vibrated, mainly in my spine, but also in my neck, head, arms and fingers" when engaged in such work. This change in perspective and energy following the arrival of serpent imagery resonates closely with the experiences that Jeanette and Ken Kelzer acknowledged after their dreams of giant serpents. All three individuals found themselves staring intently into the eyes of unusual serpents who possessed powerful healing energy but also the potential to cause harm and pain. My presentation of several snake examples should not be taken to indicate that snake imagery is common and to be expected whenever a Jungian approach is followed. Rather, by selecting similar imagery and outcomes, I have tried to impart a sense of how archetypal imagery can be suggestive of a collective unconscious.

Jung encouraged individuals to make drawings or paintings of their dreams, to sculpt them in clay, or to carve them in wood or stone. This process of attempting to vitalize dream images has been called *dream enactment* by James Hall,[42] a leading Jungian writer on dreams. One might attempt to wear clothing designed on the basis of personal dream imagery or jewelry which reminds one of a significant object from a dream. Such efforts to capture and affirm the positive energy associated with a strong dream image can serve to empower the dreamer and keep him or her in touch with this important source of unconscious inspiration. By externalizing the dream image in some graphic or plastic way, it also becomes possible to examine its gradual metamorphosis over time.

SYNCHRONICITY

Jung was challenged by the existence of phenomena which did not seem to have a casual explanation in terms of contemporary Western science. He continually reminded us that we must develop an appreciation for the mysteries of life and not attempt to force phenomena into scientific pigeonholes which could not contain them. Late in his life, he advanced the *principle of synchronicity*. This principle applies to events that occur together in time but are not causally linked. A clock might stop at the moment of its owner's death, for example. Such events might be considered coincidences, but Jung suggested that there is some other kind of order in the universe which develops parallel to the physical world; one manifestation displays itself psychically, while a related manifestation expresses itself physically in the external world. In such cases, the correspondence would be described as acausal.

As I mentioned earlier in this chapter, when Jung first pursued the descent into his own unconscious, he encountered the old wise man in the form of Philemon.

Philemon had the wings of the kingfisher with its characteristic colors. For several days Jung was engaged in painting this haunting and transfixing figure. While engrossed in this activity, he found in his garden, by the lake, a dead kingfisher. Jung

In his Red Book, Jung painted the figure of "Philemon," a wise old man whose wings were the color of a kingfisher, and who held four keys in his hands.

said that kingfishers were quite rare around Zurich and he never again found a dead one. This kingfisher had apparently been dead for only two or three days and showed no signs of external injuries.

Another bird figured in an interesting example of synchronicity with one of Jung's female patients. She said that she had fled from Freudian analysis because the analyst insistently talked about sex. She had selected Jung, she explained, because she knew he was not interested in sex. Jung replied that he felt sex could be important, but that he disagreed with Freud that it was the causative factor behind all emotional problems. After a few sessions, Jung realized that sex really was a very primary and important topic for this woman, but she ignored any comments or interpretive hints that he made in this direction. After this pattern had continued for several more weeks, Jung made up his mind that if she refused to explore the topic of sexuality at their next session, he would be forced to terminate working with her.

It was summertime and she and Jung were sitting on the lawn of his home, a setting that he frequently utilized during the warm months. After they sat down, she described a dream that was saturated with sexual material. As she concluded her report of the dream, their attention was drawn to a sparrow that had landed on the grass between them. A moment later a second sparrow noisily arrived. The second bird eagerly eyed the first one and promptly proceeded to mount it and consummate their meeting. They then both flew happily away. As soon as the birds departed, Jung and the woman looked at each other and burst out laughing. She then began, as a result of this synchronistic prompting, to discuss the sexual implications of her dream.

TELEPATHIC INFLUENCES IN DREAMS

As might be expected from Jung's interests in psychic phenomena, he was very open to considering that some dreams could be influenced by telepathy. He expressed his views on this topic as follows:

> Another dream-determinant that deserves mention is telepathy. The authenticity of this phenomenon can no longer be disputed today. It is, of course, very simple to deny its existence without examining the evidence, but that is an unscientific procedure which is unworthy of notice. I have found by experience that telepathy does in fact influence dreams, as has been asserted since ancient times. Certain people are particularly sensitive in this respect and often have telepathically influenced dreams.[43]

DREAM CREATIVITY

Jung clearly considered dreams to possess the rich variety of possibilities described in chapter 1 of this book. For Jung, the possible content to be found in dreams was a cornucopia of the most diverse topics possible:

> Dreams may contain ineluctable truths, philosophical pronounce-

ments, illusions, wild fantasies, memories, plans, anticipations, irrational experiences, even telepathic visions, and heaven knows what besides.[44]

He explained how the dreaming psyche was able to produce such diverse and new material in these words: "The images and ideas that dreams contain cannot possibly be explained solely in terms of memory. They express new thoughts that have never yet reached the threshold of consciousness."[45]

Jung frequently commented on the re-markable problem-solving potential of the unconscious mind. In his book, *Psychology and Religion*, he proposed: "The unconscious mind is capable at times of assuming an intelligence and purposiveness which are superior to actual conscious insight."[46] Similarly, in *Man and His Symbols*, he said;

The unconscious seems to be able to examine and to draw conclusions from facts, much as consciousness does. It can even use certain facts, and anticipate their possible results, just because we are *not* conscious of them.[47]

OVERVIEW

Since Jung made no effort to found a particular school of psychological thought or develop a cadre of disciples to spread his word, his viewpoints were not very well known outside Switzerland. Freud created a tightly organized international psychoanalytic society, which sponsored conventions and published journals, insuring that the world would be familiar with his theories. Jung never initiated such an active organization and recognition was much slower in arriving for him.

Jung's style of writing is often difficult to follow. He liberally intersperses foreign phrases, obscure historical facts, remote mythological references, anthropological observations, and personal anecdotes throughout his text, and his sentence structure is sometimes long and disjointed.

Academicians have shied away from Jung. They label him as a mystic, as someone so steeped in philosophy, religion, and parapsychology as to be beyond the pale of respectable psychology. Nevertheless, Jung has found increased acceptance among the general public, clinical practitioners, creative artists, and members of the clergy. His outlook on personality is definitely more optimistic than Freud's, and his emphasis upon the important integrative changes associated with the second half of life appeals to a population more and more geared to the enrichment and satisfaction which can accompany the maturing or "golden" years of life.

Jung never published a systematic book on dreams; his comments on dreams are scattered throughout his works and only recently have there been available two compilations of his observations on dreams. One of these books is an anthology containing several selections from his writings on dreams[48] and the other collects over seven hundred pages of Jung's comments on a series of thirty dreams reported by a businessman.[49] These dreams were discussed as part of a dream seminar that continued over a period of a year and a half. Jung's approach to dreams has also been described in several books written by others.[50]

Many contemporary dream therapists have incorporated various facets of Jung's approach without acknowledging, or perhaps without being aware of, their original source. Although the process of amplification may not be carried through to the level of mythological parallels, most contemporary dream workers routinely ask a dreamer to amplify and further describe any salient dream element in terms of its appearance, form, function, how it was utilized, unusual attributes, and so forth. The current tendency is to regard the manifest dream not as some crafty device to lead us astray and *conceal* its real message, as Freud contended, but rather as a communication intended to *reveal* its important message in a symbolic or metaphorical fashion. Jung wrote, "The 'manifest' dream picture is the dream itself and contains the whole meaning of the dream."[51] He argued that we must stay as close as possible to the actual dream images and consider them not as imaginary wish fulfillments, but as something that actually happened to the dreamer.

Whereas Freud discouraged his patients from writing down their dreams, almost all modern workers would encourage keeping a dream diary, as Jung advocated. Including drawings in the journal would also be suggested, as would efforts to collect personal decorations, figurines or gems that recall healing dream images. Thanks

to Jung, the importance of evaluating any given dream within the context of the dream series in which it is embedded is now taken for granted.

Another area of divergence between the Freudian and Jungian approaches can be found in the range and level of cognitive complexity that these two theorists impute to the dreaming mind. Freud denigrated the capacity of the dreaming mind to think and stated that it functioned at a very primitive and concrete level and it "does not happen to reflect reality," that the dream could "be as varied as thought during the waking state."[52] Jung, on the other hand, credited the dreaming mind with possessing skills that were sometimes superior to those of the waking mind: "It is highly probable that our dream psyche possesses a wealth of contents and living forms equal to or even greater than those of the conscious mind."[53]

In addition to the stark differences between Jung's and Freud's views of the meaningfulness of the manifest content, the importance of considering a dream's position within a series, and the utilization of amplification versus free association, they also differed sharply on other important conceptual parameters. Freud examined the dream associations for what they could tell him about the infantile sources of conflict in the past and was *regressive* in his focus, while Jung studied the dream to tell him where the dreamer was heading and was *progressive* in his outlook.

Their expectations of the symbolic content to be discovered also contrasted markedly. For Freud, "the number of subjects symbolized is not large. In dreams those pertaining to sexual life are the overwhelming majority."[54] The whole process of symbolization was conceived of in a very different way by Jung:

> Man feels himself isolated in the cosmos, because he is no longer involved in nature and has lost his emotional "unconscious identity" with natural phenomena. These have slowly lost their symbolic implications. . . . His contact with nature has gone, and with it has gone the profound emotional energy that his symbolic connection supplied.
>
> This enormous loss is compensated for by the symbols of our dreams. . . .
>
> The unconscious has preserved primitive characteristics that formed part of the original mind. It is to these characteristics that the symbols of dreams constantly refer. . . .
>
> The main task of dreams is to bring back a sort of "recollection" of the prehistoric. . . . Such recollections can have a remarkable healing effect.[55]

The theories of dream function and the methods of dream interpretation based upon these assumptions obviously reflect the personalities of the theorists who proposed them. Both Freud and Jung spent several years engaged in self-analysis and used dreams as important tools of discovery while making their inner journeys. They returned with quite different information about what sorts of materials were buried in the unconscious. Jung was clearly aware of the limitations inherent in generalizing from any single individual's experiences. He once commented to a colleague, "A man cannot transcend himself. So the fact is that Freud's, Adler's, and my psychology are all generalizations and abstractions of our own psychology."[56]

By the same token, each dream worker is attracted to the dream approach which resonates with his or her own psychology. I have never undergone a Jungian analysis nor received any Jungian training, but I have found far more helpful guidance in working with my own dreams and with the dreams of others by following a Jungian, rather than a Freudian, approach to dreams.

OTHER TWENTIETH-CENTURY DREAM THEORISTS

T o discuss all the individuals who have contributed to our knowledge of dreams as extensively as I have Freud and Jung would require a ten-volume series. A few of the other theorists who have helped to expand our awareness and understanding of dreaming and its possible significance in our lives will be briefly reviewed in this chapter. Any such selection of authors is bound to be arbitrary and would certainly differ from reviewer to reviewer, but I have chosen those whose approach I consider sufficiently promising to warrant some attention.

ALFRED ADLER

Alfred Adler, like Jung, was an early associate of Freud and at one time served as president of the Vienna Psychoanalytic Society. He resigned that position in 1911 and subsequently developed his own approach, known as Individual Psychology. In Adler's theory of personality, the role of the unconscious was minimized and man was considered to be primarily motivated by innate social drives which could be modified by culture and family experiences. He felt that individuals evolved their own unique *life style* which provided a unifying pattern around which all their behavior was organized.

Since dreams and unconscious motivation are almost synonymous, it would follow that Adler did not use dreams very extensively in his clinical practice. Unlike Freud and Jung, Adler did not provide us with any extended case illustrations clarifying the manner in which he employed dreams. He did not encourage associations to individual dream elements, but seemed to rely on a more global form of association or reaction to the dream as a whole, to illuminate the general life style. Short dreams could indicate the dreamer desired a "short cut" to his problem; a long dream might indicate the dreamer was a hesitant person considering a number of solutions to the problem. Sometimes the therapist merely interpreted the "headlines" of the dream.[1]

Adler did not share openly his own dreams or his reactions to them with his readers. The only example I have encountered was of a dream, described by one of his biographers, that occurred on the night before his first trip to America.[2] Adler was on a ship traveling to an unknown destination with all the treasurers he had acquired during his lifetime. A collision occurred, the boat sank, and everything he had was lost, but he reached the shore after a long, hard struggle. This dream suggests that Adler was aware that a difficult journey lay ahead in which many sacrifices might be necessary, but that he was confident of reaching his goal after a difficult struggle.

One of the reasons Adler may not have become very invested in his dreams is that he seemed to feel a lack of dreaming was an indicator of good psychological health. This was how Adler viewed the matter:

> We should expect, therefore, that the more the individual goal agrees with reality, the less a person dreams; and we find that it is so. Very courageous people dream rarely for they deal adequately with their situation in the day time.[3]

Nevertheless, Adler advanced some interesting conjectures about dreams. One involved his insistence that personality should be viewed as unitary; the conscious and the unconscious, in his theory, are not two different spheres of mental functioning, and "the personality is the same in dreaming life as in waking life."[4] Related to this is Adler's contention that "dreams are the product of a particular life style and, in turn, build up and enforce this style."[5] A sweeping claim for consistency is evident in this statement:

> The psychologist knows that the person's imagination cannot create anything but that which his style of life commands. His made-up dreams are just as good as those he genuinely remembers for imagination and fancy will also be an expression of his style of life.[6]

Adler believed that dreams originate in unfinished and unsolved social problems and are oriented toward the future:

> The self draws strength from the dream fantasy to solve an imminent problem for the solution of which its social interest is inadequate.... This seeking of a solution contains the "forward to the goal" and the "whither" of Individual Psychology in contrast to Freud's regression and fulfillment of infantile wishes.[7]

Adler did not give much weight to the idea that specific answers or solutions for our problems would be found in dreams.

He emphasized instead that the affect resulting from a dream would act as the springboard for subsequent action on the part of the dreamer: "The dream is extraordinarily well suited to intensify an emotion, or produce the nerve which is necessary to the solution of a particular situation."[8] The most succinct summary of his overall position is contained in the following sentence: "In dreams we produce the pictures which will arouse the emotions we need for our purposes, that is, for solving problems confronting us at the time of the dream, in accordance with the particular style of life which is ours."[9]

Adler offered the following explanations for what might be the motivations underlying "typical" dreams: Falling dreams, which he thought common among neurotics, reflect concerns about falling socially and suffering a loss of prestige. Dreams of flying are typical of forward-looking and ambitious people and leave the dreamer feeling buoyant and courageous because they portray overcoming difficulties as easy. Dreams of nudity or being scantily clad are associated with fears of exposure or being recognized as having an imperfection. Dreams of being paralyzed contain a warning that the present problem is without a solution. Traveling dreams refer to movement through life. Dreaming of a dead person indicates that the dreamer has not psychologically buried this person and is still influenced by them. If a person plays the role of spectator consistently in his or her dreams, this is probably the same role that they play in their waking life.

Samuel Lowy

Samuel Lowy set forth his views on dreaming in a 1942 book entitled *Psychological and Biological Foundations of Dream Interpretation*. He advanced a psychophysiological approach to understanding the dreaming process in which affect played a central role. Lowy contended that any idea contains both a conceptual element and an "affect-energy." Affect is a somatic factor which can lead to subjective experiences, such as joy or anger, and it also produces an alteration of organic factors, such as increased palpitation or nausea. There is a continuous, more or less steady "affect-current," as well as surges of intense affect. The task assigned to the "affective-regulative mechanism" is to enhance "somato-psychic well-being" by optimizing positive affect-currents and neutralizing undesirable aspects. For Lowy, "the dreaming-process, then, seems to be incorporated in this broader regulative mechanism."[10]

To create a unified conception of the dreaming process, Lowy included stimuli originating from both psychic and somatic sources, and proposed that they both are generated by affect. Since for Lowy, "all stimuli, impinging on the sleeper, produce dreams,"[11] he concludes that "behind every dreaming there is the whole psychosomatic life-process."[12] The dream image which enters consciousness and waking memory is "a final metabolic product of the total dreaming-process."[13] Just as metabolism produces certain concentrated material end products (for example, sugar in urine), the dream image as a metabolic end product has higher potency for depth-psychological research than the factors that went into it. The necessity to regulate affect through the creation of dream images can lead us to feel moody and miserable on some mornings because the dream phase was not properly concluded, and "a particular dream-image has not yet been brought to completion."[14]

Lowy offers the provocative proposal that it is biologically necessary that we experience dream images during sleep, but that it is not very important whether we remember them. We obtain the benefits from dreaming, even if we don't remember the images, because of its contribution to affect regulation. He suggests that if a difficult situation in waking life is not confronted, the subconscious psyche will present this reality to us in our dreams so that we can form "antibodies." As a consequence, when the difficulty actually occurs, the psyche, the nervous system, and the personality are better prepared to cope with it.

WILHELM STEKEL

Wilhelm Stekel was one of the original psychoanalytic group, but he separated from Freud in 1912 and subsequently developed a brief treatment technique he called active analytic therapy. Stekel, it will be recalled, had made a significant contribution to Freud's understanding of symbols. He placed a great deal of importance on the first dream that patients reported in therapy, as he felt it revealed their life conflict, guiding lines, and the type of resistance to be expected in therapy.

Stekel thought that dreams highlight the struggles between good and evil that exist in every person. He described "anagogic trends" in dreams, which lead to the peaks of life and contain such lofty aspirations as ethics, morality, idealism, and concerns about social communication. Opposed to these are the "katagogic trends," which lead to life at its lower levels, where sexual and egotistical impulses and instincts are dominant. Anagogic trends often appear in dreams during the later stages of successful therapy. Stekel placed considerable emphasis on religious concepts, especially fear of God and punishment for sin. He also noted that references to birth and death were frequent themes, particularly in long dreams.

When interpreting dreams, Stekel preferred to begin by simplifying the dream and attempting to abstract its main themes, much like a journalist writing the lead sentence of a news story. Emotions were similarly distilled down to their basic feelings. After the dream had been compressed, Stekel began to look for antitheses, such as active versus passive behavior, or anagogic versus katagogic trends. Within a dream series, "key" dreams would occur, which helped to unlock the meaning of more obscure dreams.

In commenting upon the types of dreams obtained in analysis, Stekel offered some insight as to the contribution that suggestion by the therapist, and acquiescence by the patient, might make to the dream that is ultimately reported:

> Patients dream in the dialect of whatever physician happens to be treating them. The dreams are "made to order" and produced in the form that will best please the analyst. That is why the dreams of a patient who is familiar with his doctor's pet theories must never be taken as confirmation of these theories. . . .
>
> Every psychotherapist who is under the dominion of an overcharged idea will tend to introduce this idea into any dream he analyzes.[15]

Stekel suggested that some dream images may reflect particular mental or physical concomitants. For example, a museum could represent the mind where memories are stored. Patients with physical symptoms may dream about their illness, as when epileptics encounter situations where they are in danger of falling, or "frigid" women dream of snowfields or ice-bound surfaces.

In Stekel's view, a strong case existed for the reality of telepathic dreaming. He claimed to have collected many examples showing that people who sleep in the same room influence each other's dreams, and, he asserted, "The literature of the subject contains various examples of the influence of one dreamer by another."[16] The existence of telepathic dreams was, he said, "indisputable,"[17] and he published a book called *Der Telepathische Traum* ("The Telepathic Dream").

THOMAS FRENCH

Thomas French advanced a "focal conflict" theory of dreams in his book *The Integrative Process in Dreams*.[18] He further elaborated his views, in collaboration with Erika Fromm, in their book *Dream Interpretation*.[19] "Focal conflict" refers to some recent problem growing out of a difficulty in interpersonal relations. The recent problem stirs up similar earlier problems from the dreamer's life, and a rather elaborate network of related problems comes to be represented in the manifest dream content.

Since the purpose of dreaming is to discover solutions to interpersonal problems, the dreamer will attempt to find a solution to his current focal problem by reviewing successful solutions to related past problems. These possible solutions are arranged in a hierarchy and make up what French calls the dream's "historical background." In order to comprehend the cognitive structure of the dream as a whole, French relies upon intuition and "empathic imagination." Dream series are preferred by French, since the dreamer's successive attempts at a solution, as reflected in the dreams, display the constellation of progressive and regressive mechanisms which link the focal problem to the dream's historical background.

ERIK ERIKSON

Erik Erikson developed a systematic approach which allowed an extensive analysis to be made of an individual dream. A latitudinal, or horizontal, analysis was made by paying attention to the following configurations of the manifest content: verbal, sensory, spatial, temporal, somatic, interpersonal, and affective. A complementary longitudinal, or vertical, approach considered some of the standard Freudian psychosexual conflicts as a means of analyzing the latent content. But Erikson also included the concepts of socialization and ego identity from his own theory of personality. Erikson provided a detailed example of his approach in connection with Freud's dream about "Irma's injection."[20]

MEDARD BOSS

Medard Boss evolved a phenomenological approach to dreams, which he described in his book *The Analysis of Dreams*. His approach was to forego all theories and hypotheses about dreams and to study the dream itself—as an actual phenomenon—to see what could be learned directly. "We cannot consider dreaming and waking as two entirely different spheres," Boss insisted.

> In reality there is no such thing as an independent dream on the one hand, and a separate waking condition on the other. . . . Any such attempt at a distinction is doomed to failure from the very beginning. For it is always the identical human being who awakens from his dreams and who maintains his identity throughout all his waking and dreaming.[21]

To get some feeling for Boss's approach, one needs to consider his response to an actual dream. Boss reported that the following dream from a young married woman occurred a few days after the first time she surrendered herself to fully accepting her husband's love. Subsequent events indicated that the dream had occurred at about the time she conceived.

> I saw a dark brown fertile field in which a plough was cutting large furrows. Suddenly I myself became the field and the sharp steel plough went easily through the length of my body and cut me into two halves. Although it hurt, it was indescribably beautiful. I experienced myself as the ploughed-up field, and the furrow as my own flesh, but it was not bleeding.[22]

Boss commented that the dreamer had previously dreamt of sexual experiences but

> this occurred while she had known merely the physical stimulation of the sexual act and not as yet love in all its richness. However, once she had experienced this love, the openness and fertility of her whole being became embodied in a freshly ploughed field.[23]

Boss also cited a remarkable series of 823 dreams obtained during a three-year analysis of an engineer in his forties who sought help because of his deep depressions and complete sexual impotence.[24] This patient maintained that before therapy began, he had only been able to remember one dream in his whole life. As he started therapy he reported a dream in which he was in a dungeon, dimly lit through a very small barred window beyond his reach. The dreamer noted that the bars were actually signs and numbers that expressed mathematical formulas. During the first six and a half months of therapy he dreamed exclusively of turbines, cyclotrons, automobiles, and airplanes. Toward the close of this period he had three dreams in which he desired to cross a bridge over a frontier river in one of his machines, but the bridge was broken and incomplete. In the next period, he dreamed about a living thing for the first time: a potted plant. During the same week he dreamed about green pine trees and red roses with sickly buds, withered leaves, and worm-infested roots.

Four months elapsed before he recalled another dream. He began to dream about dangerous and harmful insects and did so 105 times during the subsequent six months. Machines and plants occasionally reappeared. During the next six months he dreamed of toads, frogs, and snakes. One night he was frightened by a bright red snake of tremendous thickness and length. The first mammal to appear in his dreams was a mouse who quickly disappeared down a hole. Slightly later, pigs played a prominent role in his dreams for several weeks, but they eventually yielded to lions and horses.

Two years after beginning therapy he had his first dream about a human being. The dream involved a large woman wearing a long red dress, swimming in a pond far below a thick covering of ice. Six months later, he dreamed that he was dancing at a peasant gathering with a passionate woman in a red dress. In between these two dreams, there were many maternal figures. The dreamer was given a baby's bottle of milk by his grandmother, who also powdered his bottom; he committed incest with his mother, saw maternal angels guarding the Christ child, and met a gigantic blond fairy with huge breasts emitting waterfalls of milk. Although these maternal figures are reminiscent of Jung's great mother archetype, Boss firmly rejected such a conceptualization and argued against the existence of an "autonomous entity possessing its own creative and motive powers."

Boss remarked that the initial dream of this series reveals the dreamer's awareness of having become a prisoner because of his exclusive emphasis on intellectual and mathematical matters. As treatment progressed he realized that his world had long been limited to the lifeless machines with which he worked. As he began to introduce living things, starting with plants, into his dream world, his sexual potency began to improve, and he achieved complete potency when he dared to dream of lions and horses. Boss acknowledged Jung as the first to draw attention to such "phylogenetic development" of dream phenomena and the way in which increasing maturation of the dreamer's life can be reflected in serial dreams.

Boss also presented a case of a female patient who displayed the reverse pattern; that is, phylogenetic regression. In her first dream, she was with her brother, turning the pages for him while he played the piano. The dreamer heard heavy steps and saw a wild man, hairy and gorillalike, in a dark, adjoining room. When she went upstairs, she saw a noisy skeleton that became more inhuman and turned into a broomstick with a white disk for a face. The dreamer panicked and fell down the staircase into a void, but was caught by a man who carried her away. She thus regressed from the image of a close family member, to that of a gorillalike man, to a skeleton, to a broomstick, and then into a void, before her rescue by a friendly male. In her waking life, this woman was becoming cold and detached but recovered for a while, her hope revived through her love for the helpful man in her dreams. When she realized that this love was unreal, she began to withdraw again and had another dream about six months after the first.

Her second dream began in an ancient landscape. She was with some university students and went down a long staircase to a ruined city. The poet of love, Stendhal, was there and signing autographs. He gave the dreamer a drawing of her face, but where the mouth was supposed to be, he had written her first name in block letters. She and the students continued down the staircase and came to a deep ravine spanned by a small bridge in bad repair, which the dreamer crossed into a garden. A small jet-black cat moved about; instead of claws on its paws, it had leaves like daisies, but black. There was a strange flower-bed with more black cats, but "their entire bodies are leaf-like as well as their paws" and they "hardly look like cats anymore. They have already begun to be part of the plant kingdom." Next to the path were some other cats, who had turned into white clay or chalk figures. "Nearby there is a scientific institute for the investigation of this transformation of animals into plants, and from these into inorganic matter." The dreamer is shown "an inorganic structure formed out of a cat plant. It looks like a shell necklace." Boss commented on this dream:

> She notices how the forms of life
> become more and more regressive,

turning from cats into plants and then into mere calcifications and mussell-shells. She is so much involved in this observation of the retrograde process of "the living being" that in waking life, too, she is only capable of mere vegetative existence until, finally, all life disappears from her world. When during waking life her apathy had reached rock-bottom she could in fact only exist in this calcified or shell-like manner.[25]

It's interesting to observe how the imagery appearing after crossing a bridge signaled different outcomes for these two dreamers. The engineer crossed the bridge from inorganic objects into the plant world and progressed upward phylogenetically, first to animals and then to human beings. His waking life showed a parallel movement, from depression to increasing mental health and well-being. The female patient crossed the bridge from the world of human beings into the world of animals, then regressed phylogenetically downward to the world of plants and eventually to that of inorganic objects. Her waking life, too, progressively deteriorated from one of adequacy to one of increasing depression and an eventual vegetative state.

Boss attempts to look at a dream as if it were a mirror. He is not concerned with deeper layers of meaning beneath the surface; the image visible to the naked eye is a candid portrait of how the dreamer phenomenologically is experiencing his or her life at that point of time. It is an existential snapshot of how one is living one's life and of how one bears oneself toward others. The dream photograph also poses the question of how the dreamer is facing the as yet unlived possibilities of "being."

Once Boss felt he understood the dream picture—for example, a dream which revealed a woman's feeling of being the "powerless little daughter" of an "overpowering dream-mother"—he would present his view to the dreamer. In this example, he would ask her to recall any situations "in which an analogous childish dependence and unfree slavishness with respect to her mother would betray itself." For each example the dreamer brought forth, Boss would express "astonishment at the extent to which she puts up with this maternal tyranny, and even now continues to submit herself to it."[26] As a consequence, the dreamer could realize that a completely different stance was possible toward older women.

Boss also provided an example of a dream that had been interpreted by a Jungian analyst at the conclusion of his male patient's three-year analysis. In the dream, the therapist was performing life-saving surgery on the dreamer. A strong, white-haired man appeared who, out of pure love, cut out pieces of his own flesh to put into the dreamer's incisions. The Jungian analyst commented that he, as the therapist, "was only the mediator, while the actual, life-saving, and unselfish operation was to be accomplished by a higher figure of a mythological sort—by an old, strong, wise man."[27]

Boss contended there was no "higher" figure to be detected if one were to remove the "archetypal glasses" worn by the analyst at the outset. Boss asserted that this analysand should not have been released from therapy because the dream revealed several significant issues that had not been resolved. The dreamer was passively submitting to surgical treatment which "leaves the therapeutic work completely to the doctor," rather than performing the task himself. A more serious concern was that "the saving of the patient's life was brought about through a transplant from another person. . . . The healing did not occur through the regeneration of the tissue from his own body."[28]

Boss also devoted a chapter in his book to "the possibilities of 'extra-sensory' relationships in dreams." In referring to telepathic dreams, Boss discussed the experiences of a psychiatric trainee who fell ill with pneumonia one night; he dreamed that his mother was with him and he begged her to place her cool hand on his forehead. His mother, who was nine hundred kilometers away, dreamed on the same night that her son was lying in bed with a high fever and constantly asking her to cool him. The dream caused her such intense concern that she phoned his boarding house the next morning to inquire if he were seriously ill. Three years later, he broke his right leg and his mother called the next morning to ask if his injuries were serious, because she had dreamed of him lying in a hospital bed with his right leg completely bandaged. Due to her limited financial status, those were the only two long-distance calls his mother ever made.

After recounting several other impressive examples of telepathic dreams, Boss asserted:

Such dreams can no longer be honestly dismissed as mere accidents. When we find that the whole constellation of a number of dream things corresponds so exactly to a situation later met during waking life, the belief in a mere "accident" is the most impossible of all hypotheses.[29]

Boss attempted a phenomenological explanation of extrasensory dreams by describing a human being's simultaneous relation to outer and inner experiences:

Thus, it is not true that things, either of the waking or of the dream world, must first penetrate from the "outside" to the human brain, there to produce perceptions in a most mysterious manner. Quite on the contrary, man's ability to perceive things and other people is grounded in his primary openness. If so, there is no reason why man should not encounter what lies beyond the realm of his sense organs.[30]

Boss provided additional details and confirmatory evidence about Bishop Joseph Lanyi's precognitive dream of Archduke Ferdinand's assassination in Sarajevo, which I discussed in chapter 2. He emphasized that such dreams were theoretically significant, even if they do not occur very frequently: "In this respect one single verified prophetic dream could have more importance than a thousand everyday dreams."[31]

CALVIN HALL

Calvin Hall is the psychologist described in the preface who invited me to work with him for two years at the Institute of Dream Research, then located in Miami, Florida. Hall set forth his theory regarding dreams in a 1953 article entitled "A Cognitive Theory of Dreams"[32] and expanded on it in his book *The Meaning of Dreams*, published that same year and reprinted with a new introduction in 1966.

Hall's goal was to bring dream theory into the context of ego psychology by asserting that dreaming is a cognitive process. For Hall, dream images are "the embodiment of thoughts." He made a sharp distinction between perception and conception. Perception occurs when an individual *looks* at a snowy winter landscape; conception occurs when an individual *thinks* about the scene. One can only see snow in the winter, but one can think about it anytime. The invisible process of conception becomes visible when it is transformed into a dream image. To interpret a dream, one must translate the images into their referent ideas. If a content analysis is made of the manifest dream, it becomes possible to determine what kind

Calvin Hall proposed that dream images represent "the embodiment of thoughts." What the Water Brought Me *by Frida Kahlo.*

of conceptions or conceptual systems exist for the dreamer.

After examining thousands of dream reports, Hall identified the following conceptions commonly found in dreams:

Conceptions of self. The dreamer's self-conceptions are revealed by the repertoire of parts taken by the dreamer in a series of dreams. The repertoire may consist of a few roles, or it may be extensive and varied.

Conceptions of other people. Conceptions of family members, friends, and classes of people are similarly displayed through the roles these characters play in a series of dreams. Multiple conceptions of the same person are typically found.

Conceptions of the world. World-conceptions are often conveyed by the type of dream settings created by the dreamer. Are the surroundings cold and bleak or beautiful, serene, and natural? Thunderstorms or raging seas suggest a turbulent, agitated world.

Conceptions of impulses, prohibitions, and penalties. Specific ways of behaving are generally not based upon our actual impulses but on our conception of those impulses and the obstacles that stand in the way of their gratification. Prohibitions against, and restraints on, impulse gratification may be represented by the dreamer's conscience in the form of locked doors, the brakes of a car, or the interfering presence of an authority figure. If an impulse is gratified, the dreamer may express his conception of the consequences which will follow by introducing a character who punishes him or by becoming the victim of misfortune.

Conceptions of problems and conflicts. Dreams illuminate the basic predicaments of a person as that person sees them.

Dreams are a faithful pictorial record of these inner conflicts and the dreamer's attempts to resolve them.

In *The Meaning of Dreams*, Hall catalogued what he considered to be the five major conflicts to be discerned from a study of dreams: first, "the conceptual struggle which a child goes through in trying to define his feelings toward his mother and father and their feelings toward him," a conflict that "begins in early childhood," ... but may never "relax its grip completely"; second, the conflict between "the opposing ideas of freedom and security ... [which] reaches its climax during the late teens and early twenties" but also persists, "since it is hardly likely that a person will ever obtain complete freedom or complete security"; third, an ambivalence regarding sex roles, since biologically man is "both male and female, although one or the other is the dominant physical expression and is used to classify him [socially] as man or woman"; fourth, the moral conflict "between man's animal nature and the culture's expectations regarding his conduct ... [which] is largely taken up with condemning sex and aggression," as well as regulating "their expression in thought and fancy"; and finally,

> the opposing vectors of life and death ... [a] drama of conflicting biological modes, the constructive, synthesizing and assimilating processes of anabolism versus the destructive, disintegrative and decomposing processes of catabolism. ... [These biological processes provide man] with a constant flow of unconscious con-

ceptions... [Thus] the analysis of dreams gives meaning to the paradoxical assertion in the *Book of Common Prayer,* "In the midst of life we are in death."[33]

Hall considered dreams to be unequaled in their ability to discover the personal thoughts that are the real antecedents of behavior. Questionnaires are able to tap only a person's superficial and consciously available conceptions, and projective, picture-story methods contain a very limited number of possible stimulus pictures. These limitations do not apply to dreams, because dreamers make their own pictures of the conceptions of greatest current importance to them.

After classifying the typical conceptualizations and types of conflicts revealed through dreams, Hall asked, "Do the innermost thoughts in the labyrinth of the mind make their effects known in behavior?"[34] He answered:

It is clear that man's conduct is the visible embodiment of his conceptions, that behavior is the shadowing forth of deeply recessed mental states. During sleep, when the mind turns in upon itself, these recesses are explored and charted in the shape of dreams. Dreams, in effect, provide us with maps of regions which are inaccessible in waking consciousness. With these maps we are better able to follow the course of man's behavior, to understand why he selects one road rather than another, to anticipate the difficulties and obstacles he will encounter, and to predict his destinations.[35]

To help his readers learn to read these dream maps of the mind, Hall supplied verbatim reports of nearly two hundred dreams, selected to illustrate various features of the dreamer's pictorial conceptualizations. A few brief examples are given below; the dreams are in italics, followed by Hall's comments.

I dreamed that my father and I were in an old Chevrolet. I was driving but I could not seem to make the car go up a very steep hill, so my father took the wheel.

This dreamer is attempting to view herself as a person of independence but as the going gets rough she reverts to a role of dependence upon her father.[36]

I dreamed that a boyfriend came to see me and brought me a diamond engagement ring. We went for a long ride. It started at the dorm and there was a lot of snow around, but somewhere along the line the scene changed to a tropical climate.

A change in the climate is used by [this] dreamer to symbolize a change in her feelings.[37]

I was the warden at a very inefficient prison for criminals. All at once the gates to the prison opened and all the criminals tried to escape. They tried to beat me up and trample on me and I was left standing completely helpless.

If one grants that criminals in this dream symbolize the dreamer's conception of her own impulses, then the translation of the dream follows directly. The dreamer is trying to hold her impulses in check but she is not equal to the task. They break out, assault her, and leave her with a feeling of helplessness. This dream tells us that the young woman conceives of her impulses as lawless, destructive forces against which reason and conscience are powerless.[38]

I dreamed I was afloat in a rowboat, drifting without oars and wondering helplessly whether or not I would drift ashore or out to sea. I awoke still drifting helplessly with the tide and nowhere near land.

The land represents security and the open sea stands for the hazards of independence. The fact that he is without oars implies that he is not equipped to guide his life but must leave it to fate, symbolized by the tide, to take him where it will. In other words he lacks the necessary competence and confidence to solve this problem through his own efforts.[39]

I dreamed I was sentenced to death by a civil court. I walked down death row very calmly but protesting the execution as I was innocent. They strapped me into the electric chair, and pulled the switch. I awoke in a cold sweat.

If the punishment fits the crime then this young dreamer must have done something pretty bad to merit capital punishment. Protesting his innocence is an ineffectual defense because if he had been innocent he would not have had the dream.[40]

Hall and his coworkers have successfully applied his theory and method of content analysis in various projects designed to show how knowledge of an individual's dreams enables researchers to make meaningful predictions about that individual's behavior and lifestyle. These content analysis studies will be discussed in chapter 11.

Very few psychologists are aware that Hall conducted systematic studies to determine whether telepathic dreaming could be demonstrated in a laboratory setting. Some of his positive results were mentioned in the preface, and additional details of his investigation will be presented in chapter 14.

FRITZ PERLS

Frederic ("Fritz") Perls originally trained as a Freudian psychoanalyst, but he eventually came to the view that more significant therapeutic gains were made when

problems were worked on in a group setting. He developed an intensive, short-term treatment method called Gestalt therapy, which has become very popular in recent years. *Gestalt* is a German word that has been translated as meaning "whole," "pattern," or "configuration." Before his death in 1970, Perls spent several years conducting Gestalt therapy workshops at the Esalen Institute in California.

Many aspects of existentialism are reflected in Perls's approach to therapy and dreams. He was a staunch advocate of "being in the here-and-now." The task of the Gestalt therapist is to focus on what an individual is avoiding, to help the person discover the "emotional holes" in awareness, to assist the person in acting out painful situations, and to subsequently reintegrate the disowned or alienated parts into the individual's current life.

From Perls's point of view, the dream is a projection of rejected or disowned parts of the dreamer's personality. His attitude toward the dream is nicely summarized in the following quote:

> The dream is an existential message. . . . It is a message of yourself to yourself. . . . Every part, every situation in the dream . . . every aspect of it is a part of the dreamer, but a part that to some extent is disowned and projected onto others. . . . If we want to own these parts of ourselves again we have to use special techniques by which we can reassimilate those experiences.[41]

A Gestalt dream worker does not approach a dream in any standardized way. To change the dream from a past to a currently experienced reality, the therapist typically begins by requesting that the dreamer tell the dream in the present tense (I am, she is, we are, etc.). The next step might be to have the person describe various aspects of the dream and then experience those aspects as attributes of the dreamer: If someone were to dream about a colorful antique quilt, for example, they might describe themselves as attractive, soft, warm, heavy, or old, or as something that is stored away and used only when company visits. Someone whose dream involved a glass-topped patio table might describe themselves as transparent, fragile, cold, rigid, a piece of furniture, or something associated with relaxation, or as being pushed around or frequently moved. Perls believed it was essential for the dreamer not only to differentiate the parts of the dream verbally, but to actively play out each part. The dreamer must experience the dream in action so that responsibility for these actions can be owned and acknowledged.

Some therapists might therefore encourage the dreamer to become the quilt in action. The dreamer might then relax and drape himself or herself over another member of the group. In doing so, the dreamer might become aware of how it feels to provide warmth to another person or, as a clinging weight, to limit the movements of another. A dreamer trying to become the glass-topped patio table might assume a bent-over "table posture," with their hands on the floor, and experience the fear that someone could lean too hard and cause them to break into pieces or that someone could condescendingly look down and easily see through them.

The therapist observes whether the dreamer moves boldly or timidly in enacting the dream image, and also pays close attention to the dreamer's voice as various attributes of the dream characters or objects are described. Do the dreamer's vocalizations become loud and commanding, do they become barely audible, or do they take on a pleading, whiney quality?

The next step usually involves having the dreamer engage in a dialogue between different parts of the dream. A dialogue between the dreamer and the quilt, for example, might lead to the dreamer's describing how warm and comfortable he or she feels whenever the quilt is pulled up on a cold and lonely night, or the dreamer may tell the quilt how angry he or she is because of a promise to a parent to pass its "crazy quilt" pattern from generation to generation. Similarly, the therapist might encourage a dialogue between the patio table and the dreamer's spouse who appears in the dream. The table could describe its feelings of intimacy when it and the spouse interact during quiet, relaxing times, or it could angrily berate the spouse for obscuring its clear view by loading undesirable things upon it.

These dialogues are facilitated through the use of the "two chair" or "empty chair" technique. Sitting in one chair, the dreamer takes on the characteristics of part A of the dream and addresses any remarks to a nearby empty chair, as if part B of the dream were sitting there. To respond, the dreamer moves to the other chair, takes on the characteristics of part B, and answers part A as if that part were sitting in the original chair. By repeatedly shifting chairs, the distinctions between the dream parts become sharply emphasized; the dreamer may exhibit quite different postures and vocal tones when sitting in one chair, as opposed to the other.

A Gestalt approach to dreams can be helpful in working with recurrent dreams or nightmares. After a dreamer experiences an affect-laden confrontation and dialogue between himself and some threatening monster, he may experience a breakthrough in awareness which dissolves the tenacious grip of fear. Very short dreams or dream fragments can also be profitably pursued with a Gestalt approach. The therapist may emphasize the point at which the dreamer awakens from the dream in order to discover what the dreamer is trying to avoid.

If difficulty is experienced with remembering dreams, the amnesic block may sometimes be overcome by engaging in a dialogue with the lost or unavailable dreams: "Dreams, where are you?" "Dreams, why don't you come to me?" When the dialogue is reversed, the dreams might reply, "I've tried many times to visit with you recently but you always have your door locked. There's no welcome mat out for me." Or the dreams may say, "I think you're afraid of me. I promise I won't tell you anything that's not true. Why won't you let me visit you?"

An excellent collection of verbatim transcripts from a humanistically oriented Gestalt therapist can be found in *Dreams and Nightmares*.[42] Jack Downing worked with Perls for several years and was the first president of the San Francisco Gestalt Therapy Institute. In response to hypothetical questions about the meaning, symbolism, or desire to understand dreams, Downing wrote:

In Gestalt therapy we don't worry about understanding, we concentrate on *experience*. The experience becomes *discovery* which is deeper and more complete than understanding because it is not limited to the level of intellectualization as so much of therapy is. You can tell a child over and over again not to touch a hot stove and he'll nod. He understands. But only when and if he actually places a curious finger upon that hot stove does he discover what it's all about. . . .

So in Gestalt dream therapy we plunge as deeply as we can into the experience itself.[43]

Downing offered provocative titles for each dreamwork session. In one called "The Gallant State Trooper," a quiet, young school teacher describes a dream in which she was being driven in a car by a girlfriend. When the girlfriend violated some traffic rule and was spotted by a state trooper, the dreamer offered to take over the driver's seat. The trooper brought them to the police station, took them into an office, and seduced both women. The dreamer sensed this was inevitable and reported that she didn't care.

When Downing asked her what aspect of the dream was of particular interest to her, the teacher replied it was when she switched seats with her girlfriend. As the dialogue with Downing continued, she reported feeling nervous, and her legs soon began to tremble. Downing asked her to exaggerate the trembling and told her to focus upon experiencing any additional bodily sensations. After she reported a sensation of warmth in her genital area, Downing encouraged her to begin a dialogue with the state trooper and to subsequently become the state trooper. The trooper eventually indicated that he would not hurt the dreamer and they were just going "to have fun together."

Downing next asked the dreamer to lie on the floor on her back and to bend her knees so that her heels would be close to her bottom, and to then lift her bottom off the floor an inch or so. This maneuver was intended to move her into a "bioenergetic area" and eventually put a strain on the muscles in the pelvic area. He also requested that she undo her waistband and unzip her jeans so that she would have more room to move. He next encouraged her to engage in deeper breathing and to feel the breathing all through her genitals. After a while, the dreamer began to engage in rhythmic pelvic motions and soon experienced an orgasm. To facilitate further emotional expression, the dreamer was encouraged to make noises as she continued to engage in deep belly breathing. She eventually experienced five orgasms accompanied by strong body movements.

In his commentary on this workshop session, Downing remarked:

In Jean's dreamwork, I block her usual muscle patterns by putting her into a position that sets up an unusual strain on her legs and torso, making the muscles get tired. As they tire, they lose the ability to respond to the usual signals in the usual way and begin to let go all the held-back tensions at once. Jean is a well brought up, very decent young woman who learned as she grew up that sexual feelings are to be kept tightly controlled. She does this by holding back, tightening up the muscles in her thighs, vagina, and stomach. This is truly being "uptight." . . . And those muscles keep straining away until it all comes out in a dream.

The dream-Jean says, "I need more sexual release; I need to fuck. I need to make fucking movements and feel beautiful, relaxed sexual feelings. I'll dream I meet a gallant, sexy man whom I'll have to obey, so it's all right if we fuck. He makes me obey, so I don't even have to feel guilty." Through the dream-Jean's message, I guide the wake-Jean to muscle release and fuller awareness. . . . The next two days of the workshop she was open, happy, social.

This much body release unlocks the door which was locked during late childhood and adolescence. It won't be locked again unless the person chooses to do so.[44]

Lest the reader assume all Gestalt dream workshops are so earthy, I will present a few excerpts from another dreamwork session called "The Descent of the Holy Spirit." A middle-aged woman, whom he called Beatrice, described a long dream she had a few years earlier in which she was lying in a big field on a bright sunny day. When she closed her eyes, she saw an eye which became a face that eventually came to look like the face of Jesus (the dreamer was born in a Jewish family). She experienced a presence of love and unity and became filled with feelings of joy. In a later part of the dream, Beatrice recalled making a sculpted drawing of a shepherd and lambs and described having "the feeling of being part of the whole and for the first time in my life believing in something beyond myself because I had never been able to believe in God or anything beyond anything in life."

In a subsequent scene, she and several people were playing a game called "let's build a world." Everyone agreed about wanting a peaceful world, but as people cut out pieces of paper, one of the pieces had the word death on it and this piece had to be accepted and put on the table. Bombs eventually hit the world they built, and the dreamer had to say that she was dead. She was transported to a place where there were several other people, and the dreamer recognized that you are not alone where death is. She then became surrounded again by the loving feeling she had earlier experienced in the field. Beatrice reported that a year after her dream, her daughter was killed in an automobile accident.

Downing described his feelings of being overwhelmed by the power of Beatrice's dream, then engaged in some brief Gestalt dream work with her. He asked her to talk to the Christ figure and to place him in the empty chair. Beatrice reported that she saw Christ and her daughter, and experienced in her heart that they were both sitting in the same chair. Beatrice was encouraged to engage in dialogue with her daughter, and then to attempt to be her daughter, and speak as her daughter to Beatrice. After a very frank exchange of views between Beatrice and her daughter, Downing asked the dreamer what she felt in her heart. Beatrice replied that it was the "pain of not being able to reach across." Downing encouraged her to stay with the pain and experience whatever feelings occurred. Eventually the pain receded and the dreamer had an impulse to extend her arms upward. Downing encouraged her to act upon this impulse and to turn her head back, to look up, and reach her arms upward as high as she possibly could to receive God.

As the dreamer made this gesture, Downing commented, "There is a long pause, a long long pause. I sense an indescribable feeling of ecstasy, of love and peace, surrounding Beatrice and me, surrounding all of us in the room."[45] When Beatrice asked him what happened, he answered, "You have just seen or felt the descent of the Holy Spirit, the Holy Ghost, which I myself have never seen before in group work such as this."[46] Through Downing's own tear-filled eyes, he noticed that

several other people in the group were crying openly.

When Downing attempted to offer some remarks about this session, he reported:

> My professional pretensions of explanation and controlling are of little use in the face of what I can only call such "sacred moments." . . . I was able to recognize the experience for what it was—an experience transcending professional "knowledge"; an experience touching upon the supreme power, the supreme will which exists in all of us. . . .
>
> Guardians of our present intellectual age might call Beatrice "neurotic," "hysterical," "hallucinatory," "unwilling to face reality." My own experiences validate the greater reality of Beatrice's vision. There are experiences which produce happiness, wisdom, and beauty far more abundant than the concepts by which our limited personal and social lives are bound.[47]

EUGENE GENDLIN

Eugene Gendlin is a psychologist at the University of Chicago. In his book *Let Your Body Interpret Your Dreams*, Gendlin applied his theory of personality change, and his research-based therapeutic technique called "focusing," to dream work.[48] Gendlin does not present any novel theory

about why we dream or which aspects of our personality are represented in dreams, but he does offer an interesting somatic approach to working with dreams.

In reading the speculations of several dream experts, he noticed some common denominators, but each theory also had relatively unique emphases. Gendlin attempted to preserve the most useful facets of these various conceptualizations by developing a list of sixteen questions that the dreamer can ask with regard to any dream.

The only question which should be asked for every dream is the first one: "What comes to you?" This question could be varied: "What are your associations in relation to the dream?" "What comes to mind as you think about the dream?" Or the dreamer could be asked to pick a part of the dream and to indicate what comes to the dreamer in relation to that part.

The remaining questions can be grouped under five headings. Approximately a minute should be given to each of the following questions, and the order of questions can vary depending upon the response to the first question. It is not necessary to ask all of the questions.

Associations

2. *Feeling*. What did you feel in the dream? What in your life feels like some part of your dream?

3. *Yesterday*. What did you do yesterday? What were you inwardly preoccupied with yesterday, i.e., the day before the dream?

Drama

4. *Place*. What was the main place in your dream? Have you ever been in a place like that? How did it feel? What other place has felt like that?

5. *Story*. Summarize the story-plot of the dream. What in your life is like that

story? Summarize the events of the dream in two or three steps.

6. *Characters*. Who was the most important character? Were there unknown persons? Who do these people remind you of?

Working With Characters

7. *What part of you is that?* What feelings arise when you consider any particular character? What adjective could be used to describe that person? Is any part of you like that?

8. *Be that person*. Imagine yourself to be a particular dream character. How would you feel and act?

9. *Can the dream continue?* Vividly visualize the end of any important scene of the dream. How does that feel? Watch and wait for any change in images or feelings.

Decoding Techniques

10. *Symbols*. What is that kind of thing? What does that object "stand for"? What is it used for?

11. *Body analogy, especially high, low, and under*. Could something in the dream, such as a house, be an analogy for the body? Could an attic mean thoughts or being in your head, downstairs mean lower-level feelings or being grounded, a basement or underground mean the unconscious or something invisible? Odd-looking machines may be body analogies.

12. *Counterfactual*. What in the dream is specifically different from the actual situation? Why would the dream make these changes?

DEVELOPMENTAL DIMENSIONS

13. *Childhood.* What childhood memory comes in relation to the dream or any part of it? What went on in your life at that time?

14. *Personal growth.* How are you trying to develop? What do you wish you could be or do? In what way are you one-sided or not well rounded?

15. *Sexuality.* Could the dream be a story about whatever you are currently doing or feeling about sexuality?

16. *Spirituality.* What creative or spiritual potential of yours might the dream be about? Are you failing to take account of some of your human dimensions?

I have reworded slightly some of Gendlin's questions. By paying attention to these questions, the dreamer is given an excellent opportunity to review whatever features of the dream possess the most salient concerns at the time the dream is experienced. Experience is a key concept for Gendlin. He is not particularly interested in having the dreamer come to an intellectual or cognitive understanding of the dream; instead, the dreamer is urged toward experiencing a "physical felt shift" in response to the dream questions: "The basic touchstone of the method is your own bodily experience of something opening up in you."[49]

Since human nature is continually expanding and moving away from closed forms and content, the body is able to sense what is missing and seems to "know" the new whole toward which it is moving.

There is an awareness somewhere in the body as to what next step is necessary to complete this movement. This step may be represented metaphorically in the dream. Since we are generally not aware when we are dreaming, we will not make contact with this step, and that is where the focusing technique becomes relevant. By having the dreamer relax and attempt to get in touch with felt bodily senses as various elements of the dream are reviewed and reprocessed, these steps toward wholeness can be consciously experienced, allowing the dreamer to move toward a new pattern of integration.

Gendlin's approach to dreams involves two stages. In the first, the dreamer quietly contemplates each question, to discover any bodily response that may occur. The dreamer is seeking a sort of somatic "Aha" or a visceral "Eureka." This will enable the dreamer to understand "what the dream is about" but may not teach him or her anything new. To "get something new for your own development," the dreamer must move on to the second stage.

In the second stage, the dreamer attempts to sense through his or her body a "growth-direction." The dreamer is encouraged to be friendly toward any feelings that are discovered, even if these feelings are uncomfortable or disagreeable. By being open, the dreamer is in a position to experience some inward stirring and small changes, which open the way to further changes and steps.

You can feel what step is expansive and forward-moving, life enhancing, as against what feels constricting, against life, imposed on you, and closing you. Step by step you can move with this guiding sense. It keeps you on the right road. . . .

A growth step is not always easy or comfortable. It can also hurt you or make you feel anxious. But it always also feels good in a very specific way. . . .

For example, staying in a stuffy room is *more comfortable*, but going out for a walk into the cold can feel forward-moving, like fresh air! *The direction of growth often feels like fresh air.*

You can soon sense the great difference between these two kinds of feeling good. Growth feels expansive, forward-moving body energy. Comfort feels stuffy, boring after a while, limiting. Perhaps it is easier but it also has a sense of loss, giving up, giving in.

Personal growth has to do with letting your inward essence live more, expand, become freer.[50]

Gendlin advances an interesting innovation called "bias control" into a later phase of stage two. Since a new growth-direction may often involve the opposite of what we value most, he encourages the dreamer to consider what would happen if the dreamer or some other dream character were to react in a manner opposed to his or her usual behavior. This stance may allow some suppressed part of the dreamer to live for a moment, and the dreamer may determine whether a sense of freedom and power, or a reaction of fear and dislike, results. The purpose of bias control is to ensure that the dreamer doesn't prematurely jump to conclusions about the meaning of any dream and to allow the felt bodily sense to be used as a guide for exploring parameters of the dream that might otherwise be overlooked.

Gendlin's use of the body to gauge the correctness of dream inferences has some precedent in Gestalt dream work, but he has carried the principle of bodily awareness, or felt bodily sense, to a level far beyond that of any previous dream worker.

MONTAGUE ULLMAN

Montague Ullman is a psychoanalyst who has developed a democratic and nonthreatening approach to working with dreams in a group setting. In collaboration with Nan Zimmerman, a teacher, he described his technique in the book *Working with Dreams.*[51]

Ullman emphasizes two factors: safety and discovery. The "safety factor" is neces-

sary because the dreamer "is exposing a most personal and vulnerable side of himself." He needs to feel assured that at every stage of the process "control will remain in the hands of the dreamer," and in a way that "respects the privacy of the dreamer and his authority over the dream."[52] The "discovery factor" comes into play when "the group has to respond to another overriding need of the dreamer, namely, to be helped to make discoveries about himself that are difficult to make alone."[53]

There are four stages to the process that occurs in one of Ullman's dream groups. In stage 1, the dreamer volunteers a dream and the group "may ask questions to clarify the dream and to grasp it as clearly and completely as possible. Any real characters in the dream are briefly identified."[54]

In stage 2, members of the group attempt to accept the dream as if it were their own. They address comments to each other about the dream with the prefatory remark "If it were my dream," so that it is clear to everyone that whatever statements follow are to be viewed as projections of the member who is speaking, and are not necessarily valid for, or applicable to, the dreamer. Group members begin by reflecting upon the *feelings* they experience in response to the overall dream or any salient imagery within it.

If the events of the dream took place on a mountaintop, one member might say, "If it were my dream, I would have felt very anxious and frightened because I would be afraid I might lose my footing and fall off." Another member might respond, "If it were my dream, I'd feel a sense of joy and ecstasy, because I would be on top of things and have a broader perspective on what's happening around me." The dreamer does not respond at all during stage 2, but simply listens to the remarks of the other group members.

During the next phase of stage 2, the group members explore the possible *metaphorical* potential of each dream image. If the image involved "the tolling of some bells," one member might say, "If it were my dream, the tolling of bells would suggest getting married, because I always associate bells with wedding bells." Other members might associate bells tolling with death, a call to religious service, musical creativity, a community emergency such as a fire, the campus carillon from college days, or, if they recall Hemingway's novel *For Whom the Bell Tolls*, civil war. Members then attempt to find connections between the successive dream images, the metaphors they suggest, and possible life situation or concerns which might lead to such dream expression.

Stage 3, Ullman explains, "involves returning the dream to the dreamer: [the dreamer] is then invited to respond to and share to the extent he wishes how far he has come in understanding the dream. He is free to shape his responses in any manner he wishes and is given as much time as he needs without interruption."[55]

If further work is necessary, the dreamer and the group may engage in dialogue, with the goal being to help "contextualize" the dream so that the dreamer's waking life context and recent events can be connected with the dream imagery. Open-ended, "information-eliciting, not information-demanding questions" are posed to the dreamer. The dreamer is free to respond to these questions in any manner he or she chooses, or not to respond at all. Efforts are made to tie together all the information shared by the dreamer with the "projections" offered by the group members. These attempts at synthesis are called "orchestrating projections." An orchestrating projection occurs "when what the dreamer has shared is worked out in relation to all the images in the dream in proper sequence."[56]

The three stages just discussed occur within a single dream session. The dreamer then reviews the dream at home and attempts to process the information received from the session in whatever way seems helpful. When the group next meets, the dreamer is invited to share any additional thoughts or reactions that may have emerged from this private contemplation. This between-session "homework" and subsequent sharing is considered stage 4 of Ullman's approach.

Ullman has a strong conviction that a much larger population can benefit from dreams if we can overcome certain false beliefs about what they represent and how they should be worked with:

[These] include the belief that the necessary skills for dream work can come only from professional training and experience and that dream work therefore should remain exclusively in the hands of the expert, that it otherwise carries a certain danger and, finally, that dream work carried on by nonprofessionals is apt to remain at a superficial level.

... I am convinced that it need not remain a specialized tool in the hands of the expert but it can develop into a culturally sanctioned, generally available approach to a deeper understanding of the emotional side of our lives. The skills involved can be identified, learned, and applied by anyone interested enough to do so.

... Is dream work dangerous? There is the possibility of danger, but it is not intrinsic to the dream or to what the dream says to the dreamer. ... It can come from a wrong approach to the dreamer. By a wrong approach I mean one that is intrusive, one that does not respect the limits set by the dreamer, one that is conducted from an authoritarian stance, one that superimposes interpretations.[57]

For over a decade, Ullman has been offering training courses for those interested in becoming leaders of dream groups. His educational efforts have not been limited to the United States; he has been carrying out a similar program in Sweden with outstanding success.

Ullman's approach has been applied in a variety of settings in the United States, some of which are described in the book he coedited with psychotherapist Claire Limmer, *The Variety of Dream Experiences: Expanding Our Ways of Working with Dreams*.[58] Richard Jones's adaptation of Ullman's approach for use in his creative writing seminar was discussed in chapter 2.

In collaboration with Stanley Krippner, a humanistic psychologist, Ullman has also pioneered important research investigating telepathic dreaming in a laboratory setting. His successful results, documenting that individuals can dream about pictures concentrated upon by a distant "sender," will be discussed in chapter 14.

As the result of his many years of intensive and extensive involvement with dreams, Ullman has been able to discern exciting potentials in dreams that have been overlooked by those with more restricted vision:

> To end on a somewhat speculative note, I have come to look at our capacity to form these [dream] images as a way nature has of giving us the opportunity to examine whatever may be impinging on the state of our connectedness to others, for good or bad. While dreaming, we seem able to explore both the inner and the outer sources of any change in the state of these connections. It is as if, while awake, we tend to lose sight of our basic interconnectedness, focusing more on our discreteness and our separateness. Asleep, we turn our attention to the reality of our interconnectedness as members of a single species. In this sense we may regard dreaming as concerned with the issue of species-connectedness. From the perspective of where we are today it would seem that the human species can endure only if it succeeds in overcoming the fragmentation that has resulted from the play of historical forces. . . . Perhaps our dreaming consciousness is primarily concerned with the survival of the species and only secondarily with the individual. Were there any truth to this speculation it would shed a radically different light on the importance of dreams. It would make them deserving of a higher priority in our culture than they are now assigned.[59]

OVERVIEW

The limited survey presented in this chapter should make it clear that the rich ore to be found in the dark mines where dreams reside was not exhausted by the drilling and blasting efforts of Freud and Jung. Others have discovered shiny new veins or improved our ability to refine the coarse nuggets brought back by earlier techniques.

How have dream theories evolved, or techniques of dream interpretation been modified, in the decades since Freud and Jung? With regard to theory, none of the authors reviewed in this chapter accept Freud's notion that dreams act as the guardian of sleep or that they serve to discharge instinctual tensions. Lowy and, to some extent, Adler, attribute the regulation or balancing of affect to dreaming, but most of the theorists in this chapter emphasize interpersonal concerns and social relationships. The role of sexuality in dreams is not central for any of these theorists and, when considered, is not viewed in terms of the discharge of drives so much as in terms of the interpersonal context which facilitates its expression or inhibition.

Jung placed individuation, or the quest for wholeness, as the overarching urge motivating human personality and conceived of dreams as an essential source of guidance toward achieving this wholeness. This inner push toward self-actualization via dream awareness is strongly endorsed by Boss, Perls, and Gendlin. The other theorists in this chapter all embrace the idea that dreams could lead to greater emotional maturity and self-understanding, but do not focus as sharply on the concept implied in the analogy that the dream of every acorn is to fulfill its destiny as a mighty oak.

With the exception of Erikson, who retains some psychoanalytic ties with Freud, none of the theorists accept that the meaning of a dream appears in disguise and its latent content must be discovered by means of free association. They all contend that the message of the dream is imprinted in the manifest content, although it may take some sleuthing to comprehend the symbolic meaning of some dream items. The dream picture is painted with liberal use of visual metaphors.

In Freud's approach, dreams were examined for information about the past—the hidden infantile sources which had energized the dream. Other theorists have pretty much ignored the past except for French, who felt that the dream might review past solutions to problems similar to those currently confronting the dreamer. The immediate present—the current existential moment—is highlighted by Boss and Perls, who approach the dream in a completely ahistorical fashion. Mention has already been made of theorists subscribing to the acorn-oak analogy, which

implies that the dream will contain "seismological" hints or clues about emergent, soon-to-surface personality trends. Several theorists—Stekel, Boss, Hall, and Ullman—have come to the conclusion, confidently reached by Jung, and ambivalently so by Freud, that some dreams are influenced by telepathic stimuli.

None of the more recent authors seem to extol the wisdom and creative problem-solving powers of our dreaming mind to the extent that Jung did, but they all reject the low level of cognitive complexity attributed to dreams by Freud. They respect the manifest dream for the unvarnished truth it is willing to speak, if the dreamer is willing to listen, but they don't elevate it to the level of oracle.

The classical Freudian position is that all dream characters reported in psychoanalysis involve the analyst; none of the other theorists adopt this extreme position. On the other hand, the position of the Gestalt school seems equally extreme when it contends that every character and object in the dream represents the dreamer. Such a view seems far too grandiose and egotistical in my opinion, because characters with whom the dreamer also interacts in waking life are denied any objective existence—they are seen only as projections of disowned parts of the dreamer's personality, and the way they behave in the dream as not reflecting any actual attributes or personal qualities of real people. Other theorists also disagree with this aspect of the Gestalt position.

If we turn our attention to innovations in dream interpretation, we note that Stekel advocates condensing the dream down to telegraphic dimensions which preserve the main themes and emotions. Erikson and Hall elaborate a large number of elements in the manifest content which need to be systematically examined and evaluated before any conclusions can be drawn about the meaning of a particular dream.

Dialogues with dream characters in the empty-chair technique advocated by Perls can sometimes lead to insights that would not be available through simply describing another character. Exaggerating the feelings and movements present in a dream, another Gestalt technique, can also help to break through defenses which might remain intact if dreamers were simply asked to describe how they felt or what they did in the dream.

The body is used as a device for registering the validity of a possible dream inference or interpretation in Gestalt dream work and by Gendlin, who explores the salient features of a dream through his sixteen-item checklist. Bringing a somatic component into alignment with the cognitive processing of a dream seems to me a move in the right direction, because it represents a holistic approach, blending cognitive, emotional, and somatic levels of experience. When a new dream insight

resonates at all these levels simultaneously, the dreamer can be expected to take new steps to actualize that discovery in waking life.

Another comparatively recent development in dream work is having the dreamer explore the significance of a dream in a group setting. In the Gestalt tradition, the exploration is conducted, "hot seat" style, under the grilling of Perls or one of his followers, while others in the group watch silently and participate at a vicarious level. An entirely different group approach was developed by Ullman. The confrontational encounter with the group leader characteristic of Perls's work is abandoned by Ullman, who attempts to establish a gentle, protective environment in which the dreamer can comfortably share a dream. Sharing is the key principle in Ullman's approach; each member of the group shares his or her own reactions and "projections" to the various elements reported by the dreamer. Ullman's approach has become quite popular with people from all walks of life, and dream groups based upon his sharing principle have sprung up all over the United States, Canada, and Sweden.

PART 4

EXPERIMENTAL STUDIES OF DREAMING

EARLY RESEARCH APPROACHES TO DREAMS

In the preceding chapters of this book, emphasis has been placed upon the dream as a fascinating, but puzzling personal experience which occurs during sleep. People have intuitively sensed that dreams are important but have also realized that the messages they convey are ambiguous and often difficult to comprehend. Ambiguity stimulates efforts to achieve some form of mental closure, and endless speculations have arisen as to the nature and purpose of dreams. The various views of dreams put forward through the centuries have been reviewed in chapters 3 through 8, and the last three chapters have described some of the interpretive techniques that have been developed in efforts to understand how dreams relate to important psychological issues of the dreamer.

Depending on the theorist, dreams have been considered to represent intrapersonal tensions, interpersonal problems, transpersonal communications, or some combination of these. Dreams have been explored primarily in therapeutic settings; in earlier days dreams were told to shamans or priests; in the twentieth century, to psychotherapists. The correctness of a given interpretation or explanation of why a certain dream was dreamed on a particular night has been confirmed by the pronouncement of an "expert" interpreter or by a sudden "Aha" recognition by the dreamer that the explanation made sense in terms of his or her life.

All of the nineteenth- and twentieth-century theorists presented so far accepted the notion that dreams reflect unconscious needs, conflicts, and desires and therefore, if interpreted correctly, reveal much about the personality structure and character of the dreamer. Other theorists, however, conceptualized dreams as nothing but reflex responses to sensory stimuli or nothing but the by-product of cerebral disturbances resulting from chemical or hormonal somatic imbalances.

Since contemporary civilization has turned to science as the final arbiter of truth, it is natural that dreams would be subjected to examination by scientists. The remainder of this book will examine what scientists, using a variety of approaches, have found in their collective study of dreams.

The first stage of exploring any phenomenon is to collect casual observations or anecdotal information about the topic and then examine them for possible patterns or order. We'll begin by looking at anecdotal observations published between the late eighteenth century and the middle of the twentieth century.

ANECDOTAL DESCRIPTIONS OF DREAMS

In a book published in 1758, G. F. Meier described a dream of being hanged; he awoke to realize that he had fastened his nightshirt too tightly around his neck. In another dream, he was being overpowered by men who stretched him out on the ground and drove a stake into the earth between his big toe and the toe next to it. Meier woke up to find a straw sticking between these same toes.[1] *The Philosophy of Sleep*, published in 1836 by Robert Macnish, a Scottish physician, mentions a paper by a Dr. Gregory which contained observations on dreams associated with thermal stimuli. One involved Dr. Gregory himself, who applied a bottle of hot water to his feet while in bed and dreamed that he was making a journey over almost unbearably hot ground on his way to the top of Mount Etna.[2] The same stimulus induced dreams in other nineteenth-century authors of being led by Satan over the burning marl of hell; having one's feet held to a fire by a bandit; being a bear learning to dance by standing on hot iron plates; and scorching one's feet while escaping from a burning house.[3]

Macnish's book also mentioned several other dreams provoked by sensory stimuli:

> Another person having a blister [mustard plaster] applied to his head, imagined that he was scalped by a party of Indians; while a friend of mine happening to sleep in damp sheets, dreamed

that he was dragged through a stream. Another friend dreamed that he was stroking a kitten which in consequence purred most lustily. On awakening, he found that the working of the heavy machinery of a neighboring mill was slightly shaking his bed, and making the joints produce a sound like the purring of a cat.

. . . If we lie awry, or if our feet slip over the side of the bed, we often imagine ourselves standing upon the brink of a fearful precipice, or falling from its beetling summit into the abyss beneath. If the rain or hail patter against our window, we have often the idea of a hundred cataracts pouring from the rocks. . . . Should the heat of the body chance to be increased by . . . the temperature of the room, we may suppose ourselves basking under the fiery sun of Africa; or if . . . we labour under a chill, we may then be careening and foundering among the icebergs of the pole. . . .

. . . A flower being applied to the nostrils may, by affecting the sense of smell, excite powerfully the imagination, and give the dreamer the idea of walking in a garden.

If a light be brought into the room, the notion of the house being in flames perhaps invades us, and we are witnesses to the whole conflagration.[4]

These examples cover a wide range of sensory stimuli and document that their

contribution to dream imagery was fully recognized as early as 1836. Macnish did not consider that external stimuli alone motivated dreams; he also recognized the contribution of waking preoccupations:

The very circumstance of a man's dreams turning habitually upon a particular subject . . . is a strong presumption that that subject is the one which most frequently engrosses his faculties in the waking state: in a word, that the power most energetic in the latter condition is that also most active in dreams.[5]

Macnish's familiarity with the topic of dreams was quite extensive; his book also included chapters on prophetic dreams and nightmares.

Macnish gave no examples involving the sense of taste. A frequently cited taste dream was, however, recorded by Dr. William Hammond, the Surgeon General of the United States from 1862 to 1864.[6] The dreamer was a young woman who attempted to cure herself of the habit of thumb sucking by covering the offending thumb with extract of aloes one night. The lengthy dream that followed began aboard a transatlantic steamer made of wormwood. This wood has a very bitter taste and smell, and whatever the woman ate or drank aboard the ship had the flavor of wormwood. Everything she drank upon arriving in France had the same bitter taste. She eventually went to Rome to see the pope, who told her that she must make a pilgrimage to the plain where the pillar of salt stood that was Lot's wife, and she must break off and eat a piece of salt as big as her thumb. She made that trip and broke off the thumb from the figure, and as she began to eat it she awoke. The dreamer found her thumb in her mouth and realized she had sucked off all the aloes during her dream journeys.

A more pleasant taste was involved in the dream of a fifty-seven-year-old woman with a cough, whose daughter gave her some barley sugar to suck when she lay down to sleep. She dreamed she was a very little girl at a party, surrounded by laughing girls and boys she knew from her childhood. There were tarts, jellies, and an abundance of delicious sweetmeats available at the party.[7]

As I indicated earlier, many anecdotal accounts of dreams involving sensory stimuli were published. It's not clear whether all of Macnish's dream descriptions were based on factual reports, or whether some were speculations as to what dreams certain stimuli might produce. To give an indication of how typical these published reports were, I will cite a few examples involving a single sensory modality, smell, as representative of what could be presented for each sense.

The first example, published in the July 1856 issue of the *Journal of Psychological Medicine*, concerned a physician who had to stay overnight in Coventry at the residence of a cheesemonger. It was summertime and the odors from a recently unpacked barrel of "strong old American cheese" pervaded his sleeping quarters. In addition, he became aware of rats gnawing in an old wall behind the bedstead. When he finally got to sleep, the dreamer found himself in some barbarous country, charged with a political offense, and doomed to be incarcerated in a large cheese. He then became aware of an army of rats attacking the monstrous cheese which was his prison. Just as they gained entrance and began to "fix themselves in numbers upon my naked body," the dreamer awoke with throbbing temples and a sense of nausea from the extremely strong odor of cheese.

Another disturbing dream attributable to an unusual smell involved a man sleeping in a strange house who awoke in a state of exhaustion from having struggled in his dream with birds of prey, which eventually overpowered him and carried him to the gardens of the dead in India. The dreamer realized that these events were somehow connected to the story of Philip Quail, a hero somewhat like Robinson Crusoe. The dream kept recurring night after night, until the dreamer remembered that in the story of Philip Quail, a pillow stuffed with the decomposing feathers of wild birds had induced disturbing dreams for the story character. He inquired and found that the pillow upon which he had been sleeping was also stuffed with decomposing feathers. The pillow gave off a peculiar odor when his body warmed it up. His deathly dreams vanished when the pillow was changed.[8]

Corpses figured literally in a dream attributed to the wife of General Sleeman, who accompanied her husband when he was in pursuit of the Thugee in India. They had pitched their tents in an apparently ideal location, but Mrs. Sleeman had a dream in which she was haunted by the smell of dead men, and urged her husband to move their tents. When the General did so and dug up the ground beneath Mrs. Sleeman's tent, the partially decomposed bodies of fourteen victims of the Thugee were found.[9]

Pain is not usually considered a sensory stimulus but it can have an effect on dreams. A woman who awoke because of a painful sensation in her nose, caused by its resting too long on her hand, dreamed there was a peculiar epidemic going on which attacked and destroyed the bridges of its victims' noses. She was greatly affected in her dream by the agony she endured of seeing so many noseless persons, and her distress woke her.[10]

Another woman, dying following a mastectomy, dreamed that the pain associated with her surgical scars "was due to [her breast's] being uneasy with milk, and sitting to suckle her only child, dead 40 years before."[11] A patient with painful, itching skin dreamed he was stroking his dog, who enjoyed the sensations so much that the dreamer began to use his nails and intensified his efforts until he became almost breathless. He woke to find his skin lacerated and bleeding.[12]

Awareness of another's pain can also lead to strong dream imagery. When King Henry II of France attended the burning of a heretic, who was slowly drawn up and down in iron chains above a fire, infernal imagery took over his dreams. The tortured man had cast a look of excruciating agony toward the king, who turned away in horror, but in his dreams the king kept seeing the victim's face with the same look of appeal turned toward him.[13]

Although these anecdotes suggest certain things about the role of sensory stimuli, they cannot be considered scientific evidence because the observations were not made under controlled conditions. To qualify as scientific, they would have to provide a description of the stimulus, the manner in which it was applied, and the response by the subject. To avoid any bias based on the subject's expectations, the type of stimulus to be applied could not be known in advance. Let's take a look at how the study of dreams has gradually become more scientific.

EXPERIMENTAL STUDIES OF SENSORY STIMULI

Apparently the earliest systematic effort to investigate the effect of stimulus manipulation was carried out in 1831 by C. Girou de Buzareingues,[14] who was presumably a physician, as a report of his work appeared in the first volume of *The Lancet*, a British medical journal. In his first experiment, he left the back part of his head uncovered during sleep and dreamed that he was at a special outdoor religious ceremony, one of a very few occasions when members of that

faith were allowed to have their heads uncovered while worshiping. His neck felt cold during the dream scenes and also when he awoke. He reported a similar effect when he repeated the experiment several nights later. In a third experiment, he left his knees uncovered and dreamed he was traveling during the night in a stagecoach. The author observed that all travelers know it is the knees that become coldest when traveling at night in a stagecoach. The experimenter reported that none of these dreams referred in any way to the occupations of the preceding days.

An attempt to experimentally produce nightmares was described by J. Borner in his book published in 1855. Sometimes he served as the subject himself and would provoke a nightmare by burying his face in a pillow before falling asleep; when someone else served as a subject, Borner covered their mouth and part of their nostrils with bedclothes. One subject reported experiencing a nightmare in which a horrid animal seemed to be weighing him down.[15]

The following decade ushered in some experimental studies that have been classics. Alfred Maury, a French scientist, published his book *Le sommeil et les reves* ("Sleep and Dreams") in 1861, and an enlarged and revised edition was published in 1878.[16] He began by keeping a journal of his dreams and noting all the circumstances that he thought may have contributed to them. He was impressed by the role of his diet and of atmospheric conditions. Maury paid close attention to the initial images that appeared as he drifted off to sleep and advanced the term "hypnagogic hallucinations" to describe them. These images supplied the "embryogenesis" of the dream images that subsequently developed in fuller form.

Because of his reputation as a careful observer, a dream that Maury reported had a very persuasive influence on theories about the rapidity of dreams. Maury dreamed of the Reign of Terror at the time of the French Revolution; he was involved in some murders and summoned before the tribunal. Robespierre and several other famous individuals were there, and Maury was tried and sentenced to death. Accompanied by a great crowd, he was led to the place of execution and placed in position for the guillotine. He felt the knife come down, hit his neck, and sever his head from his body. Waking in terror, Maury realized that a rail over the headboard had become loose and fallen on the back of his neck, just like a guillotine.

Maury conjectured that his whole dream had taken place *after* the loose rail had fallen on his neck. It should be kept in mind, however, that this dream occurred when Maury was still a student and long before he began a serious study of dreaming. There is good evidence to suggest that the dream was probably not written down until thirteen years later, which would leave considerable room for doubt about its complete accuracy. It is also possible that Maury could have had some subliminal awareness of the precarious condition of the rail and begun dreaming all of the various events associated with the revolution long before the rail descended. Perhaps some physical action corresponded to his dreamed action of being positioned for the guillotine, agitating the bed frame and causing the rail to fall at that particular moment.

Maury later carried out several experiments in which he was the primary subject. An assistant introduced various stimuli after Maury was asleep, then later awakened him for a report of his dreaming experiences. In one experiment, he was tickled with a feather on the lips and inside the nostrils; Maury reported a dream of being punished by having a mass of pitch applied to his face and then roughly torn off, taking with it the skin from his lips, nose, and face. In another experiment, in which a piece of heated iron was held close to him, he dreamed that robbers had gotten into a house and were putting his feet to the fire to force him to reveal where the money was. After a drop of water fell on his forehead, Maury dreamed that he was in Italy drinking a particular wine and sweating profusely. In response to a burning match held close to his nostrils, Maury dreamed that he was on a ship at sea and the magazine of the ship blew up. When a bottle of eau de cologne was held to his nose, he dreamed he was in a perfumer's shop. Maury dreamed about the ringing of an alarm bell signaling that a revolution had broken out when a pair of tweezers was held near his ear and struck with a pair of scissors.

Unlike auditory and olfactory stimuli, it is very difficult to introduce visual stimuli once the subject has fallen asleep, so investigators have generally been limited to some form of immediate presleep stimulation. In his experimental work, Maury reported that when a light, surrounded with a piece of red paper, was repeatedly passed before his eyes while still awake, he dreamed of a tempest and lightning which reminded him of a storm he had encountered in the English Channel.

Another French experimenter actively studying sensory stimuli was Marquis Hervey Saint-Denys, whose work on the mechanisms of dream imagery and on lucid dreams was discussed at some length in chapter 5. He published his findings anonymously in an 1867 book. During a vacation of several weeks at Vivarais, a friend's house in the country, Saint-Denys decided to constantly smell one of his handker-chiefs impregnated with a particular perfume. After returning home, he arranged for his servant to sporadically shake a few drops of the same perfume on the Marquis's pillow after he was asleep. This was done by the servant on an irregular basis so Saint-Denys could not anticipate when it would occur. But on those nights when the servant perfumed the pillow, his master reported dreams containing images associated with Vivarais, such as mountains and chestnut trees.

Saint-Denys extended his experiments to use other scents to evoke a range of ideas. When he was painting in a certain artist's studio, Saint-Denys frequently smelled another handkerchief impregnated with a different perfume. When nocturnally exposed to a combination of the perfume associated with Vivarais and the perfume associated with the artist's studio, he dreamed he was watching an artist paint a picturesque canvas in a mountainous region similar to Vivarais. When exposed to the same combination on another occasion, Saint-Denys dreamed of being at the dining room in Vivarais, when the door opened and the artist and an attractive nude female model appeared.[17]

Taste stimuli were researched only minimally during the nineteenth century. It is difficult to introduce such stimuli after the person has fallen asleep, and there may be a strong suggestive component if they are presented to the subject before sleep. Maury did not report any results from taste stimuli, but Saint-Denys obtained successful results. While painting the statue of a beautiful woman, he kept a piece of orris-root in his mouth; when the aromatic root was passed between his sleeping lips by his servant, he dreamed of an attractive woman similar in appearance to the statue he had painted. In this case, the aroma may also have played a part in inducing his pleasant dream.

In a series of romantic "gay Parisian" experiments involving auditory stimuli, Saint-Denys, who attended balls frequently, arranged with an orchestra leader to always play a particular waltz when he danced with one partner and a different waltz whenever he danced with a second partner. Each waltz was always danced exclusively with the specific partner. He later arranged the mechanism of an alarm clock to activate a music box that could play either waltz, so that a preselected waltz would play at a set time. Whenever the waltz associated with one of his partners was played, that lady would appear in his dream, although she was not invariably seen at the dance or even dressed for dancing.[18] Confusion would result if he attempted to associate to too many tunes. He had earlier observed a similar confusion if he employed too many perfume scents.

There were several experimental studies of sensory stimuli carried out in the 1890s. George Trumbull Ladd, a founder of the American Psychological Association, considered that visual dreams which follow almost immediately after going to sleep in a dark room originate predominantly from the condition of the retina. Ladd set about using himself as a subject. He trained himself to fall asleep and wake within two to five minutes, retaining in his mind the visual images of the dreams he experienced, as well as noting the schematic patterns or arrangements of "retinal dust" which contributed to this imagery.

Ladd described being able to recall a dream involving a printed page of words and sentences clearly spread out before him. When he examined his retinal field, he claimed he could detect the minute light and dark spots arising from the activity of the rods and cones, which had arranged themselves in parallel lines extending across his retinal field. Ladd's enthusiasm for the explanatory power of his retinal dust theory is conveyed in the following quote:

If the superior psycho-physical mechanism of vision can in dream-life seize upon what is really nothing but rows of meaningless blackish spots upon the retina and can convert them into imagined pages of print which may be read with great satisfaction off hand in a dream, what is it not capable of achieving?[19]

In his article on visual dreams, Ladd mentioned that the visual centers of the brain may combine with the retina as the sources of visual dreams during the night and also wrote that he was inclined to believe "that in somewhat vivid visual dreams, the eyeballs moved gently in their sockets, taking various positions induced by the retinal phantasms as they control the dreams."[20] (Research conducted over sixty years later has indicated that movements of the eyeballs are indeed associated with dreaming, but it is the brain rather than retinal phantasms that induces these movements.)

Dreams early in the morning, Ladd said, were due to external stimuli, such as "the rays of light penetrating to the retina through the closed eyelids."[21] Some anecdotal accounts support this view. Max Simon, the French author of *The World of Dreams*, preferred to sleep in a room without curtains because in his early morning dreams he then frequently found himself in buildings "bathed in floods of dazzling light, while everything seemed animated and joyous."[22] Another dreamer found himself "stretching out his arms toward what his dream-fancy had pictured as the image of his mistress. When fully awake, this image resolved itself into the full moon."[23] It has also been suggested that the rays of the sun or glow of the moon are responsible for many of the dreams of celestial glory reported by individuals of "religious temperament."

A fairly extensive examination of presleep visual stimuli was carried out by J. Mourly Vold, a Norwegian psychologist, using himself as the primary subject. His experiments were carried out during a seven-year period and involved some three hundred exposures.[24] Before going to sleep, he would open a packet containing a number of small objects or figures cut from cardboard, place the objects upon a black or white background, and gaze at them for a specific length of time. The exposure period was generally between two and ten minutes, but he occasionally looked at them intermittently for up to half an hour.

The form, size, and color of the objects seldom remained unchanged in the subsequent dreams. For example, an object might appear in the color of the original test object, or the complementary color might dominate the entire content of the dream. The color would also often change with regard to brightness. If a small black object was placed on a white background or vice versa, light and dark images frequently alternated back and forth. It is unfortunate that no frequency figures or other type of data tabulation was reported for this extensive experimentation. A few striking examples were described, but one can't determine how typical or atypical any of the results may have been.

Mourly Vold also investigated the role of limb position and movement in dreams.[25] He used a glove, ribbon, or string to confine the muscles controlling the hands and feet. The restraining devices were applied sometimes to one side of the body and sometimes to both. Mourly Vold found that the experimentally restrained limb might be experienced in a similar position in the dream, or the whole body might be represented as performing a movement in which that limb's activity was either exaggerated or constricted. In other dreams, it might be another person or animal whose limb was affected. Sometimes the imagery was more abstract; for example, one might dream of numbers when the fingers were involved. Mourly Vold noted that we rarely dream of being in a horizontal position, which is perhaps not surprising since most of our waking life is typically spent vertically, in a sitting or standing position. Perhaps invalids who have been bedridden for many years might report dreams of being in a horizontal position.

W. S. Monroe, an American psychologist, carried out a taste experiment involving twenty women students.[26] Each woman placed a crushed clove on her tongue before going to bed for ten successive nights.

Of the 254 dreams reported, seventeen were labeled as taste dreams and eight were considered smell dreams. The burning sensation in her mouth led one woman to dream she was in a house that was on fire. Monroe also did some research on visual stimuli. He reported that his fourteen subjects who viewed designs cut from colored pieces of paper before going to sleep had an apparent increase in the frequency of colored dreams.[27]

In another study in the 1890s, J. Leonard Corning, an American neurologist credited with a role in the development of spinal anesthesia, investigated musical stimuli as a possible form of nocturnal therapy.[28] His subjects slept with a leather hood over their heads which held metallic saucers in place over each ear. Music was delivered through a long piece of tubing connected to an Edison phonograph. He hypothesized that the "sonorous stimuli" from the phonograph were "capable of inducing important changes in the metabolism of the cerebral ganglia."[29] In Corning's "vibratory plan of treatment," he found that exposure to Wagnerian compositions, as well as arpeggios and minor chords, during the drowsy state between waking and sleeping was effective in producing pleasant and transcendent dreams. Recalling these dreams, Corning claimed, made it possible "to achieve good through a kind of blending of the mentalization of day with that of the night."

Corning later added visual stimuli using a stereopticon, which consisted of two vari-colored glass disks rotated in opposite directions by a small electric motor, to produce "chromatoscopic images . . . whose ever changing forms and capricious beauty hold the attention with an ineffable enchantment." Corning felt that visual and aural stimuli in combination made a much more powerful appeal to the affective life of the subject. With extended practice, depressive moods could be overcome because "the visual and acoustic recollections arise spontaneously after a time . . . carrying joyous or tranquil moods in their train and largely displacing the kind of ideation which carries a melancholic consequent."[30]

Corning provided several case histories illustrating how his procedures had helped relieve depression and insomnia. He also claimed to have cured a twenty-year history of morbid dreams for a Mr. L. Beginning with the very first night of exposure to Corning's treatment, Mr. L's dreams changed from having been "formerly a kind of carnival of the horrible" to "agreeable visions" that brought him "comfort." According to Corning, "the experiences of the first night were repeated again and again," and by the end of the fifth week of treatment, Mr. L's dreams had an "optimistic coloring" with only a single recurrence of the "old trouble."

Corning's rotating, kaleidoscopic images did not possess any recognizable shapes or forms, but Otto Potzl developed an ingenious technique to study how a brief exposure to more realistic visual stimuli might influence our nighttime dreams.

Potzl worked with twelve subjects who were not familiar with Freudian dream analysis but who "were inclined to watch their dreams carefully and who were willing to interrupt their sleep to take notes immediately."[31] They were shown colored

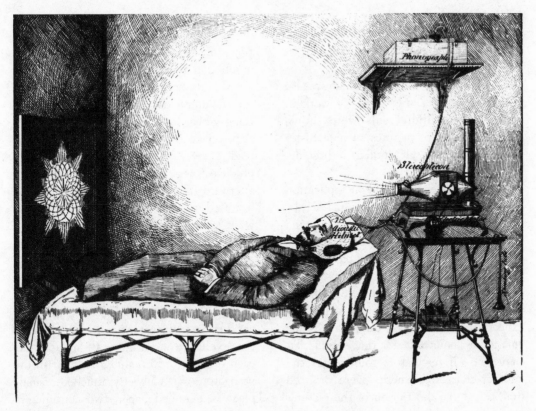

Corning's stereopticon.

slides of street scenes and landscapes using a tachistoscope, a device whose shutter speed could be set to allow only very brief exposures. After seeing an image for one-one hundredth of a second, subjects were required to describe and draw what they had seen and were asked to record in writing any dreams experienced the following night. The next day the dream was reported to the experimenter and drawings were made of the dream images.

Potzl's results indicated that these brief visual exposures were later incorporated into the dream content in an interesting fashion. The parts of the stimulus picture consciously perceived and reported immediately after the exposure were excluded from subsequent dreams, but the parts not reported were included. Potzl noted that the images underwent many transformations and distortions similar to those that Freud described as taking place during the dream work. His findings were presented to the Vienna Psychoanalytic Society in 1917 and were praised by Freud, but his work received little attention for many years. One reason for this neglect was the poor quality of Potzl's prose. As one reviewer put it,

"Potzl wrote in one of the most turgid and tormented styles ever to flow from the pen of man."[32]

Karl Abraham, a psychoanalyst, also published in 1917 the results of work in which normal individuals were shown short exposures of pictures in a tachistoscope. He found results similar to those described by Potzl.[33]

The first attempt to find an application for Potzl's work was carried out in 1931, by two psychotherapists, William Malamud and Robert Lindner.[34] They did not utilize a tachistoscope but showed pictures for thirty seconds to hospital patients receiving psychotherapy. Pictures were individually chosen for each subject, with the expectation that they would have some emotional significance for that specific patient. The investigators found that the conflict-charged elements were omitted from the initial description of the pictures but were subsequently incorporated into dreams. For example, a picture of the Madonna *nursing* an infant Christ was shown to a patient with oral conflicts involving the mother-child relationship. In the waking state, the patient incorrectly perceived the picture as showing the child not looking at the mother and pushing her breast away. In his dream that night, he was sick in bed and called a *nurse* because he was hungry. As she approached him, he felt himself shrinking to the size of a child. The nurse put her hand under his head and pulled him toward her with her other hand. She began to feed him from a white bowl that contained milk, an action that is very suggestive of nursing. This work reinforced Potzl's finding that certain elements

of the stimulus pictures would not be mentioned in the waking state because of their psychodynamic loading for the subjects, but would appear in dreams.

Malamud did some additional work, using verbal material instead of pictures.[35] A passage containing sexual symbolism was read to the patients, who attempted to reproduce what they had heard immediately afterward. The details that they omitted or distorted in those attempts at reproduction were the ones incorporated into subsequent dreams. The effect was not, however, as striking as in the studies using pictures.

The last study of sensory stimuli I'll discuss was reported in 1923 and involved another investigator who used himself as the exclusive experimental subject. On each of nearly 750 nights, the Scottish investigator A. J. Cubberly attached a small piece of gummed paper, two centimeters square, to some part of his body and recorded whatever dreams these "tensions" might produce.[36] When a "tensor" was placed upon the sole of one foot, he dreamed of people dancing rather clumsily, like rustics dancing in a barn; one woman in the center of the group was notably awkward, "as if there were lameness in one foot or the other." When a tensor was placed on his right large toe, he dreamed of climbing stairs in a building to reach a certain office, which he entered on tiptoe so as not to be discovered. A tensor positioned high on the back of his neck produced a dream in which "heads and eyes turned upwards on [an] airship" high overhead. A second dream that same night involved the dreamer leaving a shop "haughtily" because the shop assistant had been rude to him, and in a third dream, an elderly, white-moustached, "stiff-necked or poker-backed" chairman was giving a speech at a dinner. The second and third dreams were most abstract, referring to social position (being haughty and stiff-necked), rather than physical posture (looking up at an airship).

Cubberly also attempted to explore the role of "detensors." He reasoned that if increased tension influenced dream imagery, perhaps decreased tension would also affect it. For these tests, he rubbed oily substances such as glycerine or cream butter over a circular space about 3 inches in diameter. When he applied such a detensor to his buttocks, he dreamed that someone directed him to the wrong seat at a football match or the theater. When he found his own seat, someone else was sitting in it. Since Cubberly was clearly aware of the target location, having placed the tensor or detensor there himself, the role of self-suggestion could also have influenced his results.

These studies with sensory stimuli began to advance our understanding of the factors that contribute to dream imagery. If exposed to a strong sensory stimulus before sleeping, the individual generally incorporated the sensation, but not in any predictable manner. A simple stimulus-response equation was not involved; it was necessary to know something about the dreamer's background, interests, and personality dynamics in order to comprehend how the sensory stimulus would be converted into dreaming imagery.

This pattern of individual differences can be noted more clearly in those instances where the experimenter used himself repeatedly as the subject under study. Maury, for example, frequently reported calamitous incidents in response to the sensory stimuli to which he was exposed. Hervey Saint-Denys, on the other hand, seemed frequently to come up with images of beautiful and desirous women, regardless of whether auditory, olfactory, or taste stimuli were involved. And Cubberly's dream imagery was often suggestive of concerns with social status or position: people were characterized as rustics or as stiff-necked and haughty; dream locales included barns, offices, and theaters. The possibility of inferring the psychodynamics of the dreamer from patterns in individual dream imagery led to studies in the 1930s in which the defenses of the dreamer against personally threatening visual stimuli were investigated. The example of the patient with problems surrounding orality, who was exposed to the nursing Madonna and her infant, is representative of this approach.

The preceding anecdotal and experimental studies of sensory stimuli might be taken to support the viewpoint espoused by British philosopher John Locke, in 1690, that sensory inputs were the exclusive determinants of dreams. By contrast, Gottfried Leibnitz, a seventeenth-century German philosopher, had argued that ideas can exist independently of the senses. For Leibnitz, dreams could occur during sleep as expressions of ideas, without the presence of external sensations. Dreams described in the following section seem to be derived primarily from cognitive sources.

STUDIES OF SYMBOLISM

A symbol is something that represents an abstract idea or concept; a dove is a symbol of peace, for example. Dreams can be replete with symbols, and the presence of symbols is one reason dreams often seem so mysterious. The dream theorists and analysts discussed in the earlier chapters generally began with the symbols present in the dream. Investigative inquiries then attempted to ferret out what mental or emotional state of conflict, need, or desire might have instigated such a symbol in the dream. Later researchers reversed that direction, starting with the presence of a presleep emotional state and investigating what type of symbolic representations subsequently appeared in dreams.

This was the approach pursued by Herbert Silberer, a German psychiatrist.[37] He discovered that when he was very drowsy and made an intellectual effort to think of a particular topic, he would be presented with visual imagery that corresponded symbolically to the topic on which he was concentrating. He termed this transformation of thoughts into pictures an "autosymbolic" phenomenon. Silberer's paper appeared in 1909, and Freud was quick to recognize its relevance for his concept of the dream work with regards to "considerations of representability" (use of pictorial images to represent verbal expression of thoughts). Silberer used himself as the subject for his experiments and explored a wide range of concepts.

Silberer classified autosymbolic phenomena into three groups. *Material* (content) phenomena deal with representation of thought-contents. An example of this type occurred when he was concerned with improving a halting passage in an essay; an autosymbolic image emerged in which he saw himself planing a piece of wood. A more elaborate material example arose once when he was trying to discourage someone from carrying out a dangerous adventure; the symbol evolved of "three gruesome-looking riders on black horses storming by over a dusky field under leaden skies." His second group involves *functional* (effort) phenomena, which deal more with the process of consciousness than with the content, and involve concepts such as quick, easy, relaxed, successful, and so forth. For example, on one occasion when Silberer had lost the thread of his thoughts, tried to regain it, but realized he had lost the connecting link, the image emerged of a piece of typesetting with the last few lines missing. His third group deals with *somatic* phenomena, which reflect sensations associated with pain, pressure, limb position, and sensory input. An example of the somatic type appeared when Silberer had a fever and a painful irritation associated with rhinolaryngitis, which forced him to swallow saliva steadily. Each time he was about to swallow, Silberer had a picture of a bottle of water which he was supposed to swallow, but after each swallow another bottle took its place. Silberer also recognized that

Herbert Silberer investigated "auto-symbolic" phenomena by concentrating on a particular topic while in a drowsy state. His imagery changed from vague forms to symbolic imagery. Liberation by M.C. Escher. (M.C. Escher/Cordon Art-Baarn-Holland. All rights reserved)

the three types of phenomena could appear mixed in various combinations.

Another technique to investigate the effect of a mental state on later imagery is hypnotic suggestion. The first report on the systematic use of hypnosis to investigate dream imagery experimentally was published in 1911 by Karl Schroetter, a German researcher who committed suicide soon after its publication.[38] Schroetter was aware of Freud's work and attempted to explore how suggested wishes might be expressed in "experimental dreams." A male dreamer was given the suggestion to have sexual intercourse with his stepmother, but to dream it in a disguised form. In the dream reported two minutes later, the subject's father was dead and lying in a large coffin. An unfamiliar young girl entered and the dreamer became friendly and started to pat her. She resisted and said she was his sister. Then the dreamer's father suddenly stood behind him and told him something the dreamer didn't understand. Since the dreamer had no sister, the girl may have been an incestual substitute for the dreamer's stepmother. The dreamer was able to make amorous advances toward this female figure when he perceived his father as dead, but when his "sister" resisted, the father suddenly came to life and gave the dreamer some puzzling message. The dream suggestion could be considered to have been acted upon in a disguised form to some extent, because the dreamer made physical advances to a female family member, but resistance prevented any consummation of the suggested intercourse.

In another experiment, Schroetter suggested to a young woman that she dream about having a sexual experience with her girlfriend L. In this experiment, the subject was not told to dream immediately. The subject had a dream the following night, which she wrote down. In the dream, she was sitting in a small, dirty cafe holding a large French newspaper. A woman with a strong Yiddish accent twice asked her, "Don't you need anything?" The dreamer didn't answer and the woman approached her a third time. The dreamer then angrily put down the newspaper and recognized L (L is Jewish). She was holding a suitcase bearing a sticker that read, "For ladies only!" L asked the dreamer to come home with her and they went through an unfamiliar street. The dreamer found it unpleasant when L hung on to her, but put up with it. Before reaching her house, L pulled out an enormous bunch of keys and gave it to the dreamer. L explained that it was the key to her suitcase and indicated that the dreamer might like to use it, but warned her that L's husband must not find out about the key. Several other German investigators attempted to repeat Schroetter's work but were unsuccessful, which raised the question as to whether Schroetter's subjects may have been familiar with Freud's theories.

Another German investigator, Gaston Roffenstein, also used explicit sexual situations as suggestions, but was successful only with one subject, a twenty-eight-year-old uneducated nursemaid.[39] Other subjects either failed to dream or incorporated suggestions in a completely undisguised fashion. The nursemaid was instructed to dream about intercourse with her father, but to distort the dream so that it would seem innocent. She had a hypnotic dream in which her father presented her with a

bag. With it he gave her a very large key. The dreamer wondered about the key being so big and thought that it couldn't possibly fit into her bag. When the dreamer opened the bag, a snake jumped out against her mouth and she shrieked and awoke.

When it was suggested to this same nursemaid that she dream about having fellatio with her previous employer in a disguised fashion, she dreamed that while in the kitchen, she heard the bell ring and her employer calling her. She went to his room and he asked her to sit down on a chair. On the table were many bananas and the employer told her to eat. The dreamer took a banana, peeled it, began to eat it, and said it tasted fine. Before both of these dreams, the dreamer vigorously protested the suggestions and the experimenter had to assure her repeatedly that no one would understand the real meaning of the dreams.

In the two studies just mentioned, the experimenters described sexual situations to the subjects and asked them to have a hypnotic dream in which the situation was disguised. In an interesting reversal of this procedure, hypnotized subjects were presented disguised dreams of sexual situations and asked what they portrayed.[40] An eighteen-year-old hypnotized coed was told that a girl dreamed "she was packing her trunk when a big snake crawled into it. She was terrified and ran out of the room." When asked what the dream meant, the coed blushed, hesitated a second, and then said, "Well, I guess she was afraid of being seduced. The snake would be the man's organ and the trunk hers." For control purposes, the subjects were always questioned about the dream before and after hypnosis. The researchers claimed that in no instance did the subjects in the waking state make any comment comparable to that obtained under hypnosis. This ability to hypnotically translate dreams was found in about 20 percent of the subjects. It was not found in subjects who were reported to be inhibited and rigid.

Many studies of hypnotic dreams have been carried out since these early studies. More recent studies have indicated that studying hypnotic dreams is far more complicated than these rather straightforward examples may suggest. Many parameters can influence the results. It is important to know how the suggestions were presented to subjects, the depth of hypnotic trance achieved, the nature of the relationship with the experimenter, and so forth before attempting to generalize the results.

These studies of how presleep thoughts or emotional states can be transformed into visual symbols have helped to broaden an appreciation of the mind's capacity to evolve complex imagery during altered states of consciousness, such as sleep onset, hypnosis, and dreams. Sometimes the symbols seem to represent what Freud suggested—the penis is seen as a snake or key, the vagina as a suitcase—but in many other cases the symbolism is clearly idiosyncratic, a function of the dreamer's unique personality. The dreamer's previous experiences with a suggested topic, his or her defensive structure, and his or her desires are some of the factors which must be considered in any examination of dream symbolism, just as they had to be considered in the studies employing sensory stimuli. Individual differences have thus been found to be of paramount importance in any effort to understand dream imagery.

PHYSIOLOGICAL STUDIES OF DREAMING

Researchers who follow a physiological approach generally find individual differences to be a source of irritation and frustration and prefer to ignore them. Such differences interfere with their quest for the universal laws governing the functioning of nerves, glands, muscles, and organs.

Dr. Caroline Finley, who was widely decorated for her work as an operating surgeon in World War I, reported on a case in 1921 where dream content was clearly affected by endocrine therapy.[41] Finley's patient, a middle-aged woman who seemed unable to recover her strength after an at-

tack of influenza, was given an extract of whole pituitary gland each morning. After about ten days of treatment, her nighttime activities underwent a dramatic change. As soon as her head touched the pillow, she began to experience extremely pleasant dreams. The dreams generally took the form of a journey and were perceived in very bright color. The sun was shining, a familiar, dingy railroad station was now clean and bright, the fields of grain were deep yellow, and the sky was clear blue as the train moved along. The characters in her dreams were smiling or laughing. The only exception to this pattern was a dream in which she was eagerly looking forward to the birth of a child. All of these dreams gave her such pleasure that she began to anticipate going to sleep.

The pituitary extract was discontinued after three weeks and the patient was placed on an extract of suprarenal (the whole adrenal gland). After a few days of the new treatment, the character of the dreams changed. They were harder to recall, less vivid, without colors, and, without exception, unpleasant. Toward the end of the course of treatment, she would awake several times each night with a sense of horror, and muscles so tense they would ache for several minutes. The only emotions she experienced in her dreams were fear or anger. She dreamed of having violent quarrels or awaiting terrible news. In one dream, she had committed some crime and was hiding from the police. In another, there was a horribly misshapen child clinging to her neck, whose arms she was unable to loosen. The patient's daytime mood was actually more cheerful under the adrenal substance because of her increased energy level. Finley concluded her paper by saying, "It is a good example of the purely physical origin of many dreams and the emotions behind them; an aspect of the subject that has been somewhat lost sight of in the fervor of Freudian interpretation."[42]

Experimental "starvation" was the physical condition in some other studies. In an investigation reported in 1919, the subjects were two groups of twelve young men. One group had their usual caloric content reduced by one-third or one-half for a period of four months, and the other group was maintained on an even lower caloric level for three weeks. Of the twenty-four men, twenty-two reported a decrease in sexual interest, sixteen claimed a decrease in nocturnal emissions, and none of them claimed recall of any sexual dreams.[43] In a 1948 study involving thirty-six male conscientious objectors, the subjects maintained a good diet for three months (about thirty-five hundred calories), a markedly reduced diet of less than sixteen hundred calories for six months, and then a rehabilitative diet for three months. The men lost about one-quarter of their body weight during the starvation period. Sex feelings and expression were "virtually extinguished" in all but a few subjects. One subject declared, "I have no more sexual feeling than a sick oyster." According to the investigators, nocturnal emissions were absent or greatly reduced and sex dreams also were greatly reduced in number and intensity.[44]

Some observers have attempted to determine the pattern of interaction between physiological variables and dreaming that might occur during a given night. An account was published by a French physician in 1821 involving a twenty-six-year-old female subject who had lost a large portion of her skull and brain covering. He reported that when the woman was in a dreamless sleep, her brain was motionless and lay within the cranium. However, when she was agitated by dreams, her brain moved and protruded outward from the cranium. The physician commented that, "in vivid dreams, reported as such by herself, the protrusion was considerable."[45]

J. Esquirol, a French psychiatrist noted for his humanitarian attitude toward patients, spent considerable time in the 1830s sitting beside sleeping mental patients, observing their facial expressions and movements and noting their pulse and respiration. He claimed that he often knew when patients were dreaming and could predict the general nature of their dream content from this combination of behavioral and physiological indices.

Esquirol's example was followed by another French physician, Nicholas Vaschide, who published a book on sleep and dreams in 1911. Vaschide kept himself awake all night observing the movements, heart rate, and respiration of four young normal subjects. He noted facial color, amount of nasal dilation, and movements of the facial muscles, and paid particular attention to eye movements: "The muscles have their own grammar, the contractions and tremulousness of the eyelids give you messages . . . all the physiology sketches an alphabet for you."[46] Vaschide woke his subjects at various times to obtain reports of their mental activity. He found that the first few hours of sleep were generally dreamless, and that lengthy periods for which dreams were reported alternated with dreamless periods during the remainder of the night. If his subjects were not awakened, they seldom spontaneously recalled any dreams. Vaschide stated that the dream content he obtained after waking them was consistent with their previously observed physical movements, but he provided no examples to support his claims. When he explored the effect of external stimuli by playing music to his subjects, he obtained reports of music and dancing in subsequent dreams.

The next phase of research dealt with efforts to use physiological recording devices to detect correspondences between emotionality or changes in physiological status and dreams. J. MacWilliam, a physiologist at Aberdeen University, published a study in 1923 of changes in pulse, respiration, and blood pressure throughout the night.[47] He concluded that there were two distinct conditions of sleep:

> 1) undisturbed sleep, attended by lowering of blood pressure, heart and respiratory rates, etc., and 2) disturbed sleep, modified by reflex excitations, dreams, night mares, etc., sometimes accompanied by extensive rises in blood pressure, increased heart action, changes in respiration, and various reflex effects.

The most striking cardiovascular effects were found in dreams with strong emotional content, although dreams involving active movement, such as cycling, were also associated with a pronounced rise in blood pressure. Systolic blood pressure could jump from 130 mm to over 200 mm in some cases, although the technique of recording these blood pressure measurements just after waking subjects, rather than during sleep, raises doubts about their accuracy.

Acceptance of the connection between dreams and emotionality led a trio of British investigators in a different direction. They asked five subjects to describe their dreams and to free-associate to selected dream items while the investigators recorded their galvanic skin responses (GSRs). Noticeable GSRs occurred when relating to emotional dream material and associations. This was true even in one case where a subject was reacting to a dream recalled from fifteen years earlier.[48] This study was published in 1924, but I'm not aware of any efforts since then to follow up on this provocative way of highlighting emotional "hot spots" in dream interpretation.

In 1932, an American psychologist, L. Rowland, suggested that hypnotized subjects dream about various emotional words whose degree of intensity had been previously rated by judges.[49] Recordings were made of the dreaming subjects' respiration and it was found that the increase in irregularity of breathing was roughly correlated to the degree of emotional intensity assigned to each word.

An interesting study involving a group of nineteen deaf-mutes was published in 1935 by Louis Max, a psychologist from New York University. Electromyographic recordings, action-current tracings of the electrical impulses associated with muscle movements, were taken for the arm and finger muscles. When large muscular responses in this area occurred and the subjects were awakened, they almost invariably stated that they had been dreaming. Subjects awakened at times when no action current was observed in the arm and finger muscles usually reported that they had not been dreaming. On the basis of these findings, Max concluded "that *dreams in deaf-mutes tend to be accompanied by action-current responses in the finger and arm muscles.* So far as we know this is the first instance of an objective measure of detecting dreams."[50] Since deaf-mutes communicate using manual sign language, it

seemed plausible that the large action-current responses in their hands and fingers might be associated with communication activities in their dreams. When hearing subjects were studied in the same manner, Max found no changes in action currents associated with dreaming. However, when more sensitive recording devices were used by another investigator in a 1965 study, hearing subjects were found to display as much electromyographic finger activity as the deaf.[51]

On a few occasions, Max's subjects reported dreams when the arm muscles didn't show action potentials. He speculated that in those cases "the dream content was primarily visual in nature, and the seat of activity may have been in the eye muscles which at that time were not in the electrical circuit." He suggested that, had the eye muscles been monitored, he "might conceivably have registered ocular activity during these visual dreams."[52] If Max had followed up his hunch and recorded eye movements, history would have acknowledged his claim of having discovered "an objective means of detecting dreams." That honor was later bestowed upon researchers at the University of Chicago, who discovered it was in the eyes, not the hands, that the "open sesame" to the secret of dreaming activity eventually was to be found.

The preceding studies have shown that several physiological systems—involving the heart, lungs, and hand muscles—tie in with dreaming. The obvious place to focus attention if one wished to study the organ of the mind was the brain. But except for such rare cases as that of the nineteenth-century French physician whose patient had lost a portion of the skull, allowing direct inspection of the brain during sleep, scientists were frustrated in their efforts to measure brain activity. That situation changed drastically after 1930. It then became possible to detect and amplify weak electrical impulses picked up by small electrodes attached to the scalp. Small variations in brain activity could thus be recorded by means of an electroencephalogram (EEG).

The first reports using this new technology indicated that the EEG patterns during sleep and waking were quite different. By the 1940s, the EEG patterns observed during sleep had been classified and named (sometimes by letters of the alphabet), but the few researchers who attempted to link these patterns with dreaming were not very successful. *Few* should be emphasized: dreams were considered unimportant, and therefore not worthy of study, by most brain physiologists. One pair of investigators did report in 1937 that dreaming was found in the B state when the EEG recordings showed that the alpha rhythm had disappeared and low-voltage activity was present.[53] As research in the 1950s was to confirm, this finding was pretty much on target, but it was not pursued in any systematic way by either the original investigators or other researchers.

The area of sleep itself had been the subject of considerable research before the 1950s. Attempts to measure the depth of sleep were attempted as early as 1862, through plotting the figures for the intensi-

ties of sound required to awaken the sleeper at different hours of the night.[54] As work along these lines continued, there seemed to be an agreement that sleep gradually deepened after the individual fell asleep and that the deepest level was reached sixty to ninety minutes after the onset of sleep. Sleep then became somewhat lighter, but fairly regular rhythmic fluctuations occurred during the remainder of the night.

Several investigators discovered that various measures of autonomic nervous system activity also seemed to manifest rhythmic cyclic shifts during sleep. Blood volume measured by a forearm plethysmograph in an 1897 study showed distinct cycles of sixty to ninety minutes duration.[55] A team of investigators in 1944 discovered that an eighty-five-minute cycle of penile erections occurred in their male subjects during sleep, and referred to this period as a "biological hour."[56] Another investigator in 1944 observed five distinct cycles of irregular respiratory movements during an eight-hour period of sleep.[57]

The pieces of the physiological puzzle lay scattered throughout the various articles I have referred to. How they fit together would not become clear until the 1950s and 1960s. The next chapter will examine how the discovery of an objective indicator of dreaming in 1953 enabled researchers to link the previously disparate findings about sleep stages, autonomic nervous system cycles, and patterns of brain wave activity with the phenomenon of dreaming.

CHAPTER 10

CONTEMPORARY DREAM RESEARCH:

THE ERA OF

REM STUDIES

THE UNIVERSITY OF CHICAGO AND REM SLEEP

Bits and pieces of information about shifting sleep patterns and autonomic nervous system cycles had appeared in various late-nineteenth- and early-twentieth-century scientific reports. Researchers assumed that somehow these beads of information could be connected, if only they could find the conceptual thread on which to string them.

The thread gradually appeared in a series of sleep studies carried out in the laboratory of Nathaniel Kleitman, a physiologist at the University of Chicago and an internationally recognized authority on sleep. One of the medical students working in Kleitman's laboratory, Eugene Aserinsky, was observing the sleeping behavior of infants in their cribs. Aserinsky noticed that there were periods when the infants' eyes seemed to be moving for sustained periods of time. He and Kleitman decided to monitor the presence and duration of these eye movements more precisely by attaching electrodes around the infant's eyes. Having verified that these cyclic patterns of eye movement recurred in infants, they attempted to determine whether similar patterns could be found in adults.

When Aserinsky and Kleitman found clusters of adult eye movements lasting anywhere from three to fifty-five minutes, they began to consider what these patterns might mean. They speculated that the subjects might be looking at some sort of internal landscapes or events. They decided to wake the sleepers during these periods of eye movement to inquire directly whether they had been dreaming. They woke subjects twenty-seven times during these periods of rapid eye movement (REM) and found that on twenty occasions detailed descriptions of dreams were recalled. To check whether dreaming was specifically correlated with the presence of REMs, they also woke subjects twenty-three times when no REMs were present. For nineteen of these occasions, the subjects reported that they were not experiencing a dream.

Aserinsky and Kleitman also recorded the brain waves, heart rates, and respiration patterns present during these REM periods. When they looked at the overall configuration of physiological events, they found that REMs were accompanied by slightly higher heart and respiration rates and an EEG pattern showing low-voltage activity different from that usually expected in sleep.

Aserinsky and Kleitman published a two-page summary of their results in the journal *Science* on September 4, 1953.[1] That brief article would eventually lead to an outpouring of research. In 1955 they published a more detailed description of their investigative procedures and the results obtained from their original ten subjects.[2]

Having finished his dissertation, Aserinsky completed his medical training and left Chicago, but another medical student, William Dement, soon arrived. Dement had heard about the new dream research and, he later told an interviewer, "I was young and got tremendously excited" about its implications.[3] Having just finished three months of study in psychiatry, he focused his initial interest in that direction. There had been many previous speculations about the possible relation between mental illness and dreaming; Dement decided to investigate whether the new REM discoveries might help clarify some of the issues surrounding the dream life of the mentally ill.

Dement used the EEG facilities at a state hospital south of Chicago to monitor the REM periods of seventeen chronic schizophrenics, then compared their records with those obtained from seventeen medical students. Although he found no marked difference in the amount of REM dreaming between the two groups, there was a considerable difference in the quality of their dream recall and mentation. Some form of content was reported from 88 percent of the wakings for the medical students, in contrast to 60 percent for the schizophrenic group. About half of the schizophrenics reported dreams of isolated inanimate objects with no associated activity; for example, "I was dreaming of a ripped coat." When asked if anything else was involved, the patients couldn't supply further details. No dreams of this type were reported by the medical students. Dement reported his results in 1955.[4]

Since Dement was unsure what kind of EEG patterns schizophrenics might produce, he departed from the previously standard practice of spot-checking sleep activity only occasionally during the night. Instead, he turned on the EEG machine at least one minute out of every five throughout the night. Those extra yards of recording paper yielded rich dividends. Dement noted that the bursts of REM activity always made their appearance when EEG waves with a frequency of about ten cycles per second were being traced on the graph paper.

The sleep laboratory at the University of Chicago consisted of three small rooms in Abbott Hall, a gothic building at one end of the campus that housed the department of physiology, as well as a variety of experimental animals. The building could be found in the dark because of the smell of the animals. Undaunted, Dement launched into a strenuous research schedule. Recalling those early years at the Chicago sleep lab, Dement said, "They were happy to have anyone who was willing to stay up at night." And stay up at night he did! Sometimes after monitoring the EEG machine all night long, he would paste the electrodes on himself, collapse into a cot that had just been vacated, and allow his wife to monitor his REM periods. Mrs. Dement also served as a volunteer subject on some nights.

Dement published a landmark article in 1957 with Kleitman as a coauthor. The significance of the new findings was heralded by the title: "The Relation of Eye Movements during Sleep to Dream Activity: An Objective Method for the Study of Dreaming."[5] Building on the earlier study, the investigators decided to leave the EEG machine on continuously throughout the night. Their article reported on results obtained from nine adult subjects, although only five were studied very intensively. REM periods were shown by all nine subjects; the investigators estimated that their length varied from three to fifty minutes, with an average duration of about twenty minutes. These REM periods were found to occur, on average, every ninety-two minutes and to be longer later in the night. Subjects were awakened during REM periods by the sound of a ringing doorbell. Awakenings were also made during times when no rapid eye movements (NREM) were present. When subjects were asked if they had been dreaming, the dream recall rate was 80 percent for REM awakenings and 7 percent for NREM awakenings. For NREM awakenings made within eight minutes after the end of a REM period, the dream recall rate was 29 percent; if the NREM awakening followed the REM period by more than eight minutes, the recall rate plummeted to 5 percent. This indicated that dream recall faded rapidly after the REM period.

Reasoning that the length of REM periods should bear some relation to the duration of dreaming, subjects were awakened after either five or fifteen minutes of REM dreaming and asked whether they had been dreaming for a short or long period of time. Subjects were able to make this discrimination with a very high level of success. Significant correlations were also found between the duration of REM periods in minutes and the length in words of the associated dream narratives.

The researchers found that there were three cases in which only vertical eye movements had preceded the awakening. In these cases, the subjects' dreams involved action in the vertical plane, such as throwing a basketball toward a net, looking down to pick up another ball, then shooting again. There was one instance where purely horizontal movements were observed; this subject reported seeing two people throwing tomatoes at each other. Dreams reported on ten occasions, when few or no eye movements had appeared for a minute before investigators woke the subjects, involved the dreamer watching something at a distance or just staring fixedly at some object.

Dement's next article, coauthored with Kleitman, also appeared in 1957.[6] The authors studied the uninterrupted sleep patterns of thirty-three healthy adults (twenty-six men and seven women). They reported that, in a six-hour period of sleep, four REM periods would usually be seen,

ranging in duration from one to seventy-two minutes, and the amount of sleep time spent in REM activity would average about 18 percent. This percentage would be higher if an eight-hour period of sleep were considered, because REM periods became progressively longer throughout the night and a long REM period generally occurred after six hours. REM activity, they stated, was not present during the onset of sleep; subjects awakened at this time reported imagery that differed from that of actual dreams: floating, drifting, seeing flashing lights, and so forth.

Based on their all-night recordings, Dement and Kleitman proposed criteria for numerically identifying stages of sleep, and their classification system was used widely during the next decade. A study in 1967, however, indicated that there was some variation in the ways various sleep laboratories analyzed EEG records and reported results.[7] Some greater standardization was needed. A committee of experienced sleep researchers therefore published in 1968 "A Manual of Standardized Terminology, Techniques and Scoring System for Sleep Stages of Human Subjects."[8]

EEG STAGES OF SLEEP

In order to understand the findings presented in the remainder of this chapter, it may be helpful to have a few physiological terms explained briefly. You don't have to become fluent in this exotic language, but a nodding acquaintance with the terms and phrases you'll encounter most fre-

quently should make the research reports easier to follow.

An EEG tracing can be characterized with regard to its height, speed, and form. The height, or amplitude, of a wave is measured in terms of voltage and can be described as being of low voltage or high

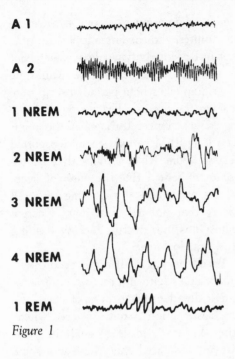

A 1

A 2

1 NREM

2 NREM

3 NREM

4 NREM

1 REM

Figure 1

voltage. The speed of a wave is measured in terms of frequency or number of cycles per seconds (cps). Almost all EEG patterns can be described by reference to these two main factors, amplitude and frequency, but descriptive terms are occasionally necessary in characterizing some distinctive EEG phenomena, for example, "spikes" or "K-complexes." There is a reciprocal relation between voltage and frequency; the higher the voltage, the slower the frequency found for a given wave form.

Samples of EEG patterns associated with the different stages of sleep are shown in figure 1. During alert wakefulness, the EEG displays low voltage with a fairly fast frequency. Such a pattern is shown in the top tracing. As relaxation and drowsiness set in, the appearance of an alpha rhythm can generally be detected. The alpha rhythm, shown in the second line, has a slightly greater amplitude than does the alert pattern and is characterized by a frequency of eight to twelve cycles per second.

A Stage 1 sleep pattern is defined by a relatively low-voltage, mixed-frequency EEG with a prominence of activity in the 2–7 cps range; sharp waves or spikes sometimes appear. Stage 2 is characterized by the presence of sleep spindles with a frequency range of 12–14 cps, shown to the left of the sample tracing, and K-complexes, in which a sharp upward wave is immediately followed by a drop in the tracing below the previous line, as shown to the far right of the sample tracing. K-complexes can be elicited in response to external stimuli, such as sudden sounds, but they also appear in response to internal stimuli that are not yet well understood.

A delta wave is a very high-amplitude, slow-frequency (1–2 cps) wave. During Stage 2 sleep, delta waves make up less than 20 percent of the EEG recording. A Stage 3 pattern contains between 20 to 50 percent delta waves. When more than 50 percent of the record consists of delta waves, it is classified as a Stage 4 pattern. The large delta waves can be seen most clearly in the Stage 4 tracing. There are thus four fairly distinct non-REM sleep stages. Stages 2, 3, and 4 are characterized by the presence of spindles, K-complexes, and delta waves, with the primary differentiation being made in terms of the relative percentage of delta waves. Stage 1 sleep is differentiated from the remaining three stages by the complete absence of spindles, K-complexes, or delta waves.

The REM state always occurs in conjunction with a Stage 1 EEG pattern. The distinction between Stage 1 non-REM and Stage 1 REM is based on the presence or absence of rapid eye movement. In addition, sharp vertex waves from the crown of the skull are more prominent in Stage 1 non-REM sleep, while Stage 1 REM sleep frequently includes a distinctive "sawtooth" wave whose shape actually resembles the teeth of a saw. A few of these saw-tooth waves are shown in the middle of the illustrated REM pattern.

The sequential unfolding of the sleep stages is shown in figure 2. As a subject moves from wakefulness through drowsiness, he or she passes through a very brief "descending" sleep, from Stage 1 down to Stage 4. After having been asleep for an hour or so, the record moves from Stage 4, back up through Stage 3, and eventually stage 1 sleep reappears, though it may only last about five minutes. Following this brief plateau, which may or may not be accompanied by eye movements, the sleeper usually returns to a period of Stage 4 sleep shorter than the first. Approximately ninety minutes after the onset of the first Stage 1 plateau the subject evidences a REM period, which may continue for approximately ten minutes. Generally the subject does not return to Stage 4 sleep, or does so only very briefly, after that REM period. The sleeper will generally spend some time in Stage 3, however, before the appearance of the next REM period. As before, this REM period begins approximately ninety minutes after the onset of the previous REM period. The typical pattern for the remainder of the night is for the subject to alternate between Stage 2 sleep and REM sleep, with the remaining REM periods also occurring at approximately ninety-minute intervals.

As the graph in figure 2 shows, most Stage 4 sleep occurs during the first third of the night. Succeeding REM periods tend to become progressively longer, and the final REM period of the night may last from twenty-five to forty-five minutes. It should be emphasized that the sleep pattern of any individual on a given night may depart from this pattern, which is based on averages obtained from a large number of young adult subjects. For the normal adult, REM sleep occupies approximately 22 percent of sleeping time, with the remainder of sleep spent in approximately the following fashion: Stage 2, 50 percent; Stage 3, 7 percent; Stage 4, 14 percent; and Stage 1 non-REM, 7 percent.

No distinctive sex differences occur in the patterning of sleep stages, but there are marked differences associated with age. A normal newborn infant spends approximately 50 percent of its sleeping time in the REM stage, and the time premature infants spend in REM sleep has been reported to be as high as 70 to 80 percent. It has been proposed that the high percent-

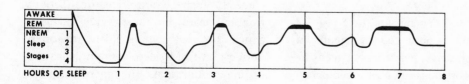

Figure 2

age of REM sleep is necessary for appropriate maturation and activation of the young child's brain; the REM percentage figure for children decreases to the level found for adults by about the fourth year. Young children also have a higher percentage of Stage 4 sleep. Growth hormone is secreted during Stage 4 sleep and seems to be necessary for the child to achieve normal stature. In elderly subjects, the percentage of REM sleep is slightly lower than for young adults, while the percentage of Stage 4 sleep is markedly decreased. If the average voltage of all of the EEG stages is examined, a progressive diminution of EEG voltage from infancy throughout the life span is found. It doesn't take much energy to generate the electrical activity of the brain. "The brain runs effectively on 20 watts of power, the amount used by an icebox light bulb."[9]

Because of its association with dreaming, the REM stage (which has also been called paradoxical sleep, activated sleep, desynchronized sleep, hindbrain sleep, and rhombencephalic sleep) became the focal point toward which the greatest research effort was directed. As investigators developed additional measuring techniques, an amazing variety of physiological correlates was found to accompany the REM state. During REM sleep, for example, changes occur in urine volume and composition[10] as well as spinal fluid pressure.[11] Examples of some of the more frequently measured physiological responses are illustrated in figure 3.

The technical name for the record of eye movements produced by means of changes in electrical potential between the retina and cornea is an electrooculogram

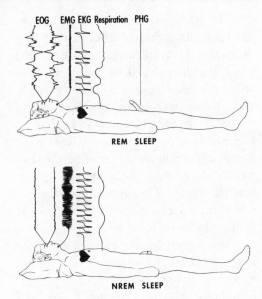

Figure 3

(EOG). The correlation of movements between the two eyes is reflected in the symmetry of the EOG tracings as the eyes dart toward or away from each other. Eye movements can also be measured with a device known as a strain gauge, which records the mechanical movement of the eyelids rather than shifting electrical potentials.[12] Subjects with lifelong blindness generally reveal no EOG activity during REM sleep, but do display eye movements when monitored with a strain gauge.[13] The EOG record during non-REM sleep would not be nearly so flat as that shown in figure 3 because the EOG tracings would also include the higher voltage electrical activity from the nearby frontal region of the brain. Since the eyes remain fairly stationary during non-REM sleep, a strain gauge recording would make it much easier to discriminate the presence of eye movements when they do occur.

If two electrodes are placed slightly less than an inch apart beneath the center of the chin, it is possible to detect electrical changes in the tonus (tension) of the nearby muscles. The resulting record of muscular activity is known as an electromyogram (EMG). As shown in the illustration, muscular tonus is generally present during non-REM sleep, but the muscles gradually relax during REM sleep. Spinal reflexes are also greatly diminished during REM sleep. As a result, major muscular movements disappear, which makes it impossible for sleeping individuals to physically act out the activities imagined in their dreams.[14]

During non-REM sleep, the heartbeat, as measured by an electrocardiograph (EKG), is fairly steady, but with the onset of REM sleep it becomes very irregular. Although the average number of heartbeats per minute increases only very slightly during REM periods, there are brief intervals during which the heart beats much faster and others during which it beats much slower; the minute-to-minute variability becomes much more pronounced. The same is true for respiration. Slow regular breathing is characteristic of non-REM sleep, but during REM sleep we change back and forth from very slow to very rapid breathing. Significant shifts in cardiac and respiratory activity, as well as in that of other organs regulated by the autonomic nervous system, are signals that emotional arousal is occurring. These barometers of emotional climate are probably associated with the often intense emotions experienced in dreams. The question of which comes first, the autonomic arousal or the dreamed activity, is a topic of considerable controversy among dream theorists.

At a practical level, some of the marked changes in physiological activity during REM periods have health implications for people who suffer from various physical ailments. Owing to the marked increase in blood flow through the brain during REM sleep, patients who experience vascular headaches are more likely to awaken with such headaches from a REM period.[15] It has been reported that ulcer patients secrete significantly more gastric acid at this time,[16] asthmatic patients are more likely to have attacks in conjunction with REM periods,[17] and cardiac patients have been found to experience more angina attacks[18] and arrhythmias[19] during REM sleep. Unfortunately, knowledge of these patterns has not led to any remedies.

REM SLEEP AND GENITAL AROUSAL

An area of psychosomatic functioning that affects all humans is genital functioning. In particular, any suspected inadequacy may provide a source of considerable concern. The first detailed laboratory study of when erections occur during sleep for male subjects was published in 1965.[20] In these first attempts to record nocturnal erection, the investigators used a thick polyvinyl tube filled with water, about "the size and shape of a doughnut," placed around the base of the penis. It was discarded because it caused too much pressure and local stimulation; one subject actually asked whether it was supposed to be "an artificial vagina." The investigators eventually decided on a more sensitive device called a mercury strain gauge, in which a thin loop of plastic tubing filled with mercury encircled the penis near the base. To insure that the recording device was not contributing to the arousal pattern, several control subjects slept nude under a thin transparent plastic sheet and were directly observed for the presence of erections, which were rated on a four-point scale for degree of tumescence (increase in size and firmness). Similar results were obtained using the gauge and visual observation. When seventeen young adult men were studied, it was found that some form of erection was present in 95 percent of the REM periods (60 percent full and 35 percent partial erections).

Many studies by other investigators also used the mercury strain gauge. A very ambitious program was undertaken by Ismet Karacan, a psychiatrist at the Baylor College of Medicine in Texas. He and his coworkers studied a total of 125 healthy boys and men ranging in age from three to seventy-nine years old.[21] All of the subjects exhibited erections during sleep. The total time spent in tumescence reached a maximum of over 190 minutes during the prepubertal years (ages ten to twelve) and gradually declined to a minimum level of less than 100 minutes for men in their sixties and seventies. The authors' only unexpected findings were the rather high amounts of erection time between ages three and nine.

Most erections occur during REM periods, but their onset may precede the REM period and they may persist for a while after the REM period ends. Some erections occurred during non-REM sleep, particularly during the prepubertal and pubertal years. The length of time between periods of tumescence becomes longer with age, increasing from approximately fifty minutes among the youngest subjects to approximately one hundred minutes for males in their sixties. Although the ability to attain and maintain full erection during REM sleep deteriorates with age, healthy subjects in their seventies were still experiencing nocturnal erections.

Recency of sexual outlet does not result in fewer erections—quite the reverse. This was studied by having ten young married men abstain from sexual activity on three occasions during a period of about ten days. Their nocturnal erections were monitored on the last night of abstinence as well as on the following night after each subject engaged in intercourse. Fewer erections and a longer period of time between erections were found on the nights following periods of abstinence in comparison to those following intercourse.[22]

A useful practical application emerged from the studies of nocturnal erections. It was found that subjects with a physical basis for impotence, such as severe diabetes or nerve damage, showed no erections during sleep, while those whose impotence stemmed from psychological causes displayed full erections during sleep. The degree of tumescence during sleep was very predictive of the degree of tumescence that a male was capable of achieving in waking life, if there were no psychological problems intervening. The psychodynamic conflicts contributing to erectile failure in waking life are bypassed in sleep. This ability to diagnose the underlying factors responsible for impotence can help physicians and marital therapists in developing the most appropriate treatment strategy for impotence.[23] Counseling for emotional problems would be recommended for males who experienced sleeping erections but were unable to achieve waking erections, while males who had no sleeping erections could be presumed to suffer from physically caused impotence and could consider the possibility of surgically implanted corrective devices to artificially restore tumescence.

It should be pointed out that nocturnal erections are not necessarily associated with erotic dream content, but rather are activated automatically by a circuit of neurological activities. Erections, however, can be diminished if anxiety is present in the accompanying dream. In one study sixteen college males were exposed to emotionally stressful movies on some nights in the lab and to neutral films on other nights; REM periods showing irregular or no erections corresponded to dreams in which significantly more anxiety was reported.[24] Another study found that anxiety or aggression in dream reports was associated with partial or absent erections.[25] In still another study, "responses of the total male genital" were evaluated by including three measures of scrotal activity.[26] One involved retractions of the testicles, which was measured by placing a large mercury strain gauge around the neck of the scrotum. Measurements of two other muscles in this

area were made by EMG recordings. The combination of these responses was labeled a scrotal complex response (SCR). SCR can occur during any stage of sleep. Mental content reports were obtained from 90 percent of the SCR awakenings. The authors reported that "awakenings preceded by an SCR response are more likely to involve anxiety-laden content."

Despite extensive investigation of erection patterns during sleep, it is apparently very unusual for any nocturnal emission, or "wet dream," to occur in a sleep laboratory. I have slept in four different laboratories and never experienced a wet dream in that setting. Calvin Hall experienced one wet dream in his home EEG laboratory in Miami, and a long-term friend experienced one in my laboratory at Virginia. Such occurrences seem to be rare in other laboratories as well. The only published reference I came across was to one subject having "a very vivid and frankly sexual dream"; just prior to emission, the article reported, the subject's respiration and heart rate accelerated "remarkably."[27] It may be that the laboratory situation inhibits dream experiences. The topic of laboratory influence will be discussed later in this chapter.

Research on the genital arousal of males during sleep can be conducted fairly simply, since erectile responses are visible to the naked eye. Such observations are impossible with females, and the lack of appropriate measuring devices has impeded research on female genital arousal. Early attempts involved efforts to measure temperature changes by means of a heat-sensitive device (thermistor) attached to a diaphragm placed within the vagina or thermistors attached to the labia, and by attempts to use clitoral strain gauges. The most recent and sophisticated efforts have employed a vaginal photoplethysmograph, an intravaginal probe that directs infrared light toward the walls of the vagina and measures the amount reflected back. The amount of reflected light varies in response to the amount of blood congested in the walls of the vagina. Greater arousal causes more congestion which leads to darker coloration and less reflected light.

A dissertation project employing this technology was carried out by Gary Rogers in my laboratory at the University of Virginia Medical School. We used a cyclindrical probe approximately five inches long and one inch in diameter enclosed by a flexible, clear rubber membrane. We reported our preliminary results at the Association for the Psychophysiological Study of Sleep convention in 1982, and a detailed article was published in 1985. Twenty normal women were studied for two nights in our laboratory. All were in their mid-twenties, were medically screened, underwent neurological assessment, blood pressure readings from several regions of their limbs, and a pelvic exam to insure that there were no gynecological abnormalities. To control for possible vascular changes associated with the menstrual cycle, all subjects were studied in the laboratory between days four and ten of their cycle. All women were judged to have normal ovulatory cycles on the basis of monthlong recordings of oral temperature.

During their first night in the laboratory, electrodes were attached for EEG, EOG, and chin EMG monitoring. An ad-ditional EMG electrode was attached to the inner thigh by a female assistant in order to detect muscle movements which might produce inaccurate readings because the subject shifted position or stretched her legs. After the subject privately inserted the probe and was settled in bed, she reclined quietly for twenty minutes of baseline physiological recording. Each subject then privately watched a ten-minute erotic film depicting a nude couple progressing from mutual massage to sexual intercourse. Immediately after the film, subjects rated their levels of sexual arousal on a seven-point scale. Another twenty-minute baseline period followed, after which subjects were asked to fantasize a sexually arousing event or situation for ten minutes. No inquiry was made as to the nature of this fantasy. After the fantasy period, subjects again rated their level of arousal and were then allowed to fall asleep. Sleep recordings were monitored all night, but not analyzed due to the high variability of first-night scores frequently found in several other studies.

The measure of genital arousal was vaginal pulse amplitude (VPA). Waking VPA scores showed highly significant changes from the baseline level for both the film and fantasy responses. There was no significant correlation, however, between the self-rated levels of arousal and the physiological levels of arousal as measured by VPA. What women reported they were experiencing was not what their bodies indicated they were experiencing. Half of these women had previously been rated as possessing high arousability and half as possessing low arousability on the basis of their test scores on a Sexual Arousability

Inventory (SAI). There were no significant differences, however, between these two groups of women on either their self-rated levels of arousal in the laboratory or their VPA scores in response to the film and fantasy stimuli.

The same recording techniques were used on the second night, but the subjects were not exposed to the presleep stimuli (film or fantasy). The VPA scores shown during REM sleep were significantly higher than those shown in the non-REM stages of sleep. There were no significant differences in VPA scores during REM sleep for the high- or low-SAI-scoring women. We summarized our results as follows:

> Nineteen out of twenty subjects in this study exhibited VPA increases during REM stage sleep that were similar to those that occurred during waking exposure to erotic stimuli and that were significantly higher than VPA levels during the other stages of sleep.[28]

Since the main focus of this study was to obtain VPA measures during uninterrupted REM periods, no awakenings were made to obtain dream reports, and almost no spontaneous reports of dreams were offered by subjects in the morning. Several other studies have found that subjects have difficulty in recalling or reporting dreams after having been exposed to emotionally arousing or threatening stimuli.[29] I have found only one brief report in which a female subject who was monitored in a sleep lab reported an orgasmic dream during a REM period.[30] It was accompanied by a marked elevation in VPA level.

Our study documented that normal young women experience a marked increase in circulatory activity in the genital area comparable to that found in males. If sufficient data could be obtained on VPA levels for a large number of normal women, it might be possible to discover whether some women suffer from insufficient circulatory activity during REM sleep, which would presumably limit their ability to experience full waking sexual satisfaction, as is the case for males who fail to achieve erections during REM periods. Awareness of this circulatory deficiency could help diminish inappropriate guilt associated with inability to respond to a sexual partner. It's probable that the same physical factors that contribute to male impotence, such as diabetes, nerve damage, or medications, could interfere with female genital arousal. No other technique is currently available to assess female "impotence."

THE ROLE OF INDIVIDUAL DIFFERENCES

The results I have presented so far are based upon averages and tend to overlook the marked individual differences among research subjects. Scientists who perform the kinds of measurements we have been discussing are likely to emphasize general traits, because their training, often in neurology, biology, or physiology, involved looking for differences between species or breeds of experimental animals, how cats differ from dogs, for example, or dachshunds from Great Danes. Psychologists or psychiatrists, on the other hand, are much more concerned with the nature of individual differences between people. They wish to discover the uniqueness of each person. So it's worth noting the preponderance of studies devoted to the physiology, as opposed to the psychology, of sleep.

The research originating at the University of Chicago generated a tidal wave of studies on the physical parameters of sleep, particularly with regard to the REM state, but only a minor ripple of research into the psychological parameters associated with dreaming. The fact that most laboratories where EEG-REM studies can be carried out are located in medical schools, rather than in psychology departments, may contribute to this imbalance.

The disproportionate emphasis given to the biological and physiological side of sleep is demonstrated dramatically by a publication called *Sleep and Dream Research: A Bibliography*, which includes over four thousand citations for the research period from 1962 to 1968. The section on "General Neurophysiology" contains 994 references, the section on "Physiology" contains 642 references, and the section on "Neurophysiology of the Visual System" contains 193 references. The section on "Phylogeny" (comparative sleep of animals) contains 128 references. By way of contrast, the section on "Special Features of Dream Recall" contains 53 references and the section on "Patterns of Dream Content" contains only 37 references. Considerably more interest was shown in animal sleep patterns than in human patterns of dream content or dream recall. After the findings were published about the erection cycle in humans, more efforts were made to discover whether a similar cycle would be shown for other mammals[31] than efforts to investigate the dreaming correlates associated with different patterns of erection.

To show how the search for general laws can lead to the ignoring of individual differences, the above-mentioned large-scale study on the frequency and duration of erections in sleep is instructive. The authors' summary indicated that the duration of tumescence peaked in prepubescent boys, while in males seventy to seventy-nine it was only about half as long. A more careful reading of their figures, however, shows that, although the average number of minutes per night of tumescence was 191 for the prepubescent group and 96 for the elderly group, some of the boys had totals under 120 minutes and some of the older men had totals over 150 minutes. Thus, although the group trends (191 minutes versus 96) present a fairly clear pattern of declining tumescence time, certain males in their seventies had considerably more tumescence time than did certain prepubescent boys.

Similarly, the second paper by Dement and Kleitman concerning cyclic variations in sleep reports that the shortest interval between REM periods was thirty-six minutes. Yet the authors claim that the cycle of ninety to one hundred minutes shows "striking" regularity. One of their tables indicates that the third REM period can begin as early as 180 minutes or as late as 340 minutes after sleep onset, and its duration can range from as short as four minutes to as long as seventy-two minutes. Such wide variations in onset and duration seem to undermine their claim for "the regularity and apparent universality" of sleep cycle patterns.

PRESLEEP INFLUENCES UPON DREAMS

MOVIES AS PRE-SLEEP DREAM STIMULI

In chapter 9 we looked at several studies in which subjects were exposed to various types of sensory stimuli, such as sounds or odors, in order to determine if they had any effect upon dreaming imagery. Such static stimuli bear little relationship to the complex moving and emotional events we encounter in our waking lives. The availability of movies enables researchers a greater opportunity to assess how presleep exposure to stimuli more closely resembling everyday life is processed in the several dreams known to occur throughout the night. Movies provide some degree of experimental control over a subject's "day-residue." Of course, film material unfamiliar to the subject can also be selected that involves subject matter expected to carry a strong emotional charge.

The first film study, reported in 1964, involved college students exposed to either a violent western film or a neutral romantic comedy.[32] Judges were unsuccessful in determining which of the films a subject had seen based on his or her dreams, except on a few rare occasions (5 percent of the cases) when the incorporated items were extremely obvious. In a similar study employing boys aged seven and eleven, a violent western and a baseball movie were shown.[33] Only 8 percent of the dreams were judged to have incorporated elements of the presleep film. These results indicated that the effects of movies were quite subtle and that dream responses would be traceable only if films had more emotional punch.

A film which might activate "castration" concerns for male subjects was employed in several studies. This black-and-white silent film, entitled "Subincision," portrays the puberty initiation ceremony of a remote Australian aboriginal group. In it four naked young men are initiated by older men in the tribe. Each initiate in turn lies on his back across the other initiates, who are on all fours, and an incision is made along the underside of his penis, from tip to scrotum, with a sharp stone. When the bleeding penis is held over a fire, the face of the initiate clearly shows his anguish.

In an initial study using this film, subjects were asked to rate how emotionally aroused they were by the film.[34] Subjects who indicated they were aroused by watching the film tended to dream about it, usually in a symbolized fashion, whereas nonaroused men did not seem to dream about the film. This methodology represents an advance over previous film-watching studies because an effort was made to evaluate how the film had affected subjects in the waking state. In another study employing this film, the degree of each subject's waking arousal was measured by physiological recordings.[35] In addition to the subincision film, subjects were shown another stressful film, showing a birth, and two neutral travelogues. Subjects who reacted with anxiety to the stressful films also showed more dream anxiety. If a subject showed increased irregularity of breathing during the first minute of the operation in the subincision film, he was designated a waking responder. The sixteen waking responders showed significantly more respiratory irregularity during REM periods following the stressful movies than they did during REM periods after the neutral films. This pattern was not shown for the twelve nonresponders.

The report involving respiratory irregularity was part of the largest systematic study of the effects of the subincision and birth films, carried out by Herman Witkin and his associates at the Downstate Medical Center in New York.[36] The subjects for this study were twenty-eight men with evening jobs, such as postal employees, who slept in the laboratory during the day. Subjects spent five sessions in the laboratory and completed a mood checklist before and after each film and after each dream report following a REM awakening. At the end of each laboratory session, the subject was asked to recall the dreams he had earlier reported and to provide associations to his experience of the film and to his dreams. At the conclusion of the laboratory sessions, a biographical interview

was conducted. Having access to this great amount of material from each subject made it possible to evaluate the interrelations between the presleep film and the subject's subsequent moods, dreams, and associations. Such an approach obviously allows individual differences to be emphasized and brings out how complex the interweaving of waking experiences and dreaming imagery can become.

One can attempt to trace the twisted thread leading from the subincision film to a specific dream narrative. In his first REM awakening, one subject reported a dream fragment in which he described being "taken for a ride" in a car. He was in the backseat of a large black car and about to be exterminated, but was not sure what he had done to merit this fate. He indicated that he was not alone in the backseat. On his mood checklist responses to the dream, the subject described himself as being jittery, fearful, and clutched up.

During his postsleep session, the subject was asked about his spontaneous recall of the dream and indicated that everything was black (all the film characters were black), and all the other people in the car were male (also matching the film). He noted he was flanked by two gentlemen in the back (corresponding to the two men holding the initiate down on his back). When the interviewer inquired about the use of the word "exterminated," the subject said that he rarely used that word and associated it with the extermination of the Jewish people during World War II. In response to further inquiry, the subject responded that he thought maybe the film involved a circumcision and later indicated that he had been shocked by the film. In follow-up comments, he indicated that he wasn't sure whether castration was involved, and had thought it might be a punishment until he realized that the people enduring the pain were not resisting. Still later, he indicated he was wondering if the young men in the film were being circumcised at that late age, but then said laughingly that he knew they weren't Jewish. During his postsleep recall, the subject had described himself in his dream as "being forcibly taken away, although I didn't *resist* or I put up no struggle." The subject had also described the initiates as not resisting. The Jewish motif acts as a powerful magnet for this subject to align several different themes. The subincision cutting is linked with circumcision, a practice connected with Judaism. The dreamer doesn't resist the fate of extermination awaiting him and doesn't understand what he has done to deserve his harsh punishment. The dreamer thus finds many parallels between his dream plight and that confronted by Jews in World War II. During his next regular sleep session at home, he complained that he had experienced one of the worst nightmares of his life, but was unwilling to divulge its contents.

Each viewer responded to the subincision film differently. Mr. A, for example, reported dreaming of two cowboys facing each other, one holding a gun on the other. The second cowboy was telling the first one that the gun he had was an old Western action gun, and he said a friend of his hadn't been very successful with that kind of gun in a contest. The dreamer saw this scene from the second cowboy's perspective, with everything blurred except the barrel of the gun pointing toward him.

The gun had a big sight on top and the dreamer's attention was drawn toward the gun sight and two winglike projections on either side of it. The dreamer's description of the gun sounds like a classic representation of the penis, with the winglike projections representing the testicles.

Whereas the first subject related to the subincision film with more of a collective concern—he was going to be "exterminated," a fate he associated with the killing of a group, by a group of black men—Mr. A structured his concern as a showdown between individual cowboys, one of whom was dressed in dark clothes. They were facing each other, and the dreamer eventually felt threatened when he saw himself staring down the barrel of the gun, held by his dark clothed rival.

Interesting responses also appeared following the birth film. This was a medical teaching film, in color, displaying the advantages of a vacuum extractor as a method of delivery. It shows the exposed vagina and thighs of a woman and the arm of an obstetrician inserting the vacuum extractor into the vagina. The obstetrician's gloved and bloody hands and arm are shown pulling periodically on a chain protruding from the vagina, and a baby is eventually delivered with a gush of blood.

In his first dream following this film, Mr. A saw a group of girls wearing white gloves sitting on park benches, carrying flowers, and trying to hide something. The dreamer earlier had been trying to catch bees and letting them go to pollinate flowers. In this first dream, it appears that the obstetrician's bloody gloves have been transformed into white gloves and birth is symbolically represented by the bees pollinating flowers.

In his second dream, Mr. A was with some other people in an airplane, like a troop carrier, flying along and looking out through a window which resembled a hole. He could see the body of the plane and a coil of wire protruding through the hole. A man was holding a loop at the end of the wire and periodically pulling it. When he pulled the wire, the door would go up and down and parachutists would drop out of the airplane. Before all the door openings, Mr. A had been talking to a baseball player, who was telling him about how many children he had. Mr. A responded by telling him how many children he had, and the baseball player then told the dreamer that everyone called the ballplayer "lover" or something similar. Mr. A and the ballplayer sat on boxes facing each other. They were on the same team, but the other man was running for some honor, such as being the best player. Mr. A acknowledged that the ballplayer was ahead of him "on the team as well as in the department of having children."

In this second dream the troop carrier, which drops parachutists when a man pulls on a wire, bears many similarities to the woman's body in the film, from which the chain-pulling obstetrician extracts a baby. The face-off between two men on "boxes" over who is the better "ballplayer," and who has the most children, mirrors the confrontation Mr. A reported with the gun-wielding cowboy following the subincision film. "Phallic rivalry" thus seems to be an important concern because it emerges fairly openly in response to both films, although the themes portrayed in them are quite different.

Sometimes a dreamer's associations can point toward material from earlier childhood that influences the subsequent imagery. Witkin and his coworkers also asked subjects to free-associate to a film while they were falling asleep.[37] To prevent the subject from hearing his own voice, white noise was fed into the subject's ears through earphones. Visual input was limited by covering the subject's eyes with halves of Ping Pong balls. This reverie state was used to monitor the associational links between the subject's thoughts and feelings after exposure to a different threatening film, a black-and-white silent film showing a mother monkey eating her dead infant. The mother is seen hauling her dead baby around, dragging it by its arms and legs, and nibbling at it.

Mr. A, whose dream responses to the other films have been described, began his reverie comments by saying, "I'm getting hungrier by the minute." He went on to indicate that he was glad the baby he saw in the movie wasn't a human baby. He then wondered what the monkey was thinking about and said it seemed she was trying to bring the baby back to life. He wondered whether the mother knew it was dead or that it was a baby. He next saw some drawings of faces and lines, a blue waterfall, and a sky with dark black clouds. He reported seeing a number of images of animals, such as a horse drawing a little buggy and a tiger with an open mouth. He then described a long green pool with stones at the bottom and, to his surprise, a frog—a blue-green frog with dark gray spots. Immediately after this he fell asleep.

During the inquiry at the end of the session, the dreamer explained that the frog in the pool of water appeared as if "it was actually before me," as opposed to how it might look if he just imagined it. In the process of associating to the elements in his reverie, he revealed that he used to be "cruel" to frogs; he would throw them across a brick-wall incinerator and kill them. "After a while frog hunting became a little scarce. I suppose they ran away when they saw me." The mother monkey's actions toward her baby apparently reminded him of his own wanton killing of frogs. Recalling his earlier cruelty was probably painful for Mr. A, and it seems as if he was trying to ward off dealing with the mother monkey's cruelty by questioning whether she really knew what she was doing.

Mr. A's dreams after the other two films prominently featured issues of rivalry and competition. The first image mentioned in his first dream following the monkey film and his reverie period involved "someone being chased." The dream figure being chased may have represented a frightened frog trying to run away from Mr. A, a baby being chased by a cruel mother, or Mr. A anxiously attempting to avoid the confrontational challenges that other men frequently posed for him.

EMOTIONS AND THEIR EFFECTS ON DREAMS

Although films can serve as a potentially strong external stimulus, there is still an artificial or distant quality to them; they take place "out there" and involve other characters rather than the dreamer. The experimenter has to assume that the film will have some personal relevance for the dreamer. A more compelling technique was used by a team of psychologists at the University of Oregon to insure that the presleep situation possessed personal relevance for the dreamer.[38] Two different types of subjects were used. One study involved five subjects who were scheduled to undergo major surgery. When the body of the dreamer, not that of some aboriginal adolescent, is going to be cut, the degree of personal relevance increases astronomically. The situation is too significant to ignore. These subjects participated in interviews, completed rating scales, responded to psychological tests, and were behaviorally observed. Dreams were collected using EEG-REM methods on four consecutive nights before the operations and three nights after the subjects were somewhat recovered from surgery. Some comparisons between two of these patients will illustrate how they handled the stress of surgery differently in both their dream and waking lives.

Al was a sixty-four-year-old retired veteran who had vascular blockages in his legs that caused coldness in his feet and reduced his mobility. He had held various jobs involving adventurous, physically demanding work, and he vigorously pursued outdoor activities after his retirement. The main threat posed by the operation was the prospect of physical debility and being forced to give up his role as an active, assertive achiever. He expressed his concept of the surgery as, "I've got something to fix and I will go in there and get it repaired and then come out."

In both his waking thoughts and his

dreams, Al represented his physical problem as a mechanical defect to be repaired, and in both he dealt with his fear by assertive activity. In his dreams, Al and others worked on repairing broken stoves, cars, trains, and septic tanks. In one dream, clogged pipes that were interfering with the activities of a work crew had to be cleared out. There were no direct references to the surgery itself, but symbolic representations were prominent. During his first preoperative night of dream recording, one of his dreams involved a family discussion about how a quarter of beef was to be cut up in order to preserve it, and a reference was made to "one of those guys that had surgery over there and how they cut them" (a patient Al had known on the ward had died in surgery the previous day).

On that first night, references were also made to Al not being able to drive successfully because there was "solid ice all across and at the bottom" of a hill: "It looked like it was a couple of two feet thick." This unusual word usage may have been a reference to Al's own two feet, because in an interview he had specifically said: "My legs are cold . . . my feet are cold all the time." Apprehension about the young doctor who would operate on his legs was apparently reflected in a dream where an unruly kid first kicked someone in the shins, then went on a rampage, "beating the hell out of a bunch of grown men" by kicking them "right under the kneecap" so that "everyone would go down." The dreamer indicated, "I, we, was all half-scared of him," but eventually the dreamer grabbed him from behind.

In his daily behavior at the hospital before the operation, the nurses saw him as "a very friendly, talkative person who derived genuine satisfaction from his social interactions." In his fourteen preoperative dreams, he interacted with others as a dream character on thirty-two occasions, but in ten postoperative dreams there were only four interactions. In nineteen of his interactions in the preoperative dreams, Al made friendly gestures and actively assisted and talked with other people, but he only talked with or assisted someone twice in his postoperative dreams. His friendly preoperative waking and dreaming activities seems to represent his efforts to mask his fears about the forthcoming operation by rallying social support from others.

Al's underlying anger at being in a dependent situation was held in check during his waking hours and expressed only indirectly, by swearing, in 86 percent of his preoperative dreams but only 20 percent of his postoperative dreams. Once he successfully survived the crisis of surgery, he vented his anger during his waking days, and the hospital records document three incidents of openly resistant postoperative behavior. The surgery also may have been conceptualized as abuse at the hands of a dominant male authority figure. In the past, Al had responded to abuse from his father by withdrawing and leaving the scene—a pattern similar to the marked reduction in social interactions he displayed in his postoperative dreams and waking life.

Mona was a forty-two-year-old housewife, and mother of four children, who had complained for several years about acute pains in her side. She delayed doing anything about the pain because she had experienced a postpartum psychosis after the birth of her last child and was afraid that a major operation would trigger a similar reaction. Mona was also apprehensive about mental illness because her mother used to threaten her children with suicide and "went into a neurosis for three years in which she never got up and did anything." A few months before her current hospitalization, Mona had undergone some minor surgery and survived with little difficulty. This experience gave her the courage to undergo an exploratory operation on her side for a suspected hernia. In her preoperative interview, when asked what concerned her the most, Mona said there were "a lot of things worse than death in this life and I think mental illness is one of them, especially if a person never recovers."

Mona usually played the role of a hard-working, dedicated, almost compulsive mother. The pain in her side had given her an excuse without which she would never have given herself permission to relax during the day. Thus, although successful surgical treatment might relieve her pain, doing so would simultaneously remove the protective role it played in her life. Two surgeons had previously refused to operate on her. No hernia was found during the current surgery, and the surgeon who removed a little fatty tissue indicated that he had some questions as to whether the symptoms were organic (physical) in origin.

Mona was awakened twelve times for dream reports during the preoperative period, but she was only able to remember two dreams and two brief fragments. On the first night, she reported a fragment involving a swinging bridge. On the third night, she was standing in the bed expressing concern about "this stuff up on my head" (electrodes), and worrying that she might unhook them. Just before her operation, Mona dreamed she had company at home and was trying to serve them. She was carrying a tray containing silverware, and as she walked down the stairs, the silverware all slipped off.

In another dream that night, she went to a doctor's office, where medicine was ordered for her daughter. When the child took the medicine, she started to break out all over and Mona had to return her to the doctor's office. Mona wanted the doctor to see the symptoms while they were still present, because she was afraid they would fade away, but the doctors were not interested. As Mona was trying to explain the doctor's lack of reaction to some friends, she stepped on some glass, "like a windowpane," which caused cuts on her feet that started to spurt blood. The doctor was now trying to hold on to a good-sized vein to stop the blood, but as Mona tried to talk to him, she continued to walk over more "broken windowpanes" and cut herself further.

Mona's fear that her surgery might leave her "unbalanced" seems to be reflected in the dream image in which she lost her balance coming down the stairs and dropped the silverware, and in her poorly coordinated walking on the broken glass, which was "all in pieces." It also would be difficult to stay balanced on a swinging bridge or standing in bed. It seems, too, that Mona was sensitive about being ignored by doctors, wanted them to see symptoms before they faded away, and eventually created a serious enough emer-

In the surgery study, one female subject feared surgery would leave her "unbalanced." She'd had dreams about losing her balance coming down the stairs. High and Low by M.C. Escher. (M.C. Escher/Cordon Art-Baarn-Holland. All rights reserved)

gency to require medical attention in her dream. Then, even as a doctor tried to help, she continued to engage in self-injurious behavior by repeatedly stepping on more windowpanes ("pains" that are invisible and can be found in every home).

The threat of instability that was so prominent in her poorly recalled preoperative dreams was almost totally absent in the nine postoperative dreams she recalled. It seems that once she accepted that she had survived the operation without becoming mentally unbalanced, she was able to put this concern aside and direct her attention to previously neglected topics. The major themes that emerged then seem to be the conflict between being an adequate mother and being free of responsibility, between being nurtured and having fun.

The stress activated in a second study might be considered a form of "emotional surgery." The subjects were four undergraduate students (two male, two female) who volunteered to participate in group therapy sessions. The group met for two hours a night, four times a week, for three weeks. During the first week they were encouraged to talk openly about themselves, to express emotions, and to interact honestly with one another. During the second and third weeks, each subject took a turn serving as the primary focus of the group for two consecutive sessions and was encouraged to be as frank as possible in expressing fears, conflicts, and memories. The group responded with questions, personal reactions, and interpretations. Subjects spent five nights in the sleep laboratory before the study began, and two nights in the laboratory following the sessions in which they were the focus of attention.

Although the four subjects had very different problems, interpersonal styles, and defenses, striking consistencies were found for each between his or her personality and the content of his or her dreams. A few examples will be given from each group member's dreams to show how they represent an effort to process the stress created in interacting with the other members and the therapist.

Hal was a socially isolated, obese young man who did not have any satisfactory peer relationships. He had never dated. After his focus session, Hal dreamed he was all alone on a raft in the ocean, but somehow taking correspondence courses. He always found food there, "sort of like it came from Heaven." In describing his dream, Hal said, "I was feeling lost and lonely, but I'd learned to cope with this by myself."

Roger was a psychology major who had been forced into a close but conflictual relationship with his mother after his father died when Roger was quite young. In the group, he tended to take on the role of therapist in relation to other members. After his focus session, he dreamed that a woman jumped into bed and started "playing peek-a-boo games where she would look at people's genital organs." Roger indicated he became embarrassed when she started to look at his genitals, but he tried to act as if it didn't make any difference to him. "Then my mother started to do the same thing and I really got upset and angry. I told her to cut it out." In another dream, in which Roger was dealing with the group, "I had the role of explainer or interpreter. . . . I was trying to explain why I thought the other people in the group had gotten the wrong idea."

Pam was an attractive woman who felt guilty because she thought she had played a role in her younger brother's being sent to a mental hospital, and she also blamed herself for the recent breakup of a longstanding relationship with her boyfriend. Pam used the group for confessing a great deal of emotion, but did so to such an extent that she overplayed the patient role. The night before her first focus session, Pam was very upset and had gone to see Roger; they eventually had intercourse that night. In one of her dreams following the first focus session, Pam had a date: "Part of the time he was Roger and part of the time the guy I'm going with." In another dream that night, Pam was trying to analyze herself and was talking to someone to "find out something about myself . . . and they couldn't help me . . . my feelings for them were very mixed up." Pam described her efforts to figure out how she felt about herself as follows: "It just reminded me of a great big thick glass and just scratching on it because you wanted to get through it or something and just being helpless." In still another dream that night, Pam was sitting in a classroom and the teacher had the therapist's personality. She had to take a psychology test, but when she put on her reading glasses "it made everything blurry and hurt my eyes." (The dreamer cried frequently during group sessions.)

The last member of the group was Jackie. She had very long hair, wore a sweatshirt, denims, and high-heeled boots, and described herself as a "nonconformist." Jackie had a seductive attitude toward the therapist. In her first focus session, Jackie revealed that she had previously gotten involved with a professor and went to a rented room with him one night, but they didn't have intercourse because of the lack of time and because she had a very small vagina. She later discovered that her vagina would need to be incised in order for her to have intercourse. After a focus session, Jackie dreamed she was talking to the therapist and he was telling the dreamer about some of his "exploits of wild drinking times." Jackie said, "I felt like we were friends." Then she and the therapist were taking turns drinking from a water fountain in the dark, but Jackie was feeling shy and apprehensive. In a different section of that same dream, Jackie was drinking at a nightclub where there were three go-go girls. Jackie felt extremely uncomfortable because the dancers seemed so hard and unreal. Jackie described the dancers as not even seeming human and said, "One of the dancers wasn't even partially clothed. . . . I was amazed at her vagina. It seemed like a little tiny, tiny hole. That's when I was most disturbed." Jackie was the only member who sought out the therapist for individual sessions after the group ended.

The results from the surgery and group therapy studies confirm countless clinical observations that stress intensifies the use of the adaptive mechanisms that people typically employ to maintain psychological equilibrium in their waking lives. These coping efforts often appear magnified in dreams. Following the focus session, Hal dealt with his loneliness by resorting to the mechanism of withdrawal and dreamed he was alone on a raft in the ocean; Jackie, who felt awkward because of her small vagina, used the mechanism of displacement

and dreamed of a go-go dancer whose genitals were far more diminutive than hers. The results of these two studies offer support for claims that dreams serve as nocturnal mirrors reflecting the concerns and adaptive patterns of waking life.

DO DREAMS REFLECT CONTINUITY OR COMPENSATION?

Does a dream about murdering someone mean that the dreamer is likely to murder that person when awake, or does it mean the opposite, that the dreamer is unlikely to commit murder because he has discharged his hostile feelings in his dreams? That question has plagued every student of dreams, but the answer remains elusive. The continuity hypothesis is that dreams act as a mirror to reflect our waking personality; the compensation hypothesis is that dreams show the reverse of our waking personality. One of the principal difficulties in selecting one hypothesis or the other lies in defining what is meant by personality and what constitutes a reflection of personality. Let me illustrate this dilemma by examining two studies frequently cited as supporting the compensatory position.

In an experiment involving social isolation, five male subjects deprived of social contact for fifteen hours subsequently reported dreams in which they had significantly more social interactions than were present on other laboratory nights.[39] It's certainly true that these subjects' dreaming activities were the opposite of that day's waking behavior and therefore apparently showed compensation. But it's also very possible that these subjects were lonely and engaged in extensive waking fantasies about being with others. If other people were "on their mind" during the day or before falling asleep, then their dreaming imagery of being with others is consistent or continuous with their waking imagery.

The other study was carried out by a colleague of mine, Peter Hauri, who worked in my laboratory for a number of years.[40] In Peter's earlier dissertation work, his subjects engaged in a different activity for six hours each day before sleeping in the laboratory: physical exercise, mental tests (study), or relaxation. When Peter's study is mentioned by others, it is generally reported that his subjects showed less physical activity in their dreams after participating in daytime physical exercise. This claim is only partially true.

After Peter's subjects were awakened, they verbalized their dream reports and rated them on several scales before returning to sleep. His subjects did rate their dreams as containing less physical activities on their exercise night, but this may have occurred because his subjects felt tired and they projected their waking tiredness onto their dream ratings without carefully considering the actual content of their dreams. When I made blind scorings of all three nights' dreams from Peter's subjects, we found that on the exercise night his subjects engaged in significantly *more* solitary physical and movement activities in their dreams than they did following the study night. These results tend to support the continuity hypothesis, because subjects who engaged in more waking physical ac-

tivity dreamed of more physical activity. The thorny question then arises as to which is the more adequate measure of physical activities in dreams: the tired subjects' quick numerical rating of their dreams, or my more extended blind scoring of their dreams?

Another finding from Peter's study deserves special mention. None of the over twenty EEG and physiological variables measured during sleep correlated very highly with the subjects' ratings of having slept soundly, but subjects claimed they slept more soundly on nights when they had not participated in an active manner in their dreams. I also rated the dreams for the amount of personal involvement that the dreamer seemed to have experienced, and confirmed that on the nights subjects judged they had slept most poorly they also showed the greatest personal involvement in their dreams. The amount of effort we expend in our dreams may have a direct bearing upon how tired or refreshed we are in the morning, and our dream moods may carry over into our morning moods.

If we are very active in our dreams, climbing mountains or struggling to figure out a difficult mental problem, we will probably wake up feeling tired. This is even more likely if our strenuous efforts fail to achieve success. If we reach our desired goal, getting to the top of the mountain or solving an intellectual task, the elation accompanying the accomplishment may override the sense of fatigue that would ordinarily be associated with the dreamed-of exertion.

The role of presleep internal states has been investigated by depriving subjects of fluids and examining their subsequent dream reports. The first EEG-REM study in 1958 by Dement and a coworker involved three subjects who restricted their intake of fluids for twenty-four hours before sleeping in the laboratory.[41] They followed this regime on five different occasions, and fifteen REM reports were obtained. The investigators reported: "In no case did the dream content involve an awareness of thirst or descriptions of actually drinking something." They reported that ten dreams seemed completely unrelated but that some relationship may have existed in five dreams. Incredibly, an example of a dream they rated as having only a "possible" relation to thirst was the following: "While watching TV I saw a commercial. Two kids were asked what they wanted to drink and one kid started yelling, 'Coca-Cola, Orange, Pepsi,' and everything." Although it is true that the subject was not actually drinking, the dream certainly seems saturated with thirst-related imagery.

Another study employed eighteen nurses who worked at night and slept in the laboratory during the day.[42] The nurses, who had been deprived of fluids and food for eight to nine hours before arriving at the lab, were presented with a salty meal before they went to sleep. This arrangement was referred to as the thirst-alone condition. The same procedure was repeated on another day, but just before each REM awakening, the nurses received a low-level, tape-recorded verbal message: "a cool delicious drink of water." This arrangement was known as the thirst-verbal stimulus condition. On another occasion there was no prior deprivation of food or fluids, and the subjects were given a nonsalty meal before sleep.

The REM reports were judged for thirst-related content using criteria much more flexible than those used in the previous study. Included on the scale were words related to thirst sensations (thirsty), thirst satisfiers (beer), foods with high water content (watermelon), water in its natural state (river), thirst activities (sip or gulp), places associated with thirst (bar or oasis), persons associated with thirst (bartender), and inanimate objects associated with thirst (glass or bottle). Use of such a scale seems warranted because presleep stimuli are very rarely directly incorporated into dreams.

The most thirst-related words occured in the thirst-verbal stimulus condition, the second most in the thirst-alone condition, and the fewest in the control condition. Subjects whose dream reports suggested drive-frustration rated themselves as thirstier and drank more fluids after their deprivation session, while subjects who had had more gratifying dreams, in which themes of drinking or eating were represented, rated themselves as less thirsty and drank fewer fluids. The results of this study can be looked at in several ways. Viewed from a compensatory perspective, the findings showed that greater deprivation of water produced more thirst-related words, but as in the social isolation experiment, it's possible that the thirsty subjects were preoccupied with thirst, making their thirst-related dream imagery continuous with their waking imagery. The other finding, involving the relation between dreams and subsequent waking behavior, is very provocative and suggests that if need gratification is obtained in a dream, there may be less need to gratify that need in waking life. Perhaps in addition to the well-recognized contribution that "day residue" plays in setting the stage for subsequent dreams, we should consider that "dream residue" may influence subsequent waking moods and behaviors.

COLOR IN DREAMS

In another study, nine subjects were deprived of exposure to certain color stimuli by wearing colored goggles during every waking moment for five to eight days. Because the goggles interfered with the passage of all but red light, the subjects almost literally were looking at the world through rose-colored glasses.[43]

All subjects reported a noticeable increase in red-orange dream objects, while the presence of blue and green imagery decreased. To identify accurately the colors in their dreams, subjects had learned over sixty color names, including such exotic varieties as "Coca-Cola" red and "interstate highway" green. The most frequently reported color was a reddish tint similar to that which the goggles produced in the waking state. On one of the goggle nights, a subject reported a dream in which the setting resembled Central Park, but said, "On the scene there was a pervading amber tint. . . . The sky was a dark, reddish brown. This is similar to the way things look through the goggles, but not exactly the same." By way of contrast, on one of the baseline nights before wearing goggles, a subject reported a dream full of varied color: "There were white mums, pink roses and sky blue petunias. On the right was a light green radiator cover. . . . The boy was wearing a white T-shirt with yellow elephants on it and green pants." The investigators reported that more than half of all the dream scenes in the goggle phase had wholly or pervasively incorporated the goggle-altered daytime experience.

When the data were analyzed by time of appearance during the night, it was found that the goggle-colored objects appeared almost entirely during the early parts of the night and all but disappeared after the third REM period. This pattern is typical of most dream studies; recent impressions are manifested most commonly at the beginning of the night. To the investigators' surprise, reports containing color-influenced imagery disappeared to almost the original baseline values on the very first night after subjects stopped wearing the goggles. This study certainly seems to support the continuity hypothesis. Subjects who lived in a red-dominated world in their waking lives also lived in a red-dominated world in their dreaming lives, at least during the early part of the night. An important clue to understanding the basis of continuity between waking and dreaming imagery was uncovered in the time-of-night effect and the washout effect as soon as subjects discontinued wearing the goggles. It appears that it is the deeply ingrained facets of waking personality that continue to shine through in dreams; brief exposures to experimental stimuli or environments have only fleeting effects on dreams unless those stimuli have a strong affective charge.

I'd like to pursue the topic of color in dreams a bit further before concluding my discussion of presleep stimuli. A large number of nonlaboratory studies have examined the frequency of color in dreams.

Although figures vary quite a bit from study to study, a spontaneous reference to color is typically made in about 20 to 25 percent of nonlaboratory dreams. But there are some interesting exceptions.

In a study describing the dreams of twenty-six deaf college students, investigators claimed that color appeared in 92 percent of the dreams of the congenitally deaf, 75 percent of the dreams of those who became deaf before age five, and only 17 percent of those whose deafness was acquired after age five, a figure comparable to that for hearing subjects.[44] The dreams of the congenitally deaf were described as characteristically being in bright color and containing primary colors in high saturation and intensity. It appears that the early and persistent deprivation of one sensory modality—hearing—led to the enhancement of another sensory modality—color perception.

Individuals for whom color perception is a significant feature of their waking lives are also sensitive to the presence of color in their dreams. A group of art students (mostly painters and a few writers), science students (majoring in physical sciences, premed, and mathematics), and engineering students turned in reports of their most recent dreams and completed a test of creativity. Color was spontaneously reported in the dreams of 50 percent of the art students, 16 percent of the science students, and none of the engineering students.[45] Even when the investigator specifically asked about the possibility of color, 45 percent of the science and engineering students denied that their dreams possessed any color qualities. The art stu-

dents reported significantly more imaginative dreams and also obtained higher scores on the test of creativity.

In another study involving female students in a creative writing class, the students chosen by their instructor as displaying greater literary inventiveness and originality of theme reported twice as many color references in their dreams as did the students with the least imaginative literary capacities. When color was used by the less-imaginative students, it was almost always in connection with clothing references,[46] while the other students were sensitive to the colors in flowers, skies, buildings and decorations. Another study found that individuals of both sexes who placed greater reliance on feelings than on thinking, reported a significantly greater percentage of color dreams.[47]

Color is more commonly reported in laboratory dreams, primarily because the investigator is able to inquire about it almost immediately after the subject is awakened. The most systematic laboratory study of color in dreams was carried out on thirty-eight subjects, who provided eighty-seven instances of dream recall from one hundred awakenings.[48] The investigators reported that distinct colors were present in 70 percent of these dreams and vague colors in an additional 13 percent. Only two subjects failed to report color in their dreams. Color responses were reported spontaneously in 25 percent of the dreams, a figure similar to that for nonlaboratory dreams, where no investigator was present to question the dreamer. A spontaneous example would be, "I saw all the girls come in and they were wearing bright red bathing suits." When subjects were questioned more carefully about their dream imagery, mention of color tripled in frequency. One woman said she dreamed she saw a bar of soap in the bathtub with a baby. When the experimenter asked what the soap looked like, she replied, "Like any bar of soap looks. It was round, it was pink, and the baby was playing with it in the bathtub." The category of "vaguely colored" dreams used by these investigators included reports in which the dream, or part of it, appeared in "vague, dull, light, or tinted colors."

An innovative approach to investigating the color characteristics of dreams was carried out by two psychologists from the University of Chicago.[49] To provide a comparison stimulus, a single photo of a young woman sitting on a couch was reproduced in 129 color variations, with different combinations of saturation and clarity (sharp versus diffuse or fogged), as well as figure versus background differences. After their REM awakenings, subjects scanned the 129 photos and selected the one which best captured the visual characteristics of their last dream scene, and also their best-remembered dream scene. The investigators claimed that subjects generally had little difficulty in matching photos to the dream scenes on the basis of their visual characteristics. Their results indicated that the recalled dream images differed most from normal waking images in their tendency toward color desaturation and loss of background clarity. The color saturation and figure-ground clarity were significantly lower for the first REM period of the night, indicating that colors get more pronounced as the night goes on. Stable individual differences were shown from night to night in the way various aspects of color were reported in subjects' dreams.

The findings from the studies just reviewed indicate that color appears in dreams with much greater frequency than is generally acknowledged. The saturation or intensity of color in dreams seems to vary along a continuum. Approximately 20 percent of color dreams display a palette of rather pale or pastel tints, similar to the effect one would get by placing a light layer of gauze over a camera lens. Such dreams apparently also display blurred edges or boundaries between objects. If attention is not quickly directed toward color elements, they seem to fade quickly, as if the daylight of waking life bleaches them away.

There are also a small percentage of dreams in which colors are greatly intensified and radiate with a bright psychedelic quality. In some of my own dreams, phosphorescent colors have glared with such Day-Glo brilliance that my attention was magnetically drawn toward them. My personal opinion is that there is often a strong correlation between the emotional significance of a dream and the intensity of the colors appearing in it. When a dream is rendered in a vivid, vibrant, Van Gogh-like style, it's calling out for immediate attention and subsequent reflection.

Although the overwhelming majority of dreams appear in color, there are situations in which the message of the dream mandates that it be conveyed in black and white. If the dreamer needs to realize that he or she is viewing some waking situation in a black-and-white, all-or-none fashion, the dream imagery may include the keyboard of a piano or the stripes of a referee's shirt. If a dreamer needs to be sensitized to how gray, confining, or confusing his or her outlook is toward life, dreams may be cast in somber, prison-gray tones or the dreamer may wander around in a fog. If dreams are pervasively black, the dreamer may be struggling with a depression that is filtering out the possibilities for color and satisfaction in his or her life.

SIGNIFICANCE OF PRESLEEP STIMULI

The presleep studies can be organized into two classes. The first class includes the film, surgery, and group therapy studies and the second, the studies involving social isolation, exercise, thirst, and colored goggles.

In the first class, subjects were placed in multidimensional, emotionally arousing situations or were selected because they were already in such situations. These subjects seldom represented or incorporated the stressful or traumatic event directly in their reported dreams. The emotional material was more typically reflected in indirect or symbolic references. Each dreamer exhibited a recognizable style and focal concerns that carried across the dreams from several nights, a "dreamprint" just as unique as a fingerprint. The examples were given of Mr. A, who brought concerns about "phallic rivalry" into several night's dreams even though exposed to different types of films, and Al, who before his surgery continually dreamed of repairing defective machines. These studies underline the importance of knowing the emotional significance of the

experimental stimulus for each subject, as well as being aware of the unique constellation of coping strategies each dreamer employs, if the role of presleep stimuli is to be evaluated.

The second class of studies exposed subjects to far milder, unidimensional stimuli, generally involving slight modifications in their physical condition. Except for the colored-goggle study, only a single night of dreaming was evaluated after exposure to the presleep stimulus, so recognizable "dreamprints" were more difficult to detect. Interpretation concerning the possible incorporation of the presleep stimulus, which often involved some form of deprivation, seemed to depend upon how sensitive the scoring system was. The investigators knew what they were looking for—evidence of fatigue, thirst, or a certain color in subsequent dreams—but might disagree as to whether they had found proof of a stimulus's influence. A clear example of this occurred in the thirst studies. Unless the subject reported personally drinking in a dream, the initial investigators concluded that the thirst condition had no effect upon later dreams, but a different investigator, willing to score thirst-related objects, such as bottles, and settings where drinking occurred, like bars, detected a significant difference between dreams following thirst-deprived and nondeprived days.

An issue related to the question of whether presleep stimuli are incorporated into dreams directly or indirectly is the question of whether dream experience is continuous with waking experience or a form of compensation for daytime lacks. It's difficult to design a study in which this issue can be straightforwardly evaluated.

The social isolation study provides a good example of the problems which arise in evaluating such studies. Although subjects didn't have *physical* access to other people, they continued to have *imaginal* access to them. To test the compensatory hypothesis, it must be shown that the lack of waking satisfaction or gratification in a selected area of functioning results in an increase of dreaming imagery involving that selected area. How can we rule out the possibility of imagined satisfaction?

Imagination can have powerful effects. As demonstrated in the study by Gary Rogers, women fantasizing about a sexually arousing situation showed a significant elevation in their measures of vaginal pulse amplitude. A male fantasizing about a sexual encounter can achieve just as firm an erection as if physical stimulation were employed. So until some way is found to eliminate imaginal activity, conclusions about the effects of presleep deprivation or other conditions to test the compensatory/continuity issue in dreams will remain uncertain.

Another troublesome measurement question arises in evaluating dream imagery for the presence of the presleep stimulus. Suppose we had a study in which subjects were exposed to presleep conditions that markedly increased their usual waking levels of hostility, and that it was found they personally engaged in less frequent hostile actions in their dreams after such a stimulus than on other nights. Such a result might suggest compensation, since an inverse relationship existed between waking and dreaming expressions of hostility. But how would the results be interpreted if it were found that all the dream characters *except for the dreamer* engaged in significantly more hostile activities in comparison to other nights? What are the relevant criteria to consider? Should it be the total number of hostile acts in the dream, regardless of who commits them, or should only the dreamer's activities be considered? Until more careful and detailed theoretical positions clarify the compensation/continuity dilemma, the answer remains up in the air.

THE EFFECTS OF STIMULI PRESENTED DURING REM SLEEP UPON DREAMS

The first experimental study using EEG-REM techniques to explore the effects of external stimuli during sleep upon dreams was undertaken in 1958 by William Dement and a psychiatric coworker, Edward Wolpert. Three external stimuli were presented during REM periods: an auditory tone, a flashing lamp shining directly on the sleeper, and a fine spray of cold water from a hypodermic syringe. The water spray was incorporated in 42 percent of the REM dream reports, the light flashes in 23 percent, and the tone in only 9 percent. The minimal results for the tone may have been due to the fact that it was a single stimulus that lasted for only five seconds, while the light continued to flash and the water remained on the subject's skin. In response to the tone, one dreamer thought a plane had crashed outside his house; the

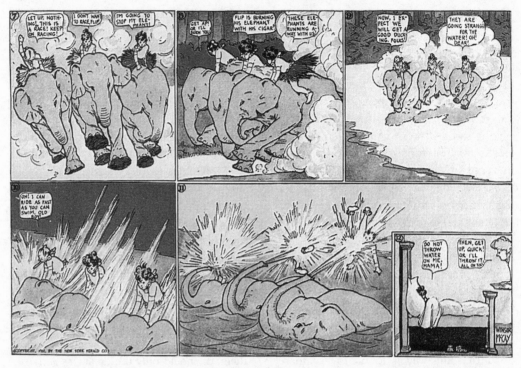

A spray of cold water was the most easily incorporated sensory stimulus in laboratory dream studies. In this adventure, from the cartoon series about Little Nemo's adventures in dream land, water thrown by Nemo's mother is incorporated into his dream.

flashing light evoked dreams of seeing lightning or shooting stars; and the water spray was associated with dreams in which there was a sudden rainfall or a roof beginning to leak.

Dement and Wolpert noticed that if a large body movement occurred, the continuity of the dream was interrupted. The presence of a body movement seemed to signal the conclusion of some specific dream activity, because the dreamer frequently reported being located in a different setting or being engaged in different activities after the body movement occurred.

The course of time in dreaming was investigated by presenting a stimulus to the subject, timing the interval between its presentation and the REM awakening, and then looking at how extensive was the dream action following the stimulus incorporation. Generalizing from the ten examples available, the researchers concluded, "The amount of dream action in the interval between the modifying stimulus and the awakening did not vary far from the amount of action that would have been expected to take place during identical time in reality."[50] There are obvious limits, of course, to this rough equivalence of dream time and elapsed time. A dream wouldn't have to last five hours, for example, for one to dream of boarding a flight in New York and deplaning in Los Angeles.

The researchers provided a good example of their timing study. Cold water had been sprayed on a subject's uncovered back after a ten-minute REM period, and they woke him thirty seconds later. In the first part of his dream, there was a complex description of acting in a play. The dreamer then described walking behind the leading lady, who collapsed: "I ran over to her and felt water dripping on my back and head. The roof was leaking. I was very puzzled why she fell down and decided some plaster must have fallen on her. I looked up and there was a hole in the roof. I dragged her over to the side of the stage and began pulling the curtains. Just then I woke up." It would have taken the subject about thirty seconds to have pulled the leading lady aside after he became aware of the roof leaking.

Another investigator administered painless shocks to the wrist and woke subjects with a buzzer either thirty seconds or three minutes later. Unusual wrist sensations were reported in 56 percent of the dreams. One subject, for example, reported he was trying to ignore someone who was tugging at his sleeve. When subjects were asked to estimate whether these wrist sensations or tinglings occurred more nearly thirty seconds or three minutes before the buzzer, he found that: "In 11 of the 12 instances where the stimulus was incorporated into the dream, subjects judged it as having occurred at a time corresponding to the actual time of the stimulation."[51]

Subjects associated short REM periods (five minutes) with short dreams and long REM periods (fifteen minutes) with long dreams. The two studies just discussed indicate that a more precise temporal correlation may be present. By using incorporation of an external stimulus into an ongoing dream as a reference point, it became possible to compare elapsed real time with elapsed dream time. The results indicate that events take about as long to unfold in a dream as they would in waking experience. This finding discounts Maury's speculation that he experienced his long and detailed guillotine dream the moment the rail of the headboard fell on his neck.

The range of stimulus conditions that could be incorporated was expanded by other investigators. When the upper part of the hospital-type bed on which they were sleeping was raised or lowered, subjects reported dreams of falling, flying, or riding a motor scooter.[52] The same report mentioned that a subject sleeping on a pad containing rubber tubing through which cold water was flowing had dreamed of getting food from a refrigerator, and when warm water was introduced, the dreamer reported experiencing a warm day. These thermal inputs had an effect upon dreams in 25 percent of the cases. A Swiss investigator exposed his subjects to three different levels of room temperature.[53] Subjects were awakened during each REM period and the next day assessed the emotional quality of their dreams. It was found that the colder room temperature increased the intensity of dream emotions and that these emotions became increasingly unpleasant.

Sixteen olfactory stimuli of various types, such as coffee, wood alcohol, roses, spoiled food, cinnamon, onions, dog feces, and hand lotion were introduced in another study for one minute after a subject had displayed a minimum of five minutes of REM sleep. The five subjects, who were reported to have a strong olfactory sense and good dream recall, were given a total of forty-eight trials during the course of fifteen nights. Incorporation was present in 22 percent of the dreams. One subject exposed to a freshly cut lemon reported the following dream: "I dreamed I was in Golden Gate Park. I was walking by some gardenias. They were just opening. All of a sudden, I could smell the gardenias, but they smelled like lemons instead of gardenias."[54]

The authors claimed pleasant stimuli were incorporated much more frequently than unpleasant stimuli. This finding surprised me because about two-thirds of dreams from normal subjects deal with unpleasant emotions or outcomes. Since dreams generally draw their material from the preceding sixteen hours of waking life, perhaps the brief experimental stimuli were able to be processed in a more positive manner because the subjects did not have time to dwell on them. Or perhaps the classification system was ambiguous: Is coffee a pleasant or unpleasant stimulus? Or cinnamon? Marked individual preferences probably exist in classifying olfactory stimuli as pleasant or not.

Two psychologists at Chicago, Alan Rechtschaffen and David Foulkes, made a frontal assault to investigate directly the role of vision upon dream imagery.[55] They selected three young adult males and taped their eyes open to discover whether stimuli presented to their open eyes during REM periods would be incorporated in dream reports. The stimuli were a coffee pot, a waving white handkerchief, a red-covered book, a card with a black X on it, and another card with the printed words Do Not Disturb. One of the experimenters quietly entered the room, held the stimulus in front of the subject's open eyes, and illuminated it with a small light for periods ranging from fifteen to seventy-eight seconds. Subjects were awakened within about ten seconds of the time the light was turned off. None of the thirty experimental trials yielded any direct perception of the stimulus object, nor was there any reference to the presence of the experimenter, who had been standing close to the subject in order to expose the stimuli. Four reports, however, included images of bright lights.

Auditory stimuli have been the most frequent class of sensory stimuli investigated. When scrambled noise was employed as a stimulus in one study, it was incorporated in 43 percent of the dream reports.[56] One of Dement's students used tape recordings of familiar sounds, such as a rooster crowing, a steam locomotive, a bugle playing reveille, a barking dog, traffic noise, and a speech by Martin Luther King, Jr. These more interesting sound stimuli influenced dream content in 56 percent of the awakenings. The locomotive sound was the most effective and traffic noise the least.[57]

The first REM study of personally meaningful verbal stimuli, carried out in 1963 by Ralph Berger, a British researcher, has become a classic in the field.[58] Berger paid careful attention to all details of his study, such as insuring that the verbal stimuli were, in fact, emotionally meaningful for the subjects. A short personal history was obtained from each of the four male and four female unmarried subjects. Among the biographical questions were inquiries about the names of the subject's current or past friends of the opposite sex. Subjects had galvanic skin responses (GSRs) recorded from the palms of their hands while a list of words, including the names elicited in the interview, were read to them. Berger selected the two names that produced the strongest GSRs and two neutral names that did not provoke any GSRs and were not known to the subjects. The neutral names had the same number of syllables, but a maximum contrast in sound to the emotional names. The tape-recorded names played to female subjects were spoken by a female voice, and those played to male subjects by a male voice. One name was presented during each REM period.

Eighty-nine dreams, approximately eleven from each subject, were obtained, and 54 percent were scored as possessing a "definite connection" to the stimulus name. Berger reported:

> There were no appreciable differences in the number of correct matchings made for emotional or neutral stimuli or in relation to the sex of the subjects, or between subjects, either when the matchings were performed by the subjects or by the independent judge.

What was intriguing about Berger's analyses were the different methods by which the incorporations were made. The most common category was labeled as "asso-

nance." This term means that there was a similarity in the sound of the stimulus name and the sound of the word in the dream narrative. In response to the stimulus word "John," one subject reported a dream about driving a car accompanied by two boys. The following words were mentioned in the report: "moved *on*," "Marchm*ont*," "going *on*." Just as a poet struggles for new words to rhyme with June and moon, it seems the dreamer's mind is trying to come up with sounds similar to the stimulus word. When the stimulus word was "Kenny," it seemed as if *K* sounds were emphasized: "I was at the *con*cert . . . some *Scots character* was—I think he was mainly a *comedian* . . . the scenery was some ro*ck* with a *crack* in it." Thus, although the objects bear no conceptual relationship to each other, the words "concert," "character," "Scots," "comedian," "rock," and "crack" all share the *K* sound found in the stimulus name Kenny. The assonance category accounted for almost twice as many incorporations as the other three groups combined.

The "association" category involved situations where the linkage could only be made because of the subject's personal associations. For example, to the stimulus word "Richard," one subject dreamed of having been to a sale at a big shop in the center of Edinburgh. This dream doesn't seem, on the surface, to be related to the stimulus word, until we learn that "Richard" was the name of the shop in the center of Edinburgh to which the dreamer had gone a day or so earlier for a sale. The "direct" category included dreams in which the stimulus name was directly mentioned in the dream report. The last category, "representation," included those cases where a subject would dream of Helen, for example, after hearing her name pronounced. When any of the incorporated stimuli appeared in the dream events, their appearance was often described as having a strange, odd, sudden, or vivid quality.

Although Berger reported that there was no difference in frequency of incorporation between meaningful and neutral verbal stimuli, a group of researchers at the V.A. hospital in Cincinnati found, in two studies, that high-meaning words (names of family and friends) were incorporated much more frequently than low-meaning names (designated by the subjects as unfamiliar).[59] One possible reason for this difference may have been that, in selecting meaningful names on the basis of elevated GSRs, Berger identified a name with negative connotations, such as that of an old boyfriend, whom the dreamer would want to avoid. If so, the subject's unconscious attitude might have been, "That's the last name I want to hear." Also, in the Cincinnati study, the names were recorded in the subject's own voice. The effects of hearing one's own voice can have a powerful influence upon the subsequent dream process.

In two studies carried out by another team of investigators, nineteen subjects, primarily psychiatric residents, were exposed to four words: fountain, pen, knee, and cap.[60] The words were recorded in the subject's own voice, and the same four words were recorded in another person's voice matched for the sex, age, and intonation to the dreamer. The rather surprising finding was that in the REM reports obtained after listening to his or her own voice, the dreamer was significantly more

active, assertive, and independent. When the dream reports followed the same words spoken in another person's voice, the dreamer was judged to be more passive and unassertive in his or her dream activities. Another striking result involved the free associations elicited just after the dream was reported. Significantly more active verbs appeared in the free associations following the presentation of the subject's own voice, while the verbs were more passive following dreams stimulated by the other person's voice. This report followed a stimulus in the dreamer's own voice:

> I was talking to someone, it was about civil rights. I used to be active in civil rights groups in Y city. I was talking with some Negro leaders about ways in which their concerns could be heard. I was trying to arrange it so that they could go to speak at the school.

In response to the same stimulus words spoken by another person, a dreamer described being in a conference with some colleagues when his supervisor walked in and attempted to put responsibility for a previous conversation on the dreamer. The dreamer was angry and afraid that the supervisor might fire him or do something to hurt his career.

As in the Berger study, neutral stimulus words were shown to affect dreams. The type of words doesn't seem to matter; who is saying them does. Hearing one's own voice in a dream seems to generate a higher level of energy and initiative. If we take the initiative to speak while awake, we immediately hear our own voice; a strong connection between decision making, action, and awareness of one's own voice is therefore forged. If we hear our own voices in dreams, it apparently calls up the other components of action and decision making. We can't hear our own voices without actively speaking, but we can hear others speaking and remain completely passive.

COMPARISON OF STIMULI INTRODUCED BEFORE AND DURING SLEEP

Visual imagery has been the preferred form for presleep sensory stimuli, but it leads to a "blind alley" when introduced during sleep. Subjects don't "get the picture" even if their eyelids are taped open. At best, subjects manage to incorporate the light associated with visual presentations, but not the details.

The preferred sensory channel for studying stimulus incorporation into ongoing dreams has been the auditory one. Neutral sounds, such as a tone, are generally briefly incorporated into the ongoing dream narrative. More meaningful or complex auditory stimuli, such as an individual's name, may have a more pervasive influence on the general emotional tone and interactions of the dreamer with other characters. The presence of a K-complex in the EEG record may indicate physiologically that the brain has reacted to the sound,[61] but it requires a sensitive evaluation technique to detect the registration of the auditory input upon the mind of the dreamer. Berger found that the most frequent indication of auditory incorporation

was the presence of assonance or "clang" associations (dish-fish-wish).

Such a response had been predicted by Carl Jung in 1918 from his word-association experiments. Finding seven times as many clang reactions during drowsiness as compared to wakeful attention, Jung speculated that "were we to succeed in producing reactions in a person sleeping, clang-reactions would certainly be the exclusive results." They were not the exclusive results in Berger's study, but they occurred twice as frequently as the other three classes of incorporation combined.

Although Berger reported that emotional stimuli were not incorporated more frequently than neutral ones, he did find that dream imagery following the incorporation of emotional names was often more complex and sometimes involved sexual imagery. When the name of his current girlfriend was spoken to one of the male subjects, he dreamed that: "a snake ... emerged out of one of the guitars and the snake snaked out and then snaked back again ... and then there was a flash ... an explosion of some kind." Several sexual symbols appear to be present in this dream: the snake as a penis, the guitar as a vaginal symbol, and the explosion as an orgasm. The guitar can be considered a vaginal symbol because it includes a curved hollow chamber with a hole in the center, and the player's hands move rhythmically back and forth across the opening.

The appearance of sexual imagery in response to minimal stimulation, the mention of a girlfriend's name, suggests that more powerful effects could be obtained if provocative comments were used, such as a girlfriend's voice requesting, "Please make love to me, John." I'm not aware of any studies that have used recordings of voices from other persons well known to the dreamer. A whole range of experimental opportunities would open up if one were to consider comparing recordings of meaningful phrases spoken by the dreamer's parents and by unfamiliar older adults, or by the dreamer's own children and unknown children. Since the dreamer's own voice noticeably increases dream activity and assertiveness, brief recordings of conversations between the research subject and significant others could be expected to be potent REM sleep stimuli. Nature stimuli have rarely been used in dream studies. The sounds of waves crashing, winds blowing, thunder booming, or animals roaring would also seem to possess considerable emotional power.

Stimuli introduced *during* REM sleep must possess considerable emotional importance to affect dream content because their exposure time is so brief. Presleep stimuli, such as films, may last for an hour or more and can be presented several hours before the subject falls asleep, allowing their emotional reverberations ample opportunity to influence subsequent dream imagery.

Through the use of modern REM technology, we now know that external stimuli do not instigate dreaming activity but do influence it. The influence may be transitory, as in the case of a bell sounding during REM sleep, or pervasive, as when an emotional film of a bloody birth is watched before sleep. No prediction can be made as to how a given subject will process stimulus material without considerable knowledge of his or her concerns and conflicts. While viewing the birth film, one subject may respond primarily to the sexual implications of seeing an exposed vagina, another to the sight of blood, another to the mother's imagined pain, and another with joy to the arrival of new life.

Within any conflict area, responses can also vary widely. If the birth film activates sexual associations, one male may feel aroused and desire to fondle the vagina; one may be embarrassed by a memory of finding blood stains on his clothing after having intercourse with a menstruating woman; and another may experience feelings of phallic inadequacy because the enlarged vagina in the film reminds him of some woman who made derogatory comments about the size of his penis. Before we can speculate what the mirror of dreams will show, we need to know something about the person who will be standing before it.

DREAMING OUTSIDE REM SLEEP

The research findings reviewed so far in this chapter have been based on waking subjects from REM sleep. It has been widely assumed that dreaming is exclusively associated with REM periods.

Dreaming and REM sleep have been considered to be so synonymous that some authors have referred to REM sleep as "D" sleep, to indicate that it was the stage of sleep in which dreaming occurred. Although early investigators reported a small percentage of dream reports from non-REM sleep, they concluded that the content was merely remembered from a preceding REM period. REM sleep was held in such an exalted position as to be termed "a third state of human existence": there was the waking state, the sleeping state, and the REM state.

The black-and-white view equating REM sleep with dreaming began to be revised around 1960. In a study by a group of investigators at the Downstate Medical Center in New York in 1959, subjects were classified as dreamers or nondreamers on the basis of a questionnaire.[62] They found that subjects classified as dreamers, on the average, reported content more often after non-REM awakenings (53 percent) than did nondreamers after REM awakenings (46 percent). This pattern became more pronounced as the night progressed; dreamers reported more content from non-REM awakenings during the last four hours of sleep (67 percent) than during the first four hours (17 percent).

David Foulkes, in his 1960 doctoral dissertation at Chicago, focused attention on non-REM reports; he published his results in a 1962 article entitled "Dream Reports from Different Stages of Sleep."[63] That article drastically changed subsequent theorizing about mental activity during sleep. The eight subjects in Foulkes's study were awakened four times each night, once a week, for seven weeks. Awakenings were made after various durations of REM sleep, as well as during various stages of non-REM sleep. When subjects were awakened, they were asked if they had been dreaming. If they indicated they had not been dream-ing, they were then asked, "Was anything going through your mind?" Following REM awakenings, subjects typically reported that they had been dreaming, following non-REM awakenings, that they had been "thinking."

Foulkes gave the following example of a typical thinking report after a non-REM awakening of an IRS employee: "I was thinking of tax exemption and it skipped around to something else." When the experimenter asked what the subject had been thinking about the tax exemption, he replied, "Oh, one of the points made in the class . . . was that you had to provide over half of the support of a person in order to claim them as dependents." This sounds very similar to what the subject might have replied during his waking hours if a friend had said, "A penny for your thoughts." The content was what might be expected from an IRS employee whose mind was wandering or who was engaged in some form of reverie.

After subjects reported their mental activity, they were asked a number of questions concerning their imagery—whether other people were present, whether color was seen, the nature of the setting, if the subject engaged in physical activity, and whether the content seemed coherent. Subjects completed a Dream Information Survey the next morning and were asked to rate the intensity of the various dimensions associated with their imagery. Foulkes concluded that REM reports were longer, displayed more intense visual imagery, and showed a higher degree of integration and continuity; specifically, the dreamer often engaged in physical movement, several scene shifts occurred, and the dreamer displayed more emotional involvement. The non-REM reports seemed to involve more recent events or daytime concerns of the subject without too much distortion, although some of them did sound very dreamlike.

Several other papers soon appeared confirming and extending Foulkes's findings.[64] There was agreement that non-REM imagery started to take on more "dreamy" aspects during the latter part of the night; a late non-REM report might resemble a REM report from early in the night. Nevertheless, the two types of reports could be successfully discriminated when judges were given a REM and a non-REM report by the same subject from approximately the same time of night.[65] The exact nature of the cues employed by the judges was not specified. If they considered, in a composite fashion, the qualities of vividness, distortion, elaboration, and degree of visual hallucinatory quality, they were able to pick out the REM from the non-REM reports with about 90 percent accuracy.

Foulkes further pursued his interest in the various kinds of mental activity present during sleep by exploring the mentation that occurs in the very first stages of sleep. He and a psychiatrist from Chicago, Gerald Vogel, woke subjects approximately six times during the beginning phases of sleep when various patterns of EEG and EOG activity were observable.[66] They were interested in the presence of alpha activity and slow eye movements (SEMs) in association with descending Stage 1 EEGs. After subjects gave their reports of mental activity, they were asked many of the same questions about the nature of their imagery as in Foulkes's non-REM study.

Foulkes and Vogel found that some kind of mental content was present in over 95 percent of the awakenings. Over 80 percent of these reports contained visual imagery, while auditory and bodily imagery each occurred in about 25 percent. These reports from the hypnagogic state, that is, the period when the subject was falling asleep, generally seemed emotionally flat, with mildly positive and mildly negative feelings appearing about equally often. When falling asleep, subjects initially reported a loss of volitional control, followed by a loss of awareness of their immediate environment; in the final stage of the experience, there was an increased sense that the experienced events were actually happening in the "real" world. In other words, the subjects accepted the "hallucinatory" imagery because the people and events seemed real to them. Individual differences in mental experiences during the hypnagogic period were much larger than those found in REM-period dreaming.

When Foulkes and Vogel tabulated the percentage of "dreamlike" reports (those referring to a dramatic episode which seemed to the subject to be "really" happening), about 75 percent of the descending Stage 1 and about 40 percent of the alpha activity awakenings yielded "dreams." Subjects were often active participants in these dreams and made frequent references to other people being present. Some of the hypnagogic dreams seemed to occur during a fairly short time span; the imagery seemed more like a succession of snapshots than a movie. The authors suggested that the label, "dreamlet," could be applied to some hypnagogic content. This study indicated that, despite the differences between REM-period dreams and hypnagogic "dreams," there were many striking similarities. The list of products produced by our sleeping mind was thus extended to include dreams, dreamlets, extensive thought patterns, and many hybrid combinations of these mental experiences.

A new conceptualization of the mind's activity during sleep was now required. The previous model, suggested by the early Chicago work, held that dreams emerged abruptly at regular intervals during sleep and were nonexistent in the interim periods. The non-REM and sleep onset findings, however, indicated that there is no period during sleep in which our mind is "blank"; some kind of mental activity is always occurring. This mental activity varies along broad continua of reality, vividness, and descriptive detail, with extremely subtle differences discernible when a moment-by-moment analysis is attempted. A few peaks can be detected, but they rise almost imperceptibly from a background of many smaller peaks and uninterrupted activity.

Foulkes and some coworkers explored personality factors associated with sleep onset in another study involving thirty-two subjects (sixteen males and sixteen females).[67] Each subject slept one night in the laboratory and was awakened seven times. Four of these awakenings were made during either descending Stage 1 EEG or alpha EEG with SEMs. Three REM sleep awakenings were also made. After subjects indicated what they were able to recall, they were asked about the hallucinatory quality of their visual imagery and were asked to classify their state of wakefulness

or sleep just before the experimenter called their name.

Judges rated the reports for aggressive and sexual content as well as for whether the dream seemed pleasant or not. Very little manifest aggressive or sexual content was found in either the hypnagogic or REM reports, and both types were rated similarly on the degree of pleasantness. In addition, all reports were rated on a scale of Dreamlike Fantasy (DF). A score of 0 was given for no content reported, a score of 1 when the subject felt something was going through his mind but reported no content, a score of 2 for everyday conceptual content, and so on. The highest score, of 7, was given for perceptual content that was hallucinatory, bizarre or unusual, and dramatic. The DF scale has been used widely by other investigators and by Foulkes in almost all his later studies. Foulkes wanted an instrument that would detect minimal levels of mentation. It might be said analogically that the DF scale attempts to rate how much heat or light is associated with sleep mentation. At the lowest level would be an ignited paper match, then a wooden match, a small twig, a big twig, and so on, up to the dream level represented by a roaring bonfire. It ignores content areas, themes, interactions, and emotions and is concerned only with degrees of cognitive activity.

It was found that DF scores of 6 or 7, the most dreamlike ratings, were applied to 69 percent of the REM awakenings and 39 percent of the hypnagogic awakenings. Most of the hypnagogic reports received an average DF score of 4, which indicated that the imagery was everyday, undramatic, and nonhallucinatory. Not only were REM reports more likely to receive very high scores (6 or 7), but 18 percent of the REM awakenings received very low scores (0 or 1). It should be pointed out that no-content reports are common when subjects have been exposed to very emotional material; some of their nonremembered REM dreams may have been so emotional that they were blocked from conscious recall, which would help account for the surprising number of very low scores from REM period awakenings.

Subjects also completed some personality tests, which included a Picture-Story Test. Significant correlations were found between the hypnagogic DF scores and scores on the Picture-Story Test, a finding which suggests that waking fantasy production is related to hypnagogic mentation. After examining the overall scores on the psychological tests, the researchers proposed that: "Hypnagogic dreamers tended to have greater social poise, to be more self-accepting, to be less rigidly conforming to social standards, and to be more adept at producing voluntary waking fantasy than did the hypnagogic non-dreamers." They also pointed out that strong similarities existed between the rigid "authoritarian personality" syndrome and the characteristics of individuals who seemed unable to spontaneously enter into lively hypnagogic imagery.

It may be difficult for some people to let go and relinquish control of their thoughts and feelings. These individuals could find surrendering to sleep and the "things that go bump in the night" to be a disturbing experience. Thus, individual differences are more prominent in the hypnagogic state. Some readily plunge into the night's oceanic waters, while others struggle against the insistent tide, desperately clinging to rocks or pilings. Adrift after leaving shore, we are all captured by the pirates of sleep and become involuntary passengers on a boat that sails along exotic coastlines and enters foreign ports. We seem to differ more in the way we leave the land of wakefulness than in our behavior aboard the ship of sleep.

The boundaries staked out by previous dream researchers between various types of mental experience have often been contested and frequently redrawn. Most non-REM researchers had awakened subjects during Stage 2 sleep, when there was a minimal presence of delta waves. It was assumed that significant mental activity disappeared when delta waves were prominent. This assumption was tested and found to be untenable by a husband and wife research team who woke their twenty-one subjects from both Stage 2 and Stage 4 sleep.[68] The average DF score for Stage 2 reports was 2.8 and for Stage 4 reports, 2.4. This difference was not significant, suggesting that both stages of sleep usually produce low-level cognitive activity. If mental activity with a DF score of 5.5 or higher is considered to be a "dream," the percentage of dreams was 27 percent for Stage 2 and 20 percent for Stage 4 reports. Subjects had been allowed five minutes of sleep in each of these two stages of sleep. The authors concluded, "Stages 2 and 4 differ negligibly in parameters of recall and content when time in stage is controlled."

William Zimmerman, from the University of Chicago, attempted to discover whether physiological factors, like personality factors, might be associated with different types of mental activity during sleep.[69] In order to differentiate light and deep sleepers, he gradually increased the loudness of a tone until it awakened a sleeper. The point at which this occurred was called the auditory awakening threshold (AAT).

Subjects who could be roused easily (low AAT) were called light sleepers, and sixteen of them were compared with sixteen subjects classified as deep sleepers (high AAT). All subjects were awakened for two REM and two non-REM reports during the later part of the night. After completing their reports, subjects answered a questionnaire about various dimensions of their mental experiences. No differences were found between the light and deep sleepers on any aspects of their REM mentation, but the light sleepers reported dreaming after 71 percent of their non-REM awakenings, while only 21 percent of the deep sleepers reported dreaming after their non-REM awakenings. Among the light sleepers, the differences between REM and non-REM reports were very minor, and they generally classified themselves as dreaming when awakened from either stage of sleep. It was only the deep-sleepers who were likely to label their non-REM reports as involving thinking. Thus predicting when a thinking report could be expected took more than just knowledge of what sleep stage had been interrupted; it was also necessary to know whether a subject was a light or deep sleeper.

Since the light sleepers had faster heart and respiration rates, higher body temperatures, and more body movements and awakenings during sleep than the deep sleepers, Zimmerman suggested that there might be underlying differences in their levels of central nervous system functioning. He hypothesized that dreaming occurs when the level of cerebral arousal exceeds a certain critical point, and that levels below this point might be sufficient only to sustain thinking. If the light sleepers were displaying elevated levels of cortical arousal during sleep, it would be easier for them to engage in dreaming while in non-REM sleep, while the deep sleepers required the active cortical arousal boost of being in REM sleep to enter the dreaming state. Zimmerman suggested that more dream reports should be expected from the hypnagogic period, too, because it is so close in time to wakefulness, when cerebral arousal would also be high.

Excited by the implications of Zimmerman's work, two other researchers at the University of Chicago followed up on his AAT findings.[70] Subjects were studied for an average of ten nights, rather than for just one night. These researchers discovered that auditory awakening threshold levels decreased markedly from night to night and also decreased within each individual night. They found that the frequency of Stage 2 reports of dreaming was associated not with AAT, but with the subjects' own assessments of their depth of sleep before being awakened. If subjects judged that they had been in a deep sleep before a Stage 2 awakening, they were significantly more likely to give a report of having been dreaming. Another new variable, subjective depth of sleep, now had to be considered in the search for the elusive criteria to indicate the presence of dreaming.

One interesting result that emerged

from this study was the finding that Stage 2 reports which were close together in time tended to produce greater similarity in manifest content. Below are the Stage 2 reports from one subject along with his judgments as to the type of mentation involved.

1:25 A.M. (dreaming) I was selling hockey sets ... those hockey sets with little toy men that you move by turning handles on the side of the box ... except these became real people. It looked like it was going to be a rough game ... that somebody was going to be hurt.

1:50 A.M. (dreaming) I was watching a hockey game on TV with some other people.

6:55 A.M. (dreaming) I was at the house of these girls I know and I was asking about the rent ... and then I was thinking about Professor M's course which hasn't met yet this quarter.

7:17 A.M. (thinking) I was thinking about Professor M's course in political science, which I am signed up for. The course is being canceled. I was thinking about what to do.

This subject's early Stage 2 reports involved hockey and the later ones were concerned mostly with Professor M's course. Sometimes a single theme seems to characterize the dreams of an individual who has strongly entrenched waking interests. Calvin Hall and I reported that 30 percent of the fifty lab dreams of a sports car buff contained references to sports cars, 36 percent of the thirty-six dreams of an avid football fan dealt with football, and 23 percent of the lab dreams of another subject dealt with situations involving the color guard to which he belonged.[71]

Unless an investigator knows a great deal about the waking interests and conflicts of an individual subject, it may be difficult to find connections between dreams on any given night or across nights. For example, William Dement and Edward Wolpert obtained thirty-eight sequential nights of dreams from eight subjects and reported that on only seven of these nights were there any indications of similarity in plot or details.[72] The conclusions they reached would apply to most of the studies carried out in this area: "For the most part, each dream seemed to be a self-contained drama relatively independent of the preceding or following drama."[73]

As was evidenced in the presleep studies, if one has sufficient background information and knowledge about current life events for a given subject, it may be possible to detect symbolic connections across separate dreams. Multiple laboratory awakenings were made for fifteen nights with one psychotherapy patient. The researchers claimed that all of the dreams on a particular night were concerned either with the same conflict or with a limited number of conflicts.[74] They supported their claim by discussing this patient's dreams from two nights in great detail. They noted that earlier dreams during the night often dealt with the experimental situation and that the nine dreams for which a temporal setting of childhood or adolescence was reported occurred after 4:30 A.M.

This tendency toward regression to

earlier time periods as the night continues was first studied by Paul Verdone from the University of Chicago.[75] In an oversimplified version of sleeping events, the first dream of the night would be expected to deal with material from the preceding twenty-four-hour period, while the next REM report would deal with events from the preceding month. The third REM report would deal with events from several years ago and the fourth REM period would involve childhood scenes or the dreamer being much younger in age.

It appears as if our dreaming mind identifies some current problem or conflict related to the previous day, then attempts systematically to trace the earlier developmental events associated with that issue. A conflict involving authority figures, for example, might be represented in the first dream by an argument with the boss at work, in a succeeding dream by a misunderstanding with a high school teacher, and in a later dream by the dreamer as a younger child being scolded by his or her father. Dreams then progress toward more contemporary times in the last REM period before awakening, as if the dreamer were preparing to exit from the dreaming state to confront the present realities outside the bedroom. Though oversimplified, this is a basically accurate description of a general pattern that seems to be expressed in many sequential dream series I have encountered.

Studies involving the AAT technique emphasized the depth of sleep or the level of cortical arousal as important variables in understanding sleep mentation. Other workers pursued different avenues in their attempts to localize the mechanisms underlying the various forms of mental activity that emerge during sleep.

There has been increasing interest in recent years in the different forms of mental activity associated with the two hemispheres of the brain. The left hemisphere is associated with logical, rational, linear thinking such as occurs in solving arithmetic problems, while the right hemisphere is associated with global perception of visual and auditory imagery such as would be involved in appreciating a painting or listening to a symphony. The right hemisphere therefore seems more likely to be more active during dreaming activity, and the left hemisphere to be more active during non-REM thinking episodes.[76]

Data supporting the hypothesis that the right cerebral hemisphere is active during REM sleep was obtained by some Italian investigators.[77] Right-handed subjects were given a tactile recognition test which involved touching a target shape with the index and middle fingers of each hand, then searching for this shape among three other choices. After waking from REM sleep, the subjects were more successful in making this discrimination with their left hand than they had been in the waking state, or following non-REM awakenings. Since the left hand is controlled by the right hemisphere, this finding indicates that the right hemisphere was active in REM sleep. The investigators also examined the level of dream recall from laboratory awakenings and from dream diaries kept at home. For both lab and home data, the high dream recallers presented a left-hand superiority on the tactile recognition test after REM sleep, showing that subjects with more active right hemisphere arousal had greater dream recall.

It was not the side of the brain, but the frequency of brain wave activity which interested a team of Israeli investigators.[78] They attempted to manipulate brain waves by exposing their sleeping subjects to "flickering photic stimulation," that is, a bright light turned rapidly on and off at certain predetermined rates. Subjects awakened during sleep onset, during a REM period, and under three different conditions from Stage 3 EEG supplied reports concerning their mental activities. One Stage 3 EEG awakening occurred after five minutes' exposure to light flashing at a rate of twenty-six flickers per second (FPS), another after five minutes' exposure to a light flickering at the frequency of the subject's own alpha waves, and the third when no stroboscope had been involved. Judges blindly rated these reports for the percentage of experiences which were dreamlike. These figures were 85 percent from REM, 85 percent from sleep onset, 25 percent from regular Stage 3, and 18 percent from Stage 3 awakenings with 26 FPS. A surprising finding was that the judges rated 93 percent of the Stage 3 reports obtained when subjects were exposed to a stroboscope flashing at their own alpha frequency as dreamlike—a higher percentage figure than that for even REM awakenings. Subjects not only reported a higher percentage of dreams when thus stimulated during Stage 3 sleep; they also responded with more imaginative stories to stimulus cards when stimulated by a stroboscope set at their own alpha frequency in a waking state.

In the studies just reviewed, the investigators made an effort to uncover some form of physiological index which could be correlated with the presence of dreaming or of thinking. These studies were not concerned with the specific content mentioned when a physiological marker was present, but primarily with classifying the obtained sleep report as one that more resembled dreaming or more resembled thinking. The opposite goal is pursued in studies of "psychophysiological parallelism," which attempts to correlate specific forms of mental imagery with specific forms of physiological activation. No cause and effect relationship is proposed; the relationship is simply one of correlation between a physiological change and a psychological change.

If subjects are awakened after REM bursts, their images are generally visual in nature, but if they are awakened after intervals of no eye movements during REM sleep, their reports are more conceptual in nature and are similar to those obtained from non-REM stages of sleep. Claims made in earlier studies, that the direction of eye movements were related to the direction of visual activity in the dream, have generally not been supported in later studies.[79] Since eye movements occur both in fetuses[80] and in humans without any cerebral cortex, it would be difficult to expect any precise relationship to exist between directions of eye movement activity and specific dreaming visualizations. Directional correspondence can be found occasionally if the eye movements are extremely distinctive, if the dreamer's recall is very detailed, and if the dreamer is asked about the visual imagery present in the very last ten to twenty seconds before awakening.

In one study in which electrodes were

attached to subjects' limbs, it was possible to detect a correspondence between muscle activity and dream imagery involving the use of a particular limb. For example, reaching for a jacket was associated with EMG activity from an arm, and in a dreamer who reported jumping over a line, EMG activity was shown for the leg, trunk, and arm muscles. These correspondences were shown in only a few subjects, however.[81] In a similar study by another investigator, subjects awakened after lower extremity EMG activity reported corresponding dream activity, such as running or kicking, while awakenings after upper extremity movements showed more dream activity involving the upper body.[82] Electrodes attached to the chin and lip areas of female undergraduates detected significant lip and chin EMG activity during conversational dreams, but not during visual dreams.[83] Similarly, reports of greater than usual listening activities in dreams corresponded to more activity of the middle ear muscles as measured by a device placed within subjects' ears.[84]

Emotionality in dreams has been assessed by several measuring techniques. It is known that emotionally stressful situations induce elevated levels of plasma free fatty acids (FFA). A significant correlation was found between the amount of anxiety in dreams and the level of FFA after fifteen minutes of REM sleep.[85] Awakenings after both REM and non-REM sleep are more likely to yield reports of dreams that are emotional and vivid and involve physical activity, if there is an elevated rate and variability of respiration. "Respiratory content" was more likely to be reported if there was a marked reduction in breathing.

For example, when one dreamer reported that she was an actress who was being choked, the respiratory record showed an interval of about fifteen seconds during which no breathing had taken place.[86] Nocturnal angina occurs mainly during REM sleep and the associated dreams contain either anxiety or physical effort.[87]

Peter Hauri and I looked at several different physiological variables in relation to reports of mental activity.[88] Our data came from Peter's dissertation on the effects of activity before sleep, which was discussed in connection with presleep stimuli. I scored the REM reports for levels of emotionality, physical activity, and the dreamer's involvement as an actor in the dream. Our most sensitive indicator was the amount of heart rate variability during the last six minutes of REM sleep preceding the awakening. There were significant positive correlations between this measure and each of the three dream dimensions. The next most sensitive indicator was the variability of skin potential fluctuations occurring during the last minute before awakening. Individual differences were prominent. Of the fifteen subjects, nine showed a clear, positive association between dream emotionality and heart rate variability, five showed no association, and one actually demonstrated a reverse trend.

We also looked at non-REM reports.[89] Since these reports were generally briefer, it was difficult to evaluate them separately for selected content measures, so a composite rating was made for the amount of emotionality, vividness of visual imagery, and extent of activity. Pairs of non-REM reports were selected so that one report had received a high composite content rating, and the other a low composite rating. The only physiological measure which differentiated between these sets of pairs was the amount of heart rate variability shown during the six minutes before each non-REM awakening. These results indicate that heart rate variability was a better predictor of the nature of mental activity than was knowledge of sleep stage. A non-REM report with marked heart rate variability contained content with more emotionality and activity than did a REM report with minimal heart rate variability.

It would be inappropriate to assume that all people respond to stress or emotionality with the same organ system. For some, cardiac activity may be emphasized, for others, breathing patterns may be affected, while still others may perspire excessively. It would, therefore, be important to know which organ system is the most likely to respond to emotionality. It is also important to determine whether different organ systems are activated for different kinds of emotionality. A particular individual might respond to aggression with changes in heart rate, to sexual imagery with changes in breathing, and to anxiety with increased levels of perspiration. Subjects should be tested in the waking state to determine which organ system responds to the particular emotion under study if a more careful examination of psychophysiological parallelism is to be made.

RELEVANCE OF PHYSIOLOGICAL MODELS OF DREAMING

The results of the studies on psychophysiological parallelism may seem to offer a promising beginning to charting the domains of the dreaming mind, but no less an authority than David Foulkes made the following devastating evaluation of work in this area:

> Psychophysiological correlational research now appears to offer such a low rate of return as not to be a wise place for dream psychology to continue to commit its limited resources. . . . Dreaming is a mental process and it must be studied as

we now study other mental processes. Whatever brain events *accompany* dreaming, what the dream *is* is a mental act.[90]

Foulkes recently turned his attention toward a cognitive approach to understanding dreams and organized his views into a book entitled *Dreaming: A Cognitive-Psychological Analysis*. In his introductory chapter, Foulkes states, "It is my assumption that the sleeping mind is not functionally distinct from the waking mind; hence dreaming does not depend on mental processes or systems that are in any way unique to sleep.[91] Foulkes is willing to dispense with the unconscious and with any effort to specify the physiological bases of dreaming. The content of dreams fails to interest him. "My primary concern is with *how* we are thinking when we're dreaming, rather than with *what* we are thinking when we're dreaming."[92] Foulkes rejects the notion that dreams contain "particular messages or gems of wisdom which, if interpreted correctly, can help us to set our lives aright."[93] He is very cynical about dream interpretation: "What's sought in dream interpretation doesn't exist . . . there's no more underlying meaning in dreaming than there are angels who might sit on the heads of pins."[94] Foulkes proposes that dream research would be significantly advanced if greater attention were given to structural linguistics, which is concerned with the forms (processes) of language. For Foulkes, awareness of the rules governing language acquisition would best further our understanding of nocturnal cognition.

In summarizing the research on REM sleep another renowned researcher, William Dement, declared, "Never before in the history of biological research has so much been known about something from a descriptive point of view, with so little known at the same time about its function."[95] Harry Hunt, a Canadian psychologist, cautions that it may be unrealistic for us to expect to understand the function of dreaming:

I do not know if we will find true *functions* of dreaming, any more than we have been able to for hu-

man existence. A self-referential, self-transforming system like the human mind will evolve its uses as creatively and unpredictively as it evolves its structures.[96]

Hunt emphasizes that there are so many different types of dreaming that it would be difficult to discover a single common physiological denominator that would successfully account for their "multiplicity" of uses:

There do seem to be distinct types of dreaming, each with its own line of articulation emerging out of ordinary true-to-daily-life dreams: a lucid-control line, a Freud-type pressure-discharge line, a Jung-type archetypal-mythological line, and perhaps a problem solving line and a Robert Louis Stevenson-type creative story line. It may be *because* dreaming (and human life) has no fixed function that it is open to so many different *uses*.[97]

Hunt's view proposes that dreams are very multifaceted in nature and can possess many levels of meaning.

According to two British researchers, Francis Crick and Graeme Mitchison, neither of whom has spent any time in a sleep laboratory, dreams are meaningless.[98] For Crick, a physicist who won a Nobel Prize for his work on the DNA molecule, and Mitchison, a neurochemist, the process which takes place in REM sleep is "reverse learning." During REM sleep, they assert, the brain attempts to rid itself of excessive memory or "parasitic" modes of behavior, the reverse of the acquisition of new information involved in learning. This insures that the brain will not accumulate too much useless clutter. These researchers state that memory is stored in neural nets and that there is a limit to what these nets can store before the system begins to "misbehave." If we remember our dreams too frequently, they will interfere with this process of unclogging the neurocircuitry, and presumably could have negative consequences for our well-being.

Thus, Crick and Mitchison argue, "we dream in order to forget." In a later paper, they indicate that this earlier slogan was too strong a statement, because some people assume they meant the function of REM sleep is to delete *all* the elements of our unconscious dreams from memory.[99] "If we had to produce alternative slogans, we might suggest, 'we dream to reduce fantasy,' or 'we dream to reduce obsession.' "[100] They elaborate this view as follows:

> Reverse learning is unlikely to remove completely the interaction of related ideas and concepts but merely to reduce their interaction, so that, as a result, the system becomes less imaginative and more prosaic in its behaviour.[101]

Whereas Foulkes contends that the sleeping mind is not functionally distinct from the waking mind, Crick and Mitchison argue, "There is a special process related to memory which operates in REM sleep and is in a loose sense the opposite of what happens when we are awake."[102] With regard to dream content, Crick and Mitchison assert that their theory "provides a good explanation of the nature of the bizarre intrusion. It has nothing useful to say about the narrative."[103]

The theory which has attempted to be the most inclusive with regard to incorporating physiological discoveries about dreams is the "activation-synthesis hypothesis" proposed by J. Allan Hobson and Robert McCarley from the Harvard Medical School. They feel they have refuted Freud's dream hypothesis, because Freud proposed that psychological processes instigated dreams and determined their formal characteristics, whereas in their hypothesis, physiological processes, such as those they have recorded in their lab, are the primary instigators of dreams and the primary determinants of their formal characteristics (distortion, bizarreness, discontinuity, and incoherence).[104]

The main tenets of the activation-synthesis hypothesis are that cells deep in the pontine area of the brain stem are *activated*, generating REM sleep and randomly stimulating the forebrain, which then *synthesizes* dreams by using stored memories to make sense of the incoming random neural firing. Barraged with all this random stimulation, the forebrain seeks out anything in the memory system which remotely resembles the erratic input, and thereby creates the distortion and incoherence common in dreams.

Hobson has described the latest development of the activation-synthesis hypothesis in detail in his recent book *The*

Dreaming Brain. My reading of the book gives me the impression that Hobson is ambivalent about how to treat dreams. On one page, he says, "The study of dreams is the study of a model of mental illness."[105] And on another page,

> Dreaming not only is worthy of participatory enjoyment but has the function of providing us with an opportunity to understand ourselves better. In this view, dreaming is, after all, a message from the gods in the most prophetic sense.[106]

Hobson's dilemma perhaps arises because, as director of the neurophysiology laboratory at the Massachusetts Mental Health Center, he has a tendency to reduce dreams to their existence as biochemical events in the brain, but having kept a dream diary for several years, he also has a keen understanding of dreams as imaginative creative events. As he says,

> Anyone who has kept a dream journal will understand the sybaritic and delight-enhancing function of dreaming. Dreams are truly marvelous. Why not simply enjoy them? ... It seems to me irreverent and inappropriate to reduce this pleasurable function of dreams to the derivation of an instinct. Dreaming may reflect instincts, but it also reflects creative imagination: both serve science as well as art.[107]

After diagramming and describing the many intricate pathways and connections between neural systems and interrelated biochemical processes, Hobson attempts to place these findings into a larger perspective. He reminds us that even after thirty years of intense scientific effort, psychologists accuse physiologists of being reductionistic, while physiologists accuse psychologists of being dualistic and mystical. The reason for the continuation of these disputes, he explains, is that we still have an unclear and inadequate picture of the human mind. "This battle for the mind will be won no more easily by the forces of pure materialism than by those of pure idealism," Hobson says, but he proposes a solution:

> A clear and adequate picture may emerge only through a progressive and liberal extension—upward—of materialistic knowledge to the level of information processing, so as to lay bare the creative, multi-leveled, open-loop nature of the brain-mind. At the same time, psychology must become much more detailed, clear, and precise, so that it can be fitted—downward—upon the schemata of the material structures and dynamics.[108]

One certainly can't fault Hobson for the apparent reasonableness of his proposal; it is a rational compromise between a materialistic and a mental approach and provides a warm feeling of optimism that the differences will someday be bridged between these two sides of the issue. I myself am less optimistic. I have no doubt that considerable progress will be made in advancing our knowledge of the neurophysiological properties of the brain and that new information regarding the psychological principles underlying association, symbolism, and memory will be forthcoming, but I think an irreconcilable Grand Canyon will always remain between these two competing explanatory constructs, regardless of what advances are made.

I find myself much more drawn toward the unitary point of view put forth by Gordon Globus, a professor of psychiatry and philosophy at the University of California at Irvine, in his fascinating recent book *Dream Life, Wake Life*.[109] In his preface, Globus acknowledges that his book may seem strange or incomprehensible to those who do not "honor" their dreams. In a recent article in the new journal *Dreaming*, Globus encourages other dream researchers to learn to honor their dreams: "Until the new scientists of dreams conduct a searching intense inquiry into their own dream life they are vulnerable to the charge of narrow-mindedly missing what is obvious."[110]

Globus indicates in his book that he opposes the mechanistic view of Hobson and McCarley and states that his approach is an existential phenomenological one. He also disagrees with Freud's theory, which he characterizes as a "compositional theory" because Freud considered dream life to represent a composite of memory traces from waking life. Globus argues, "When we turn to our own dream lives then we find *authentically novel* elements

that cannot be plausibly explained by the compositional theory."[111] The world of our dreaming life is spontaneously formed as a whole and not as a secondary derivative of the world of our waking life:

> The dreaming life-world is created *de novo*. Thus our dreams are first-hand creations, rather than put together from residues of waking life. *We have the capacity for infinite creativity*; at least while dreaming, we partake of the power of immanent Spirit, the infinite Godhead that creates the cosmos. In waking, we "contract away from infinity" as Wilber says, and take a Heideggerian "fall" into a limited life-world.[112]

Despite the occasional tinges of mysticism, such as characterize the above statement, Globus is not some wild-eyed, mantra-chanting visionary. He has spent research time in a sleep lab. He displays incredible erudition and maneuvers with great agility among various theoretical positions and empirical findings to fashion a truly interdisciplinary product. To anchor his proposal that we have the capacity for infinite creativity, he reviews scientific evidence from several sources. He refers, for example, to the latest discoveries about the immune system, when an antigen such as a virus invades the body, an antibody appears which matches and neutralizes its potential harmful effects. It had previously been assumed that the antibody was newly manufactured in response to the antigen. Recent discoveries, however, indicate that an almost infinite variety of antibodies already exist and are available for multiplication. The antibodies are prepackaged, so to speak, before the antigen ever arrives. This line of defense is "enfolded" in the system and "unfolded" in response to invasion by a virus or bacteria. Just as infinite creativity to maximize physical well-being is enfolded in the immune system, infinite creativity to maximize psychological well-being is enfolded in the dreaming system.

Globus also discusses the new optical information technology that includes holography. One application of holography is in making the three-dimensional images seen on plastic charge cards, but it has less familiar aspects as well. A unique property of the hologram is that the image of the entire object can be reproduced from just a small piece of the hologram. The information of the whole is contained in a part. We are all familiar with examples from nature where the structure of the whole is contained in a part. A tiny acorn contains the information needed to assemble all the roots, trunk, branches, and leaves of a mighty oak tree. Globus also refers to David Bohm, a theoretical physicist at the University of London and a former colleague of Einstein, who has expanded upon the implications of the hologram model to suggest that the information of the entire universe is contained in each of its parts. The world is not put together from separate units, but is seamlessly joined in an indivisible whole of pattern, process, and interrelatedness. My own acceptance of the wholeness of the universe and my rejection of the view that we possess separate minds (as opposed to brains) while dreaming, is reflected in the title of this book—*Our Dreaming Mind*. The pronoun "our"

conveys the concept of collective ownership, and using the word "mind" in its singular form emphasizes that dreaming experiences unfold from a single source.

Bohm makes a distinction between what he calls the "explicate" order and the "implicate" order of the physical universe. The explicate order is what we see, and the processes of which we are aware. This leads to a perception of, and belief in, separate minds in isolated bodies. The implicate order is the invisible enfolded reality that underlies the external manifestations. For Bohm, the entire universe has to be understood as a single, indivisible whole:

> Deep down the consciousness of mankind is one ... and if we don't see this it's because we are blinding ourselves to it. ... If we don't establish these absolute boundaries between minds, then ... it's possible they could ... unite as one mind.[113]

By referring to the work on the immune system, the holographic process, and the implicate order of the physical universe, Globus weaves together an argument suggesting that all world possibilities are enfolded in the "object." Psychological reality, therefore, becomes an unfolding that requires no direct interaction with the surrounding environment. In his epilogue, Globus explains what he has attempted to do: "My basic endeavor here has been to use dreaming for philosphical purposes, and at the same time maintain psychoanalytic, biological, cognitive, existential and transpersonal understandings."[114]

DOES THE LABORATORY CONTEXT CREATE DREAM MUTATIONS?

It is impossible to observe an ongoing dream as it is experienced by the dreamer. We cannot preserve the rich cornucopia of dream elements that tumble across the stage of the dreamer's mind on film or videotape. Even if we could, we would not be able to subjectively experience the dreamer's unique feelings and reactions to his or her unfolding dream drama. The only trace of that evanescent event we have to work with is the dreamer's imprecise verbal or graphic representation of what transpired. The distinction between the internal dream and the external dream report was nicely delineated nearly a century ago by Sir Samuel Wilks: "The dreamer merely forms a mental picture, and the *description* of it he calls his dream."[115] Dream researchers are forced to recognize that some form of distortion will always be present whenever they work with dream reports and treat them as reasonable facsimiles of the impalpable, ethereal originals.

A large number of social factors influence the reporting of dreams. Dreams are told differently to different people at different times. In one of the earliest explorations of this issue, one male and one female patient spent several nights in a laboratory being awakened for REM dream reports; they were also later interviewed by their psychiatrists.[116] Perhaps because his psychiatrist did not specifically ask for dreams, the male patient failed to report to

him twenty-seven of the thirty-four dreams recalled in the laboratory setting. He told the dreams that emphasized his heterosexuality and omitted those with homosexual connotations. The psychiatrist for the female patient did ask for dreams, but thirteen of the fifty-four she recalled in the laboratory were not shared with her psychiatrist. The female subject did not report competitive dreams involving her and the male experimenter to the experimenter, but did report them to her therapist; conversely, she reported to the experimenter, but not to her therapist, dreams involving erotic feelings about the therapist. The omission of important dreams and dream details seemed related to the presence of major interpersonal conflicts with that person.

The study just described involved both a male experimenter and a male psychiatrist. In another study, a male college student and a female nurse slept in a dream laboratory, but on some nights the experimenter was a female technician-student and on the other nights a male psychiatrist.[117] The nurse's dreams seemed focused on dependency issues. Her dreams reported to the male physician frequently included situations in which the nurse was with a doctor who was taking care of her patients' needs in a satisfactory manner, but in the dreams she reported to the female experimenter, she cast doctors in a more negative light, as unavailable to meet patients' needs. When the male subject reported his dreams to the male experimenter, he was frequently performing before others: conducting an orchestra, playing a concert, or taking a test on complicated machinery before some doctors. With the female experimenter, the dreams dealt with experiences in which the subject was, or could be, hurt, such as being in a combat zone, having a bloody nose, or being laughed at by women.

Serving as a subject in a dream laboratory can be a very anxiety-provoking experience. Having directed two sleep and dream laboratories and served as an experimental subject in four such laboratories, I can attest that the laboratory bed can sometimes seem like a bed of nails. Our lab personnel would comment that some subjects displayed such initial tension that it appeared the only parts of their body touching the bed were the backs of their heads and the backs of their heels. It would, therefore, be surprising if this unfamiliar and alien atmosphere did not intrude into subjects' dreams and influence their content.

The first investigators to examine the effects of the laboratory setting studied five male and five female subjects at the Cincinnati V.A. Hospital in 1962.[118] The investigators wished to examine how anxiety might be related to the experimental setting by noting references to the presence of the male experimenter, the sleeping room, and the monitoring equipment. The investigators concluded that features of the experiment were represented in an obvious way in one-third, and in a disguised manner in another third, of the reported dreams.

The anxiety engendered by participating in the study was probably increased because these normal subjects were also administered three different drugs (a sedative, a tranquilizer, and an antidepressant). The experimenter was variously pictured in dreams as being seductive, particularly by the women, and sadistic, particularly by the men, and by both sexes as inefficient, incompetent, and even menacing, appearing to some as a drug pusher who was going to make addicts of the subjects. Sleeping in the small cubicle, which had only one door to the outside, led to dreams of being trapped in a confining situation and having difficulty breathing. Subjects also expressed apprehension concerning communication being cut off and the experimenter not being able to hear the subject. The experimental equipment was frequently dreamed about as causing injury—electrocution occurring through the EEG wires, or skin or body parts being pulled off because the electrodes had been glued on too firmly.

The money subjects received for participating in the study was also incorporated into their dreams in interesting ways. One woman, for example, dreamed of being sold as a "wife" to a man, and other women dreamed about prostitution. The effects were different for males, several of whom dreamed of working in stores as salesmen or servicemen where their pay was slow in coming or did not come at all.

The researchers were surprised that such strong effects were produced, because the subjects didn't display noticeable overt anxiety while participating in the study. They concluded:

> It is clear in this study that neither reassurance about the apparatus nor repeated episodes of exposure to the apparatus were sufficient to decrease anxiety about the experimental situation, even over a period of four weeks. Surface cooperativeness and surface placidity may well hide massive fear and anxiety reactions which would affect physiological, biochemical and, of course, psychological measurements.[119]

In another study dreams from fourteen male and eight female dreamers were evaluated for the presence of the laboratory situation. At least one overt reference to the experimental situation was found in 30 percent of the 219 dreams collected. This figure did not drop from the first five nights to the second five nights. Qualitative analysis revealed that the experiment was perceived as threatening by females, while males viewed it as annoying and exhibitionistic.[120]

Dement and other researchers have contended that the effect of the laboratory situation is not a very long-lasting one. Combining data from three different laboratories, they reported that the experimental situation appeared in 34 percent of dreams reported during the first laboratory night, whereas the percentage on all other nights averaged 19 percent. They claimed that "much of the influence exerted by the experimental situation in determining the manifest content of laboratory dreams is

eliminated after one night's exposure."[121] It should be emphasized, however, that the majority of their subjects (forty of seventy-seven) slept only one night in the lab, and twenty spent only two nights. The sample also included twelve subjects who had slept in the lab previously without being awakened for REM reports; these subjects presumably had undergone some adaptation to the laboratory environment and should have found it less threatening.

Women had significantly more dreams about the experimental situation than men on the first night. The investigators suggested that first night dreams more often reflected fear of the apparatus or concern about the subject's performance, while later dreams dealt with issues related to the developing experimenter-subject relationship. The first two dream excerpts below come from women's first-night dreams and the latter two from later nights.[122]

> I dreamt that I was lying here and something went wrong so that any second I was going to be electrocuted. I wanted to tear the wires off but suddenly realized that my hands were tied. I was very relieved when you woke me up.
>
> The experimenter was talking to Dr. X. Some young man was leaving the laboratory. After he left the experimenter smirked at Dr. X and Dr. X smirked back.

> I said I was very hungry and you went and got some ice cream. Then you fed it to me with a spoon. I felt very contented.

Then the two other girls who were going to be subjects wanted to know what was going on. The doctor wanted them to take off their clothes so he could examine them. They were very upset because they thought he was going to try to seduce them. I know this was ridiculous because he was a very nice young man and wouldn't think of such a thing.

Despite the obvious contributions that the laboratory situation made to the REM reports typified above, the Dement group concluded that "dream material elicited by the REM technique can be utilized as a valid sample of typical dream life."[123]

A Japanese investigator studied REM reports from twenty college students and fourteen psychiatrists and found that 21 percent of the reported dreams were related to the laboratory situation.[124] A group of Swiss investigators obtained five hundred REM dreams from forty-four dreamers and found the laboratory situation represented in 25 percent of the dreams.[125] Researchers in Spain from the Universidad Anahuac had subjects wear inverting prisms, which caused them to see the world upside down, for five hours before bedtime. They also employed a control group who did not wear the prisms. The prism effect was not incorporated, but the laboratory situation was incorporated for both groups. Because the effects of the laboratory situation were so much more powerful than the prism effects, these researchers "question[ed] the usefulness of pre-sleep stimuli to study dream origin" in the laboratory.[126]

LABORATORY VERSUS HOME DREAMS

The obvious next step was to compare whether dreams from the same subjects differ when obtained under sleep laboratory conditions and under natural conditions at home. Twelve male subjects slept in the University of Chicago laboratory for a total of ten nights each and contributed an equal number of home dreams for comparative purposes. The dreams reported at home included more sexuality and aggressive interactions in which the dreamer was involved; in laboratory dreams, the subjects more often reported witnessing the aggressive interactions of others. Because of the curtailment of the direct expression of sexuality and aggression in the laboratory dreams, the researchers proposed that the experimental situation had an inhibiting effect upon the dreamer.[127]

Another study involved six female subjects who reported dreams from home and laboratory awakenings. No sexual act was reported in the fifty-one laboratory dreams but three were reported in the fifty-one home dreams. Home dreams also contained more hostile/violent elements. The investigator characterized home dreams as "spicier" and concluded, after comparing various studies of home versus laboratory dreams, that the results "favor the collection of home dreams for quantitative dream-content studies aimed at furthering our understanding of unconscious fantasies and symbolism."[128]

Calvin Hall and I studied fifteen male subjects who had slept an average of twenty-five nights (as few as five, and as many as forty-eight nights) in our laboratory at the Institute of Dream Research.[129] The "laboratory" situation for our study was actually a very benign and nonthreatening one, because it was Calvin's home, a comfortable private house located close to the bay in Miami. We had modified one of the downstairs bedrooms for EEG monitoring and made every effort to create an informal homelike ambience.

Subjects were allowed three nights to adjust to the sleeping arrangements before being awakened for a dream report. Subjects were awakened only once per night for a REM report on the next four nights. Despite the nonthreatening setting and the three adjustment nights, 22 percent of the dreams during the subsequent four nights were scored as experimental situation (ES) dreams. Subjects were awakened several times for REM reports later in the study. Of the 559 dreams collected overall in this informal laboratory, 14 percent contained some feature of the experimental situation. The criterion for scoring an ES dream was the same as that employed by the Dement group. Of 150 dreams from nights twenty-five through thirty-one, 9 percent were still scored as ES dreams. The percentage of ES dreams was higher on nights when multiple, as opposed to single awakenings, were made.

When the 269 home dreams in our study were compared with laboratory dreams, we found the home dreams had a greater amount of aggression, friendliness, sex, success, failure, misfortune, and good fortune. We interpreted these dream scores as reflecting a greater dramatic quality in the home dreams. In discussing these results in another paper, Calvin indicated that we weren't prepared to accept Dement's conclusion that REM dreams were a valid sample of dream life:

> Although there is no way of knowing at the present time what "typical dream life" is like, it is a plausible assumption that it will not be found in a laboratory setting no matter how normal the environment provided the subject.[130]

David Foulkes and a graduate student, Robert Weisz, at the University of Wyoming attempted to provide uniform sampling conditions for home and laboratory dreams.[131] They studied twelve young adult males who spent two nights dreaming in a laboratory and two nights dreaming at home. In both conditions, the subject was awakened by an alarm clock at 6:30 A.M. and reported any dreams he could remember into a tape recorder. A total of twenty laboratory and eighteen home dream reports was collected. Even under these "uniform sampling conditions," the investigators reported that "elements relating to the experimental situation appeared in 50 percent of the dreams retrieved in the laboratory and in 6 percent of the dreams reported at home."[132] This difference was statistically significant. The dreams were also rated on six dimensions and it was found that, "under comparable sampling conditions, home and laboratory dreams differed significantly in manifest aggressive content, with home dreams containing more aggression."[133] Home dreams also had much higher ratings for sexuality. After reviewing the results of other investigators, as well as the results from their own study,

Weisz and Foulkes acknowledged "the consistent finding of significantly greater manifest impulse in home dreams,"[134] but they nevertheless doggedly concluded that "there is apparently nothing in a laboratory setting that renders its dreams *inherently* unrepresentative for the study of many important questions relating to the nature of dream content."[135]

Some Japanese investigators used a portable "dream detector," which an earlier study had shown could reliably detect frequent eye movements during periods when the EMG records showed a lack of muscle tonus. This portable machine could be utilized in a home setting without the experimenter being present. Their subjects were five male psychiatrists. They were awakened both at home and in the laboratory for REM reports, at home by the portable device, and also recorded their dreams at home for two weeks without the device. Laboratory related content was present in 73 percent of the lab dreams, 6 percent of the home REM-detected dreams, and 4 percent of the home dreams. The laboratory dreams were significantly less bizarre, with fewer sexual and emotional elements.[136]

The largest-scale systematic comparison of laboratory dreams to home dreams that I am aware of was carried out by Subhash Bose as part of his dissertation research at Andhra University in India.[137] Home reports were obtained from fifty normal college-age males by the diary method for a period of five nights. Subjects subsequently spent five nights in a laboratory and were awakened for successive REM reports. They also slept an additional five nights in the laboratory without any REM

awakenings, but were asked to report any recall of dreams in the morning.

There were 245 dreams reported from home, 586 from REM awakenings, and 352 from morning recall after laboratory nights without awakenings. The experimenters appeared in none of the home dreams, but in 59 of the laboratory dreams. Home reports had fewer settings and human characters, but more animal characters than lab reports; home reports contained more elements of the dreamer as befriender, more sexual interactions, and more emotional content than lab reports; and there were more descriptive elements in home reports than laboratory reports.

Subjects who sleep in the laboratory are exposed to a rather unique environment. They are sleeping "in public": in a small, dark, unfamiliar bedroom often located in a hospital, with mysterious electrical gadgets attached to their bodies, scrutinized by an invisible scientist, whose voice on an intercom wakes them without warning and asks them to divulge the personal content of their dreams so that it can be permanently recorded. By way of contrast to this "Big Brother is watching you" setting, subjects at home sleep in familiar, comfortable surroundings and are awakened only when their own internal monitor decides the time is right. They are not under external scrutiny. In addition to the pervasive effect upon the verbal dream report, it seems that the laboratory can affect physiological responses. As was mentioned earlier, it is extremely rare for a "wet dream" to occur in a laboratory setting.

There are advantages and disadvantages to each method of obtaining dream reports. The two obvious advantages of the laboratory method are that it is possible to obtain a large number of dream reports in a very short span of time, and the effects of various experimental manipulations upon the dreaming process can be evaluated. The disadvantage is that the unnatural laboratory setting and presence of a scrutinizing experimenter produces dream reports that differ in several important respects, such as social interactions and emotional content, from those which would be spontaneously recalled after waking from a night's sleep at home.

There has been an active controversy over which class of dreams should be studied if one wishes to make inferences about the dreamer's personality. Some scientists insist that the only acceptable way to obtain dreams for research on personality is to awaken subjects repeatedly throughout the night for their REM reports. According to them, this constant dipping of the nets into the ocean of dreams will insure that all the dreaming material from that night is retrieved, and that inferences about the subject's personality will be based upon the full catch of dreams. Others see that version as a kind of fish story. The views of the prolaboratory scientists, however, prevailed so strongly that studies employing only home dreams were not accepted for presentation at the annual meetings of the Association for the Psychophysiological Study of Sleep for many years.

Researchers like Calvin Hall and myself, who might be classified as "dream naturalists," would argue that spontaneously recalled dream reports from a natural setting are preferable to study, because those are the ones our dreaming mind has selected as relevant and worthy of personal review by the dreamer at that particular time.

I once estimated that when the costs of the laboratory equipment, laboratory space, and laboratory personnel salaries were taken into account, it costs at least one hundred dollars to secure each REM-awakened dream report. When compared to a penny or so for pen and paper to secure each home dream report, the gargantuan cost doesn't seem justified by the reports obtained. Except for highly specialized needs, the ten-thousand-fold difference in price for the name brand dream seems excessive; the generic home dream has much to recommend it.

The lab report told to an experimenter is far more likely to be edited for socially acceptable content and laden with extraneous elements derived from the experimental laboratory conditions. Home reports can be influenced if specialized instructions are given, but if open-ended instructions similar to those to be described in the next chapter are provided, the resultant dream report can offer a revealing look at the dreamer's experiential world. The view of that inner world may still be a somewhat selected and distorted one, but the corrective lenses are much thinner than those which have to be prescribed for examining REM-awakened laboratory dreams. It has been observed by clinically oriented researchers that it is much more difficult to obtain associational material for lab dreams than for spontaneously recalled home dreams, perhaps because the REM-awakened dreamers feel less connected with the dreams "plundered" from them by manipulative experimenters.

Which method of securing dreams will best predict the dreamers' waking personality remains a question for further research.

Until the final answer is found, I have opted for the use of home dreams, and almost all the material to be discussed in the remainder of this book, except for the chapter on telepathic dreams, will come from that source.

THE DIMENSIONS OF DREAMS

WHAT'S IN A DREAM?

THE USE OF

CONTENT ANALYSIS

D reams that were recalled in the subject's usual sleeping environment were labeled "home dreams" in the last chapter to indicate that they had not been influenced by any experimental environment or procedure. This chapter will be concerned with the kinds of dreams we experience every night and will introduce a method for examining them in a systematic fashion.

Just as the REM researchers had to develop objective tools to detect and measure the physiological indicators associated with dreaming, tools also had to be developed to measure and quantify the elements found in spontaneous dream reports. Some of the problems involved in assessing the relevance of dream imagery were raised in the last chapter. In the thirst studies, for example, what types of dream imagery could be taken to indicate an effect produced by water deprivation? This chapter will present the measurement approach Calvin Hall and I developed to quantitatively analyze the content of dreams.

STUDIES OF DREAM CONTENT BEFORE 1950

The earliest systematic study of dream content I have found cited is an 1838 article in German by G. Heermann, who studied the dream imagery of one hundred blind subjects.[1] Visual imagery was absent in the dreams of the fourteen persons who lost their sight before age five, variable for those whose blindness began between the fifth to seventh year, and present for all subjects who became blind after the seventh year. Visual dreams were maintained in some cases for over fifty years after the onset of blindness.

In 1888 another investigator studied the dreams of two hundred subjects in institutions for the blind in Philadelphia and Baltimore.[2] Of the fifty-eight subjects who were totally blind, none of the thirty-two who became blind before age five saw in their dreams, visual imagery was variable for the six subjects who lost their sight between the fifth and seventh years, and visual dreams were present for all twenty subjects who became blind after their seventh year. This investigator had been unaware of Heermann's research when he started his own work, but the results of these two large-scale studies were amazingly similar. The developmental stage between the fifth and seventh years was the critical period that separated nonvisual recallers from those who continued to have visual imagery in their dreams. Both of these early studies also reported that visual imagery progressively faded as the subjects became older. Individual differences were prominent, however.

The first systematic investigation of sensory imagery in the dreams of subjects without specific sensory impairments was reported in 1893 by Mary Calkins, a psychologist from Wellesley College.[3] Dr. Calkins later became the first female president of the American Psychological Association. Based on several hundred dream reports contributed by herself and a male subject, she found that the most frequent type of dream imagery was visual and the second most common, auditory. She concluded that there was an essential continuity of waking and dreaming life, because she was able to discover some evident connection with waking experience in 89 percent of the dreams. She also reported that reasoning was present in some dreams:

> Not only imagination but real thought occurs in dreams though the fact is often denied. The frequency of conversation in dreams might be looked upon as a proof of the lower stages, conception and judgment, of thought activity, for both are necessary to the use and combination of words. . . . Not only do we form judgments in our dreams sometimes correctly though often incorrectly, but we carry on whole trains of reasoning.[4]

Calkins's approach was continued by two of her students, Sarah Weed and Florence Hallam, who obtained 381 dreams from six females.[5] They reported that 85 percent of the dreams involved visual imagery, 68 percent auditory, 11 percent tactile (touch), 7 percent olfactory (smell), and 6 percent gustatory (taste). The majority of dreams were classified as unpleasant in emotional quality. In decreasing order of frequency, these unpleasant emotions were perplexity and hurry, discomfort and helplessness, fear, anger, disappointment, and shame. The degree of overall unpleasantness varied considerably between subjects.

A 1905 study that asked fifty-five female students in an introductory psychology course to record their dreams on six successive mornings reported similar findings.[6] The 287 dreams recorded were classified with regard to sensory imagery. Visual imagery was mentioned in 63 percent of the reports, auditory imagery in 26 percent, tactile imagery in 8 percent, and motor imagery such as falling, running, or flying in 5 percent. Taste and smell imagery appeared in only about 1 percent of the dreams. The researcher reported that emotional reactions were described in 11 percent of the dreams but in only two of the thirty-one dreams were the reactions pleasurable. The students were able to account for some connection between their preceding daytime experiences and the dream content in over 55 percent of their dreams.

One investigator administered a questionnaire to eighty-one male and eighty-nine female students in psychology courses and reported that over ninety-six percent of subjects reported that visual imagery was more frequent in their dreams than auditory imagery.[7] Two-thirds indicated their belief that they did think in their dreams. By far, the most frequent subject matter was that of "frustrated effort"; nearly 90 percent of the subjects acknowledged such dreams. Over two-thirds of the subjects reported their dreams were complicated rather than simple, and 93 percent reported that they usually participated actively in their dreams. An interesting finding was that women were inclined to tell their dreams to friends almost twice as often as men.

One researcher used interviews to obtain information about dreaming experiences from twenty-five male and twenty-five female college students.[8] The male subjects were questioned by a male interviewer and female subjects by a female interviewer. All the interviewees were friends of the interviewers. The overwhelming majority of the subjects reported being the chief actor in their dreams, and a majority reported that they experienced recurrent dreams. Women were far more likely to realize consciously that they were dreaming. Seven women reported that they were able to purposely wake themselves to get rid of a bad dream, while only one male reported this ability. Many more types of fear dreams were reported by women, while men were more likely to report pleasant dreams. For example, fear of pursuit was mentioned by twenty-three women and fear of burglars by sixteen women, but no male subjects reported either of these fears. Men's most frequent fear dream was of falling, but only eight men acknowledged such dreams, while twenty females reported falling dreams. Almost all the women reported their dreams had some relation to a love affair, particularly when it was at its height, whereas only one male reported any relationship between a love affair and his dreams. Perhaps the male subjects felt that they had to maintain a "macho" image with their male interviewers; they were afraid of almost nothing and not sentimental or overly involved in romantic concerns.

An excellent review of various studies carried out on dreams up to the middle of the twentieth century was published in 1953 by Glenn Ramsey, a psychologist at the University of Texas.[9] A total of 121 titles appeared in his reference list. On the basis of his extensive review, Ramsey evaluated the research on dreams up to that time. He indicated that dream researchers needed to follow certain basic scientific practices if the potential of their work was to be realized. They should design their experiments in ways that would allow other researchers to repeat the study and check its results. They should emphasize quantitative rather than anecdotal data and should publish their basic data along with the conclusions they drew from it, so that other investigators could evaluate the findings and test other possible interpretations of the data. It was also essential, he noted, to use control groups, especially when asserting "that particular groups . . . have characteristic dreams." He also offered the following observations:

> More precise definitions are needed in selecting and classifying various aspects or characteristics of dreams. Some of the contradictory findings appear to be artifacts of the classificatory treatment of data rather than actual characteristics of dreams. . . .
>
> A survey of past studies on dreaming probably gives one of the best examples in the field of psychology for the need of statistical controls and treatment of data. . . .
>
> The subject of dreaming is considered relevant to the dynamics of behavior by many practicing psychiatrists and psychologists. Even academic psychologists who are interested in thought and imagery processes find that dreaming is a phenomenon of importance to them. The psychologist with his research orientation and research abilities could undoubtedly help advance the knowledge of dreaming from the present speculative and descriptive stage and give it a more experimental and quantitative basis.[10]

HORTON'S INVENTORIAL RECORD FORMS

Since his review was so thorough, it is surprising that Ramsey overlooked the "inventorial record forms" published by psychologist Lydiard Horton in 1914.[11] Horton's interest in objectification and a statistical approach to the study of dreams was clearly stated in his opening paragraphs:

> The method to be described is for those workers in psychology who may wish to reach agreement as to a given case of dream analysis by the application of objective, that is to say, statistical methods. . . .
>
> The dream inventory is nothing more than a systematic and clean-cut enumeration of the principal items entering into a given dream phantasy. . . .
>
> The inventory is not only an enumeration and a catalogue of items to be accounted for, but it is also a classification of the elements in a dream.[12]

Horton's *Dream Analysis Record* consisted of four pages. Page A, the "Narrative Page," provided space for a preliminary record of the dream narrative along with supplementary details. Page B was the "Inventory Page" and itemized five classes of elements: (1) scenery and settings; (2) characters; (3) stage properties, such as clothing and other objects; (4) situations or the plot and action; and (5) attitudes of characters, including the dreamer, with regard to postures and emotional tone. Page C, the "Association Page," requested that the dreamer give attention to each of the individual items previously listed and "ask yourself what it makes you think of." Page D was the "Recent Impressions Page," which asked the dreamer to note any conversations, books read, and so forth during the twenty-four-hour period preceding the dream and to search for "any recent impression or event

that seems similar or related to the dream." In this last section the dreamer was also requested to note any external or internal stimuli which may have influenced the dreamer's condition while asleep.

In discussing how he came to develop his inventory, Horton indicated,

> This standard is based on the expected need of classification as arrived at after experiment with two hundred dreams of normal people, and, to finish off, an experiment in classifying "Alice" [in Wonderland]. Thereafter, the classification of "Alice" was treated as a model and guide in the matter of listing items taken from actual dreams. . . . It is, then, the existence of a common standard of this kind which gives to the dream inventory its objective character, and which tends to make the items in different dreams reasonably comparable. With this beginning assured, we may look for some validity in the statistics of individual differences in dreams.[13]

In his article, Horton gave some brief examples of how elements from the dreamlike story of Alice would be categorized in his system, and he also demonstrated how it was employed in his attempt to analyze the possible meaning of a dream from a young girl. Horton later published a series of theoretical articles in which he attempted to explain various dream mechanisms, but he never published any statistical tabulations utilizing his classification system.

CALVIN HALL'S CONTENT APPROACH

Ramsey's strongly worded call for dream researchers to develop and apply some system of classifying dream content so that it could be evaluated in an objective and quantitative fashion had already been put into practice by Calvin Hall, the individual most responsible for making giant strides in the area of dream content analysis since the middle of the twentieth century.

As I pointed out in chapter 8, Hall wanted to translate his cognitive theory of dreams[14] and dream symbols[15] in such a way that the frequency of certain dream images could be numerically tabulated, in order to discover what conceptions and preoccupations of the dreamer might lie behind such images. Hall decided to utilize the technique of content analysis to realize his objective. He indicated that content analysis offered the following benefits: it provided

> methods in which the bias of the analyst is at least minimized, in which the essential operations can be made explicit and the conclusions thereby more easily replicated, and in which the findings can be communicated in meaningful numbers.[16]

During his tenure at Western Reserve University, from 1937 to 1957, Hall and his graduate students collected thousands of dream reports from college students and other populations. He prepared a seventeen-page mimeographed "Manual for Dream Analysis" in 1949, which was used by several of his graduate students in their theses and dissertations on various dream topics. Although it was not specifically cited, this manual was employed by Hall in preparing a short popular article in 1951 for *Scientific American* entitled "What People Dream About."[17]

Hall's findings in this article were based upon dreams from essentially normal people. Dreams had been recorded by subjects on a printed form which requested them "to write down your dream in as complete detail as you are able to." Information concerning the setting or settings of the dream; the age, sex, and relationship of the characters to the dreamer; the dreamer's emotions and extent of participation; and the dreamer's awareness of color was also requested.

To determine the most common settings, Hall examined a thousand adult dreams and tabulated a total of 1,328 different settings. The most frequent scene was a part of a home or other building; this appeared in 24 percent of dreams. A conveyance such as an automobile appeared in 13 percent of the dreams. There were eight other categories of settings, such as recreational places, outdoor areas, streets, and shops. When the setting was part of a dwelling, it was most often the living room, followed in order by the bedroom, kitchen, stairway, and basement. Most of the scenes reported in these dreams were reasonably familiar to the dreamer, but Hall commented that work-oriented settings such as offices, factories, and classrooms were only minimally represented.

To tabulate the characters appearing in dreams, Hall utilized 1,819 dreams from subjects between the ages of eighteen and twenty-eight. In 15 percent of these dreams, the only character was the

Of all activities occurring in dreams, movement like walking or running is the most common. Nude Descending a Staircase, No. 2 by Marcel Duchamp.

dreamer. In dreams in which other characters appeared, 43 percent of them were identified as strangers, 37 percent as friends or acquaintances, and 19 percent as family members, relatives, or in-laws. When the characters were identified with regard to sex, Hall found that men dream about other men twice as often as they do about women, whereas women dream almost equally about both sexes. When the age of the characters was considered, Hall reported that people dream most often about other people of approximately their own age.

To examine the types of activities in dreams, Hall classified 2,668 actions from a thousand dreams. The most common category of activity involved movements, such as walking, running, or other change in bodily position (34 percent), and the next most common involved talking (11 percent), followed by sitting and watching (7 percent each). Common waking activities such as typing, cooking, and fixing things were hardly ever reported in dreams. Interactions between characters were classified from a sample of 1,320 dreams. Hostile acts outnumbered friendly ones 448 to 188. Emotions felt by the dreamers were also classified, and Hall concluded that 64 percent of all dream emotions were negative or unpleasant, involving emotions such as apprehension, anger, or sadness. Paradoxi-

cally, Hall noted that in the judgment of the dreamers themselves, the dreams as a whole were rated pleasant much more often than unpleasant. Dreams may have been rated as pleasant overall because the dreamers enjoyed the flights of fancy and participation in surreal experiences that dreams provide and chose to overlook the individual events that were accompanied by unpleasant emotions.

Over three thousand dreams were surveyed for the presence of color. Hall found that 29 percent of the dreams were in partial or full color, with 31 percent of women and 24 percent of men reporting color. Individual differences were marked; many people reported never experiencing color in their dreams, while a few individuals stated that all of their dreams were in color.

After Hall founded the Institute of Dream Research in 1961, he began to systematize his efforts for a content analysis approach to dreams. During 1962, he prepared a mimeographed set of six technical manuals for classifying various dream elements, and he and Bill Domhoff used some of them to publish three articles in 1963 on aggression, friendliness, and the sexual identity of characters in dreams. These three articles will be discussed in the next chapter, where age and sex differences in dream content are reviewed.

THE HALL-VAN DE CASTLE SCALES

When I joined Calvin at the Institute of Dream Research in 1964, I arrived with a background of clinical and research experi-

ence in scoring and validating projective tests of personality. We decided to collaborate on the task of amplifying his mimeographed technical manuals for classifying different dream elements and prepared a book presenting an expanded set of scoring rules for various dream scales. Below are some remarks from the preface to our book, *The Content Analysis of Dreams*:

> [This] is the first book devoted to describing how the investigation of dreams can be approached in an objective quantitative fashion. We hope that it will do for dreams quantitatively what Freud's book did for them qualitatively. . . .
>
> . . . For the first time, a comprehensive system of classifying and scoring the contents of reported dreams has been described and made available to the dream investigator. An important empirical contribution is provided through the extensive normative material based upon 1,000 dreams that is included in this book.[18]

Normative material refers to the availability of information based upon data obtained from a large number of individuals. Reference to normative data is made implicitly when we say that the average American male is so many inches tall, weighs a certain number of pounds, and watches a given number of hours of football on TV annually. The use of actuarial tables by life insurance companies to calculate health risks or longevity is an explicit example of using normative materials, or simply "norms."

Our book contained a chapter explaining the reliability of our scoring system, in which we demonstrated that it is possible for two independent judges to obtain very similar scores when using the scales we developed. Several appendices were included in our book: One listed alphabetically the 1,170 objects mentioned in our sample of one thousand dreams, along with their frequencies for male and female dreamers. Another appendix, intended to increase familiarity with our scales for potential users, presented a detailed discussion as to how ten sample dreams would be scored within our system. A third appendix described how our classification system could be transferred to punched cards, so that the data could be mechanically tabulated and evaluated by computer. The final appendix suggested a dream report form that other investigators might wish to adapt for their research studies. In addition to name, age, sex, and date of the report, the dreamer would be asked the following:

> Please describe the dream exactly and as fully as you remember it. Your report should contain, whenever possible, a description of the setting of the dream, whether it was familiar to you or not, a description of the people, their sex, age, and relationship to you, and of any animals that appeared in the dream. If possible, describe your feelings during the dream and whether it was pleasant or unpleasant. Be sure to tell exactly what happened during the dream to you and the other characters.

The norms presented in our book were obtained from a content analysis of one thousand dreams collected from undergraduate students at Western Reserve University and Baldwin Wallace College in Ohio during the years 1945 to 1950. These students had recorded their dreams as part of various class projects using assigned code numbers so that their identity was known only to the class instructor. Five dreams were picked from each of one hundred male and one hundred female dream series. A dream series would contain ten to twenty dreams. The selection procedure was random, except that any dream report of less than fifty words or more than three hundred words was rejected.

Basically, our scoring system consists of sixteen "empirical" scales and three "theoretical" scales, the latter derived from psychoanalytic theory, with an elaborate but precise form of notation that researchers can use to describe dreams. To give some idea of the comprehensiveness of the system, a brief explanation will be given of each of the various scales.

The Settings scale is used to describe the type of location in which the events take place. The major distinctions involve classifying the locale as an indoor or outdoor setting and indicating the degree of familiarity that the setting has to the dreamer. Sixteen different scores are possible for settings.

The Objects scale is used to categorize any tangible objects that appear in dreams. Buildings are included under an architectural heading and are further broken down into subtypes: houses or other "residential" dwellings; "vocational" buildings, such as factories or offices; and buildings or rooms used for "entertainment," such as restaurants or movie theaters. Other object clas-

sifications refer to things found in the household, used for travel, or used for communication, such as a book or radio. Twenty-four different object categories are found on this scale.

The people, mythological figures, or animals appearing in dreams are scored on the Characters scale. With the exception of animals, each character is classified with regard to four components: whether a single character or a group of characters is represented; the sex of the character (male, female, or indefinite); the character's relationship to the dreamer (family member, relative, known character, etc.); and age of the character (adult, teenager, child, or baby). Hundreds of different character combinations can be represented by this schema.

Three different groupings of social interactions are scored: Aggression, Friendliness, and Sex. The scoring is similar for all three types of interactions. The character who initiates the interaction is recorded first and the recipient character second. Various subclassifications within each social interaction grouping are also included. For example, eight classifications of aggression are scored. It is also possible to indicate whether the interaction was spontaneously initiated or occurred as a response to some previous action.

The Activities scale indicates which types of activities—physical, verbal, visual, auditory, and so forth—are involved and which character carries out these activities. Two scales, included under an Achievement Outcomes grouping, indicate whether characters succeed or fail in coping with problem situations encountered in the dream. Similarly, two scales included under the Environmental Press grouping indicate which characters experience misfortune or good fortune in the dream. A misfortune is any adversity that befalls characters as a result of external circumstances over which they have no control, as the result of fate or bad luck. A good fortune would be scored for a dream character who won a lottery or benefited from some other form of good luck.

Five different types of Emotions are scored and an indication is made as to which character experiences these emotions. The types of descriptive terms used by the dreamer in referring to things (big, small, old, ugly, fast, cold, etc.) are included in the Modifiers scale. The Temporal scale contains scores for occasions when the dreamer indicates concern with time factors, while the Negative scale includes instances in which the dreamer uses words such as no, not, never, and so forth.

The theoretical scales were included in our book to illustrate how one could construct scales for measuring any psychodynamic construct that can be defined in an objective fashion. The Castration Complex grouping, for example, includes three scales, designed to measure castration anxiety, castration wish, and penis envy in dreams. The Orality grouping includes two scales: one devoted to instances of oral incorporation such as eating, while the other refers to oral emphasis and includes mention of oral body parts like the lips or tongue and related oral activities, such as kissing. The other theoretical scale is a Regression scale for scoring instances when the dreamer mentions persons, locations, or activities that were associated with an earlier part of his or her life.

An extremely negative and, in our opinion, stunningly inaccurate, sloppy review of our book appeared by a member of the Chicago research establishment.[19] For example, he criticized us for failing to review the work of others, even though we had a fifty-eight-page chapter entitled "Scales of Content Analysis Devised by Others." He also stated that our "norms appear to have very little utility for present and, future dream research." I'm happy to report that our norms have, in fact, shown considerable utility and our system of content analysis has been the one most extensively used by contemporary researchers in studies involving dream content. The precision and detail of our normative material, along with the impressive reliability figures we have provided for the various scales, are the major reasons other researchers have been drawn to our system.

Not only were Hall and I able to obtain high levels of agreement when we independently scored the various scales in our system, but other researchers also have obtained high levels of scoring agreement between two different judges or raters. When ten of our scales were used by two Canadian judges to score 849 dreams, their percentages of agreement ranged from 84 percent to 94 percent for the various scales.[20] When all of our scales were used to score 200 dreams by two Indian judges, their percentages of perfect agreement were often higher than Hall and I obtained.[21] One investigator[22] was particularly interested in using our Activities scale. He reported reliability figures of .98 for physical activities, .98 for movement activities, and .99 for total activities. Our scoring rules therefore appeared to be clearly enough stated so that other investigators could use them to score dreams in an objective manner, and in a manner that would be consistent from one judge or rater to another.

It would also be important to know whether the frequency of various scoring categories that we reported for our sample of dreamers would be similar to those obtained from other groups of dreamers. A group of researchers[23] collected 418 dream reports from twenty-six male and thirty-nine female introductory psychology students at the University of Cincinnati, that were similar in length to our normative group. After these dream reports were scored for the presence of over thirty different kinds of characters, the researchers concluded: "The accompanying table shows a striking similarity of character frequency between the Cincinnati dreams and those reported by Hall and Van de Castle."

A larger scale comparison was carried out with fifty-three male and sixty-nine female students in psychology classes at the University of Richmond in Virginia.[24] Each student contributed an average of about five dreams, making a total number of 263 male dreams and 340 female dreams. These dreams were scored for the presence of characters; aggressive, friendly, and sexual interactions; misfortunes; settings; and clothing and weapons. A few differences were found between these two college groups. The Richmond students had a higher proportion of familiar characters than did their Western Reserve counterparts. The characters in the Richmond dreams showed somewhat less friendliness and less reference to clothing. There were

no differences on seven different scores of aggression or on misfortunes or the percentage of outdoor settings. Overall, the scores were surprisingly similar from these two student samples even though they had been obtained thirty years apart. Sex differences were also examined in the study, and the investigators concluded that "sex differences or lack of them in all [twenty] content categories used in this study have remained the same in dreams collected from college students in 1950 and 1980."[25]

Another researcher in California recently (1991) scored five hundred dreams from one hundred female college students at the University of California at Berkeley. A total of fifty-four categories was employed, but very few significant differences were found when they were compared to our female normative tables. The researcher concluded that "the norms do seem to be surprisingly stable."[26]

One particularly intriguing use of content analysis methodology was devised by Hall in conjunction with Bill Domhoff from the University of California at Santa Cruz.[27] They applied the methodology to an analysis of twenty-eight of Freud's dreams and thirty-one of Jung's. There were many similarities in what these two famous psychiatrists dreamed about, but there were also some clear differences. Hall and Domhoff attempted to relate some of the differences to information known about these two prominent men. There were more characters in Freud's dreams than Jung's, which fits in with Jung's interest in spending considerable time alone in Bollingen at his lake retreat. There were, however, more family members in Jung's dreams, which corresponds with his social life being centered around his family. Although both men had about the same amount of friendliness in their dreams, in Freud's dreams the friendliness was nearly always initiated by another person, while Jung was always the one who initiated the friendliness to others in his own dreams. Various biographical sources indicate that Freud did expect others to come to him.

The pattern of aggressive and friendly interactions with male and female characters was notably different. Most male dreamers have more aggressive interactions with male characters and friendly interactions with female characters. Jung's dreams followed this pattern, but Freud's manifested the opposite order; he displayed more aggression with females and more friendliness with males. Quite a bit of biographical data is available to support the assessment that Freud had a negative attitude toward women, while he had several intense friendships with men.

Encouraged by the results of the Freud and Jung dream analyses, Hall and another collaborator analyzed thirty-seven dreams from the diaries and letters of Franz Kafka.[28] They found seven major themes, such as bodily preoccupation, body disfigurement, and an emphasis on clothing. Consulting various biographical material, they found that these themes were amply reflected in his waking life. Kafka was very concerned about his body and continuously worried about his health and how his body compared to that of other men. He was excessively interested in clothes, and his diaries were filled with descriptions of what types of clothing people were wearing. His dreams also demonstrated a great interest in looking at and witnessing others' behaviors. Kafka acknowledged that he was an "eye-man" in his waking life.

Hall's next project did not involve a famous person, but his subject, "Norman," was an unusual individual. Alan Bell was a psychologist who had worked with Norman as a patient and in the process had obtained a large number of dreams from him. Bell contacted Hall to see if Hall would be willing to create a profile of Norman's personality based only on his dreams. Knowing only his age (early thirties) and sex, Hall used our scoring system to analyze 1,368 dreams from this individual. It soon became apparent from examining these dreams that the dreamer had been institutionalized for molesting children. Hall compared the various elements in Norman's dreams with our norms for male dreamers, then read through the dreams to see if there were any predominant themes that might have been missed by our scoring system.

Operating on the assumption that the frequency of occurrence of a dream element or theme directly represented the dreamer's preoccupation with that topic in waking life, Hall prepared a detailed psychological profile of this individual. One conjecture was that this man preferred to look at the genitals of little girls. The presence of women with beards and penises led to another prediction that the dreamer suffered from gender confusion. Hall also paid attention to the underrepresentation of certain dream elements that would be expected to be present. Since there were no references to a father, Hall speculated that Norman's father either was absent or that Norman had suffered some traumatic experience in connection with him. On the basis of other dream material, Hall predicted that Norman had been sexually abused by his father when he was a child.

Bell later provided biographical information concerning the dreamer; further information was obtained from records at various institutions where Norman had been confined and from psychological tests. Norman himself wrote several letters providing additional information in response to questions raised by Hall after the dream analysis was completed. In their book on Norman, *The Personality of a Child Molester*, Bell and Hall give many examples of Norman's dreams and a description of his background and test scores.[29] The numerous "blind" statements by Hall, based only on dream material, were in striking agreement with what documentary information subsequently revealed about Norman's history, personality dynamics, and sexual behavior. It was learned, for example, that Norman had been forced to perform fellatio on his father for several years, beginning around age four, which confirmed Hall's surmise regarding sexual abuse.

Many other examples of marked correspondences between the dream series of widely different individuals and the facts of their waking lives are provided in *The Individual and His Dreams* by Hall and Vernon Nordby.[30] After a case-by-case demonstration of the continuities between dreams and waking life, the authors include a lengthy section explaining how our content analysis system can be used to help individuals analyze their own dreams. A detailed, step-by-step procedure is given to guide the person aspiring to obtain better self-understanding through dreams. I am a

biased observer, of course, but I feel that such abundant case history material powerfully demonstrates our system's utility for carrying out character and personality analysis on the basis of manifest dreams.

Content analysis is illuminating in a number of different ways. By pointing out differences and similarities between the dreamer's scores and the norms we have developed, it can help to define an individual's uniqueness with considerable precision. It can also be used, as I describe in some of my own writings, to explore the symbolic or theoretical significance of a selected dream element.[31] An example of this approach is a large-scale study that I carried out to explore the significance of animal figures in dreams.[32]

Dream theorists have offered several speculations as to the meanings which might be attributed to animal figures in dreams. Freud proposed that "wild beasts . . . represent passionate impulses of which the dreamer is afraid, whether they are his own or those of other people."[33] In a later paragraph describing how many specific animals, such as snakes, fish, and cats, are used as genital symbols, Freud stated, "Small animals and vermin represent small children—for instance, undesired brothers and sisters."[34] Ernest Jones, Freud's biographer, said, "Analytical experience has shown that the occurrence of animals in a dream regularly indicates a sexual theme, usually an incest one."[35] Wilhelm Stekel claimed, "The danger of approaching insanity expresses itself in dreams of . . . a sudden attack by a wild beast."[36] Another theorist proposed that being bitten by an animal may be a symbol of "pangs of conscience."[37] Nandor Fodor, a psychoanalyst who emphasizes birth trauma, suggested that being swallowed by a voracious animal was a portrayal of our intense fear of birth.[38] Medard Boss observed, "In subjective interpretation a dream tortoise would signify the tortoiselike and armored character of the dreamer himself."[39]

It's obvious from this limited selection that several theoretical views have been advanced regarding the significance of animal figures in dreams. I began my own research into this subject matter with a quantitative analysis of how often animal figures appeared in adult dreams and which animals were the most common. I examined two thousand dreams from female college students and two thousand dreams from male college students. There were 149 female and 151 male dreams containing at least one animal figure. This represents a frequency of 7.5 percent animal dreams for each sex. The seven most common animals for adults were dogs (66), horses (59), cats (27), birds (27), snakes (24), fish (21), and insects (20).

I also examined the dreams of 721 children aged four to sixteen for the presence of animal figures. There were 383 girls and 358 boys in this sample. The frequency for each animal figure at each age level was tabulated for girls and boys. Animal figures were present in 39.4 percent of dreams from the four- and five- year-old children and the percentage steadily dropped for each subsequent age grouping (six- and seven-year-olds, 35.5 percent; eight- and nine-year-olds, 33.6 percent; ten- and eleven-year-olds, 29.8 percent; twelve- and thirteen-year-olds, 21.9 percent; and fourteen- through sixteen-

year-olds, 13.7 percent). Boys had higher animal percentage figures at ages four through six (44 percent, versus 34 percent for girls), while girls had higher figures at ages nine through 11 (36 percent, versus 26 percent for boys). Overall, animal figures appeared in 29 percent of the combined girls' dreams and 29.6 percent of the combined boys' dreams. There were more than three times as many animal figures in the dreams of children as there were in the dreams of adults. The seven most frequent animal figures for children were dogs (30), horses (28), cats (15), snakes (15), bears (14), lions (13), and monsters (Wolfman) (13).

If the frequencies for all animal figures are considered, it is clear that children dream more frequently of large and threatening wild animals, while college students dream more often of pets and domesticated or small animals. Bears, lions, tigers, gorillas, elephants, bulls, dinosaurs, dragons, and monsters accounted for 27 percent of the animal figures in children's dreams but only 7 percent of the animal figures in adult dreams. This collection of wild animals appeared more frequently (forty-four times) in boys' dreams than in girls' dreams (twenty-seven times). Several theorists have suggested that these large, threatening animals may represent parental figures in the dreams of children.

An interesting sex difference was found in the types of animal figures. Women and girls reported significantly more mammals, while men and boys reported significantly more nonmammals. What could account for this difference? Since mammals are biologically, behaviorally, and conceptually more similar to humans—since humans, in fact, are mammals—people who report more mammals in dreams should also be inclined to report more human characters. In our normative tables, Hall and I found that women report significantly more human characters than men (1,423 versus 1,180). Individuals who give mammal responses on the Rorschach Inkblot Test are considered to have greater acceptance of their own emotions.[40] Our normative tables indicate that women describe their personal emotions in dreams more often than men (351 times, versus 241 for men). Thus, women may dream more about mammals because they are more preoccupied with, and socially accepting of, humans and humanlike characters, and because they display more emotional self-acceptance. Conceptualized in this fashion, mammals may represent greater social and emotional maturity. It's also possible that females may identify at some deeper level with other forms of life that nurse their young with mammary glands.

An interesting confirmation for the suggestion that a higher level of animal phylogenetic development might be associated with a higher level of social and emotional maturity was provided in the two dream series reported by Medard Boss that were discussed in chapter 8.[41] One series involved an engineer who moved from the world of inanimate objects to the plant world and gradually through progressively more phylogenetically developed animals in his dreams as his mental health improved. The other series involved a woman who regressed in her dreams from the world of highly developed animals down to the plant world and finally to the level of

inanimate objects as her mental health deteriorated.

To investigate what further meanings might be attached to animal figures in dreams, I carried out a "contingency analysis" to determine what other elements are present when animal figures appear in dreams. Simply stated, I tried to answer the question, What other dream content is found when an animal shows up? I examined four groups of dreams from American college students. The first group consisted of 907 dreams (454 from males, 453 from females) in which all the characters were humans. The remaining three groups, totaling 150 dreams, varied in terms of how predominant animal figures were. The first animal group consisted of 54 dreams in which both human and animal characters appeared, but the number of human characters was greater. In the second animal group, an equal number of human and animal characters appeared in each of the 40 dreams. The third animal group contained 56 dreams in which either only animal characters, or at least more animal characters than human characters, were present. Each of the three groups of animal dreams included an equal number of male and female dreams.

The assumption underlying this grouping of dreams was that if animal figures in dreams do represent some unusual affective or cognitive component of mentation, there should be progressive changes in dream scores as the predominance of animal figures increases. Various dream scores from our system of content analysis were employed to test this assumption. Several significant findings emerged. Dreams became progressively shorter as animal figures

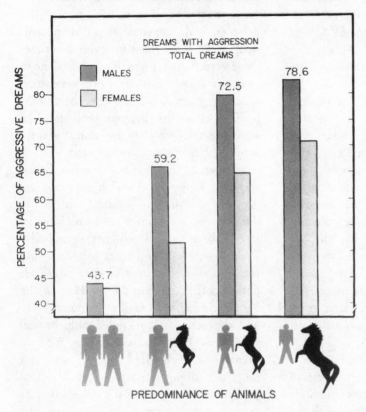

PERCENTAGE OF DREAMS WITH AGGRESSIONS IN
RELATIONSHIP TO PREDOMINANCE OF ANIMAL CHARACTERS

The percentage of aggressive dreams increases for both sexes as the presence of animal figures increases.

predominated. Since anxious dreams can cause premature awakenings, it is possible that there was something sufficiently threatening about animal dreams to cause the dreamer to abort such dreams quickly.

There was a marked and progressive increase in the percentage of aggressive dreams as animal figures predominated. For the human only category, the figure was 44 percent; for the more human than animal category, it was 59 percent; for the equal human and animal category, it was 73 percent; and for the more animal than human category, it was 79 percent. Not only were

there more aggressive dreams but, within the dreams, the number of aggressive acts associated with each dream character also increased markedly. In the human only category, there were twenty-eight aggressive acts for every one hundred characters; in the equal human and animal category, the figure rose to thirty-eight aggressive acts per one hundred characters; and in the more animal than human category, there were fifty-six aggressive acts per one hundred characters.

As the predominance of animal figures increased, there was a steady increase in the presence of misfortunes, apprehension, and apparently disorientation, because an increase occurred in the proportion of unfamiliar and distorted settings. Efforts to cope with challenges posed within the dream also progressively increased as animal figures predominated.

When asked to judge the sex of animals on an association test, subjects reported that 73 percent were male. This finding led to additional analysis; the number of male characters present was found to increase with the predominance of animal figures.[42] This association between males and animals may be reflected in such everyday statements as "He behaved like an animal"; seldom do we hear "She behaved like an animal." If an association between a woman and an animal occurs, it is generally in reference to a natural maternal instinct to nourish and protect her young.

Striking differences appeared when a close examination was made of aggressive and friendly interactions in dreams involving only humans versus dreams involving animals. In the human only category, the dreamer received friendliness almost as often as aggression from other characters, but animals in dreams attacked the dreamer on forty-seven occasions and acted friendly on only two. If another character was to initiate some interaction with the dreamer, there was a 44 percent chance that it would be friendly if the other character was human, but only a 4 percent chance if that character was an animal.

Animals behaved the same way toward both sexes. They attacked male characters twenty-three times more often than they extended friendliness, and they attacked females twenty-four times more often. The dreamer's response to the animal varied somewhat according to the sex of the dreamer. Male dreamers attacked the animal twenty-three times for every five times they were friendly; female dreamers, however, attacked animals only seventeen times for every ten times they befriended it. The sex of the dreamer, therefore, had some influence on how the animal was reacted to but not on how it acted.

An effort to determine whether the association between animal figures and aggression in dreams would hold for a different age level was made by Rick Seidel in his master's thesis, which I supervised.[43] Rick analyzed dreams from fifty boys and fifty girls eleven and twelve years old. Each child contributed one dream. Half of the dreams contained at least one animal figure and the other half included only human characters. These two contrasting types of dreams were matched by age, sex, and length of dream report. Aggression was present in 74 percent of the animal dreams but in only 44 percent of the nonanimal dreams. Aggression was always physical when an animal was involved, but only 30 percent of the time in the nonanimal dreams. Rick also looked for possible sex differences. He found that for boys, animal figures were strongly and positively associated with aggression, particularly physical aggression, but the association was much weaker for girls. Girls displayed significantly more friendly interactions in all their dreams and this sometimes included those involving animal characters.

These quantitative analyses suggest that animal figures in dreams represent the unacceptable and frightening impulses that reside within our personalities, as claimed by several clinicians, including Freud. In short, animal figures portray the animal side of our nature. These results indicate a very strong relationship between animal figures and aggression, particularly physical aggression. We can try to appease animals when they appear in our dreams, but they generally act in ways that cause us distress and fear. Our attempts to tame our animal urges are usually not very successful.

Since animals seemed to signify unbridled emotional expression, I predicted that they would appear less frequently in laboratory dreams, because the laboratory situation seems to inhibit the frank expression of hostile and sexual feelings. I expected that the sanitized laboratory situation would not provide a sufficiently earthy environment to support the presence of animal figures. I utilized the data that Hall and I had collected in our study of laboratory versus home dreams, where dreams were obtained from the same fifteen male subjects under both conditions. To obtain an index of animal "density," I divided the number of animal characters by total characters (human and animal characters combined). The animal density figure was 3.9 percent for 506 REM dreams and 7.4 percent for 264 spontaneously recalled home dreams from the same subjects. In his dissertation, involving fifty Indian male college students, Subhash Bose also found more animal characters and a higher animal density figure in spontaneously recalled home dreams than in REM dreams. Dream animals seem to come out and roam more frequently in a natural home environment than in an artificial laboratory environment.

The percentage of animal figures decreases as the dreamer's age increases. This finding is theoretically significant: animal imagery may represent an immature, less-developed or less-differentiated form of cognitive structure. That is the interpretation given to a high percentage of animal imagery on the Rorschach Inkblot Test. When I analyzed the laboratory dreams from the study by Hall and myself, I found another line of evidence to suggest an association between animal figures and more regressive modes of mental activity. More animal characters were present during the second and third REM periods, the time of night when dream imagery is more likely to involve childhood settings and earlier temporal references. Animal figures thus seemed to be more frequent when the dreamer returned to an earlier developmental period in his or her life.

Animal imagery may also be related to sexual maturity. I obtained several hundred dreams from female nursing students in Miami, as well as information regarding their menstrual histories. I divided them into three maturity groups on the basis of when they had reached menarche (first period). The most sexually immature group (those not reaching menarche until age thirteen or later) had the highest percentage of animal dreams, those reaching menarche at the "normal" age of twelve had an intermediate animal percentage, while the most sexually mature group (those reaching menarche by age eleven or younger) had the lowest percentage of animal dreams.

We've seen that age and sex can be important variables to consider when attempting to understand the significance of animal figures in dreams. What about the contribution of culture? Do animal figures in dreams vary from culture to culture, or are there some dream animals which appear in all cultures?

I examined cross-cultural dreams in Calvin Hall's files to obtain some answers to these questions. We had dreams from Australian aborigines, natives on South Pacific islands, Hopi and Kwakiutl Indians, and Peruvians. The only type of animal figure to appear in the dreams of *all* these cultural groups was some form of bird. The other animal figures were particular to each culture: kangaroos in Australian aborigine dreams, fish and aquatic animals in dreams of natives living near water, and snakes in the dreams of desert-dwelling natives. Lions and elephants were reported only by Peruvian adolescents who were attending school. Except for the Peruvians, many of the animals were reported in the context of hunting or fishing, although animals were often cast in an attacking role throughout all these cultural groups.

In chapter 10, which dealt with laboratory approaches to dreaming, I indicated that considerable advances have been made toward understanding the biology and temporal patterning of dreaming. Objective physiological indicators are now available to indicate *when* we are dreaming. The material presented in this chapter has demonstrated that the use of objective content analysis approaches can broaden our understanding of *what* we dream about. We now know what types of dream elements are generally found in the dreams of normal adults, that these elements are remarkably similar from one region of the United States to another, and that they have not changed very much over a period of several decades.

Several examples were provided in this chapter of the power of content analysis to make accurate inferences about a given individual's waking personality and preoccupations based on an examination of the frequency of various elements in his or her dreams. By means of some analyses carried out on animal dreams, it has also been shown that content analysis can help to clarify the possible theoretical meaning or significance associated with the presence of a particular dream element. The tools provided by content analysis, particularly the scales that Calvin Hall and I developed, can enable a dream researcher to report results in an objective, quantified fashion that can be independently evaluated by other investigators. The measurements of a night's dream content can actually be assessed more reliably than can measurements of a night's EEG tracings.

Our system of content analysis is not the only one available. Well over a hundred separate scales have been developed by others for selected purposes.[44] The chief advantages to be obtained in using our scales are that they cover almost all the elements to be found in dreams, they have been shown to have high agreement between two raters on their scoring, and they present extensive normative material.

In the next chapter, we will look at how dreams change over the life span and how differences in sexual and social roles influence the material to be found in our dreams.

DREAMS THROUGHOUT THE LIFE SPAN:

THE EFFECTS OF GENDER, SOCIETY,
STRESS, AND AGING

A succinct summary of the factors that influence dream content was given nearly 150 years ago by P. Jessen, a German psychologist:

The content of a dream is invariably more or less determined by the individual personality of the dreamer, by his age, sex, class, standard of education, and habitual way of living, and by the events and experiences of his whole previous life.[1]

Many of the variables mentioned by Jessen will be examined in this chapter. We'll look at the way developmental changes are processed by human beings, how dreams can mirror the world as viewed by men and women, and we'll also consider the role of stress and unresolved tensions in creating disturbing dreams.

BIRTH DREAMS

Some say the most meaningful point at which to begin a discussion of dreams as they relate to an individual's development is his or her birth. Nandor Fodor, a psychoanalyst, has written extensively about the trauma of birth and its long-lasting effects, which may be manifested in dreams for many decades.[2] He gives an example of a woman who was born with the umbilical cord tightly wound around her neck and later had recurrent dreams of being strangled. Another individual sustained a head injury while being born and reported anxious dreams about being scalped.

Carol Warner, whose anima dreams were described in chapter 7, experienced a dream in which she was in an enclosed body of water that drained through a narrow opening. The dreamer felt pressure and found it difficult to breathe as she was drawn through this opening. She emerged in a flat area feeling very frightened and alone. She was aware of a commotion nearby, where a group of lifeguards was attending to a prone victim. Troubled by her dream, Carol speculated that it might have been a birth dream. She asked her mother if there had been any complications surrounding her birth, and found out that during the delivery her mother had temporarily stopped breathing and had to be revived by the professional staff. Carol explained that there had always been some indefinable tension between her and her mother that had never been resolved successfully, even though she and her mother

had separately and jointly engaged in psychotherapy to explore their impasse.

Once she learned about the traumatic events surrounding her birth, Carol could better understand why her mother might have ambivalent feelings about her and behave in such a way as to make Carol feel abandoned or ignored. Indeed, when she arrived in the world Carol had been neglected physically by everyone because attention had to be directed toward her mother's emergency situation. Her mother, on the other hand, recognized during the course of her conversations with Carol that she had never expressed the anger she felt at her daughter for nearly causing her death. Once the two of them processed the implications of Carol's dream, the previous tension seemed to dissolve and the mother-daughter relationship became much more satisfying for both of them.

Jane English, a physicist, explores how her own arrival in the world, via a caesarean delivery, affected her self-concept and ways of relating to others in her intriguing book *Different Doorway: Adventures of a Caesarean Born*.[3] English presents many of her dreams and drawings to illustrate the various phases of uncovering and integrating information and feelings about the particulars of her birth. In the dream that led to her journey of discovery, she was lying drugged and unable to move on her back on a high table. Her mother was lying on top of her and raped her. The dreamer felt overwhelmed, physically and psychologically, and gave up. Then she felt resentment. When Jane saw her mother standing by a wall, she went over and tore her belly open with her hands and felt great rage as she killed her. She next walked into an empty room and then arrived in a room full of strangers, who eventually brought her gifts. She realized that it was her birthday party.

English feels that the memory of her birth was expressed in symbolic language. Since her in utero existence was wholly and exclusively identified with that of her mother, English believes that the helplessness and traumatic invasion she experienced in her dream represented the anesthetization and opening of her mother's body when she was born. She felt the empty hall was the nursery and the strangers were the various people who handled her on the day of her birth. One of her later dreams was similar; she was being clutched by a huge black female demon that lay on top of her. The dreamer was aware of a membrane stretched over her that trapped her until someone on the other side poked a hole in it. Her therapist conjectured that the membrane represented the amniotic sac.

Although it may sound implausible to many people, there is increasing evidence that "how one is born seems to be closely related to one's general attitude toward life."[4] One of the pioneer investigators in this area is Stanislav Grof, a psychiatrist who worked with Jane and wrote the foreword to her book. How one is born— uncomplicated or difficult vaginal delivery, nonlabor caesarean section, or emergency caesarean section—may significantly affect one's outlook. Grof proposes that the ex-

treme pressure, and feelings both of pain, fear, suffocation, helplessness, and rage, as well as excitement and ecstasy, can combine to provide the most intense experience a human being ever goes through. These imprinted traumatic memories can have profound and lasting effects, but are often difficult to recover because they could not be verbally processed at the time they occurred.

It may be possible to recapture some of the tactile, movement, or other somatic sensations associated with intrauterine life and birth through dream imagery. Calvin Hall developed a theoretical scale that attempted to measure the presence of such imagery in dreams.[5] He thought that the prenatal amniotic environment could be represented by images of being in dark or watery places. He also looked for reports of being in enclosed structures, which suggest the cramped amniotic envelope that encases the fetus and limits its range of motions, becoming more restrictive as the fetus grows. The process of birth could be portrayed by images of being squeezed, suffocating, or leaving an enclosure. It would be interesting to compare whether scores on this scale vary among individuals who have experienced different forms of delivery. The symbolic process of "rebirthing" has become increasingly popular as a therapeutic technique. Hall and English both referred to several books which contain extensive information about prenatal influences on individual development. New scientific information in this area is presented at the annual international conferences held by The Pre- and Perinatal Psychology Association of North America.

Children's Dreams

Skipping ahead a few years, let's take a look at how children's dreams change as they increase in age. Several large-scale studies, some involving hundreds of children's dream reports, have been carried out and their findings cataloged.[6] Unfortunately, various researchers studied different populations of children, both normal and disturbed, used different methods to obtain dream reports, and evaluated their results differently, so it is very difficult to make comparisons across these studies. There has been considerable disagreement as to how often unpleasant dreams occur and whether children's dreams represent simple wish fulfillments, as Freud claimed. Perhaps the only consistent finding is that animal figures are fairly common in children's dreams.

A popular book called *Your Child's Dreams*, by Patricia Garfield, contains many interesting examples of dreams from fairly young children.[7] Her material was collected from 109 American schoolchildren and 11 children from India. The majority of these children were between five and eight years old. Garfield characterizes dreams as "good" or "bad." Of the 158 bad dreams, 77 involved the child's being chased or attacked by some threatening figure; in 28 dreams the child sensed danger—when, for example, a ghost or monster was nearby—but was not actually threatened. The next most frequent category involved either the dreamer or an-

other character's being injured or killed, but without any dream villain being specified and where the cause seemed accidental (26 dreams). These three categories accounted for about 73 percent of all the bad dreams. There were only 89 good dreams. The most frequent category involved the child simply having a good time, playing games or with toys, taking trips to interesting places, or engaging in holiday activities (30), while the next most frequent included situations where the child received some gift or appealing object or already had desirable possessions (15). These two categories accounted for 50 percent of the good dreams reported.

Sex differences were obvious in many dream categories. Animal figures were prominent in the dreams collected by Garfield, and she devotes a chapter to discussing their significance. She also has an excellent chapter in which parents are given many helpful suggestions for dealing with children's bad dreams. (Anne Wiseman, an expressive therapist, also offers many excellent suggestions for helping children deal with troubling dreams in her book *Nightmare Help: A Guide for Parents and Teachers*.)[8]

David Foulkes, whose laboratory work was mentioned in chapter 10, also conducted a long-term study of children's dreams. His results are discussed at length in his book *Children's Dreams: Longitudinal Studies* and summarized in other sources.[9]

Foulkes's observations come from two studies in which children's dream reports were collected from laboratory awakenings over a five-year period. One group of fourteen children was studied from ages three years to nine years and the other group of fourteen children from ages nine to fifteen years. These children were awakened for both REM and non-REM reports; home dreams were collected by parents. In addition, psychological testing was carried out and interviews conducted with the child, as well as parents and teachers, concerning the child's activities. Although there were relatively few subjects, they were studied very extensively and systematically. Additional subjects had to be added to replace children who dropped out.

Foulkes is very dogmatic about the merits of home versus sleep-laboratory dreams: "The only reliable and representative evidence we now have ... about children's dreams has come (or will come) from laboratory investigations of physiologically monitored dream periods."[10] Foulkes claimed his subjects' home and laboratory dreams were not systematically different from each other. But in light of the prevalence of bad dreams in Garfield's study and in review studies, which estimate that 25 percent of children experience "current" nightmares, it seems surprising when Foulkes claims that "children's dreams generally are not particularly frightening or unpleasant. The child who falls asleep is not thereby cast into a sea of poorly socialized impulses or terrifying fantasies beyond her or his feeble control." He goes on to observe that "the typical child dream is much like the typical REM dream of the young adult," which involves a coherent account of a realistic situation, with characters caught up in ordinary activities and preoccupations.[11]

My reasons for doubting the representativeness of dreams that take place in the laboratory were elaborated in chapter 10 and won't be repeated here. Foulkes says his results offer reassurance that children are not preoccupied with disturbing dreams. Maybe if every child slept in a laboratory every night, parents wouldn't hear about disturbing dreams, but Foulkes's statement seems to ignore the troubling scary dreams that erupt with volcanic fury in children's own bedrooms. It's not only contemporary children, living in an age of potential nuclear warfare, who are frightened by their nightmare visions. A sixteenth-century Belgian physician gave terrifying dreams ninth place in a list of fifty-two diseases afflicting children (A disturbance in gastrointestinal functioning was thought to be the cause). A sixteenth-century English pediatrician wrote:

> oftentimes it happeneth that the chyld is afraid in ye slepe & somtymes waketh sodainly, & sterteth, somtyme shriketh and trembleth, whiche effect commeth of the arysing of stynkyng vapours out of ye stomake into the fantasye.[12]

It is difficult to condense the mass of material Foulkes accumulated from his sample of approximately forty children. Normative data was obtained from nine laboratory nights per year during years one, three, and five of the longitudinal study. During each of these laboratory years, fifteen REM awakenings, nine non-REM awakenings, and three sleep-onset awakenings were scheduled. A total of 2,711 awakenings was made and 1,151 sleep mentation reports collected.

The REM reports of three- and four-year-old children are generally only a sentence or two in length, and no report exceeded fifty words. Most of the dream activity is carried out by other characters, and animal figures are relatively predominant. In commenting on the animal characters, Foulkes stated, "Contextual evidence does support the idea that children's dream animals either are family figures or the child's own 'animal' drives."[13] The three-year-old who had the largest number of animal dreams was reported to show assertive behavior in his waking life and to have a reputation for quarrelsomeness. No significant sex differences were observed at this age level.

At ages five and six, dream reports double in length and there is an observable increase in physical and interpersonal activities within the dreams. The dreamer as a character, however, remains relatively passive in dealing with the other dream characters. Sex differences begin to emerge: male strangers and untamed animals appear more frequently in boys' dreams, while friendly interactions and happy outcomes appear in girls' dreams. "The girls' dreams are 'nice' ones, while those of the boys seem more preoccupied with conflict."[14] Foulkes seems to accept, for this age level, Calvin Hall's finding that male strangers in dreams may be symbols of the oedipal father.[15]

At ages seven and eight, the dreamers

A NIGHTMARE STANDING ON THE DREAMER'S BED THAT FRIGHTENS HER. SHE CAN SEE BUT NOT FEEL IT

A child's drawing of a nightmare.

become more active participants in their own dreams. Boys' dreams become more like those of girls and include family members and other boys of similar ages. These characters now appear more often than animal figures, and the preoccupation with male strangers drops out. Girls similar in age to the dreamer appear more often in girls' dreams than in boys' dreams.

From age nine to age twelve, the dreamer's involvement in the dream scenarios becomes more active, and interaction with peers becomes more prominent as family characters decline. Peer characters tend to be of the dreamer's own sex, and friendly social activity, as well as dream pleasantness, increases. Sex differences appear with regard to the type of social interactions; manifestly aggressive behavior in dreams decreases for girls, while it increases for boys, so that late preadolescent boys have roughly twice as many dreams containing aggressive acts as do their female counterparts. Working out issues of sex-role identity is an important concern for the preadolescent. Boys are exploring what it means to be a "man" in their dreams, and they focus upon athletic activities and male pursuits, such as hunting. Girls display more concern with learning domestic skills and improving their social relations.

Adolescent dreams, from age thirteen to age fifteen, seem more troubled. The settings become more vague, and character distortion is more noticeable. Other characters are increasingly described as angry, social behavior becomes less satisfying, and there are fewer happy interpersonal outcomes. The girls' dreams suggest that this is a somewhat easier time for them than it

is for the boys. Foulkes presents evidence from studies of waking behavior to document that achieving sex-role identity is harder for boys because they have to renounce their early childhood identification with the mother, whereas this requirement is not imposed on girls. He also points out that impulses involving aggression and sexuality appear to be stronger in male children and may be more difficult to learn how to manage while growing into adulthood. Drawing on some of his other laboratory studies, Foulkes reports that the proportion of hostile to friendly interactions is greater in the dreams of working-class adolescent boys than in those of middle-class adolescent boys.

A medical student, Donna Kramer, and I looked at one hundred spontaneously recalled home dreams from children in each of three age groups: two to five years, six to nine years, and ten to twelve years. Each group contained dreams from an equal number of boys and girls. The dreams of the younger children had been reported to parents or teachers and recorded by them. In most cases only one dream had been obtained per child.

When the three hundred children's dreams were compared with the adult norms reported by Hall and me, several significant differences were found. The children dreamed of significantly more parents and other family members, significantly fewer unfamiliar characters, and had significantly more animal characters. More references to nature were found in children's dreams, and there were more implements such as toys and weapons. Children had significantly fewer references to objects of transportation such as automobiles.

From the descriptions in the children's dreams, it was much more difficult to determine whether their dream background was indoor or outdoor, and their settings were more frequently unfamiliar ones.

Significant differences were also present in their social interactions. Children had more dreams with aggression; the aggression was characteristically physical and almost always directed toward the child. Children seemed to perceive that everyone treated them as punching bags. Less friendliness overall appeared in children's dreams, particularly those of boys. Fear-related emotions were expressed twice as often by children as by adults, and children's dreams seldom had an outcome in which either failure or success was achieved. The colors of dream elements are reported significantly more often by children.

Our results seem to support the continuity hypothesis: the children's dreams were reasonably reflective of their waking lives. Their social world was lived out primarily through family interactions, and although they often felt themselves the targets of hostile remarks and actions, they were relatively helpless to redress the imbalance of power between themselves and others. The world outside their home is not well articulated or differentiated, and except for the presence of a few friends, it also conveys an atmosphere of threat and possible harm. Children do not possess much confidence that they will be able to influence the outcome of the external events in which they participate.

GENDER DIFFERENCES IN DREAM CONTENT

Several interesting sex differences were present in our study of children's dreams. At each of the three age levels, girls' dreams were significantly longer and included more familiar characters and references to clothing. Girls had more dreams with friendly interactions and were more often the recipients of friendly interactions from others. They reported more dreams with emotions and described their dreams in greater detail, using a wider range of adjectives, particularly those referring to color. These differences were consistent across all three age levels, indicating that sex differences manifest in dreams at the earliest stages of development and remain in place into adulthood. Whether this is due to nature or nurture—to hormones or to the way children are directed into sex roles by adults' choices of toys, books, and behavior—remains an open question.

The dreams of adolescents have not been extensively investigated. In one dissertation, dreams were recorded at home for a week by twenty-seven females and seventeen males who were fifteen or sixteen years old. These dreams were compared with dreams from thirty-one female and twenty-three male college students on various Hall–Van de Castle scales. The investigators reached the following conclusions:

The manifest dream content appeared similar for the high school and college students—for setting, dream characters, dream objects, outcome, social interaction, and positive emotion. The groups differed significantly in two areas. The older group expressed more stress in dreams on four of the 14 variables which measured stress, and the dream reports from the high school students were fewer in number, shorter, diffuse, and lacked detail as measured by the descriptive scales. Seven significant sex differences were found. Females reported more dreams than males, and their dream reports contained more female characters, friends, friendly interactions, references to food, and internal pressure. College males expressed more aggression than college females.[16]

Sex differences in dreams have been demonstrated by several studies involving children and adolescents. These studies have usually involved spontaneously recalled home dreams, which may be preferable if one wishes to study the natural world of sex differences. David Foulkes, who insists that the laboratory is the only appropriate setting within which to study children's dreams, has not been very successful in discovering sex differences, stating, "By and large, however, children's dreams do not seem to differ markedly in form or substance according to the gender of the dreamer (at least for the sort of dream features we've been discussing here)."[17] Besides the artificial effect of the

laboratory, sex differences may be minimized in Foulkes's findings because he isn't examining or scoring relevant dream features.

Sex differences in dreams have been more widely studied in adults. Researchers rang door bells in Cincinnati and asked the persons answering the door whether they would be willing to describe a recent dream.[18] From three hundred people asked in this stratified random sample, 182 dreams were obtained, and more women than men reported a dream. Women's dreams had significantly more indoor settings, characters, home and family themes, friendly interactions, and emotions. Men's dreams had significantly more aggression, castration anxiety, and successful achievement outcomes. These researchers found some differences with regard to socioeconomic status and race, but the sex differences were so pervasive that they concluded, "We see a reaffirmation that anatomy is destiny, for the single most important factor in determining dream themes is the sex into which one is born."[19]

Calvin Hall and Bill Domhoff found that the percentage of male characters is higher in male dreams than in female dreams.[20] (The calculation excluded characters of unspecified sex—"someone"—or number—"a crowd.") Hall and Domhoff termed this difference "ubiquitous" because it appeared in each of eleven groups of various ages and ethnic backgrounds, including two from non-Western cultures. They examined 3,874 dreams collected from 1,399 male dreamers and found that male characters appeared in 64 percent overall. Male characters appeared in only 52 percent of the 3,064 dreams that had been collected from 1,418 females.

A few subsequent studies, using primarily non-Western groups, questioned whether this sex difference really was ubiquitous. Hall published another article in which he greatly expanded the number and variety of dreamers analyzed.[21] He considered dreams obtained from five different groups of college students in the United States and seven groups of college students from other countries, such as India and Nigeria; dreams from children and adolescents in the United States and six other countries; and dreams from several nonstudent adult populations, including climbers from an American Mount Everest expedition. Anthropological collections of dreams from ten different cultures, including Hopi Indians and Australian aborigines, were added to the dream pool, as were twelve series of at least a hundred dreams each obtained from American adults, and dreams from three different dream laboratories—one in Scotland, one in Chicago, and one in Cincinnati.

Results from each of these many groups, including nearly 3,000 male and 1,850 female dreamers, were tabulated. It was thus possible to make comparisons between males and females for thirty-five distinct groups. Overall, male characters appeared in 65 percent of male dreams and 50 percent of female dreams. Six of the groups, all from outside the United States, yielded inconclusive results concerning the percentage of male characters in men's versus women's dreams. The differences in the percentage of male characters were highly significant for the other twenty-nine groups. Hall concluded:

The sex difference occurs in groups on every continent; in a diversity of cultures, from the more "advanced" to the more "primitive"; in all age groups; in dreams collected in the laboratory, in the classroom, and in the field by many different investigators over a period of 30 years.[22]

In an effort to explain the meaning of this "ubiquitous" sex difference, Hall proposed that the frequency of occurrence of a dream element or theme was a direct measure of the strength of a dreamer's preoccupation with that theme or element. A preoccupation with male characters indicates that they are either a source of pleasure or a source of anxiety and conflict for the dreamer. Hall turned to Freud's theory of the male and female Oedipus complex to account for male dreamers' greater preoccupation with other male characters. For both sexes, the father is seen as the original intruder in the loving relationship with the mother; these conflicts continue for the boy and are displaced to other males in later life.

Although Hall found highly significant differences in the overall percentage of male figures between male and female dreamers, there can be individual self-explanatory exceptions to this general finding. In one study involving college students from India, it was found that the more close friends of the opposite sex the dreamer had, the more often opposite sex figures appeared in their dreams. Sex ratio of dream characters was viewed by these investigators as related to the social experience of the dreamer, rather than to the gender of the dreamer or to the Oedipal conflict.[23] In another study, using dreams from college students in New York City and Peru, the percentage of male characters was higher in American male dreams than American female dreams, but Peruvian males had a lower percentage of male characters than Peruvian females did. One explanation offered for this finding was that Peruvian males were said to start dating girls approximately one year earlier on average than American males, and as a result might have been involved with the opposite sex for a longer period of time.[24] A Canadian study reported that working mothers had a higher proportion of male characters and vocational settings in their dreams than did homemakers.[25] A recent study found that subjects interested in stereotypically masculine activities were more likely to dream of male characters regardless of their own gender.[26]

I made an effort to evaluate social familiarity with the opposite sex to sex ratios in dreams by examining some of my data dealing with the effects of birth order on dream content.[27] I assumed that this data could provide some index of familiarity with opposite sex siblings. The subjects were the nursing students in Miami who participated in the menstrual cycle study mentioned in the last chapter. Those with two siblings were divided into four groups, and four dreams, balanced for time phases during the menstrual cycle, were selected from each subject's folder. Among the nine women with an older brother, 59 percent of dream characters were male; for the seven women with a younger brother the figure was 54 percent; and for the twelve women with only sisters it was 49 percent.

An older brother should provide greater familiarity with male interaction and companionship because he's been there since the dreamer's birth and is by the order of births the superior figure. In contrast, a younger brother might not arrive until several years later and would be given less recognition. These data indicate that the more dominant the fraternal influence a female dreamer experiences, the higher the percentage of male figures in her dreams. I also examined data from five subjects who had no siblings. These women had a male percentage figure of 49 percent. More female characters than male characters appeared in the dreams of five of the twelve subjects with just sisters, but in only one of the sixteen subjects with a brother.

More evidence that social climate may influence the sex ratio in women's dreams comes from Walter Ritter's doctoral dissertation at Columbia University.[28] Two groups of fifteen female university students who initially turned in three dream reports per subject, were found to have a similar percentage of male characters. After these baseline dreams were collected, a young male experimenter met individually with each subject twice a week to discuss her nine subsequent dream reports. The fifteen women in the M (male) group were reinforced with subtle positive verbal comments when they described the presence of male characters in their dreams, while the fifteen women in the F (female) group were reinforced when they described the presence of female characters. There was a significant increase in the percentage of male dream figures for the M group after these individual sessions, but no increase in the percentage of female dream figures for the F group. None of the subjects indicated any awareness of the experimental manipulations when questioned after the study was completed.

Ritter's subjects may have developed some positive "transference" to him. He stated that "a substantial portion of their dreams dealt with sexual matters" and went on to conclude:

> The positive result for the M group may have been a complex result of the fact that a young male experimenter showed an interest in the sexual activities of young, unmarried women, as reflected in their dreams. By ignoring the sexual element in the F groups, an inadvertent mild negative reinforcement may have obscured or somehow reduced the positive reinforcement for female figures.[29]

Ritter made the obvious suggestion that the study should be repeated with a female experimenter to assess the degree to which the sex of the experimenter rather than the verbal reinforcement influenced the results.

When Hall and I tabulated the results for our normative tables, significant sex differences were found on almost every one of our dream scales. Since the dream reports of women are longer, various proportion scores were computed to minimize this factor. Women have proportionately more indoor and familiar settings and mention more dwellings and household articles. When a residential structure is referred to, women are more likely to call it a home, whereas men call it a house. The clothing, jewelry, and facial characteristics of dream characters are described in greater detail by women. More people appear in women's dreams, these characters are generally familiar to them, and the dreamer is more likely to interact with these characters on an individual basis. More family members, relatives, children, and babies appear in women's dreams, and women have more dreams in which there are friendly encounters. The friendly interactions occur with familiar characters, and more friendly interactions occur with male characters than with female characters. Verbal activities are featured more prominently in women's dreams, and the dreamer is more likely to be talking to other women. More emotions are reported in women's dreams, and adjectives describing the color, attractiveness, or evaluative qualities (good and bad) of dream elements are more common.

In male dreams, outdoor and unfamiliar settings prevail. Men report more implements, such as weapons and tools, and make more references to cars, roads, and streets. Men's dreams have more groups of characters, and the characters are more frequently unknown to the dreamer and described with regard to their occupational status. Males report aggressive dreams only slightly more frequently than females, but their aggressive dreams contain a much higher percentage of physical aggression. Male dreamers initiate physical aggression three times more often than women. This aggression is directed toward other males and toward characters unfamiliar to the dreamer. The dreamer is also attacked more frequently by males and by unfamiliar characters. If the dreamer receives friendliness from another character, it is more likely to be from a character who is unfamiliar. More sex dreams are reported by men, and their partners are usually unknown, attractive women somewhat resembling those in *Playboy* centerfolds. Men engage in more physical activities in their dreams and have more dreams in which failure or success is involved. Men pay more attention to the physical dimensions (small or large) of elements in dreams.

Hall and Bill Domhoff have also made a larger-scale analysis of social interactions in terms of sex and age patterns. They examined 3,049 dream reports collected from 1,940 males and females ranging in age from two to eighty for the presence of aggressive interactions.[30] Aggression levels were almost equally high for both young boys and girls between two and twelve years of age, but after age twelve levels of aggression decreased for females.

In male sexual dreams, female partners are generally described as beautiful and with well-developed figures, but their personal identities are very vague. Le Viol (The Rape) by Rene Magritte.

Adolescent and young adult males maintain the same high levels of aggression characteristic of younger boys and have an aggressive encounter with about one out of every four characters in their dreams. Adolescent and young adult females have an aggressive encounter with only about one out of every seven characters in their dreams. The level of aggression drops off somewhat for male dreamers between the ages of thirty and eighty. Females in the thirty-to-eighty age range have aggressive encounters with only about one out of every twenty-five characters in their dreams.

The category of physical aggression includes situations in which a character is chased, hit, or killed by another character. A percentage figure for physical aggression can be computed with reference to the number of total aggressions, which include verbal aggressions, threats, and rejections.

The greatest percentage of physical aggression is found for children between two and twelve years of age and is much higher for boys than girls. During the turbulent years from twelve to eighteen, about 48 percent of the aggression in the dreams of both male and female adolescents is physical, but after the age of eighteen, physical aggression represents approximately 65 percent of the aggression in male dreams and 35 percent of that in female dreams. If a familiar character is involved the dreamer initiates more physical aggression than he or she receives, but when a stranger is involved the dreamer receives more physical aggression than he or she initiates. For both male and female dreamers, physical aggression is more frequent with male characters than with female characters.

Although female dreamers do not dream of themselves being involved in physical aggression nearly so often as they dream of men in that context, there are no clear sex differences in the frequency with which women and men report observing or witnessing physical aggressions between other characters in their dreams. It appears that women can watch physical aggression far more easily than they can participate in it. Noticeable individual differences are present in the frequency with which dreamers become involved with aggressive interactions. Some dreamers report no aggressions in their dreams, whereas other dreamers might engage in a fight or quarrel with two out of every three characters in their dreams.

This same data pool of dream reports was also analyzed by Hall and Domhoff for the presence of friendliness.[31] There were over twice as many acts of aggression (1,490) found in these dreams as there

were acts of friendliness (711). Many of the aggressive acts were physical in nature and quite violent, but most of the friendly acts consisted of mild expressions of friendliness, such as greeting someone, shaking hands, paying a compliment, or doing some small favor. It was very rare to encounter a major act of friendliness, such as saving a life or protecting someone from danger. More friendliness was found in male dreams, and male dreams were three times more likely to display this friendliness toward female than male characters. Women were only slightly inclined to show more friendliness to male than to other female characters unless the males were familiar to them. Children and young women were more apt to receive friendliness than to initiate it. The lowest incidence of friendliness was found in children's dreams and the dreams of those over the age of thirty. It was mentioned in chapter 11 that almost all of the significant sex differences Hall and I found in the dream scores of college students from the 1940's were also significant in the 1980 study involving the home dreams of 122 college students in Richmond, Virginia. The scores reported in our norms for females were also extremely similar to those found in 1991 when five hundred home dreams from one hundred California female college students were tabulated.

An effort was made in 1983 to examine sex differences in the laboratory dreams of eleven male and eleven female university students in a Cincinnati sleep lab.[32] The male subjects dreamed of significantly more male characters and strangers as well as more energetic activities, and they used more adjectives describing dream elements as large, but the usual differences in social interactions were not found. The investigators concluded that the "sexual revolution" was beginning to show its effects. In view of the handful of subjects involved, as well as the consistent finding that social interaction scores are muted in laboratory dreams, the authors' conclusions should be viewed as dubious.

Another recent study examined dreams mailed in by 220 men and women in response to an advertisement on a nationally televised show.[33] Respondents were promised a computerized analysis of a personal dream for a nominal fee. Some of these subjects were teenagers, and several were over sixty years old. One third of the respondents sent in recurring dreams, and some sent in dreams they had experienced as children. Since subjects were paying for an "analysis" of their dreams, they were likely to select some particularly salient or unusual dream instead of their most recent dream, which was the type of dream considered in the other studies done on sex differences. The type of subjects, class of dreams, and method of obtaining dreams, therefore, was markedly different in this study than in any of the others on sex differences.

Several sex differences found in other studies were not manifested in this study, but women did dream of more family members, children, and babies and have more indoor settings in their dreams than did men. Although these researchers reported that the patterns of aggression did not distinguish men from women, they found that it did distinguish between residents of different geographical areas. Dreamers from the East Coast were more likely to be the aggressor (40 percent) than those from the Midwest (10 percent). West Coast dreamers were the aggressors 22 percent of the time.

The significance of gender differences in relation to family and occupational roles has recently been investigated by Monique Lortie-Lussier and her colleagues at the University of Ottawa. In their first study, home dreams were collected from thirty middle-class French-Canadian mothers of preschoolers, half of whom were homemakers and half wage earners. The wage earners reported more male characters, fewer indoor settings, and more unpleasant emotions, while the homemakers reported more friendly interactions but also more misfortunes and overt hostility.[34] In their second study, dreams from eighteen single female college students were compared with nineteen wage-earning mothers of young children. The students' dreams incorporated familiar characters drawn from their circle of friends and family, while the mothers' dreams incorporated characters related to both home and work, such as husbands, children, and work colleagues. Physical aggression with men and autonomous problem solving were reported more often by mothers, and the students reported more affiliative and romantic concerns.[35]

In their 1992 paper, Lortie-Lussier and her colleagues analyzed two home dream reports from each of thirty-two mothers at home, thirty-two mothers employed outside the home, and thirty-two employed fathers.[36] The average age of the employed parents was thirty-four and the average age of the mothers at home was thirty-seven. Most of the participants had received university degrees. In comparison to the employed parents, the homemakers reported significantly more family and child characters, indoor settings, and misfortunes, while the employed parents reported more vocational characters. The employed mothers described more vocational characters than the employed fathers.[37] The researchers also attempted a thematic analysis and found that the number of family-centered dreams was forty-eight for 25 homemakers, seventeen for 16 fathers, and fifteen for 13 wage-earning mothers (sixty-four dreams were examined for each group). Dreams with work-related themes were reported by three homemakers, nine fathers, and eighteen dual-role mothers.

The authors made several observations about the significance of their results with regard to the current changing social scene. They noted that "the fathers' involvement with their children in many of their dreams could be a sign of changes in family responsibilities resulting from women's new occupational roles."[38] They also observed, "The professional role might still be problematic for women, but its enactment more often gave the dual-role mothers a more self-assured sense of control over dream events than the full-time mother role did."[39] They mentioned that a "converging self-concept structure" may be emerging, because friendliness was more prevalent in the dreams of both sexes than in earlier studies by Hall and Domhoff; also, aggression was less prevalent in men's dreams and more prevalent in women's

dreams than in past studies. The investigators cautioned against premature generalization based on their studies because only small samples of middle-class Canadians were involved, but I would support their conclusion:

> Questions about gender differences should be reframed to take into account role and developmental changes that have not received the attention they deserve. Then research can uncover different strata of dream structure and functioning which can have varying degrees of sensitivity to environmental factors, to personality, and to gender.[40]

In her 1988 master's thesis, involving thirty college students in California who contributed 804 home dreams, Veronica Tonay found that although males reported more aggressive acts per dream than did females, "there were no significant relationships between the aggressive/victim role of the dreamer and gender."[41] As in previous studies, women dreamed more about individuals than groups and men reported experiencing fewer emotions pertaining to themselves. If the "sexual revolution" is affecting dreams, it appears to be in terms of women becoming more assertive and less willing to allow themselves to be victimized.

A different approach to content was used by C. Brooks Brenneis, who examined differences in "ego modalities" between men and women.[42] Some theorists have suggested that the male mode is one of intrusion and the female mode is one of incorporation and inclusion. Brenneis developed a checklist to score for the presence of these presumed stylistic differences in dreams. It was found that the dreams of female college students had more indoor settings and contained a greater number of people who were familiar to the dreamer, particularly parents. The male students usually played the central role in their own dreams, which were characterized by "two pivotal issues, motion and separateness." Brenneis summarized the patterns he found as follows:

> Fewer people appear in [men's] dreams and are more often unfamiliar, unknown, or nameless people defined only by their presence or by the actions in which they are involved. These men view themselves not in terms of familiarity or community, but rather in terms of a fixed boundary between themselves and others. . . . Only on rare occasions does this boundary give way so that the male dreamer can allow a figure other than himself to play out the central role in his dream. The male . . . sees himself alone in an alien world.
>
> Female ego modalities cluster about the issue of intimacy. . . . Sensory appreciation, physical closeness, and familiar company all set in a stable enclosure are important facets of this. In their dreams, women create an atmosphere of personal closeness full of people they know and can refer to by name, a closeness demonstrated in their greater tendency to allow

others to act as the central figure in their dreams. . . .

Of special note is the tendency for women's dreams to be organized around contained spaces which seem to facilitate the occurrence of intimacy and sensory immediacy more than the relatively unbounded expanse of male dreams.[43]

Another study carried out by Brenneis and a coworker employed the ego modality checklist with Chicano and Anglo college students from the University of New Mexico.[44] The researchers reported that the dreams of women in both cultural groups were characterized by "(1) the depiction of enclosed and firmly localized settings, and (2) the more frequent inclusion of other characters and characters who can be designated as familiar." They acknowledged differences between women in the two groups but indicated that these patterns "mark off some fundamental aspect of feminine experience." The environment in men's dreams, they said,

> tends to be exposed and unfixed. By exposed, we mean out in the open, unprotected by structures and enclosures; by unfixed, we mean unlocalized and not precisely demarcated. It is a more fluid and potentially risky or dangerous environment . . . [which] presents itself to the men as demanding and challenging, re-

Women dream of indoor settings and interior details more often than men do.

quiring greater robust physical exertion from its characters.[45]

Although these investigators used a different conceptual model and scoring system, their findings are remarkably similar to those that Hall and I reported earlier in our normative tables.

The emphasis given to enclosed spaces by these investigators prodded me to look through the list of objects that Hall and I reported to see whether sex differences would be found in the frequencies for enclosed areas. I indicated earlier that women report more dwellings in their dreams. Ignoring residential structures, women still had approximately 180 buildings—dormitories, schools, hospitals, and hotels—in their dreams, while men had only about 90 of these buildings. There were more rooms

(about 180) in women's dreams than in men's (about 140). Women also reported small enclosed structures within their rooms (closets, desks, dressers, drawers, boxes, suitcases) over three times more frequently than men. Enclosed bodies of water (lakes, pools, ponds) also appeared about three times as frequently in women's dreams as in men's.

This combination of dream scores reveals that women's dreams do contain more enclosed spaces or areas with discrete boundaries. These architectural or landscape features could represent more structured and demarcated environments if they were conceptualized in terms of living space. For Freud, these enclosed areas could serve as symbolic representations of internal female sexual organs, such as the uterus or vagina.

SEX-ROLE ORIENTATION AND DREAM PATTERNS

If women possess different internal landscapes and anatomical structures than men do, is it reasonable to assume that "anatomy is destiny"? We have seen in the research by Lortie-Lussier that when women have careers outside the home after college, some of their dream scores resemble those typically reported by males.

I found that some of the dream scores of first-year female nursing students in Miami showed differences when evaluated with regard to the women's level of masculine or feminine identification. These fifty-one students turned in dreams throughout the semester they were in my course, using a code name for anonymity, and also completed some psychological tests, which included a question asking who they would like to be if they could change their identity for a day. Those who chose both a masculine code name (Tonto, King George) and a masculine preference for their one-day identity (John Glenn) were rated as having a "masculine" identification; those who chose both a feminine code name (Mona Lisa, Scheherazade) and one-day identity (Elizabeth Taylor) were rated as having a "feminine" identification. Dreams from the eighteen students with masculine ratings were compared with dreams from the nineteen students with feminine ratings. The "feminine" group reported significantly more indoor settings and children and babies in their dreams. This pattern was the same as that found for Lortie-Lussier's older homemaker group,

although all of the nursing students were single and their average age was nineteen.

My data based upon nursing students brings up the issue of how sexual identification or sex role may affect gender differences in dream content. Sex roles have been defined in terms of "agency" and "communion."[46] Agency qualities include surgency (self-expansion, assertiveness, competition), instrumentality (mastery, problem solving), and libido (raw sexuality). The communion-based complex of behavioral styles includes social cooperation (altruism, helping), passive social connectiveness (reunion, receiving support), and eros (expressions of warmth, affection). When nine nights of REM reports were obtained from twelve males and eight females aged eleven to thirteen years old, the male dreams were rated as primarily characterized by agency and female dreams as primarily communal.[47]

David Cohen, from the University of Texas, evaluated twenty-seven male and thirty-two female dreamers on the basis of their sex-role orientation.[48] He used femininity scores on a standard psychological test to categorize college students as "masculine" or "feminine." Each subject contributed two dreams which were rated for the presence of agency and communion. This male dream, for example, was rated high on agency: "I dreamt that I was some kind of merchant dealing with both sides in the American Civil War. I took my payments in sex with northern and southern women." This dream displays the flamboyant, libidinal, exploitive quality associated with agency. Another male dream was rated high on communion, because of its expression of aesthetic interest and emotion rather than self-assertive reaction to rebuff: "I see G and L in Hermann Park in Houston. I want G to go to the Winnipeg Royal Ballet with me that night. She already has tickets to go to some other club. I blow it off and am somewhat disappointed."

Four subgroups were formed: fifteen masculine males, twelve feminine males, seventeen feminine females, and fifteen masculine females. Cohen found that "masculine" subjects, regardless of gender, had dreams with significantly more scores for agency than communion and more often had aggressive dreams, particularly dreams involving physical aggression, than did "feminine" subjects. He pointed out that the effects of sexual identification on dream scores were consistently larger than the effects of gender, especially in males. If the dimensions were combined, the differences became quite marked. For example, 53 percent of the masculine male group engaged in physical aggression in their dreams, while only 12 percent of the feminine females did.

Cohen also found that more of the subjects with sex-role orientation contrary to their gender had more unpleasant dreams when compared to subjects whose sex-role orientation was congruent with their gender. This relation between unpleasantness and lack of sex-role congruence held only for dreams involving some form of aggression. If the analysis was limited to only those subjects whose dreams included aggression, 75 percent of the subjects whose sex-role orientation was different from their gender had unpleasant dreams, but only 25 percent of those whose sex role was congruent with their gender had unpleasantness in their dreams. On the basis of his results, Cohen suggested that a sex-role orientation contrary to gender stereotype is more disturbing for males than females. He commented that in our culture it is generally more distressing for adults to witness the behavior of a sissy than that of a tomboy.

Perhaps individuals might be less susceptible to societal judgments about sex role if they possessed a high level of positive self-concept. One investigator looked at the differences between male and female subjects who had scored high and low on a psychological test intended to measure personality integration (PI).[49] High-PI women were more active and aggressive in their dreams than high-PI men were in theirs; conversely, the men were more detached and passive in their dreams. The high-PI women were also more actively involved in friendly interactions in their dreams than the high-PI men and more often took the initiative as the befriender. Since the high-PI subjects were displaying patterns of social interaction not congruent with their gender identity, one might expect them to have experienced the unpleasantness in their dreams that Cohen found in his study, but no such findings were reported by the investigator. It did indeed seem to be the case that a greater degree of personality integration was sufficient to insulate these subjects from feeling uncomfortable about deviating from the norm in their development of a more androgynous personality structure.

What types of dreams might be expected from individuals who display a preference for a sexual partner of the same sex? When the most recent dreams from a group of homosexual males were compared to dreams from heterosexual males, the homosexual dreams had several scores that would more typically be found in women's dreams.[50] They had significantly more indoor settings and marginally significant differences in the direction of having more individual characters and less aggression directed toward them.

Stanley Krippner, a humanistic psychologist, and some coworkers used our scales to evaluate the dreams of ten preoperative male transsexuals.[51] Transsexuals are persons who feel so strongly they have the mind and personality of the opposite sex that they are willing to undergo surgical and hormonal treatment to change their gender. Four times as many males as females request sex reassignment. Subjects maintained dream diaries for several months and their first three dreams were used for content analysis. The investigators compared the transsexuals' dream scores with those reported in our normative tables. My discussion of the transsexuals' dreams is based upon the figures published by these investigators but, in many cases, I've computed scores to bring out information not mentioned in their monograph.

Transsexual subjects were similar to the normative male group in that they rarely dreamed about household items, but they were also like the normative females in that they rarely dreamed about money or streets. References to clothing appeared much more frequently in the transsexuals' dreams than in either normative group. Many transsexuals spontaneously engage in cross-sex dressing because they wish to be socially acceptable as a member of the opposite sex and not to achieve erotic stimulation, as is sometimes true for transvestites. Male transsexuals frequently have to undergo a year's "trial" of dressing like a woman before a gender conversion operation will be scheduled. Clothing, therefore, becomes an important part of the process of obtaining the hoped-for surgical procedure.

The transsexuals had more than twice as many unfamiliar settings and twice as many characters of indefinite sex in their dreams as either normative group. Unfamiliar settings suggest feelings of being lost or disoriented, which are feelings to be expected in someone who is on the verge of such a major life change. The greater frequency of characters with an indefinite sexual identification would also be expected from persons who are in rebellion against their own sexual identity. Transsexuals had significantly more dreams about groups than our male normative or female dreamers, which may relate to the fact that their social life is often limited to groups of fellow transsexuals until their operation is completed and they can seek out individualized relationships.

An examination of the transsexuals' patterns of friendliness in their dreams helps to expand this speculation. In our normative tables, based upon 500 dreams, males have far fewer friendly acts (250) than aggressive acts (402), and women also report slightly fewer friendly acts (308) than aggressive acts (337). The transsexuals, however, in the thirty dreams studied had fifty friendly acts but only twenty aggressive acts. They definitely appear to be more preoccupied with friendliness than aggression. Their number of aggressive acts per dream is below that for males and identical to that for females. The transsexuals' proportion of friendly acts per dream is almost three times higher than that for either normative group. The transsexual, however, has less personal involvement in these friendly acts and instead reports witnessing them more often than our male or female dreamers. It seems as if the transsexual wishes he could experience more friendliness, but feels as if he can only watch. This inability to initiate or develop friendly interactions may arise because the transsexual does not identify with the assertive, initiative-taking role typically expected from males. In the transsexuals' dreams, 52.7 percent of the characters were male, a figure very similar to that found for female dreamers. Several transsexuals actually dreamed of themselves as women.

A successful outcome to a dream activity was scored five times more often in males' dreams generally than in transsexuals' dreams; failure also was five times more common in the normative male dreams. These scores indicate that this group of transsexuals was not motivated to attempt any mastery of events. The lack of achievement motivation may spring from the transsexual's failure to identify himself as an adult; 12.5 percent of the human characters in the transsexuals' dreams were teenagers or children, while the corresponding figure was only 4.2 percent for the male and female groups combined. Some transsexuals feel that their entry into an adult world is delayed until successful completion of their operation. One transsexual explained that he had changed his birth date to the date of his operation because that was "the day I finished being born."

Not only were transsexuals less likely to struggle toward external achievements, they also reported significantly less internal cognitive activity than either sex in the normative tables. They apparently didn't like to focus on negative features; there wasn't a single example of a dream element being described as bad or ugly, although they used significantly more positive adjectives (good, pretty, attractive) than either sex to describe dream elements.

Only limited information is available about female transsexual dreams. In the one study I could find, the authors reported:

> In the imagery of sleep dreams, five patients reported that they were male, dressed as a male, acting as a male and making love as a male. One of these also dreamt sometimes of being a woman. Two of these four reported waking just before achieving a sexual climax. None reported a sexual climax while dreaming.[52]

These analyses of male homosexual and transsexual dreams certainly bear strong testimony to the importance of considering not just gender but sex-role orientation when discussing sex differences in dreams. Coupled with findings from other studies in which sex-role orientation was shown to be an important discriminator in dream scoring patterns, the data support the view that the statement "anatomy is destiny" is an incomplete explanation of sex differences in personality as reflected in dreams. Other factors, such as age, vocation, cultural milieu, amount of opposite sex contact, availability of suitable role models, and, as we've been discussing, sex-role orientation, to name a few, must be considered in addition to the anatomical differences in external genitalia and internal bodily spaces.

BIRTH ORDER, SOCIAL CLASS AND DREAM CONTENT

Birth order is another factor in the content of dreams and can override even gender as a determinant. I indicated earlier that the greater the fraternal influence a female dreamer experiences in her life, the higher the percentage of male characters in her dreams. When birth order for male dreamers was examined by another investigator, it was found that first-born male college students had more themes of "positive interaction" than did younger siblings.[53] In my birth order study, I found that first-born females dreamed of more aggressive characters and more aggressive interactions with strangers than did younger siblings. Middle-born females (with at least one older and one younger sibling) had more friendly characters and more strangers performing friendly acts toward the dreamer. In comparison to men, women generally report more children and babies in their dreams, but last-born women, the "babies" of their own families, had fewer children and babies in their dreams than women in other birth order positions.

Social class is another variable affecting dream content. It too can sometimes override the expected influence of gender. In dreams obtained from high school students in Detroit, more aggression was reported by girls and by lower-class students.[54] When the effects of social class and gender were combined, it was found that lower-class girls expressed more aggression in their dreams than middle-class girls or boys of either class.

These findings are included to emphasize how complicated the discussion of sex differences can become. If one wished to isolate the "pure" effects of gender on dream content, it would be necessary to control for the effects of a large array of variables, including those just discussed— sex-role orientation, birth order, and social class. If such variables can't be controlled, conclusions should be based on studies of an extremely large number of dreamers in order to balance out the contributions these uncontrolled variables could make to dream patterns.

Except for the study involving the Detroit high school students, the role of social class has been almost ignored in dream research. It was considered in the Cincinnati door-to-door study in which individuals from a stratified random sample were asked to describe a recent dream.[55] An index of social class status was based upon education, income, and occupation. There were significantly more human characters in the dreams of the lower socioeconomic groups than in those of the upper middle class. The researchers speculated that lower-class subjects were more likely to experience crowding within their home and working environments, which might contribute to a greater density of people in their dreams. The lower classes dreamed significantly more often of home and family members than did the upper-middle-class group. The alert reader may have noticed that the dream scores reported for members of lower socioeconomic classes involving character density, family members, and homes are also those typically associated with females—another lower-status group in our society. Greater anxiety and misfortune were present in the dreams of lower-status subjects. The misfortunes were of the "environmental barrier" type, in which some obstacle is encountered.

Unpleasantness in Dreams

One does not, however, have to be in a lower socioeconomic status to have dreams in which an environmental barrier leads to misfortune or causes frustration or concern on the part of the dreamer. In fact, negative or unpleasant dreams are far more common among almost all dreamers than are positive dreams. In our normative tables, Hall and I showed that more dreams contain aggression than friendliness, failure rather than success, and misfortune rather than good fortune.

To obtain an overall index of "unpleasantness," I added together the number of dreams with aggression, failure, or misfortune and the number of times the dreamer expressed feeling apprehensive, sad, angry, or confused and came up with a total of 1,409 unpleasant elements. In comparison, there were 687 dreams with friendliness, success, good fortune, or feelings of happiness. Thus, it could be said that two-thirds of dreams are unpleasant in nature.

Many people are surprised to learn that the majority of dreams are unpleasant. Since most people don't share dreams with others on a regular basis, they tend to assume that their own dreams are more negative, troubling, bizarre, and unusual than those experienced by others. Knowing that other people also frequently have disturbing dreams may be a source of relief to those who might worry that their dreams indicate some psychological disturbance or abnormality. But other individuals may use this information as an excuse to distance themselves from their dreams. "I have enough problems and unpleasantness in my everyday waking life, why would I want to expose myself to further unpleasant events and emotions in my dreams?" they may say. "If dreams were likely to offer relief, I might make a more active effort to cultivate them, but why deliberately pursue doom and gloom?"

I would respond that by paying attention to the troubling events in our dreams, we improve our long-range chances of reducing stress and anxiety in our waking life. Dreams tell us things that we need to know to function more effectively when we're not dreaming. They inform us about conditions which require remedial action and often give us hints as to which plans might be most successful. Checking in with our dreams for an assessment of our emotional welfare is similar to checking in with a doctor for an assessment of our physical welfare. Would it make sense to avoid regular physical checkups because they might reveal high blood pressure or diabetes? The great feature about dreams is that you don't have to make an appointment; they'll come to you on a regular basis, and for free, and all they ask in return is that you pay attention to them. To demystify some of the most common dreams, let's look at a few and discuss what they might be trying to tell the dreamer.

Typical Dreams

If you do pay attention to your dreams, it's very probable that there are some typical experiences you will encounter. Several questionnaire surveys have inquired as to whether the respondents had ever experienced particular types of dreams. The two types most frequently acknowledged are dreams of falling and those in which the dreamer is attacked or pursued. When two thousand Army selectees were asked "Have you ever in your life dreamed that you were falling?" and "Have you ever in your life dreamed that you were in some sort of danger from someone or something trying to get at you, hurt you, or chase you, and you find it difficult to get away?" 81 percent of the respondents indicated they had experienced either one or both types of dreams.[56]

Calvin Hall asked these same questions of 517 college students.[57] He found that 93 percent of the males and 98 percent of the females indicated they had had one or both dreams. When Hall made a content analysis of 106 dreams about being attacked, he found that both men and women typically dreamed of an unprovoked physical attack by a man or group of men, to which the dreamer responded by fleeing, waking up, or other actions of a passive, escapist nature. It is very rare that the dreamer actively resists or fights back. Hall concluded that the dream of being attacked represents the dreamer's self-conception as a weak, passive, inferior, or helpless person at the time when the dream appeared.

In my experience, such dreams sometimes seem to represent anxieties concerning the harmful intentions of others toward the dreamer, but in some cases the person in the attacking role represents a projected and disowned part of the dreamer's personality. If you have several such dreams in quick succession, you should ask yourself if some family member, fellow employee, or person in your social group has been unusually critical toward you recently. If such a person can be identified, try to step back and see the situation through

Falling dreams are very common. Most people have experienced them at some time or another. Phaeton by Hendrik Goltzius. (The Metropolitan Museum of Art, Harris Brisbane Dick Fund, 1953. [53.601.338 (5)])

their eyes. Could they have a valid reason for being angry at you? Is there anything you can do to ease this interpersonal tension? If you can't fathom their motive, take a risk and discuss your dream with them.

Ask them why they think you had this dream and, if they're aware of any tension between the two of you, whether they have any suggestions to reduce it. If you fail to find an external nemesis, gaze into your own internal mirror. Is there some saboteur lurking in the shadows that makes you trip over your own feet or, worse yet, shoot yourself in the foot? If you can catch a glimpse of this other punitive you, the nay-sayer that keeps telling the positive you that you're inadequate or not entitled, then you can ask yourself, What needs are served by his or her continued existence? What would it be like to live more freely, without having to nourish this internal parasite? If you don't feel strong enough to banish this part of yourself, is there some sort of truce or compromise that can be negotiated?

The attacker can sometimes be an animal. In Western society, we are generally not at risk of attack from wild animals during our waking life, and the appearance of an animal attacker is likely to symbolize our fears of being overwhelmed by our own animal impulses and desires or those of someone else. In another culture, attack by a wild animal might be a realistic waking concern. When three hundred Bushmen from South-West Africa were asked to relate some dream they had experienced, sixty-two percent of their disturbing dreams involved being threatened by an animal, but only fifteen percent dealt with threats of violence from human characters.[58] If the attacker in your dream is an animal, you may get some clues about its presence by asking yourself what attributes you associate with that animal. Is it an animal that bites, strangles, or stomps its victims? Can you link that attribute with yourself or someone you know?

In falling dreams the height from which a dreamer falls can vary considerably. One dreamer described being in outer space observing the moon, planets, and stars, when he suddenly had the sensation of rapidly falling and experienced extreme fear over what would happen when he hit earth. Since the Bushmen are not familiar with space flight, or even with mountains or tall buildings, their most common experience of falling involves pits or wells.

Several explanations have been offered to account for falling dreams. Downward motion is considered to have negative connotations: Hell is down below and we'll descend to there if we are sinful; we "fall down" on the job if we fail in our work performance; we "land" in the gutter if we don't behave correctly. In a falling dream, we no longer have our feet "on the ground," we have "lost our balance," and there is generally nothing we can do in the dream to control our rapid descent or alter our expected demise. Falling dreams, consequently, are generally considered to represent situations in which the dreamer feels in danger of losing status, respect, security, or emotional stability. If you experience an increasing number of falling dreams, you should ask yourself if any of these situations might apply to you and then begin to explore ways of "rising" to the challenge. Falling dreams are usually terminated by an abrupt awakening on the part of the dreamer before hitting the ground, although some individuals have developed the ability to decelerate their fall so that they float slowly downward or hover in space. By discovering ways to take greater control of your waking life and improve your self-confidence, you can diminish the frequency of falling dreams.

When over one thousand readers of *Psychology Today* responded to the magazine's request for information about their dreams, the most frequently mentioned typical dreams were of being chased or falling. A surprising 39 percent of the respondents claimed to be able to sometimes control the course or outcome of their dreams.[59] In questionnaire surveys on typical dreams, data was obtained from college students in California,[60] Alabama,[61] Kentucky, and Japan.[62] In all these college populations, a slightly higher percentage of women reported having had dreams of falling. Some theorists have speculated that a woman who dreams of herself as being a "fallen woman" may be concerned with issues concerning morality and sexual behavior. Another study has reported that women report falling dreams more frequently when they are actually "falling asleep."[63] It's unclear whether a metaphorical meaning should be attached to such an experience or whether it represents the subjective sensation of releasing control during the process of sleep onset.

The contrast to the falling dream is obviously the flying dream. Just as downward movement carries negative associations, upward movement conveys positive associations. We "go up" to Heaven, "climb" the ladder of success, and aspire to "upper-class" status. In Freud's phallocentric universe, flying dreams are associated with erections, but although their experiences of sexual arousal are different, women report as many flying dreams as do males. Various postures may be assumed in a flying dream: Superman-style with arms straight ahead; airplane-style with arms at right angles to the dreamer's body; flapping one's arms like bird's wings; or hands on hips, in sort of an Irish jig fashion.

The emotions associated with flying in dreams are generally extremely positive and exhilarating. Many people report that the "high" from a flying dream will last for several days. The satisfaction accompanying the sensation of flying is derived from the feeling of having complete control of one's own actions, changing one's direction at will, and encountering no roadblocks. The sky is, literally, the limit when flying. Flying also affords the dreamer new perspective on situations that might not be easy to view from a lower level. The aerial view of a city is quite different from the street-level view. Individuals who enjoy "being on the top" experience flying dreams more often than those who have a hard time "getting off the ground" in their everyday activities.

Since the voluntary control of the dreamer reigns supreme in a flying dream, the dreamer can often choose to expand feelings of self-control by turning the dream into a lucid dream, in which the events of the dream are programmed at will by the dreamer. Lucid dreams will be discussed at greater length in chapter 15. A flying dream in which the dreamer is only able to achieve a limited elevation or a brief flight, or encounters obstacles such as power lines, would suggest that the dreamer's aspiration level in some waking task exceeds his or her current ability. Some flying dreams may arise simply as an occupational by-product. When I asked some hang-gliding instructors at Kitty Hawk, North Carolina, the site of the Wright brothers' original flight, about their dream lives, they told me that they frequently dreamed of flying but without their hang-glider being present.

The typical dream of appearing nude or inappropriately dressed in a social setting was discussed in chapter 7. In contrast to Freud's exhibitionistic interpretation of such dreams, I believe they represent the dreamer's concern about what others would think of the dreamer if they could really see him as he actually is.

Examination dreams are another category of frequently experienced dreams. There are many types of examination dreams. The prototypical one involves the dreamer's taking an examination and discovering that the questions are incomprehensible, the writing instrument defective, the allotted time inadequate, or the examination otherwise impossible to pass. Sometimes the dreamer arrives too late for the examination or is not able to find the place where it is being held.

The term "examination dream" is also used to describe situations in which the dreamer has to deliver a talk and is speechless, is in the cast of a play and can't remember the lines, or in some other way fails to perform in a satisfactory way in a public situation. The common denominator in all these dreams is that the dreamer feels poorly prepared or deficient in knowledge or techniques and therefore fears the judgment of an authority figure or his peers. We all experience occasional uncertainty about our intellectual ability, comprehension of factual material, or mastery of vocational skills. Examination dreams are most likely to appear when we doubt our ability to satisfy some task master who could mete out serious consequences if we fail.

Some dream themes may be typical only for a selected population. When a group of one hundred mentally retarded adolescents in a training school were asked what they dreamed about most often, the most common response was "home" and "going home"[64] Such a theme is certainly not hard to understand for a group of subjects living away from their homes.

Other "typical" dreams are more difficult to understand. One of these is the dream in which the dreamer experiences his or her teeth falling out or crumbling. This dream seems to be more common among women. One "feminine" interpretation for this dream is that it refers to giving birth: a small object is expelled from an orifice of the dreamer's body, resulting in pain and bleeding. This corresponds to the folk belief that a woman loses a tooth for every baby she bears, which may be based on the notion that the developing embryo depletes the level of calcium in the mother's body. Freud offered a more "masculine" interpretation for this dream; since teeth are usually lost by "pulling them," he considered that dreams with a "dental stimulus" represented adolescent masturbation for males.

A belief held in many non-Western cultures, as well as some segments of our own culture, is that the loss of a tooth symbolizes the death of a family member. The central teeth refer to the parents and the peripheral ones more distant relatives. Based on this folk belief, it has been proposed that the loss of a tooth in a dream represents an unconscious wish for the death of a relative. An ancient Egyptian papyrus dating back to about 2000 B.C., gives the reverse interpretation: if a man dreams of his teeth falling out, the dreamer will die through the action of his relatives.

One psychoanalyst suggested that losing teeth in dreams represents a desire to become a toothless, helpless baby and to be taken care of at a level where sex is not a problem.[65] For another theorist, the loss of teeth in dreams symbolizes the fear of aging, since we lose our teeth when we get older.[66] If the mouth can be used to make biting remarks or deliver sarcasm, and clenched teeth can connote anger, the loss of teeth may represent a "dropping out" or releasing of verbal hostility. A physiological explanation has also been advanced. The sensation of losing teeth may occur because the small muscles in the gums and tongue become active during REM sleep at the same time the large chewing muscles of the jaw become inactive.

In the only research study I am familiar with involving this topic, the researchers advertised for and located fourteen people who had recurrent dreams of lost teeth and compared them with fourteen people who had recurrent dreams of flying.[67] On the basis of psychological tests,

the researchers concluded that people with recurrent dreams of losing their teeth are more anxious and tend to worry and be upset about things. They have lower self-esteem, tend to be critical of themselves, and feel more helpless in dealing with life's events. It was not clear whether this conclusion was based on the data from the psychological tests in isolation, or on comparison with the other dreamers. Since the "frequent flyers" would be expected to show optimism, self-confidence, and calmness, any group compared with them would likely come up with less flattering and more negatively toned qualities.

An orthodontist told me that several of his patients who are concerned about orthodontal disease, which could cause them to lose their teeth, frequently experience dreams of losing their teeth. So sometimes our dreams are simply lifelike representations of our waking anxieties and experiences and don't need to be examined for deep metaphorical meaning.

RECURRENT DREAMS

Typical dreams are those that a large percentage of people experience at least once in their life. A recurrent dream is one that appears on a fairly frequent basis for an individual dreamer. It is, of course, possible for a recurrent dream to involve a typical theme, such as when a person repeatedly dreams of being attacked or chased. Most recurrent dreams are disturbing and generally are first experienced in childhood or

early adolescence.[68] Repetitive dreams are likely to be more pleasant the later in life they first occur.[69] One survey of several hundred adults found that 64 percent of female and 55 percent of male subjects reported one or more repetitive dreams, while another study of 350 adults found that 70 percent of females and 65 percent of males reported repetitive dreams.[70] Thus, approximately two-thirds of adults experience some form of repetitive dream, and most seem to be associated with stressful events. An understanding of repetitive dreams is not likely to be forthcoming from any laboratory study. One group of investigators recruited self-reported recurrent dreamers to study in a sleep laboratory, but only one recurrent dream was produced throughout the complete study.[71]

Freud showed very little interest in recurrent dreams and indicated, "I have never myself experienced one."[72] Physiological theorists who claim that dreaming represents purely random neuronal firing are also uninterested in recurrent dreams but have a difficult time explaining how the same well-formed and constructed dream can keep reappearing for weeks, months, or years. The odds against such a pattern being random would be astronomical.

Jung, unlike Freud and the physiologists, attached great significance to recurrent dreams and indicated they were "of specific importance for the integration of the (overall) psyche."[73] In his view, recurrent dreams indicate that some focal conflict remains unresolved. It is as if the psyche serves as a benign bill collector who patiently sends statements about an unpaid debt until the account is settled.

The consensus among clinicians is that a recurrent dream will cease once the underlying psychological issue has been resolved. Rosalind Cartwright developed a questionnaire to evaluate recurrent dreams and suggested that the cessation of a recurrent dream might "be a useful indicator of an improved ability to cope with the waking situation."[74] Evidence to support such a view was obtained by two Canadian researchers who recruited three types of dreamers from newspaper and radio announcements in Montreal.[75] One group, the recurrent dream group (RD), was composed of people who were currently experiencing a recurrent dream and had been for at least six months. A past-recurrent dream group (PRD), was composed of people who had experienced a recurrent dream for at least six months as adults but had not done so for at least the past year. A nonrecurrent dream group (NRD) was composed of people who reported never having experienced a recurrent dream in their adult life. All participants completed an extensive battery of psychological tests and also recorded dreams at home for fourteen consecutive nights.

The average duration of current recurrent dreams was 8.2 years, while the past recurrent dream had lasted for an average of 3.2 years. The three groups of dreamers contained mostly women, who were similar in age, education, and socioeconomic status. None of the subjects reported being in therapy, either in the present or in the past.

The highest level of psychological well-being was found for the PRD group, whose members had ceased experiencing previously recurrent dreams. Not only did the PRD group achieve significantly higher scores than the other two groups on the psychological test measuring well-being, but their dream content scores, which were based on several of our scales, showed more friendly interactions, positive affects, and successes and good fortunes than those for the other two groups. The RD group not only continued to suffer from their recurrent dreams but their other dreams contained "larger proportions of aggressive, anxious, and dysphoric dream content, relative to the other two groups."[76] Those individuals who had resolved or mastered their recurrent dreams, and presumably the underlying issues that caused those dreams, were able to achieve a higher level of well-being than those who had never experienced a recurrent dream. It's as if the PRD group had been forced to exercise their mental muscles more strenuously to overcome some deficit and were consequently more fit than those who hadn't been challenged to exercise so vigorously.

As I mentioned earlier, sometimes a recurrent dream can involve a typical dream. The following example of a recurrent dream combines two such typical themes. "Harold" first experienced this dream when he was about five years old and reexperienced it up through middle age. Its most recent occurrence was just a month before he shared it in a dream workshop led by Jeremy Taylor. Taylor discusses Harold's dream in a chapter on recurrent dreams in his recent book *Where People Fly and Water Runs Uphill: Using Dreams to Tap the Wisdom of the Unconscious*. This chapter contains the best clinical discussion of recurrent dreams that I have encountered. This is the dream Harold reported to a dream group comprising people who shared a strong concern with spiritual development:

I am fleeing in absolute terror, running through a barren landscape, pursued by something so horrible I cannot bring myself even to look back and see who or what it is. I run flat out through the sand and rocks with a horrible pursuer right behind me until I come to a big deep chasm that blocks my path of escape. There is a frail looking rope suspension bridge hanging across the chasm. I plunge onto the swaying rope bridge with the thought that if I can just make it to the other side, I may be able to grab a quick look back and get a glimpse of who or what is pursuing me . . . but before I can get across to the other side, the rope bridge snaps, and I end up falling through space . . . [and] this falling always wakes me up in terror, my heart pounding.[77]

This recurrent dream clearly involves both typical pursuit and typical falling themes. I can only give a few of the highlights from Taylor's detailed discussion of this dream. Harold had been raised a devout Catholic and imagined that he would eventually become a priest. However, at about the age of five, according to Taylor, he became disillusioned as to the spiritual validity of certain church dogmas. Harold later explored many other religions and spiritual traditions, but always ended up disillusioned as he became more acquainted with the dogma of the new church and the personal failings and hypocrisies of its leaders. But he had never made the conscious connection between his disillusionment at age five and the onset of this recurrent dream.

As the group processed his dream, Harold recognized in the imagery a very strong metaphor for the intensity of his religious striving. He entered into each new religious exploration intending to temporarily withhold judgment about what he would find. The frail rope bridge of his dream appeared to represent this "suspension of disbelief," but each time it snapped when his attitude could no longer be maintained. Harold further realized that his search for spiritual truth was a central focus of his life and that at some level he agreed to suffer this frightening recurrent dream because he was unwilling to give up his hope of finding the spiritual confirmation he sought. The "barren landscape" seemed to serve as a metaphor for his feelings toward a harsh patriarchal Christian tradition which failed to grant full spiritual equality to women, focused upon sin, and prohibited spontaneous and enjoyable sexual expression.

Harold concluded that the mention in his dream of "the other side" seemed to refer to death. He realized that, at one level, his goal in reaching the other side was to see God, because he believed that this was an opportunity afforded to the recently deceased. Harold recognized that he did at times long for death, hoping it would provide the spiritual certainty he sought. This exploration gave Harold a completely new perspective on this dream, which he had previously felt occurred on a purely random basis. The vivid images of the barren landscape, horrible pursuer, deep chasm, frail bridge, and the other side are all powerful metaphors that lend themselves fairly readily to amplification in the Jungian sense.

Here is a more puzzling recurrent dream from the same chapter in Taylor's book. The dreamer, "Mary," said that she had experienced this dream, in more or less the same form, "for as long as she could remember." It appeared several times a year and resurfaced a few days before this workshop. She indicated that she had been unable to relate any waking experiences to her dream, which she recounted as follows: "A disembodied close-up view of a wooden surface painted white. The paint is just beginning to blister and bubble."

Whenever Mary had this dream she became overwhelmed with feelings of despair, anguish, and terror, and at a level far more intense than when she experienced these emotions in her waking life. It's easy to understand why Harold would feel terror because of the relentless pursuer and his falling into the deep chasm. But why would Mary's very sparse imagery create such overwhelming, disturbing feelings? She explained that when she awoke from this recurrent dream, the feelings of misery and terror would remain with her for some time, then eventually ebb away and be replaced by feelings of anger, confusion, and frustration.

Mary considered her dream to be "totally meaningless and pointless." Taylor, however, felt certain that the dream contained a great deal of meaning and pointed toward some important truth for Mary. Taylor holds this view toward recurrent dreams generally:

> Recurrent dreams tend to be about the deeper layers of the dreamer's personal "myth"—that essential, archetypal, symbolic story that a

person tends to act out, over and over again in various forms, over the course of his or her entire life. Recurrent dreams, particularly recurrent dreams with particularly strong affect, such as Mary's dream of the "blistering paint," often turn out to be concise metaphoric statements of as-yet-unfulfilled aspects of the dreamer's fundamental "life task," or the "deepest value conflict" in his/her life, not just in the moment, but over the entire span of time that the dream has been recurring.[78]

In the group work with Mary's dream, it was suggested that maybe she had grown up in a repressed home where the spontaneous expression of feelings was not allowed and had to be covered up with white paint. If strong emotions began to bubble up, the thin veneer of social politeness might blister and possibly peel away. The family image would be tarnished if feelings trapped beneath the surface heated up and became visible.

Mary was stunned by these comments but recognized their validity. Suddenly she found herself flooded with previously repressed memories about specific incidents of physical abuse and emotional trauma from her childhood. These were memories that had been totally blocked from awareness during the intervening years. She realized that she had internalized the adult fears that her family's social position would be destroyed if someone were to find out the family's guilty "secrets" about her

abuse. Mary was therefore expected to "whitewash" them. Although this technique of coping with the abuse may have been necessary during childhood, it was no longer appropriate and was preventing her from feeling comfortable with emotional expression and intimacy.

As a result of these insights, Mary began to talk about the family situation with her adult siblings and found out that each one had been abused, but had suffered in silence and guilt because they had assumed they had been the only one. As a result, the family members experienced tremendous relief, although this was accompanied by feelings of grief and anger. Once the members began to exchange honest communication, the whole family's pattern of neurotic behavior began to change.

Harold and Mary felt that they obtained very significant benefits through exploring the meanings of their dreams. Taylor feels that such benefits are potentially available to all of us. Here is how he characterizes the potential payoff from working with your dreams:

The single most important thing to understand about dreaming is that *all dreams come in the service of health and wholeness.* Every dream is a completely natural and spontaneous instinctive expression, welling up from your unconscious depths, directed toward bringing conscious awareness to neglected or repressed aspects of your experience. The greater awareness of these inadequately appreciated elements of your life that comes from paying more attention to your dreams always turns out to foster psychological and emotional growth and increasing maturity, creative expression, and developing awareness of your life's fullest potentials.[79]

TRAUMATIC DREAMS

In Mary's case, the original trauma behind her richly metaphorical dream was traceable to her family's effort to paint over the corrosive incidents that took place within the home. Traumatic events occurring in adulthood can also have a strong influence upon dreams and are more likely to be represented in a realistic fashion. In an article published at the end of World War I, the author stated that he regarded "the recurrence of 'terror dreams' as the outstanding symptom of the anxiety neurosis of warfare."[80] Another author from this same era noted, "The dream is always the same, always of the enemy . . . a dream of the charge, of the bursting shell, of the bayonet thrust!"[81] This author made the interesting observation that the same battle nightmare recurred when soldiers were going under or coming out of anesthesia and usually related to a surprise attack. A concern with the enemy is clear in a dream reported by an American Marine during the 1991 Gulf war: "I am the first into the trenches. I throw a grenade, but it doesn't explode. I zero in on an Iraqi. He is also aiming at me, but I pull the trigger first."[82] The recurrent nightmares of Vietnam veterans have been studied fairly extensively. These veterans reexperience terrifying imagery in their dreams which closely parallels the wartime events they initially experienced.

It helps therapeutically if there is an opportunity to discuss these traumatic dreams in groups with other veterans who are experiencing similar dreams. After a period of time, the intensity of traumatic dreams declines and their content gradually changes and incorporates other elements. If new stressors appear, even if they are quite different in content—marital conflicts, for example—the war scenes can return with all of their associated pain and anxiety. One group of investigators has provided many examples of this response and concludes that "the Vietnam experience serves as a metaphor to express the difficulties."[83] Watching a movie or TV show about fighting in Vietnam can also reactivate combat dreams.

Life-threatening situations outside of the battlefield may also find their way into dreams. In one survey, 155 subjects reported that they had been involved in a serious accident in which a person was killed or seriously injured.[84] Dreams about the accident were reported by 36 percent of the subjects, and over half of those who reported them described recurring stereotyped dreams of the events. One man said that redreaming the accident always happened "after a close call in driving." A woman reported that in her dream she takes the place of the woman whom she killed in the automobile accident.

Responses to earthquakes were examined in this same study. Since students from southern California were involved, 88 percent of them had experienced at least one earthquake. There had been a particularly strong earthquake about two years before the study was undertaken. Emotional reactions to this event varied. Some found it thrilling, while others reported undifferentiated excitement or feelings of indifference. An unpleasant reaction was reported by 31 percent of the men and 49 percent of the women. Over 40 percent of those with an unpleasant reaction subsequently dreamed about their experiences, and over 70 percent of them stated that the emotion was the same in the dream as in the earthquake experience.

Traumatic dreams were also experienced by the survivors of the Buffalo Creek disaster in West Virginia, where a sudden Appalachian flood killed 125 people and left 4,000 homeless. In these dreams, the agony associated with the disaster was relived in all its intensity immediately after it occurred. Gradually the initial terror began to diminish and the dreams had a less painful outcome and eventually became modified. In later dreams, the subject matter shifted from the flood to earlier crises, such as separation, abandonment, or guilt that had been successfully coped with by the dreamer. The researchers offered this explanation for the shift in dream themes:

Dreams of long-past stresses that had been mastered provided reassurance to the survivors that they could overcome the recent trauma . . . dreams that are characteristic of traumatic neuroses attempt to neutralize the overwhelming anxiety of the traumatic event by recalling successful past adaptations to difficult situations.[85]

A different form of traumatic dream was experienced by Czech refugees who fled to Switzerland during the Cold War.[86] When one hundred of them were interviewed by another Czech refugee, fifty-six percent reported having dreamed about being back in their Soviet-dominated homeland and being unable to escape again. Most of the refugees left during a brief period when "tourist trips" were allowed but they never returned. The failure to return is a crime punishable with several years of forced labor in a penitentiary. Their most frequent dream themes expressed the need to hide or concerns about being recognized and arrested. These dreams were not posttraumatic in the strictest sense because they didn't replay events that the dreamer had actually experienced, such as being discovered by the police, but their repetitive nature and the terror associated with them would seem to qualify them as a special form of traumatic dream. These refugees were obviously undergoing continuing stress and ambivalence because of their simultaneous desire to return home and fear of the consequences if they did so. Some of the dreams, however, were classic traumatic dreams and dealt with dramatic events, such as crawling over mine fields at the border and being shot at.

NIGHT TERRORS AND NIGHTMARES

Just as the distinctions between REM, non-REM, and sleep-onset reports can become rather blurred, the various categories of dreams subsumed under the heading of "nightmare" can also fade into each other. For many people, the term is used in a generic way to describe a "bad" dream or a dream associated with overwhelming anxiety and apprehension. For sleeping researchers, the term "nightmare" is too vague and nonspecific to be useful. They prefer to use at least two different categories for these dreams: REM anxiety dreams and night terrors. As its name implies, a REM anxiety dream is a dream with anxiety-producing content that is reported after a REM awakening. The dream is more likely to be experienced during the latter part of the sleep cycle and the dreamer usually has quite detailed recall of its content. A night terror, on the other hand, occurs during the first two hours of sleep, is associated with Stage 4 sleep, and generally yields minimal or no recall of its content. If any recall exists, it generally involves a single frightening image such as "I was choking" or "There was something heavy on my chest." A scream frequently precedes the awakening from a night terror and the subject may be disoriented for ten or twenty minutes following the awakening.

Many researchers are hesitant to consider a night terror as a genuine dream and view it as a cognitive effort to describe a sudden shift in physiological status, rather than as an attempt by the unconscious to process psychological conflicts. In a night terror tremendous autonomic nervous system changes take place very rapidly, the pulse and respiratory rates sometimes doubling. Because the awakening is so abrupt and involves such extraordinary shifts in the autonomic nervous system, night terrors have been classified as "disorders of arousal."[87] Sleepwalking sometimes follows the onset of a night terror. The night terror does not depict a symbolic drama involving sequential imagery from which the sleeper gradually awakens, but seems to be a description of acute somatic sensations associated with respiratory or cardiac distress.

Night terrors are most common in children, and their frequency decreases as the child grows older. Research suggests a somatic factor may be responsible for many cases of night terror. An 1899 article in the *British Medical Journal* reported that seventeen out of thirty cases of night terrors were associated with early heart disease.[88] After their adenoids were removed, twenty-two out of twenty-three children who had been suffering night terrors immediately ceased to do so.[89] Another study that investigated children with night terrors claimed that early childhood cerebral damage was found in 50 percent of the ninety children in the group and pathological EEG findings were present in 59 percent.[90] Further, if indirect, evidence for non-psychological explanations for night terrors is that adults who suffer from night terrors do not seem to share any other similarities with regard to personality characteristics (although a few of them have been described as somewhat tightly controlled).

The most extensive studies of frequent nightmares have been made by Ernest Hartmann, who published his findings in a book called *The Nightmare*. Hartmann is a psychiatrist and the director of a sleep laboratory at Lemuel Shattuck Hospital in Boston. Advertisements were placed in several Boston newspapers to recruit subjects who had experienced at least one nightmare per week for at least the past six months. Most of the thirty-eight adults selected for the original study had suffered from nightmares since childhood. These subjects were interviewed in considerable depth about their nightmare history and the content of their nightmares. Eleven of these subjects were studied in the sleep laboratory for four nights.

Screaming, temporary disorientation, and minimal recall of content occur with night terrors. The Scream by Edvard Munch.

The investigators also conducted a second study and selected an additional twelve subjects who reported at least one nightmare per week and had a lifelong history of nightmares. They compared this group to another group of twelve subjects who had frequent vivid dreams but no nightmares, and a third group of twelve individuals who had neither nightmares nor vivid dreams. They found that the nightmare sufferers differed greatly from the vivid and nonvivid dreamers, but resembled very closely the thirty-eight nightmare sufferers in the original study. Hartmann's conclusions about nightmare sufferers therefore involve the entire group of fifty subjects from the two studies.

The most common nightmare theme was of being chased. As a child, the dreamer could recall nightmares in which he or she was chased by a monster or some other large and frightening creature. Later on, the pursuer was more likely to be a large, unidentified man or a group of frightening people, such as Nazis. In addition to being attacked, the dreamer often experienced feelings of pain and helplessness. A few of the women had nightmares in which members of their families were in danger and the dreamer was unable to help them.

These researchers also studied Vietnam veterans suffering from posttraumatic stress disorders. They found that their nightmares were repetitive replayings of actual experiences they had encountered while in service. This carbon-copy type of repetitive dreaming was pointed out earlier, in the section on traumatic dreams. The imagery reported by the civilians with a lifelong history of nightmares did not have this quality. Each nightmare was different, although the themes were frequently similar. There was a marked absence of explicit sexual content in the nightmares of both civilians and veterans. Periods of stress accompanying school or work problems or strained personal relationships increased the frequency of nightmares. When not experiencing nightmares, the nightmare sufferers reported vivid and detailed dreams which often included very bright colors and distinctive sounds. In addition, tactile sensations were often present, and sensations which are usually absent in other people's dreams, such as pain, taste, and smell, were also experienced. Several nightmare sufferers described dreams in which they were some other character, such as a member of the opposite sex, or an animal. The intense emotional feelings experienced in the dream frequently continued after the dreamer awakened. Thus, even when not experiencing nightmares, the unusual contents and sensations in the dreams of the nightmare sufferers put them in a class by themselves.

None of the nightmare sufferers held ordinary blue- or white-collar jobs. They frequently had musical or artistic careers or were teachers. They also did not fit society's sex-role stereotypes: there was not a single tough, macho man or a woman who saw her role as marrying and having children. Their personal relationships were often stormy, and they tended to become overinvolved in relationships quickly, which then led to difficult, painful separations. Adolescent years had been particularly difficult for them and one third of them had attempted suicide or had thought very seriously about it. Two-thirds of them had sought psychotherapy at some time in their life.

What came as a surprise was that these nightmare sufferers had not experienced any obvious traumatic events in their childhood, nor were any family patterns found which might have been related to the nightmares. The only significant finding to emerge from the interviews about childhood was that the nightmare sufferers saw themselves as different from other children and perceived themselves as more sensitive, artistic, easily hurt, and fragile.

After considering all of the detailed information he had acquired on nightmare sufferers, Hartmann proposed that the most meaningful way to differentiate them from other types of dreamers was to describe them as having "thin boundaries":

> I am led to characterize persons with frequent nightmares in terms of unusual openness, defenselessness, vulnerability, and difficulty with certain ego functions. The term I come up with that describes them best is "thin boundaries," thin in many realms, including sleep-wake boundaries, ego boundaries, and interpersonal boundaries. I examine twenty different ways in which we use the term boundaries and find that in all senses persons with frequent nightmares have thinner or more permeable boundaries than most people. It appears that having thin boundaries, as opposed to heavy rigid boundaries, may be related to being more artistic, more aware of one's own inner feelings and those

of others, and it may also make one more vulnerable to some types of mental illness.[91]

It appears from various research studies that there are three primary kinds of individuals who experience nightmares. One group involves individuals with "thin" boundaries who have had a history of chronic nightmares since their childhood or early adolescence. These individuals continue to suffer nightmares on an almost weekly basis. Their nightmares have some recurrent themes but are still quite individualized. Hartmann speculates that a genetic basis may underlie their predisposition to experience vivid emotions and imagery in their dreams and painful sensitivity in their waking life. The frequency of nightmares will diminish somewhat for these individuals if they are in a stable environment, but they will probably continue to suffer these harrowing nighttime experiences throughout their lives.

Another group suffers from traumatic nightmares set into motion by having to deal with a catastrophic situation (military combat), a natural disaster (a flood or an earthquake), or a life-threatening encounter with a vicious attacker, such as a rapist or potential murderer. In such cases, the traumatic events are repeated without much variation on almost a nightly basis. In time, the nightmares will become less frequent and new features will gradually be incorporated as some old features gradually disappear. The recovery process may be speeded up by discussing the nightmares with others who have experienced similar trauma. Those who live through an event in which others die often suffer "survivor guilt," and it can be similarly beneficial to discuss these feelings with others who are struggling with the same issues.

The third group experiences nightmares related to stress at school, work, or home or in an ongoing relationship; these stresses do not threaten the dreamer with loss of life or dismemberment, but they do threaten his or her self-esteem and interpersonal security. When confronted by such upsetting situations, the individual may become somewhat "thin-skinned" for a time and experience a troubling nightmare.

When 1,006 representative households in the Los Angeles metropolitan area were surveyed about sleep problems, 11 percent of the respondents reported being troubled by nightmares.[92] Women are more likely to respond to newspaper advertisements recruiting nightmare sufferers,[93] and among Canadian university students more women than men acknowledged they are frequently troubled by nightmares.[94] We often feel reduced to childish helplessness when encountering the many frightening figures that may appear in our nightmares. In his book *Nightmares and Human Conflict* the psychiatrist John Mack comments:

> Whether the dreamer is threatened by an ancient demon, a vampire, a lobster, a fairy story monster, a robot, or an atomic ray, his experience is in each instance like that of a helpless child confronted by powerful forces with which he is unable to deal effectively.[95]

Just as a fever indicates something may be developing physically which deserves medical attention, a nightmare should alert one to the possibility that something is amiss psychologically. Responding to the emergency message—attending to problem conditions in waking life or changing aspects of one's underlying mental attitude—can serve to inoculate the dreamer against experiencing even more intense future symptoms.

Several approaches have been developed to dealing with the stress of nightmares.[96] Achieving insight into the metaphorical meaning of the nightmare can loosen its grip on both the dreaming and waking self, such as when Mary realized that the blistering white paint represented the repressed emotions surrounding her childhood abuse. Another approach encourages the dreamer to gain conscious control over the dream events as was described by the nineteenth-century Frenchman Hervey Saint-Denys. He fixed his eyes on a frightening pursuing monster and thereby caused it to slow down and change into a floating bundle of rags. If Harold, for example, could develop such lucidity and turn around to see who was pursuing him as he fled across the rope bridge, he might be able to permanently dispatch his life-long recurrent nightmare (if the revelations arrived at in the group were not sufficient to do that). In other cases, a behavioral approach may be indicated.[97] If someone had nightmares about encountering a spectral figure in a cemetery, the therapist might encourage the individual to approach a cemetery in waking life and to walk farther and farther into it over a period of days or weeks until he or she reached the middle. If the dreamer encountered no spectral figure, he or she should be able to "deep six" this nightmare.

DREAMS AND AGING

We all have various crises to deal with as we move through life. Aging is a particularly difficult challenge for many, but dreams can be of great assistance in dealing with the issues we face as we enter the second half of life. C. Brooks Brenneis, the researcher who investigated "ego modalities" in Chicano and Anglo dreams, has also examined the developmental aspects of aging in women.[98] He compared the dreams of adolescent, young adult, and older adult (ages forty to eighty-five) women matched for education and family economic status. The settings in older women's dreams seemed to be more restricted and less familiar. They also had the fewest characters. These characters were less likely to be identified with regard to gender and were more frequently family members or relatives of the dreamer. The dreamer herself was less likely to be a central figure in her dream events and aggressive dream encounters were less frequent. Sexual themes, however, were not significantly less frequent in the dreams of the older women.

Brenneis noticed an overriding theme of scarcity in the dreams of the older women. This could manifest as being frustrated at facing a long line for food or running out of ingredients in preparing meals at home. The dreamer was also frequently frustrated through interference or disruption by others when she was in the process of preparing food. Brenneis speculated that the scarcity may reflect a perceived limitation of resources previously available from others, while the interference with preparing food for others may reflect a limitation on the dreamer's perceived ability to provide for others. These food-related themes did not appear in the dreams of the younger women and perhaps indicates metaphorically that the older women feel less able to nurture and to get nurturing support.

Dreams from fifty-two patients from a home for the aged in New York City, with a median age of eighty, also were described as "preoccup[ied] with loss of resources."[99] The investigators characterized the dreamers as weakened, lost, frustrated, vulnerable, and threatened by a loss of previous control over environmental events. One dreamer reported, "There are all sorts of roads that criss-cross and I cannot find my way." Another dreamer wanted to go to the toilet and tried a dozen toilets, but all of them were locked up; concern over the ability to take care of his own bowel functioning in an independent fashion may have led to this dream. Sexual content appeared fairly often, but in men's dreams it was usually in a context of anxiety and failure, whereas in women the dreams depicted passive, pleasurable gratification of dependent needs.

Some of these elderly patients suffered from varying levels of senility, and their dreams tended to be repetitive. Their dreams did not deal very much with day residue, but seemed to emphasize the "lost resources." One man, in his dreams, was baking bread but was missing salt. A woman was looking for an apartment for her sister and herself but couldn't find one. Initially, these dreamers enjoyed the relationship provided by the psychiatrist collecting the dreams. After the man had been asked about his dreams several times, he began baking magnificent bread without any missing ingredients, and the woman who had vainly sought an apartment soon found a perfectly acceptable one in her dreams. The psychiatrist, however, interacted only minimally and did not offer any comments about the dreams or provide any other kind of emotional support. As disappointment over expectations for a fuller relationship set in, the bread again soured for the baking dreamer and the woman's new apartment was discovered to have a large hole in the floor.

The same investigators also obtained dreams from a group of noninstitutionalized elderly dreamers living in New York City, whose median age was sixty-nine.[100] Dreamers who were leading active and self-sufficient lives generally reported elaborate, active dreams that related to daily events. The concern about lost resources, however, was evident in many dreams, particularly among one group of dreamers who were members of a day center rather than living independently in their own homes. There seemed to be a desire for some kind of reassurance that security and nurturant needs would be met. One seventy-year-old woman reported, "It's very embarrassing for a woman my age, but I had a sexy dream with a rich, young man who was very nice and who was going to 'keep' me."[101] A few senile patients reported the

same types of repetitive dreams as those in the institutionalized group in the earlier study. The investigators suggested that dreams might prove to be a sensitive indicator of cerebral organic disease.

It's understandable that elderly individuals would develop anxieties over the availability of monetary resources and the continuity of material necessities, such as food, clothing, and shelter. In fact, it would seem surprising if these characteristic waking concerns were not reflected in dream content unless the elderly dreamers were in robust good health, had a strong social network available for emotional support, and had adequate financial reserves. In a study of thirty-seven elderly women, with an average age of seventy-four years, who lived in very comfortable private retirement homes in Virginia, it was found that, in comparison to college women, they experienced more enjoyment and less anger and fear in their dreams.[102] The retirement years may not have been so stressful for these women because they all came from reasonably high economic strata. But financial security isn't everything.

Old age is considered to be a fairly secure stage of life in Finland because the elderly have access to a comparatively good pension and health care system.[103] But their dreams don't necessarily suggest pleasure in this stage of life. A group of eighty seventy-five-year-olds living in Helsinki were interviewed concerning their dreams. Some form of dream report was obtained from about 75 percent of the individuals interviewed (though most of the subjects did not consider dreams to be very important in their life). Some classical nightmares were reported in which the dreamer was threatened or trying to escape, and several nightmares also involved work themes: tools were lost, work could not be completed or was unsuccessful, the work place was foreign or foreign people were there. Only one work-related dream was experienced as positive. The authors considered that these dreams represented a means of going through the sorrow connected with retiring. Dreamers returned to their workplaces only to see that their skills and knowledge had become old-fashioned. One man who previously owned a food store reported dreaming of being at his store but finding the goods mixed up. It was impossible for him to sell anything, although the store was full of customers, because he was alone, with nobody to help him. Such a dream can be considered to fit the "lost resources" category, because the dreamer had lost the skills necessary to successfully handle his business affairs.

One in four of the Finnish subjects reported having recently dreamed about their childhood homes, parents, and siblings. Such dreams were usually experienced as pleasant, since the dream gave them contact with significant family members, many of them now dead. In addition to these dreams about childhood scenes and family members, there were also a few dreams in which a friend's death or the dreamer's own sickness was predicted. Dreams spanned intervals of time ranging from the past to the future and seemed to help the dreamer to gain a wider perspective on his or her own life's activities.

Dreams dealing with sexuality persist into old age. In the American studies already described, the authors mentioned that sex dreams were reported by several of their subjects. Only a few cases of sexual dreams were reported in the Finnish study, but an Italian study found that half of the twelve subjects, with an average age of seventy-three, reported recent erotic dreams.[104] Erotic dreams were also reported by 36 percent of seventy-four men from Philadelphia whose average age was seventy-one.[105] Kinsey reported that wet dreams still occurred for males over sixty, and the occurrence of wet dreams among males in their seventies was reported in another study.[106] This study also found that 45 percent of the REM periods were categorized as showing full or moderate erections for eighteen healthy subjects aged seventy-one to ninety-six.

David Gutmann, a psychologist, has proposed that some developmental changes for males can be characterized in terms of ego mastery styles. He obtained dream reports from highland Maya subjects in Mexico and found that there were differences in mastery style between young (thirty to forty-nine years old) and old (fifty to ninety years old) men. The young men exhibited a more achievement-oriented, active stance toward life events, while the older men showed greater passivity, a kind of resigned accommodation to the world rather than an attempt to change it.[107] Gutmann and a coworker carried out a similar study with Navajo males. They found that the dreamer played an active role in eighty-eight percent of the dreams of younger men (ages thirty-five to fifty-four), while 60 percent of the older men (ages fifty-nine to ninety-five) played a passive role or were absent in their dreams.[108] A forty-one-year-old man re-

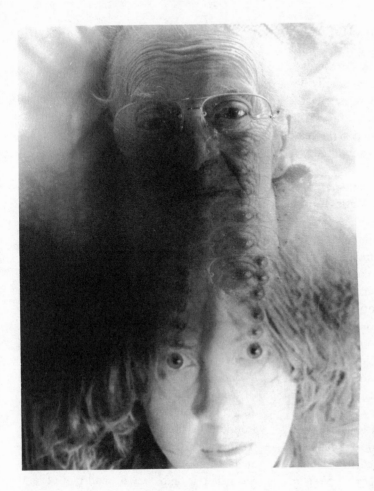

In the dreams of the elderly there is frequently a temporal regression to earlier periods of the dreamer's life.

ported, "I usually dream about riding horses or walking on the edge of the cliff." A sixty-two-year-old man reported "I usually dream about the horses, sheep, and cattle, how I used to handle them in the past." This same older dreamer also dreamed of ripe, or fully aged, cantaloupes in the garden. The only subjects to report indoor settings were older males. This may have simply reflected the fact that these less-active men were spending more time indoors, or it might suggest a psychological turning inward. Since indoor settings are more frequently reported by women, integration of masculine and feminine components may also have been signified.

A hospice worker told me about the dreams of a dying patient she was attending, which showed a reduction in feelings of empowerment or intact body identity. During the final two weeks of this man's life, the dreamer progressively shrank in physical stature until he had almost reached the height of a small child just before his death. A woman dying of cancer had recurring dreams of being on the bank of a river and seeing a hand beckoning from the other side. As the days passed, the width of the river gradually decreased until, a few days before her death, it had narrowed to a tumbling spring which she knew she could step across easily.[109] The river apparently symbolized the river of life for this woman.

Erik Erikson, a psychoanalyst, proposed that issues of special concern to older individuals were those of "generativity" (relationships between different generations) and "integrity" (managing the prospect of death).[110] A linkage between older and younger generations is shown in a dream reported by a seventy-six-year-old man three days before his death: "A bouncy baby was in the room, one year old. It was smiling at me. I love and I admire it and place it on the shelf. Then an old-looking baby is shaking its fists at me."[111]

A concern with generativity was also apparent in the following dream reported by Robert Macnish. I referred to the third edition of his book *Philosophy of Sleep* in chapter 9. Macnish was thirty-five years old at the time of this 1836 edition and he died in 1837. There was no mention in the book that Macnish was in poor health and I'm not sure how soon he died after experiencing this remarkable dream:

I dreamed that I was converted into a mighty pillar of stone, which reared its head in the midst of a desert, where it stood for ages, till generation after generation melted away before it. Even in this state, though unconscious of possessing any organs of sense, or being else than a mass of lifeless stone, I saw every object around— the mountains growing bald with age—the forest trees drooping in decay; and I heard whatever sounds nature is in the custom of producing, such as the thunderpeal breaking over my naked head, the winds howling past me, or the ceaseless murmur of streams. At last I also waxed old, and began to crumble into dust, while the moss and ivy accumulated upon me, and stamped me with the aspect of hoar antiquity.[112]

In a series of dreams from a male bachelor dying of cancer, the dreamer found a connection with an earlier generation.[113] In one dream, the man saw a picture of his great-grandfather and tried to make a silhouette of him with ice-cream salt on the ground. The dreamer associated making ice cream with his childhood. In another dream from the same night, the dreamer was negotiating to buy a small plot of land but was running into zoning problems. In his associations, the dreamer indicated that he had been thinking of buying a plot of land where he hoped to cultivate a large garden when he left the hospital. This land would subsequently be given to the public as a place where people could rest quietly and perhaps children could play. These two dreams could be considered to deal with generativity, but the latter also confronts the patient's death (the small plot of ground can be viewed as his grave). After he had been hospitalized and was no longer able to walk, he had a dream which also seemed to presage his forthcoming death:

A shadowy stranger, dressed darkly, stands by my bedside. I find I can walk. He leads me out of the hospital to a place I've never been to before. He is somehow very comforting. I am extremely interested in what he shows me—but now I don't remember what it was.

In his last dream, a few days before his death, he was in a room with two acquaintances who were enjoying themselves and playing a record. The dreamer said, "It is as if I am a ghost; they cannot see me." When the record ended, the turntable kept spinning and the dreamer found himself very angry and shouted, "It's all over. Turn it off." But they couldn't hear him and kept talking and laughing. The patient had become increasingly impatient with being sick, being paralyzed, and having to endure so many of the indignities of his illness, and in his waking life he wished for things to be over. This desire seemed to be reflected in his request for the uselessly spinning record to be stopped.

The dreams of the dying often contain imagery that suggests a continuation of life at some other level of existence, or at least the wish for it. Marie-Louise von Franz, who worked with Jung for more than three decades, wrote an intriguing but difficult book entitled On Dreams and Death. She commented:

All of the dreams of people who are facing death indicate that the unconscious, that is, our instinct

world, prepares consciousness not for a definite end but for a profound transformation and for a kind of continuation of the life process which, however, is unimaginable to everyday consciousness.[114]

Dr. von Franz presents several fascinating dreams in which the dreamer seems to experience death as a rebirth into a new plane of existence. Two weeks before her death, a seventy-four-year-old woman dying from cancer and experiencing stomach cramps, had the following dream:

The dreamer was lying across the opening of a cement pipe about one meter wide, whose upper edge pressed painfully against her stomach. The pipe itself was stuck into the earth. She knew that she had to emerge from it headfirst and intact into another land.[115]

The image of emerging headfirst from the opening of a pipe strongly suggests birth and the intact emergence into another land a rebirth, implying the continuation of existence at another level. Dr. von Franz speculated that the dreamer was lying across the opening because she was still making an effort to put her affairs in order and was not yet in a position to make her descent into the other existence. Other investigators who have studied near death experiences report the almost universal experience of passing through some sort of tunnel before arriving at a new state of existence.

The spiritual beliefs of the dreamer obviously play an important role in whether death will be faced with terror or with faith that there is something more "beyond." Dr. von Franz described the dream of a totally irreligious woman who was committed to a rationalistic-materialistic attitude toward the world. In her dream, the woman is in a courtyard. On one side of it are garbage men who say that she cannot get out; another man mentions that there could be a revolving door through which he might get the dreamer out, but she is fearful it might be a trap and so she remains walking in a circle along the walls of the courtyard with the garbage men. In her dream, the woman is tortured by the fear of not being able to find her way home.

In contrast to the preceding dream, in which it seems the dreamer's body will be relegated to garbage men, is this dream of another woman, who died the day following its appearance:

> She sees a candle lit on the windowsill of the hospital room and finds that the candle suddenly goes out. Fear and anxiety ensue as the darkness envelops her. Suddenly, the candle lights on the other side of the window and she awakens.[116]

Although there is some momentary fear and anxiety in this dream, the dreamer recognizes that the candle will light again on the other side of the window after it goes out. This reassurance allowed the woman to die "completely at peace."

One theorist has proposed that a "life review" is one of the necessary activities engaged in by the elderly.[117] A superb example of a life review was described in the chapter on Jung: John Sanford's father experienced a dream in which all the key events in his life from his childhood onward were reviewed. His dream concluded with the image of a light shining on the other side of a window, similar to the image of the candle in the dream just discussed. The light in the dream of Sanford's father became a brilliant path on which he began to walk and then disappeared. He died a week later.

We have gone full course during this chapter. It began with dreams of birth, progressed through dreams associated with childhood and adolescent development, recognized the troubling and emotional imagery which can break through into dreaming awareness at various stressful points in adult life, and concluded with dreams of the aged. The dreams that I have selected from individuals approaching death seem to signal not the demise of the dreamer, but only the completion of a cycle, with life continuing along a path of light to a new birth or existence beyond the clay-covered grave. This chapter has suggested that if we are mindful of our dreams, the difficult course which we traverse during our life can be much less harsh and anxiety-producing. When we are ready to see and listen, dreams can offer us, like the fictive specters of Christmas past, present, and future in the dreams of Scrooge, a helpful perspective on where we have been and the possibilities which lie ahead.

PART 6

THE TWILIGHT ZONE OF DREAMS

C H A P T E R 1 3

SOMATIC CONTRIBUTIONS TO DREAMS

I n the preceding chapters of this book, dreams have been discussed primarily from a psychological point of view. Their origin has been attributed to unfinished emotional business and their function ascribed to promoting self-awareness. But we all surely exist and experience life at more than just an emotional level.

In this chapter on somatic contributions, we will look at how dreams may alert us to disturbed physiological functioning of organ systems. Researchers who study REM sleep in a laboratory setting are very sensitive to the influence of biochemical and physiological factors when they attempt to account for the presence or absence of dreaming, but they dismiss the possibility that dreams could provide a diagnostic index of the dreamer's physical health. I think rejection of that possibility represents a serious oversight on the part of contemporary investigators, and I hope that the numerous examples of diagnostic and prodromal dreams presented in this chapter will encourage more active attention to this topic. Since scant North American and European material is available, I will begin by referring to work carried on in Russia by Vasily Kasatkin, then move on to other special classes of biologically based dreams, such as healing dreams, before closing with a review of my own work in the area of dreams during the menstrual cycle and during pregnancy.

KASATKIN'S RESEARCH IN RUSSIA

Calvin Hall's counterpart in Russia is Vasily Kasatkin, a psychiatrist at the Leningrad Neurosurgical Institute. Kasatkin was born in 1912, and his dream career also spanned four decades. In his book *Theory of Dreams*, published in 1967, Kasatkin described his findings based on 10,240 dreams obtained from twelve hundred subjects.[1] Unfortunately, this book has not been translated into English, but a brief summary of it has been reported in French.[2]

Kasatkin relied upon home dreams for his data. In addition to describing their dreams, subjects noted their health, their activities during the preceding day, their emotional tone, environmental conditions such as temperature or other external stimuli, and the sensations felt in various parts of their body. Kasatkin rejected psychoanalytic interpretations and directed his attention to the manifest content of the dream, which he felt depended upon interior physiological stimuli, possibly external sensory stimuli, and social environment. Kasatkin also concluded that dream content is closely determined by the dreamer's life conditions and reflects the dreamer's age, sex, social and cultural class, profession, and ethnic group. He was aware that dreams change from one stage of life to the next and gave many examples to document such changes.

According to Kasatkin, sex differences are apparent in dreams from the age of six years; young boys dream about games such as fighting and playing war, while young girls dance and play with dolls. These differences become more pronounced with age and are demonstrated, for example, by the emphases women give to items such as clothing and to feelings. Kasatkin claims that it is fairly simple to identify the sex of the dreamer by the content of his or her dreams.

Kasatkin also asserted that one can confidently deduce the cultural level of the dreamer and that geographical influences shape the way languages, customs, clothing, and food appear in dreams. Dreams will change if the dreamer changes profession or moves to another region. Kasatkin collected a large number of dreams from soldiers representing the many different nationalities that comprised the USSR. During the first year of service the soldiers' dream content varied widely because their dreams contained many elements of their past lives, but gradually common traits began to appear in their dreams, and by the third year, it became difficult to distinguish the dreams of the Russians from those of, for example, Ukrainians, Tatars, and Uzbeks.

One notable departure from findings with American subjects is Kasatkin's emphasis on professional or work activities in dreams. In his study of ten thousand American dreams, Calvin Hall reported that "the world of dreams does not duplicate the work-a-day world" and that work activities were very seldom described in dreams. Kasatkin seems to regard professional activities as one of the chief determinants of dream content, since 67 percent of his subjects dreamed in a fairly precise manner of their occupation. Perhaps the emphasis given to working activities in the dreams of these Soviet subjects reflects their limited possibilities for individual expression or for pursuing more gratifying and sensual pursuits in their daily waking lives.

When I was in Moscow in August 1991 for the "Dreaming in Russia" conference, I led a small workshop in which both Soviet and American dreamers participated. Valery, a Russian psychologist from Leningrad, shared a dream in which he was standing by the side of a road observing an endless mass of people with downcast eyes slowly moving along a dusty road. The procession seemed to stretch to the horizon in both directions, and no one in the massive column seemed to be aware that there was an open gate next to the dreamer which led to wide fields and green pastures. The dreamer acknowledged ambivalent feelings in his dream; he was glad he was not part of the collective group, but he also felt some internal pressure to join them. The title Valery gave to his dream was *Homo Sovieticus*, because he felt it portrayed the collective mentality of the typical Soviet citizen. He was aware of a faint glow of

light in their eyes, however, which suggested a potential for greater animation and vitality. This dream was shared during the week that the Soviet political structure was toppling in Moscow. The other Soviet members of our dream group agreed that the shuffling human herd accurately characterized how most members of Soviet society ordinarily behaved. A society in which individuality is submerged or barely discernible in a collective group, and identity is predicated almost exclusively upon professional activities, may help to explain Kasatkin's findings of a heavy emphasis upon work-related themes in the dreams of his Soviet subjects.

Even with the emphasis upon occupational dreams, Kasatkin's conclusions that a demonstrable correspondence exists between the dreamer's life conditions and the manifest content of dreams is consistent with the continuity hypothesis accepted by most American researchers. Kasatkin, however, carries the continuity hypothesis to a biological and physiological level that has been almost totally neglected in contemporary American research. A lengthy chapter in his book is devoted to the types of dreams associated with physical illness.

Kasatkin concluded that the modifications produced in dreams by physical illnesses vary according to the duration of the illness, its seriousness, and its location, but that some common features can be distinguished: (1) illness is associated with an increase in dream recall; (2) illness causes dreams to become distressful and to include nightmarish or violent images of war, fire, blood, corpses, tombs, raw meat, garbage, dirty water, or references to hospitals, doctors, and medicines (frightening feelings were associated with these images in 91 percent of the dreams, but pain was experienced in only 9 percent); (3) these dreams generally appear before the first symptoms of the illness; (4) dreams caused by illness are longer than distress dreams caused by ordinary annoyances and persist throughout the night and throughout the duration of the illness; (5) the content of the dreams can reveal the location and the seriousness of the illness.

Kasatkin was interviewed in Leningrad by two American writers for the *National Enquirer* in 1975. Under a bold front-page headline, "Dreams Are Saving Lives," the article quoted Kasatkin as saying, "By correctly interpreting dreams we've been able to discover and treat serious illnesses long before they would be diagnosed by any traditional means. We have been able to save many lives."[3] Symptoms that follow dream warnings, he noted, vary from two weeks for a heart attack to a year or more for mental illness. Repeated dreams of body wounds "are among the most serious and they invariably indicate a very dangerous illness such as cancer, liver trouble, kidney or heart disease."

In this article, Kasatkin gave an example of a physician who had a recurring dream that one of his young patients was being attacked by muggers. The doctor tried to help the patient in his dream but couldn't. Finally, he saw the patient lying in the street with a long wound across his stomach, his right kidney lying detached from his body. Kasatkin noted that it was actually the doctor's own right kidney that was seriously infected. Dreams, Kasatkin explained, "are sentries that watch over our health. There are nerves coming to the brain from every part of the body—and they relay the signals of impending illness that the subconscious translates into dreams."

PRODROMAL DREAMS

The concept of a close correspondence between physical illness and dream content did not originate with Kasatkin. It has a long tradition dating back to the early Greeks, who gave great emphasis to the ideal appearance and functioning of the human body. Aristotle wrote that the "beginnings of diseases and other distempers which are about to visit the body . . . must be more evident in the sleeping than in the waking state." Hippocrates, the father of Greek medicine, also proposed that some dreams had the potential to indicate diseases, humoral imbalances, or other physical conditions, such as overeating. Galen, a second-century Greek physician, also stressed the ability of dreams to foretell impending illnesses. In his book *Prophecy in Dream* he mentions the case of a man who dreamed that his leg was turned to stone and who developed a paralysis of this leg a few days later.

Several diagnostic dreams preceding illness are reported by Artemidorus. Arnald of Villanova, a physician in the Middle Ages, compared dreams to magnifying glasses which could detect the small beginnings of physical illness. He described the case of a man who dreamed on two successive occasions that his ear was being beaten with a stone. Soon afterward, he developed a serious inflammation of the ear on the same side as he had been beaten in his dream.

Dreams which herald the onset of a physical illness were classified by M. Macario around the middle of the nineteenth century as "prodromic," a term which is still employed today.[4] He used the term "symptomatic" to describe those dreams which occurred during the course of a disease after it had been detected. Macario cited a prodromal dream involving a minister of justice who dreamed that he suffered from apoplexy (stroke) and died of this condition three days later. Macario himself dreamed of a pain in his throat, awoke feeling well, but later that day developed severe inflammation of his throat. Many other writers during the latter part of the nineteenth century also emphasized the close relationship between

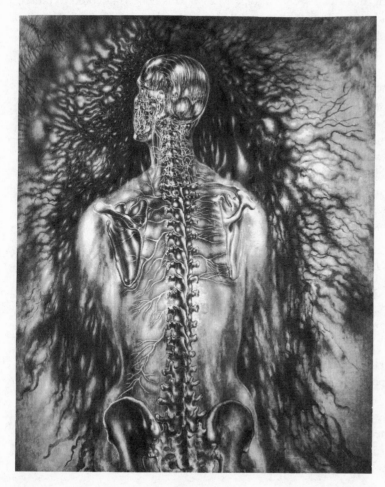

In prodromal dreams, imagery is often influenced by physical symptoms. Anatomical Painting by Pavel Tchelitchew. (Collection of Whitney Museum of American Art, New York)

dream content and the condition of various bodily organs. For example, an 1890 book by A. Dochmasa was entitled *Dreams and Their Significance as Forebodings of Disease.*

Many examples of dreams preceding the onset of cancer have been published. One author traces a link between dreams, disturbing emotions, lowered functioning of the immune system, and increased susceptibility to cancer. He claims the images in dreams can symbolize the type of cancer and its location and gives the example of a woman who had recurrent nightmares of dogs tearing at her stomach a few months before she was diagnosed with stomach cancer. She died three months after the diagnosis was made.[5]

Bernard Siegel, a cancer surgeon at the Yale School of Medicine who has written two popular books on self-healing, described the case of a journalist who had a dream in which torturers were placing hot coals beneath his chin. He felt the heat start to sear his throat and screamed in desperation as "the coals gnawed his larynx."[6] He awoke very disturbed and received a long-distance call from his girlfriend, who had just experienced a horrible dream of being with him in a bed filling with blood. In a later dream, medicine men stuck hypodermic needles into what he called his "neck brain." The journalist felt sure these dreams indicated something was wrong in his throat. He had difficulty, however, persuading his physician to take seriously his concern that his dreams might mean he was developing cancer in his throat. But a physical checkup confirmed the presence of cancer in his thyroid gland, which is located near the larynx.

In the February 1983 issue of the *Dream Network Bulletin,* Dr. Siegel reported that a patient with breast cancer dreamed her head was shaved and the word cancer written on it. She awoke with the knowledge that her cancer had metastasized (spread) to her brain, even though no physical signs or symptoms were then present. Three weeks later her dream diagnosis was confirmed.

Daniel Schneider, a psychoanalyst and neurologist, wrote a book called *Forewarning Cancer Dreams and the Bioplasma Concept.* Most of this book is devoted to tables, graphs, and mathematical equations intended to support Schneider's bioplasma theory, which proposes to explain certain aspects of biological functioning through analogies to modern physics. He asserts that "bioplasma" in each cell of the body sends signals "via chemical and other 'codes' " to a "paraconscious" mind and that this communications system provides the basis for dreams warning of impending disease.[7] Schneider presents several examples of forewarning cancer dreams. One is a repetitive dream from a heavy smoker who dreams he is in the army in a combat area and attempts to take cover in the hollow trunk of a large tree. He hears machine-gun fire and looks down to see "the bullets are reaching the tree and cutting me in half methodically going from the left side of my lower chest to the right, clear across my body."[8] A checkup revealed a small tumor on the left lower lobe of his lung, but it had not yet metastasized. Another patient who had a rapidly metastasizing neoplasm of the gall bladder dreamed that his "entire body exploded, shattering into a thousand fragments."[9]

In a journal article, Schneider presented a dream from a patient with coronary heart disorder who had received news of a severe setback in his financial affairs on the previous day. In his dream he was on a stage receiving tremendous applause, which he acknowledged with a bow. He then opened his violin case and took out, not a violin, "but a machine gun and swiftly I put the muzzle to my mouth and rat-a-tat-tat I blow my brains out. . . . I fall to the ground." The patient woke from his dream and experienced a massive heart attack a few minutes later.[10] The loud, rhythmic "rat-a-tat-tat" heard in his dream suggests a markedly accelerated heart rate.

Another author described the case of a fifty-year-old male who dreamed some guests shot at him at a palace reception. The dreamer felt the bullets pierce his heart and saw blood flow out. Other dream events then occurred, and at its conclusion the dreamer felt as if a bomb exploded. The dreamer had experienced an arterial infarct (heart blockage) during this dream.[11] Kasatkin reported the case of a recently widowed woman who dreamed that she was sitting on her husband's grave in the cemetery when two skeletal hands came out of the grave and grabbed her. One grabbed her at the throat, and the fingers of the other hand pierced deep into her flesh near her heart. She awoke choking and had a mild cardiac arrest.

In the cases just reviewed, the heart-related imagery was surprisingly specific. Individuals with heart problems are also more likely to project heart content into their waking imagery, as shown by a study employing ink-blot stimuli. The investigator presented three cards, each of which bore a somewhat heart-shaped ink blot in either red or blue ink, and asked subjects to describe what they saw. Student nurses who had reported cardiac symptoms, such as a pain in their chest or their heart skipping a beat, reported seeing either significantly more or significantly fewer heart images than a group of nurses not reporting such cardiac symptoms.[12] Subjects with cardiac abnormalities were thus either acutely aware of cardiac stimuli or they denied their presence.

Many people attempt to cope with illness by denying its existence. When a psychiatrist asked a group of patients with neurological disorders to dream about their sickness so that their dreams could be discussed the following day, he found that almost all the patients seemed motivated by a desire to deny the fact that they were ill. They frequently replied, "I do all I can *not* to think about my sickness by day; why should I plague myself with thoughts about it at night?"[13]

Kasatkin recorded some dreams of patients with tuberculosis. A medical student, for example, dreamed she was lying on the earth when it began to give way under her, forming a cavity. The sides of the earth then began to fall on top of her body, compressing her chest and producing a feeling of suffocation. Kasatkin reported that this dream had been recorded two months before the onset of her illness. Another tubercular patient, who developed pleurisy in her left lung, described a dream in which a mountain slide fell on her chest, and when she tried to crawl through a small opening, the left side of her chest was too large to squeeze through.

Just as compressed chest imagery was

present in the dreams of tubercular patients, the dreams of ulcer patients depicted some injury to the stomach. The night before he experienced a perforated ulcer, a twenty-nine-year-old man had a dream in which he was eating pizza and his stomach "broke open."[14] A forty-year-old man who had a recurrent dream about a rat gnawing in the lower right part of his abdomen was eventually diagnosed as having a duodenal ulcer.[15] After a successful operation for the ulcer, this dream no longer recurred.

Heat imagery was featured in some cases when inflammation was present. Medard Boss described a patient who dreamed on three successive nights about a Balinese demon of disease who forced her to sit on an overheated central-heating pipe, which caused her to experience burning pain between her legs. She was subsequently diagnosed as suffering from acute cystitis.[16] A woman who dreamed that a stranger threw oil over her and set it on fire came down with typhoid fever three days later.[17]

Various types of gastrointestinal disorders have also been reflected in dreams. Sometimes the onset of symptoms immediately followed the dreams. Kasatkin reported the case of a man who dreamed he was in an apartment littered with feces and dirty water. In a second dream that same night he was in a restroom that was dirty with feces. Later in the dream, he was caught by an enemy who hit him on the head with a rifle butt and another who bayoneted him in the abdomen. The dreamer awoke with dysentery, a headache, and a pain in his lower abdomen. Kasatkin noted that in gastrointestinal disturbances

with a slow onset, the repetitive dreams may involve visions of spoiled food, intestinal worms, or raw fish. He cited many examples involving rotting or decomposing fish.

There are many interesting examples of how disturbed cerebral conditions followed rapidly after dreams in which imagery involving the head was featured. A seventeen-year-old girl dreamed that a man broke through her bedroom window and shot her on the left side of her head. She woke up with a severe migraine headache on the left side.[18] Another woman dreamed she was taking a walk when a storm broke out. A bolt of lightning struck her head and turned her around several times before she fell down. She also woke with a migraine headache.[19] In a nineteenth-century dream, a woman's deceased father appeared and told her that during his lifetime he had to wear a crown, which he then placed on her head. She felt the weight and tightness of the crown around her brow and realized that its rim was studded on the inside with sharp points that pierced her forehead and drew blood. After she awoke, she recalled that her father had been subject to epileptic convulsions before being cured by surgery. As she began to tell the dream to her sister, she suddenly gave a shriek and fell to the floor in an epileptic convulsion. A week later the dream was repeated and was followed by another attack. After undergoing treatment, both the dream and the attacks ceased.[20]

A neurologist reported on the dreams of a twenty-one-year-old woman who was in good health. One night she experienced several dreams which emphasized the theme of immobility. In one, she became a living statue of stone, and in another she fell into a sleep so deep she couldn't be awakened. She awoke the next morning a victim of sleeping sickness (encephalitis lethargica).[21] Patricia Garfield reported that a woman in her sixties dreamed for several months of characters who were ominously still. In one, the seated people in a kitchen seemed to be waxlife figures, and in another, corpses sat upright in an undertaker's parlor. This woman was later discovered in a deep coma. Her diagnosis was myxedema coma, a potentially fatal condition resulting from an underactive thyroid gland.[22] The immobile characters in this woman's dreams represented her own condition of slowed metabolism.

Medard Boss described a different outcome for a twenty-five-year-old woman who experienced repetitive dreams that her family members turned into stone statues. Although she appeared to be "the picture of mental and physical health" at the time these dreams began, she developed severe catatonia (schizophrenia with rigid posture) ten days after the fourth repetition of her dream. Her immobility was remarkably similar to the petrification of her family members in her dreams.[23]

Visual problems were foreshadowed for a women who both saw and felt "wiggly, incandescent worms of all colors" crawling over her eyelids. She developed retinitis (inflamed retina) two days later, accompanied by intense pain and flashes of light.[24]

Association can account for some unusual premonitory images in dreams. A man who had suffered from severe inflammation of the eyes while in Egypt, suddenly began, ten years later, to dream regularly of scenes from Egypt. He could not explain these Egyptian dreams, but soon after their appearance he again developed inflammation of his eyes.[25] The learned association between scenes of Egypt and inflamed eyes was apparently unconsciously activated when incipient signs of eye trouble began to develop again. Another interesting example was reported by Alan Moffitt, a former president of the Association for the Study of Dreams. Moffitt was allergic to animals, and whenever he petted a cat his eyes and sinuses would swell up and he couldn't breathe. When he was about nine years old, he had a dream in which a cat had been rubbing itself over him. After awakening, he experienced a full-blown allergy attack.[26] In these last two dreams, an organ system was not depicted, but the imagery was intimately associated with the previous presence of a disturbance in a specific organ system.

Dreams almost seem to serve as X rays in some cases. An American researcher reported the case of a woman who, for nearly a year, repeatedly dreamed that a woman resembling a nurse held a lighted candle toward the dreamer's left leg. At first the nurse did not burn the dreamer, but as the dreams continued, the nurse came closer and did seem to burn the dreamer. Eventually, the woman began to feel a little pain in her left shin; soon after, she developed an infection in the bone marrow of her left leg which required an operation.[27]

The examples which have been cited will, I hope, serve as a prod to stimulate more attention to prodromal dreams by American researchers. Laboratory investigators have found that brief external sensory stimuli, such as heat or sprays of cold water, and possibly the electrodes or other recording devices attached to the dreamer's body, can be incorporated into an ongoing dream. If such fleeting stimuli can cause detectable changes in dream content, it certainly seems plausible and logically consistent that continuously active physical stimuli within the dreamer's body should also instigate recognizable images that correspond at a manifest level to the dreamer's inner somatic environment. It is clear, in any case, that some connection exists between the physical condition in our bodies and what appears on the monitoring screen of our dreaming mind. Many examples of psychophysiological parallelism were cited in chapter 10, which documented how changes in respiratory rates, for example, were associated with dreams of suffocation or drowning, and changes in the middle ear with increased auditory imagery in dreams.

Robert Smith, a psychiatrist at the Michigan State University College of Human Medicine, has carried out two studies to investigate a possible biological role in dreaming. In one study, forty-nine medical inpatients reported dreams occurring within the preceding twelve months to an interviewer. Most of these patients had cardiovascular disease, but some were suffering from pulmonary disease, infections, or other general medical problems. The state of their health was evaluated six months after they were discharged from the hospital. Dreams were scored for the presence of "death," which included references to graveyards, funerals, wills, or conditions such as the heart stopping. Another dream category dealt with separation and included references to disruptions of personal relationships or displacement from the home. Smith found a significant association between death references in the dreams of males and a subsequent deterioration in their medical condition, while women's medical condition deteriorated when their dreams contained references to separation.[28]

In his second study, Smith obtained dreams from forty-eight patients who were undergoing cardiac catheterization. Most of these patients had cardiac problems, but a few had cancer or diabetes. He found the severity of cardiac dysfunction was related to the number of dream references to death for males and to separation for women. Smith concluded that "these dreams had a warning function, signaling the presence of severe biological impairment. If a useful intervention occurred as a result of these warnings, the dreams would have an adaptive meaning or function."[29]

DREAMS ASSOCIATED WITH MEDICAL RECOVERY

Patricia Garfield, author of several popular books on dreams, has written an excellent book on the relationship between dreams and bodily functioning. After she broke her left wrist in a fall and had to have it rebroken surgically because the bones were healing incorrectly, she became very aware of how the medical course of her recovery was being expressed in her dreams. In her book *The Healing Power of Dreams*,[30] Garfield presents some drawings of her dreams to illustrate how the imagery reflected the underlying status of her physical recovery. She also provides useful examples of how individuals can attempt to program dreams to assist in their own healing process.

I have also had indications of my health status register in my dreams. In the summer of 1982, I experienced a heat stroke while trying to set a personal record for a ten-mile run. Somewhere between the ninth and tenth mile, I collapsed and awoke in an ambulance. After my whole body was packed in ice in the emergency room, my temperature came down to about 104 degrees. Had someone not found me on the cross-country trail, my brain would very soon have taken on the consistency of cooked oatmeal because the midday temperature and humidity were extremely high. After an overnight hospitalization I was released, but felt extremely weak physically and was very fuzzy mentally. My body had been so severely traumatized that I could not recall any dreams for four nights. In the first dream I remembered, I was involved in some sort of telepathy study with two colleagues and was in charge of collating the stimuli. However, everything was going so fast that I said the procedure had to stop because the reliability of my work was breaking down. I was then sorting through a box containing hardware, trying to find some nuts and bolts. I felt this dream reflected my difficulty in trying to achieve any mental concentration, and I recognized I needed to slow down and attend to the basic "nuts and bolts" of physical recovery.

Two nights later, I dreamed I was at a banquet celebration where music was playing. A performer was onstage making sensational skiing moves, including going up the side of a wall. I was at another platform, but making only very minimal motions. In my waking life, I had been feeling considerable apprehension over whether I would be able to run again and was going "up the wall" with anxiety. I feared that I might have to be restricted to very minimal movements on my Nordic Trac, a stationary cross-country exercise machine that I had previously used. In a later dream that night, the tempo of my activities increased; I was running and turned a corner and started to accelerate. At that point in my dream, I remembered that I had promised my doctor I wouldn't attempt running for quite a while, so I stopped running in the dream. I felt encouraged by this later dream's indication that I would eventually "turn the corner" and be able to resume running, but I also realized I should progress slowly and not overdo any physical activities.

About ten days after my heat stroke, I had a dream in which three puddles of blood spilled on the floor. (Earlier that day three tubes of blood had been drawn to determine how my recovery was going.) As I was cleaning up the blood, a small frog appeared. For me, a frog has always been associated with a special spiritual and healing quality, and I have accepted a frog as representing my "totem animal" or "spirit guide." After waking from this dream, I felt positive that the blood analyses would indicate I was out of danger and that the various metabolic indices would be at normal levels. A few days later when I received the results, my dream-inspired diagnosis proved correct.

My metabolism had stabilized, but I knew from the previous dreams that I still should not push myself too hard. I eventually began to take very brief walks, extended them to longer walks, and about two months later was able to jog slowly for a few dozen yards. Approximately a year later, I returned and completed that same ten-mile course, but I made sure that I had a companion with me this time in case I were to overextend myself and experience any physical problems.

No prodromal dream had preceded my physical collapse because I had been in excellent health. All my physical organ systems were in good shape before the run; it was my overly large ego that was the disturbed organ system. I had chosen a humid, ninety-seven-degree day to run, did not have adequate water available during the run; and had stupidly refused to accept the physical limitations that apply to a fifty-four-year-old man. I suffered nearly fatal consequences for my arrogance.

I have also experienced dreams which indicated that I was at risk because my physical condition was not up to par. I once flew from Lima, Peru, which is at sea level, to Cuzco, almost eleven thousand feet above sea level. The plane trip lasted one hour, and there wasn't sufficient time to acclimate to the change in altitude. Members of our group, who were planning eventually to visit Machu Picchu, were told to stay in our hotel rooms for a while and not to engage in any vigorous physical activity. Any exertion could cause slight dizziness, because our lungs were not yet

able to obtain sufficient oxygen in the rarefied atmosphere at that altitude. During an afternoon nap at the hotel, I dreamed that I was trying to walk down some wide ancient stone corridors, but kept stumbling and bouncing off the walls as if intoxicated. I paid attention to that dream and decided to delay any extended walking tours of Cuzco until after returning from Machu Picchu. Markedly unpleasant dreams or nightmares have been reported to be typical for individuals suffering from chronic exposure to high altitudes.[31]

Edgar Cayce, the "Sleeping Prophet," was able to go into a self-induced trance and provide "readings," or answers to questions asked of him, while in this altered state. During his lifetime, he gave approximately fourteen thousand readings, many of which related to dreaming. A two-volume work has been compiled which provides information on his readings dealing with dreams. Biographical data was supplied for each person for whom a dream reading was given, along with a chronological listing of the person's dreams and Cayce's interpretation of each dream.[32] Cayce suggested that many dreams were related to improper diet, incorrect posture, or predisposition to some illness. He apparently made many accurate diagnoses of physical disorders from dreams and suggested a wide variety of treatments to cure these ailments. The Association for Research and Enlightenment, an educational and research organization devoted to disseminating Cayce's views on dreams and other topics, has existed for several years in Virginia Beach, Virginia.

Health Remedies in Dreams

The necessary ingredients for cure are sometimes prescribed in dreams. Pliny's *Natural History* contains an account concerning Ptolemaus, who was dying of a poisoned wound. His friend, Alexander the Great, dreamed that a dragon appeared holding a certain plant in its mouth and said that the plant would cure Ptolemaus. Soldiers were sent to obtain the plant and they found it in the place seen in Alexander's dream. Ptolemaus and many others suffering from the same affliction were healed by this plant. In the seventeenth century, Sir Christopher Wren, the famous architect, was very feverish and had a difficult time urinating. A physician was planning to engage in bloodletting, but Wren asked him to defer his treatment for another day. That night he dreamed he was in a place where palm trees grew and a woman in an unusual costume reached up and gave him some dates. The next day he sent for dates and they cured him of the uncomfortable symptoms.[33]

A woman, who had been on antibiotics for over a year after an operation, was suffering from a chronic vaginal yeast infection which failed to respond to traditional medical treatment. Taking some advice from a friend, she began to take large doses of folic acid (a vitamin of the B complex). In a few days she developed cramps and had a dream in which she was in her kitchen moving bowls of "acid" around but wondering what to do with them. In another part of the dream, she gave a kitten some brown bread with yeast and strawberries in it and the kitten gobbled it up. After reflecting on this dream, the woman decided that the bowls of acid referred to the folic acid and she stopped taking it, but began to take yeast tablets because the kitten in her dream seemed to relish yeast. This woman's cramps disappeared almost immediately, and in a few days her yeast infection showed remarkable improvement.[34]

Some individuals have had dreams warning them to avoid the effects of cigarette smoking. William Dement, whose pioneering work in the early days of REM research were described in chapter 10, had been a heavy cigarette smoker who consumed up to two packs a day. He had a dream in which he saw an X ray of his chest and realized that the entire right lung was cancerous. A colleague conducted a physical examination in his dream and detected wide-spread metastases in his lymph nodes. Dement experienced deep anguish in his dream. He knew his life was at an end and that he would never see his children grow up and that all of this could have been avoided if he had quit cigarettes when he first learned of their carcinogenic potential. When he woke up from his vivid dream, he experienced incredible joy and relief and felt that he was reborn and given a chance to alter the direction of his life. He immediately stopped smoking.[35]

DREAMS ASSOCIATED WITH SPONTANEOUS HEALING

In the health-related dreams discussed so far, the dreamer was given guidance as to changes in diet or behavior patterns that would facilitate recovering better health. Some people have reported dreams in which healing spontaneously occurred while they were dreaming. Patricia Garfield gives an example of a woman who had suffered severe migraine headaches for nearly forty years, which immobilized her for about a week three to five times a year. During one of these painful episodes, when the headaches had continued for two or three days, the woman lay down for a nap and had a long dream that she was with an old woman, this woman's husband and their son. The dreamer was taking care of the old woman, who was dying, but wanted to leave to take care of her own family. Since there was no one else to care for the old woman, the dreamer decided to stay with her until she died. After her funeral, the old woman's husband and son came to visit the dreamer, who was suffering from a migraine. The two men stood by her bed, and the son indicated that because she had been so kind to his mother he would help her. He laid his hand on her forehead and said she would never experience another migraine headache. When the dreamer awoke her headache had vanished, and she was still symptom-free at the time she described her dream to a friend over a year and half later.[36]

N. Ahmad, the author of a quaintly titled book, A Peep into the Spiritual Unconscious, indicated that he had been suffering from severe attacks of colic for approximately nine months and was hospitalized for this condition. After several days of extreme pain, he had a dream in which Muhammad offered him a large glass of milk with a piece of bread in it. Muhammad raised the glass to the dreamer's mouth and the dreamer sipped a little of it, believing it was intended as a remedy for his colic. Ahmad awoke with a very sweet taste in his mouth. When a medical attendant came to visit him that morning, he was surprised to see Ahmad so much improved. At the time of writing his book eight years later, Ahmad reported that he never experienced another attack of colic after this dream.

A physician, who was an editor of a health journal, was very ill with acute bronchitis which had been occurring every winter and spring for several years. He was depressed because he was afraid his condition might become chronic. He experienced a dream in which he saw his sister, who had been dead for more than twenty years. She said, "Do not worry about your health, we have come to cure you; there [is] much yet for you to do in this world." She then vanished and his brain seemed electrified, as if by a shock from a battery, and the sensation spread downward over his entire body. He awoke, found himself well, and never again had an attack of the disease.[37]

A woman from Virginia suffered most of her life from a lower back problem, which worsened after her children were born. This woman acknowledged complaining a great deal, which she felt was as irritating to others as a child's complaints can sometimes be to adults. She had a dream of being in a kitchen where the floor had black and white tiles. The dreamer was feeding ice cream to a friend's little girl, who was sitting in a high chair. As the child began to eat, her head slumped over on her shoulder and the dreamer said, "I think she is dead." The dreamer was only slightly upset, however, because at that very instant her lower back "felt like a hot iron had been set off at the base of her spine." The thought went through her mind in her dream that she was healed. When she awoke her lower back was quite hot and so was the bed in the area where her spine touched the bed. The dreamer wrote me that she had not experienced any further pain in her back in the years since having her healing dream. The imagery in her dream suggests that perhaps the healing was associated with the demise of her childlike attitude of complaining (sitting in a high chair) and of looking at her physical condition in such a black and white fashion.

A dream experienced by a twenty-four-year-old female patient also caused a marked change in attitude. She was in the hospital with a serious illness that required the presence of a rubber tube in her nose. She was constantly complaining to the hospital staff and had developed a reputa-tion as the most difficult patient they could remember for a long time. One day when she had been particularly nasty, constantly criticizing the staff, she took an afternoon nap. She had a dream in which Jesus appeared, and as the dreamer looked at him, she noticed that blood was coming from his nostrils. He looked at the dreamer compassionately and said, "I have suffered. Can't you suffer a little bit, too?" The dreamer said yes. From the time she awoke, the staff noticed an astounding change of attitude on her part. She ceased her chronic complaining and everyone subsequently commented upon her extremely cooperative behavior.[38]

Light sometimes figures in healing dreams. A former student of mine told me of a healing dream that she had experienced when suffering from a disabling bronchial infection. This was her dream:

I saw a sudden spot of light and watched as it came closer to me, growing in intensity and size. It grew until it covered me, felt hot in the center of my chest, made my eyes burn with its brightness and gave me the feeling that I was being healed.

This woman was able to get out of her sick bed the next day and deal successfully with a family crisis that required tremendous physical effort.

Janice Baylis, who has written two books on how to work with dreams, described a healing dream of her own. She had been experiencing a great deal of difficulty and pain in her right eye and made an appointment for an eye examination.

The day before her exam, she stayed home from work because of the intensity of the pain. During an afternoon nap, she had the following dream:

> I am looking at a bubble of water on our patio. A fish is swimming in it. . . . The bubble changes to a spotted light with a dark center. It begins to move toward me. I am very glad that I am going to be immersed in that light. As the light reaches me I feel a tingling, electrified sensation strongly centered in my right eye.[39]

When the dreamer awoke the pain in her right eye was gone, and it checked out fine in the exam the following day.

With the exception of Smith's prospective studies, all of the examples I have cited have been based on retrospective accounts and are therefore subject to the vagaries of selective memory, embellishment, and incomplete observation. I cannot vouch for the accuracy of Kasatkin's work or that of my various other sources. My objective in collating this material is to suggest that the cumulative weight of so many impressive anecdotal accounts would seem to warrant serious consideration by open-minded investigators.

The material reviewed so far offers suggestive evidence that organic disturbances that are not picked up in waking consciousness can sometimes be represented meaningfully in our dreams. Some dreams involve a specific organ, such as the heart or throat, while others may indicate that the overall metabolic condition of the dreamer is out of balance. Dream imagery that reflects an underlying somatic condition can be referred to as "oneirosomatic" imagery.

Many people may feel that their dreams are not likely to show much oneirosomatic imagery because they are basically in good health. But it is possible that normal shifts in endocrine levels or hormonal balances can be reflected in the dreams of healthy people. Dreams during a woman's menstrual cycle, for example, display marked shifts in content due to changes in internal hormonal levels and externally visible events, such as the onset of her period.

DREAMS DURING THE MENSTRUAL CYCLE

In 1964 I collected over 450 dreams from approximately fifty first-year nursing students in Miami. To protect anonymity, each woman selected a code name and used it on her dream reports, which were dated with regard to her menstrual cycle, throughout the three-month study. At the time these dreams were obtained, birth control pills were not yet generally available.

Although no student reported a dream in which she was actually menstruating, there were several dreams in which menstruation was symbolized through references to bloody female anatomy. "Andria" reported a dream in which she could see the underside of the thighs of a terminally ill patient: "It was a solid mass of bloody flesh." "U of M" reported watching a classmate operating on her young sister on a kitchen table and noticed color: "red and pink of the blood and flesh from the long incision she had made on her sister's side." "Mac 4021" was getting some shots from classmates, and one of them wound up doing this incorrectly. The dreamer described her reaction: "It really hurt. I was bleeding." In another dream "Kahlil" saw:

> a dismembered very bloody corpse of a young woman with blond, curly, short hair. . . . Someone said that there was a hatchet murderer loose in the area. Then I saw another corpse in the same condition, but this one had reddish brown, short, curly hair.

These four dreams took place either on the first or second night after the onset of the dreamer's menstrual period. On the third night after her menses began, "Old Taylor" dreamed that a captain in the army was standing next to her, "holding a test tube of blood. I turned to him and said I would like to see his white blood count." On the fourth night after her period began, Mac 4021 dreamed about a disaster of some sort that seemed like a train wreck. A small boy was covered with all kinds of tubes, and after he died the dreamer said, "I remember emptying the bottles of scarlet secretions."

In the dreams occurring shortly after the beginning of the dreamer's periods, blood appears in fairly large quantities and is visible on a female dream character's body, whereas in the dreams later in the period, the amount of blood is limited, is associated with male characters, and

appears at a distance in impersonal containers.

The color red appeared in another interesting context during menstrual dreams. Two dreamers described red chairs, another a rose-colored chair, another a rocking chair with red and brown cushions, and yet another a big red sofa. These red seats could represent either the menstruating women's bottoms or their fear of leaving a visible red mark if they sat on furniture without adequate protection.

The only direct reference to activities associated with menstruation was a menstrual dream from "Pepsi," who indicated, "I was in the bathroom changing sanitary protection when I heard my mother's footsteps." The use of sanitary napkins is also suggested in "Dale's" dream. Dale was in a big room with a dirt floor, and as long as she and some classmates kept their feet off the ground, they would be safe during an upcoming war: "We were going to make slings out of blankets, tie them to pegs on the wall, and sit in them during this war. This was going to be a horrid experience. . . . We started practicing stringing ourselves up."

Several theorists have suggested that the human body can be portrayed in dreams through images of a house or other architectural structure. Rooms within a house can then be conceptualized as representing various regions or structures within the body. Major changes are going on in a woman's uterus during menstruation, and she may be more sensitive to internal regions or anatomical divisions within her body at this time: womb awareness may be translated into room awareness. There were significantly more references to rooms during menstrual periods than at any other cycle phase. Some support for the notion that a room could represent the womb is shown in a menstrual dream of "Mrs. D. B.," which took place in a big house with a baby and a little girl: "One room was called the X ray room, there was a room off that (secret) and it was furnished all in pink, very feminine. The little girl knew of this room and showed it to me." Another menstrual dreamer noted, "My room was filled with children."

An emphasis on uterine functioning is also revealed in other dream themes during menstruation. Three dreamers gave birth to babies, and another was cuddling and breast-feeding a baby. There were more references to children and babies during the menstrual period than during any other cycle phase. As indicated, some menstrual dreams emphasized the birth of a baby, but there were also many dreams of sick, injured, or deformed children. These imperfect babies or children may represent the dreamer's unconscious awareness that the presence of menstrual blood indicates the absence of a potential baby. One poet has suggested that the womb mourns its failure to create new life each month by shedding tears of blood. Death was a fairly common theme in menstrual dreams. Characters were murdered, committed suicide, died from illnesses, or were seen in coffins.

Birth and death, representing the beginning and end of life, appear to be closely linked during menstruation. So too does another pair of opposites: feminity and masculinity. Menstruation is undeniably one activity which differentiates the two sexes. Some women may never be-

come pregnant, but all women will menstruate. Menstruation can be considered the hallmark of femininity and a time when women's special biological functioning is emphasized. It's interesting to observe that this is also the time when the themes of marriage, weddings, and engagements also become prominent in dreams.

Four dreamers described receiving engagement rings from their boyfriends during their menstrual dreams. Others found themselves mysteriously married to men they didn't know. "Miss Understood" dreamed, "I was in a dark kitchen with a man I thought of as my husband. . . . He had no face. He was tall and had dark hair. I was very much in love with him." Another mysterious marital partner appeared in Mrs. D. B.'s dream: "I was sitting in a cafeteria . . . when I saw a colored man come in. I jumped up and ran over to him and took him by the hand, and said, 'come on, honey, let's go home.'" At other points in her dream, Mrs. D. B. refers to this man as "my husband" and reports "sitting in the cafeteria again [with] a tiny colored baby in my arms." "Tall Texan" was asked out to lunch by a familiar male, but an unfamiliar, nice-looking young man said she couldn't go because she was his wife. "I did not even know him although I did not deny that I was his wife."

These menstrual dreams of being wed to mysterious strangers or receiving engagement rings from boyfriends may represent an attempt to incorporate masculine elements at this time of heightened femininity; a fusion of feminine and masculine energy may be seen as enabling the woman to achieve increased psychic vitality and power. Many non-Western societies endow the menstruating woman with mysterious and powerful energy, and efforts are made to isolate her to insure that she will not use these magical powers to cause crops to wither, hunts to fail, or food to turn bad. Although contemporary Western males may consider confining women to menstrual huts to be silly or superstitious, many nevertheless support the idea that anyone who experiences menstruation and its attendant hormonal changes should not be elected to the White House or allowed other positions of influence.

Other patterns of social interaction in dreams throughout the menstrual cycle will be presented later in this section. First I'd like to further consider how dream imagery may represent alterations in organ systems that occur during the cycle. Reference has already been made to the increased incidence of rooms, blood, children and babies, and death in menstrual dreams, which may indicate heightened attention to the uterus. But many women also experience definite somatic changes in the days immediately preceding their periods. Quite a few women experience premenstrual water retention, and water references in dreams at this time generally involved large bodies of water, such as oceans or seas, in contrast to the rivers or creeks that are more typical during the menstrual period. The premenstrual dreamers frequently reported swimming and two of them dove to considerable depths before returning to the surface. One dream character nearly drowned when pulled through the water behind a speed boat, and another described waves at high tide. One dreamer pulled handfuls of fish from the sea, and another saw a round bowl of water with a goldfish

in it. Concern with releasing water retention was shown in Mrs. D.B.'s dream. She was walking in a hospital when "I looked into one of the rooms and saw a woman who looked as if she were in pain. I walked over and lifted up the covers and saw that her water had broken." Another dream referred to Niagara Falls.

Edema (swelling) or abdominal distention is suggested by the image of a "big enormous red balloon" that was blown up by three people in one dream, including the dreamer. Another dreamer felt she was fat, which made her dress too tight. Andria reported unpleasant abdominal sensations in a dream in which she was sitting in the cockpit of a small airplane and realized it was going into a steep descent: "I knew I was going to have the same terrible feeling and sensation throughout my body, particularly in my stomach. . . . I crossed my arms tightly over my gastric region, closed my eyes and braced myself." Stomach imagery appeared in quite a different form for another dreamer. Tall Texan was on the balcony of a tall building when she heard birds singing and had the sudden insight that "pushing my navel would allow me to fly also."

During the premenstrual phase, there is a change in the endometrium or uterine lining. Vasospasms occur which lead to the breakdown or shedding of tissues. Vasospasms may underlay a premenstrual dream in which "Marshmellow" described some explosions. In her dream, student nurses were administering painful skin tests to her in unusual places, such as her back, buttocks, and perineum. Later in this same dream, she became suspicious that "something was wrong down at the shack. There

Dreams of collapse and destruction are more common before a woman's menstrual periods. All Soundings Are Referred to High Water by Kay Sage.

were a couple of explosions. We crept through the woods toward the shack ... there was another explosion." The shedding of the endometrium may also be represented by the collapse or destruction of architectural structures. In a dream reported by "Miss Informed," a huge tractor trailer crashed into a church, causing bricks to start falling from the top: "It looked like the entire church would tumble down." "Jersey Cow" told of a dream in which people had to abandon a "rotten,

dark and dirty two story boat" because "it started to burn."

The endometrium is thicker and its surface more spongy or "wrinkled" before it sloughs off and menstrual bleeding is initiated. Several premenstrual dreams referred to the need to iron wrinkled clothing. "McWein" reported, "I was in the bathroom ironing." The "Worldly Philosopher" dreamed, "I was living in the backwoods in an old shack. I was going to iron my uniform when some men relatives came ...

[but] it was time to go to class and I wasn't even ready. So I was running around trying to iron my apron." A concern with lateness and a need for ironing was also present in this dream from "Sweet Pea": "Everyone was running around trying to get ready and I was getting nervous because I was afraid I would be late. My cap was all wrinkled and out of shape ... my uniform that I was to wear wasn't ironed."

Having considered these examples of oneirosomatic imagery from the premenstrual phase, I'd like also to examine the role psychological factors can play in shaping dream imagery throughout the menstrual cycle. Menstruation can be associated with many somatic complaints, such as cramps and backaches. For some women, the sight of blood may be associated with injury or may raise concerns that something is wrong with their bodies. I therefore attempted to develop a "somatic concern" score for dreams which assessed references to (1) hospitals; (2) anatomical and sexual body parts, such as bones, tissue, and genitals; and (3) medications or medical equipment, such as hypodermic needles. This somatic concern score was higher during the menstrual period than at any other cycle phase.

A woman's attitude toward her period seems to be a critical determinant of how much somatic concern is expressed. When asked to indicate on a questionnaire what slang term they used to refer to their period, those nursing students who answered with "the curse," "falling off the roof," "on the rag," or similar terms were classified as having a negative attitude toward menstruation. Those referring to their periods as "my secret friend," "my monthly visitor,"

"Mother Nature calling," or similar terms, were classified as having a positive attitude toward menstruation. Significantly higher somatic concern scores were found in the menstrual dreams of the women with negative attitudes than those with positive attitudes. A more careful analysis indicated that the differences became extremely minor during the later part of their periods, but were very pronounced during the first two days of menstrual flow. For those with negative attitudes, 15 percent of all the objects described in their dreams during the first two days were in this "somatic concern" category, whereas the score was less than 2 percent for the women with positive attitudes toward menstruation.

Another questionnaire item asked whether the women had experienced a major childhood illness that required hospitalization. Women with such hospitalization experience had higher somatic concern scores during their menstrual periods than those women who had not. These differences were accentuated if the analyses were restricted to dreams from just the first two days of the period.

Some interesting nondream data is available to support the idea that women become more concerned with somatic functioning during their menstrual periods. Mothers take their children to the doctor more often just before and during their menstrual period than at any other time during the month.[40] Not only are children brought in more frequently at this time, but the children who are brought in are less ill, and have been ill for a shorter period of time, than those brought in during other phases of the cycle.

Women who had a childhood illness

requiring hospitalization not only have a higher somatic concern score during the first two days of their menstrual periods, but they also report more aggression from other characters directed toward them at this time. The types of characters appearing in their dreams are also more unusual or bizarre during the first two menstrual days; they report more dead and imaginary characters and more characters who become transformed into other characters. These differences in aggressive patterns and types of characters are not significant during the later days of their periods. The appearance of menstrual bleeding seems to trigger distant traumatic memories for these women, who presumably felt afraid, confused, and physically vulnerable as children in a hospital environment, but they adapt fairly quickly to the recurrent stress it poses and react to the later days of their period no differently than other women.

The "average" female dreamer engages in very different types of social interactions with males and females during her period than during other times of her cycle. There were 152 male and 141 female characters present during the menstrual period and 515 male and 450 female characters present during the nonmenstrual phases. The dreamer initiated a social (aggressive or friendly) encounter with 45 percent of the males during her period, but with only 31 percent of the males at other times. A social encounter was initiated with 33 percent of the women during her period, but only 22 percent during the remainder of her cycle. In contrast, she was the recipient of a social interaction from 29 percent of the male characters during her period, but this figure increased to 42 percent dur-

ing the remainder of her cycle. She was the recipient of a social interaction from 21 percent of the female characters during her period and 24 percent at other times.

During her period a consistent pattern is revealed; the dreamer initiates many more social interactions with members of both sexes than she receives. This suggests that the average menstruating woman perceives herself as being more socially isolated at that time than at other phases of her cycle. Differences between social interactions during various cycle-phases can become even more complex if personality variables are considered. For example, women with a negative attitude toward menstruation initiate far more aggression toward male characters during their menstrual periods than do those women with a positive attitude toward menstruation.

If nonmenstrual dreams are examined more closely, very different patterns appear for dreams occurring before ovulation and those occurring after ovulation. During the preovulative phase, it might be said that women's dreams have a somewhat "masculine" quality. The dreamer is more likely to be in an outdoor setting that is unfamiliar, and implements are frequently mentioned. The percentage of male characters is higher at this time, and the dreamer initiates aggression toward males and unfamiliar characters. The dreamer also becomes involved in significantly more activities. All of these dream patterns are typically associated with male dreamers.

If masculine-toned dreams are more goal-oriented and "agentic," then the goals during this cycle phase seem to be receiving attention from males and becoming more closely and romantically involved with them. This desire is clearly shown in a dream from Jersey Cow:

> I was riding around and I came to a pier where a bunch of cute guys were. They all talked to me and paid a lot of attention to me, but they all began leaving as if I wasn't even there. This really upset me and I was really hurt. RL (my boyfriend) was there but I didn't care. I wanted the other guys there, too.

This interest in cultivating multiple relationships with men also appears in a dream from "Scheherazade." She accepted a date with John, the brother of a friend:

> We went out during the time he was at home and I appeared to like him very much. He told me he loved me, but it seemed like my present boyfriend was still in the picture, but I didn't care about that. I enjoyed going out with John.

The same theme is present in the dream of "Desiree":

> My boyfriend (DM) was going to spent the night. We were in bed together and fell asleep. We had a fight later and he left me. I slept then with another boy whom I didn't recognize. I woke up in the morning by myself and I saw DM out the window. I tried to pretend I didn't see him but he saw me

looking at him. He came in and we made up.

Dreamers seem to be preoccupied with attracting men during the preovulative phase. Boyfriends are prominent characters, but unfamiliar male characters are also more common that at any other cycle phase. One dreamer was excited about meeting a cute boy in Rome and another dreamer by having a blind date with a West Pointer.

The highest level of estrogen secretion occurs during the preovulative phase. The presence of this hormone in other mammals is associated with estrus, or "being in heat." It is at this time that the female animal will accept mating with the male. There are more dreams with sex during this phase than any other. The dreamer actually doesn't show much initiative with regard to the sexual activities, but she seems to send out the message that "I'm interested and I'm available." Her receptivity is signaled by the fact that the male characters she introduces into her dreams are more than twice as likely to initiate a friendly encounter toward her as an aggressive one. The dreamer has some form of social interaction with 82 percent of all the male characters in her dreams at this time. Perhaps because her "mating" interest is so focused on involvement with males as she approaches her time of maximum fertility, the dreamer may see other women as rivals. She initiates less friendliness to other women now than during any other cycle phase.

Estrogen levels start to decline just before ovulation begins, and during ovulation there is a sudden surge of luteinizing hormone (LH), associated with sharp changes in body temperature. Since I had no measures of body temperature, I estimated when ovulation occurred by counting back fourteen days from the onset of the subsequent menstrual period. I examined dreams from the night of presumed ovulation, as well as the night before and after, for dream elements which might correspond to the sudden and dramatic peak in LH.

In several dreams, some catastrophic event had happened or was about to happen. "King George" reported, "A Miami police department car with wailing siren sped by" to deal with a medical emergency. Earlier in her dream, she was "making some kind of shelter to protect myself." "Fruit Basket" "heard an alarm telling us the earthquake was to start" and wanted to find protection behind a cement block wall. In Mac 4021's dream, she "was running down a dark road. There was a huge black cloud chasing me, and it was catching up with me even though I was running as fast as I could." One can only speculate whether sudden internal reproductive shifts, such as the marked thickening of cervical mucus and the bursting of the Graafian follicle in response to the LH surge, have a corollary in dream imagery involving sudden natural disasters.

A shift in views toward maternity during ovulation was indicated by the dreamer's transferring childbearing roles to older women rather than assuming the role herself. "Beatle Bob" dreamed that "my mother (41) had a baby—a boy. She came home from the hospital the day the baby was born and she let me take care of the baby." Another dreamer had a roommate whose mother also had a brand-new baby.

Ovulation occurs at mid-cycle and functions like a railroad switch that moves the dreamer to a new set of tracks. Males, for example, no longer seem so appealing. One dreamer described Neanderthal men and another reported "a huge, hairy, almost monsterlike man." One dreamer was "chased by mean-looking men," another had "Spanish-looking" men follow her and "pull out their guns," and another happily followed a man whom she knew, but when they came to a dark alley he suddenly struck her, and the dreamer "heard the quick click of a switchblade knife." These dreams strongly suggest that the dreamer is no longer inclined to play the "dating game."

The dreamer now begins to gravitate toward other women and moves away from the aloofness or minimal friendliness that characterized her during the preovulative phase. Female vitality, previously dormant, has new life breathed into it. "CB2010" reported a dream in which "a female was brought in on a stretcher. A doctor gave her mouth to mouth respiration. After a long period of time the girl came to and sat up."

After ovulation, high levels of progesterone are secreted, and the tendencies toward merger with feminine energy which began to emerge with ovulation intensify. In the following postovulative dream, Miss Understood describes a feeling of awe and reverence in the presence of an older woman who seems to radiate some goddesslike power, and she reaches out to make physical contact with her:

My dorm room was located in the hospital. We were told of a mysterious patient in the room across the hall from me. I remember thinking to myself that it was a man and that he was going to die for some unknown reason. Later, during the day, we were told that we could visit this patient only if we didn't stay long. We had to march past him in a single file line. As I entered the room, in line with the other girls, I noticed the room was very dark and gave the appearance of being a holy place. As I neared the patient, I was surprised to find the patient was a woman, not a man. When I approached her, I held her hands in mine even though I knew she did not understand me well, but she smiled at me. She was a very elderly woman around 70 and had medium length, white hair, and very beautiful eyes. They portrayed kindness, understanding, greatness and compassion. . . . I left the room feeling good and knowing that I would be back to visit the woman again.

A similar theme was present in "Midsummer Night's Dream," who developed an increased appreciation for her mother's nurturing role and, like Miss Understood, reached out to make physical contact with a compassionate older woman. When she recognized that her mother was not feeling well and had a temperature, she put her to bed and kept her forehead cool with a cloth: "I remembered all the times she had taken care of me and my brothers and sisters when we had the mumps and all the

other things kids catch." Her dream seemed to involve bridging a generational gap. "Dandelion," too, bridged a generational gap, by casting her female teachers in new roles:

> I and several other girls were boarding a train to attend some important Girl Scout event. . . . [Later] we were gathered around a huge modern hotel and my nursing instructors were Girl Scout leaders. There were small holes in the ground and they were making us plant flowers in these. Then I found myself coming back to the dormitory from this trip. . . . I went to the bulletin boards (there were two instead of one) and here I got so many messages that I could barely carry them. I remember one strange thing on the bulletin board that's not really here. It was a list of really strange words and the heading said: "What are the Boy Scout words for these?"

Dandelion came back from her trip, which connected her with past (Girl Scouts), present (nursing instructors), and future (planting flowers) aspects of femininity, and recognized that she had received many messages. She wonders whether males encounter similar experiences and what the comparable male responses would be—"What are the Boy Scout words for these?" This cycle phase serves to raise many questions about the meaning of feminine experiences and what messages are being communicated. More references to objects of communication are present at this phase of the cycle than at any other time.

Awareness of a potential for growth emerges in Dandelion's dream through planting flowers; other women dreamed of a beautiful garden, bushes, green weeds on a log, fields of wheat, tall trees, and a dark forest during the postovulative phase. At the same time the dreamer shows awareness of "Mother Nature," she also becomes sensitive to her own body: there are more references to the dreamer's body at this phase of the cycle than at any other time. Her "somatic awareness" score is almost as high as it was during the menstrual period. In contrast to the active adventurous "masculine" style she displayed before ovulation, the dreamer now becomes more passive and withdrawn. More indoor and familiar settings are described than at any other time, which may represent the dreamer's efforts to provide a structured, familiar psychological space while she engages in introspective questioning and processing of her changing modes of relating to males and females.

The dreamer has social interactions, aggressive or friendly, with 57 percent of the female dream characters during the postovulative phase, compared to 43 percent during preovulation. The reverse is true concerning male characters. The dreamer interacts socially with only 51 percent of the male dream characters after ovulation, compared to 82 percent during the preovulative and 85 percent during the premenstrual phases.

The nature of the dreamer's postovulative relationship to other women is a complex one. She is more likely to be friendly to a female character whom she knows or who is older. Dreamers are thus most likely to display friendliness toward their mother or another maternal figure. Although the dreamer may not initiate friendliness to peer-age females, she is frequently in the company of her roommates or classmates, and more women of all types are now present in her dreams. There are more aggressive interactions with other female characters at this cycle phase, and the dreamer receives slightly more aggression from other women than she initiates toward them. This seems to be the time during which a woman sorts out her own personal parameters as to what it means to be a woman and struggles to define that in terms of social dimensions not related to her childbearing potential. Children and babies appear far less frequently at this phase than at any other time.

After ovulation, males recede into comparative insignificance while the woman sorts out the various facets of her femininity. Disinterest in marriage seems implicit in a dream from "Wet Feet": "I saw a beautiful wedding gown. I tore it apart and made a beautiful semi-formal with it." If dreamers do become romantically involved with males, they frequently are men who seem appealing because of their professional identity rather than their personal attractiveness. Dating or romantic partners included two doctors, a dentist, and a medical technician.

Males do not possess the same libidinal quality for the dreamer as before ovulation, and the dreamer seems to view herself as having parity with males. She is friendly to males about as often as they are friendly to her, and she also exchanges aggression with them at an equal level. This pattern might be characterized as, "I'll do unto you as you do unto me."

The importance of males may even be downgraded in areas like pregnancy. Dreamers who delivered babies during their menstrual period dreams did so in the presence of a caring boyfriend. Maternity therefore was linked with paternity in such dreams. "Gypsy" was the only dreamer who had a baby during the postovulative phase. In her dream she had been in a gab session with her roommate and some other girls. One of these girls said that it looked like Gypsy was pregnant. This is how Gypsy described what happened next:

I looked, but nothing was unusual, or abnormal. They told me to take it easy because I was having pains, but I really wasn't. I started jumping up and down to show them I wasn't, and all of a sudden I had a baby girl with a lot of dark hair. . . . Then we conspired to find a way to keep the baby in the dorm without anyone knowing about it.

There was not a hint of male energy present anywhere in this dream. The dreamer miraculously delivered a baby girl in the presence of an exclusively female group of onlookers and they plotted to keep the mysterious happening a secret.

In dreams during the premenstrual phase, interpersonal relationships are very ambivalent, unsatisfying, and often involve triangular relationships with feelings of jealousy. A high density of male characters appear, but they are frequently dating other women and leaving the dreamer be-

hind. Perhaps because of the water retention discussed earlier, the dreamer may feel self-conscious about her appearance. Insecurity and emotional lability are apparent, and she becomes extremely dependent. References to food and oral-related imagery are markedly higher than at any other cycle phase.

Sexual encounters generally had an unfortunate outcome in premenstrual dreams. One dreamer was in the backseat of a car engaged in sexual relations when she was caught by her mother; the dreamer became frightened and "everything went black." Another was kissed several times by a good-looking man who gave her a "passion mark," and when she returned to her dorm everyone laughed at her. Another was in bed on her honeymoon: "We started to have a relationship, but it wouldn't fit. We tried and tried but it just wouldn't. We then didn't know what to do." After another dreamer gave a physical to an ex-boyfriend, she found out that he had a very weak heart and could die any minute. "Then I thought about all of the times that we had made love and that he could have died while we were doing that and it would have been my fault." Intercourse was fatal for another character in one woman's dream. She was told Cassius Clay (Muhammad Ali) was having intercourse one too many times and he just died in the act.

It is critical in any study of women's dreams to take the menstrual cycle into account, because dream scores can shift so dramatically from one phase to another. Unless a large number of female dreamers are utilized in any adult study of gender differences, to cancel out phase differences, it's quite possible that the results could be biased by an overrepresentation of dreamers from a particular phase of the cycle. Consider, for example, the question of how frequently the dreamer initiates or receives friendly interactions from others. During her period, the dreamer initiates friendliness in 69 percent of the cases, but receives it in only 31 percent of the cases; during preovulation, she initiates friendliness in only 35 percent of the cases, but receives it from 65 percent of the other characters; during postovulation, she initiates friendliness 50 percent of the time and receives it 50 percent of the time from others; while during the premenstrual phase, she initiates friendliness to others 54 percent of the time and receives it from them 46 percent of the time. These results for friendly interactions represent only two dream scores and I tabulated dozens of scores from each dream.

Many variables can have an effect upon dream scores during the menstrual cycle. I indicated earlier that scores are influenced by a woman's health history (presence or absence of childhood hospitalization) and her attitude toward menstruation (positive versus negative). Dream scores during the menstrual period also differed between women judged to have a "feminine" orientation and those deemed to be "masculine." During their periods, feminine dreamers had more mothers, relatives, and individual characters than did masculine dreamers. Feminine dreamers also had more friendly interactions with a wide variety of characters during their periods, had less physical aggression present, and also had less "somatic concern" than masculine dreamers. To make a bad pun,

feminine dreamers seemed better able to "go with the flow" during their periods and were less stressed. Significant differences between feminine and masculine dreamers were also evident at other phases of their cycles.

I presented some of these findings in outline form over twenty years ago.[41] My results are fairly similar to those found by Theresa Benedek for women in psychoanalysis whose levels of estrogen and progesterone secretion were medically assessed.[42] A few other studies have been carried out in this area, but they have generally involved a small number of subjects, a limited number of poorly defined dream scores, or comparisons in which all nonmenstrual dreams are grouped together.

I think the significance of the changing pattern of dreaming during the menstrual cycle has not been appreciated by either women or men. Just as the moon goes through phases when it appears to be full and bright but gradually diminishes to a narrow crescent shape only to return again to its state of illuminated wholeness, so too does a woman manifest a waxing and waning of various personality traits during her lunar-cycle dreams.

Depending upon which cycle phase is emphasized, a woman deals with issues of birth and death, union with the anima and animus archetypes, assertiveness or receptivity from others, extroversion or introversion, independence or dependency, as well as several other polarities. She does not remain fixated on any issue, but encounters each, processes it, and leaves it behind until that phase of her cycle returns again. A woman is forced continually to confront these contrasting experiences because of her own complicated internal shifts in hormone levels. It's as if she were programmed by nature to insure that she will face in her dreams all the bipolarities of "being," and thus will have the opportunity to develop a well-rounded, balanced, and harmonious perspective on the realms of the intrapersonal, interpersonal, and transpersonal. Through the ebb and flow of her hormonal tides, a woman is placed in a unique position to mirror the subtle balance that prevails in nature when we let it unfold without trying to block it or control it.

Western males have been driven to conquer and control nature, rather than seeking peaceful coexistence and learning to accept things as they are. In their book *The Goddess Within*, Jennifer and Roger Woolger have commented:

> Our whole culture—with its endless violence, homeless people on the streets, colossal nuclear arsenals, and global pollution—is sick. It is sick because it is out of harmony with itself; it suffers from

Throughout their menstrual cycle, women's dreams reflect their hormonal and emotional fluctuations. My Room Has Two Doors *by Kay Sage.*

what the Hopi Indians call *koyaanisqatsi*, which is rendered in English, "crazy life, life in turmoil, life out of balance." What is missing is the feminine dimension in our spiritual and psychological lives; that deep mystical sense of the earth and her cycles and of the very cosmos of a living mystery. We have lost our inner connection to that momentous power that used to be called the Great Mother of us all.[43]

Along similar lines, Elinor Gadon in her book *The Once and Future Goddess* has observed:

> In the late twentieth century there is a growing awareness that we are doomed as a species and planet unless we have a radical change of consciousness. The re-emergence of the Goddess is becoming the symbol and metaphor for this transformation of culture.[44]

Our society's attitude toward women and menstruation has been on a level not much beyond that associated with the menstrual huts and taboos prevalent in non-Western societies. Rather than ostracizing women, the physical manifestations of their hormonal fluctuations, and the corresponding varied but balanced dream imagery, we should accept and honor this eternal renewal of the feminine principle, which is so badly needed in our masculine-dominated culture.

I am reminded of my experiences among the Cuna Indians of Panama, where a young girl's first period is the occasion for a joyous four-day celebration by all the people of her island and the nearby islands. They revere the Earth Mother and believe she came to create humans and all of the land and sea animals through the power of her menstrual functioning. On each day of the world's creation, she menstruated a different color blood and various creatures flowed forth from her womb. During my eight trips to visit among the Cuna, I never saw a child hit or even scolded, never encountered a psychotic or physically assaultive adult, and never saw a hungry or neglected elderly person. The Cuna lifestyle has much to recommend it and is obviously shaped by many influences. Perhaps one factor is their deep respect for the Earth Mother's creative powers expressed through the changing colors of her menstrual flow. This metaphor may contribute to a fuller appreciation of the importance of honoring the feminine goddess principle in Cuna culture and thereby serve as a possible link to the desirable social outcomes described above.

Dreams during Pregnancy

Dreams may be shaped in response to the many somatic changes a woman experiences during pregnancy. It is a time during which oneirosomatic dreams flourish. I became interested in pregnancy dreams in 1966 after reading over a large number of

Pregnant women often report dreams in which buildings appear distorted or tilted.
Balcony *by M.C. Escher. (M.C. Escher/Cordon Art-Baarn-Holland. All Rights Reserved)*

them volunteered by women in North Carolina. I presented a paper at the American Psychological Association in 1967 comparing one hundred dreams obtained from fourteen of these pregnant women with the five hundred female dreams in the normative tables that Hall and I published. This is the summary from that presentation:

Pregnant women dream more of architectural objects. If one accepts that houses may symbolize the body image, this may represent heightened concern over somatic changes occurring within them during pregnancy. References to the baby are extremely common and occur in approximately one third of all dreams after the fifth month. The actual delivery is not very often mentioned and the baby is frequently born as if by magic, or sometimes the woman's mother obligingly has it for her. Once born, the baby usually possesses unusual physical characteristics such as weighing 5 ounces or else tipping the scales at 35 pounds, or can walk or talk at birth. Anxiety about the baby being born dead, deformed or injured is quite apparent in many of these dreams.

I began to wonder whether pregnant women subsequently experienced any of the dire events pictured in their dreams. Could dreams communicate diagnostic information about a woman's medical condition during pregnancy? I collected some more dreams, with follow-up data, from pregnant women and briefly discussed my results in a few publications.[45] Several popular articles in women's and parents' magazines referenced my findings, and mentioned my interest in hearing from readers who had had dreams that contained information about the course of their pregnancies. I received responses from over two hundred women, who contributed in excess of four hundred dreams describing unusual experiences associated with their pregnancy outcomes. These dreams are obviously a very biased sample, but they do provide some impressive accounts of prodromal dreams and dreams that appeared close to the time of conception.

The premise throughout this chapter is that changes in organ systems or tissues can be recognized by the dreaming mind and translated into appropriate oneirosomatic imagery. How small of a physiological shift can be detected? Is it possible that changes at the time of conception could cause enough of a shift to be telegraphed to a woman in her dreams? Daniel Schneider, whose "bioplasma" theory was discussed earlier in this chapter, contends that there are dreams in which "the impregnation changes which take place at the time of fertilization signal almost immediately to the 'receiving paraconscious.' "[46] He gives an example of a conception dream from a young married woman that he felt combined the symbols of the impregnated uterus and the pulsing image of the heart:

There was an open shoe-box. Suddenly a purring, lively kitten with a pink ribbon tied around its neck jumped into the box. Immediately the sides of the shoe-box began to fold over by themselves. They apparently developed a zipper which automatically zipped the shoe-box tight. I could feel the frightened kitten beating in and against the side of the box.

Several reports are available from women who claimed to remember distinctive dreams occurring around their time of conception. For example, Elena B. (women who wrote me in response to a popular media article are identified by first name and last initial), an eighteen-year-old single woman, shared this dream:

I was in my room but there were no windows or doors. I heard my girlfriend call me from my kitchen. I was suddenly in the hallway with her putting a loaf of unbaked bread into an oven. We then walked into the kitchen where I started rinsing out leaves of lettuce in the sink which was full of water. I realized that the water had dead and half dead centipedes floating in it.

Elena indicated that a friend of hers had a book on dreams and when they looked up the symbols of the doorless, windowless room, the unbaked bread, the oven, and the dead centipedes, they realized that every symbol pointed to pregnancy or the womb. The book translated the centipede as "the pitter-patter of little feet" and classified dead insects as "un-

wanted children." Elena decided to get a pregnancy test and found out that she was indeed pregnant. She aborted her pregnancy shortly after that.

These two dream examples involve objects being placed in boxlike containers. My wife, Susanna, had a conception dream of being in a department store looking for a baby thermometer and discovering a round indoor swimming pool in which a woman and a dolphin were playing. After watching them for a while, Susanna decided to enter the pool and join in their playful antics. Since I was sixty-three when she experienced this dream, we weren't sure that the obvious pregnancy-related symbols really indicated that her body had taken the plunge into maternity, but subsequent testing validated the accuracy of her dream. Shortly after my sixty-fourth birthday, Susanna and I celebrated the arrival of our beautiful, healthy, nine-pound daughter, Parker Mary.

References to new plant growth appeared in several conception dreams. Nancy M. dreamed she was engaged in a contest with some other girls that involved rowing across a river in half of an orange shell. As Nancy was rowing, she discovered a magic seed, which she placed in the orange shell. This seed grew very fast and eventually formed a plant. In Nancy's dream, the orange shell makes an excellent symbol for the uterus and the fast-growing magic seed nicely represents the fertilized egg. Another woman dreamed about strawberry seedlings that she was eventually going to pick.[47] A thirty-seven-year-old woman, who for three years had been trying unsuccessfully to conceive, dreamed of looking down and seeing huge, ripe bunches of grapes growing from her belly.[48] She knew she had finally conceived. In chapter 8, Medard Boss provided a conception dream in which the woman dreamed she became a dark, brown, fertile field that was being plowed.[49]

Another powerful symbol associated with femininity and fertility appeared in a dream experienced by a married woman who had been delaying her efforts to conceive until she and her husband had more money. In the following dream, she seems to surrender and become absorbed in an almost mystical union with nature:

I'm staring at a dark, starless sky. Slowly I look over my right shoulder and a huge, full moon overwhelms my vision. I can't see anything else, but I'm not concerned. The moon gives off a glowing aliveness. I absorb a feeling of complete benevolence from this moon, and I face it head-on.

Looking again, I see that there's a smaller moon racing within the large moon. Clouds are crossing back and forth in front of the little moon. Together the two moons produce a sense of total innocence and wonder. I accept the clairvoyance, the inner light, the brightness that exist.

When this woman awoke from her dream, she told her husband that she was pregnant and that the child was a girl. A subsequent test confirmed that she was pregnant, and she did have a girl.[50]

Conception is not always conveyed by symbols of growth and development, such as bread baking or fruit ripening. Sometimes a child itself appears, but in such a special context that the dreamer recognizes she is functioning at a new level biologically. Susan G. and her husband had been patients of an infertility specialist for two years, and during that time she had repeated dreams about getting pregnant. This is how she described those dreams:

There was always something wrong when the child was delivered. The child was too tiny to be held. The child was too large to be held. The child was only a doll. . . . There was always something that prevented me from "mothering" the child.

Then abruptly in February, the dreams changed. I vividly remember awaking from a dream with a warm sense of fulfillment. I had, for the first time, held my baby. It was a real, complete child that I had held.

The dream had to occur within hours of conception. I never again had a dream about a child I could not "mother."

Peggy A. already had two teenage sons and she thought she was unable to have any more children. A few weeks before her pregnancy was diagnosed, she had an inspiring dream:

I found myself on a small hospital bed in a strange place. The room was completely white, and I saw nurses in white uniforms. Someone appeared with a child wearing a purple dress. She seemed to be at least one year old and her features were very pretty. A soft voice tells me, "This child will be yours." I began to groan and beg, "Take her away. I don't want her." In that instance a voice boomed from above me: "YOU MUST HAVE THIS CHILD." I cried out, "No, please. I don't want her, please take her away."

Peggy awoke shivering and crying and wondered why she would reject this pretty little girl in her dream when she wanted one so much. After her pregnancy was diagnosed, Peggy had to make a tormenting decision because she had a nerve injury which required at least sixteen aspirins daily for the pain. She was told that this could cause her not only to hemorrhage, but to give birth to a hemophiliac baby. In Peggy's letter she said that she had picked up the phone countless times to call for an abortion, but would sit down and cry instead. "The dream haunted me and I heard the voice constantly tell me: 'YOU MUST HAVE THIS CHILD,' and I saw the little face I had denied. Finally I gave in and decided I would have this child." Peggy delivered a healthy daughter who "is the most perfect angel on earth." She added that her daughter did wear a little purple dress home that her father had chosen for her.

In another dreamer's case, no symbols indicated the nascent life within her womb. Kathy C. just "knew" physically that she was pregnant. Many incidents surrounding her son's birth and postnatal de-

velopment were apparently foretold in her dreams, but I'll only describe what she wrote about the events leading up to her discovering that she had conceived. Kathy's mother had taken DES, which caused several abnormalities in Kathy's reproductive system. Kathy had one growth on her uterus removed and she was told that she would be unable to have any children unless some blockage in her fallopian tubes was surgically removed. She had the following dream: "There were two of 'me.' The 'me' I saw told me I was pregnant. I argued and said it wasn't possible. The other 'me' insisted and kept saying 'You're pregnant.' The arguing kept continuing." About three weeks later, Kathy underwent several tests for pregnancy and they all turned out positive. Her doctor refused to believe these results and insisted upon a second round of tests, which again confirmed that she was pregnant.

It was the absence of certain dream imagery which made Michele H. aware that she was pregnant. Since her letter contained so many examples of the oneirosomatic hypothesis I am advancing in this chapter, I will quote several sections from it:

For some time now I have believed that a woman's dreams can be affected by hormonal levels, not only during pregnancy, but on a monthly basis. After the birth of my first child, I began to experience the same dream every month, approximately 3 to 4 days before the onset of menstruation. In the dream I would be using the bathroom and I would find blood on the toilet paper. The dream occurred with such regularity that I began to accept it as assurance that I was not pregnant. Then one month the dream did not occur, and a few weeks later it was confirmed that I was pregnant.

During the nine months of my second pregnancy, I dreamed labor had begun and that upon arriving at the hospital I took a leisurely walk through a beautiful garden and then delivered a baby girl whom I named Kathy. During my first birth, labor lasted 28 hours and I had expected that things would be just as difficult the second time. A few weeks after this dream I had a very easy and unmedicated labor. I gave birth to a baby girl whom we named Erin Kathleen. A few months later, the monthly dreams heralding menstruation returned.

My third pregnancy ended with an early miscarriage, I had no dreams that I felt related to the pregnancy.

My fourth pregnancy also ended in miscarriage. At approximately ten weeks, I dreamed that I lost the baby. The dream was remarkably close to the actual event, even to such details as what I was wearing, my surroundings at the time of miscarriage, etc.

My next pregnancy began with some very promising signs. A sonogram revealed twins. At approximately six weeks into the pregnancy, however, I had a dream that would reoccur several times. I was lying in a bathtub when the water began to turn red with blood that was coming from me. At 14 weeks I hemorrhaged and was taken to the hospital where I miscarried.

My sixth and last pregnancy began with some ominous signs, but since there were no bad dreams I was heartened. At seven months, I had a dream that scared me badly. I dreamed I was lying on a long narrow table in a tiled room. I was aware that I was having the baby, but I was also aware that I had not gone into labor. My doctor and a nurse were working over my abdomen. I had the impression of lots of blood, blood on me, blood on the doctor. It seemed there was blood everywhere, but for some reason I could see very little of it. At two weeks past my due date, my doctor attempted to induce labor. Two days of I.V. with pitocin did not produce labor. We elected for a cesarean and I delivered a healthy baby girl. I believe that the scene in my dream was the cesarean. Within five months after the birth, the dream signaling the onset of menstruation returned.

I do firmly believe that my dreams were my body's way of communicating to me events that were about to transpire. I do also believe that anyone could experience the same if they would just open themselves to it.

In Michele's remarkable series of dreams she was given an indication that she had conceived when her usual premenstrual dreams failed to appear, she was warned about an impending miscarriage, and she received information as to how two of her labor experiences would go. It is small wonder that Michele developed a firm belief that her dreams were her body's way of communicating to her events that were about to transpire.

Several other women also described prodromal dreams that preceded miscarriages.

Blood-related imagery was present in two disturbing dreams that Freda T. experienced about three months into her first pregnancy. This was her first dream:

My mother and grandmother were at my house. I was taking a bath when all of a sudden, the bath water got all bloody. I cried for my mother to come. We let the water out of the tub and there lying by the drain was a baby. Even though it was only about 4 inches long, it was perfectly formed, just like a newborn. I started to cry.

A week later, Freda had another unsettling dream: "I lost the baby in the doctor's office while he was giving me a pelvic exam, but it wasn't a baby this time. It was only a red mass about fist size." Three days later, Freda went in for a pelvic examination and the doctor expressed his concern that she might lose the baby during his examination. An hour after the pelvic exam, Freda miscarried.

Theresa T. wrote that her first four pregnancies had resulted in miscarriages between the twelfth and fourteenth week.

During Theresa's fifth pregnancy she dreamed she had a baby boy, and everything about him was normal except that he had "this wooly, strawlike hair that stuck out all over his head." During the fourth month of pregnancy, it was determined through blood tests and ultrasound that her baby boy had anencephaly (lack of skull development) and the pregnancy had to be terminated. The head area beyond the eyebrow had not developed.

Carolyn P. shared a dream that foretold the time frame within which her miscarriage would occur. Her first two pregnancies were normal, but she miscarried during her third pregnancy. During her fourth pregnancy, Carolyn dreamed she was miscarrying but could not go to the hospital until her kindergartner returned home from school. When she told the dream to her husband, he said she was only upset because of the previous miscarriage and, besides, their daughter had not started school yet. Three weeks later, the daughter was in school and Carolyn went into labor, but couldn't leave for the hospital until her daughter arrived home. Carolyn was five months pregnant at the time and said she believed "the dream was a way of preparing me for what was to come."

One of Brenda T.'s dreams foreshadowed a sad event. When she was three months into her first pregnancy, she had this ominous dream: "I told several of my friends and relatives I was pregnant, but as I told each one they would say nothing and simply turned their backs toward me." The next afternoon Brenda began to spot and was admitted to the hospital. A day and a half later she miscarried.

Brenda also had a happy event foretold in a dream. Six and a half months into her second pregnancy, Brenda dreamed she was riding home in a car from her local hospital with a baby wrapped in a white blanket with patterns in blue and some other color. On the morning following her dream, Brenda received an excited call from her mother, who had retrieved from the attic the baby blanket in which Brenda had been brought home from the hospital twenty-six years before. She brought the blanket with her when she picked up Brenda to take her for a doctor's appointment. Brenda's doctors told her she might have to enter a hospital in a nearby city and remain until the baby's birth because unanticipated problems were developing. Brenda, however, was not troubled by this information because of her dream of the night before. Brenda had a son by natural childbirth in her local hospital. He was taken home in their car wrapped in Brenda's own baby blanket, which was white with blue and pink rabbits and ducks on it.

Dannett M. experienced a pair of dreams with contrasting outcomes during two of her pregnancies. Dannette was not particularly aware of any dreams during her first two normal pregnancies. However, about three months into her third pregnancy she had the following chilling dream:

My infant baby was lying on an examination table awaiting the checkup by the doctor. The doctor entered the room with a nurse and

began gently probing my baby. He told the nurse that he would discontinue the checkup because the baby was too cold.

Within a month, the baby died in the womb and was surgically removed. But approximately one month before the due date for her next child, Dannette had a very different dream:

I was sitting with a group of friends in the middle of someone's living room. I was holding my infant who appeared to be about three months old. My baby was smiling and cooing and trying to amuse my friends. It wanted everyone there to love it. It had a beautiful smile and beautiful disposition.

This dream created a feeling of strong optimism for Dannette, and she told her husband that she was not at all worried about the outcome of this pregnancy. She delivered a son whom she characterized as "a very well adjusted, cheerful little *ham*. His personality matches the baby in the dream closely."

Diana A. also had a dream about a cold baby. Diana had had two previous normal pregnancies, but during the seventh month of her third pregnancy she had this troubling dream:

I was coming home from doing some shopping. My mother had stayed to watch my newborn baby. When I got there, I asked her where the baby was. She told me she had put him in the refrigerator because she didn't know what to do with him when he started crying. I took him out and noticed that his skin was all blue and his body was very stiff, like frozen.

When Diana's mother heard the dream "she looked really worried and scared because she had always believed that dreams mean something." Diana laughed at her mother's reaction and said that the doctor had told her everything was looking good. But when she went in for a checkup two weeks before her due date, the doctor couldn't find any heartbeat and told Diana that her baby girl was dead. The umbilical cord had wrapped around the baby's neck and strangled her. In closing, Diana wrote: "To this day, I think back and wish I had read your article a few months before. I don't know if anything could have been done, but I'm sure I would have insisted on more frequent checkups. I never again will have any doubts about dreams."

Barbara C. had "funny feelings like something was going to happen" after this dream: "I was in the hospital with other women. There were babies on a table and I went over to my baby and he fell off the table and I never saw him again." Acting in response to her dream, Barbara discouraged her husband from his plans to put things in layaway. Two weeks later, she went into premature labor and bled heavily before her son was born. At the time of delivery, he wasn't breathing on his own, and after two hours he was rushed to a medical center in a neighboring town. Four days later he died at the medical center from circulatory problems.

Sometimes the information conveyed in a dream is uncannily accurate. Louise B. stated in her letter that she had this dream on August 15: "I dreamed I became pregnant and in the dream I was carrying twins, a boy and a girl. The babies' grandmother poisoned me—to kill the babies. The attempt to kill both failed—the girl lived and the boy died." Louise wrote that approximately eight months after her dream, she delivered, by C-section, a healthy girl weighing six pounds, eleven ounces, and a six-pound-five-ounce boy who was born dead.

Eleanor M.'s first and third pregnancies were perfectly normal, and there were no memorable dreams associated with them. However, during the seventh month of her second pregnancy, she experienced two very disturbing dreams on the same night. In her first dream she had boarded a troop ship, and she and another girl were exploring the interior. After they had walked up a wide, elegant, white marble staircase, Eleanor became terrified, "because on that landing was a small white marble coffin on a pedestal." Eleanor screamed and woke herself up. She described her other dream that night as follows:

I am going to a funeral parlor with a friend. I do not know the deceased. We were walking to the far end of a long, narrow room. Their friend was at the end. On both sides were other caskets. I am walking last in our group when, suddenly, there was a movement to my left. I look around and there against the wall is a child's mahogany coffin with half glass on top. What had caught my eye was movement inside that coffin. It would seem that a young boy's body was raised on a partial ledge. Some gases or fluids remaining in the body had caused the movement and the body fell to the bottom of the coffin.

Eleanor wrote that she had screamed with the first dream and became hysterical with the second one. "From that point on I was sure that my baby's life was in jeopardy." Her baby was due on November 20, but he was born on November 1 with an underdeveloped stomach. By the age of two months, he weighed little more than he had at birth. The doctor advised Eleanor to admit him to the hospital because there was nothing more that she could do at home. A month later he was still dying. Finally an experimental diet was tried, which reversed his condition and saved his life.

A dream sent in by Denise C. contained imagery associated with the umbilical cord wrapped around the baby's neck. Denise did not recall any dreams associated with her first successful pregnancy. During her second pregnancy, she had this brief dream: "My grandfather, who has been dead for 26 years, handed me a white legal size envelope with a large paper clip attached to the left hand side of this envelope." Denise's second daughter was born three weeks premature with a birth weight of five pounds, five ounces. She was born with the umbilical cord wrapped around her neck six times with a true knot. She was placed in the neonatal intensive care right after Denise's emergency C-section. Her daughter was not expected to live, but

did eventually survive. If the white envelope represented the fetus, then "the large paper clip" attached to it could reflect the umbilical cord wrapped around her daughter's neck.

During her first pregnancy, Susan H. had pleasant dreams and delivered a healthy boy. During the second trimester of her second pregnancy, Susan had "horrible dreams that my baby would be born with grotesque birth-defects, such as severe clubbing or missing limbs, but the ones I remember most were of my baby having its face severely disfigured." During the last trimester of her pregnancy, Susan dreamed of complications with a very long, hard delivery. She had a troubling recurrent dream of "My baby being stillborn." Susan's daughter was born with a bilateral cleft lip and palate. She also had respiratory distress and neonatal asphyxia as a result of having the cord wrapped around her neck twice and around one of her legs twice. In her letter, written ten months after her daughter's delivery, Susan indicated that her daughter has severe respiratory problems and has been in the hospital more than she has been home. Her daughter was suffering from apnea, severe seizures, heart problems, and pneumonia. Susan's doctors have diagnosed her daughter's brain damage as being terminal.

I've offered enough detailed dreams and personal histories to have made a strong case that some dreams of pregnant women can possess oneirosomatic imagery. The unconscious mind of the pregnant woman seems able to monitor and detect biochemical imbalances, tissue abnormalities, or structural defects in the uterine environment and communicate an awareness

Dreams during pregnancy typically offer images of the developing fetus and the changing body. They can even reflect the physical growth and health of the baby. Conscious Dreaming by Fariba Bogzaren.

of disturbed functioning through dream imagery, which is sometimes fairly literal, sometimes symbolic.

How early can such cues be transmitted from a uterus undergoing acute physiological distress? In several of the examples I recounted of miscarriage, the information seemed available by the second or third month of gestation. I also provided many case histories in which women recognized, through their dreams, that a particular pregnancy, out of several they had experienced, was different and might have later problems. Dreams can sometimes act as nocturnal sonograms and relay visual images that bear a symbolic resemblance to the mysterious events transpiring in the mother's womb.

Another investigator who has also worked with dreams from pregnant women arrived at a similar conclusion. In her doctoral dissertation, involving dreams from sixty-seven pregnant women, Patricia Maybruck concluded:

Those of our subjects who dreamed of physical complications prior to the onset of symptoms appeared to have experienced an unusual sensitivity to the physiological aspects of their pregnancy. . . .

Despite the rarity of such dreams in the present study's data, the notion that the gravida's [pregnant woman's] dreams can be significant diagnostic tools appears warranted. . . . Most of our subjects who reported dreams that indicated physiological aspects of pregnancy outcome did, in fact, exhibit these symptoms or physiological traits after they dreamed of them. Thus it appears that, were physicians to heed the possibility that the gravida's dreams may indicate undetected complications, it is possible that the warning would be useful.[51]

In a later publication, Maybruck reported the following:

Subjects in my own studies have reported dreams which appeared symbolic of stillbirth and other complications that had not yet been detected by their physicians. At least 5% of all the pregnant women I've studied have reported dreams they believed were predictive of complications during labor and delivery. For example, three women who had stillbirths reported nightmares that clearly depicted the baby as being born dead. Two women reported dreams of unexpected complications, and in both cases these abnormalities did arise, causing attending physicians to feel compelled to perform C-sections. Since all these women reported their seemingly predictive dreams to me after the tragic outcomes, there is no absolutely valid data showing that their dreams were, in fact, predictive.[52]

The accounts I have presented suffer from the same problem of being primarily retrospective in nature. There were a few in which the unfortunate outcome was not known at the time the dreamer sent her first account to me and was only verified by means of my follow-up letters. However, the sheer number of accounts I received adds weight to the proposition that *some* dreams during pregnancy can be predictive of the outcome portrayed in them. I wish to emphasize the word *some* in that last sentence because I would not want any readers of this book to become unduly alarmed if they were to experience disturbing dreams during their pregnancy. Disturbing dreams are par for the course in pregnancy. It must be kept in mind that I requested dreams from pregnant women who had unusual experiences associated with their pregnancies, and my request appeared in several popular magazines and newspapers. The combined readership probably included hundreds of thousands of women who had been pregnant at some time. I am presenting these dreams as additional evidence, along with the examples of prodromal and healing dreams and the data from dreams during the menstrual cycle, that somatic disturbances can be recognized by our dreaming mind and communicated in appropriate oneirosomatic imagery.

Not only are disturbing dreams common during pregnancy, there is some evidence to support the idea that they can be associated with the favorable outcome of shortened labor time. When recent dreams obtained from seventy healthy, young women who were pregnant for the first time were scored for the presence of anxiety, an interesting finding emerged:[53]

[Anxiety] was present in over 80 percent of the dream reports of those who subsequently delivered in less than 10 hours, but was scorable in only 25 percent of the dreams of the prolonged labor group (over 20 hours). The women who were intermediate in frequency of anxiety themes were also intermediate in length of labor.

These dreams were obtained during the third trimester. Overt themes of babies, labor, and delivery rooms were present in about one-third of the dreams from all the subjects, but did not bear any relation to the length of labor. The investigators, at the University of Cincinnati, offered this speculation:

We found that pregnant women in whom anxiety and threat themes are missing from their dreams are more likely to undergo prolonged labor due to inefficient uterine action than their counterparts whose

dreams contain anxiety and threat. This supports the hypothesis that the function of the dream is an attempt to master, in fantasy, an anticipated stress in waking life. . . .

We hypothesize that for some women the anticipated trauma of childbirth is too great to be allowed even symbolic or displaced expression in dreams. . . . Such women are tenser both psychologically and physiologically than the women who have used dreaming as a psychologic immunization to prepare themselves for the approaching confinement. . . .

Dreaming can function to mobilize and integrate adaptive mechanisms and thus perform a major function in coping with one of the important stresses in a woman's life.[54]

Maybruck had collected 1,048 dreams from her sixty-seven volunteers and claimed that 70 percent of these dreams were unpleasant and indicated anxiety on the part of the dreamer. She labeled 40 percent of the pregnant dreams as nightmares. She reported that the frequency of nightmares was not related to the length of labor but discovered that "those women who were assertive in their nightmares had significantly shorter labors than did those who were consistently victimized in such dreams."[55] Among the women who had short labor (less than ten hours), 94 percent had been assertive in at least one of their nightmares. In the long-labor group (more than eleven hours), 70 percent of the women had allowed themselves to be victimized in all their nightmares.

Because negatively toned dreams are so numerous, a pregnant woman generally should not attach great significance to a dream from which she awakens in a state of anxiety. What seemed to characterize the dreams sent in to me by women who had experienced predictive dreams was a quality of vividness and tenacity that put them in a class by themselves. Many of these women claimed that they remembered their predictive dreams as vividly many years later as they did when they first experienced them. It is the dreams which seem to leave an indelible imprint on the dreamer which may need to be given further consideration for their possible prodromal quality. If the dreamer absolutely cannot shake the dream off, then it may be an important diagnostic dream.

All dreams during pregnancy deserve some attention, but not just to discover one that may be prodromal in nature. Much of the material I gathered in connection with pregnant women's typical dreams was included in a book by Eileen Stukane entitled *The Dream Worlds of Pregnancy*.[56] Perhaps the way I can summarize these common themes is to quote from my foreword to her book:

> An expectant mother's dreams, in part, reflect her changing body image, her concern about the birth and health of her baby, her assessment of her ability to care for her child, her uncertainty about how another life would affect her marriage, and an apprehension about what her future would be like once the baby was born.
>
> Since so many tension-laden issues interact during pregnancy, the resulting dreams are extraordinary. These nine months are a time when psychic as well as physiologic stimuli are translated into fascinating visual metaphors during sleep. . . . Women appalled by their expanding waistlines dreamed of husbands who no longer felt amorous, women fearful about labor had their mothers enter their dreams to substitute for them in the delivery room, and women hesitant to interrupt their professional careers managed to forget where they had left their dream babies.

In that foreword I expressed my gratitude to the men and women who had allowed me to review their dream lives (Stukane's book also contains dreams of expectant fathers). I can only repeat my appreciation here and hope that these examples will inspire both parents and investigators to examine the content of such dreams more closely. By doing so, mothers- and fathers-to-be may enrich the mutual transition they are experiencing.

CHAPTER 14

PARANORMAL DREAMS:

PSYCHIC CONTRIBUTIONS

TO DREAMS

A dream which correctly represents unlikely future events is called a precognitive dream. A telepathic dream is one in which the dreamer becomes aware of someone else's current mental state. In a clairvoyant dream, the dreamer obtains information about the location or physical properties of some distant object, but not from someone else's mind. Precognitive, telepathic, and clairvoyant dreams are referred to as paranormal or psi (psychic) dreams. Paranormal dreams clearly pose a challenge to current scientific conceptions as to how things are supposed to work in the world. But several prominent dream theorists, such as Freud, Jung, Stekel, and Boss, have strongly asserted the existence of paranormal dreams.[1]

A GRISLY PRECOGNITIVE DREAM

Walter Franklin Prince, a psychologist and Episcopal minister, experienced a very striking precognitive dream, which, unlike most such dreams, involved a stranger. His dream occurred on the night of November 27, 1917, and he told it to his wife

In paranormal dreams, the dreamer seems to sense someone else's thoughts, or even observe faraway events. (Odilon Redon, French, 1840–1916, Guardian Spirit of the Waters, charcoal on paper, 1878, 46.6 x 37.6 cm, David Adler Collection, 1950. Photograph © 1993, The Art Institute of Chicago. All rights reserved.)

and his secretary the next morning, before the tragic events foreseen in it unfolded.

Prince dreamed that he had in his hand a small paper, with an order printed in red ink for the execution of the bearer, a slender woman with blond hair about thirty-five years old. The woman appeared to have brought the execution order to Dr. Prince voluntarily and indicated her willingness to die, if only he would hold her hand. After he examined the execution order, the lights went out and it was dark. Prince could not determine how the woman was put to death, but he soon felt her hand grip his and knew that the deed was being carried out. Then he felt one of his hands on the hair of her head, which was loose and severed from her body, and he felt the moisture of blood. The fingers of his other hand were caught in the woman's mouth, which opened and shut several times. Prince was horrified at the thought of the severed but living head. Then the dream faded.

Two days later the local newspaper, *The Evening Telegram*, carried an article describing how a Mrs. Sara Hand, at approximately 11:15 on the night of November 28, had deliberately placed her head in front of the wheels of a train that had stopped in a Long Island Railroad Station, so that the wheels would pass over her neck and decapitate her when it started. Near the body was a new butcher knife and cleaver, which Hand had apparently intended to use for her self-decreed "execution" before deciding to lay across the railroad tracks. In her handbag nearby, a letter was found with this message:

Please stop all trains immediately. My head is on the track and will be run over by those steam engines and will prevent me from proving my condition. . . . My head is alive and can see and talk, and I must get it to prove my case to the law. No one believed me when I said I would never die and when my head was chopped off I would still be alive. Everyone laughed and said I was crazy, so now I have proved this terrible life to all.

Please have all trains stopped to save my head from being cut in fragments. I need it to talk to prove my condition and have the doctor arrested for this terrible life he put me in.[2]

Hand, who fit the physical description in Dr. Prince's dream, had been mentally disturbed since the death of her young daughter a few months earlier. Dr. Prince's dream could be considered precognitive, since Hand carried out her own execution the next night. The dream could also be considered telepathic, since she seemed to be planning her death when she purchased the butcher knife and cleaver on November 27. The dream dealt with a highly unlikely event: an unfamiliar woman decapitating herself in the darkness to prove that her head could continue to live, and talk, after being severed from her body. Prince's dream also contained many prominent references to *hands*.

DREAMS OF NATURAL DISASTERS

At age 23, before he became famous as Mark Twain, Samuel Clemens dreamed he saw a metal coffin resting on two chairs in his sister's sitting room. As he approached the coffin, he saw the body of his brother Henry. One detail in particular caught his attention: a bouquet of white flowers, with one crimson flower in the center, lying on Henry's chest. A few days later, a Mississippi riverboat blew up and many of the passengers and crew were killed instantly. Henry had been one of the crew members. When Clemens rushed to the scene of the accident, in Memphis, he found his brother lying unconscious on a mattress in an improvised hospital. There was some hope that his brother might pull through, but on the sixth night he died. When Clemens arrived at the room which was being used as a temporary morgue, he found that most of the dead were lying in plain wooden coffins, but there was one metal coffin lying on two chairs. Henry's struggle to survive had inspired such interest among the Memphis ladies that they had taken up a special collection and bought a metal casket for him. As Clemens approached his brother's casket, an elderly woman entered the room carrying a large bouquet of white flowers, in the center of which was one crimson rose, and laid them on Henry's chest.

Sometimes several people seem to "tune in" to an impending disaster which involves a large number of victims.[3] Through diligent investigation, Ian Stevenson, a psychiatrist at the University of Virginia, collected corroborated reports of nineteen individuals who anticipated the sinking of the Titanic in 1913.[3] Several of these involved dreams, and one individual dreamed twice that he saw the Titanic floating keel upward, with passengers and crew swimming about in the water. However, he did not cancel his passage because of the dreams, but eventually did so because of a change of business plans.

On October 21, 1966, a massive coal-tip slid down a mountainside and engulfed the Welsh mining village of Aberfan, killing 144 persons, mostly school children. In response to an appeal the following week in a national newspaper, an English psychiatrist, J. Barker, obtained a large number of reports from respondents who felt they may have received paranormal information concerning this tragedy.[4] After all claims were carefully checked out, thirty-five cases remained which Dr. Barker considered worthy of confidence. In twenty-four cases, the respondents had related the information to someone else before the landslide occurred. Dreams figured in twenty-five of the accounts. In one, the dreamer saw, spelled out in large, brilliant letters, the word ABERFAN. In another, a telephone operator from Brighton talked helplessly to a child, who walked toward her, followed by a billowing cloud of black dust or smoke.

Apparently the clearest precognitive dream was that of a young girl, Eryl Mai

Jones. She often tried to tell her mother about her dreams, but her mother tended to dismiss them. One morning, however, Eryl Mai got her mother to listen to one of her dreams. In her dream, "We go to school but there is no school there; something black has come down all over it."

She told her mother, "I'm not afraid to die, Mommie. I'll be with Peter and June." When the huge slag deposit slid down on the school two days later, Eryl Mai, Peter, and June were among the 118 children crushed or buried alive.

ANECDOTAL ACCOUNTS

The largest collection of anecdotal accounts of paranormal dreams was collected by Dr. Louisa Rhine, the wife of Dr. J. B. Rhine, who established the famous Duke Parapsychology Laboratory. Louisa Rhine collected over seven thousand accounts of alleged ESP experiences from readers who responded to appeals published in various popular media. The majority of the accounts involved dreams and most were precognitive in nature. Her files included 433 precognitive dreams dealing with events that could have been altered if the dreamer had taken steps to do so, but such an effort was made in only 30 percent of these cases. Many of the dreams sent to her are discussed in her book *Hidden Channels of the Mind*.[5] Numerous other books containing anecdotal accounts of paranormal dreams have been published.[6] Death looms as the most prominent theme and is present in over 50 percent of anecdotal psi dreams, with accidents and injuries following next, in order of prominence. Women outnumber men nearly two to one as dream percipients (receivers), while men are dreamed about in approximately 60 percent of the cases. Close blood ties are involved in about 50 percent of the dreams, although spouses and personal friends are also frequently involved.

Paranormal dreams are described as being unusually vivid and intense, and they have a particularly tenacious quality to them after the dreamer awakens. Sometimes the scenario and characters are pictured fairly accurately. Louisa Rhine stated that dreams contain a greater amount of complete information about the event in question than do impressions received in the waking state. Most psi dreams, however, are psychologically edited so that details are variously distorted or displaced or obscured by personal symbols and metaphors.

DREAMS IN A THERAPEUTIC SETTING

Spontaneous psi dreams generally deal with highly charged topics and characters to whom the dreamer has important emotional ties. Since disturbing material is encountered so commonly in therapy, and since the therapist, because of transference, has an exaggerated emotional significance for the patient, it is not surprising that many paranormal dreams occur in the therapeutic situation and most have the therapist as the central figure. An excellent collection of dreams arising from therapy has been compiled in a book called *Psychoanalysis and the Occult*.[7]

Jule Eisenbud, a psychoanalyst, observed many psi dreams in his practice and discussed them in his book *PSI and Psychoanalysis*.[8] Several pages are often required to trace the links that exist between the dreams, various events in the analyst's life, and the stage of transference present at the time of the dream, but it is not difficult to understand the following example. One evening Eisenbud had to phone his daughter in California to ask her to put off her planned visit to their home in Denver. He had a chance to work with a particularly interesting patient, a woman with an unusual disorder who would only be available for a week. He did not wish to pass up this opportunity and planned to put her up in his home. That night one of his current patients had the following dream:

> I came into your office and found a child of about three who didn't speak at all but who looked as if she were your daughter. You indicated to her somehow that you were busy. No words were exchanged. She knew that she wasn't approved of, as if you had said, "Go home, I have no time for you."

Eisenbud explained that the patient who presented the dream had probably felt rejected herself by the analyst and could therefore identify with his own disappointed daughter. The dreamer may also have felt jealous and threatened because the new patient would represent another, feminine competitor for the analyst's attention.

Another analyst, Geraldine Pederson-Krag, reported a series of dreams from a male patient who seemed to zero in on her whenever she was struggling with issues that made her uncomfortable.[9] She gave two examples involving money. Dr. Pederson-Krag was feeling some distress because she had been receiving "professional courtesy" from a colleague for medical treatment and had decided she should express her appreciation with a gift. However, she kept putting it off and found herself feeling guilty for failing to carry through on her plan. Her patient had a dream about a gray-haired, bustling hostess whose personality reminded him of Dr. Pederson-Krag. The hostess appeared very pleasant, but the dreamer didn't care for her because she explained to a physician that she was entitled to professional courtesy.

A few days later, Dr. Pederson-Krag and her children met a friend for dinner at a restaurant. When the bill came, Dr. Pederson-Krag's share was something over six dollars, while the friend's was only two dollars, but he insisted on paying for Dr. Pederson-Krag. She felt uneasy because she felt this might imply a relationship that she did not wish to encourage. Despite the friend's protest, she paid her own share. That night the same patient dreamed that he was taking "my girl" out to dinner; she ate about seven dollars' worth of food, while his meal came to only two dollars. The dreamer remembered feeling very angry but saying nothing about the sums of money involved. The dreamer had thus shifted his analyst from being a hostess in the earlier dream to being his "girl."

British analyst W. H. Gillespie reported several examples of paranormal dreams.[10] On a particular night after Dr. Gillespie had engaged in intercourse, he fell asleep and had this very brief dream: "I had two stumps and artificial legs." The following day, a young female patient came in and told him she had an extraordinary "supernatural" dream the preceding night. In the first part of her dream, she was going up and down in a shaft full of moving staircases. Most of the time she was going down but now and then she was suddenly wafted up. The patient, who was a virgin, explained that she felt a frightening, but exciting, feeling which she felt vaguely was related to sex. In the second part of her dream, she was going to analysis but it was in a place with gardens and shrubs. There was a man there sitting cross-legged on a platform selling vegetables and flowers. The dreamer suddenly realized he had only two stumps; his legs had been cut off above the knees. The man lifted up a cabbage and she was surprised to see under it two corn cobs. The analyst interpreted the cabbage and corn cobs as a display of the male genitals, but the corn cobs could also have possibly represented the two artificial legs. The correspondence between the two dreams of a man with two stumps was much more striking than any reference the symbolic staircase dream may have had to the analyst's waking intercourse. Dr. Gillespie was initially reluctant to share his observations, but acknowledged that "analysts should be the last people to reject unwelcome new facts just because they are unwelcome."

Paranormal dreams seem to surface most readily in the analytic setting when the patient feels neglected by the therapist or when one of the therapist's unresolved problems is activated in the therapeutic encounter. Therapists have been reluctant to publish accounts of paranormal dreams from their practices for several reasons. They may wish to avoid negative reactions from skeptical scientific colleagues who reject the idea that any paranormal dreams occur. But admitting a patient's psi dream also implies that the therapist had been ignoring the patient so badly that the patient had to resort to paranormal fireworks to regain the therapist's attention. If the dream is in response to some unresolved problem of the therapist, the therapist would then have to acknowledge the problem publicly and share whatever intimate details were necessary to make dynamic sense of the patient's dream.

QUESTIONNAIRE SURVEYS

David Ryback, a clinical psychologist in Atlanta, based his book *Dreams That Come True* on a questionnaire administered to 433 undergraduate students. The students were asked for information about dreams and provided written accounts of personal dreams that dealt with the future.[11] A surprising 67 percent of the students reported some type of paranormal dream. Many were not very convincing, such as dreams about a lost dog that returned, but several contained a considerable amount of detail about unlikely events that did eventually occur. Ryback attempted to corroborate these dreams by interviewing the subjects and contacting others who might be able to verify the dreamer's account. He estimated that about 8 percent of the dreams he obtained could reasonably be considered paranormal.

Questionnaire surveys inquiring about psychic experiences and dreams have been carried out with a wide range of populations. Walter Franklin Prince, who experienced the grisly dream involving Mrs. Hand, mailed a questionnaire to several thousand individuals whose names appeared in *Who's Who in America*. A total of 430 persons in this distinguished group acknowledged some form of ESP experience, and dreams were involved in approximately 25 percent of them.[12] Questionnaires have been administered to nearly twenty-five hundred eighth-grade students in northern India, approximately two hundred university students in west Africa, and approximately three hundred students at the University of Virginia. About one out of six of the eighth-grade students and one out of three of the university students indicated they had experienced a paranormal dream at some time during their life.

PARAPSYCHOLOGY AND THE SCIENTIFIC ESTABLISHMENT

I have presented a review of anecdotal material and a survey of questionnaire studies on paranormal dreams in a chapter in the *Handbook of Parapsychology*.[13] This handbook describes the relationship of parapsychology to other fields of investigation and summarizes the research methodologies and findings which have emerged in these fields. The field of parapsychology continues to generate conflicts. Many scientists think that science would be thrown into a state of chaos if the findings which seem to be at such marked variance with how the real world supposedly works, were accepted. Other scientists are stimulated by the same data because they realize parapsychology opens new perspectives on the human mind and spirit.

In 1957 the Parapsychological Association was formed. It is an international association of researchers devoted to using the scientific method to advance our understanding of the mysterious and challenging realms associated with apparent paranormal abilities. Almost all members possess doctoral degrees and their research results are published in peer-reviewed scientific journals. For several years, the Parapsychological Association (P.A.) attempted unsuccessfully to gain membership to the American Association for the Advancement of Science (AAAS). Finally, in

1969, when the AAAS was again debating the P.A.'s application, Margaret Mead stood up and said:

> For the last ten years we have been arguing about what constitutes science and scientific method and what societies use it. We even changed the By-Laws about it. The P.A. uses statistics and blinds, placebos, double blinds and other standard scientific devices. The whole history of scientific advancement is full of scientists investigating phenomena that the establishment did not believe were there. I submit that we vote in favor of this association's work.[14]

Dr. Mead's argument carried the day and the P.A. became officially affiliated with the AAAS. The first symposium given by the P.A. was at a meeting in Chicago in 1970. I served as the chairperson for that symposium; I also served as the president of the P.A. that year. In the introductory remarks for that symposium, Gardner Murphy, a former president of the American Psychological Association, stated:

> In the half century in which I have tried to observe and evaluate the situation in parapsychology there has been a very notable increase in sophistication in the experimental procedures devised. . . . It will take much time and labor, but in both quantitative and qualitative terms the experimental analysis of dream telepathy is now a problem of such urgency that a mature science can no longer handle it either by ignoring it or denying it. Fortunately, organized science has at last begun to recognize the need to look straight at the experimental data and their interpretation.[15]

EXPERIMENTAL STUDIES OF PARANORMAL DREAMS

How have scientists tried experimentally to investigate paranormal dreams? Probably the earliest published account of an experimental effort to paranormally influence a dream was reported in 1819 by H. M. Weserman.[16] The experimenter attempted to project his "magnetic influence" into the dreams of friends at a distance and claimed five successful experiments. In one of them, Weserman sent a message to an elderly woman that she would dream about the funeral procession of a deceased friend of the experimenter. When he checked with her the next day, she reported she had dreamed about a funeral procession, but it was the experimenter who was the corpse. Weserman noted that "there was thus a slight error." In all the studies to be reviewed, it will be found that there is often a "slight error"; very rarely does a receiver, or percipient, report a dream that exactly duplicates the stimulus the sender, or agent, was trying to transmit.

In 1895, an Italian psychiatrist, Dr. G.

Ermacora, published a paper entitled "Telepathic Dreams Experimentally Induced."[17] The percipient was a four-year-old girl, Angelina, and the agent was her cousin, a medium with a child trance personality named Elvira. When Angelina visited this medium in Venice, Ermacora would come to the medium's home at night and place her in a trance. He would then ask Elvira to transmit some topic for Angelina to dream about. Ermacora would then leave the house and return the next morning to check on the results.

In the early stages of research, the medium herself would ask the child about her dreams, but later the medium's mother carried out the questioning before the medium awoke. One night, part of the message to be transmitted was that Angelina was to be a goatherd grazing goats on a hillside. Angelina dreamed she was in a high place, with a stick in her hand, among a lot of dogs with horns on their heads. On another night, the suggestion involved Angelina being with Dr. Ermacora at the church of San Marco and meeting Elvira there, who would be dressed in pink with a white handkerchief round her head. They would then all go into a tent and be shown a tiger. Angelina's dream mirrored all details of the suggestion except she said the final action

was, "We all went together to a little house, where there was an animal like a cat, but larger, and not really a cat." Although a large number of dreams incorporated details of the scenarios selected by Ermacora, the experimental procedures were lax on so many critical points, that one cannot accept the findings with any degree of confidence. To Ermacora's credit, however, quite a few nights were noted when complete failure occurred.

A Viennese psychotherapist, Wilfred Daim, used a random pairing of a color and a geometrical symbol as target materials.[18] Daim concentrated on the stimulus early in the morning and the intended percipient wrote down his dreams before the therapist checked the results. Daim claimed that in 75 percent of their trials, the target material was directly reflected in the dream content. The percipient often reported an intrusive element in his dreams. In one instance, Daim concentrated on a red triangle and the dreamer reported a three-cornered red fir tree suddenly appeared in an ongoing dream about music and soldiers. Since the therapist was aware of the target when questioning the percipient, and was the one who assessed the trials' success, this study also has some obvious shortcomings.

The Maimonides Project on Paranormal Dreams

The most systematic study of paranormal dreams in a laboratory setting was initiated by Montague Ullman in 1962. Ullman established a dream laboratory at Maimonides Hospital in Brooklyn, where he was chairman of the psychiatry department.

With the help of a graduate student, he worked out the details of a protocol that served as the basis for all later studies. Stanley Krippner, a psychologist, joined the laboratory in 1964 when the first formal studies were beginning. Ullman and Krippner worked together for nearly ten years investigating some of the parameters involved in paranormal dreaming. They published a large number of scientific articles and summarized their findings in a popular book entitled *Dream Telepathy*, published in 1973. An updated edition was published in 1989.[19]

The basic experimental design was as follows: The percipient's sleep stages were monitored after he or she went to sleep in a locked, sound-insulated bedroom. The agent attempted to "send" a target stimulus to the percipient during the night. A third person, the monitor, watched the EEG tracings all night long to detect the percipient's REM periods. The nature of the target picture given to the agent by the experimenter was not known to anyone at the time of the experiment.

The target stimulus was randomly selected from among hundreds of colored art reproductions of paintings or sculptured works, which had been individually sealed in manila envelopes well in advance of the experiment. The same target picture was used for the entire night. The experimenter left the laboratory once the agent had received the sealed envelope and was locked into his or her bedroom. The agent's room in the first studies was thirty-two feet away from the room where the percipient was sleeping, later it was ninety-eight feet away, and still later it was fourteen miles away. No sensory contact between the agent and the percipient occurred once the experiment was under way.

When the monitor saw that a REM period had begun, he signaled the agent, via a one-way buzzer, to insure that the agent was awake and concentrating upon the target picture. After ten or fifteen minutes of REM activity, the monitor woke the percipient via an intercom and asked the percipient to describe his or her dreams in as much detail as possible for the tape recorder. At the conclusion of each REM recording, the percipient returned to sleep and the agent was signaled to also return to sleep. The pattern was repeated throughout the night for each REM period.

The experimenter returned the following morning to question the percipient regarding the content of any dreams that had been reported to the monitor. These inquiries were tape recorded. The experimenter was still unaware what picture had served as the target. The percipient would then usually be shown a collection of eight art reproductions, one of which was a duplicate of the target picture the agent had attempted to transmit. The percipient looked over the pictures and ranked them from 1 (the most likely target picture) to 8 (the least likely). The percipient also assigned a confidence rating, from 1 to 100 points, for each picture in terms of how closely it matched the content or emotions of his or her dreams. The set of eight pictures and the transcripts of the night's dreams were also sent to outside judges for independent evaluation. This procedure enabled the experimenters to evaluate statistically the likelihood of correctly matching the percipient's dreams and the target picture.

A study generally consisted of a series of eight nights of dreaming. There were thirteen major studies carried out, and in nine of the thirteen, statistically significant results favoring a psi explanation were found. In chapter 10, when I reviewed the role of presleep stimuli on dream content, it was obvious that a great deal of distortion, displacement, and transformation of imagery took place even when the subject viewed a film before falling asleep (e.g., dreaming about birds and bees in response to a birth film). At Maimonides, no physical stimulus was shown to the percipient; the only stimulus available was the distant target picture and the agent's mental imagery. Sometimes the correspondence between the target picture and a dream image would be based upon a similarity in form (a full moon represented by a crystal ball, or a pencil by a telephone pole), in material composition (a lake representing a swimming pool or an ice cube representing an iceberg), or in color (red wine substituted for blood, or green book pages for money). Similarities in texture might lead to a marshmallow being portrayed as a soft pillow or a rock as a lump of metal. Puns and plays on words also occurred: if the target picture contained a few coins, the percipient might dream of a change; if intercourse were depicted, of a screw.

In order to give the reader a feeling for the types of correspondences involved, I will give examples from some of my dreams when I served as a percipient for an eight-night study at Maimonides. Before doing that, let me share some background material to place my participation in a clearer context.

MY LABORATORY EXPERIENCES AS A TELEPATHIC DREAMER

In the preface, I mentioned the boxing dream that I experienced when Calvin Hall attempted to "transmit" the Muhammad Ali boxing match and the skiing dream I had when he "sent" skiing imagery. Calvin attempted to influence my dreams during the nights I was sleeping in our laboratory a total of 17 times. He concluded that some representation of the intended target material was detectable on thirteen of those occasions, for a success rate of 76 percent. Calvin was so impressed by his successes with me and five other male subjects that he published a paper entitled "Experiments on Telepathically Influenced Dreams" in a German publication.[20] He also discussed his procedure in a chapter for a proposed book, which he had not completed at the time of his death. This description of his testing procedure is from that chapter:

> After the subject fell asleep and prior to the beginning of a REM period, the experimenter [Hall] began to "send" a message to the subject. These messages consisted of activities such as cutting down a tree, watching a prize fight, skiing, watering the lawn, playing the

piano, getting a haircut, and so forth. The experimenter made a list of such topics beforehand, wrote each topic on a slip of paper, and sealed it in an envelope. From twenty envelopes which had been shuffled, one was selected at random, and opened *after* the subject had fallen asleep. The experimenter thought about the topic, pantomimed it, and drew pictures of it. He tried to implant it in the mind of the sleeping subject. All of the activities of the experimenter were done silently. Sending was continued during a REM period until the subject was awakened. The awakening was done by the experimenter going into the bedroom and calling the subject's name. He then started the tape recorder and the subject transcribed the dream if he could remember one. There was no communication between the experimenter and the subject until the end of the transcription when the experimenter asked some standard questions about the dream. These questions had nothing to do with the topic that was being sent. . . . In all of the cases except one, the subject did not know that any sendings were being made. In the one case where he did, he had no idea of what was being sent. Nor did the experimenter know what was to be sent until after the subject had fallen asleep and the envelope was opened.

Hall made the following comments about the dream of the boxing match:

Several things will be noted about the incorporation into the dream of the topic. First, it was a very direct reproduction of what the experimenter was thinking about and pantomiming. Second, the boxing episode was inserted into the dream and appeared to have no connection with what went before it and what followed it. This inserted quality is also what one finds when a sleeping person is stimulated by a sound, a light, or drops of water. It appears that the subject received the message in the middle of a dream which was interrupted in order to incorporate the subliminal stimulus and then returned to the main dream again. Third, the subject's personal involvement in the action by standing up and throwing a few imaginary punches may have reflected the experimenter's rather spirited but silent pantomiming in the next room. These experiments were then conducted with five other subjects on whom a total of 121 presentations of stimulus material was made. In 56 of these presentations, some correspondence was noted between the material that was sent and the contents of the dreams that were reported. These correspondences were not usually as close as those observed in the prize fight dream.

Hall gave some examples of the correspondences that resulted from his efforts to "send" impressions to other subjects during their REM periods. Hall used an axe one night as a prop in his efforts to pantomime chopping down a coconut tree. The subject dreamed about using a knife to chip some organic growth from something that resembled the interior of a acorn squash. The yellow chips were about an inch and a half thick. We can see in this example the substitution of a knife for the axe and an acorn squash for a coconut. The chips would be similar to what might result from chopping down a tree. Hall gave additional examples from some other subjects:

(1) The stimulus topic was that of broiling a steak. The dream contained a reference to an outside barbecue unit. (2) The experimenter was thinking about finding money and the subject reported a dream in which his father's company was going bankrupt and his father was trying to design an airplane that would make a lot of money. (3) The stimulus material was climbing a mountain. The subject dreamed that his girlfriend was pedaling a bicycle up a very steep hill with snow on it. (4) The experimenter thought about a tooth being extracted, and the dream included the image of a ferocious tiger with a huge, cavernous mouth.

After Ullman and Krippner heard of Calvin's results with me, they invited me to participate as a dream subject at the Maimonides Laboratory. I accepted their offer. The first of my experimental sessions began on January 5, 1967, and my participation ended forty-four weeks later. During this time, I served as the percipient for a total of eight nights and earned the honorary title "The Prince of the Percipients." A chapter bearing that title appears in their *Dream Telepathy* book and describes my participation in considerable detail.

The randomly selected target for my first night was *Discovery of America by Christopher Columbus*, by Salvador Dalí. This painting depicts the young Columbus in a dream sequence about his future voyage across the Atlantic. The Virgin Mary is shown on a banner borne by Columbus as he walks forward on the beach. He wears a white transparent robe through which one can see the nipples of his breasts. Behind him are his ship, a church, some priests, and several altar boys in white robes bearing crosses.

Among the dream images described in my REM reports that night were references to "some fairly youngish male figure," "a woman from Atlantic City or Atlantic Beach," "the theme of motherhood," "a big Mass," "people dressed in white robes," and "semi-transparent pajamas through which you could still see her nipples." The following morning, before seeing the pool of eight pictures, I said, "people were wearing the kind of little white frocks that altar boys wear" and indicated that the target picture would deal with "something of national importance, something of historical significance."

The next experimental night was February 2. The target picture was *The Wine*

Taster by Van Delft. It shows a Dutch couple in old-fashioned dress, with the man wearing a large black hat and holding a bottle. The woman is seated at a table with a colorful flower design on it and is drinking a glass of wine. The floor is covered with black and white tiles in a checkerboard pattern. Some of my dream images from that night referred to a "night club cabaret scene," "a Toulouse-Lautrec poster and a fellow . . . dressed in the clothing of that era . . . wearing a black derby hat," "a black-and-white checked coat," "I was taking a glass of water to take this pill," and "a flower field."

The first two nights were carried out with a young female agent. For the third night, March 15, the agent was Monte Ullman. The target picture was Henri Rousseau's *Repast of the Lion*, which depicts a jungle setting and, in a small central area of the foreground, a lion whose jaws encircle the head of a smaller, striped animal.

My dreams that night contained a great deal of aggression, including a reference to a murderess, giving karate chops, and nearly strangling someone. Dogs were mentioned in my second REM report and in my third REM report I described "two puppies . . . the two of them had been sort of fighting . . . their jaws were open and you could see their teeth . . . where they snap at each other," "an outdoor setting."

The next experimental session was on May 17, over two months later; a new female agent was used on that night and the remaining nights. The target picture was *Kathak Dancing Girls* by an unknown artist in India. It portrays two women in bright, striped costumes dancing in a meadow. An oval shape circles these women and golden starlike objects are scattered through a blue sky outside this oval.

In my dream imagery that night I mentioned that it would be a "foreign land," "there were striped black and yellow bees . . . you could only see two of them," "one of the people . . . has a striped suit on . . . which might be like the bees and the stripes they had on," "there was a little bit of vegetation," "the sky seemed to be full of stars and the stars had a sort of golden color to them." Associating to the image of bees, I said that they "were communicating to the other bees where the direction of the honey would be, the way they wiggled their tails, the way they did their dance."

On June 27, the target picture was Giorgio de Chirico's *The Enigma of Fate*. It contains a tall triangular painting with a giant hand from the wrist down in the foreground. The hand is touching a black-and-white checkerboard. In the center is a tall brick building, and in the background are two two-story buildings.

There were several references to hand imagery in my dreams that night: "I turned to look at my wristwatch," "my hands were wet," "you told me to push this button . . . I remember pushing and my finger being wet or my thumb being wet . . . and you were going to push the button," "playing football inside . . . it was touch football . . . we had to touch the other wall for a touchdown." I also said it was as if it had "something to do with a giant" and that "there were two stories in the building."

The target picture for September 9 was Paul Cézanne's *Trees and Houses*. The painting shows a tiny pair of joined houses on a hillside. In the foreground a series of leafless trees rise from some clay-colored soil. Behind the trees is a narrow stream or road, and ruts or gullies can be seen between the trees. No people appear in the picture.

My recall for this evening was sparser than on any other night. However, the imagery I did report stressed the presence of houses and the lack of people. In my first REM report I said, "something about a house." In my fourth REM report, I indicated, "there was a house . . . there were no people involved." Describing the imagery in more detail, I said, "It was just this isolated house that seemed very small in size, either like a doll house or a toy house." In a later REM report I described "dingy buildings . . . one street which was empty." In my final report I referred to a "dirt road . . . very deep dirt ruts in the road . . . sort of orange clay of the dirt road." I also referred to "a lonely shack sitting upon a hillside."

The target picture for the session on October 23 was *Gangster Funeral* by Jack Levine. The picture portrays a dead gangster lying in his coffin; the edge of the casket is bordered with silk or satin. The gangster is seen from the top of his balding head, and only the top half of his body can be seen. Near the foot of the coffin is a police officer. To the right of the coffin is a group of older male mourners; one female figure is holding a handkerchief over half of her face and only one eye is visible. The dominant gangster wears a brown suit and greyish vest. Near the top of the picture are two windows.

In contrast to the previous session, I characterized my dreams on this night as being very "people dominated." The de-

ceased gangster figure may have been represented when I described "a portrait, or a bust or cameolike picture—it seems to be centrally located with maybe a little bit of border around it." I also referred to "one guy [who] seemed to be sort of lying down on a bed" and to a person "in his early 40's . . . who had partial thinning of hair, or baldness." In my comments the next morning, I noted, "I could see him from chest up; waist up." In one REM report I said, "I looked into the room . . . from one of the windows. . . . It seemed like there were maybe six people in there . . . one girl in particular seemed to have an eye turned toward me. It seemed like just the one eye turned toward me, the other was not." I also described a policeman and a character who "had on a vest which was not exactly matching the suit."

My final night as a subject at Maimonides took place on November 26. The target picture was *Man with Arrows and Companions* by Bichitr. It shows an outdoor setting in India with three men sitting on the ground a few feet apart from each other. All three are wearing tunics with cloth sashes around their waists and some type of cloth turban wound around their heads. Two of the men have short sleeves with their arms showing. The man on the far left is playing a stringed musical instrument like a mandolin, the figure on the far right has a bow in his lap with the tip extending up from his shoulder, a taut bowstring across his chest and an arrow in his hand. The man in the lower center has a stick with a notch at its tip, which looks like a gun, over his shoulder and a large blanket by his feet, tied together with several large knots. There is a stake in the background around which a rope is wrapped, and in the right foreground is a bag with a cord coiled around the top extending away from the bag. At the top of the picture, three old tree trunks support the rafter of a primitive shelter.

I will discuss this night's results in more detail, because they have been referred to by two authors, who came to opposite conclusions regarding the significance of my dream imagery in relation to the target picture. First, let me describe some of the material I reported during my REM period awakenings and the comments I made the following morning before seeing the pool of the eight art reproductions.

My first REM report included these images:

Man with Arrows and Companions, *one of the target pictures for the Maimonides experiment*

The first image seemed to be sort of a bedroll . . . straight ahead of me were three men . . . equally distant apart from each other. They were dressed . . . in short-sleeved shirts and berets. . . . I believe they were holding rifles . . . as if the rifle butt were resting on the ground . . . there was an image of a rope . . . a setting that's foreign or rural or western.

In my next REM report, I said:

It started being focused on rope again . . . a short length of a rope . . . the image now seemed to be the rope was in a direct line for a very short distance, then there was three or four coils of rope, then the rope came down in a straight line again . . . earlier there was kind of a circular loop image . . . the words came to mind "The Oxbow Incident" . . . the image I had with the hanging . . . an old withered tree with an arm branch and this guy swinging from the rope . . . the words came through which are the tunes to a folk song.

During my next awakening, I said someone was "being pulled out of the water by a rope around their leg." I also referred to "an object, the same as a shield, but it was very small, and coming out of each corner was a coiled spring and it seemed to be like some of the rope images that had been there earlier." During a later REM report, I described a "hammock in which there were an awful lot of suspended strings, and this image was of this knife cutting one of the strings . . . this isolated knife sawing through this fairly thick string or cord." In summarizing my imagery for the night I noted, "Certainly what kept coming through time and time again was some kind of concern with rope or with string or cord." I guessed the target picture showed "a scene of Western life involved. People dressed up in cowboy suits with guns. . . . Somewhere in the picture rope imagery appears in a very prominent or conspicuous way."

The following morning, I selected the *Man with Arrows and Companions* as my first choice and indicated my confidence rating for that choice was 100 points, the maximum which could be given. This was considered a "direct hit" because it was the correct target picture out of the eight possibilities. Both outside judges also ranked this picture as their number one choice.

Here's how my responses for that last night were evaluated in two different popular books. Elizabeth Hall in *Possible Impossibilities* recognized that "like other dreamers, Van de Castle transformed the pictures in his dreams." She described the target picture and was aware that I had reported six dreams that night, "four of which included ropes or strings or cord." Hall went on to state:

The dreamer apparently picked up the weapons, the musical instrument, the cloth bundle, and the three hatted men, but the strings on the instrument, the bowstring, and the rope combined to overpower his dreams. In a third

dream, a drowned person was pulled from the water by a rope, and yet another included a hammock with lots of "suspended strings."[21]

However, John Grant, the British author of *Dreamers*, seemed unable to comprehend the way the studies were evaluated and labeled them "a statistically hilarious procedure." He didn't seem to realize that "blind" outside judges ranked the transcripts of all the night's dreams against a pool of eight pictures—only one of which duplicated the target picture. This enabled precise statistical evaluations to be made with regard to the odds of selecting the correct target picture by chance. This is how he described my final night:

The dreamer involved was Robert Van de Castle, the team's star at the telepathic art. . . . He got the three men, all right, but in a Wild West scene (a pun on "Indians"?); the three were standing rather than, as in the picture, seated. They were wearing berets, and all held rifles with the butts resting on the ground beside them. A bedroll featured. One of the main elements of the *dream-scene* was a rope—but the only rope in the picture features merely as an obscure detail; to be fair, Van de Castle thought that a collection of strings (the stringed instrument?) was important, too.

But all this isn't desperately impressive. I think we're justified in politely forgetting about the rope, even though Van de Castle was insistent that it dominated his dream. We're left with the three human figures, the roll of cloth, the strings on the instrument, and the stick that looks a little bit like a rifle. Yet Van de Castle gave this dream a rating of 100%: it was a "direct hit"!

Distortions of fact like this—whether deliberate or unconscious—do not help one to decide whether or not such phenomena as dream-telepathy actually exist.[22]

It's unclear to me in Grant's remarks why "we're justified in politely forgetting about the rope" when rope imagery was featured so prominently in several of my dreams and in the target picture. I'm also not sure what the "distortions of fact" are. The selection was called a "direct hit" because it was the correct choice of the eight available pictures, not because the dream imagery was an exact reproduction of the target picture. Grant also kept mentioning my *dream* as if only a *single* dream were available for consideration, rather than a collection of dreams obtained throughout the night. It was the *consistency* of the rope or string imagery from dream to dream which forced me to examine the pool of eight pictures for the one in which rope or string imagery was most prominent. The *Man with Arrows and Companions* clearly had the most obvious examples (stringed musical instruments, bowstring, strings around the bag, rope around the stake, as well as the looped sashes and head coverings). My dreams and the target picture also shared a number of other features: the

three men, the rural setting, folk tunes, the bedroll, and so forth.

A very thorough and scholarly review of the Maimonides research program was published in the *American Psychologist* by Irvin L. Child, the chairperson of psychology at Yale University. He carefully described the procedures and results and independently evaluated the statistical significance of the overall findings. Child concluded:

> The outcome is clear. Several segments of the data, considered separately, yield significant evidence that dreams (and associations to them) tended to resemble the picture chosen randomly as target more than they resembled other pictures in the pool.[23]

Dr. Child devoted several pages of his article to documenting how the Maimonides research program has been misrepresented or ignored in books by psychologists that could be expected to cover the topic of paranormal dreams. This is how he evaluated what had been written:

> Some of those books engage in nearly incredible falsification of the facts about the experiments; others simply neglect them. I believe it is fair to say that none of these books has correctly identified any defect in the Maimonides experiments other than ones relevant only to the hypothesis of fraud or on inappropriate statistical reasoning (easily remedied by

new calculations from the published data).[24]

One of the more flagrant examples of inaccurate and biased reporting has been that by E. M. Hansel, a leading British critic of parapsychology. He had earlier published a book ruthlessly attacking the field and in a revised edition added a chapter describing the new experiments on telepathy in dreams.[25] He devoted one page to describing the basic method used at Maimonides and limited his discussion of nine successful experiments to a single paragraph, but he devoted nearly eight pages to his discussion of the "unsuccessful" Van de Castle replication. He was referring to an eight-night study where I served as a subject at the University of Wyoming for David Foulkes and a graduate student, Edward Belvedere.[26] I had agreed to be a subject there to see if my previously successful results could be repeated in his laboratory.

Foulkes, whose cognitive approach to dreams was described earlier in this book, agreed that he would try to conduct his study with conditions as similar to those at Maimonides as possible. There were, however, many dissimilarities between the two studies. The emotional climate was markedly different at the two laboratories. At Maimonides, I felt welcomed by the staff; they made me feel like a visiting sultan. When I arrived in Wyoming during the middle of the winter, both the weather and the staff were extremely cold.

I had sent a letter before my arrival indicating that it would be acceptable to use color photographs instead of art reproductions, but that the pool of pictures to be used each night should be selected so that each one would be as different as possible from the others. Upon my arrival, I found that they had selected mostly black-and-white photos and the pictures in each pool often did not differ much from each other.[27]

After my first two nights, I strongly expressed my disappointment about the similar themes in the pools of pictures. Foulkes then requested that his assistant make more of an effort to introduce variety into the remaining pools, but I felt the assistant, Robert Weisz, whose research on lab versus home dreams was cited in chapter 10, still included very similar images in each pool. For example, on night six, the target picture was a black-and-white close-up of a nursing infant, whose mother was shown nude from the waist up. One of the pictures in that pool showed a man, who was nude from the waist up, kissing a woman; another showed several people drinking at a party with some beverage bottles displayed. All three pictures could be considered to feature oral themes. On night seven, the target picture was again a black-and-white photograph of a nursing infant whose mother was nude from the waist up. This time the images in the pool included a young man's face, shown in close-up, with lips parted close to a woman's face; a waterfront dock with a bottle of wine and some fruit; a dragonfly eating a leaf; a group of cheering sports spectators with open mouths; and a young girl playing a flute. These six pictures all seemed to contain prominent oral themes or mouth imagery.

The number of potential agents was also limited. At Maimonides, I could choose from a large number of people that worked at the hospital. At Wyoming, the selection of potential agents available during the between-semesters break was much more narrow. No successful results were obtained with the initial agent, so I shifted to a woman who worked as a laboratory assistant for Foulkes and we were quite successful on two nights.

On the first successful night, the target picture was a black-and-white photo showing six preteen boys and a girl laughing and strutting in drum-major fashion across a large grassy area. They were in single file and several were carrying batons with small balls on the ends. Throughout my various REM reports there were references to children playing, some small steel balls with a horn, four or five teenagers in a row, a girl parading around, a bunch of kids cutting the grass, and so forth. My guess about the target picture was:

The overriding thing during the night was the constant kid reference, they were either as boy scouts or as young kids or as teenagers . . . or this last of young kids who were perhaps 9 or 10 years old . . . so I would look for the picture that involved a group of boys either playing baseball or some other sport . . . there should be quite a few boys not just an isolated one, there should be at least a half a dozen of them or so.

I gave the target picture a ranking of 1 and so did two independent judges. I began to feel some optimism that perhaps I might be able to achieve some positive results in spite of the difficult conditions. I teamed up with the same agent three nights later, which was the longest interval between Wyoming sessions (the shortest interval between sessions at Maimonides was twenty-eight days). The target picture was a black-and-white photo of a woman, apparently a mental patient, sitting with her head and arms on top of her knees, which are drawn up to her chest. She is sitting on a wide, wooden bench in front of a high plaster or cement wall with paint peeling from the ceiling.

In my first REM report, I described "an old, wooden chair. . . . I had the Negro girl try and sit on this and it just wasn't a very good fit . . . underground subway tracks . . . with the high, like concrete sides, along either side." In my second REM report, I mentioned, "We entered into this building . . . and there were various seats possible . . . this girl said that she would like to sit in these other kinds, which looked like church pews and she sat there." In my third REM report, I referred to "looking around inside the house. There were some problems with it, it was an older house and there were some cracks in the ceilings." On the basis of these various dream images, my guess about what the target picture would show was:

a somewhat unusual building . . . the one dream had the church pews . . . an unusual something in the way of buildings or the interior of them. . . . As far as people . . . I see it more as one anticipating more people arriving but as yet they had not ... you'd notice the number of empty seats more than you would the full ones. I don't think the picture would convey any set emotion ... the picture would not be particularly unusual as far as the color.... There isn't very much activity in there.... The people are either just sitting there, or perhaps implied conversation, but I don't get any feeling of great motoric activity at all.

I gave the target picture a rank of 1 and so did one of the judges, but the other judge gave it a rank of 6, which seems surprising in view of my summary comments.

I now began to feel real hope that I could pull this experiment out of the fire. The overall results would be statistically significant if I managed to choose the correct target picture one more time. I then encountered the two back-to-back nights with the target pictures of the nursing infants and all the other oral-related themes in the pools of pictures. Everything now depended on the final night. If I were to give the target picture a rank of 1, the experiment would be published as a success; if not, it would be published as a failure. The agent with whom I had obtained the two very successful nights decided she did not want to participate for the final night. I had to return to working with the initial agent, with whom I had been completely unsuccessful. I felt I would give it my best effort, however, and see if I could turn things around with her.

On the basis of my dream imagery throughout the night, I made the following guess about what the target picture would show for that final night:

> It would deal with a foreign culture or people from a foreign culture ... [or] it may be something like a hippy culture within America which would be sort of like a foreign culture.... If I were to look for the unifying ones [themes], it would be the element of exotic or foreign culture, faraway places kind of thing ... the clothing is going to be somewhat unusual ... somewhat distinctive and different.

My guess that a foreign culture or subculture, faraway places, and distinctive clothing were all involved would have enabled me to select a single corresponding picture fairly readily if the pool had been sufficiently varied, but, as usual, it was not. The pictures were: a postcard from Austria showing a bare-breasted woman in peasant costume with a child near a thatched-roof house; a photo of two dark-skinned women with many bracelets, wearing saris or long shawls over their heads and shoulders; a street scene in the French Quarter of New Orleans, with black musicians entertaining tourists; a street scene in a ghetto, with two black teenagers in shorts in front of an open fire hydrant; a street scene in Latin America with a priest wearing a long lace cassock and a man holding a fringed umbrella over him; a crowd of Asians with the men wearing long gowns slit at the side; a young man wearing a black leather jacket, carrying a guitar case, and walking down some railroad tracks with a companion wearing a plaid jacket; and the Milky Way or some other galaxy. I felt quite confident that the target picture was *not* the Milky Way (which it wasn't), but there was such an overabundance of ethnic material in the other pictures that I was not successful in picking the target picture, and the study was published, and widely referred to, as a failure to show any evidence of ESP when laboratory conditions were well controlled by the investigators.

Hansel did not accurately describe the details of my participation at Maimonides. He stated that I "slept in the [Maimonides] Dream laboratory on eight *successive* nights"(italics mine).[28] In fact, it took me forty-four weeks to complete the series at Maimonides, because the studies were spaced from four to eleven weeks apart. I had told Foulkes that "my usual morning-after reaction at Maimonides was that of experiencing a headache and a feeling of being a little giddy or becoming unglued." There is an important psychological difference when one has at least a month to recuperate between these exhausting nights of constantly being awakened and struggling to recall every item of dream imagery, and when one has only a single day to recuperate, as happened on four occasions at Wyoming. The eight experimental sessions there were completed within a fourteen-day period. However, Hansel makes no mention of this when he describes "the essential differences in procedures"[29] between the two laboratories.

Hansel also claimed that Edward Belvedere, who was a graduate student of Foulkes's and whose academic affiliation was listed as the University of Wyoming

on their article, was from the Maimonides Laboratory. He apparently wanted it to sound as if there were a sympathetic experimenter on the scene. Hansel makes the clear, but inaccurate, implication that the experimental conditions at Maimonides were not well controlled and implies that any evidence for ESP evaporates if stringent conditions are imposed. Foulkes, however, offered the following interesting remarks when he reflected back upon his study:

> The replication attempt was unsuccessful. In retrospect, we may have erred too much on the side of "scientism" to the exclusion of creating conditions in which telepathy might reasonably (if it exists at all) be expected to flourish. It proved hard to escape the role of protector of scientific purity or guardian of the scientific morals. Were we sympathetic and encouraging observers, or scientific detectives out to prevent a crime from being committed before our very eyes? . . . Particularly revealing personally was a brief moment in intrapsychic panic when it seemed as though some telepathic influence might be "coming through"—how could it be? Where had I failed to prevent a sensory leakage? Our subject [Van de Castle] clearly felt himself "on trial" before a not entirely sympathetic jury, and we also could not totally avoid the feeling that we too were on trial, with a favorable verdict for the subject raising

doubts as to the scrupulosity of our judgment process. There is no place for sloppy dream research, whether on telepathy or anything else. But being rigorous is a different matter from insecurely flaunting one's rigor as we may have done in our first study.[30]

Foulkes later reported that he had "experienced a personally impressive instance of apparent telepathy in another laboratory study ostensibly unrelated to ESP." He had been studying children's dreams and one night was writing a review of an article on the effects of thirst on the sleep cycle. His attention was caught by a sentence that read: "The cheese and crackers bedtime snack added a new and seemingly unnecessary aspect to the deprivation condition." His subject entered a REM period and when Foulkes awoke her she reported a dream in which a man came to her house and had a snack and asked the dreamer's father if he wanted a beer. Her father decided he wanted one even though he was a strict teetotaler. The dreamer then noticed three boxes of crackers, and one box had a little piece of cheese between the crackers.

Foulkes noted that this girl had had no dreams of thirst-cheese-crackers in any of the other twenty-five nights they had observed her dreams, nor had "this particular combination of elements ever occurred in the hundreds of dreams we have collected from other children in the same study." Foulkes admitted,

An experience such as this keeps alive one's spark of interest in telepathic dreams, whatever the out-

come of his own more formal experiments. It also raises some interesting questions about those experiments. Here, two entirely unself-conscious persons seemed unwittingly to have made some contact. The atmosphere was quite in contrast to the highly self-conscious "we're-all-on-trial" environment of our first formal replication study. The laboratory setting *can* change and distort the phenomena under study, it *does* limit generalizations to everyday life, it quite often *does* force trivial reductions of essential human phenomena.[31]

We might label Foulkes's thirst-cheese-crackers stimulus as nonintentional, because he had no conscious plans to transmit such a message. It seemed as if the stimulus configuration originated somewhere in his preconscious mind. I have encountered many examples of preconscious conflicts being indirectly "sent" by an agent, who would confess to them the next morning after learning that his or her "secrets" had surfaced in my dream reports. These cases parallel the clinical examples discussed earlier where patients zeroed in on the unresolved emotional issues of their therapists.

On one experimental night when an agent had been preoccupied with her feelings toward a previous therapist and her brand-new therapist, I had several references in my REM reports to comparisons between therapists. Another agent had very conflicted feelings one night about whether she should attend Mass the next day. That night one of my REM reports was about Christ being nailed to a cross and his side being slashed by a vicious soldier. On many other nights, personal concerns of the agents were reflected in my dream reports, which were "direct hits" with regard to the agents' personal problems but, unfortunately, complete misses in reference to the target pictures.

Once the telepathic gates are opened up, transmissions may not be limited to just the agent. For example, on the night when *Kathak Dancing Girls* was the target picture, I felt guilty because I was looking at Dr. Krippner's (the experimenter) expense account statements in my dream, and it seemed they pertained to California. Scrawled below the figures was something to the effect of "This was not enough money; $25.00 more needed to be raised." Somehow I knew in the dream that the money had already been raised and the problem corrected. Krippner had made a lecture trip to California two months earlier, but I didn't know that in totaling up his expenses, he discovered he was twenty-five dollars short of breaking even. One of his sponsors had quietly come up with a check for the additional amount but told him to keep the transaction secret.

The staff at Maimonides Hospital also investigated precognitive dreams and obtained significant evidence of their existence under well-controlled laboratory conditions. The percipient, Malcolm Bessent, a British sensitive, attempted to dream precognitively about a situation that he would experience the following morning. After the tape recordings of Bessent's dreams from the night had been removed from the laboratory, an assistant completely unfamiliar with the content of the dreams randomly selected a scenario from a large number of possible stimuli. The chosen situation was then acted out for the percipient. Judges were later presented transcripts of the percipient's dreams from the preceding night and descriptions of eight different possible situations to which the subject might have been exposed. They were able to correctly match Bessent's dream reports to the situation he later experienced to a statistically significant degree. Two successful experimental series, each lasting for eight nights, were carried out.

The experiences Bessent was exposed to during the second series were sequences of slides accompanied with music or sounds that corresponded to the images. The experimenter who selected the targets was completely unfamiliar with the content of the preceding night's dreams.

One morning, for example, the slide sequence that Bessent saw involved birds. No particular type of bird was emphasized; the images included birds on water, on land, and in the air, and Bessent listened to the sounds of bird calls. On the preceding night, Bessent had reported dreams in which deep blue was important, had mentioned the sea or sky, and had said that the target would be of emotional interest to Bob Morris, a friend who had done his doctoral dissertation on bird behavior. Bessent added that Bob Morris had "taken me out to see his sanctuary where all the birds are kept." He mentioned various types of birds he had seen there and concluded, "I just have a feeling that the next target material will be about birds."

I have carried out some limited studies

on paranormal dreaming in my own laboratory. When we studied a pair of identical female twins, one gave a REM report about a crowded English pub with beer mugs when her sister looked at a target picture of a crowded cabaret with a musician and people drinking. On another night we studied a pair of identical male twins. One brother looked at a target picture of a large waterfall. His twin dreamed that we had installed a shower in his room during the night and reported hearing the sounds of the water splashing and seeing a woman standing in the shower.

I served as an agent one night when the target picture was of a boxing match between a black boxer and a white boxer. The research at Maimonides had achieved greater success when the agent attempted to experience the target stimulus in more than one sensory modality, so I tried to get into this boxing atmosphere as fully as possible. I imagined myself as one of the boxers: threw some strong punches at a pillow, snorted through my nose a few times, pranced around an imaginary ring, and made bobbing motions with my head. Then I tried to become the other boxer, punching myself in the stomach and ribs. I tried to hear the excitment of the crowd and feel the anxiety of a fighter risking injury. In one of her REM periods, the percipient reported:

> I was working at some sort of an Olympic game that was played with a really heavy metal ball. . . . They played it with sort of a paddle and metal balls about the size of a small bowling ball, about duck-pin size, and banged it across

something like a tennis court. I don't know why they all didn't get killed, the ball kept coming across and they looked so heavy . . . it was a very dangerous-looking game . . . the men were wearing shorts and shirts . . . this game kind of scared me. I was afraid one of the balls might hit me.

I had the opportunity for a few brief naps between rounds of shadowboxing. I recorded three dreams of my own from these napping episodes. In one, I was looking at a newspaper, and on the left side of the front page was a photograph showing Tony Zale, a former middleweight champion knocking someone down. The caption indicated it was a second-round knockout. A question arises as to whether my conscious efforts to behave like a boxer initiated the percipient's dream, or whether my dream about a boxing event was the more potent stimulus. Perhaps a percipient's dream imagery resonates more easily to an agent's dream imagery than to the agent's waking imagery.

In one of my other dreams that night, I was with several people in a large laboratory going from one room to another. The percipient dreamed she was in a room with a friend who was doing an experiment and the friend went to another part of the laboratory. I also dreamed about a dog barking, and the percipient had a dream with a dog in it. Still another dream involved my wife taking a car trip with other people, including Dr. L. My wife met a man with whom she talked about music. The percipient dreamed about being on a car trip with other people and was later talking to

Dr. L. She also dreamed about a woman who got up and sang on something like "The Ed Sullivan Show." The surprising number of dream-to-dream correspondences suggests that it may be easier for two dreaming minds to develop a sort of synchronicity than it is for a dreaming mind to connect with a waking mind.

Further evidence in support of this idea was reported by Alan Rechtschaffen, a well-known sleep researcher from the University of Chicago. He noticed that there was often an impressive degree of correspondence between dreams occurring at about the same time when two subjects were sleeping in his laboratory. He described the most striking example:

In the first dream, one subject dreamt about students singing in Russian, and the other subject dreamt about students doing some kind of interpretive singing. In the second dream, the first subject was taking a violin lesson and the other subject was learning a guitar melody. In the third dream, the first subject was watching a James Cagney gangster movie, and the other subject reported a dream about a recent gangster movie, *Bonnie and Clyde*.[32]

After observing a few other examples of simultaneous dreams, Rechtschaffen remarked, "We became very excited. We thought that maybe the question is not so much what do dreams mean, but whose dream are you having?"[33] Rechtschaffen decided to use hypnosis to investigate the possibility of simultaneous dreaming more carefully. Before the agent went to sleep for the night, he was placed in a hypnotic trance and told that during the night he would have a certain dream.

Rechtschaffen indicated that his initial work was very encouraging. The first night this procedure was used, the hypnotized agent was told to dream of the death of Martin Luther King, Jr., and of the fear of riots. The agent subsequently dreamed that King had been shot, somebody threw a rock, and they were afraid a riot would start. The percipient, who had not received any suggestions, dreamed of a black policeman who was beating another man, and he was afraid that somebody would throw a brick and start a riot. On another night, the hypnotized agent was told to dream he was in an amusement park having a very good time. He dreamed about riding on a merry-go-round. The percipient dreamed of people laughing and running in circles, and of "grinning, funny-looking horses."

In the next stage of research, Rechtschaffen explored simultaneous waking hypnotic dreams. He again got very good results during his initial work. His procedure was to hypnotize two subjects, tell each one, "When I give you the signal you will have a dream of ten minutes' duration. You will wake up after ten minutes and tell us the dream." The subject who served as the agent was given a specific suggestion as to what he should dream; the other subject, the percipient, who was at the opposite side of the building on a different floor, did not receive any suggestion. On occasion, this procedure achieved dramatic results. Here is Rechtschaffen's account of the most impressive of these simultaneous dreams:

> The topic suggested to our first subject (agent) was, "You are falling and unable to stop." The subject dreamt he was in a third floor apartment in a big city. He was highly dissatisfied, and the atmosphere was somewhat tragic. In the apartment below there was a girl playing a flute and dancing. She was pregnant. The subject slipped off the windowsill and floated down. As he floated down, the girl threw him an orange. He threw her a book, *The Wasteland*. Suddenly the building vanished.
>
> The other subject (percipient) had this dream: He was in New York City in 1928. There was music in the background: they were playing "Rhapsody in Blue" and "I Can't Get No Satisfaction." Suddenly all the buildings collapsed because of the depression. He saw a bicycle pump, inserted it into the buildings, and they sprang to life (using his words). Then he found himself dancing on the keys of a piano, and then jumping on a trampoline which turned into a tangerine. And following that, he found himself floating upside down in the hallway.[34]

It will be worthwhile to highlight some of the correspondences between these two dreams by listing them (see table).

AGENT'S DREAM	PERCIPIENT'S DREAM
1. Big city	New York City
2. Dreamer was highly dissatisfied	Music: "I Can't Get No Satisfaction"
3. Atmosphere was somewhat tragic	Music: "Rhapsody in Blue"
4. A girl plays a flute and dances	Background music; dreamer dances on the keys of a piano
5. Girl was pregnant	Dreamer inserts a bicycle pump into buildings causing them to "spring to life"
6. Dreamer floats down	Dreamer floats upside down
7. The girl throws him an orange	The trampoline turns into a tangerine
8. The buildings vanish	The buildings collapse

The suggested topic with another agent was: "You fall in love with a beautiful girl in the spring . . . you walk in the wind and sun and are filled with bliss." He subsequently reported an idyllic dream: he was with a beautiful girl on a beautiful day; the sun was out and it was just the right temperature. The percipient, who had received no instructions about what to dream, reported the following dream:

I was in this swanlike boat in a lake, and I saw a really beautiful girl. The boat went over to where she was . . . there were angels singing. . . . The girl was very beauti-

ful. She had long blond hair and it was very sunny and nice out.[35]

Rechtschaffen felt that the greatest successes were achieved using emotional topics with which physical sensations were associated. He observed that "hits," when they occurred, were quite impressive and quite easy to detect. He indicated, "When you simply have judges matching a dream against a suggested topic, a hit does not reveal the degree of the hit. A simple matching procedure does not take into account the very unlikely probability of such a specific correspondence."[36]

DREAM NETWORK BULLETIN TELEPATHY PROJECT

Another personal experience sustains my belief that the dream-to-dream or unconscious-to-unconscious connection may carry a more powerful charge than an agent's conscious attention upon a target picture. When I was a coeditor of the *Dream Network Bulletin*, we decided to carry out a telepathy project. Readers were notified that on the night of November 17, 1985, I would focus on a target picture at my home in Charlottesville, Virginia. They were invited to dream on that night about the target picture. A total of twenty-seven percipients mailed in letters describing their dream experiences that night.

Stimuli corresponding to three levels of my consciousness may have possibly served as the target material that night. The *conscious* level involved my concentrating upon the target picture, which

was a black-and-white photograph of a Cuna Indian woman from Panama standing in front of a council house with slatted, wooden walls and a thatched palm roof. Standing on a large metal pot behind her was a young boy with his hands around a wooden pole. A *preconscious* level was represented by free associations I had written about this photo, which included mention of an alcoholic beverage drunk at puberty ceremonies and the music and dancing that accompany other religious ceremonies held in the council house. The third, *unconscious* level would be represented by my dreams. I woke up three times during the night and recorded several long dreams.

Several of the dreams sent included images corresponding to the photograph: specific clothing, such as a short-sleeved blouse and unusual ankle jewelry, like that

The target picture that the author concentrated on for the Dream Network Bulletin *telepathy project.*

the Cuna Indian woman wore; foreign locations; and children. Several dreams mentioned elements included in my written associations, such as music and dancing; and three dreamers mentioned alcoholic beverages. However, the most striking and specific correspondences were to my dreams.

One woman, Claudia B. from Brooklyn, who was a complete stranger to me, managed to pick up on the target photo, my associations, and my dreams as well. With regard to the target picture, she mentioned her young daughter, hands on a

structure of beams and poles, wooden sliding doors, and a building with an unusual-looking roof.

With reference to my associations, Claudia described a reception room with low benches along the walls where many young women were excitedly getting ready for the first meeting of a church choir, which required a special dress. The council house has low benches along the wall, and the first meeting of the young women sounds similar to my associations regarding puberty ceremonies. I also had written that the thatched palm roof provides good protection from the rain; Claudia dreamed she heard rain beginning and realized she didn't have an umbrella.

I was really amazed at the correspondences between the imagery in our dreams. My first dream involved a fishing scene: I was sometimes on a boat and sometimes on shore. The man I was with caught two large flounder and a woman insisted that I put them on top of a boat and gut them. I attempted to cut the fish open with a razor blade. Some blood came out; the fish's face turned into a man's face and he was bleeding. I told him to rinse his face with water and said I would need his advice as to how to cut around his ears and nose. Here is an excerpt from Claudia's first dream:

> I am outdoors, perhaps on the deck of a ship ... mounting the fresh, whole wet skin of a small whale or whale's head (fish-sized) on a board, for artistic and maybe ritual purposes. After removing one eye (the only one, it's a side view) with the knife I'm using, I hear a conversation. . . . (All of this could be influenced by a recent waking experience of washing flounder for cooking, but not removing their heads). I feel a kinship, or sympathy, with the whale, which at some point transforms into a person. The wet, stretched, mounted skin is now of a man's face, reddish-brown. . . . I don't seem to notice the change from the whale.[37]

The odds against two strangers on the same night dreaming of being on a boat

cutting open a fish and having the face of the fish turn into a bloody man's face are astronomical, and that both dreamers mentioned flounder delivers the coup de grace to any notion that the correspondences are mere coincidence.

My next dream involved providing drinks that cost forty-one cents each for a group of students working on a project. There was also something about a mother dividing a cake or other dessert into two portions. In Claudia's next dream she had stolen some money with several other people and offered to count another person's share. She wrote down figures which were an "odd amount of dollars and cents." Claudia's daughter was with her and asked the others to count out a share with "equal demoninations." In her next dream, Claudia described a group of people watching a film depicting college students and an instructor working on an art project.

Rita Dwyer, the recent president of the Association for the Study of Dreams, also seemed to "tune in" to the bloody incision of my first dream. She saw an animal face and an animal with an open wound that she wanted to sew up or heal before too much blood was lost. A water setting and a boat had also figured in my first dream. Other dreamers mentioned an ocean, a sea, a river, pools of water, an ocean trip, a boat, a yacht, oars for a rowboat, fishhooks, and a hook.

In my last dream, there was a crowd of people in a slanted auditorium, and some board members and I were sitting down to eat at a table on the main floor or lecturing area. A total of eleven dreamers made references to activities taking place at a different elevation: in a grandstand, high in a theater, on a stage, in a balcony, and so forth. One dreamer described a meeting in a civic auditorium. The board members were also reflected; one dreamer described the chairman of a group trying to decide on a meeting time, three dreamers had politicians present (President Eisenhower in one case), and another had a manager present. Tables were mentioned by four ences.

In another scene of my last dream, I was using a hose to water down a pile of leaves. Watering activities may have shown up in some dreams. Two of the nine male dreamers reported urinating in their dreams and one woman dreamed that something like tea was being splashed or dripped on the rippled pages of a magazine. (Urine was not mentioned even once in the thousand dreams used for our norms.)

There were also many overlapping items among the twenty-seven dreamers that were not represented in my dreams or associations. For example, items like apples and potatoes, which according to our norms would be expected to appear less than once in three hundred dreams, appeared in the dreams of two or more dreamers, suggesting that these dreamers were also tuning in to each other.

Some form of shared dreaming, therefore, apparently occurred on the night of November 17, 1985, when all of these dreamers were invited to "drop in" on me in Charlottesville. Not only did some of them pick up on my dreams and the stimulus photo on which I had focused before sleeping; they also established contacts among themselves. It seemed we all became midnight swimmers in a common cosmic sea. Projects in which individuals attempt to meet and interact with each other in dreams have been described by several other authors.[38]

DREAM HELPER CEREMONY

My initial motivations as a subject at the Maimonides lab involved strong narcissistic and egotistical needs to be the most successful percipient ever and to "leave behind a performance record that would be unbeatable." After the death of my son, I found that my values underwent some definite changes, and I became much more interested in spiritual matters. In the preface, I briefly described how Henry Reed and I developed a dream helper ceremony to direct telepathic dreaming toward service and healing. Rather than determining who could most successfully dream about a target picture, the goal in the dream helper ceremony is to dream collectively about a target person's problem and to help that person find a solution to the problem.

The telepathic dreamers are called dream helpers. Before retiring for the night, these dream helpers gather around the designated target person and engage in some activity to create a feeling of bonding. They might meditate, pray, sing together, or sit silently holding hands. It's useful if the target person can loan some personal object—jewelry, a photograph, or an article of clothing—to each dream helper. Wearing that object or having it by the bedside will enable each dream helper to feel a special connection with the target person when they go to sleep that evening. The target person does not disclose, or even hint at, the nature of the problem for which he or she is seeking guidance.

The dream helpers renounce the right to experience any personal dreams that night and dedicate all their dreaming activity to being of service to the target person. They ask to be used as a psychic vehicle to achieve understanding and healing for the target person. At home they might not make the special effort to record every one of their dreams for themselves, but since they have dedicated all of their dreams to the target person, they work diligently to maximize their dream recall during the night. They don't want to cheat the target person out of the dreams to which they are entitled. The next morning, the dream helpers gather again with the target person, and each one describes in detail the dreams remembered from the preceding night. A fascinating pattern emerges as the warp of one dreamer's images is laid against the woof of another's and dream strand after dream strand is woven into the rich collective tapestry.

In one of our ceremonies, the dream helpers reported a black car driving into the town of White Hall, someone being hesitant to accept an Oreo cookie, someone ordering an ice cream cone with one scoop of chocolate and one of vanilla, someone noticing the black and white keys on a piano keyboard, and Martin Luther King, Jr., preaching in front of the White House. With each successive report, the theme of black and white became more predominant. Several dreams also dealt with family dissension and parental lectures about obedience.

The target person, a white woman, was very surprised by these dreams. Most of the dream helpers were strangers to her and none were aware that she was dating a black man and struggling with the question of how to deal with the negative reaction she anticipated from her family. One of the helpers dreamed that his watch was slow, and another about seeing a movie in slow motion. As the dream helpers discussed these dreams about slow motion, they suggested to the dreamer that she might move slowly in bringing up this relationship to her parents until she was sure she wanted to continue it.

The group was astonished and delighted at what they had accomplished. They felt they had been so successful because they were not attempting to gain anything for themselves; they were engaged in a healing service nourished solely from a sense of love. Everyone benefited and felt energized by their participation. The target person was deeply touched by the obvious sense of caring that the group communicated to her. Although she had not verbalized the problem she sought help with, the dream helpers had been able to comprehend her problem, empathize with her feelings, and reflect on how she might lessen the anguish her conflicts generated.

Seldom does any single dream helper grasp the full significance of the target person's problem. Like the proverbial blind men and the elephant, one describes the tail, one the leg, one the trunk, one the tusks, one the ears; but only when these discrete bits of information are assembled it is possible to grasp the nature of the elephant.

The dream helper ceremony can be a very powerful technique for uncovering ordinarily hidden issues. It should not be attempted unless everyone is fully committed to dealing with whatever emotional issues are uncovered. The target person's problem should not be something trivial (What sort of car should I buy?). It should be some emotional concern that one might discuss with a very trusted friend or counselor in the hope of reaching a better understanding of the overall problem.

For one dream helper ceremony, the target woman's question, which she revealed after all the helpers' dreams had been reported, dealt with whether to enter some new, as yet undetermined, vocation. Almost every dream helper reported dreams of extreme violence: wild animals were involved, someone was hit on the head with a hammer, and other acts of aggression were mentioned. There were also several mother-daughter dreams with disturbing content; one had a mother duck and several drowned baby ducks. When I asked the target person why she thought there was so much violence in these dreams and why the troubled mother-daughter relationships were portrayed, she broke down and confessed that her mother, who had been a psychiatric patient, had been quite violent and cruel to her when she was younger. Her mother had once

tried to drown her in a tub of boiling water, which helped explain the image of the drowned baby ducks. The subsequent group discussion suggested that maybe the target person needed to resolve this old issue with a therapist before moving on to a new vocation.

During one dream helper weekend, we had so many participants that we divided up into two groups, with Henry leading one group and me leading the other. We discerned that although each of the target persons was a female of about the same age, education, and socioeconomic status, the dreams of the two helper groups diverged widely. The dreams for target person A were right "on target," but did not apply to target person B at all, and the dreams for target person B were amazingly specific to her problem but had no pertinence for target person A. It seemed as if each target person were a psychic magnet attracting only dream filings of a very specific metal.

I think the dream helper ceremony is a convenient way for an open and interested person to observe psi in action and to experience the inner personal and collective power that results from shared awareness.

If the time ever comes when we all agree to use the formidable power of our dreaming mind as dream helpers for each other, we will witness a positive change in planetary consciousness greater than the negative change in planetary consciousness following the dropping of the first atomic bomb.

FINDING OUR INNER LIGHT:

LUCID AND SPIRITUAL

DREAMS

Our society often relies upon the vision of material reality revealed to us by scientists. But scientists' opinions, like all opinions, are fallible. Conclusions are based on the information available at a particular time, which is never complete, and are affected by personal and cultural expectations and prejudices and by beliefs about what constitutes valid evidence. Thomas Edison, for example, said in 1897, "I prefer to devote my time to objects which have some commercial value. At best, airships would be only toys." In a report made to President Harry S. Truman in 1945, Dr. Vannever Bush, the president of the Carnegie Institution, stated unequivocally, "The atom bomb will never go off and I speak as an expert on explosives."

Many scientists have steadfastly rejected the possibility of paranormal dreams. Yet the evidence presented in the preceding chapter, based upon the REM monitoring techniques of a modern sleep laboratory, seems to me to be scientifically valid and to suggest that paranormal dreams sometimes occur.

The study of lucid dreams has also faced much scientific skepticism. In a lucid dream, the dreamer becomes consciously aware that he or she is dreaming and is able to access the conscious attributes of memory and volition while participating in the events and emotions of the ongoing dream. As far back as the fourth century B.C., Aristotle commented: "Often when one is asleep, there is something in consciousness which declares that what then presents itself is but a dream."[1] Other testimonials to the existence of lucid dreams have been offered throughout the ages, but REM-oriented scientists have strongly discounted such claims. By definition, they explain, an individual cannot be simultaneously conscious and dreaming: you can be one or the other, but definitely not *both* at the same time. At best, such tales might represent brief intervals of wakefulness during REM periods in which the individual consciously elaborates or distorts elements from the preceding REM experience.

In this chapter, I'll review some highlights from the history of lucid dreaming, discuss experimental efforts to examine their validity in modern sleep laboratories, and speculate on the special significance that lucid dreams hold for us in our efforts to understand the full range of consciousness that can be developed in the dreaming state.

THE HISTORY OF LUCID DREAMING

An excellent review of the history of lucid dreaming is provided in the book *Lucid Dreaming* by Stephen LaBerge, a psychologist at the Stanford University Sleep Research Center.[2] The first description of a lucid dream experience was described in a letter written by Saint Augustine in 415. He recounted two dreams experienced by Gennadius, a former Roman physician. As a young man, Gennadius was troubled by doubts about the existence of life after death. He experienced a dream in which a youth of "remarkable appearance and commanding presence" told Gennadius, "Follow me." They came to a city where Gennadius began to hear "sounds of a melody so exquisitely sweet as to surpass anything he had ever heard." When Gennadius asked his guide about this mu-

sic, he was told, "It is the hymn of the blessed and the holy."

On the following night, the same youth appeared to Gennadius and asked the dreamer whether he recognized him. Without the slightest uncertainty, Gennadius replied that he knew him well. The youth then asked Gennadius where they had met before. Gennadius promptly described the previous dream and the exquisite music he had heard. His dream guide then inquired whether Gennadius had encountered these experiences while in sleep or while awake, and Gennadius answered, "In sleep." The youth confirmed that Gennadius had seen these things in his sleep and pointed out that Gennadius was again seeing in his sleep. His dream teacher inquired about the location of

Gennadius's body at that moment, and Gennadius answered, "In my bed." The youth then explained what was happening:

> Asleep and lying on your bed, these eyes of your body are now unemployed and doing nothing, and yet you have eyes with which you behold me, and enjoy this vision, so, after your death, while your bodily eyes shall be wholly inactive, there shall be in you a life by which you shall still live, and a faculty of perception by which you shall still perceive. Beware, therefore, after this of harboring doubts as to whether the life of man shall continue after death.[3]

After this remarkable dream, Gennadius no longer doubted the continuity of life after death.

As early as the eighth century A.D., Tibetan Buddhists pursued the cultivation of dream lucidity. Achieving mastery of lucid dreams was considered a prerequisite to seeking enlightenment. As a monk increased the frequency of lucid dreaming and developed the ability to modify his dream imagery by willing it to change, he gradually recognized the illusory nature of the dream. This awareness similarly enabled the adept to recognize the waking world as an illusion. The monk would then recognize consciousness, which continues in both waking and dreaming states, rather than coarse, material existence, as reality. The steps to follow toward this elevation in consciousness are clearly delineated in an English translation by W. Evans-Wentz

of a classic book, *Tibetan Yoga and Secret Doctrines*.[4]

Islam also encouraged its followers to train themselves in the skills of lucid dreaming. A twelfth-century Spanish Sufi, Ibn El-Arabi, proclaimed the "greatest master" in the Arab world, exhorted his followers: "A person must control his thoughts in a dream. The training of this alertness ... will produce great benefits for the individual. Everyone should apply himself to the attainment of this ability of such great value."[5]

It's obvious from these three accounts that lucid dreams were granted a special status in early Christianity, Tibetan Buddhism, and Islam. But by the nineteenth century, lucid dreams came under increasing scientific scrutiny. The most imposing figure of this era was the Frenchman Hervey Saint-Denys, whose explorations were discussed in chapter 5. His countryman Yves Delage also carried out studies in lucid dreaming. There is some historical controversy over who first classified dreams associated with simultaneous conscious awareness as lucid dreams. Saint-Denys used the term *rêve lucide* in 1867 to describe those dreams in which "I had the sensation of my situation."[6]

The person generally credited with proposing the term "lucid dream" was the Dutch psychiatrist Frederik Van Eeden. He used the term to describe dreams in which he was fast asleep yet had "full recollection of [his] day-life, and could act voluntarily." In 1913 Van Eeden presented a paper to the Society for Psychical Research on 352 lucid dreams collected between 1898 and 1912.[7] He had carried out various experiments to test the parameters of his lucid dreams. He marveled at the fact that he could shout and sing very loudly in his lucid dreams, but his wife lying next to him in the bed never heard him utter a sound.

In England, Hugh Calloway, who wrote under the pen name Oliver Fox, had independently discovered lucid dreaming in 1902. He was a sixteen-year-old student of science and electrical engineering when he experienced his first lucid dream. It involved a scene with tall trees at the corner of a road and a nearby bay. He felt the quality of his ongoing dream change profoundly when he realized that he was dreaming:

> Instantly, the vividness of life increased a hundred-fold. Never had sea and sky and trees shone with such glamorous beauty; even the commonplace houses seemed alive and mystically beautiful. Never had I felt so absolutely well, so clear-brained, so inexpressibly *free*! The sensation was exquisite beyond words; but it lasted only a few minutes and I awoke.[8]

Fox called such dreams "dreams of knowledge," because one had in them the knowledge that one was really dreaming. In such dreams, Fox felt "free as air, secure in the consciousness of my true condition and the knowledge that I could always wake if danger threatened."[9]

Until recently, lucid dreams were a neglected topic in the United States. It took some accounts of "sorcery" for the public to recognize that lucid dreams could be a valuable ally in seeking personal growth and that they could be cultivated through

training. Carlos Castenada introduced this concept in describing his alleged experiences with the Yaqui sorcerer, Don Juan. The authenticity of Castenada's accounts, however, has been the subject of considerable controversy.[10] In Castenada's third book about his apprenticeship to Don Juan, *Journey to Ixtlan* (1972), he reports being taught to achieve a state of lucid dreaming. Castenada is told to look at his hands in his dreams in order to awaken his consciousness within the dream. Don Juan explains that anything can be used as a device if you have chosen it in advance and seek to find it in your dreams, but the dreamer's hands are convenient "because they'll always be there." He further explained that when his hands begin to change their shape, the dreamer must move his sight away from them, pick something else, and then return to looking at his hands. With the ability to direct awareness toward prechosen objects in his dreams, the dreamer can become "accessible to power." With this power, "you can change things; you may find out countless concealed facts; you can control whatever you want."

Several other popular books also focused attention on lucid dreaming. Patricia Garfield had a chapter on lucid dreams in *Creative Dreaming* (1974). She wrote that the lucid dreamer would have an "unbelievable freedom from all restrictions of body, time, and space":

> When you become lucid you can do *anything* in your dream. You can fly anywhere you wish, experience love-making with the partner of your choice, converse with

friends long dead or people unknown to you; you can see any place in the world you choose, experience all levels of positive emotions, receive answers to questions that plague you, observe creative products, and, in general, use the full resource of the material stored in your mind. *You can learn to become conscious during your dreams.*[11]

In *The Dream Game*, published in 1976, Ann Faraday made this claim for lucid dreams:

This remarkable state of consciousness is in my view one of the most exciting frontiers of human experience. . . . In fact, one of the most thrilling rewards of playing the dream game is that this type of consciousness, with its feeling of "other worldliness," begins to manifest itself much more frequently as self-awareness grows through dream work.[12]

In one of her papers, Faraday described an "extra-ordinary" ecstatic lucid dream of flying and surging through walls and ceilings after an emotional breakthrough.[13]

SENSORY ENHANCEMENT IN LUCID DREAMS

Lucid dreams are often distinguished by the enhanced sensory imagery that appears in them. In the dream I cited, Oliver Fox referred to sea, sky, and trees shining with "glamorous beauty" and even commonplace houses seeming "mystically beautiful." In another colorful lucid dream described by Fox, there was "a culminating vision of a gigantic peacock, whose outspread tail filled the heavens."[14]

In his fifth-century lucid dream, Gennadius heard "a melody so exquisitely sweet as to surpass anything he had ever heard, a hymn of the blessed and holy." Celestial music is still experienced by twentieth-century lucid dreamers, but in the case of Stephen LaBerge he was himself the source of the hymn. After recognizing he was lucid, he decided to seek "The Highest" within him. After flying high in the clouds and noticing various religious symbols, he rose still higher and encountered a mystical realm full of love. He described what next transpired:

My mood had lifted to corresponding heights, and I began to sing with ecstatic inspiration. The quality of my voice was truly amazing—it spanned the entire range from deepest bass to highest soprano—and I felt as if I were embracing the entire cosmos in the resonance of my voice. As I improvised a melody that seemed more sublime than any I had heard before, the meaning of my song revealed itself and I sang the words, "I praise Thee, Oh Lord!"[15]

Changes in kinesthetic sensations are common in lucid dreams, and exhilarating flying dreams are often recounted. These aerial journeys are described as blissful, but sometimes bliss can be associated with more down-to-earth activities. After Patricia Garfield learned to become lucid in her dreams, "I began experiencing dream orgasms of profound intensity. . . . I found myself bursting into soul- and body-shaking explosions."[16]

The vividness and intensity of the visual and auditory images suggest a heightened awareness of the external environment in lucid dreams. Awareness of self also seems to be heightened. If dreaming is considered to be an altered state of consciousness, then lucid dreams can be considered an altered state of dreaming.

But even if thousands of lucid dreamers were to solemnly swear that they were telling the truth, the whole truth, and nothing but the truth, skeptical scientists would insist on more proof. Verbal testimonials from dreamers simply constitute hearsay, which is not accepted as evidence. For the white-coated doubting Thomases, ink tracings of sleeping EEG activity on polygraph paper during a "conscious" lucid dream would be needed before they would begin to consider them as legitimate.

LABORATORY STUDIES OF LUCID DREAMING

The task posed for advocates who accepted the reality of lucid dreams was to devise some technique whereby a lucid dreamer could signal to the observing scientist that he or she was experiencing lucidity. Since the hallmark of dreaming was considered to be the presence of rapid eye movements, the prolucid researchers decided to use the presence of REM to their advantage. They reasoned that if the sleeping subject could develop conscious awareness in a dream, he or she could then make very specific voluntary movements of the eyes which would be distinguishable from the involuntary eye movements found in an ordinary REM period. The stage was then set to see if this stratagem would work.

On April 12, 1975, Alan Worsley, a longtime British lucid dreamer (he had discovered he could wake himself from frightening dreams at age five by shouting "Mother!") had the usual REM monitoring equipment attached to him by Keith Hearne, a fellow graduate student interested in parapsychology. They were utilizing a sleep lab at Hull University in England, and Worsley had been instructed to move his eyes from left to right a certain number of times if he became aware that he was experiencing a lucid dream. Later that night, Worsley experienced a lucid dream, remembered the signal he was to give, and made the specified eye movements. The EEG pen tracings, an objective record of Worsley's physiological activity, indicated both that he was fully asleep in a REM period and that he gave the prearranged ocular signal. Worsley was awakened and reported an unmistakable lucid dream. Hearne delayed publishing his results, apparently because he wished to obtain more substantial documentation and to seek financial support for his work.

Unaware of Hearne's work, Stephen LaBerge and his colleagues at the Stanford University Sleep Lab conducted essentially the same experiment two years later, with LaBerge serving as the lucid dreamer. LaBerge also succeeded in making the required ocular signals during REM sleep. Objective laboratory evidence had now been obtained on both sides of the Atlantic to confirm that lucid dreams did, indeed, exist.

LaBerge was able to recruit several other lucid dreamers, who were also able to produce prearranged ocular signals during REM periods and to describe mental events that corresponded to the experience of a lucid dream. These early experiments were part of LaBerge's doctoral dissertation. He described his results in a paper he sent to the prestigious journal *Science* in 1980. One of the anonymous reviewers thought it was an excellent report that succeeded in validating lucid dreaming under laboratory conditions, and gave it his highest recommendation for publication. The other reviewer, however, found it "difficult to imagine subjects simultaneously both dreaming their dreams and signaling them to others" and therefore recommended that the paper be rejected. The editors decided in favor of the latter opinion.

In June 1981, LaBerge presented four papers on lucid dreaming at the annual Association for the Psychophysiological Study of Sleep meeting in Hyannis Port, Massachusetts. I had been selected by the meeting organizers to serve as the official discussant for LaBerge's papers. I found his experimental designs carefully conceived and the data from his interrelated studies very impressive. In my remarks to the assembled sleep researchers, I shared these views and said that the only reasonable conclusion was that a firm case had been made for the existence of lucid dreaming under controlled laboratory conditions. The audience members also seemed to be impressed. LaBerge was very pleased by my comments and those from the audience. He wrote, "After all the resistance we had encountered, I was at first surprised and then gratified to observe the positive response my presentations received."[17] A new frontier of research on consciousness in sleep had arrived. Other labs, including my own at the University of Virginia Medical School, began to study lucid dreams.

For his dissertation in clinical psychology, Joe Dane, a student of mine, chose to use hypnosis as a technique to induce lucid dreams.[18] His subjects consisted of thirty highly hypnotizable females who were able to recall at least one dream a month but reported that they had not previously experienced a lucid dream. Fifteen of the subjects were hypnotized; the remaining fifteen served as controls. All the subjects received strong verbal encouragement about the possibility of experiencing lucid dreams.

The fifteen subjects who were hypnotized were told that hypnosis would help them connect with the deep level of the unconscious from which dream life originates. They were encouraged to descend, via the image of a descending elevator, to a deeper level of awareness and to identify a personal symbol that would represent lucidity for them. They were told that they would be able to recognize that they were in a lucid state when they saw their personal symbol in their dreams. Dane's level of lucid dream induction for previously nonlucid dreamers is the highest ever reported in a laboratory setting. After only one night in the lab, fourteen of the fifteen hypnotic subjects had experienced at least one lucid dream. Even seven of the control subjects had at least one lucid dream, but their lucid signals and dreams were more likely to occur during non-REM sleep.

It probably should be emphasized that the control subjects were not hypnotized during their night in the laboratory, but previous testing had revealed them to be highly hypnotizable. Dane found that the subjects who had been exposed to the hypnotic instructions had lucid dreams with more intensity, personal relevance, and involvement and that their lucid dreams in the lab tended to last longer than those of subjects in the control group. Perhaps of more relevance, the hypnotic-suggestion group had more lucid dreams at home after their exposure to the laboratory condition. Special placement of electrodes around the eyes enabled Dane's subjects to signal lucidity with eye movements that produced square-topped EOG tracings. The EOGs usually seen during REM periods are rather spiky or jagged. Before they fell asleep, Dane instructed his subjects to practice making a specific pattern of left and right eye movements to insure that they comprehended the instructions and to check that the EOG placement was recording accurately. He told them that when they achieved lucidity in a dream, they should make the same pattern of left and right eye movements to confirm that they had achieved lucidity.

Subjects were told that if they failed to demonstrate this special signal every thirty seconds, they would be awakened for a dream report. Subjects thus had to remember the signal they had learned while awake, and also had to remember to demonstrate it at the onset of lucidity and again at least once every thirty seconds if they wished to continue their lucid dream. In a different study by Dane, involving experienced lucid dreamers, one subject was able to periodically signal that he was lucid for a period of eleven minutes!

TECHNIQUES FOR DEVELOPING LUCIDITY

Joe Dane's results were extremely impressive in terms of the high percentage of subjects who achieved lucidity with only a single night's training. However, these subjects were all highly hypnotizable and all women. Evidence has been marshaled by Jayne Gackenbach that women have a greater "propensity to dream lucidly."[19]

Gackenbach speculates that the "neuroelectrical organization" of the female brain predisposes women to achieve consciousness more easily during dreaming. But even someone not highly hypnotizable or not female can probably achieve lucidity in dreams with sufficient motivation. It has been found that the regular practice of

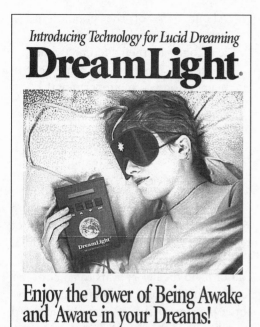

Stephen LaBerge's DreamLight.

meditation, for example, improves one's ability to recall dreams. Not only is recall for dreams in general improved, but Gackenbach and some coworkers have reported that meditators tend to have more lucid dreams.[20] Other benefits are also associated with meditation, such as a reduction in stress, but you might feel that meditation is not your thing. Alternative routes to becoming a lucid dreamer are also available.

Earlier in this chapter, I mentioned that Don Juan told Castenada to focus on his hands while dreaming if he wished to develop "power" in his dreams. This suggestion was followed up in a novel way by Gary Rogers, a student of mine whose dissertation on vaginal vasocongestion during REM periods was described in chapter 10. Simply dreaming of one's hands does not

necessarily guarantee that lucidity will follow. The critical ingredient is establishing a connection between hand awareness in dreams and the "Aha!" recognition of lucidity.

Gary decided to use his hands as a cueing device for achieving awareness of possible lucidity by setting the alarm system on his wrist watch to go off every ninety minutes during the day, the length of time between onset of REM periods. When the alarm sounded, Gary would gaze intently at his hands for a few minutes and ask himself whether he was awake or dreaming while doing so. After two days of constantly making this waking inquiry every ninety minutes, Gary experienced his first lucid dream when he gazed at his dream hands, asked himself whether he was dreaming, and recognized that he was. It seemed that when Gary entered a REM period at home, his "conditioned response" to examine his hands every ninety minutes was unconsciously triggered and he was able to determine that he was dreaming.

LaBerge has developed a method called the MILD technique (Mnemonic Induction of Lucid Dreams). The procedure involves waking up from a dream, visualizing yourself back in that same dream, seeing yourself becoming lucid, and telling yourself, "Next time I'm dreaming, I want to recognize I'm dreaming." LaBerge claims that with practice using his MILD technique, he was able to have lucid dreams on any night he wished.

LaBerge has also developed a mechanical device called the DreamLight. It consists of a Lone Range–style mask that picks up eye movements with an infrared detection device. When a miniature computer counts enough eye movements to determine that a REM period is probably occurring, flashing red lights are turned on within the mask. Awareness of the flashing red lights then acts as a signal to the dreamer that a REM period is occurring, and the dreamer can use that information to achieve lucidity.

The recognition of inconsistency is the most common factor leading to awareness of dreaming. Something strikes the dreamer as so bizarre or implausible to be possible only in a dream. Flying is often mentioned as such a stimulus, since we obviously don't go about like birds in our waking lives. Encountering an extraterrestrial figure or a pink elephant could serve the same purpose if the dreamer took a moment to reflect upon the liklihood of such a creature existing.

Many people achieve lucidity without undertaking any of the training procedures just described. Jayne Gackenbach, on the basis of various surveys she has conducted, makes the following estimate:

About 58% of the population have experienced a lucid dream at least once in their lifetime, while about 21% report it with some frequency (one or more per month). Additionally, 13% of dreams recalled on the morning after and recorded in dream diaries are likely to be lucid.[21]

Lucid dreams are apparently quite common in childhood. In one study of ten-, eleven-, and twelve-year-old children, Deborah Armstrong-Hickey reported, "Recall of lucid dreams appears to go down, at least in this sample, as children age. Sixty-three percent of the 10-year-olds reported monthly lucid dreams, 58% of the 11-year-olds, and 36% of the 12-year-olds."[22] It is unfortunate that our culture doesn't provide more reinforcement for children to develop and expand their capacity for lucid dreaming.

USING LUCID DREAMS THERAPEUTICALLY

Many people have found that they can employ lucid dreams to deal with some troubling conflict. In the hypnotic study that Joe Dane carried out in my laboratory, one of the hypnotic subjects had been experiencing a long-standing recurrent nightmare involving a particular frightening male figure. Following her experience in the laboratory, this figure appeared in several dreams, but each time he did, the dreamer was able to become lucid. The first time he appeared in her dreams at

home, her immediate response was to turn and yell at him to scare him away. She did the same thing the second time he appeared. The third time he appeared, she was gratified to report that her response had been more creative in that she had materialized a bag of "magic darts" to throw at him. Interestingly, once she decided she was ready to experiment with how she encountered this figure, rather than simply scaring him away, he no longer appeared in her dreams. In yet another lucid dream, the same subject was able to enlist a dream figure's help in holding some male attackers at bay until the police could arrive. When the attackers began shooting at her, she materialized a crash helmet for herself and turned their bullets into popcorn balls!

Most clinicians who have worked with lucid dreams would have suggested a different approach to dealing with a menacing dream figure than that used by this woman during her first experience with lucidity. She would be commended for developing the courage and self-confidence to confront this frightening figure, but would be urged to interact with him in order to understand who or what he might represent in her life. To simply banish him, eliminates the possibility of discovering why he kept reappearing and what made him frightening. What inner quality made his external appearance so frightening?

If we adopt a Gestalt viewpoint toward a lucid dream, the various figures we encounter can be conceptualized as components of the dreamer's personality. It would thus be unwise to kill or harm some threatening figure in a lucid dream. To murder a dream character would be to commit a form of intrapsychic suicide. When lucid, the dreamer should engage menacing figures in a dialogue that begins by asking who they are or why they are there in the dream. Such a dialogue can often lead to impressive insights about the role that these split-off parts of our selves play in preventing us from moving on to greater maturity. A character with menacing green eyes might turn out to represent the dreamer's jealousy, or a fire-breathing dragon, the dreamer's hotheadedness.

When such a dialogue succeeds, the previously threatening dream character may get smaller, become more friendly, or disappear.

If initial efforts at dialogue are not productive, the lucid dreamer may choose to fly away from the menacing figure for the time being and try again in a later dream. The dreamer might also ask another dream figure for assistance, as Joe Dane's subject did when she enlisted the assistance of a dream figure to help hold her male attackers at bay. If the events of the dream become too overwhelming or accelerate at an uncomfortable speed, the lucid dreamer is also able to "put on the brakes" by voluntarily waking up. One technique to facilitate waking from a lucid dream is to stare fixedly at any single object for a few seconds.

When, in a lucid dream, an unacceptable and previously invisible aspect of one's personality is externalized as a recognizable character that one can confront consciously, exciting opportunities for self-examination and eventual integration open up. As the old walls separating our inner subsystems come tumbling down, our living chambers are greatly expanded and previously dissociated energy sources can contribute to further growth.

Some dreamers have applied lucidity to overcoming phobias. One man who was very fearful of heights used his lucid dreams of flying to gradually rise higher and higher. As he became able to ascend further in his dreams without discomfort, his waking apprehension gradually decreased. A woman with a long-term fear of bugs decided in a lucid dream to shrink herself to such a degree that cockroaches seemed ten feet tall. She felt safe because she knew she could retain control in her dream. She looked at a cockroach close up and "we had a nice talk." The dreamer next "dreamt myself into being a bug so I could see what it was like. . . . I looked at this bug and saw him the way that other bugs must see him."[23] The dreamer reported that when she woke up she wasn't afraid of bugs anymore and could pick one up if she had to.

Taking on the identity of another dream character to view the situation from the perspective of that character has been advocated as a helpful approach to some problems by Paul Tholey, a West German psychologist who began studying lucid dreaming in 1959. He has provided some fascinating accounts of the types of interactions that can occur between characters in a lucid dream. One can create new dream characters while lucid; when dreamers are angry or afraid, for example, they can blow out the anger or fear through their mouths and thereby create a dream character that corresponds to the emotion.

Tholey has proposed that a higher form of lucidity is attained when all the dream characters display lucidity. The usual progression is that the dreamer's dream ego becomes lucid first and the other dream figures attain lucidity as the dream progresses. If the dream ego is able to convince the other characters that they are in a dream, a deeper level of communication between the dream characters is established. He describes an interesting dream in which this usual sequence was reversed; another dream figure became lucid and persuaded the dream ego that she too was lucid.

In his example, the dreamer had forced herself through a gray and slimy mass.[24] It was unpleasant but she felt it was necessary if she was to advance further. In a brightly lit place in the midst of the slime, the dreamer recognized Mr. Spock from the television series *Star Trek*. Mr. Spock told the dreamer that she shouldn't worry about what happened because she was dreaming. The dreamer didn't believe him and asked about the gray, slimy mass through which she had just passed. He replied that the dreamer had just passed through her own brain or mind. The dreamer was skeptical. Mr. Spock told her that he would jump up and remain suspended in midair to prove to her that they were part of a dream. When he successfully remained suspended, the dreamer finally became convinced that she was dreaming. Her newfound mentor continued to show and tell the dreamer many incredible things and eventually explained "the meaning of my path in a very plausible manner." In his comments on this dream, Tholey suggests that "the dream character of Mr. Spock may be characterized as standing for the so-called internal self-helper (ISH) who gives important advice to the dreamer for her dream and daily lives."[25]

The concept of an ISH is a familiar one to most therapists who work with patients experiencing multiple-personality disorder (MPD). The ISH typically knows the age, gender, and emotional characteristics of each alternate personality as well as the nature of the interrelationships among them. Many MPD therapists value the almost omniscient knowledge an ISH seems to possess and welcome them into the role of cotherapist in the quest for eventual integration. One experienced MPD therapist prefers the term "Center" and speculates that the knowledge and abilities displayed by a Center transcend normal human limitations.[26] The names taken by ISHs or Centers often have a spiritual association, such as "Angela," "Grace," or "Faith." In one MPD patient that I worked with, the Center took the name of "Katherine," which was this patient's Catholic confirmation name. During my contact with Katherine, I witnessed more paranormal phenomena in a few weeks than I had during a thirty-year professional career in parapsychology, and the phenomena were much clearer and stronger than what I was accustomed to observing in a parapsychology laboratory. I therefore found Tholey's comments concerning ISHs to be of great interest, since he apparently based his statements on his research into lucid dreams and not on any contact with MPD patients. Katherine once told me that it was possible for a Center to create helpful or healing dreams and that many more dreams originated from this source than our contemporary society ever suspected. In discussing "this important component of lucid dreaming," Tholey made the following observations:

> One often finds an ISH at a place which is difficult to reach and which can be brightly lit (as in the example with Mr. Spock), or which is situated high up. There are examples in which one has to climb to the top of a mountain where one meets an ISH who calls

himself a monk, a guru, or possibly a psychotherapist. Others pass themselves off as guardian angels or helpful ghosts.[27]

Tholey's work indicates that considerable interaction between various internal dream characters can take place in a lucid dream. Is it possible that interactions between different individuals can take place in lucid dreams? In Celia Green's book *Lucid Dreams*, this British parapsychologist describes a case in which a mother was experiencing a lucid dream and tried to communicate with her son. She felt contact had been made and told him, "I can't stay long; I am feeling muzzy." When she met her son the next day for lunch, he repeated the words to her before she brought the topic up and said he heard them in a lucid dream. Green said the woman's son confirmed this story.[28]

Green also cites another example from Oliver Fox. Fox had been spending the evening with two friends, Slade and Elkington. After a discussion on dreams, they agreed to meet at Southampton Common in their dreams that night. Fox dreamed he met Elkington there that night, but Slade was absent. He and Elkington greeted each other in the dream and commented on Slade's absence. When Fox saw Elkington the next day, he asked him if he had dreamed. Elkington replied that in a dream he had met and greeted Fox on the Common and that he and Fox had commented on Slade's absence. When Slade was contacted the next day, he indicated that he had not dreamed at all. Fox mentions that he and Elkington were unable to repeat this small success.

ARE THERE RISKS ASSOCIATED WITH LUCID DREAMING?

Everything I have said so far suggests that lucid dreams can have incredible power, and we all know that power can be abused. In the case of lucid dreaming, it is not others who would be negatively affected; misuse of the power would be a form of self-abuse. What cautions should be exercised by individuals wishing to develop their lucid dreaming skills?

Just as we shouldn't attempt to break records running before we have fully mastered walking, we need to be careful about embarking on too ambitious a program of self-growth or development before we have decided on a direction and the goals to be attained. One of Joe Dane's subjects found herself frustrated because she couldn't control the rain in her dream. She then found herself in a train station, but the characters there ignored her when she asked when the next train left. She finally encountered a character who told her, "Well, that depends on where you want to go." An alternative answer, incorporating a pun on the dream imagery, might have been, "What do you want to train for?" This dreamer was overemphasizing "getting somewhere" before she had determined where she was or where she might want to go. As a consequence, she was frustrated and going nowhere. She was also frustrated because she couldn't change the weather, but that's as inappropriate a goal in dreams as in waking life: major disappointments can be expected. A more reasonable goal would be to learn to adapt successfully to the weather, to react more creatively. Perhaps, in the rain, she could have summoned a figure like Gene Kelly to go singing and dancing with her.

Jung proposed that the unconscious moves in the direction of individuation and transcendence, but such development requires a long gestation. Movement doesn't occur in a linear fashion; high tide is reached only after many waves advance and recede. The wisdom of the unconscious has its own way of modulating or regulating the intensity of experiences that it might be expected to absorb at any given time. Sometimes the unconscious simply refuses to cooperate with conscious requests it judges to be against the subject's self-interest or moral codes. A hypnotized subject, for example, will not carry out instructions to murder or rob if such activities would not be acceptable in waking life. Here is a dramatic example of the unconscious failing to honor a dreamer's wishes:

> As in many previous dreams, Harry, the dreamer, is cornered on a beach with no way to turn, menaced by awesome forces. As in many previous dreams, in this one, Harry begins to shout, "Harry, Harry, remember Harry, this is only a dream." This device had worked in previous nightmares, awakening the sleeper. In this

dream, however, a great, booming voice roared back at him, "The hell it is, Harry. The hell it is." The dreamer subsequently awakened, terrified.[29]

There seems to be a strong consensus among experienced lucid dreamers that the term "dream control" is not really very accurate, because the conscious mind cannot actually control the unconscious mind. In Jeremy Taylor's words:

The dream remains autonomous and is *not* under the *control* of, or at the disposal of, the conscious will. The archetypal elements that are the foundation of the dream are so much older, so much wiser, and so much stronger and more subtle than even the most disciplined, habitual lucid consciousness that "control" of the dream state is simply impossible. At best—and it is pretty good!—all that lucidly dreaming ego consciousness can do is increase conscious *influence* in the dream.[30]

Ken Kelzer expressed a similar view: "The lucid dreamer, at best, is able to *take charge of* his personal experience within the dream but is not actually able to *control* the dreamscape itself to any great extent."[31]

Too frequent journeys into lucidity may have troubling side effects for individuals who are not "well grounded" in other areas of their life. Since the usual distinctions between wakefulness and dreaming are obliterated during lucidity, such individuals have reported that frequent experiences with lucidity were leading to confusion, because they couldn't reliably recognize what state they were in during their waking hours. Good mental balance is required to insure that the boundaries between conscious/unconscious, waking/sleeping, and lucid/nonlucid states do not become too fuzzy. In a series of studies, Jayne Gackenbach has actually found that successful lucid dreamers display greater ability on tasks involving physical balancing skills.[32] There appears to be an important interrelationship between emotional, cognitive, and physical balance.

LIGHT AND SPIRITUALITY IN LUCID DREAMS

Light is often associated with the divine. We metaphorically locate heaven, the habitat of divine personages, high in the sky, a region from which we expect light to steadily emanate. During the day, we expect sunlight, and during the night, moonlight. Divine figures are described as suffused in radiant light, and artists paint halos around the heads of holy people and angels to indicate that the light dwelling within them is so powerful it can be seen externally.

People reporting near-death experiences (NDEs) customarily have some kind of encounter with light. Raymond Moody, a former colleague in my department at the University of Virginia, has compiled information from hundreds of individuals

In transcendent, lucid dreams, the dreamer often experiences bright light, the sensation of floating or flying, and encounters spiritual beings. *Queen Katharine's Dream* by William Blake. *(National Gallery of Art, Washington D.C., Rosenwald Collection)*

who have undergone near-death experiences and described those findings in his book *Life after Life*. After the sensation of leaving their body and viewing it from above, these individuals move on and recognize "the spirits of relatives and friends who have already died, and a loving warm spirit of a kind . . . never encountered before—a being of light—appears before him."[33] Other NDE researchers, such as psychologist Kenneth Ring, have also described the unfolding of various stages during this experience. Of relevance here is the description of the last two: "The hallmark of the fourth stage is a brilliant light of exceptional beauty; and the last stage is one in which the subject experiences himself as 'entering the light.' "[34]

A linkage between near-death experiences and lucidity experiences has been suggested by several researchers. Jayne Gackenbach reports, for example, "Two studies have found that people who have NDEs are more likely to experience dream lucidity."[35]

When light appears in a lucid dream the dreamer typically reports some form of transcendent experience, and the feelings associated with its presence are usually labeled as extremely joyful, exhilarating, and sometimes transforming. The appearance of light in a lucid dream seems to be associated with an evolution of consciousness or awareness to a very high level.

In a lucid dream reported by Oliver Fox, the presence of light symbolized the evolution of humankind and civilization. He described the sudden appearance of "a roadway of golden light stretching from earth to zenith," and in this shining haze appeared "countless coloured forms of men and beasts, representing man's upward evolution through different stages of civilization."[36] For Patricia Garfield, the presence of light represents the evolution of her own personal growth. She draws an analogy between the necessity of sunlight for tree branches to grow and the importance of an inner light to personal growth. In her autobiographical *Pathway to Ecstasy*, she extends her tree analogy:

> Our psychic growth . . . is recorded . . . in the pattern of past dreams. We can trace it well, observe old wounds, follow the circuitous routes of passage we have taken until now. We, too, reach toward sunlight to nourish our growth. If our world is too crowded, if the dark is too solid, we end up stunted and shriveled. We, too, must have light to survive. Only, for us, the life-giving light is internal as well as external.
>
> I have watched with wonder this inner light emerging through the twisting evolution of my own dreams. . . .
>
> . . . For some three years I had noticed that my lucid dreams would often contain imagery of light. Now, this is not simply the general change in quality—the brightening of images or the translucency of colors—but also there is a specific *source* of light. . . . The light often takes the form of a line or a crack, such as illumination gleaming from underneath a closed door or shining through a space like a window. . . . Often the

light I notice in lucid dreams seems to reflect from the sparkles of moon-light or sunlight upon the waves of ocean or river, or from the moon itself.[37]

Other experienced lucid dreamers have come to associate luminescence with an increase in mystical feelings or a union with the divine. Scott Sparrow, a psychologist in Virginia Beach associated with the Association for Research and Enlightenment, recounts many personal examples of dreams with luminescence in *Lucid Dreaming: Dawning of the Clear Light*. He describes how his lucid dreams have evolved toward a closer relationship to what he calls the "inner Light." Sparrow suggests that the aim of lucid dreaming is to seek and become one with the light, which to him represents "the Divine." The association between light and the divine is made clear in this passage:

> This experience of light and energy seems to be universally recognized in the literature on meditation and contemplative prayer as actual communion between the individual and the Divine. Whether or not this is an *objective* truth, its ubiquitous occurrence lends credence to its essential importance.[38]

The process of surrender facilitates Sparrow's experience with the inner light:

> This stage of the lucid dream during which the dreamer may enter an illuminated state is referred to in the Tibetan text as the "Dawning of the Clear Light." It is a stage in which the dreamer turns his attention to the Source motivating the dream images. . . .
>
> . . . Yet as the Light becomes visible, the dreamer realizes that the independence and the interests of self must be relinquished if the Light is to approach and to become an inner experience. The pre-eminent demand placed upon the dreamer as he stands at this threshold is to *surrender*.
>
> . . . The concept of surrender becomes the key to inner illumination *and* creative expression in the world.[39]

George Gillespie, a minister and Sanskrit scholar, has written a useful review of light in lucid dreams.[40] In discussing various categories of light in his lucid dreams, he concludes that the category he labels "fullness of light" is, in at least some respects, comparable to the Tibetan account of the clear light. He describes his efforts to understand the significance of his luminescent dreams:

> It did not occur to me at first, during waking analysis, to consider the God of my lucid dream experiences to be the God I pray to and worship when awake. But I did eventually accept on faith that the experiences of the fullness of light

were what they seemed to be—experiences of the God who transcends body, mind, dream imagery, dreamless sleep imagery, unconscious processes and God archetype.[41]

Fariba Bogzaran, a transpersonal psychologist in California, was aware that she had experienced numerous lucid dreams following incubation tasks centered around wanting to be in the presence of the "Great Spirit." She found she experienced the divine differently in each lucid dream and her curiosity as to how other people experienced it in their lucid dreams evolved into her master's thesis. Thirty-five subjects participated in her project. Bogzaran developed a questionnaire to un-

cover the lucid dreamer's concepts of the divine and their experience of the divine in their lucid dreams. These concepts were categorized as either personalized, such as encountering a figure like Christ or Buddha, or impersonalized, when the divine was considered to be all-encompassing, energy, formless, and so on. She found that 83 percent of the subjects who believed in the divine as a person encountered a personalized divine presence in their lucid dreams, while 87 percent of the subjects who believed in an impersonal divine experienced the divine in forms other than a person in their lucid dreams. Bogzaran's results definitely indicate that one's preconceptions or expectations have a strong influence upon the form in which the divine will appear to the lucid dreamer.[42]

SOME FINAL WORDS ON LUCIDITY

It is difficult to summarize such a complex topic as dream lucidity. When Joe Dane and I developed a questionnaire to discriminate potentially successful lucid dreamers from nonlucid dreamers, we found that subjects with a spirit of adventure, who wished to explore the unknown and had a rich curiosity about the ranges of human experiences, were excellent candidates for lucidity and also tended to be good hypnotic subjects. Perhaps you can decide from this brief description whether an adventure into lucidity would appeal to you or would leave you rather indifferent. The choice is obviously yours, but before turning away from lucid dreaming, you might

want to consider what Ken Kelzer has claimed are its benefits:

Lucid dreaming can provide people with a natural experience of ecstasy. In this context I refer to the experience as "natural" because it is not induced by drugs or chemicals of any kind. Rather, lucid dreaming seems to be induced primarily by a particular combination of emotional readiness and willingness to enter the lucid state. The ecstasy that I refer to seems to run the whole gamut of human possibilities, from intense sensual delights, indescribable orgasms and pleasures, to peak-spiritual experiences and everything that people can possibly imagine.

. . . I have come to appreciate more clearly that human beings need ecstasy in one form or another. . . . Without ecstasy the human ego, both individually and collectively, soon becomes bound and limited within some ordinary set of experiences that ultimately proves to be too confining.[43]

In closing this chapter, I would like to leave the reader with an insightful comment from Richard Bach: "There was always light shining in the darkness for those who dared to open their eyes at night."

AFTERWORD

I magine a group of long-haired people, clad in furs and wearing necklaces of animal teeth, huddled about a fire with a star-filled sky overhead. An old man is getting ready to speak and the others look intently toward him because they know his knowledge is vast and his counsel can be trusted. This ancient teacher and storyteller, the custodian of the tribe's oral history, says:

Tonight, I, Netsua, will tell you how dreams came to our great-great-grandfathers and grandmothers who lived before the great-great-grandfathers and grandmothers we remember. In the beginning, Wosun, the maker of all things, gave to some of his children fins; to others he gave feathers; and to those with four legs he gave fur. Wosun gave the gift of two eyes to all his children, those who swam in the water, flew in the sky, or walked upon the land.

When Wosun gave eyes to his children, he made it possible for our brothers, the animals, to see far away things clearly if Yonti, the sun, or Weemu, the moon, were above. But for the two-leggeds, it was different. When Weemu, the moon, came out of her cave at night, the two-leggeds could not see things that were far away like the owl could. But Wosun wanted his people to know that he had not forsaken them, for he loved them very much, so he gave the two-leggeds the most special gift of all—the gift of being able to see clearly with their eyes closed.

When the dark blanket of night lay heavily upon them, Wosun would appear to the two-leggeds and instruct them about everything they needed to know. In dreams, he taught them how to make weapons and hunt for food, showed them new tools, told them which medicines to use when they were sick, announced who should be their chiefs, and gave them warnings when danger approached. He brought other two-leggeds with him, so that the dreamer could enjoy being with his family and other companions. But he also sometimes brought evil two-leggeds with him, so that the dreamer might be reminded to beware of them when he awoke.

To further show his love for the two-leggeds, Wosun gave them tongues so that they could tell each other about what they had seen at night. And that is how I, Netsua, the eldest elder of the tribe, can tell you about the special gift of clear-seeing at night that Wosun gave to his people. Remember what I have told you and teach your children and your children's children to be always grateful for the way Wosun's light shines within his people at night.

I feel a strong bonding with the mythical figure of Netsua. I know as he circled among the members of his tribe around the campfire on other nights, he would tell them about dreams their ancestors had recounted, remind them of dreams that had led to different ways of doing things for the tribe, and repeat what he had heard from the elders of the various clans about their views on dreams. His hope would be that by presenting all the knowledge he had accumulated about dreams from his own experiences and the information he had learned from others regarding their beliefs and discoveries, his people would come to appreciate more deeply, and use more frequently, the gift of "clear-seeing at night" that had been given to them by Wosun.

As a modern-day stand-in for Netsua, I have attempted in this book to repeat and update the material that he shared during his many nocturnal talks about dreams. In this book, the dreams of our ancestors have been honored and the dreams that have influenced so many aspects of our culture have been cited. The views of the Freudian, Jungian, and other clan leaders have been described.

I have also gone into considerable detail about how twentieth-century scientists have learned to measure the physiological factors which may accompany dreams and the ways in which the content of dreams may be associated with different lifestyles, social experiences, and emotional traumas. In the last section of the book, the "twilight zone" of dreams has been explored. What seem to be new areas of "discovery"— prodromal, telepathic or paranormal, and lucid dreams—are looked at in terms of the scientific evidence confirming their validity. I suspect that Netsua and his tribal members already were strongly convinced of their validity, because they believed firmly in their dreams and acted upon the messages received in them.

Netsua's followers knew that when their bodies were not functioning properly, they had disturbing symbols in their dreams, such as fires or bloody organs, which alerted them to their imbalanced physical condition. When family members discussed their dreams in the morning, they often discovered they had shared the same unusual dreams or that their dreams informed them about events taking place at considerable distances, such as when a relative had died. And they had dreams in which they flew, found themselves standing triumphantly on brightly lit mountain tops, or encountered Wosun or radiant beings of light, who seemed very powerful and knowledgeable and silently communicated unconditional love to the dreamer.

It may be hard for some contemporary citizens of our twentieth century, surrounded by metal skyscrapers, concrete highways, and asphalt parking lots to relate to the image of Netsua clad in animal skins. But his message is timeless and of critical importance. Our response should not depend upon whether he strikes us as sartorially correct.

Scientists in white laboratory coats have estimated that in a normal life span we will each experience a hundred thousand dreams. We individually and collectively need those dreams now, more than ever, if we are to cope successfully with the many complicated problems facing us in the twenty-first century. Jeremy Taylor, a minister whose examples of recurrent dreams were discussed in chapter 12 and who has seen the power of dream work in churches, hospitals, and prisons, has made an eloquent plea for our generation to utilize the creative power of dreams for improving the course of our future history:

The problems we face in the twentieth century may appear initially to be different from the problems of previous generations, but honest examination reveals that they are simply the age-old problems ... magnified to world-shattering proportions by the increasing power and efficiency of our contemporary technology and social organization. ... We can no longer escape the knowledge that interior lives and our external circumstances reflect each other—that planetary ecology and psychology are inextricably intertwined, and that the solutions to our personal and collective dilemmas must be sought simultaneously. Throughout our history as a species the dream has been a primary vehicle for the evolution and unfolding of human consciousness and increasing self-awareness. In the contemporary struggle to evolve ourselves, in this "race between education and disaster," as Bertrand Russell called it, we can no longer afford to ignore the creative potential inherent in each individual—a potential embodied in our dreams, and released consciously when we remember and work with our dreams.[1]

We can all use those hundred thousand priceless, but free, opportunities for "clear-seeing at night" to encounter ourselves at a deeper level, to comprehend better our social interactions with others, and to explore humankind's relation to transpersonal sources of energy. Dreams can serve to dispel the lonely illusion of separateness we maintain during waking hours and reveal the many levels of interconnectedness which exist between us. These benefits can be reaped by starting to share our dreams with each other and learning to develop a greater appreciation of the power of our dreaming mind.

DREAM RESOURCES

T he Association for the Study of Dreams is a nonprofit international organization promoting an awareness and appreciation of dreams in both professional and public arenas. Any appreciator of dreams is welcome to join. ASD sponsors an annual summer convention, at which a wide range of papers bearing upon dreams is presented. Also available at the convention are a large number of workshops devoted to learning techniques for working with dreams. Members receive a quarterly newsletter and a quarterly professional journal, *Dreaming*. Also available are brochures on such topics as how to start a dream group. For further information write to ASD, P.O. Box 1600, Vienna, Virginia 22183.

Dream Network is a quarterly journal exploring dreams and myth. Its goal is "to demystify dream work and to integrate dream-sharing into our lives for the enhancement of our culture." Information about ongoing dream groups is provided.

Write to Dream Network, 1137 Power-house Lane, Suite 22, Moab, Utah 84532.

Night Visions is a quarterly publication whose purpose "is to delve behind the images of our dreams and to seek that reality which they represent." A dream topic, such as lucidity, healing, or mystical experiences in dreams, is featured in each issue. For further information, write to Night Vision, P.O. Box 402, Questa, New Mexico 87556.

Lucidity (formerly *Lucidity Letter*) is an annual publication of the Lucidity Association containing research and clinical articles as well as personal experiences dealing with lucid dreams. Write to Lucidity, 8703 109th Street, Edmonton, Alberta, T6G 2L5 Canada.

The Lucidity Institute is an organization directed by Stephen LaBerge. It offers a newsletter, *Night Light*; lectures; workshops; and correspondence courses dealing with lucidity. Write to Lucidity Institute, 2555 Park Boulevard #2, Palo Alto, California 94306.

WORKING WITH YOUR OWN DREAMS

D reams are a powerful alternative state of consciousness that gives us access to realms of being and imagination available in no other way. If we fail to integrate them into our lives, we are neglecting what may be our most potent natural resource for personal and collective change. And the amazing thing is that the benefits are free! They don't cost a penny and you don't have to pay any taxes on them. To gain access to them, you don't have to exert any physical energy, as you would for an aerobics class, your forehead will never glisten with a single drop of perspiration, your joints will never ache from assuming some uncomfortable yoga posture, and you won't require any special workout clothing—just your nightie, pj's, or birthday suit. The only mental energy required is that of paying attention to the dreams that are given to you, repeatedly throughout each and every night, and being willing to consider the possible messages they convey. Right now, even as you read this, the director, producer, casting manager, and writers are hard at work creating the late-night show that will be staged for you, exclusively, tonight. Are you willing to take some notes on tonight's show to remind you about the fascinating scenarios your staff comes up with?

You can start your preparation today by finding a suitable notebook or diary to record those dreams tomorrow morning. Place it on your nightstand or under your pillow tonight when you retire. After getting into bed, review what sort of day you had and pay particular attention to any unresolved emotions that stirred you up. In what ways could it have been a better day? After completing this review, relax as fully as possible and earnestly petition your inner source of dream enlightenment to provide you with dreams tonight—dreams that will highlight the nature of your current concerns, help you to understand better their origins, and show you possible ways to diminish their negative impact and to move toward greater personal satisfaction and fulfillment.

When you wake up during the night or in the morning, don't open your eyes immediately. Lie very still and try gently to recall any imagery that may have been present as you awoke. Were you in some building or unusual location? Was anyone else present? Did you notice something unusual in your surroundings? Were you or another character engaged in some activity? Did you awaken with a strongly felt emotion? If you can recall any specific image (D), try to reconnect it with whatever event or activity preceded it (C), and what preceded that (B), and what preceded that (A), tracing it back as far as you are able. Once you have re-created these DCBA

sequences of events or images, rehearse them a few times before opening your eyes and recording the dream in its ABCD order. Describe the dream as fully as you can without crossing out any words. How you wrote it initially may have some significance when you later try and understand it. When you have time, read through the dream with the goal of extracting its main theme or essence and coming up with a title or headline that represents its story. Examples might be: Too Many Weeds in My Garden; The Garbage in the Living Room; or Frightened by an Obese Stranger.

As you read it over, look for similarities in details between what happened in your dream and in your waking life. Were things in your dream distorted? Was the bedroom smaller and more confining, the boss changed in physical stature, some character's behavior more appealing or more repulsive? If you encountered a character in your dream that you haven't seen or spoken to for many years, try to enumerate in your mind the most outstanding qualities you associated with that person: arrogance, generosity, self-indulgence, violent temper, or whatever you recall. This character's presence in your dream suggests that you were dealing with those qualities in some way the preceding day.

Take any puzzling images in your dreams and use the techniques of free association (Freud), amplification (Jung), or dialoguing (Gestalt) to extend your understanding of its significance. Go over Gendlin's sixteen questions (chapter 8) to flesh out the structure of your dream. If your dream has a compelling emotional quality to it, it may be helpful to represent it graphically through sketches with colored pencils or crayons, or through assembling a collage of pictures cut from magazines.

Many other creative ways of exploring your dreams, such as inspirational writing or poetry projects, can be found in Henry Reed's *Getting Help From Your Dreams*.[1] For those wishing a deeper immersion into their dream life, Henry has also published *Dream Solutions*, arranged in diary form and containing detailed exercises to be completed each week for a month.[2] This book was specifically designed and tested to be able to help people interpret their dreams for the purpose of creative problem solving.

As you begin to experience the personal rewards of your dream explorations, your dream journal will achieve a special place in your life. Honor its importance by creating personalized art work for its cover and adding meaningful poetry selections to its pages. Review your journal at regular intervals to note how your life patterns are changing and to discover any overlooked precognitive dreams. Good journeying!

For readers interested in receiving consultation about their dreams through the mail, the author will provide a thirty-minute audiotape commentary on two dreams for a reasonable fee. Write for a brochure to: Dreams, P.O. Box 3048, University Station, Charlottesville, Virginia 22903.

NOTES

PREFACE

1. E. Aserinsky and N. Kleitman, "Regularly Occurring Periods of Eye Motility, and Concomitant Phenomena During Sleep," *Science* 118 (1953):273–74.

2. C. Hall, *The Meaning of Dreams* (New York: Harper and Row, 1953).

3. C. Hall and R. Van de Castle, *The Content Analysis of Dreams* (New York: Appleton-Century-Croft, 1966).

4. R. Van de Castle, "Animal Figures in Fantasy and Dreams," in *New Perspectives on our Lives with Companion Animals*, ed. A Katcher and A. Beck (Philadelphia: University of Pennsylvania Press, 1983), 148–73.

5. R. Van de Castle, "Psi Abilities in Primitive Groups," in *Surveys in Parapsychology: Review of the Literature With Updated Bibliographies*, ed. R. White (Metuchen, N.J.: Scarecrow Press, 1976).

6. R. Van de Castle, "An Investigation of Psi Abilities Among the Cuna Indians of Panama," in *Parapsychology and Anthropology: Proceedings of an International Conference*, ed. A. Angoff and D. Barth, 80–97 (New York: Parapsychology Foundation, 1974).

7. R. Van de Castle, "Dreams and Menstruation," *Psychology* 4 (1968):374–75.

8. R. Van de Castle and P. Kinder, "Dream Content During Pregnancy," *Psychophysiology* 4 (1968):375.

9. E. Stukane, *The Dream Worlds of Pregnancy* (New York: William Morrow, 1985).

10. R. Van de Castle and T. Smith, "Dream Content and Body Build," *Sleep Research* 1 (1972):115.

11. I. Stevenson, *Twenty Cases Suggestive of*

Reincarnation, 2d ed. (Charlottesville: University Press of Virginia, 1974); Cases of the Reincarnation Type, vol. 1, Ten Cases in India (Charlottesville: University Press of Virginia, 1975).

12. C. Hall, "Experimente Zur Telepathischen Beeinflussung von Traumen" [Experiments on Telepathically Influenced Dreams], Zeitschrift fur Parapsychologie und Grenzgebeite der Psychologie 10 (1967):18–47.

13. M. Ullman, S. Krippner, and A. Vaughan, Dream Telepathy (New York: Macmillan, 1973) and Dream Telepathy: Explorations in Nocturnal ESP, 2d ed. (Jefferson, N.C.: McFarland, 1989).

14. R. Van de Castle, "ESP in Dreams: Comments on a Replication 'Failure' by the Failing Subject," in Dream Telepathy: Explorations in Nocturnal ESP, ed. M. Ullman, S. Krippner, and A. Vaughan, 2d ed. (Jefferson, N.C.: McFarland, 1989).

15. H. Reed, "Sundance: Inspirational Dreaming in Community," in Extrasensory Ecology: Parapsychology and Anthropology, ed. J. Long, 155–87 (Metuchen, N.J.: Scarecrow Press, 1977); "Dreaming for Mary," in Getting Help From Your Dreams (New York: Ballantine, 1989).

Chapter 1

1. L. Yutang, The Wisdom of Laotse (New York: Random House, 1948).

2. G. Bullett, "The Other 'I,' " in The World of Dreams, ed. R. L. Woods (New York: Random House, 1947), 920.

3. Ibid., 921.

4. Ibid.

5. B. Inglis, The Power of Dreams (London: Paladin; Grafton, 1987), 6.

6. H. Keller, "The World I Live In," in The World of Dreams, ed. R. L. Woods (New York: Random House, 1947), 26.

7. Ibid., 927.

8. Ibid.

9. Ibid., 930–31.

10. S. Clemens, "Dream Body Lives After Death," in The World of Dreams, ed. R. L. Woods (New York: Random House, 1947), 884–85.

11. B. Inglis, The Power of Dreams (London: Paladin; Grafton, 1987), 17.

12. H. Ellis, The World of Dreams (Boston: Houghton Mifflin, 1911), 280.

13. F. Greenwood, Imagination in Dreams and Their Study (London: Lane, 1894), 94.

14. Ibid., 186–87.

15. H. Ellis, The World of Dreams (Boston: Houghton Mifflin, 1911), 279.

16. Ibid., 186–87.

17. G. Gorer, Africa Dances: A Book About West African Negroes (New York: Knopf, 1935).

18. J. Dunne, An Experiment with Time (New York: Macmillan, 1927).

Chapter 2

1. J. A. Garraty and P. Gay, eds. The Columbia History of the World (New York: Harper and Row, 1972).

2. A. Breton, Manifestoes of Surrealism (Ann Arbor: University of Michigan Press, 1969).

3. K. Kovacs, "José Luis Borau on Movies and Dreams," Dreamworks 2, no. 1 (1981):64.

4. M. Kinder, "The Dialectic of Dreams and Theater in the Films of Ingmar Bergman," Dreamworks 5 (1988):186.

5. C. Saura, "Carlos Saura: A Conversation," Dreamworks 2, no. 1 (1981):62.

6. M. Kinder, "The Art of Dreaming in Three Women and Providence: Structures of the Self," Film Quarterly 31 (1977):10–18.

7. O. Welles, "Conversations With Filmmakers on Dreams," Dreamworks 3, no 1 (1981):56.

8. J. Cocteau, "The Process of Inspiration," in The Creative Process, ed. B. Ghiselin (Berkeley: University of California Press, 1952).

9. W. Archer, On Dreams, ed. T. Besterman (London: Methuen, 1935), 173.

10. B. Inglis, The Power of Dreams (London: Paladin; Grafton, 1987), 15.

11. A Sonnet, *The Twilight Zone of Dreams* (Philadelphia: Chilton, 1961), 129.

12. G. Johnson, "Music in Dreams," in *Dreams Can Point the Way*, ed. V. Bass (Sugar Land, Tex.: Miracle House Books, 1984).

13. A. Sonnet, *The Twilight Zone of Dreams* (Philadelphia: Chilton, 1961), 130.

14. A. Hock, *Reason and Genius* (New York: Academic Press, 1960).

15. J. Morris, *The Dream Workbook* (Boston: Little, Brown, 1985), 126.

16. H. Ellis, *The World of Dreams* (Boston: Houghton Mifflin, 1911), 276–77.

17. B. Inglis, *The Power of Dreams* (London: Paladin; Grafton, 1987) 10.

18. J. Grant, *Dreamers* (Bath: Ashgrove Press, 1984), 82–83.

19. R. Stevenson, "A Chapter on Dreams," in *The World of Dreams*, ed. R. L. Woods (New York: Random House, 1947), 878.

20. Ibid., 872.

21. Ibid., 876–77.

22. Synesius, "Dreams Take the Soul to 'The Superior Region,'" in *The World of Dreams*, ed. R. L. Woods (New York: Random House, 1947), 137.

23. R. Megroz, *The Dream World: A Survey of the History and Mystery of Dreams* (New York: Dutton, 1939), 156.

24. Ibid., 159.

25. J. Howell, "Just Plain Bill," *High Times*, March 1985, 36.

26. R. P. Warren, "To the Editor," *Dreamworks* 2(1981) 128.

27. J. Kerouac, *Book of Dreams* (San Francisco: City Lights Books, 1961).

28. F. Kafka, *Diaries* (New York: Schocken Books, 1965), 2:77.

29. Ibid., 1:73.

30. C. Hall and R. Lind, *Dreams, Life, and Literature: A Study of Franz Kafka* (Chapel Hill: University of North Carolina Press, 1970).

31. B. Inglis, *The Power of Dreams* (London: Paladin; Grafton, 1987), 10.

32. G. Greene, *Ways of Escape* (London, 1982), 210–11.

33. B. Inglis, *The Power of Dreams* (London: Paladin; Grafton, 1987), 11–12.

34. N. Fruman, *Coleridge: The Damaged Archangel* (London: Allen and Unwin, 1972), 335–38, 551–69.

35. J. Masefield, "The Woman Speaks," in *Such Stuff as Dreams*, ed. B. Hill (London: Rupert Hart-Davis, 1967), 168.

36. M. Voltaire, "Somnambulists and Dreamers," in *The World of Dreams*, ed. R. L. Woods (New York: Random House, 1947), 230.

37. J. Goethe, "Conversations of Goethe With Eckerman," in *The World of Dreams*, ed. R. L. Woods (New York: Random House, 1947), 239.

38. B. Hill, *Gates of Horn and Ivory: An Anthology of Dreams* (New York: Taplinger, 1967), 125.

39. R. Jones, "Dream Reflection as Creative Writing," in *The Variety of Dream Experience: Expanding Our Ways of working With Dreams*, ed. M. Ullman and C. Limmer (New York: Continuum, 1987), 155.

40. Ibid., 164–65.

41. A. Van Vogt, "Dreaming and Writing," *Dreamworks* 2 (1981):137.

42. F. Blomefield, "The Swaffham Tinker," in *The World of Dreams*, ed. R. L. Woods (New York: Random House, 1947), 378–80.

43. T. White, "The College," in *Such Stuff as Dreams*, ed. B. Hill (London: Rupert Hart-Davis, 1967), 9–10.

44. S. Bradford, *Harriet Tubman: The Moses of Her People* (Gloucester, Mass.: Peter Smith, 1981).

45. M. Gandhi, *An Autobiography: The Story of My Experiments With Truth* (Boston: Beacon Press, 1957).

46. D. Kearns, *Lyndon Johnson and the American Dream* (New York: Harper and Row, 1976).

47. R. de Becker, *The Understanding of Dreams and Their Influence on the History of Man* (New York: Hawthorn Books, 1968), 78–79.

48. K. Hollenbeck, "Patton: Many Lives, Many Battles," *Venture Inward*, September–October 1989, 5, 12–14.

49. L. Farago, *Patton: Ordeal and Triumph* (New York: Dell, 1965), 254.

50. M. Kelsey, *Dreams: The Dark Speech of

the Spirit (New York: Doubleday, 1968), 124–26.

51. R. de Becker, *The Understanding of Dreams and Their Influence on the History of Man* (New York: Hawthorn Books, 1968), 30–31.

52. Ibid., 76.

53. Ibid., 69.

54. UPI release, August 31, 1975.

55. R. de Becker, *The Understanding of Dreams and Their Influence on the History of Man* (New York: Hawthorn Books, 1968), 50–56.

56. B. Inglis, *The Power of Dreams* (London: Paladin; Grafton, 1987), 52–53.

57. J. D. Hughes, "The Dreams of Alexander the Great," *Journal of Psychohistory* 12 (1984):168–92.

58. R. de Becker, *The Understanding of Dreams and Their Influence on the History of Man* (New York: Hawthorn Books, 1968), 75.

59. Ibid., 62.

60. Ibid.

61. K. Craig, *The Fabric of Dreams* (New York: Dutton, 1918).

62. M. Boss, *The Analysis of Dreams* (New York: Philosophical Library, 1958), 186–87.

63. B. Hill, *Gates of Horn and Ivory: An Anthology of Dreams* (New York: Taplinger, 1967), 21–22.

64. W. Lamon, "Abraham Lincoln's Dream Life," in *The World of Dreams*, ed. R. L. Woods (New York: Random House, 1947), 383–85.

65. *Dreams and Dreaming* (Alexandria, Va.: Time-Life Books, 1990), 137.

66. Ibid.

67. J. Kirsch, *The Reluctant Prophet* (Los Angeles: Sherbourne Press, 1973), 30.

68. Ibid., 54–55.

69. R. de Becker, *The Understanding of Dreams and Their Influence on the History of Man* (New York: Hawthorn Books, 1968), 80.

70. G. Price, *I Knew These Dictators* (London: Harrop, 1937).

71. J. Grant, *Dreamers* (Bath: Ashgrove Press, 1984), 153–54.

72. C. Beradt, *The Third Reich of Dreams* (Chicago: Quadrangle Books, 1968), 52.

73. Ibid.

74. R. de Becker, *The Understanding of Dreams and Their Influence on the History of Man* (New York: Hawthorn Books, 1968), 85.

75. B. Kedrov, "On the Question of Scientific Creativity," *Voprosy Psikologii* 3 (1957): 91–113.

76. *Brain/Mind Bulletin*, July 28, 1986.

77. W. Dement, *Some Must Watch While Some Must Sleep* (San Francisco: W. H. Freeman, 1972).

78. L. Talamonte, *Forbidden Universe* (New York: Stein and Day, 1975).

79. *Brain/Mind Bulletin*, July 28, 1986.

80. W. Dement, *Some Must Watch While Some Must Sleep* (San Francisco: W. H. Freeman, 1972).

81. S. Krippner and W. Hughes, "Dreams and Human Potential," *Journal of Humanistic Psychology* 10 (1970):1–20.

82. M. Fagen, ed. *A History of Engineering and Science in the Bell System: National Service in War and Peace (1925–1975)* (Murry Hill, N.Y.: Bell Telephone Laboratories, 1978).

83. W. Kaempffert, *A Popular History of American Invention*, 2 vols. (New York: Scribners, 1924).

84. B. Hill, *Gates of Horn and Ivory: An Anthology of Dreams* (New York: Taplinger, 1967), 22–23.

85. M. de Manaceine, *Sleep: Its Physiology, Pathology, Hygiene, and Psychology* (New York: Charles Scribner's, 1897), 314–15.

86. W. Newbold, "Sub-Conscious Reasoning," *Proceedings of the Society for Psychical Research* 12 (1886):11–20.

87. M. de Manaceine, *Sleep: Its Physiology, Pathology, Hygiene, and Psychology* (New York: Charles Scribner's, 1897), 314–15.

88. A. Teillard, *Spiritual Dimensions* (London: Routledge and Kegan Paul, 1961).

89. R. de Becker, *The Understanding of Dreams and Their Influence on the History of Man* (New York: Hawthorn Books, 1968), 42–45.

90. Ibid., 45–47.

91. E. B. Tylor, *Primitive Culture*, 2 vols. (London: John Murray, 1873).

92. H. Ellis, *The World of Dreams* (Boston: Houghton Mifflin, 1911), 211.

CHAPTER 3

1. T. Allison and H. Van Twyver, "The Evolution of Sleep," *Natural History* 79 (1970):56–65.

2. L. Mumford, *Technics and Human Development* (New York: Harcourt Brace Jovanovich, 1966), 48–51.

3. A. Marshack, *The Roots of Civilization* (New York: McGraw-Hill, 1972), 117–19, 283.

4. A. Oppenheim, "The Interpretation of Dreams in the Ancient Near East with a Translation of an Assyrian Dream-Book," *Transactions of the American Philosophical Society* 46, pt. 3 (1956):179–373.

5. A. Oppenheim, "Mantic Dreams in the Ancient Near East," in *The Dream and Human Societies*, ed. G. von Grunebaum and R. Caillois (Los Angeles: University of California Press, 1966).

6. A. Oppenheim, "The Interpretation of Dreams in the Ancient Near East with a Translation of an Assyrian Dream-Book," *Transactions of the American Philosophical Society* 46, pt. 3 (1956):179–373.

7. 1 Kings 3.

8. Numbers 12:6.

9. Genesis 28.

10. Daniel 2:1–34; Genesis 41.

11. S. Lorand, "Dream Interpretation in the Talmud," *International Journal of Psychoanalysis* 38 (1957):92–97.

12. M. Spero, "Anticipations of Dream Psychology in the Talmud," *Journal of the History of the Behavioral Sciences* 11 (1975):374–80.

13. H. Brugsch-Bey, "The Dream of King Thutmes IV," in *The World of Dreams*, ed. R. L. Woods (New York: Random House, 1947).

14. E. Wallis-Budge, *Egyptian Magic* (London: Paul, Trench, and Trubner, 1899).

15. A. Gardiner, *Hieratic Papyri in the British Museum*, no. 3, *The Dream Book* (London: British Museum, 1935).

16. D. Coxhead and S. Hiller, *Dreams: Visions of the Night* (London: Thames and Hudson, 1981).

17. J. Lincoln, *The Dream in Primitive Cultures* (London: Cresset Press, 1935).

18. B. Laufer, "Inspirational Dream in Eastern Asia," *Journal of American Folklore* 44 (1931):737–41.

19. M. Palmer, ed., *T'ung Shu: The Ancient Chinese Almanac of Life* (Boston: Shambala, 1986).

20. B. Laufer, "Inspirational Dream in Eastern Asia," *Journal of American Folklore* 44 (1931):737–41.

21. K. Das Gupta, *The Shadow World: A Study of Ancient and Modern Dream Theories* (Delhi: Atma Ram, 1971), 54.

22. Ibid., 56.

23. Ibid., 54.

24. R. L. Woods, ed., *The World of Dreams* (New York: Random House, 1947), 54–56.

25. C. Meier, "The Dream in Ancient Greece and Its Use in Temple Cures (Incubation)," in *The Dream and Human Societies*, ed. G. von Grunebaum and R. Caillois (Los Angeles: University of California Press, 1966).

26. A. Aristides, *Aristides*, trans. C. Behr, 4 vols. (Cambridge, Mass.: Harvard University Press, 1973).

27. N. Parsifal-Charles, *The Dream*, 2 vols. (West Cornwall, Conn.: Locust Hill Press, 1986).

28. E. Edelstein and L. Edelstein, *Asclepius: A Collection and Interpretation of the Testimonies*, 2 vols. (Baltimore: Johns Hopkins University Press, 1945).

29. L. Bonuzzi, "About the Origins of the Scientific Study of Sleep and Dreaming," in *Experimental Study of Human Sleep: Methodological Problems*, ed. G. Lairy and P. Salzarulo (Amsterdam: Elsevier Scientific, 1975), 192.

30. H. McCurdy, "The History of Dream Theory," *Psychological Review* 53 (1946):225–33.

31. Galen, *On the Usefulness of the Parts of the Body*, 2 vols. (Ithaca, N.Y.: Cornell University Press, 1968).

32. N. MacKenzie, *Dreams and Dreaming* (London: Aldus Books, 1965), 51–52.

33. Lucretius, "Spirits Possess Our Bodies

When We Sleep," in *The World of Dreams*, ed. R. L. Woods (New York: Random House, 1947), 188.

34. Cicero, "Argument Against Taking Dreams Seriously," in *The World of Dreams*, ed. R. L. Woods (New York: Random House, 1947), 199.

35. Ibid., 204.

36. Artemidorus, *Oneirocritica: The Interpretation of Dreams*, trans. R. White (Torrance, Calif.: Original Books, 1975).

37. Ibid., 21.

38. Ibid., 209.

39. Ibid., 189.

40. Ibid., 198.

41. Ibid., 137.

42. Ibid., 183.

43. Ibid., vii.

CHAPTER 4

1. G. von Grunebaum, "Introduction: The Cultural Function of the Dream as Illustrated by Classical Islam," in *The Dream and Human Societies*, ed. G. von Grunebaum and R. Caillois (Los Angeles: University of California Press, 1966), 11.

2. T. Fahd, "The Dream in Medieval Islamic Society," in *The Dream and Human Societies*, ed. G. von Grunebaum and R. Caillois (Los Angeles: University of California Press, 1966), 361.

3. Ibid., 351.

4. S. Oberhelman, *The Oneirocriticon of Achmet: A Medieval Greek and Arabic Treatise on the Interpretation of Dreams* (Lubbock: Texas Tech University Press, 1991), 245.

5. T. Fahd, "The Dream in Medieval Islamic Society," in *The Dream and Human Societies*, ed. G. von Grunebaum and R. Caillois (Los Angeles: University of California Press, 1966), 360.

6. G. von Grunebaum, "Introduction: The Cultural Function of the Dream as Illustrated by Classical Islam," in *The Dream and Human Societies*, ed. G. von Grunebaum and R. Caillois (Los Angeles: University of California Press, 1966), 20.

7. *Jewish Encyclopedia* (New York: Funk and Wagnalls, 1925), 4:654 ff.

8. M. Maimonides, *The Guide for the Perplexed* (London: Routledge and Kegan Paul, 1951), 225.

9. L. Savary, P. Berne, and S. Williams, *Dreams and Spiritual Growth* (New York: Paulist Press, 1984), 39.

10. M. Kelsey, *Dreams: The Dark Speech of the Spirit* (New York: Doubleday, 1968), 255.

11. Ibid., 256–57.

12. Ibid., 256.

13. H. McCurdy, "The History of Dream Theory," *Psychological Review* 53 (1946):231.

14. A. Fitzgerald, *The Essay and Hymns of Synesius of Cyrene* (London: Oxford University Press, 1930).

15. M. Kelsey, *Dreams: The Dark Speech of the Spirit* (New York: Doubleday, 1968), 142.

16. Ibid., 103.

17. Ibid., 243.

18. Ibid., 242.

19. Ibid., 245.

20. Ibid., 246.

21. Ibid.

22. Ibid.

23. Ibid., 159.

24. Ibid., 153.

25. W. Stahl, *Macrobius: Commentary on the Dream of Scipio* (New York: Columbia University Press, 1952).

26. T. Aquinas, "Is Divination Unlawful?" in *The World of Dreams*, ed. R. L. Woods (New York: Random House, 1947), 148.

27. F. Seafield, *The Literature and Curiosities of Dreams*, 4th ed. (London: Lockwood, 1869), 105.

28. M. Kelsey, *Dreams: The Dark Speech of the Spirit* (New York: Doubleday, 1968), 171.

29. Ibid., 283.

30. Ibid., 300.

31. Ibid., 290.

32. Ibid., 291.

33. Ibid.

34. P. Meseguer, *The Secret of Dreams* (Westminster, Md.: Newman, 1960), 220.

35. F. Seafield, *The Literature and Curiosities*

of Dreams, 4th ed. (London: Lockwood, 1869), 106.

36. Ibid., 107.

37. P. Meseguer, *The Secret of Dreams* (Westminster, Md.: Newman, 1960), 211, 213, 214.

38. T. Hobbes, Excerpt from *Leviathan*, in *The World of Dreams*, ed. R. L. Woods (New York: Random House, 1947), 215.

39. T. Browne, "On Dreams," in *The World of Dreams*, ed. R. L. Woods (New York: Random House, 1947), 218–19.

40. A. Ratcliff, *A History of Dreams* (Boston: Small, Maynard, 1923), 196–97.

41. D. Hartley, "Observations on Man," in *The World of Dreams*, ed. R. L. Woods (New York: Random House, 1947), 400.

42. L. Whyte, *The Unconscious Before Freud* (New York: Basic Books, 1960), 115.

CHAPTER 5

1. A. Ratcliff, *A History of Dreams* (Boston: Small, Maynard, 1923).

2. H. Ellenberger, *The Discovery of the Unconscious* (New York: Basic Books, 1970), 207.

3. R. L. Woods, ed., *The World of Dreams* (New York: Random House, 1947), 497.

4. F. Seafield, *The Literature and Curiosities of Dreams*, 4th ed. (London: Lockwood, 1869).

5. Ibid., 51.

6. H. Ellenberger, *The Discovery of the Unconscious* (New York: Basic Books, 1970), 209.

7. R. L. Woods, ed., *The World of Dreams* (New York: Random House, 1947), 241.

8. M. Boss, *The Analysis of Dreams* (New York: Philosophical Library, 1958), 25–26.

9. S. Freud, *The Interpretation of Dreams* (New York: Basic Books, 1953), 359.

10. H. Saint-Denys, *Dreams and How to Guide Them* (London: Duckworth, 1982), 34.

11. Ibid., 128.

12. Ibid., 38.

13. Ibid., 128.

14. Ibid.

15. Ibid., 129.

16. Ibid., 131.

17. Ibid.

18. Ibid., 133.

19. Ibid., 134.

20. Ibid., 133.

21. Ibid., 134.

22. Ibid., 76–77.

23. Ibid., 108, 109.

24. Ibid., 109.

25. Ibid., 144.

26. Ibid., 37.

27. Ibid., 111.

28. Ibid., 93.

29. Ibid., 25.

30. Ibid., 56.

31. Ibid., 63.

32. Ibid., 154.

33. S. Freud, *The Interpretation of Dreams* (New York: Basic Books, 1953), 60.

34. S. LaBerge, *Lucid Dreaming* (New York: Ballantine, 1986), 34.

35. F. Hildebrant, *Der Traume und Seine Verwerthung fur's Leben* (Leipzig: Reinboth, 1875), 51.

36. Ibid., 55, 56.

37. S. Freud, *The Interpretation of Dreams* (New York: Basic Books, 1953), 63, 67.

38. M. de Manaceine, *Sleep: Its Physiology, Pathology, Hygiene, and Psychology* (New York: Charles Scribner's, 1897), 274.

39. Ibid., 313.

40. Ibid., 317–18.

41. J. Sully, *Illusions: A Psychological Study*, 4th ed. (New York: Appleton, 1897).

42. J. Sully, "The Dream as a Revelation," *Fortnightly Review* 59 (1893):360–65.

43. F. Myers, *Human Personality and Its Survival of Bodily Death*, ed. S. Smith (New Hyde Park, N.Y.: University Books, 1961), 23.

44. Ibid., 26.

45. Ibid., 27.

46. Ibid., 84–85.

47. Ibid., 85.

48. Ibid., 113.

49. Ibid., 7.

50. G. Murphy and R. Ballou, eds., *William James on Psychical Research* (New York: Viking, 1960), 218.

51. H. Ellenberger, *The Discovery of the Unconscious* (New York: Basic Books, 1970), 314.

52. H. Vande Kemp, "The Dream in Periodical Literature: 1860–1910: From *Oneirocritica* to *Die Traumdeutung* via the Questionnaire" (doctoral dissertation, University of Massachusetts, 1977), University Microfilms, 77–15, 131, and "The Dream in Periodical Literature: 1800–1910," *Journal of the History of the Behavioral Sciences* 17 (1981):88–113.

53. H. Vande Kemp, "The Dream in Periodical Literature: 1860–1910: From *Oneirocritica* to *Die Traumdeutung* via the Questionnaire" (doctoral dissertation, University of Massachusetts, 1977), University Microfilms 77–15, 10, 16.

54. Ibid., 56.

55. F. Cobbe, "Dreams as Illustrations of Unconscious Cerebration," *MacMillan's Magazine* 23 (1871):512–23.

56. H. Vande Kemp, "The Dream in Periodical Literature: 1860–1910: From *Oneirocritica* to *Die Traumdeutung* via the Questionnaire" (doctoral dissertation, University of Massachusetts, 1977), University Microfilms 77–15, 81.

57. Ibid., 18.

58. B. Inglis, *The Power of Dreams* (London: Paladin; Grafton, 1987), 181.

59. R. Emerson, *Lectures and Biographical Sketches* (Cambridge: Riverside Press, 1883), 7–8.

CHAPTER 6

1. L. Whyte, *The Unconscious Before Freud* (New York: Basic Books, 1960), 66.

2. H. Ellenberger, *The Discovery of the Unconscious* (New York: Basic Books, 1970), 463.

3. S. Freud, "Some Additional Notes Upon Dream Interpretation as a Whole," in *Sigmund Freud: Collected Papers*, ed. J. Strachey, vol. 5 (1925; New York: Basic Books, 1959), 171–72.

4. Ibid., 172–73.

5. Ibid., 173.

6. A. Adler, "On the Interpretation of Dreams," *International Journal of Individual Psychology* 2 (1936):4.

7. E. Jones, *The Life and Work of Sigmund Freud*, vol. 2, *Years of Maturity, 1901–1919* (New York: Basic Books, 1955), 443.

8. S. Freud, "New Introductory Lectures on Psychoanalysis," in *Sigmund Freud: Complete Works*, ed. J. Strachey, vol. 22 (London: Hogarth, 1933), 4.

9. S. Freud, *The Interpretation of Dreams* (New York: Basic Books, 1953), 591.

10. Ibid., 96.

11. D. Gelman, "Finding the Hidden Freud," *Newsweek*, 1981, 64–70.

12. W. Stewart and L. Freeman, *The Secret of Dreams: A Key to Freudian Dream Analysis* (New York: Macmillan, 1972), 96.

13. Ibid., 20.

14. Ibid., 10.

15. Ibid., 15.

16. Ibid., 20.

17. Ibid., 13.

18. S. Freud, *The Interpretation of Dreams* (New York: Basic Books, 1953), 63.

19. Ibid.

20. Ibid.

21. W. Wolff, *The Dream: Mirror of Conscience.* (Westport, Conn.: Greenwood Press, 1973)

22. S. Freud, *The Interpretation of Dreams* (New York: Basic Books, 1953), xxiii.

23. Ibid., xxv.

24. Ibid., 93.

25. Ibid.

26. H. Ellenberger, *The Discovery of the Unconscious* (New York: Basic Books, 1970), 783–84.

27. S. Freud, *The Interpretation of Dreams* (New York: Basic Books, 1953), 93.

28. Ibid., xxvii–xxviii.

29. Ibid., xxxii.

30. E. Jones, *The Life and Work of Sigmund Freud*, vol. 2, *Years of Maturity, 1901–1919* (New York: Basic Books, 1955), 112.

31. S. Freud, *The Interpretation of Dreams* (New York: Basic Books, 1953), 344.

32. H. Nagera, ed., *Basic Psychoanalytic Concepts on the Theory of Dreams*, vol. 2 (New York: Basic Books, 1969).

33. Ibid., 92.

34. S. Freud, "Some Additional Notes

Upon Dream Interpretation as a Whole," in *Sigmund Freud: Collected Papers*, ed. J. Strachey, vol. 5. (1925; New York: Basic Books, 1959), 150.

35. S. Freud, "Introductory Lectures on Psychoanalysis," in *Sigmund Freud: Complete Works*, ed. J. Strachey, vol. 15 (London: Hogarth, 1916–1917), 222.

36. S. Freud, *The Interpretation of Dreams* (New York: Basic Books, 1953), 350.

37. E. Jones, *The Life and Work of Sigmund Freud*, vol. 2, *Years of Maturity, 1901–1919* (New York: Basic Books, 1955), 134.

38. S. Freud, "Introductory Lectures on Psychoanalysis," in *Sigmund Freud: Complete Works*, ed. J. Strachey, vol. 15 (London: Hogarth, 1916–1917), 168.

39. Ibid., 153.

40. S. Freud, *The Interpretation of Dreams* (New York: Basic Books, 1953), 354–59.

41. Ibid., 358.

42. Ibid., 241.

43. Ibid., 245.

44. Ibid.

45. Ibid., 249.

46. Ibid., 394.

47. Ibid., 395.

48. Ibid.

49. Ibid.

50. Ibid., 385.

51. Ibid., 387.

52. Ibid., 396.

53. Ibid., 403–4.

54. Ibid., 99.

55. Ibid., 100–101.

56. Ibid., 103–4.

57. S. Freud, "Remarks Upon the Theory and Practice of Dream Interpretation," in *Sigmund Freud: Collected Papers*, ed. J. Strachey, vol. 5 (1923; New York: Basic Books, 1959), 137.

58. Ibid., 141.

59. Ibid., 138.

60. S. Freud, "Some Additional Notes Upon Dream Interpretation as a Whole," in *Sigmund Freud: Collected Papers*, ed. J. Strachey, vol. 5 (1925; New York: Basic Books, 1959), 152.

61. Ibid., 150–51.

62. Ibid., 155.

63. Ibid.

64. S. Freud, *The Interpretation of Dreams* (New York: Basic Books, 1953), 553.

65. R. Jones, *The New Psychology of Dreaming* (New York: Grune and Stratton, 1970).

66. S. Freud, *On Dreams* (New York: Norton, 1952), 70.

67. S. Freud, "Remarks Upon the Theory and Practice of Dream Interpretation," in *Sigmund Freud: Collected Papers*, ed. J. Strachey, vol. 5 (1923; New York: Basic Books, 1959), 146.

68. G. Devereux, ed., *Psychoanalysis and the Occult* (New York: International Universities Press, 1953).

69. Ibid., 57.

70. Ibid., 58.

71. Ibid., 59.

72. Ibid., 76.

73. Ibid.

74. Ibid., 77.

75. Ibid.

76. Ibid., 86.

77. Ibid., 77.

78. Ibid., 86.

79. Ibid., 89.

80. Ibid., 91.

81. Ibid., 95.

82. Ibid., 108.

83. Ibid.

84. Ibid.

85. E. Jones, *The Life and Work of Sigmund Freud*, vol. 2, *Years of Maturity, 1901–1919* (New York: Basic Books, 1955), 375.

86. Ibid., 395.

87. Ibid.

88. E. L. Freud, ed., *Letters of Sigmund Freud*, trans. T. Stern and J. Stern (New York: Basic Books, 1960).

89. E. Jones, *The Life and Work of Sigmund Freud*, vol 3, *The Last Phase, 1919–1939* (New York: Basic Books, 1957), 392.

90. Ibid., 385.

91. Ibid., 391.

92. Ibid., 392.

93. S. Freud, *The Interpretation of Dreams* (New York: Basic Books, 1953), 108.

94. S. Freud, "New Introductory Lectures on Psychoanalysis," in *Sigmund Freud: Complete Works*, ed. J. Strachey, vol. 22 (London: Hogarth, 1933), 10.

95. Ibid., 9.

96. E. Jones, *The Life and Work of Sigmund Freud*, vol. 2, *Years of Maturity, 1901–1919* (New York: Basic Books, 1955), 382–84.

97. Ibid., 421.

98. Ibid.

99. S. Freud, *The Interpretation of Dreams* (New York: Basic Books, 1953), 111.

100. E. Jones, *The Life and Work of Sigmund Freud*, vol. 2, *Years of Maturity, 1901–1919* (New York: Basic Books, 1955), 419.

101. S. Freud, *The Interpretation of Dreams* (New York: Basic Books, 1953), 163.

102. Ibid., 120–21.

103. Ibid., 397.

104. Ibid.

105. Ibid., 397–98.

106. Ibid., 270.

107. H. Ellenberger, *The Discovery of the Unconscious* (New York: Basic Books, 1970), 467.

CHAPTER 7

1. C. Jung, *Memories, Dreams, Reflections* (New York: Vantage Books, 1965), 149.

2. Ibid., 361–62.

3. V. Brome, *Jung: Man and Myth* (New York: Atheneum, 1978), 149.

4. C. Jung, *Memories, Dreams, Reflections* (New York: Vantage Books, 1965), 155–56.

5. Ibid., 158.

6. S. Freud, "A History of the Psycho-Analytic Movement," in *Sigmund Freud: Complete Works*, ed. J. Strachey, vol. 14 (London: Hogarth, 1914), 43.

7. C. Jung, *Memories, Dreams, Reflections* (New York: Vantage Books, 1965).

8. Ibid., 5.

9. L. van der Post, *Jung and the Story of Our Time* (New York: Pantheon, 1975), 174.

10. V. Brome, *Jung: Man and Myth* (New York: Atheneum, 1978), 252.

11. Ibid., 289.

12. C. Jung, *Memories, Dreams, Reflections* (New York: Vantage Books, 1965), 161.

13. C. Jung, *Man and His Symbols* (Garden City, N.J.: Doubleday, 1964), 67.

14. C. Jung, *Memories, Dreams, Reflections* (New York: Vantage Books, 1965), 180–81.

15. C. Warner, "The Positive Animus: Its Evolution in a Woman's Dreams," paper presented at meeting of the Association for the Study of Dreams, Marymount College, Virginia, 1987.

16. V. Brome, *Jung: Man and Myth* (New York: Atheneum, 1978).

17. Ibid., 178–79.

18. Ibid., 179.

19. C. Jung, *Dreams*, trans. R. F. C. Hull (Princeton, N.J.: Princeton University Press, 1974).

20. C. Jung, *Dream Analysis: Notes of the Seminar Given in 1928–30*, Bollingen series, vol. 99 (Princeton, N.J.: Princeton University Press, 1984).

21. J. Sanford, *Dreams: God's Forgotten Language* (New York: J. B. Lippincott, 1968).

22. Ibid., 59–60.

23. C. Jung, *Collected Papers on Analytical Psychology* (New York: Moffat and Yard, 1917), 468.

24. S. Freud, *The Interpretation of Dreams* (New York: Basic Books, 1953), 357.

25. C. Jung, *Dream Analysis: Notes of the Seminar Given in 1928–30*, Bollingen series, vol. 99 (Princeton, N.J.: Princeton University Press, 1984), 251.

26. Ibid., 251–52.

27. Ibid., 261.

28. K. Kelzer, *The Sun and the Shadow* (Virginia Beach, Va.: A.R.E. Press, 1987).

29. Ibid., 119.

30. Ibid., 120.

31. Ibid., 123.

32. G. Krishna, *Kundalini: The Evolutionary Energy in Man* (Boulder: Shambala, 1971).

33. K. Kelzer, *The Sun and the Shadow* (Virginia Beach, Va.: A.R.E. Press, 1987), 123.

34. C. Jung, *Dream Analysis: Notes of the Seminar Given in 1928–30*, Bollingen series, vol. 99 (Princeton, N.J.: Princeton University Press, 1984).

35. C. Jung, *Dreams*, trans. R. F. C. Hull (Princeton, N.J.: Princeton University Press, 1974), 27.

36. Ibid., 34.

37. Ibid., 52.

38. C. Jung, *The Symbolic Life: Miscellaneous Writings*, Bollingen series, vol. 17 (Princeton, N.J.: Princeton University Press, 1976), paragraph 469.

39. C. Jung, *Alchemical Studies*, Bollingen series, vol. 13 (Princeton, N.J.: Princeton University Press, 1967), paragraph 469.

40. C. Jung, *Man and His Symbols* (Garden City, N.J.: Doubleday, 1964), 99.

41. D. Sander and N. Churchill, "Serpent as Healer," *Shaman's Drum* 10 (fall 1987): 32–34.

42. J. Hall, *Clinical Uses of Dreams: Jungian Interpretation and Enactments* (New York: Grune and Stratton, 1977).

43. C. Jung, *Dreams*, trans. R. F. C. Hull (Princeton, N.J.: Princeton University Press, 1974), 47–49.

44. Ibid., 95–96.

45. C. Jung, *Man and His Symbols* (Garden City, N.J.: Doubleday, 1964), 38.

46. C. Jung, *Psychology and Religion: West and East*, Bollingen series, vol. 11 (Princeton, N.J.: Princeton University Press, 1958), 45.

47. C. Jung, *Man and His Symbols* (Garden City, N.J.: Doubleday, 1964), 78.

48. C. Jung, *Dreams*, trans. R. F. C. Hull (Princeton, N.J.: Princeton University Press, 1974).

49. C. Jung, *Dream Analysis: Notes of the Seminar Given in 1928–30*, Bollingen series, vol. 99 (Princeton, N.J.: Princeton University Press, 1984).

50. M. Mahoney, *The Meaning in Dreams and Dreaming* (New York: Citadel Press, 1966); M. Matoon, *Applied Dream Analysis: A Jungian Approach* (Washington, D.C.: Washington and Sons, 1978); J. Hall, *Clinical Uses of Dreams: Jungian Interpretation and Enactments* (New York: Grune and Stratton, 1977); J. Hall, *Jungian Dream Interpretation: A Handbook of Theory and Practice* (Toronto: Inner City Books, 1983).

51. C. Jung, *Dreams*, trans. R. F. C. Hull (Princeton, N.J.: Princeton University Press, 1974), 97.

52. S. Freud, "Introductory Lectures on Psychoanalysis," in *Sigmund Freud: Complete Works*, ed. J. Strachey, vol. 15 (London: Hogarth, 1916–1917), 222.

53. C. Jung, *Dreams*, trans. R. F. C. Hull (Princeton, N.J.: Princeton University Press, 1974), 95–96.

54. S. Freud, "Introductory Lectures on Psychoanalysis," in *Sigmund Freud: Complete Works*, ed. J. Strachey, vol. 15 (London: Hogarth, 1916–1917), 153.

55. C. Jung, *Man and His Symbols* (Garden City, N.J.: Doubleday, 1964), 95–99.

56. M. Matoon, *Applied Dream Analysis: A Jungian Approach* (Washington, D.C.: Washington and Sons, 1978), 110.

CHAPTER 8

1. Alexandra Adler, *Guiding Human Misfits* (London: Faber and Faber, 1948).

2. P. Bottome, *Alfred Adler* (London: Faber and Faber, 1939).

3. A. Adler, "On the Interpretation of Dreams," *International Journal of Individual Psychology* 2 (1936):9.

4. A. Adler, *What Life Should Mean to You* (New York: Capricorn, 1931), 19.

5. Ibid., 99.

6. H. Ansbacher and R. Ansbacher, eds., *The Individual Psychology of Alfred Adler* (New York: Basic Books, 1956), 359.

7. Ibid.

8. A. Adler, *What Life Should Mean to You* (New York: Capricorn, 1931), 99.

9. A. Adler, "On the Interpretation of Dreams," *International Journal of Individual Psychology* 2 (1936):6.

10. S. Lowy, *Psychological and Biological Foundations of Dream Interpretation* (London: Paul, Trench, and Trubner, 1942), 174.

11. Ibid., 176.

12. Ibid.

13. Ibid., 177.

14. Ibid., 178.

15. W. Stekel, *The Interpretation of Dreams* (New York: Grosset and Dunlap, 1962), 13–14, 512.

16. Ibid., 552.

17. Ibid.

18. T. French, *Integration of Behavior*, vol. 2, *The Integrative Process in Dreams* (Chicago: University of Chicago Press, 1954).

19. T. French and E. Fromm, *Dream Interpretation* (New York: Basic Books, 1964).

20. E. Erikson, "The Dream Specimen of Psychoanalysis," *Journal of the American Psychoanalytic Association* 2 (1954):5–56.

21. M. Boss, *The Analysis of Dreams* (New York: Philosophical Library, 1958), 207.

22. Ibid., 156.

23. Ibid., 158.

24. Ibid., 113–14.

25. Ibid., 166.

26. M. Boss, "Dreaming and the Dreamed in the Daseins Analytical Way of Seeing," in *On Dreaming: An Encounter With Medard Boss*, ed. C. Scott (Chico, Calif.: Scholars Press, 1982), 12.

27. Ibid., 31.

28. Ibid., 14.

29. M. Boss, *The Analysis of Dreams* (New York: Philosophical Library, 1958), 207.

30. Ibid., 184.

31. Ibid.

32. C. Hall, *The Meaning of Dreams* (New York: McGraw-Hill, [1953b] 1966).

33. Ibid., 222–25.

34. Ibid., 225.

35. Ibid., 230.

36. Ibid., 23.

37. Ibid., 51.

38. Ibid., 106.

39. Ibid., 136.

40. Ibid., 161.

41. F. Perls, "Four Lectures," in *Gestalt Therapy Now*, ed. J. Fagan and I. Shepherd (Palo Alto: Science and Behavior Books, 1970), 27.

42. J. Downing and R. Marmorstein, eds., *Dreams and Nightmares* (New York: Harper and Row, 1973).

43. Ibid., 11.

44. Ibid., 40–41.

45. Ibid., 73.

46. Ibid., 74.

47. Ibid., 74–75.

48. E. Gendlin, *Let Your Body Interpret Your Dreams* (Wilmette, Ill.: Chiron Publications, 1986).

49. Ibid., 1.

50. Ibid., 54–55.

51. M. Ullman and N. Zimmerman, *Working With Dreams* (New York: Dellacorte Press/ Eleanor Friede, 1979).

52. M. Ullman, "The Experimental Dream Group," in *The Varieties of Dream Experience*, ed. M. Ullman and C. Limmer (New York: Continuum, 1987), 4.

53. Ibid.

54. Ibid., 5.

55. Ibid., 7.

56. Ibid., 8.

57. M. Ullman, Introduction, in *The Variety of Dream Experiences*, ed. M. Ullman and C. Limmer (New York: Continuum, 1987), ix.

58. M. Ullman and C. Limmer, eds., *The Varieties of Dream Experience* (New York: Continuum, 1987).

59. M. Ullman, "The Dream Revisited: Some Changed Ideas Based on a Group Approach," in *Dreams in New Perspective*, ed. M. Glucksman and S. Warner (New York: Human Sciences Press, 1987), 129–30.

CHAPTER 9

1. S. Freud, *The Interpretation of Dreams* (New York: Basic Books, 1953), 24.

2. R. Macnish, *The Philosophy of Sleep*, 3d ed. (Glasgow: MM'Phun, 1836), 54.

3. M. de Manaceine, *Sleep: Its Physiology, Pathology, Hygiene, and Psychology* (New York: Charles Scribner's, 1897), 259–60.

4. R. Macnish, *The Philosophy of Sleep*, 3d ed. (Glasgow: MM'Phun, 1836), 54–60.

5. Ibid., 69–70.

6. J. Gulliver, "The Psychology of

Dreams," *Journal of Speculative Philosophy* 14 (1880): 206–8.

7. L., "On a Particular Class of Dreams Induced by Food," *Journal of Psychological Medicine and Mental Pathology* 11–12 (1858):575–96.

8. B. Richardson, "The Physiology of Dreams," *Asclepiad* 9 (1892):129–60.

9. W. Walsh, *The Psychology of Dreams* (New York: Dodd, Mead, 1920), 175.

10. F. Seafield, *The Literature and Curiosities of Dreams*, 4th ed. (London: Lockwood, 1869), 263.

11. A. MacFarlane, "Dreaming," *Edinburgh Medical Journal* 36 (1890):717.

12. Ibid., 718.

13. F. Scholz, *Sleep and Dreams* (New York: Funk and Wagnalls, 1893), 61.

14. R. Macnish, *The Philosophy of Sleep*, 3d ed. (Glasgow: MM'Phun, 1836), 55–56; *Lancet* 1 (1831–1832):921–22.

15. J. Borner, *Das Alpdrucken, Sein Begrundung und Verhutung* (Würzburg, 1855), 8–9, 27.

16. A. Maury, *Le sommeil et les reves* (Paris: Didier Edition, 1861; 2d ed., 1878).

17. H. Saint-Denys, *Dreams and How to Guide Them* (1867; London: Duckworth, 1982), 112–14.

18. Ibid., 122–23.

19. G. T. Ladd, "Contributions to the Psychology of Visual Dreams," *Mind* (1892), 304; see R. L. Woods, ed., *The World of Dreams* (New York: Random House, 1947), 511–15.

20. G. T. Ladd, "Contributions to the Psychology of Visual Dreams," *Mind* (1892), 303.

21. Ibid., 302.

22. P. Simon, *Le monde des reves* (Paris: Alcon, 1888), chap. 2.

23. J. Sully, *Illusions: A Psychological Study*, 4th ed. (New York: Appleton, 1897), 140.

24. M. de Manaceine, *Sleep: Its Physiology, Pathology, Hygiene, and Psychology* (New York: Charles Scribner's, 1897), 258–59.

25. H. Warren, "Sleep and Dreams," *Psychological Review* 4 (1897):549–53.

26. W. Monroe, "A Study of Taste Dreams," *American Journal of Psychology* 10 (1899): 326–27.

27. W. Monroe, "Note on Dreams," *American Journal of Psychology* 9 (1897):413–14.

28. J. Corning, "The Use of Musical Vibrations Before and During Sleep—Supplementary Employment of Chromatoscopic Figures—A Contribution to the Therapeutics of the Emotions," *Medical Record* 55 (1899):79–86.

29. Ibid., 82.

30. Ibid., 83.

31. O. Potzl, "The Relationship Between Experimentally Induced Dream Images and Indirect Vision," *Psychological Issues* 2, monograph 7 (1960):47.

32. C. Fisher, "Introduction: Preconscious Stimulation in Dreams, Associations, and Images," *Psychological Issues* 2, monograph 7 (1960):1.

33. M. Small, "Dreams," *Psychological Bulletin* 7 (1920):346–49.

34. W. Malamud and R. Lindner, "Dreams and Their Relationship to Recent Impression," *Archives of Neurology and Psychiatry* 25 (1931):1081–99.

35. W. Malamud, "Dream Analysis: Its Application in Therapy and Research in Nervous and Mental Disease," *Archives of Neurology and Psychiatry* 31 (1934):356–72.

36. A. Cubberly, "The Effects of Tensions of Body Surface Upon Normal Dreams," *British Journal of Psychology* 13 (1923):243–65; see R. L. Woods, ed., *The World of Dreams* (New York: Random House, 1947), 819–27.

37. H. Silberer, "Report on a Method of Eliciting and Observing Certain Symbolic Hallucination-Phenomena" (1909), in *Organization and Pathology of Thought*, ed. D. Rapaport (New York: Columbia University Press, 1951).

38. K. Schroetter, "Experimental Dreams" (1911), in *Organization and Pathology of Thought*, ed. D. Rapaport (New York: Columbia University Press, 1951).

39. G. Roffenstein, "Experiments on Symbolization in Dreams" (1924), in *Organization and Pathology of Thought*, ed. D. Rapaport, 249–56 (New York: Columbia University Press, 1951).

40. L. Farber and C. Fisher, "An Experimental Approach to Dream Psychology

Through the Use of Hypnosis," *Psychoanalytic Quarterly* 12 (1943):202–16.

41. C. Finley, "Endocrine Stimulation as Affecting Dream Content" (1921) in *The World of Dreams*, ed. R. L. Woods (New York: Random House, 1947), 437–42.

42. Ibid., 442.

43. W. R. Miles, "The Sex Expression of Men Living on a Lowered Nutritional Level," *Journal of Nervous and Mental Disease* 49 (1919):208–24.

44. J. Franklin et al., "Observations of Human Behavior in Experimental Semistarvation and Rehabilitation," *Journal of Clinical Psychology* 4 (1948):28–45.

45. R. Macnish, *The Philosophy of Sleep*, 3d ed. (Glasgow: MM'Phun, 1836), 42.

46. J. A. Hobson, *The Dreaming Brain* (New York: Basic Books, 1988), 71.

47. J. MacWilliam, "Some Applications of Physiology to Medicine. III. Blood Pressure and Heart Action in Sleep and Dreams: Their Relation to Haemorrhages, Angina, and Sudden Death," *British Medical Journal* 2 (1923): 1196–1200.

48. A. Ikin, T. Pear, and R. Thouless, "The Psycho-Galvanic Phenomenon in Dream Analysis," *British Journal of Psychology* 15 (1924): 23–44.

49. L. Rowland, "The Relation of Judgments of Excitement Value to Certain Bodily Changes Shown During Hypnotic Dreams," *Proceedings of the Oklahoma Academy of Sciences* 12 (1932):92.

50. L. Max, "An Experimental Study of the Motor Theory of Consciousness. III. Action-Current Responses in Deaf-Mutes During Sleep, Sensory Stimulation and Dreams," *Journal of Comparative Psychology* 19 (1935):482.

51. J. Stoyva, "Finger Electromyographic Activity During Sleep: Its Relation to Dreaming in Deaf and Normal Subjects," *Journal of Abnormal Psychology* 70 (1965):343–49.

52. L. Max, "An Experimental Study of the Motor Theory of Consciousness. III. Action-Current Responses in Deaf-Mutes During Sleep, Sensory Stimulation and Dreams," *Journal of Comparative Psychology* 19 (1935):481.

53. H. Blake and R. Gerard, "Brain Potentials During Sleep," *American Journal of Physiology* 119 (1937):692–703.

54. E. Kohlschutter, "Messungen der Festigkeit des Schlafes," *Zeitschrift uber Rationalistisch Medizin* 17 (1862):209–53.

55. W. Howell, "A Contribution to the Physiology of Sleep Based Upon Plethysmographic Experiments," *Journal of Experimental Medicine* 2 (1897):313–45.

56. P. Ohlymeyer and H. Huellstrung, "Periodische Vorgaenge im Schlaf," *Pfluegers Archiv* 248 (1944):559–60.

57. G. Magnussen, *Studies on Respiration During Sleep: A Contribution to the Physiology of the Sleep Function* (London: H. K. Lewis, 1944).

CHAPTER 10

1. E. Aserinsky and N. Kleitman, "Regularly Occurring Periods of Eye Motility, and Concomitant Phenomena during Sleep," *Science* 118 (1953):273–74.

2. E. Aserinsky and N. Kleitman, "Two Types of Ocular Motility Occurring in Sleep," *Journal of Applied Physiology* 8 (1955):1–10.

3. E. Diamond, *The Science of Dreams* (New York: Doubleday, 1962), 105.

4. W. Dement, "Dream Recall and Eye Movement During Sleep in Schizophrenics and Normals," *Journal of Nervous and Mental Disease* 122 (1955):263–69.

5. W. Dement and N. Kleitman, "The Relation of Eye Movements during Sleep to Dream Activity: An Objective Method for the Study of Dreaming," *Journal of Experimental Psychology* 53 (1957):339–46.

6. W. Dement and N. Kleitman, "Cyclic Variations in EEG during Sleep and Their Relation to Eye Movements, Body Motility, and Dreaming," *Electroencephalography and Clinical Neurophysiology* 9 (1957):672–90.

7. L. Monroe, "Inter-Rater Reliability of Scoring EEG Sleep Records," *Psychophysiology* 4 (1968):370–71 (abstract).

8. A. Rechtschaffen and A. Kales, eds., *A Manual of Standardized Terminology, Techniques and Scoring System for Sleep Stages of Human*

Subjects (Public Health Service, U.S. Government Printing Office, 1968).

9. J. A. Hobson, *The Dreaming Brain* (New York: Basic Books, 1988), 289.

10. A. Mandell et al., "Dreaming Sleep in Man: Changes in Urine Volume and Osmolality," *Science* 151 (1966):1558–60.

11. R. Cooper and A. Hulme, "Intra-Cranial Pressure and Related Phenomena During Sleep," *Journal of Neurology, Neurosurgery and Psychiatry* 29 (1966):564.

12. B. Baldridge, R. Whitman, and M. Kramer, "A Simplified Method for Detecting Eye Movements During Dreaming," *Psychosomatic Medicine* 25 (1963):78–82.

13. J. Gross, J. Byrne, and C. Fisher, "Eye Movements During Emergent Stage 1 EEG in Subjects With Life-long Blindness," *Journal of Nervous and Mental Disease* 141 (1965):365–70.

14. R. Hodes and W. Dement, "Depression of Electrically Induced Reflexes ('H-reflexes') in Man During Low Voltage EEG 'Sleep,' " *Electroencephalography and Clinical Neurophysiology* 17 (1964):617–29.

15. J. D. Dexter and E. Weitzman, "The Relation Between Nocturnal Migraine, Cluster Headaches and Sleep Stage," paper read at meeting of the Association for the Psychophysiological Study of Sleep, Boston, 1969.

16. R. Armstrong et al., "Dreams and Gastric Secretions in Duodenal Ulcer Patients," *New Physician* 14 (1965):241–43.

17. E. Hartmann, *The Biology of Dreaming* (Springfield, Ill.: Charles Thomas, 1967), 118–19.

18. J. Nowlin et al., "The Association of Nocturnal Angina Pectoris with Dreaming," *Annals of Internal Medicine* 63 (1965):1040–46.

19. G. Rosenblatt, E. Hartmann, and G. Zwilling, "Cardiac Irritability During Sleep and Dreaming," *Journal of Psychosomatic Research* 17 (1973):29–134.

20. C. Fisher, J. Gross, and J. Zuch, "Cycle of Penile Erections Synchronous With Dreaming (REM) Sleep," *Archives of General Psychiatry* 12 (1965):29–45.

21. I. Karacan et al., "The Ontogeny of Nocturnal Penile Tremescence," *Waking and Sleeping* 1 (1976):27–44.

22. I. Karacan, R. Williams, and P. Salis, "The Effect of Sexual Intercourse on Sleep Patterns and Nocturnal Penile Erections," *Psychophysiology* 7 (1970):338 (abstract).

23. I. Karacan, "Clinical Value of Nocturnal Erection in the Prognosis and Diagnosis of Impotence," *Medical Aspects of Human Sexuality* 4 (1970):27–34.

24. I. Karacan et al., "Erection Cycle during Sleep in Relation to Dream Anxiety," *Archives of General Psychiatry* 15 (1966):183–89.

25. C. Fisher, "Dreaming and Sexuality," in *Psychoanalysis: A General Psychology: Essays in Honor of Heinz Hartman*, ed. R. Lowenstein et al., 537–69 (New York: International Universities Press, 1966).

26. Anita I. Bell and C. Stroebel, "The Scrotal Sac and Testes During Sleep: Physiological Correlates and Mental Content," in *Sleep: Physiology, Biochemistry, Psychology, Pharmacology, Clinical Implications*, 380–84 (Basel: Karger, 1973); Anita I. Bell, "Male Anxiety During Sleep," *International Journal of Psycho-analysis* 56, no. 4 (1975):455–64.

27. F. Snyder, "Sleep and Dreaming: Progress in the New Biology of Dreaming," *American Journal of Psychiatry* 122 (1965): 377–391.

28. G. Rogers et al., "Vaginal Pulse Amplitude Response Patterns During Erotic Conditions and Sleep," *Archives of Sexual Behavior* 14 (1985):339.

29. D. Goodenough, "Some Recent Studies of Dream Recall," in *Experimental Studies of Dreaming*, ed. H. Witkin and H. Lewis (New York: Random House, 1967), 135–40.

30. S. LaBerge, W. Greenleaf, and B. Kedzierski, "Physiological Responses to Dreamed Sexual Activity during Lucid REM Sleep," *Psychophysiology* 20 (1983):454–55.

31. E. Hartmann, *The Biology of Dreaming* (Springfield, Ill.: Charles Thomas, 1967), 26.

32. D. Foulkes and A. Rechtschaffen, "Presleep Determinants of Dream Content: Effects of Two Films," *Perceptual and Motor Skills* 19 (1964):983–1005.

33. D. Foulkes et al., "Dreams of the Male

Child: An EEG Study," *Journal of Abnormal Psychology* 72 (1967):457–67.

34. G. Collins, L. Davison and L. Breger, "Dream Function in Adaptation to Threat: A Preliminary Study," paper presented at meeting of the Association for the Psychophysiological Study of Sleep, Santa Monica, 1967.

35. D. Goodenough et al., "The Effects of Stress Films on Dream Affect, on Respiration, and Eye-Movement Activity During Rapid-Eye-Movement Sleep," *Psychophysiology* 12 (1975): 313–20.

36. H. Witkin and H. Lewis, "Presleep Experiences and Dreams," in *Experimental Studies of Dreaming*, ed. H. Witkin and H. Lewis (New York: Random House, 1967).

37. H. Witkin, "Influencing Dream Content," in *Dream Psychology and the New Biology of Dreaming*, ed. M. Kramer (Springfield, Ill.: Charles Thomas, 1969).

38. L. Breger, I. Hunter, and R. Lane, "The Effect of Stress on Dreams," *Psychological Issues* 7, monograph 27 (1971). New York: International Universities Press.

39. P. Wood, "Dreaming and Social Isolation" (doctoral dissertation, University of North Carolina, 1962).

40. P. Hauri, "Evening Activity, Sleep Mentation, and Subjective Sleep Quality," *Journal of Abnormal Psychology* 76 (1970):270–75.

41. W. Dement and E. Wolpert, "The Relation of Eye Movements, Body Motility, and External Stimuli to Dream Content," *Journal of Experimental Psychology* 55 (1958):543–53.

42. E. Bokert, "The Effects of Thirst and a Related Verbal Stimulus on Dream Reports," *Dissertation Abstracts* 28, 4753B (1968):122–31.

43. H. Roffwarg et al., "The Effects of Sustained Alterations of Waking Visual Input on Dream Content," in *The Mind in Sleep: Psychology and Psychophysiology*, ed. A. Arkin, J. Antrobus, and S. Ellman (Hillsdale, N.J.: Lawrence Erlbaum, 1978).

44. J. Mendelson, L. Siger, and P. Solomon, "Psychiatric Observations on Congenital and Acquired Deafness: Symbolic and Perceptual Processes in Dreams," *American Journal of Psychiatry* 116 (1960):883–88.

45. N. Schecter, G. Schmeidler, and M. Staal, "Dream Reports and Creative Tendencies in Students of the Arts, Sciences, and Engineering," *Journal of Consulting Psychology* 29 (1965):415–21.

46. J. Adelson, "Creativity and the Dream," *Merrill Palmer Quarterly* 6 (1960):92–97.

47. R. Suinn, "Jungian Personality Typology and Color Dreaming," *Psychiatric Quarterly* 40 (1966):659–66.

48. E. Kahn et al., "Incidence of Color in Immediately Recalled Dreams," *Science* 137 (1962):1054–55.

49. A. Rechtschaffen and C. Buchignani, "Visual Dimensions and Correlates of Dream Images," *Sleep Research* 12 (1983):189.

50. W. Dement and E. Wolpert, "The Relation of Eye Movements, Body Motility, and External Stimuli to Dream Content," *Journal of Experimental Psychology* 55 (1958):550.

51. D. Koulack, *To Catch a Dream* (Albany: State University Press of New York, 199), 44.

52. B. Baldridge, "Physical Concomitants of Dreaming and the Effect of Stimulation on Dreams," *Ohio State Medical Journal* 62 (1966):1271–79.

53. A. Ziegler, "Dream Emotions in Relation to Room Temperature," in *Sleep: Physiology, Biochemistry, Psychology, Pharmacology, Clinical Implications* (Basel: Karger, 1973).

54. K. Trotter, K. Dallas, and P. Verdone, "Olfactory Stimuli and Their Effects on REM Dreams," paper presented at meeting of Association for the Study of Dreams, Marymount College, Virginia, 1987.

55. A. Rechtschaffen and D. Foulkes, "Effect of Visual Stimuli on Dream Content," *Perceptual and Motor Skills* 20 (1965):1149–60.

56. C. Bradley and R. Meddis, "Arousal Threshold in Dreaming Sleep," *Physiological Psychology* 2 (1974):109–10.

57. W. Dement, *Some Must Watch While Some Must Sleep* (San Francisco: W. H. Freeman, 1972).

58. R. Berger, "Experimental Modification of Dream Content by Meaningful Verbal Stimuli," *British Journal of Psychiatry* 109 (1963): 722–40.

59. L. Kinney, M. Kramer, and M. Scharf, "Dream Incorporation: A Replication," *Sleep Research* 11 (1982):105.

60. V. Castaldo and P. Holzman, "The Effects of Hearing One's Own Voice on Dream Content: A Replication," *Journal of Nervous and Mental Disease* 148 (1969):74–82.

61. H. Fernandez, "Evoked K-Complexes in the Early Stages of Sleep and Their Relation to Visual Images," *American Journal of EEG Technology* 9 (1969):18–21.

62. D. Goodenough et al., "A Comparison of 'Dreamers' and 'Nondreamers': Eye Movements, Electroencephalograms, and the Recall of Dreams," *Journal of Abnormal and Social Psychology* 59 (1959):295–302.

63. D. Foulkes, "Dream Reports from Different Stages of Sleep," *Journal of Abnormal and Social Psychology* 65 (1962):14–25.

64. J. Herman, S. Ellman, and H. Roffwarg, "The Problem of NREM Dream Recall Reexamined," in *The Mind in Sleep: Psychology and Psychophysiology*, ed. A. Arkin, J. Antrobus, and S. Ellman (Hillsdale, N.J.: Lawrence Erlbaum, 1978).

65. L. Monroe et al., "Discriminability of REM and NREM Reports," *Journal of Personality and Social Psychology* 2 (1965):456–60.

66. D. Foulkes and G. Vogel, "Mental Activity at Sleep Onset," *Journal of Abnormal Psychology* 70 (1965):231–43.

67. D. Foulkes, P. S. Spear, and J. D. Symonds, "Individual Differences in Mental Activity at Sleep Onset," *Journal of Abnormal Psychology* 71 (1966):280–86.

68. R. Tracy and L. Tracy, "Reports of Mental Activity from Sleep Stages 2 and 4," *Perceptual and Motor Skills* 38 (1974):647–48.

69. W. Zimmerman, "Sleep Mentation and Auditory Awakening Thresholds," *Psychophysiology* (1970):540–49.

70. R. Watson and A. Rechtschaffen, "Auditory Awakening Thresholds and Dream Recall in NREM Sleep," *Perceptual and Motor Skills* 29 (1969):635–44.

71. C. Hall and R. Van de Castle, *The Content Analysis of Dreams* (New York: Appleton-Century-Croft, 1966).

72. W. Dement and E. Wolpert, "Relationships in Manifest Content of Dreams Occurring on the Same Night," *Journal of Nervous and Mental Disease* 126 (1958a): 568–78.

73. R. Van de Castle, "Temporal Patterns of Dreams," in *Sleep and Dreaming*, ed. E. Hartmann (Boston: Little, Brown, 1970).

74. W. Offenkrantz and A. Rechtschaffen, "Clinical Studies of Sequential Dreams. I. A Patient in Psychotherapy," *Archives of General Psychiatry* 8 (1963):497–508.

75. P. Verdone, "Temporal Reference of Manifest Dream Content," *Perceptual and Motor Skills* 20 (1965):1253–68.

76. P. Bakan, "Dreaming, REM Sleep and the Right Hemisphere: A Theoretical Integration," *Journal of Altered States of Consciousness* 3 (1977–1978):285–307.

77. C. Violani et al. "Dream Recall as a Function of Individual Patterns of Hemispheric Lateralization," *Sleep Research* 12 (1983):190.

78. I. Lewin et al., "The Induction of a Quasi-Dreaming Mental State by Means of Flickering Photic Stimulation," in *Sleep: Physiology, Biochemistry, Psychology, Pharmacology, Clinical Implications* (Basel: Karger, 1973).

79. A. Rechtschaffen, "The Psychophysiology of Mental Activity during Sleep," in *The Psychophysiology of Thinking*, ed. F. McGuigan and R. Schoonover (New York: Academic Press, 1973).

80. J. Birnholz, "The Development of Human Fetal Learning," *Science* 222 (1983): 516–18.

81. E. A. Wolpert, "Studies in Psychophysiology of Dreams," *AMA Archives of General Psychiatry* 2 (1960):231–41.

82. G. Russel et al., "The Relationship of Small Limb Movements during REM Sleep to Dreamed Limb Action," *Psychosomatic Medicine* 37 (1975):147–59.

83. F. J. McGuigan and R. G. Tanner, "Covert Oral Behavior during Conversational and Visual Dreams," *Psychonomic Science* 23 (1971):263–64.

84. H. Roffwarg, J. Herman, and S. Lamstein, "The Middle Ear Muscles: Predictability of Their Phasic Activity in REM Sleep

from Dream Material," *Sleep Research* 4 (1975):165.

85. L. Gottschalk et al., "Anxiety Levels in Dreams: Relation to Changes in Plasma Free Acids," *Science* 153 (1966):654–57.

86. J. A. Hobson, J. A., F. Goldfrank, and F. Snyder, "Respiration and Mental Activity in Sleep," *Journal of Psychiatric Research* 3 (1964).

87. J. Nowlin et al., "The Association of Nocturnal Angina Pectoris with Dreaming," *Annals of Internal Medicine* 63 (1965):1040–46.

88. P. Hauri and R. L. Van de Castle, "Psychophysiological Parallels in Dreams," *Psychosomatic Medicine* 35 (1973):297–308.

89. R. Van de Castle and P. Hauri, "An Investigation of Psychophysiological Correlates of NREM Mentation," *Psychophysiology* 7 (1970):330.

90. D. Foulkes, *A Grammar of Dreams* (New York: Basic Books, 1978):99.

91. D. Foulkes, *Dreaming: A Cognitive-Psychological Analysis* (Hillsdale, N.J.: Lawrence Erlbaum, 1985).

92. Ibid., 4.

93. Ibid., 14.

94. Ibid., 191.

95. W. Dement, "Discussion of F. Snyder, *Toward an Evolutionary Theory of Dreaming*," *American Journal of Psychiatry* 123 (1966):136.

96. H. Hunt, "Some Relations Between the Cognitive Psychology of Dreams and Dream Phenomenology," *Journal of Mind and Behavior* 7 (1986):226.

97. Ibid.

98. F. Crick and G. Mitchison, "The Function of Dream Sleep," *Nature* 312 (1983):101.

99. F. Crick and G. Mitchison, "REM Sleep and Neural Nets," *Journal of Mind and Behavior* 7 (1986):229–50.

100. Ibid., 234.

101. Ibid., 237.

102. Ibid., 229.

103. Ibid., 232.

104. J. A. Hobson and R. W. McCarley, "The Brain as a Dream State Generator: An Activation-Synthesis Hypothesis of the Dream Process," *American Journal of Psychiatry* 134 (1977):1335–48.

105. J. A. Hobson, *The Dreaming Brain* (New York: Basic Books, 1988).

106. Ibid., 9.

107. Ibid., 297–98.

108. Ibid., 297.

109. G. Globus, *Dream Life, Wake Life* (Albany, N.Y.: State University of New York Press, 1987).

110. G. Globus, "Dream Content: Random or Meaningful?" *Dreaming* 1 (1991):27–40.

111. G. Globus, *Dream Life, Wake Life* (Albany, N.Y.: State University of New York Press, 1987), 21.

112. Ibid.; the reference within the quote is to K. Wilber, "Physics, Mysticism and the New Holographic Paradigm," in *The Holographic Paradigm and Other Paradoxes*, ed. K. Wilber (Boulder: Shambala, 1982).

113. D. Bohm, *Wholeness and the Implicate Order* (Boston: Routledge and Kegan Paul, 1980).

114. G. Globus, *Dream Life, Wake Life* (Albany, N.Y.: State University of New York Press, 1987), 178.

115. H. Ellis, *The World of Dreams* (Boston: Houghton Mifflin, 1911), 214.

116. R. Whitman, M. Kramer, and B. Baldridge, "Which Dream Does the Patient Tell?" *Archives of General Psychiatry* 8 (1963):277–82.

117. R. Fox et al., "The Experimenter Variable in Dream Research," *Diseases of the Nervous System* 29 (1968):698–701.

118. R. Whitman et al., "The Dreams of the Experimental Subject," *Journal of Nervous and Mental Disease* 134 (1962):431–39.

119. Ibid., 438.

120. B. Domhoff and J. Kamiya, "Problems in Dream Content Study with Objective Indicators," *Archives of General Psychiatry* 11 (1964):519–32.

121. W. Dement, E. Kahn, and H. Roffwarg, "The Influence of the Laboratory Situation on the Dreams of the Experimental Subject," *Journal of Nervous and Mental Disease* 149 (1965):129.

122. Ibid., 128–29.

123. Ibid., 131.

124. E. Fukuma, "A Study of Dreams by Using 'REMP-Awakening Technique'— Psychophysiological Study of Dreams in Normal Subjects: The First Report," *Psychiatria et Neurologia Japonica* 71 (1969):960–79; English summary, 1026–27.

125. B. Meier and I. Strauch, "The Phenomenology of REM-Dreams: Dream Settings, Dream Characters, Dream Topics, and Dream Realism," paper presented at conference of the Association for the Study of Dreams, Chicago, 1990.

126. M. Corsi-Cabrera et al., "Effect of Distorted Visual Input on Dream Content," *Sleep Research* 11 (1982):112.

127. B. Domhoff and J. Kamiya, "Problems in Dream Content Study with Objective Indicators," *Archives of General Psychiatry* 11 (1964):519–32.

128. B. Domhoff, "Home Dreams versus Laboratory Dreams," in *Dream Psychology and the New Biology of Dreaming*, ed. M. Kramer (Springfield, Ill.: Charles Thomas, 1969), 215.

129. C. Hall and R. Van de Castle, *Studies of Dreams Reported in the Laboratory and at Home*, Institute of Dream Research monograph series, no. 1 (Felton, Calif.: Big Trees Press, 1966).

130. C. Hall, "Representation of the Laboratory Setting in Dreams," *Journal of Nervous and Mental Disease* 144 (1967):206.

131. R. Weisz and D. Foulkes, "Home and Laboratory Dreams Collected Under Uniform Sampling Conditions," *Psychophysiology* 6 (1970): 588–96.

132. Ibid., 593.

133. Ibid., 594.

134. Ibid.

135. Ibid., 596.

136. T. Okuma, E. Fukuma, and K. Kobayashi, "Dream Detector and Comparison of Laboratory and Home Dreams Collected by REMP-Awakening Technique," in *Advances in Sleep Research*, ed. E. D. Weitzman, 2:223–31 (Bronx, N.Y.: Spectrum Publications, 1975).

137. V. S. C. Bose, "Dream Content Transformations: An Empirical Study of Freud's Secondary Revision Hypothesis" (doctoral dissertation, Andra University, Waltair, India, 1982).

CHAPTER 11

1. G. Heerman, "Beobachtungen und Betrachtungen uber die Traume der Blinden," *Monatschrift fur Medizin, Augenheilkunde und Chirurgie* (Leipzig) 1 (1838):116–80.

2. J. Jastrow, "Dreams of the Blind," *New Princeton Review* 5 (1888):18–34.

3. M. Calkins, "Statistics of Dreams," *American Journal of Psychology* 5 (1893):311–43.

4. Ibid., 325.

5. S. Weed and F. Hallam, "A Study of Dream Consciousness," *American Journal of Psychology* 7 (1896):405–11.

6. W. Monroe, "Mental Elements of Dreams," *Journal of Philosophy* 2 (1905):650–52.

7. W. Middleton, "Nocturnal Dreams," *Scientific Monthly* 37 (1933):460–64.

8. R. Husband, "Sex Differences in Dream Content," *Journal of Abnormal and Social Psychology* 30 (1936):513–21.

9. G. Ramsey, "Studies of Dreaming," *Psychological Bulletin* 50 (1953):432–55.

10. Ibid., 450–52.

11. L. Horton, "Inventorial Record Forms of Use in the Analysis of Dreams," *Journal of Abnormal Psychology* 8 (1914):393–404.

12. Ibid., 394–95.

13. Ibid., 397.

14. C. Hall, "A Cognitive Theory of Dream Symbols," *Journal of General Psychology* 48 (1953):169–86.

15. C. Hall, *The Meaning of Dreams* (New York: Harper and Row, 1953; McGraw-Hill, 1966).

16. C. E. Osgood, "The Representation Model and Relevant Research Methods," in *Trends in Content Analysis*, ed. I. de Sola Pool (Urbana: University of Illinois Press, 1959), 34.

17. C. Hall, "What People Dream About," *Scientific American* 184 (1951):60–63.

18. C. Hall and R. Van de Castle, *The Content Analysis of Dreams* (New York: Appleton-Century-Croft, 1966), x.

19. L. Monroe, "Review of *The Content*

Analysis of Dreams," *Contemporary Psychology* 12 (1967):607.

20. R. Brown and D. Donderi, "Dream Content and Self-Reported Well-Being Among Recurrent Dreamers, Past-Recurrent Dreamers, and Nonrecurrent Dreamers," *Journal of Personality and Social Psychology* 50 (1986):612–23.

21. V. S. C. Bose, "Dream Content Transformations: An Empirical Study of Freud's Secondary Revision Hypothesis" (doctoral dissertation, Andra University, Waltair, India, 1982).

22. P. Newton, "Recalled Dream Content and the Maintenance of Body Image," *Journal of Abnormal Psychology* 76 (1970):134–39.

23. M. Riechers, M. Kramer, and J. Trinder, "A Replication of the Hall–Van de Castle Character Scale Norms," paper read at meeting of the Association for the Psychophysiological Study of Sleep, Santa Fe, New Mexico, 1970.

24. C. Hall et al., "The Dreams of College Men and Women in 1950 and 1980: A Comparison of Dream Contents and Sex Differences," *Sleep* 5 (1982):188–94.

25. Ibid., 190–93.

26. V. Tonay, "California Women and Their Dreams: A Historical and Sub-Cultural Comparison of Dream Content," *Journal of Imagination, Cognition, and Personality* 10 (1991): 85–99.

27. C. Hall and B. Domhoff, "The Dreams of Freud and Jung," *Psychology Today*, June 1968.

28. C. Hall and R. Lind, *Dreams, Life, and Literature: A Study of Franz Kafka* (Chapel Hill: University of North Carolina Press, 1970).

29. A. Bell and C. Hall, *The Personality of a Child Molester: An Analysis of Dreams* (Chicago: Aldine Atherton, 1971).

30. C. Hall and V. Nordby, *The Individual and His Dreams* (New York: Signet, 1972).

31. R. Van de Castle, "Some Problems in Applying the Methodology of Content Analysis to Dreams," in *Dream Psychology and the New Biology of Dreaming*, ed. M. Kramer (Springfield, Ill.: Charles Thomas, 1969).

32. R. Van de Castle, "Animal Figures in Fantasy and Dreams," in *New Perspectives on our Lives With Companion Animals*, eds. A. Kacher and A. Beck, (Philadelphia: University of Pennsylvania Press, 1983).

33. S. Freud, *The Interpretation of Dreams* (New York: Basic Books, 1953), 410.

34. Ibid., 357.

35. E. Jones, *On the Nightmare* (New York: Grove, 1959), 70.

36. W. Stekel, *The Interpretation of Dreams* (New York: Grosset and Dunlap, 1962), 421.

37. E. Gutheil, *The Handbook of Dream Analysis* (New York: Grove, 1960).

38. N. Fodor, *New Approaches to Dream Interpretation* (New York: Citadel Press, 1962).

39. M. Boss, *The Analysis of Dreams* (New York: Philosophical Library, 1958), 49.

40. G. Booth, "Organ Function and Form Perception: Use of the Rorschach Method with Cases of Chronic Arthritis, Parkinsonianism and Arterial Hypertension," *Psychosomatic Medicine* 8 (1948):367–85; H. Linton, "Rorschach Correlates of Response to Suggestion," *Journal of Abnormal and Social Psychology* 49 (1954):75–83.

41. M. Boss, *The Analysis of Dreams* (New York: Philosophical Library, 1958).

42. W. S. Gill, "Animal Content in the Rorschach," *Journal of Projective Techniques and Personality Assessment* 31 (1967):49–56.

43. R. Seidel, "The Relationship of Animal Figures to Aggression and Ego Immaturity in the Dreams of Eleven and Twelve Year Old Children" (master's thesis, University of Virginia, Department of Foundation of Education, 1984).

44. C. Winget and M. Kramer, *Dimensions of Dreams* (Gainesville: University Press of Florida, 1979).

CHAPTER 12

1. S. Freud, *The Interpretation of Dreams* (New York: Basic Books, 1953), 8.

2. N. Fodor, *New Approaches to Dream Interpretation* (New York: Citadel Press, 1962).

3. J. English, *Different Doorway: Adventures of a Caesarean Born* (Point Reyes Station, Calif.: Earth Heart, 1985).

4. Ibid., 1.

5. C. Hall, "Are Prenatal and Birth Experiences Represented in Dreams?" *Psychoanalytic Review* 54 (1967a): 157–74.

6. C. Winget and M. Kramer, *Dimensions of Dreams* (Gainesville: University Press of Florida, 1979), 291–96.

7. P. Garfield, *Your Child's Dreams* (New York: Ballantine, 1984).

8. A. Wiseman, *Nightmare Help: A Guide for Parents and Teachers* (Berkeley, Calif.: Ten Speed Press, 1989).

9. D. Foulkes, *Children's Dreams: Longitudinal Studies* (New York: John Wiley, 1982); also D. Foulkes, "Children's Dreams," in *Handbook of Dreams: Research, Theories and Applications*, ed. B. Wolman (New York: Van Nostrand Reinhold, 1979); *Dreaming: A Cognitive-Psychological Analysis* (Hillsdale, N.J.: Lawrence Erlbaum, 1985).

10. D. Foulkes, "Children's Dreams," in *Handbook of Dreams: Research, Theories and Applications*, ed. B. Wolman (New York: Van Nostrand Reinhold, 1979), 131.

11. Ibid., 147.

12. J. Mack, *Nightmares and Human Conflict* (Boston: Little, Brown, 1970), 4–5.

13. D. Foulkes, "Children's Dreams," in *Handbook of Dreams: Research, Theories and Applications*, ed. B. Wolman (New York: Van Nostrand Reinhold, 1979), 150.

14. Ibid., 153.

15. C. Hall, "Strangers in Dreams: An Empirical Confirmation of the Oedipus Complex," *Journal of Personality* 31 (1963):336–45.

16. M. Howard, "Manifest Dream Content of Adolescents," *Dissertation Abstracts International* 39, 8–13 (1979):4103.

17. D. Foulkes, *Dreaming: A Cognitive-Psychological Analysis* (Hillsdale, N.J.: Lawrence Erlbaum, 1985), 133.

18. C. Winget, M. Kramer, and R. Whitman, "The Relationship of Socio-Economic Status and Race to Dream Content," *Psychophysiology* 7 (1972):325–26.

19. Ibid., 206.

20. C. Hall and B. Domhoff, "A Ubiquitous Sex Difference in Dreams," *Journal of Abnormal and Social Psychology* 9 (1963b): 259–67.

21. C. Hall, " 'A Ubiquitous Sex Difference in Dreams' Revisited," *Journal of Personality and Social Psychology* 46 (1984):1109–17.

22. Ibid., 1115.

23. A. Grey and D. Kalsched, "Oedipus East and West: An Exploration via Manifest Dream Content," *Journal of Cross-Cultural Psychology* 2 (1971):337–52.

24. S. Urbina and A. Grey, "Cultural and Sex Differences in the Sex Distribution of Dream Characters," *Journal of Cross-Cultural Psychology* 6: (1974): 358–64.

25. M. Lortie-Lussier, C. Schwab, and J. De Konick, "Working Mothers vs. Homemakers: Do Dreams Reflect the Changing Roles of Women?" *Sex Roles* 12 (1985):1009–21.

26. J. Wood, D. Sebba, and R. Griswold, "Stereotyped Masculine Interests as Related to the Sex of Dream Characters," *Sleep Research* 18 (1989):133.

27. R. Van de Castle, "Dream Content and Birth Order," *Sleep Research* 1 (1972):126.

28. W. Ritter, "Verbal Conditioning and the Recalled Content of Dreams," *Dissertation Abstracts* 24, no. 9 (1964):3840.

29. Ibid., 45.

30. C. Hall and B. Domhoff, "Aggression in Dreams," *International Journal of Social Psychiatry* 9 (1963):259–67.

31. C. Hall and B. Domhoff, "Friendliness in Dreams," *Journal of Social Psychology* 62 (1964):309–14.

32. M. Kramer, L. Kinney, and M. Scharf, "Sex Differences in Dreams," *Psychiatric Journal of the University of Ottawa* 8 (1983):1–4.

33. K. Rubenstein, "How Men and Women Dream Differently," in *Dreamtime and Dreamwork*, ed. S. Krippner, 135–42 (Los Angeles: Jeremy Tarcher, 1990).

34. M. Lortie-Lussier, C. Schwab, and J. De Konick, "Working Mothers vs. Homemakers: Do Dreams Reflect the Changing Roles of Women?" *Sex Roles* 12 (1985):1009–21.

35. N. Rinfret, M. Lortie-Lussier, and J. De Konick, "The Dreams of Professional Mothers and Female Students: An Exploration of Social Roles and Age Impact," *Dreaming* 1 (1991): 179–91.

36. M. Lortie-Lussier et al., "Beyond Sex Differences: Family and Occupational Roles' Impact on Women's and Men's Dreams," *Sex Roles* 26 (1992):79–96.

37. Ibid., 88–89.

38. Ibid., 91.

39. Ibid., 92.

40. Ibid., 94.

41. V. Tonay, "Behavioral Continuity and Affective Compensation: Personality Correlates of Dream Recall and Content" (master's thesis, University of California, Berkeley, 1988).

42. C. B. Brenneis, "Male and Female Ego Modalities in Manifest Dream Context," *Journal of Abnormal Psychology* 76 (1970):434–42.

43. Ibid., 440–41.

44. C. B. Brenneis and S. Roll, "Dream Patterns in Anglo and Chicano Young Adults," *Psychiatry* 39 (1976):280–90.

45. Ibid., 285–86.

46. D. Bakan, *The Duality of Human Existence* (Chicago: Rand McNally, 1966).

47. E. Turpin, "Correlates of Ego-Level and Agency-Communion in Stage REM Dreams of 11–13 Year Old Children," *Journal of Child Psychology and Psychiatry and Applied Disciplines* 17 (1976):169–80.

48. D. B. Cohen, "Sex Role Orientation and Dream Recall," *Journal of Abnormal Psychology* 82 (1973):246–52.

49. J. Thomas, "The Relationship Between the Manifest Content of Dreams and Personality Integration," *Sleep Research* 10 (1981):166.

50. C. Winget and R. Farrell, "A Comparison of the Dreams of Homosexual and Non-Homosexual Males," *Psychophysiology* 9 (1972):119.

51. S. Krippner et al., "Content Analysis of 30 Dreams from 10 Pre-Operative Male Transsexuals," *Journal of the American Society of Psychosomatic Dentistry and Medicine*, monograph supplement no. 2 (1974), 3–23.

52. J. Money and J. G. Brennan, "Sexual Dimorphism in the Psychology of Female Transsexuals," in *Transsexualism and Sex Reassignment*, ed. R. Green and J. Money (Baltimore: Johns Hopkins University Press, 1969), 145–46.

53. C. Ward et al., "Birth Order and Dreams," *Journal of Social Psychology* 90 (1973):155–56.

54. J. Buckley, "The Dreams of Young Adults" (Sociological Analysis of 1,133 Dreams of Black and White Students), *Dissertation Abstracts International* 31, 7-A (1971):3635.

55. C. Winget, M. Kramer, and R. Whitman, "The Relationship of Socio-Economic Status and Race to Dream Content," *Psychophysiology* 7 (1972):325–26.

56. I. Harris, "Observations Concerning Typical Anxiety Dreams," *Psychiatry* 11 (1948): 301–9.

57. C. Hall, "The Significance of the Dream of Being Attacked," *Journal of Personality* 24 (1955):168–80.

58. K. Achte and T. Schakir, "A Study of the Dreams of a Group of Bushmen," in World Psychiatric Association Symposium on the Psychopathology of Dream and Sleeping, ed. K. Achte and T. Tamminen, *Psychiatria Fennica Supplementum* (Auranen, Forssa, Finland, 1985).

59. E. Stark, "To Sleep, Perchance to Dream," *Psychology Today*, October 1984, 16.

60. L. Gahagen, "Sex Differences in Recall of Stereotyped Dreams, Sleep-Talking, and Sleep-Walking," *Journal of Genetic Psychology* 48 (1936):227–36.

61. M. de Martino, "Sex Differences in the Dreams of Southern College Students," *Journal of Clinical Psychology* 9 (1953):199–201.

62. R. Griffith, O. Miyagi, and A. Tago, "The Universality of Dreams: Japanese vs. Americans," *American Anthropologist* 60 (1958):1173–79.

63. D. Schacter and H. Crovitz, " 'Falling' While Falling Asleep: Sex Differences," *Perceptual and Motor Skills* 44 (1977):656.

64. M. de Martino, "Some Characteristics

of the Manifest Dream Content of Mental Defectives," *Journal of Clinical Psychology* 10 (1954):175–78.

65. S. Lorand, "On the Meaning of Losing Teeth in Dreams," *Psychoanalytic Quarterly* 17 (1948):529–30.

66. J. M. Schneck, "Loss of Teeth in Dreams Symbolizing Fear of Aging," *Perceptual and Motor Skills* 24 (1967):792.

67. F. Coolidge and D. Bracken, "The Loss of Teeth in Dreams: An Empirical Investigation," *Psychological Reports* 54 (1984):931–35.

68. P. Robbins and F. Houshi, "Some Observations on Recurrent Dreams," *Bulletin of the Menninger Clinic* 47 (1983):262–65.

69. R. Cartwright, "The Nature and Function of Repetitive Dreams: A Survey and Speculation," *Psychiatry* 42 (1979):131–37.

70. R. Cartwright and I. Romanek, "Repetitive Dreams of Normal Subjects," *Sleep Research* 7 (1978):174; C. Browman and L. Kapell, "Repetitive Sexual Dream Content of Normal Adults," *Sleep Research* 11 (1982):115.

71. G. Klein et al. "Recurrent Dream Fragments and Fantasies Elicited in Interrupted and Completed REM Periods," *Psychophysiology* 7 (1971):331–32.

72. S. Freud, *The Interpretation of Dreams* (New York: Basic Books, 1953), 190.

73. C. Jung, in G. Adler, ed. *C. G. Jung: Letters*, Bollingen series, no. 95 (Princeton: Princeton University Press, 1973), 1:93.

74. R. Cartwright, "The Nature and Function of Repetitive Dreams: A Survey and Speculation," *Psychiatry* 42 (1979):136.

75. R. Brown and D. Donderi, "Dream Content and Self-Reported Well-Being Among Recurrent Dreamers, Past-Recurrent Dreamers, and Nonrecurrent Dreamers," *Journal of Personality and Social Psychology* 50 (1986):612–23.

76. Ibid., 619.

77. J. Taylor, *Where People Fly and Water Runs Uphill* (New York: Warner Books, 1992), 178–79.

78. Ibid., 173.

79. Ibid., 12.

80. W. Turner, "The Bradshaw Lecture on Neuroses and Psychoses of War," *Lancet* 2 (1918): 613–17.

81. G. Crile, *A Mechanistic View of War and Peace* (New York: Macmillan, 1915).

82. R. Wilkinson, "Anatomy of a Cakewalk," *Newsweek*, March 11, 1991, 48.

83. M. Kramer, L. Schoen, and L. Kinney, "Nightmares in Vietnam Veterans," *Journal of the American Academy of Psychoanalysis* 15 (1987):79.

84. L. Gahagen, "Sex Differences in Recall of Stereotyped Dreams, Sleep-Talking, and Sleep-Walking," *Journal of Genetic Psychology* 48 (1936):227–36.

85. J. Titchner and F. Kapp, "Family and Character Change at Buffalo Creek," *American Journal of Psychiatry* 133 (1976):298.

86. Z. Cernovsky, "Interpretations of the Refugee Nightmare," *ASD Newsletter* 3, no. 3 (1986).

87. R. Broughton, "Sleep Disorders: Disorders of Arousal?" *Science* 159 (1968):1070–78.

88. G. Little, "The Causation of Night-Terrors," *British Medical Journal*, August 19, 1899.

89. I.-G. Agrell and A. Axelsson, "The Relationship Between Pavor Nocturnus and Adenoids," *Acta Paedopsychiatrica* 39, pt. 3 (1972): 46–53.

90. E. Kurthe, I. Gohler, and H. Knaapa, "Untersuchungen uber den Pavor Nocturnus bei Kindern" [Research regarding night terrors in children], *Psychiatrie, Neurologie, und Medizinische Psychologie* 17 (1965):1–7.

91. E. Hartmann, *The Nightmare* (New York: Basic Books, 1984), 7–8.

92. E. O. Bixler et al., "Prevalence of Sleep Disorders in the Los Angeles Metropolitan Area," *American Journal of Psychiatry* 136 (1979):1257–62.

93. A. Kales et al., "Nightmares: Clinical Characteristics and Personality Patterns," *American Journal of Psychiatry* 137 (1980): 1197–1201; E. Hartmann et al., "Who Has Nightmares? The Personality of the Lifelong

Nightmare Sufferer," *Archives of General Psychiatry* 44 (1987):49–56.

94. D. Belicki and K. Belicki, "Nightmares in a University Population," *Sleep Research* 11 (1982):116.

95. J. Mack, *Nightmares and Human Conflict* (Boston: Little, Brown, 1970), 13.

96. G. Halliday, "Direct Psychological Therapies for Nightmares: A Review," *ASD Newsletter* 2 (1985).

97. M. Hersen, "Nightmare Behavior: A Review," *Psychological Bulletin* 78 (1972):37–48.

98. C. B. Brenneis, "Developmental Aspects of Aging in Women: A Comparative Study of Dreams," *Archives of General Psychiatry* 32 (1975):429–35.

99. M. Barad, K. Altschuler, and A. Goldfarb, "A Survey of Dreams in Aged Persons," *Archives of General Psychiatry* 4 (1961): 419–24.

100. K. Altschuler, M. Barad, and A. Goldfarb, "A Survey of Dreams in the Aged," *Archives of General Psychiatry* 8 (1963):33–37.

101. Ibid., 50.

102. J. Howe and K. Blick, "Emotional Content of Dreams Recalled by Elderly Women," *Perceptual and Motor Skills* 56 (1983):31–34.

103. K. Achte, P.-L. Malassu, and M. Saarenheimo, "Sleeping and Dreams of 75-Year-Old People Living in Helsinki," in World Psychiatric Association Symposium on the Psychopathology of Dream and Sleeping, ed. K. Achte and T. Tamminen. *Psychiatria Fennica Supplementum* (Auranen, Forssa, Finland, 1985).

104. M. Stromba-Badiale, A. Ceretti, and G. Forni, "Aspetti del Sonno nel Soggetto Anzians e Molto Anziano" [Aspects of Sleep in Old and Very Old Subjects], *Minerva Medica* 70 (1979):2551–54.

105. J. Freeman, "Sexual Capacities in the Aging Male," *Geriatrics* 16 (1961):37–43.

106. E. Kahn and C. Fisher, "REM Sleep and Sexuality in the Aged," *Journal of Geriatric Psychiatry* 2 (1969):181–99.

107. D. Gutmann, "Aging Among the Highland Maya: A Comparative Study," *Journal of Personality and Social Psychology* 7 (1967): 28–35.

108. A. Krohn and D. Gutmann, "Changes in Mastery Style with Age: A Study of Navajo Dreams," *Psychiatry* 34 (1971):289–300.

109. J. Grant, *Dreamers* (Bath: Ashgrove Press, 1984), 16.

110. E. Erikson, "Identity and the Life Cycle," *Psychological Issues*, monograph 1 (1959).

111. M. Barad, K. Altschuler, and A. Goldfarb, "A Survey of Dreams in Aged Persons," *Archives of General Psychiatry* 4 (1961): 421.

112. R. Macnish, *The Philosophy of Sleep*, 3d ed. (Glasgow: MM'Phun, 1836), 96.

113. H. Greenberg and H. Blank, "Dreams of a Dying Patient," *British Journal of Medical Psychology* 43 (1970):355–62.

114. M.-L. von Franz, *On Dreams and Death* (Boston: Shambala, 1986), 156.

115. Ibid., 57.

116. Ibid., 64.

117. R. Butler, "The Life Review: An Interpretation of Reminiscence in the Aged," *Psychiatry* 26 (1963):65–76.

CHAPTER 13

1. V. N. Kasatkin, *Teoriya Snovidenii* [Theory of Dreams] (Leningrad: Meditsina, 1967), 352.

2. E. Ellenberger and H. F. Ellenberger. "Recherches Recentes en Russie sur les Reves," *L'Union Medicale du Canada* 104 (1975): 1667–76.

3. W. Dick and H. Gris, *National Enquirer*, March 18, 1975, 8.

4. F. Seafield, *The Literature and Curiosities of Dreams*, 4th ed. (London: Lockwood, 1869) 270–71.

5. R. A. Lockhart, "Cancer in Myth and Dream: An Exploration into the Archetypal Relation Between Dreams and Disease," *Spring* 1 (1977):1–26.

6. B. Siegel, *Peace, Love and Healing* (New York: Harper and Row, 1989), 64–65.

7. D. Schneider, *Revolution in the Body-Mind. I. Forewarning Cancer Dreams and the Bioplasma Concept* (Easthampton, N.Y.: Alexa Press, 1976).

8. Ibid., 7.

9. Ibid., 9.

10. D. Schneider, "Conversion of Massive Anxiety into Heart Attack," *American Journal of Psychotherapy* 27 (1973):360–78.

11. A. Ziegler, "A Cardiac Infarction and a Dream as Synchronous Events," *Journal of Analytical Psychology* 7 (1962):142–43.

12. W. Cassell, "Responses to Ink-Blot Configurations Resembling the Heart," *Journal of Projective Techniques and Personality Assessment* 33 (1969):123–26.

13. L. Linn, "The Suggestion to Dream About Sickness," *Journal of Hillside Hospital* 3 (1954):154–65.

14. H. Warnes and A. Finkelstein, "Dreams That Precede a Psychosomatic Illness," *Canadian Psychiatric Association Journal* 16 (1971):317–25.

15. E. Mitchell, "The Physiological Diagnostic Dream," *New York Medical Journal* 118 (1923):417.

16. M. Boss, *The Analysis of Dreams* (New York: Philosophical Library, 1958), 160.

17. J. Jewell, "The Psychology of Dreams," *American Journal of Psychology* 16 (1905):9.

18. H. Warnes and A. Finkelstein, "Dreams That Precede a Psychosomatic Illness," *Canadian Psychiatric Association Journal* 16 (1971):319.

19. E. Gutheil, "Dreams as an Aid to Evaluating Ego-Strength," *American Journal of Psychiatry* 12 (1958):338–57.

20. H. Vande Kemp, "The Dream in Periodical Literature: 1860–1910: From *Oneirocritica* to *Die Traumdeutung* via the Questionnaire" (doctoral dissertation, University of Massachusetts, 1997), University Microfilms 77–15, 279.

21. O. Sacks, *Awakenings* (New York: Dutton, 1983), 67–79.

22. P. Garfield, *The Healing Power of Dreams* (New York: Simon and Schuster, 1991), 108–9.

23. M. Boss, *The Analysis of Dreams* (New York: Philosophical Library, 1958), 162–63.

24. E. Mitchell, "The Physiological Diagnostic Dream," *New York Medical Journal* 118 (1923):417.

25. M. de Manaceine, *Sleep: Its Physiology, Pathology, Hygiene, and Psychology* (New York: Charles Scribner's, 1897), 292–93.

26. *ASD Newsletter* 6, no. 2 (1989):9.

27. E. Mitchell, "The Physiological Diagnostic Dream," *New York Medical Journal* 118 (1923):416.

28. R. Smith, "The Meaning of Dreams: The Need for a Standardized Dream Report," *Psychiatry Research* 13 (1984):267–74.

29. R. Smith, "Evaluating Dream Function: Emphasizing the Study of Patients with Organic Disease," in *Cognition and Dream Research*, ed. R. Haskell, (*Journal of Mind and Behavior*, 7 (2–3) 1986), 206.

30. P. Garfield, *The Healing Power of Dreams* (New York: Simon and Schuster, 1991).

31. E. Van Liere and J. Stickney, *Hypoxia* (Chicago: University of Chicago Press, 1963).

32. E. Cayce, *Dreams and Dreaming: The Edgar Cayce Readings*, comp. M. Peterson (Virginia Beach, Va.: Association for Research and Enlightenment, 1976).

33. B. Hill, *Gates of Horn and Ivory: An Anthology of Dreams* (New York: Taplinger, 1967).

34. J. Baylis, "Sleep On It!" *Sundance Community Dream Journal* 2 (1978):152.

35. W. Dement, *Some Must Watch While Some Must Sleep* (San Francisco: W. H. Freeman, 1972), 102

36. P. Garfield, *The Healing Power of Dreams* (New York: Simon and Schuster, 1991), 200.

37. F. Myers, *Human Personality and Its Survival of Bodily Death*, ed. S. Smith (New Hyde Park, N.Y.: University Books, 1961), 86–87.

38. E. Sechrist, *Dreams: Your Magic Mirror* (New York: Cowles, 1968).

39. J. Baylis, *Sleep On It! The Practical Side*

of Dreaming (Marina del Rey, Calif.: De Vorss and Co., 1977).

40. R. Tuch, "The Relationship Between a Mother's Menstrual Status and Her Response to Illness in Her Child," *Psychosomatic Medicine* 37 (1975):388–94.

41. R. Van de Castle, *The Psychology of Dreaming* (Morristown, N.J.: General Learning Press, 1971), 40.

42. T. Benedek, *Psychosexual Factors in Women* (New York: Ronald Press, 1952).

43. J. Woolger and R. Woolger, *The Goddess Within: A Guide to the Eternal Myths That Shape Women's Lives* (New York: Ballantine, 1987).

44. E. Gadon, *The Once and Future Goddess* (New York: Harper and Row, 1989).

45. R. Van de Castle and P. Kinder, "Dream Content During Pregnancy," *Psychophysiology* 4 (1968):375; R. Van de Castle, *The Psychology of Dreaming* (Morristown, N.J.: General Learning Press, 1971).

46. D. Schneider, *Revolution in the Body-Mind. I. Forewarning Cancer Dreams and the Bioplasma Concept* (Easthampton, N.Y.: Alexa Press, 1976), 17.

47. J. Smith, "Dream Baby," *Sundance Community Dream Journal* 3 (1979):150–59.

48. P. Garfield, *Women's Bodies, Women's Dreams* (New York: Ballantine, 1988), 173

49. M. Boss, *The Analysis of Dreams* (New York: Philosophical Library, 1958), 156.

50. E. Stukane, *The Dream Worlds of Pregnancy* (New York: William Morrow, 1985), 15.

51. P. Maybruck, "An Exploratory Study of the Dreams of Pregnant Women" (doctoral dissertation, Saybrook University, San Francisco, 1986), 188–89.

52. P. Maybruck, "Pregnancy and Dreams," in *Dreamtime and Dreamwork*, ed. S. Krippner (Los Angeles: Jeremy Tarcher, 1990), 151.

53. C. Winget and F. Kapp, "The Relationship of the Manifest Content of Dreams to Duration of Childbirth in Primaparae," *Psychosomatic Medicine* 34 (1972):313–20.

54. Ibid., 317–18.

55. P. Maybruck, "Pregnancy and Dreams," in *Dreamtime and Dreamwork*, ed. S. Krippner (Los Angeles: Jeremy Tarcher, 1990), 149.

56. E. Stukane, *The Dream Worlds of Pregnancy* (New York: William Morrow, 1985).

Chapter 14

1. S. Freud, "Dreams and Telepathy" (1922), in *Psychoanalysis and the Occult*, ed. G. Devereux (New York: International Universities Press, 1953), 86; C. Jung, *Dreams*, trans. R. F. C. Hull (Princeton, N.J.: Princeton University Press, 1974), 47; W. Stekel, *The Interpretation of Dreams* (New York: Grosset and Dunlap, 1962), 552; M. Boss, *The Analysis of Dreams* (New York: Philosophical Library, 1958), 182.

2. G. Murphy, *Challenge of Psychical Research* (New York: Harpers, 1961), 36.

3. I. Stevenson, "Seven More Paranormal Experiences Associated with the Sinking of the Titanic," *Journal of the American Society of Psychical Research* 59 (1965):211–24; see also I. Stevenson, "Precognition of Disasters," *Journal of the American Society of Psychical Research* 64 (1970):187–210.

4. J. Barker, "Premonitions of the Aberfan Disaster," *Journal of the Society for Psychical Research* 44 (1967):169–81.

5. L. Rhine, *Hidden Channels of the Mind* (New York: William Sloane, 1961).

6. E. Gurney, F. Meyers, and F. Podmore, *Phantasms of the Living*, 2 vols. (London: Trubner, 1886); C. Flammarion, *The Unknown* (New York: Harper, 1900); W. Prince, "Human Experiences," *Bulletin of the Boston Society for Psychic Research* 14 (1931):5–328; O. Stevens, *The Mystery of Dreams* (New York: Dodd, Mead, 1949).

7. G. Devereux, ed., *Psychoanalysis and the Occult* (New York: International Universities Press, 1953).

8. J. Eisenbud, *PSI and Psychoanalysis* (New York: Grune and Stratton, 1970).

9. G. Pederson-Krag, "Telepathy and Re-

pression," *Psychoanalytic Quarterly* 16 (1947): 61–68.

10. W. Gillespie, "Extrasensory Elements in Dream Interpretation," in *Psychoanalysis and the Occult*, ed. G. Devereux (New York: International Universities Press, 1953).

11. D. Ryback, *Dreams That Come True* (New York: Doubleday, 1988).

12. W. Prince, "Human Experiences," *Bulletin of the Boston Society for Psychic Research* 14 (1931):5–328.

13. R. Van de Castle, "Sleep and Dreams," in *Handbook of Parapsychology*, ed. B. Wolman (New York: Van Nostrand Reinhold, 1977).

14. W. Bowles and F. Hynds, *Psi Search* (San Francisco: Harper and Row, 1978).

15. G. Murphy, "Introductory Address," in *Technique and Status of Modern Parapsychology: AAAS Symposium*, ed. D. Dean (Newark, N.J.: Newark College of Engineering Press, 1971), 3.

16. J. Eisenbud, *Psi and Psychoanalysis* (New York: Grune and Stratton, 1970), 55.

17. G. Ermacora, "Telepathic Dreams Experimentally Produced," *Proceedings of the Society for Psychical Research* 11 (1895):235–308.

18. W. Daim, "Studies in Dream-Telepathy," *Tomorrow* 2 (1953):35–48.

19. M. Ullman, S. Krippner, and A. Vaughan, *Dream Telepathy* (New York: Macmillan, 1973); *Dream Telepathy: Explorations in Nocturnal ESP*, 2d ed. (Jefferson, N.C.: McFarland, 1989).

20. C. Hall, "Experimente zur Telepathischen Beeinflussung von Traumen [Experiments on Telepathically Influenced Dreams]," *Zeitschrift fur Parapsychologie und Grenzgebeite der Psychologie* 10 (1967b): 18–47.

21. E. Hall, *Possible Impossibilities: A Look at Parapsychology* (Boston: Houghton Mifflin, 1977), 127.

22. J. Grant, *Dreamers* (Bath: Ashgrove Press, 1984), 135.

23. I. L. Child, "Psychology and Anomalous Observations: The Question of ESP in Dreams," *American Psychologist* 40 (1985):1223.

24. Ibid., 1228.

25. E. M. Hansel, *ESP and Parapsychology: A Critical Reevaluation* (Buffalo: Prometheus, 1980).

26. E. Belvedere and D. Foulkes, "Telepathy and Dreams: A Failure to Replicate," *Perceptual and Motor Skills* 33 (1971):783–89.

27. R. Van de Castle, "ESP in Dreams: Comments on a Replication 'Failure' by the Failing Subject," in *Dream Telepathy: Explorations in Nocturnal ESP*, ed. M. Ullman, S. Krippner, and A. Vaughan, 2d ed. (Jefferson, N.C.: McFarland, 1989).

28. E. M. Hansel, *ESP and Parapsychology: A Critical Reevaluation* (Buffalo: Prometheus, 1980), 245.

29. Ibid., 246.

30. M. Ullman, S, Krippner, and A. Vaughan, *Dream Telepathy* (New York: Macmillan, 1973), 236.

31. Ibid., 238.

32. A. Rechtschaffen, "Sleep and Dream States: An Experimental Design," in *Psi Favorable States of Consciousness*, ed. R. Cavanna, 87–120 (New York: Parapsychology Foundation, 1970), 89.

33. Ibid., 89.

34. Ibid., 91.

35. Ibid., 92.

36. Ibid.

37. R. Van de Castle, "The D.N.B. Telepathy Project," *Dream Network Bulletin* 5, no. 1 (1986), 6.

38. L. Magallon and B. Shor, "Shared Dreaming: Joining Together in Dreamtime," in *Dreamtime and Dreamwork*, ed. S. Krippner (Los Angeles: Jeremy Tarcher, 1990).

CHAPTER 15

1. Aristotle, *On Dreams*, ed. R. Hutchings, Great Books of the Western World, vol. 8 (Chicago: Encyclopedia Brittanica, 1952), 703–6.

2. S. LaBerge, *Lucid Dreaming* (New York: Ballantine, 1986).

3. M. Kelsey, *Dreams: The Dark Speech of*

the Spirit (New York: Doubleday, 1968), 264–65.

4. W. Evans-Wentz, *Tibetan Yoga and Secret Doctrines* (London: Oxford University Press, 1958).

5. I. Shah, *The Sufis* (London: Octagon Press, 1984).

6. C. den Blanken and E. Meijer, "An Historical View of *Dreams and the Ways to Direct Them*, by Marie-Jean-Leon Lecoq, le Marquis d'Hervey-Saint-Denys," *Lucidity* 10, nos. 1–2 (1991):314.

7. F. Van Eeden, "A Study of Dreams," *Proceedings of the Society for Psychical Research* 26 (1913):431–61.

8. O. Fox, *Astral Projection* (New Hyde Park, N.Y.: University Books, 1962), 32–33.

9. Ibid., 34.

10. R. DeMille, *Castenada's Journey: The Power and the Allegory* (Santa Barbara: Capra Press, 1976).

11. P. Garfield, *Creative Dreaming* (New York: Simon and Schuster, 1974), 143.

12. A. Faraday, *The Dream Game* (New York: Harper and Row, 1976), 263.

13. A. Faraday, "Once Upon a Dream," *Voices* 14 (1978):67–76.

14. O. Fox, *Astral Projection* (New Hyde Park, N.Y.: University Books, 1962), 90.

15. S. LaBerge, *Lucid Dreaming* (New York: Ballantine, 1986), 271.

16. P. Garfield, *Pathway to Ecstasy* (New York: Holt, Rinehart and Winston, 1979), 44.

17. S. LaBerge, *Lucid Dreaming* (New York: Ballantine, 1986), 73.

18. J. Dane and R. Van de Castle, "A Comparison of Waking Instruction and Posthypnotic Suggestion for Lucid Dream Induction," *Lucidity* 10, nos. 1–2 (1991):209–14.

19. J. Gackenbach, "Women and Meditators as Gifted Lucid Dreamers," in *Dreamtime and Dreamwork*, ed. S. Krippner, 244–51 (Los Angeles: Jeremy Tarcher, 1990).

20. J. Gackenbach, R. Cranson, and C. Alexander, "Lucid Dreaming, Witnessing Dreaming, and Transcendental Meditation Technique:

A Developmental Relationship," *Lucidity Letter* 5, no, 2 (1986):34–40.

21. J. Gackenbach, "An Estimate of Lucid Dreaming Incidence," *Lucidity*, 10, nos. 1–2 (1991):7.

22. D. Armstrong-Hickey, "A Validation of Lucid Dreaming in School Age Children," *Lucidity* 10, nos. 1–2 (1991):250–54.

23. J. Gackenbach and J. Bosveld, *Control Your Dreams* (New York: Harper and Row, 1989), 91–92.

24. P. Tholey, "Overview of the Development of Lucid Dream Research in Germany," *Lucidity* 10, nos. 1–2 (1991):349.

25. Ibid.

26. C. Comstock, "Internal Self Helpers or Centers," *Integration* 3 (1987):3–12.

27. P. Tholey, "Overview of the Development of Lucid Dream Research in Germany," *Lucidity* 10, nos. 1–2 (1991):349.

28. C. Green, *Lucid Dreams* (London: Hamish Hamilton, 1968), 110.

29. H. S. Sullivan, *Conceptions of Modern Psychiatry* (New York: William Alanson White Psychiatric Foundation, 1940), 34.

30. J. Taylor, *Where People Fly and Water Runs Uphill* (New York: Warner Books, 1992), 218.

31. K. Kelzer, *The Sun and the Shadow* (Virginia Beach, Va.: A.R.E. Press, 1987), 213.

32. J. Gackenbach and J. Bosveld, *Control Your Dreams* (New York: Harper and Row, 1989), 172.

33. R. Moody, *Life After Life* (Atlanta: Mockingbird Books, 1977), 24.

34. G. Gabbard, S. Twenlow, and F. Jones, "Do 'Near-Death Experiences' Occur Only Near Death?" *Journal of Nervous and Mental Disorders* 169 (1981):375–77.

35. J. Gackenbach and J. Bosveld, *Control Your Dreams* (New York: Harper and Row, 1989), 129.

36. O. Fox, *Astral Projection* (New Hyde Park, N.Y.: University Books, 1962), 90.

37. P. Garfield, *Pathway to Ecstasy* (New York: Holt, Rinehart and Winston, 1979; rev. ed., New York: Prentice Hall, 1989), 204–5.

38. G. S. Sparrow, *Lucid Dreaming: Dawning of the Clear Light* (Virginia Beach, Va.: A.R.E. Press, 1982), 51.

39. Ibid., 12–13.

40. G. Gillespie, "Light in Lucid Dreams: A Review," *Dreaming* 2 (1992):167–80.

41. Ibid., 171.

42. F. Bogzaran, "Experiencing the Divine in the Lucid Dream State," *Lucidity* 10, nos. 1–2 (1991):169–76.

43. K. Kelzer, *The Sun and the Shadow* (Virginia Beach, Va.: A.R.E. Press, 1987), 232.

AFTERWORD

1. J. Taylor, *Dream Work* (New York: Paulist Press, 1983): 18–19.

APPENDIX B

1. H. Reed, *Getting Help from Your Dreams* (New York: Ballantine, 1989)

2. H. Reed, *Dream Solutions* (San Rafael, CA.: New World Library, 1991)

BIBLIOGRAPHY

Achte, K., P.-L. Malassu, and M. Saarenheimo. 1985. Sleeping and Dreams of 75-Year-Old People Living in Helsinki. In World Psychiatric Association Symposium on the Psychopathology of Dream and Sleeping, ed. K. Achte and T. Tamminen. *Psychiatria Fennica Supplementum.* Auranen, Forssa, Finland.

Achte, K., and T. Schakir. 1985. A Study of the Dreams of a Group of Bushmen. In World Psychiatric Association Symposium on the Psychopathology of Dream and Sleeping, ed. K. Achte and T. Tamminen. *Psychiatria Fennica Supplementum.* Auranen, Forssa, Finland.

Adelson, J. 1960. Creativity and the Dream. *Merrill Palmer Quarterly* 6:92–97.

Adler, A. 1931. *What Life Should Mean to You.* New York: Capricorn.

———. 1936. On the Interpretation of Dreams. *International Journal of Individual Psychology* 2:3–16.

Adler, Alexandra. 1948. *Guiding Human Misfits.* London: Faber and Faber.

Adler, G., ed. 1973. *C. G. Jung: Letters.* Vol. 1, 1906–1950. Bollingen series, no. 95. Princeton: Princeton University Press.

Agrell, I.-G., and A. Axelsson. 1972. The Relationship Between Pavor Nocturnus and Adenoids. *Acta Paedopsychiatrica* 39 (pt. 3):46–53.

Allison, T., and H. Van Twyver. 1970. The Evolution of Sleep. *Natural History* 79:56–65.

Altschuler, K., M. Barad, and A. Goldfarb. 1963. A Survey of Dreams in the Aged. *Archives of General Psychiatry* 8:33–37.

Ansbacher, H., and R. Ansbacher, eds. 1956.

The Individual Psychology of Alfred Adler. New York: Basic Books.

Aquinas, T. 1947. Is Divination Unlawful? In *The World of Dreams*, ed. R. L. Woods. New York: Random House.

Archer, W. 1935. *On Dreams.* ed. T. Besterman. London: Methuen.

Aristides, A. 1973. *Aristides.* Trans. C. Behr. 4 vols. Cambridge, Mass.: Harvard University Press.

Aristotle. 1952. On Dreams. Ed. R. Hutchings. Great books of the Western World, vol. 8. Chicago: Encyclopædia Brittanica.

Armstrong, R., et al. 1965. Dreams and Gastric Secretions in Duodenal Ulcer Patients. *New Physician* 14:241–43.

Armstrong-Hickey, D. 1991. A Validation of Lucid Dreaming in School Age Children. *Lucidity* 10 (1–2):250–54.

Artemidorus. 1975. *Oneirocritica: The Interpretation of Dreams.* Trans. R. White. Torrance, Calif.: Original Books.

Aserinsky, E., and N. Kleitman. 1953. Regularly Occurring Periods of Eye Motility, and Concomitant Phenomena During Sleep. *Science* 118:273–74.

———. 1955. Two Types of Ocular Motility Occurring in Sleep. *Journal of Applied Physiology* 8:1–10.

Bakan, D. 1966. *The Duality of Human Existence.* Chicago: Rand McNally.

Bakan, P. 1977–78. Dreaming, REM Sleep, and the Right Hemisphere: A Theoretical Integration. *Journal of Altered States of Consciousness* 3:285–307.

Baldridge, B. 1966. Physical Concomitants of Dreaming and the Effect of Stimulation on Dreams. *Ohio State Medical Journal* 62:1271–79.

Baldridge, B., R. Whitman, and M. Kramer. 1963. A Simplified Method for Detecting Eye Movements During Dreaming. *Psychosomatic Medicine* 25:78–82.

Barad, M., K. Altschuler, and A. Goldfarb. 1961. A Survey of Dreams in Aged Persons. *Archives of General Psychiatry* 4:419–24.

Barker, J. 1967. Premonitions of the Aberfan Disaster. *Journal of the Society for Psychical Research* 44:169–81.

Bass, V. 1984. ed. *Dreams Can Point the Way.* Sugar Land, Tex.: Miracle House Books

Baylis, J. 1977. *Sleep On It! The Practical Side of Dreaming.* Marina del Rey, Calif.: De Vorss and Co.

———. 1978. Sleep On It! *Sundance Community Dream Journal* 2:149–65.

Belicki, D., and K. Belicki. 1982. Nightmares in a University Population. *Sleep Research* 11:116.

Bell, A., and C. Hall. 1971. *The Personality of a Child Molester: An Analysis of Dreams.* Chicago: Aldine Atherton.

Bell, Anita I. 1975. Male Anxiety During Sleep. *International Journal of Psycho-analysis* 56 (4):455–64.

Bell, Anita I., and C. Stroebel. 1973. The Scrotal Sac and Testes During Sleep: Physiological Correlates and Mental Content. In *Sleep: Physiology, Biochemistry, Psychology, Pharmacology, Clinical Implications*, 380–84. Basel: Karger.

Belvedere, E., and D. Foulkes. 1971. Telepathy and Dreams: A Failure to Replicate. *Perceptual and Motor Skills* 33:783–89.

Benedek, T. 1952. *Psychosexual Factors in Women.* New York: Ronald Press.

Beradt, C. 1968. *The Third Reich of Dreams.* Chicago: Quadrangle Books.

Berger, R. 1963. Experimental Modification of Dream Content by Meaningful Verbal Stimuli. *British Journal of Psychiatry* 109:722–40.

Birnholz, J. 1983. The Development of Human Fetal Learning. *Science* 222:516–18.

Bixler, E. O., et al. 1979. Prevalence of Sleep Disorders in the Los Angeles Metropolitan Area. *American Journal of Psychiatry* 136:1257–62.

Blake, H., and R. Gerard. 1937. Brain Potentials During Sleep. *American Journal of Physiology* 119:692–703.

Blomefield, F. 1947. The Swaffham Tinker. In *The World of Dreams*, ed. R. L. Woods. New York: Random House.

Bogzaran, F. 1991. Experiencing the Divine

in the Lucid Dream State. *Lucidity* 10 (1–2):169–76.

Bohm, D. 1980. *Wholeness and the Implicate Order*. Boston: Routledge and Kegan Paul.

Bokert, E. 1968. The Effects of Thirst and a Related Verbal Stimulus on Dream Reports. *Dissertation Abstracts* 28 (4753B):122–31.

Bonuzzi, L. 1975. About the Origins of the Scientific Study of Sleep and Dreaming. In *Experimental Study of Human Sleep: Methodological Problems*, ed. G. Lairy and P. Salzarulo. Amsterdam: Elsevier Scientific.

Booth, G. 1948. Organ Function and Form Perception: Use of the Rorschach Method with Cases of Chronic Arthritis, Parkinsonianism and Arterial Hypertension. *Psychosomatic Medicine* 8:367–85.

Borner, J. 1855. *Das Alpdrucken, Sein Begrundung und Verhutung*. Würzburg.

Bose, V. S. C. 1982. Dream Content Transformations: An Empirical Study of Freud's Secondary Revision Hypothesis. Doctoral dissertation. Andra University, Waltair, India.

Boss, M. 1958. *The Analysis of Dreams*. New York: Philosophical Library.

———. 1982. Dreaming and the Dreamed in the Daseins Analytical Way of Seeing. In *On Dreaming: An Encounter with Medard Boss*, ed. C. Scott. Chico, Calif.: Scholars Press.

Bottome, P. 1939. *Alfred Adler*. London: Faber and Faber.

Bowles, W., and F. Hynds. 1978. *Psi Search*. San Francisco: Harper and Row.

Brachfeld, F. 1951. *Come Interpretare i Sogni*. Milan: Garganti.

Bradford, S. 1981. *Harriet Tubman: The Moses of Her People*. Gloucester, Mass.: Peter Smith.

Bradley, C., and R. Meddis. 1974. Arousal Threshold in Dreaming Sleep. *Physiological Psychology* 2:109–10.

Breger, L., I. Hunter, and R. Lane. 1971. The Effect of Stress on Dreams. *Psychological Issues* 7 (monograph 27). New York: International Universities Press.

Brenneis, C. B. 1970. Male and Female Ego Modalities in Manifest Dream Content. *Journal of Abnormal Psychology* 76:434–42.

———. 1975. Developmental Aspects of Aging in Women: A Comparative Study of Dreams. *Archives of General Psychiatry* 32:429–35.

Brenneis, C. B., and S. Roll. 1976. Dream Patterns in Anglo and Chicano Young Adults. *Psychiatry* 39:280–90.

Breton, A. 1969. *Manifestoes of Surrealism*. Ann Arbor: University of Michigan Press.

Brome, V. 1978. *Jung: Man and Myth*. New York: Atheneum.

Broughton, R. 1968. Sleep Disorders: Disorders of Arousal? *Science* 159:1070–78.

Browman, C., and L. Kapell. 1982. Repetitive Sexual Dream Content of Normal Adults. *Sleep Research* 11:115.

Brown, R., and D. Donderi. 1986. Dream Content and Self-Reported Well-Being Among Recurrent Dreamers, Past-Recurrent Dreamers, and Nonrecurrent Dreamers. *Journal of Personality and Social Psychology* 50:612–23.

Browne, T. 1947. On Dreams. In *The World of Dreams*, ed. R. L. Woods. New York: Random House.

Bruce, H. 1915. *Sleep and Sleeplessness*. New York: Little, Brown.

Brugsch-Bey, H. 1947. The Dream of King Thutmes IV. In *The World of Dreams*, ed. R. L. Woods. New York: Random House.

Buckley, J. 1971. The Dreams of Young Adults (Sociological Analysis of 1,133 Dreams of Black and White Students). *Dissertation Abstracts International* 31 (7-A):3635.

Bullett, G. 1928. The Other "I." In *The World of Dreams*, ed. R. L. Woods. New York: Random House.

Butler, R. 1963. The Life Review: An Interpretation of Reminiscence in the Aged. *Psychiatry* 26:65–76.

Caillois, R., ed. 1963. *The Dream Adventure*. New York: Orion Press.

Caire, J. 1981. A Holographic Model of a Psychosomatic Pattern: Freud's Specimen Dream Reinterpreted. *Psychotherapy and Psychosomatics* 36:132–42.

Calkins, M. 1893. Statistics of Dreams. *American Journal of Psychology* 5:311–43.

Cartwright, R. 1979. The Nature and Function of Repetitive Dreams: A Survey and Speculation. *Psychiatry* 42:131–37.

Cartwright, R., and I. Romanek. 1978. Repetitive Dreams of Normal Subjects. *Sleep Research* 7:174.

Cassell, W. 1969. Responses to Ink-Blot Configurations Resembling the Heart. *Journal of Projective Techniques and Personality Assessment* 33:123–26.

Castaldo, V., and P. Holzman. 1969. The Effects of Hearing One's Own Voice on Dream Content: A Replication. *Journal of Nervous and Mental Disease* 148:74–82.

Cayce, E. 1976. *Dreams and Dreaming: The Edgar Cayce Readings*. Comp. M. Peterson. Virginia Beach, Va.: Association for Research and Enlightenment.

Cernovsky, Z. 1986. Interpretations of the Refugee Nightmare. *ASD Newsletter* 3 (3).

Child, I. L. 1985. Psychology and Anomalous Observations: The Question of ESP in Dreams. *American Psychologist* 40:1219–30.

Cicero. 1947. Argument Against Taking Dreams Seriously. In *The World of Dreams*, ed. R. L. Woods. New York: Random House.

Clemens, S. 1947. Dream Body Lives After Death. In *The World of Dreams*, ed. R. L. Woods. New York: Random House.

Cobbe, F. 1871. Dreams as Illustrations of Unconscious Cerebration. *MacMillan's Magazine* 23:512–23.

Cocteau, J. 1952. The Process of Inspiration. In *The Creative Process*, ed. B. Ghiselin. Berkeley: University of California Press.

Cohen, D. B. 1973. Sex Role Orientation and Dream Recall. *Journal of Abnormal Psychology* 82:246–52.

Collins G., L. Davison and L. Breger. 1967. "Dream Function in Adaptation to Threat: A Preliminary Study." Paper presented at meeting of the Association for the Psycholphysiological Study of Sleep, Santa Monica.

Comstock, C. 1987. Internal Self Helpers or Centers. *Integration* 3:3–12.

Coolidge, F., and D. Bracken. 1984. The Loss of Teeth in Dreams: An Empirical Investigation. *Psychological Reports* 54:931–35.

Cooper, R., and A. Hulme. 1966. Intra-Cranial Pressure and Related Phenomena During Sleep. *Journal of Neurology, Neurosurgery and Psychiatry* 29:564.

Corning, J. 1899. The Use of Musical Vibrations Before and During Sleep—Supplementary Employment of Chromatoscopic Figures—A Contribution to the Therapeutics of the Emotions. *Medical Record* 55:79–86.

Corsi-Cabrera, M., et al. 1982. Effect of Distorted Visual Input on Dream Content. *Sleep Research* 11:112.

Coxhead, D., and S. Hiller. 1981. *Dreams: Visions of the Night*. London: Thames and Hudson.

Craig, K. 1918. *The Fabric of Dreams*. New York: Dutton.

Crick, F., and G. Mitchison. 1983. The Function of Dream Sleep. *Nature* 312:101.

———. 1986. REM Sleep and Neural Nets. *Journal of Mind and Behavior* 7:229–50.

Crile, G. 1915. *A Mechanistic View of War and Peace*. New York: Macmillan.

Cubberly, A. 1923. The Effects of Tensions of Body Surface upon Normal Dreams. *British Journal of Psychology* 13:243–65.

Daim, W. 1953. Studies in Dream-Telepathy. *Tomorrow* 2:35–48.

Dane, J., and R. Van de Castle. 1991. A Comparison of Waking Instruction and Posthypnotic Suggestion for Lucid Dream Induction. *Lucidity* 10 (1–2):209–14.

Das Gupta, K. 1971. *The Shadow World: A Study of Ancient and Modern Dream Theories*. Delhi: Atma Ram.

de Becker, R. 1968. *The Understanding of Dreams and Their Influence on the History of Man*. New York: Hawthorn Books.

de Manaceine, M. 1897. *Sleep: It's Physiology, Pathology, Hygiene, and Psychology*. New York: Charles Scribner's.

de Martino, M. 1953. Sex Differences in the Dreams of Southern College Students. *Journal of Clinical Psychology* 9:199–201.

———. 1954. Some Characteristics of the Manifest Dream Content of Mental Defectives. *Journal of Clinical Psychology* 10:175–78.

Dement, W. 1955. Dream Recall and Eye Movement during Sleep in Schizophrenics and Normals. *Journal of Nervous and Mental Disease* 122:263–69.

———. 1966. Discussion of F. Snyder, *Toward an Evolutionary Theory of Dreaming*. *American Journal of Psychiatry* 123:136–42.

———. 1972. *Some Must Watch While Some Must Sleep*. San Francisco: W. H. Freeman.

Dement, W., E. Kahn, and H. Roffwarg. 1965. The Influence of the Laboratory Situation on the Dreams of the Experimental Subject. *Journal of Nervous and Mental Disease* 149:119–31.

Dement, W., and N. Kleitman. 1957a. Cyclic Variations in EEG during Sleep and Their Relation to Eye Movements, Body Motility, and Dreaming. *Electroencephalography and Clinical Neurophysiology* 9:672–90.

———. 1957b. The Relation of Eye Movements during Sleep to Dream Activity: An Objective Method for the Study of Dreaming. *Journal of Experimental Psychology* 53:339–46.

Dement, W., and E. Wolpert. 1958a. Relationships in Manifest Content of Dreams Occurring on the Same Night. *Journal of Nervous and Mental Disease* 126:568–78.

———. 1958b. The Relation of Eye Movements, Body Motility, and External Stimuli to Dream Content. *Journal of Experimental Psychology* 55:543–53.

DeMille, R. 1976. *Castenada's Journey: The Power and the Allegory*. Santa Barbara: Capra Press.

den Blanken, C., and E. Meijer. 1991. An Historical View of *Dreams and the Ways to Direct Them*, by Marie-Jean-Leon Lecoq, le Marquis d'Hervey-Saint-Denys. *Lucidity* 10 (1–2):311–22.

Devereux, G., ed. 1953. *Psychoanalysis and the Occult*. New York: International Universities Press.

Dexter, J. D., and E. Weitzman. 1969. The Relation Between Nocturnal Migraine, Cluster Headaches and Sleep Stage. Paper read at meeting of the Association for the Psychophysiological Study of Sleep. Boston.

Diamond, E. 1962. *The Science of Dreams*. New York: Doubleday.

Dick, W., and H. Gris. 1975. *National Enquirer*, March 18, 8.

Domhoff, B. 1969. Home Dreams versus Laboratory Dreams. In *Dream Psychology and the New Biology of Dreaming*, ed. M. Kramer. Springfield, Ill.: Charles Thomas.

Domhoff, B., and J. Kamiya. 1964. Problems in Dream Content Study with Objective Indicators. *Archives of General Psychiatry* 11:519–32.

Downing, J., and R. Marmorstein, eds. 1973. *Dreams and Nightmares*. New York: Harper and Row.

Dreams and Dreaming. 1990. Alexandria, Va.: Time-Life Books.

Dunne, J. 1927. *An Experiment with Time*. New York: Macmillan.

Edelstein, E., and L. Edelstein. 1945. *Asclepius: A Collection and Interpretation of the Testimonies*. 2 vols. Baltimore: Johns Hopkins University Press.

Eisenbud, J. 1947. The Dreams of Two Patients in Analysis Interpreted as a Telepathic Reve a Deux. *Psychoanalytical Quarterly* 16:39–60.

———. 1970. *PSI and Psychoanalysis*. New York: Grune and Stratton.

Ellenberger, E., and H. F. Ellenberger. "Recherches Recentes en Russie sur les Reves," *L'Union Medicale du Canada* 104:1667–76.

Ellenberger, H. 1970. *The Discovery of the Unconscious*. New York: Basic Books.

Ellis, H. 1911. *The World of Dreams*. Boston: Houghton Mifflin.

Emerson, R. 1883. *Lectures and Biographical Sketches*. Cambridge: Riverside Press.

English, J. 1985. *Different Doorway: Adventures of a Caesarean Born*. Point Reyes Station, Calif.: Earth Heart.

Erikson, E. 1954. The Dream Specimen of Psychoanalysis. *Journal of the American Psychoanalytic Association* 2:5–56.

———. 1959. Identity and the Life Cycle. *Psychological Issues* (monograph 1).

Ermacora, G. 1895. Telepathic Dreams Experimentally Produced. *Proceedings of the Society for Psychical Research* 11:235–308.

Evans-Wentz, W. 1958. *Tibetan Yoga and Secret Doctrines.* London: Oxford University Press.

Fagen, M., ed. 1978. *A History of Engineering and Science in the Bell System: National Service in War and Peace (1925–1975).* Murry Hill, N.Y.: Bell Telephone Laboratories.

Fahd, T. 1966. The Dream in Medieval Islamic Society. In *The Dream and Human Societies,* ed. G. von Grunebaum and R. Caillois. Los Angeles: University of California Press.

Faraday, A. 1976. *The Dream Game.* New York: Harper and Row.

———. 1978. Once Upon a Dream. *Voices* 14:67–76.

Farago, L. 1965. *Patton: Ordeal and Triumph.* New York: Dell.

Farber, L., and C. Fisher. 1943. An Experimental Approach to Dream Psychology Through the Use of Hypnosis. *Psychoanalytic Quarterly* 12:202–16.

Fernandez, H. 1969. Evoked K-Complexes in the Early Stages of Sleep and Their Relation to Visual Images. *American Journal of EEG Technology* 9:18–21.

Finley, C. [1921] 1947. Endocrine Stimulation as Affecting Dream Content. In *The World of Dreams,* ed. R. L. Woods. New York: Random House.

Fisher, C. 1960. Introduction. Preconscious Stimulation in Dreams, Associations, and Images. *Psychological Issues* 2 (monograph 7): 1–40.

———. 1966. Dreaming and Sexuality. In *Psychoanalysis: A General Psychology: Essays in Honor of Heinz Hartman,* ed. R. Lowenstein et al., 537–69. New York: International Universities Press.

Fisher, C., J. Gross, and J. Zuch. 1965. Cycle of Penile Erections Synchronous with Dreaming (REM) Sleep. *Archives of General Psychiatry* 12:29–45.

Fitzgerald, A. 1930. *The Essay and Hymns of Synesius of Cyrene.* London: Oxford University Press.

Flammarion, C. 1900. *The Unknown.* New York: Harper.

Fodor, N. 1962. *New Approaches to Dream Interpretation.* New York: Citadel Press.

Foulkes, D. 1962. Dream Reports from Different Stages of Sleep. *Journal of Abnormal and Social Psychology* 65:14–25.

———. 1978. *A Grammar of Dreams.* New York: Basic Books

———. 1979. Children's Dreams. In *Handbook of Dreams: Research, Theories and Applications,* ed. B. Wolman. New York: Van Nostrand Reinhold.

———. 1982. *Children's Dreams: Longitudinal Studies.* New York: John Wiley.

———. 1985. *Dreaming: A Cognitive-Psychological Analysis.* Hillsdale, N.J.: Lawrence Erlbaum.

Foulkes, D., and A. Rechtschaffen. 1964. Presleep Determinants of Dream Content: Effects of Two Films. *Perceptual and Motor Skills* 19:983–1005.

Foulkes, D., P. S. Spear, and J. D. Symonds. 1966. Individual Differences in Mental Activity at Sleep Onset. *Journal of Abnormal Psychology* 71:280–86.

Foulkes, D., and G. Vogel. 1965. Mental Activity at Sleep Onset. *Journal of Abnormal Psychology* 70:231–43.

Foulkes, D., et al. 1967. Dreams of the Male Child: An EEG Study. *Journal of Abnormal Psychology* 72:457–67.

Fox, O. 1962. *Astral Projection.* New Hyde Park, N.Y.: University Books.

Fox, R., et al. 1968. The Experimenter Variable in Dream Research. *Diseases of the Nervous System* 29:698–701.

Franklin, J., et al. 1948. Observations of Human Behavior in Experimental Semistarvation and Rehabilitation. *Journal of Clinical Psychology* 4:28–45.

Freeman, J. 1961. Sexual Capacities in the Aging Male. *Geriatrics* 16:37–43.

French, T. 1954. *Integration of Behavior.* Vol. 2, *The Integrative Process in Dreams.* Chicago: University of Chicago Press.

French, T., and E. Fromm. 1964. *Dream Interpretation*. New York: Basic Books.

Freud, E. L., ed. 1960. *Letters of Sigmund Freud*. Trans. T. Stern and J. Stern. New York: Basic Books.

Freud, S. [1914–1962.] A History of the Psycho-Analytic Movement. In *Sigmund Freud: Complete Works*, ed. J. Strachey, vol. 14. London: Hogarth.

———. [1916–1917–1963.] Introductory Lectures on Psychoanalysis. In *Sigmund Freud: Complete Works*, ed. J. Strachey, vol. 15. London: Hogarth.

———. [1922] 1953. Dreams and Telepathy. In *Psychoanalysis and the Occult*, ed. G. Devereux. New York: International Universities Press.

———. [1923] 1959. Remarks Upon the Theory and Practice of Dream Interpretation. In *Sigmund Freud: Collected Papers*, ed. J. Strachey, vol. 5. New York: Basic Books.

———. [1925] 1959. Some Additional Notes Upon Dream Interpretation as a Whole. In *Sigmund Freud: Collected Papers*, ed. J. Strachey, vol. 5. New York: Basic Books.

———. [1933–1966.] New Introductory Lectures on Psychoanalysis. In *Sigmund Freud: Complete Works*, ed. J. Strachey, vol. 22. London: Hogarth.

———. 1952. *On Dreams*. New York: Norton.

———. 1953. *The Interpretation of Dreams*. New York: Basic Books.

Fruman, N. 1972. *Coleridge: The Damaged Archangel*. London: Allen and Unwin.

Fukuma, E. 1969. A Study of Dreams by Using "REMP-Awakening Technique"—Psychophysiological Study of Dreams in Normal Subjects: The First Report. *Psychiatria et Neurologia Japonica* 71:960–79; English summary, 1026–27.

Gabbard, G., S. Twenlow, and F. Jones. 1981. Do "Near-Death Experiences" Occur Only Near Death? *Journal of Nervous and Mental Disorders* 169:375–77.

Gackenbach, J. 1990. Women and Meditators as Gifted Lucid Dreamers. In *Dreamtime and Dreamwork*, ed. S. Krippner, 244–51. Los Angeles: Jeremy Tarcher.

———. 1991. An Estimate of Lucid Dreaming Incidence. *Lucidity* 10 (1–2):232–33.

Gackenbach, J., and J. Bosveld. 1989. *Control Your Dreams*. New York: Harper and Row.

Gackenbach, J., R. Cranson, and C. Alexander. 1986. Lucid Dreaming, Witnessing Dreaming, and Transcendental Meditation Technique: A Developmental Relationship. *Lucidity Letter* 5 (2):34–40.

Gadon, E. 1989. *The Once and Future Goddess*. New York: Harper and Row.

Gahagen, L. 1936. Sex Differences in Recall of Stereotyped Dreams, Sleep-Talking, and Sleep-Walking. *Journal of Genetic Psychology* 48:227–36.

Galen. 1968. *On the Usefulness of the Parts of the Body*. 2 vols. Ithaca, N.Y.: Cornell University Press.

Gandhi, M. 1957. *An Autobiography: The Story of my Experiments With Truth*. Boston: Beacon Press.

Gardiner, A. 1935. *Hieratic Papyri in the British Museum*. No. 3, *The Dream Book*. London: British Museum.

Garfield, P. 1974. *Creative Dreaming*. New York: Simon and Schuster.

———. [1979] 1989. *Pathway to Ecstasy*. New York: Holt, Rinehart and Winston; rev. ed., New York: Prentice Hall.

———. 1984. *Your Child's Dreams*. New York: Ballantine.

———. 1988. *Women's Bodies, Women's Dreams*. New York: Ballantine.

———. 1991. *The Healing Power of Dreams*. New York: Simon and Schuster.

Garraty, J. A., and P. Gay, eds. 1972. *The Columbia History of the World*. New York: Harper and Row.

Gelman, D. 1981. Finding the Hidden Freud. *Newsweek*, 64–70.

Gendlin, E. 1986. *Let Your Body Interpret Your Dreams*. Wilmette, Ill.: Chiron Publications.

Gill, W. S. 1967. Animal Content in the Rorschach. *Journal of Projective Techniques and Personality Assessment* 31:49–56.

Gillespie, G. 1992. Light in Lucid Dreams: A Review. *Dreaming* 2:167–80.

Gillespie, W. 1953. Extrasensory Elements in

Dream Interpretation. In *Psychoanalysis and the Occult*, ed. G. Devereux. New York: International Universities Press.

Globus, G. 1987. *Dream Life, Wake Life*. Albany, N.Y.: State University of New York Press.

——. 1991. Dream Content: Random or Meaningful? *Dreaming* 1:27–40.

Goethe, J. 1947. Conversations of Goethe With Eckerman. In *The World of Dreams*, ed. R. L. Woods. New York: Random House.

Goodenough, D. 1967. Some Recent Studies of Dream Recall. In *Experimental Studies of Dreaming*, ed. H. Witkin and H. Lewis, 135–40. New York: Random House.

Goodenough, D., et al. 1959. A Comparison of "Dreamers" and "Nondreamers": Eye Movements, Electroencephalograms, and the Recall of Dreams. *Journal of Abnormal and Social Psychology* 59:295–302.

——. 1975. The Effects of Stress Films on Dream Affect, on Respiration, and Eye-Movement Activity During Rapid-Eye-Movement Sleep. *Psychophysiology* 12:313–20.

Gorer, G. 1935. *Africa Dances: A Book About West African Negroes*. New York: Knopf.

Gottschalk, L., et al. 1966. Anxiety Levels in Dreams: Relation to Changes in Plasma Free Acids. *Science* 153:654–57.

Grant, J. 1984. *Dreamers*. Bath: Ashgrove Press.

Green, C. 1968. *Lucid Dreams*. London: Hamish Hamilton.

Greenberg, H., and H. Blank. 1970. Dreams of a Dying Patient. *British Journal of Medical Psychology* 43:355–62.

Greenberg, R. 1981. Dreams and REM Sleep: An Integrative Approach. In *Sleep, Dreams and Memory*, ed. W. Fishbein. New York: Spectrum Publications.

Greene, G. 1982. *Ways of Escape*. London.

Greenwood, F. 1894. *Imagination in Dreams and Their Study*. London: Lane.

Grey, A., and D. Kalsched. 1971. Oedipus East and West: An Exploration via Manifest Dream Content. *Journal of Cross-Cultural Psychology* 2:337–52.

Griffith, R., O. Miyagi, and A. Tago. 1958. The Universality of Dreams: Japanese vs. Americans. *American Anthropologist* 60:1173–79.

Grinstein, A. 1968. *On Sigmund Freud's Dreams*. Detroit: Wayne State University Press.

Gross, J., J. Byrne, and C. Fisher. 1965. Eye Movements During Emergent Stage 1 EEG in Subjects with Life-long Blindness. *Journal of Nervous and Mental Disease* 141:365–70.

Gulliver, J. 1880. The Psychology of Dreams. *Journal of Speculative Philosophy* 14:206–8.

Gurney, E., F. Meyers, and F. Podmore. 1886. *Phantasms of the Living*. 2 vols. London: Trubner.

Gutheil, E. 1958. Dreams as an Aid to Evaluating Ego-Strength. *American Journal of Psychiatry* 12:338–57.

——. 1960. *The Handbook of Dream Analysis*. New York: Grove.

Gutmann, D. 1967. Aging Among the Highland Maya: A Comparative Study. *Journal of Personality and Social Psychology* 7:28–35.

Hall, C. 1951. What People Dream About. *Scientific American* 184:60–63.

——. 1953a. A Cognitive Theory of Dream Symbols. *Journal of General Psychology* 48:169–86.

——. [1953b–1966] *The Meaning of Dreams*. New York: McGraw-Hill.

——. 1955. The Significance of the Dream of Being Attacked. *Journal of Personality* 24:168–80.

——. 1963. Strangers in Dreams: An Empirical Confirmation of the Oedipus Complex. *Journal of Personality* 31:336–45.

——. 1967a. Are Prenatal and Birth Experiences Represented in Dreams? *Psychoanalytic Review* 54:157–74.

——. 1967b. Experimente zur Telepathischen Beeinflussung von Traumen [Experiments on Telepathically Influenced Dreams]. *Zeitschrift fur Parapsychologie und Grenzgebiete der Psychologie* 10:18–47.

——. 1967c. Representation of the Laboratory Setting in Dreams. *Journal of Nervous and Mental Disease* 144:198–206.

——. 1969. Normative Dream-Content Studies. In *Dream Psychology and the New Bi-*

ology of Dreaming, ed. M. Kramer. Springfield, Ill.: Charles Thomas.

———. 1984. "A Ubiquitous Sex Difference in Dreams" Revisited. Journal of Personality and Social Psychology 46:1109–17.

Hall, C., and B. Domhoff. 1963a. Aggression in Dreams. International Journal of Social Psychiatry 9:259–67.

———. 1963b. A Ubiquitous Sex Difference in Dreams. Journal of Abnormal and Social Psychology 96:278–80.

———. 1964. Friendliness in Dreams. Journal of Social Psychology 62:309–14.

———. 1968. The Dreams of Freud and Jung. Psychology Today, June.

Hall, C., and R. Lind. 1970. Dreams, Life, and Literature: A Study of Franz Kafka. Chapel Hill: University of North Carolina Press.

Hall, C., and V. Nordby. 1972. The Individual and His Dreams. New York: Signet.

Hall, C., and R. Van de Castle. 1965. An Empirical Investigation of the Castration Complex in Dreams. Journal of Personality 33:20–29.

———. 1966a. Studies of Dreams Reported in the Laboratory and at Home. Institute of Dream Research monograph series, no. 1. Felton, Calif.: Big Trees Press.

———. 1966b. The Content Analysis of Dreams. New York: Appleton-Century-Croft.

———. 1967. An Answer to Monroe's Review of The Content Analysis of Dreams. Contemporary Psychology 12.

Hall, C., et al. 1982. The Dreams of College Men and Women in 1950 and 1980: A Comparison of Dream Contents and Sex Differences. Sleep 5:188–94.

Hall, E. 1977. Possible Impossibilities: A Look at Parapsychology. Boston: Houghton Mifflin.

Hall, J. 1977. Clinical Uses of Dreams: Jungian Interpretation and Enactments. New York: Grune and Stratton.

———. 1983. Jungian Dream Interpretation: A Handbook of Theory and Practice. Toronto: Inner City Books.

Halliday, G. 1985. Direct Psychological Therapies for Nightmares: A Review. ASD Newsletter 2.

Hammond, W. 1982. Sleep and Its Derangements. New York: De Capo.

Hansel, E. M. 1980. ESP and Parapsychology: A Critical Reevaluation. Buffalo: Prometheus.

Harris, I. 1948. Observations Concerning Typical Anxiety Dreams. Psychiatry 11:301–9.

Hartley, D. 1947. Observations on Man. In The World of Dreams, ed. R. L. Woods. New York: Random House.

Hartmann, E. 1967. The Biology of Dreaming. Springfield, Ill.: Charles Thomas.

———. 1984. The Nightmare. New York: Basic Books.

Hartmann, E., et al. 1987. Who Has Nightmares? The Personality of the Lifelong Nightmare Sufferer. Archives of General Psychiatry 44:49–56.

Hauri, P. 1970. Evening Activity, Sleep Mentation, and Subjective Sleep Quality. Journal of Abnormal Psychology 76:270–75.

Hauri, P., and R. L. Van de Castle. 1973. Psychophysiological Parallels in Dreams. Psychosomatic Medicine 35:297–308.

Heermann, G. 1838. Beobachtungen und Betrachtungen Uber die Traume der Blinden. Monatschrift fur Medizin, Augenheilkunde und Chirurgie (Leipzig) 1:116–80.

Herman, J., S. Ellman, and H. Roffwarg. 1978. The Problem of NREM Dream Recall Reexamined. In The Mind in Sleep: Psychology and Psychophysiology, ed. A. Arkin, J. Antrobus, and S. Ellman. Hillsdale, N.J.: Lawrence Erlbaum.

Hersen, M. 1972. Nightmare Behavior: A Review. Psychological Bulletin 78:37–48.

Hildebrant, F. 1875. Der Traume und Seine Verwerthung fur's Leben. Leipzig: Reinboth.

Hill, B. 1967. Gates of Horn and Ivory: An Anthology of Dreams. New York: Taplinger.

Hobbes, T. 1947. Excerpt from Leviathan. In The World of Dreams, ed. R. L. Woods. New York: Random House.

Hobson, J. A. 1988. The Dreaming Brain. New York: Basic Books.

Hobson, J. A., F. Goldfrank, and F. Snyder. 1964. Respiration and Mental Activity in Sleep. Journal of Psychiatric Research 3:79–90.

Hobson, J. A., and R. W. McCarley. 1977. The Brain as a Dream State Generator: An Activation-Synthesis Hypothesis of the Dream Process. *American Journal of Psychiatry* 134:1335–48.

Hock, A. 1960. *Reason and Genius*. New York: Academic Press.

Hodes, R., and W. Dement. 1964. Depression of Electrically Induced Reflexes ("H-reflexes") in Man During Low Voltage EEG "Sleep." *Electroencephalography and Clinical Neurophysiology* 17:617–29.

Hollenbeck, K. 1989. Patton: Many Lives, Many Battles. *Venture Inward*, September–October, 5, 12–14.

Horton, L. 1914. Inventorial Record Forms of Use in the Analysis ot Dreams. *Journal of Abnormal Psychology* 8:393–404.

Howard, M. 1979. Manifest Dream Content of Adolescents. *Dissertation Abstracts International* 39 (8–13):4103.

Howe, J., and K. Blick. 1983. Emotional Content of Dreams Recalled by Elderly Women. *Perceptual and Motor Skills* 56:31–34.

Howell, J. 1985. Just Plain Bill. *High Times*, March.

Howell, W. 1897. A Contribution to the Physiology of Sleep Based Upon Plethysmographic Experiments. *Journal of Experimental Medicine* 2:313–45.

Hughes, J. D. 1984. The Dreams of Alexander the Great. *Journal of Psychohistory* 12:168–92.

Hunt, H. 1986. Some Relations Between the Cognitive Psychology of Dreams and Dream Phenomenology. *Journal of Mind and Behavior* 7:213–28.

———. 1989. *The Multiplicity of Dreams: A Cognitive Psychological Perceptive*. New Haven, Conn.: Yale University Press.

Husband, R. 1936. Sex Differences in Dream Content. *Journal of Abnormal and Social Psychology* 30:513–21.

Ikin, A., T. Pear, and R. Thouless. 1924. The Psycho-Galvanic Phenomenon in Dream Analysis. *British Journal of Psychology* 15:23–44.

Inglis, B. 1987. *The Power of Dreams*. London: Paladin; Grafton.

Jastrow, J. 1888. Dreams of the Blind. *New Princeton Review* 5:18–34.

Jaynes, J. 1976. *The Origin of Consciousness in the Breakdown of the Bicameral Mind*. Boston: Houghton Mifflin.

Jewell, J. 1905. The Psychology of Dreams. *American Journal of Psychology* 16:1–34.

Jewish Encyclopedia. 1925. Vol. 4. New York: Funk and Wagnalls.

Johnson, G. 1984. Music in Dreams. In *Dreams Can Point the Way*, ed. V. Bass. Sugar Land, Tex.: Miracle House Books.

Jones, E. 1955. *The Life and Work of Sigmund Freud*. Vol. 2, *Years of Maturity, 1901–1919*. New York: Basic Books.

Jones, E. 1957. *The Life and Work of Sigmund Freud*. Vol 3, *The Last Phase, 1919–1939*. New York: Basic Books.

———. 1959. *On the Nightmare*. New York: Grove.

Jones, R. 1970. *The New Psychology of Dreaming*. New York: Grune and Stratton.

———. 1987. Dream Reflection as Creative Writing. In *The Variety of Dream Experience: Expanding Our Ways of Working with Dreams*, ed. M. Ullman and C. Limmer. New York: Continuum.

Jung, C. 1917. *Collected Papers on Analytical Psychology*. New York: Moffat and Yard.

———. 1958. *Psychology and Religion: West and East*. Bollingen series, vol. 11. Princeton, N.J.: Princeton University Press.

———. 1964. *Man and His Symbols*. Garden City, N.J.: Doubleday.

———. 1965. *Memories, Dreams, Reflections*. New York: Vantage Books.

———. 1967. *Alchemical Studies*. Bollingen series, vol. 13. Princeton, N.J.: Princeton University Press.

———. 1974. *Dreams*. Trans. R. F. C. Hull. Princeton, N.J.: Princeton University Press.

———. 1976. *The Symbolic Life: Miscellaneous Writings*. Bollingen series, vol. 17. Princeton, N.J.: Princeton University Press.

———. 1984. *Dream Analysis: Notes of the Seminar Given in 1928–30*. Bollingen series, vol. 99. Princeton, N.J.: Princeton University Press.

Kaempffert, W. 1924. *A Popular History of American Invention*. 2 vols. New York: Scribners.

Kafka, F. 1965. *Diaries*. Vol. 1, trans. J. Kresh; vol. 2, trans. M. Greenberg. New York: Schocken Books.

Kahn, E., and C. Fisher. 1969. REM Sleep and Sexuality in the Aged. *Journal of Geriatric Psychiatry* 2:181–99.

Kahn, E., C. Fisher, and L. Lieberman. 1969. Dream Recall in the Normal Aged. *Journal of the American Geriatric Society* 17 (12):1121–26.

Kahn, E., et al. 1962. Incidence of Color in Immediately Recalled Dreams. *Science* 137:1054–55.

Kales, A., et al. 1980. Nightmares: Clinical Characteristics and Personality Patterns. *American Journal of Psychiatry* 137:1197–1201.

Karacan, I. 1970. Clinical Value of Nocturnal Erection in the Prognosis and Diagnosis of Impotence. *Medical Aspects of Human Sexuality* 4:27–34.

Karacan, I., R. Williams, and P. Salis. 1970. The Effect of Sexual Intercourse on Sleep Patterns and Nocturnal Penile Erections. *Psychophysiology* 7:338 (abstract).

Karacan, I., et al. 1966. Erection Cycle During Sleep in Relation to Dream Anxiety. *Archives of General Psychiatry* 15:183–89.

———. 1976. The Ontogeny of Nocturnal Penile Tumescence. *Waking and Sleeping* 1:27–44.

———. 1986. Uterine Activity During Sleep. *Sleep* 9:393–97.

Kasatkin, V. N. 1967. *Teoriya Snovidenii* [Theory of Dreams]. Leningrad: Meditsina, 352.

Kearns, D. 1976. *Lyndon Johnson and the American Dream*. New York: Harper and Row.

Kedrov, B. 1957. On the Question of Scientific Creativity. *Voprosy Psikologii* 3:91–113.

Keller, H. [1908–1947.] The World I Live In. In *The World of Dreams*, ed. R. L. Woods. New York: Random House.

Kelsey, M. 1968. *Dreams: The Dark Speech of the Spirit*. New York: Doubleday.

Kelzer, K. 1987. *The Sun and the Shadow*. Virginia Beach, Va.: A.R.E. Press.

Kerouac, J. 1961. *Book of Dreams*. San Francisco: City Lights Books.

Keys, A., et al. 1950. *The Biology of Human Starvation*. Minneapolis: University of Minnesota Press.

Kinder, M. 1977. The Art of Dreaming in *Three Women* and *Providence*: Structures of the Self. *Film Quarterly* 31:10–18.

———. 1988. The Dialectic of Dreams and Theater in the Films of Ingmar Bergman. *Dreamworks* 5:186.

Kinney, L., M. Kramer, and M. Scharf. 1982. Dream Incorporation: A Replication. *Sleep Research* 11:105.

Kirsch, J. 1973. *The Reluctant Prophet*. Los Angeles: Sherbourne Press.

Klein, G., et al. 1971. Recurrent Dream Fragments and Fantasies Elicited in Interrupted and Completed REM Periods. *Psychophysiology* 7:331–32.

Koestler, A. 1964. *The Act of Creation*. New York: Macmillan.

Kohlschutter, E. 1862. Messungen der Festigkeit des Schlafes. *Zeitschrift uber Rationalistisch Medizin* 17:209–53.

Koulack, D. 1991. *To Catch a Dream*. Albany: State University Press of New York.

Kovacs, K. 1981. José Luis Borau on Movies and Dreams. *Dreamworks* 2 (1):64.

Kramer, M., L. Kinney, and M. Scharf. 1983. Sex Differences in Dreams. *Psychiatric Journal of the University of Ottawa* 8:1–4.

Kramer, M., L. Schoen, and L. Kinney. 1987. Nightmares in Vietnam Veterans. *Journal of the American Academy of Psychoanalysis* 15:67–81.

Krippner, S. ed. 1990. *Dreamtime and Dreamwork*. Los Angeles: Jeremy Tarcher.

Krippner, S., and W. Hughes. 1970. Dreams and Human Potential. *Journal of Humanistic Psychology* 10:1–20.

Krippner, S., et al. 1974. Content Analysis of 30 Dreams from 10 Pre-Operative Male Transsexuals. *Journal of the American Society* of Psychosomatic Dentistry and Medicine, monograph supplement no. 2, 3–23.

Krishna, G. 1971. Kundalini: The Evolutionary Energy in Man. Boulder: Shambala Publications.

Krohn, A., and D. Gutmann. 1971. Changes in Mastery Style with Age: A Study of Navajo Dreams. Psychiatry 34:289–300.

Kurthe, E., I. Gohler, and H. Knaapa. 1965. Untersuchungen uber den Pavor Nocturnus bei Kindern [Research Regarding Night Terrors in Children]. Psychiatrie, Neurologie, und Medizinische Psychologie 17:1–7.

L. 1858. On a Particular Class of Dreams Induced by Food. Journal of Psychological Medicine and Mental Pathology 11–12:575–96.

LaBerge, S. 1986. Lucid Dreaming. New York: Ballantine.

———. 1988. Induction of Lucid Dreams Including the Use of the Dream Light. Lucidity Letter 7(2):15–21.

LaBerge, S., W. Greenleaf, and B. Kedzierski. 1983. Physiological Responses to Dreamed Sexual Activity During Lucid REM Sleep. Psychophysiology 20:454–55.

Ladd, G. T. 1892. Contributions to the Psychology of Visual Dreams. Mind, 299–304.

Lamon, W. 1947. Abraham Lincoln's Dream Life. In The World of Dreams, ed. R. L. Woods. New York: Random House.

Laufer, B. 1931. Inspirational Dream in Eastern Asia. Journal of American Folklore 44:737–41.

Le Guin, U. 1980. Commentary. Dreamworks 1:156–57.

Lewin, I., et al. 1973. The Induction of a Quasi-Dreaming Mental State by Means of Flickering Photic Stimulation. In Sleep: Physiology, Biochemistry, Psychology, Pharmacology, Clinical Implications. Basel: Karger.

Lincoln, J. 1935. The Dream in Primitive Cultures. London: Cresset Press.

Linn, L. 1954. The Suggestion to Dream About Sickness. Journal of Hillside Hospital 3:154–65.

Linton, H. 1954. Rorschach Correlates of Response to Suggestion. Journal of Abnormal and Social Psychology 49:75–83.

Little, G. 1899. The Causation of Night-Terrors. British Medical Journal, August 19.

Lockhart, R. A. 1977. Cancer in Myth and Dream: An Exploration into the Archetypal Relation Between Dreams and Disease. Spring 1:1–26.

Loewi, O. 1960. An Autobiographical Sketch. Perspectives in Biology and Medicine 4:3–25.

Lorand, S. 1948. On the Meaning of Losing Teeth in Dreams. Psychoanalytic Quarterly 17:529–30.

———. 1957. Dream Interpretation in the Talmud. International Journal of Psychoanalysis 38:92–97.

Lortie-Lussier, M., C. Schwab, and J. De Konick. 1985. Working Mothers vs. Homemakers: Do Dreams Reflect the Changing Roles of Women? Sex Roles 12:1009–21.

Lortie-Lussier, M., et al. 1992. Beyond Sex Differences: Family and Occupational Roles' Impact on Women's and Men's Dreams. Sex Roles 26:79–96.

Lowy, S. 1942. Psychological and Biological Foundations of Dream Interpretation. London: Paul, Trench, and Trubner.

Lucretius. 1947. Spirits Possess Our Bodies When We Sleep. In The World of Dreams, ed. R. L. Woods. New York: Random House.

Lynd, B. 1976. Dreams and Healing. Sundance Community Dream Journal 1:18–26.

MacFarlane, A. 1890. Dreaming. 3 parts. Edinburgh Medical Journal 36:499–512, 616–24, 712–19, 817–25, 900–10, 993–99.

Mack, J. 1970. Nightmares and Human Conflict. Boston: Little, Brown.

MacKenzie, N. 1965. Dreams and Dreaming. London: Aldus Books.

Macnish, R. 1836. The Philosophy of Sleep. 3d ed. Glasgow: MM'Phun.

MacWilliam, J. 1923. Some Applications of Physiology to Medicine. III. Blood Pressure and Heart Action in Sleep and Dreams: Their Relation to Haemorrhages, Angina, and Sudden Death. British Medical Journal 2:1196–1200.

Magallon, L., and B. Shor. 1990. Shared Dreaming: Joining Together in Dreamtime.

In *Dreamtime and Dreamwork*, ed. S. Krippner. Los Angeles: Jeremy Tarcher.

Magnussen, G. 1944. *Studies on Respiration During Sleep: A Contribution to the Physiology of the Sleep Function*. London: H. K. Lewis.

Mahoney, M. 1966. *The Meaning in Dreams and Dreaming*. New York: Citadel Press.

Maimonides, M. 1951. *The Guide for the Perplexed*. London: Routledge and Kegan Paul.

Malamud, W. 1934. Dream Analysis: Its Application in Therapy and Research in Nervous and Mental Disease. *Archives of Neurology and Psychiatry* 31:356–72.

Malamud, W., and R. Lindner. 1931. Dreams and Their Relationship to Recent Impression. *Archives of Neurology and Psychiatry* 25:1081–99.

Mandell, A., et al. 1966. Dreaming Sleep in Man: Changes in Urine Volume and Osmolality. *Science* 151: 1558–60.

Marshack, A. 1972. *The Roots of Civilization*. New York: McGraw-Hill.

Masefield, J. 1967. The Woman Speaks. In *Such Stuff as Dreams*, ed. B. Hill. London: Rupert Hart-Davis.

Matoon, M. 1978. *Applied Dream Analysis: A Jungian Approach*. Washington, D.C.: Washington and Sons.

Maury, A. 1861. *Le sommeil et les reves*. Paris: Didier Edition; 2d ed., 1878.

Max, L. 1935. An Experimental Study of the Motor Theory of Consciousness. III. Action-Current Responses in Deaf-Mutes During Sleep, Sensory Stimulation and Dreams. *Journal of Comparative Psychology* 19:469–86.

Maybruck, P. 1986. An Exploratory Study of the Dreams of Pregnant Women. Doctoral Dissertation. Saybrook University, San Francisco.

———. 1989. *Pregnancy and Dreams*. Los Angeles: Jeremy Tarcher.

———. 1990. Pregnancy and Dreams. In *Dreamtime and Dreamwork*, ed. S. Krippner. Los Angeles: Jeremy Tarcher.

McCurdy, H. 1946. The History of Dream Theory. *Psychological Review* 53:225–33.

McGuigan, F. J., and R. G. Tanner. 1971. Covert Oral Behavior During Conversational

and Visual Dreams. *Psychonomic Science* 23:263–64.

Megroz, R. 1939. *The Dream World: A Survey of the History and Mystery of Dreams*. New York: Dutton.

Meier, B., and I. Strauch. 1990. The Phenomenology of REM-Dreams: Dream Settings, Dream Characters, Dream Topics, and Dream Realism. Paper Presented at Conference of the Association for the Study of Dreams, Chicago.

Meier, C. 1966. The Dream in Ancient Greece and Its Use in Temple Cures (incubation). In *The Dream and Human Societies*, ed. G. von Grunebaum and R. Caillois. Los Angeles: University of California Press.

Mendelson, J., L. Siger, and P. Solomon. 1960. Psychiatric Observations on Congenital and Acquired Deafness: Symbolic and Perceptual Processes in Dreams. *American Journal of Psychiatry* 116:883–88.

Meseguer, P. 1960. *The Secret of Dreams*. Westminster, Md.: Newman.

Middleton, W. 1933. Nocturnal Dreams. *Scientific Monthly* 37:460–64.

Miles, W. R. 1919. The Sex Expression of Men Living on a Lowered Nutritional Level. *Journal of Nervous and Mental Disease* 49:208–24.

Mitchell, E. 1923. The Physiological Diagnostic Dream. *New York Medical Journal* 118:416–17.

Money, J., and J. G. Brennan. 1969. Sexual Dimorphism in the Psychology of Female Transsexuals. In *Transsexualism and Sex Reassignment*, ed. R. Green and J. Money. Baltimore: Johns Hopkins University Press.

Monroe, L. 1967. Review of *The Content Analysis of Dreams*. *Contemporary Psychology* 12:607.

———. 1968. Inter-Rater Reliability of Scoring EEG Sleep Records. *Psychophysiology* 4:370–71 (abstract).

Monroe, L., et al. 1965. Discriminability of REM and NREM Reports. *Journal of Personality and Social Psychology* 2:456–60.

Monroe, W. 1897. Note on Dreams. *American Journal of Psychology* 9:413–14.

———. 1899. A Study of Taste Dreams. *American Journal of Psychology* 10:326–27.

———. 1905. Mental Elements of Dreams. *Journal of Philosophy* 2:650–52.

Moody, R. 1977. *Life After Life*. Atlanta: Mockingbird Books.

Morris, J. 1985. *The Dream Workbook*. Boston: Little, Brown.

Muller, F. M. 1884. *The Sacred Books of the East*. Vol. 15, *Brhadarnyaka-Upanishad*. Oxford: Clarendon Press.

Mumford, L. 1966. *Technics and Human Development*. New York: Harcourt Brace Jovanovich.

Murphy, G. 1961. *Challenge of Psychical Research*. New York: Harpers.

———. 1971. Introductory Address. In *Technique and Status of Modern Parapsychology: AAAS Symposium*, ed. D. Dean. Newark, N.J.: Newark College of Engineering Press.

Murphy, G., and R. Ballou, eds. 1960. *William James on Psychical Research*. New York: Viking.

Myers, F. 1961. *Human Personality and Its Survival of Bodily Death*. Ed. S. Smith. New Hyde Park, N.Y.: University Books.

Nagera, H., ed. 1969. *Basic Psychoanalytic Concepts on the Theory of Dreams*. Vol. 2. New York: Basic Books.

Newbold, W. 1886. Sub-Conscious Reasoning. *Proceedings of the Society for Psychical Research* 12:11–20.

Newman, J. 1948. Sriniwasa Ramaniyan. *Scientific American* 78:54–57.

Newton, P. 1970. Recalled Dream Content and the Maintenance of Body Image. *Journal of Abnormal Psychology* 76:134–39.

Nowlin, J., et al. 1965. The Association of Nocturnal Angina Pectoris with Dreaming. *Annals of Internal Medicine* 63:1040–46.

Oberhelman, S. 1991. *The Oneirocriticon of Achmet: A Medieval Greek and Arabic Treatise on the Interpretation of Dreams*. Lubbock: Texas Tech University Press.

Offenkrantz, W., and A. Rechtschaffen. 1963. Clinical Studies of Sequential Dreams. I. A Patient in Psychotherapy. *Archives of General Psychiatry* 8:497–508.

Ohlymeyer, P., and H. Huellstrung. 1944. Periodische Vorgaenge im Schlaf. *Pfluegers Archiv* 248:559–60.

Okuma, T., E. Fukuma, and K. Kobayashi. 1975. Dream Detector and Comparison of Laboratory and Home Dreams Collected by REMP-Awakening Technique. In *Advances in Sleep Research*, ed. E. D. Weitzman, 2:223–31. Bronx, N.Y.: Spectrum Publications.

Oppenheim, A. 1956. The Interpretation of Dreams in the Ancient Near East with a Translation of an Assyrian Dreambook. *Transactions of the American Philosophical Society* 46 (pt. 3):179–373.

———. 1966. Mantic Dreams in the Ancient Near East. In *The Dream and Human Societies*, ed. G. von Grunebaum and R. Caillois. Los Angeles: University of California Press.

Osgood, C. E. 1959. The Representation Model and Relevant Research Methods. In *Trends in Content Analysis*, ed. I. de Sola Pool. Urbana: University of Illinois Press.

Palmer, M., ed. 1986. *T'ung Shu: The Ancient Chinese Almanac of Life*. Boston: Shambala.

Parsifal-Charles, N. 1986. *The Dream*. 2 vols. West Cornwall, Conn.: Locust Hill Press.

Pederson-Krag, G. 1947. Telepathy and Repression. *Psychoanalytic Quarterly* 16:61–68.

Perls, F. 1970. Four Lectures. In *Gestalt Therapy Now*, ed. J. Fagan and I. Shepherd. Palo Alto: Science and Behavior Books.

Potzl, O. 1960. The Relationship Between Experimentally Induced Dream Images and Indirect Vision. In *Preconscious Stimulation in Dreams, Associations, and Images. Psychological Issues* 2 (monograph 7):41–120.

Price, G. 1937. *I Knew These Dictators*. London: Harrop.

Prince, W. 1931. Human Experiences. *Bulletin of the Boston Society for Psychic Research* 14:5–328.

Rainville, R. 1988. *Dreams Across the Lifespan*. Boston: American.

Ramsey, G. 1953. Studies of Dreaming. *Psychological Bulletin* 50:432–55.

Ratcliff, A. 1923. *A History of Dreams*. Boston: Small, Maynard.

Rechtschaffen, A. 1970. Sleep and Dream States: An Experimental Design. In *Psi Favorable States of Consciousness*, ed. R. Cavanna, 87–120. New York: Parapsychology Foundation.

———. 1973. The Psychophysiology of Mental Activity during Sleep. In *The Psychophysiology of Thinking*, ed. F. McGuigan and R. Schoonover. New York: Academic Press.

Rechtschaffen, A., and C. Buchignani. 1983. Visual Dimensions and Correlates of Dream Images. *Sleep Research* 12:189.

Rechtschaffen, A., and D. Foulkes. 1965. Effect of Visual Stimuli on Dream Content. *Perceptual and Motor Skills* 20:1149–60.

Rechtschaffen, A., and A. Kales, eds. 1968. *A Manual of Standardized Terminology, Techniques and Scoring System for Sleep Stages of Human Subjects*. Public Health Service, U.S. Government Printing Office.

Reed, H. 1977. Sundance: Inspirational Dreaming in Community. In *Extrasensory Ecology: Parapsychology and Anthropology*, ed. J. Long, 155–87. Metuchen, N.J.: Scarecrow Press.

———. 1989. Dreaming for Mary. In *Getting Help from Your Dreams*. New York: Ballantine.

———. 1991. *Dream Solution*. San Rafael: CA.: New World Library.

Rhine, L. 1961. *Hidden Channels of the Mind*. New York: William Sloane.

Richardson, B. 1892. The Physiology of Dreams. *Asclepiad* 9:129–60.

Riechers, M., M. Kramer, and J. Trinder, 1970. A Replication of the Hall–Van de Castle Character Scale Norms. Paper Read at Meeting of the Association for the Psychophysiological Study of Sleep, Santa Fe, New Mexico.

Rinfret, N., M. Lortie-Lussier, and J. De Konick. 1991. The Dreams of Professional Mothers and Female Students: An Exploration of Social Roles and Age Impact. *Dreaming* 1:179–91.

Ritter, W. 1964. Verbal Conditioning and the Recalled Content of Dreams. *Dissertation Abstracts* 24 (9):3840.

Robbins, P., and F. Houshi. 1983. Some Observations on Recurrent Dreams. *Bulletin of the Menninger Clinic* 47:262–65.

Roffenstein, G. [1924] 1951. Experiments on Symbolization in Dreams. In *Organization and Pathology of Thought*, ed. D. Rapaport, 249–56. New York: Columbia University Press.

Roffwarg, H., J. Herman, and S. Lamstein. 1975. The Middle Ear Muscles: Predictability of Their Phasic Activity in REM Sleep from Dream Material. *Sleep Research* 4:165.

Roffwarg, H., et al. 1978. The Effects of Sustained Alterations of Waking Visual Input on Dream Content. In *The Mind in Sleep: Psychology and Psychophysiology*, ed. A. Arkin, J. Antrobus, and S. Ellman. Hillsdale, N.J.: Lawrence Erlbaum.

Rogers, G., et al. 1985. Vaginal Pulse Amplitude Response Patterns During Erotic Conditions and Sleep. *Archives of Sexual Behavior* 14:327–42.

Rosenblatt, G., E. Hartmann, and G. Zwilling. 1973. Cardiac Irritability During Sleep and Dreaming. *Journal of Psychosomatic Research* 17:29–134.

Rowland, L. 1932. The Relation of Judgments of Excitement Value to Certain Bodily Changes Shown During Hypnotic Dreams. *Proceedings of the Oklahoma Academy of Sciences* 12:92.

Rubenstein, K. 1990. How Men and Women Dream Differently. In *Dreamtime and Dreamwork*, ed. S. Krippner, 135–42. Los Angeles: Jeremy Tarcher.

Rubin, R. 1953. A Possible Telepathic Experience During Analysis. In *Psychoanalysis and the Occult*, ed. G. Devereux. New York: International Universities Press.

Russel, G., et al. 1975. The Relationship of Small Limb Movements During REM Sleep to Dreamed Limb Action. *Psychosomatic Medicine* 37:147–59.

Ryback, D. 1988. *Dreams That Come True*. New York: Doubleday.

Sacks, O. 1983. *Awakenings*. New York: Dutton.

Saint-Denys, H. 1982. *Dreams and How to Guide Them*. London: Duckworth.

Sander, D., and N. Churchill. 1987. Serpent as Healer. *Shaman's Drum* 10 (fall):30–36.

Sanford, J. 1968. *Dreams: God's Forgotten Language*. New York: J. B. Lippincott.

Saura, C. 1981. Carlos Saura: A Conversation. *Dreamworks* 2 (1):62–63.

Savary, L., P. Berne, and S. Williams. 1984. *Dreams and Spiritual Growth*. New York: Paulist Press.

Schacter, D., and H. Crovitz. 1977. "Falling" While Falling Asleep: Sex Differences. *Perceptual and Motor Skills* 44:656.

Schecter, N., G. Schmeidler, and M. Staal. 1965. Dream Reports and Creative Tendencies in Students of the Arts, Sciences, and Engineering. *Journal of Consulting Psychology* 29:415–21.

Schneck, J. M. 1967. Loss of Teeth in Dreams Symbolizing Fear of Aging. *Perceptual and Motor Skills* 24:792.

Schneider, D. 1973. Conversion of Massive Anxiety into Heart Attack. *American Journal of Psychotherapy* 27:360–78.

———. 1976. *Revolution in the Body-Mind. I. Forewarning Cancer Dreams and the Bioplasma Concept*. Easthampton, N.Y.: Alexa Press.

Scholz, F. 1893. *Sleep and Dreams*. New York: Funk and Wagnalls.

Schroetter, K. [1911] 1951. Experimental Dreams. In *Organization and Pathology of Thought*, ed. D. Rapaport. New York: Columbia University Press.

Seafield, F. 1869. *The Literature and Curiosities of Dreams*. 4th ed. London: Lockwood.

Sechrist, E. 1968. *Dreams: Your Magic Mirror*. New York: Cowles.

Seidel, R. 1984. The Relationship of Animal Figures to Aggression and Ego Immaturity in the Dreams of Eleven and Twelve Year Old Children. Master's Thesis. University of Virginia, Department of Foundation of Education.

Shah, I. 1984. *The Sufis*. London: Octagon Press.

Siegel, B. 1989. *Peace, Love and Healing*. New York: Harper and Row, 64–65.

Silberer, H. [1909] 1951. Report on a Method of Eliciting and Observing Certain Symbolic Hallucination-Phenomena. In *Organization and Pathology of Thought*, ed. D. Rapaport. New York: Columbia University Press.

Simon, M. 1888. *Le monde des reves*. Paris: Alcon.

Small, M. 1920. Dreams. *Psychological Bulletin* 17:346–49.

Smith, J. 1979. Dream Baby. *Sundance Community Dream Journal* 3:150–59.

Smith, R. 1984. The Meaning of Dreams: The Need for a Standardized Dream Report. *Psychiatry Research* 13:267–74.

———. 1986. Evaluating Dream Function: Emphasizing the Study of Patients with Organic Disease. In *Cognition and Dream Research*, ed. R. Haskell. *Journal of Mind and Behavior* 7 (2–3).

Snyder, F. 1965. Sleep and Dreaming: Progress in the New Biology of Dreaming. *American Journal of Psychiatry* 122:377–391.

Snyder, F. 1970. The Phenomenology of Dreaming. In *The Psychodynamic Implications of the Physiological Studies on Dreams*, ed. H. Madow and L. Snow. Springfield, Ill.: Charles Thomas.

Sonnet, A. 1961. *The Twilight Zone of Dreams*. Philadelphia: Chilton.

Sparrow, G. S. 1982. *Lucid Dreaming: Dawning of the Clear Light*. Virginia Beach, Va.: A.R.E. Press.

Spero, M. 1975. Anticipations of Dream Psychology in the Talmud. *Journal of the History of the Behavioral Sciences* 11:374–80.

Stahl, W. 1952. *Macrobius: Commentary on the Dream of Scipio*. New York: Columbia University Press.

Stark, E. 1984. To Sleep, Perchance to Dream. *Psychology Today*, October, 16.

Stekel, W. 1962. *The Interpretation of Dreams*. New York: Grosset and Dunlap.

Stevens, O. 1949. *The Mystery of Dreams*. New York: Dodd, Mead.

Stevenson, I. 1965. Seven More Paranormal Experiences Associated with the Sinking of the Titanic. *Journal of the American Society of Psychical Research* 59:211–24.

———. 1970. Precognition of Disasters. *Journal*

of the American Society of Psychical Research 64:187–210.

———. 1974. *Twenty Cases Suggestive of Reincarnation*. 2d ed. Charlottesville: University Press of Virginia.

———. 1975. *Cases of the Reincarnation Type*. Vol. 1, *Ten Cases in India*. Charlottesville: University Press of Virginia.

Stevenson, R. [1892] 1947. A Chapter on Dreams. In *The World of Dreams*, ed. R. L. Woods. New York: Random House.

Stewart, W., and L. Freeman. 1972. *The Secret of Dreams: A Key to Freudian Dream Analysis*. New York: Macmillan.

Stoyva, J. 1965. Finger Electromyographic Activity During Sleep: Its Relation to Dreaming in Deaf and Normal Subjects. *Journal of Abnormal Psychology* 70:343–49.

Stromba-Badiale, M., A. Ceretti, and G. Forni. 1979. Aspetti del Sonno nel Soggetto Anzians e Molto Anziano [Aspects of Sleep in Old and Very Old Subjects]. *Minerva Medica* 70:2551–54.

Stukane, E. 1985. *The Dream Worlds of Pregnancy*. New York: William Morrow.

Suinn, R. 1966. Jungian Personality Typology and Color Dreaming. *Psychiatric Quarterly* 40:659–66.

Sullivan, H. S. 1940. *Conceptions of Modern Psychiatry*. New York: William Alanson White Psychiatric Foundation.

Sully, J. 1893. The Dream as a Revelation. *Fortnightly Review* 59:354–65.

———. 1897. *Illusions: A Psychological Study*. 4th ed. New York: Appleton.

Synesius. 1947. Dreams Take the Soul to "the Superior Region." In *The World of Dreams*, ed. R. L. Woods. New York: Random House.

Talamonte, L. 1975. *Forbidden Universe*. New York: Stein and Day.

Taylor, J. 1983. *Dream Work*. New York: Paulist Press.

———. 1992. *Where People Fly and Water Runs Uphill*. New York: Warner Books.

Teillard, A. 1961. *Spiritual Dimensions*. London: Routledge and Kegan Paul.

Tholey, P. 1988. A Model for Lucidity Training as a Means of Self-Healing and Psychological growth. In *Conscious Mind, Sleeping Brain: Perspectives on Lucid Dreaming*, ed. J. Gackenbach and S. LaBerge, 263–87. New York: Plenum Press.

———. 1991. Overview of the Development of Lucid Dream Research in Germany. *Lucidity* 10 (1–2):340–60.

Thomas, J. 1981. The Relationship Between the Manifest Content of Dreams and Personality Integration. *Sleep Research* 10:166.

Titchner, J., and F. Kapp. 1976. Family and Character Change at Buffalo Creek. *American Journal of Psychiatry* 133:295–99.

Tonay, V. 1988. Behavioral Continuity and Affective Compensation: Personality Correlates of Dream Recall and Content. Master's Thesis. University of California, Berkeley.

———. 1991. California Women and Their Dreams: A Historical and Sub-Cultural Comparison of Dream Content. *Journal of Imagination, Cognition, and Personality* 10:85–99.

Tracy, R., and L. Tracy. 1974. Reports of Mental Activity from Sleep Stages 2 and 4. *Perceptual and Motor Skills* 38:647–48.

Trotter, K., K. Dallas, and P. Verdone. 1987. Olfactory Stimuli and Their Effects on REM Dreams. Paper Presented at Meeting of Association for the Study of Dreams, Marymount College, Virginia.

Tuch, R. 1975. The Relationship Between a Mother's Menstrual Status and Her Response to Illness in Her Child. *Psychosomatic Medicine* 37:388–94.

Turner, W. 1918. The Bradshaw Lecture on Neuroses and Psychoses of War. *Lancet* 2:613–17.

Turpin, E. 1976. Correlates of Ego-Level and Agency-Communion in Stage REM Dreams of 11–13 Year Old Children. *Journal of Child Psychology and Psychiatry and Applied Disciplines* 17:169–80.

Tylor, E. B. 1873. *Primitive Culture*. 2 vols. London: John Murray.

Ullman, M. 1987a. Introduction. In *The Variety of Dream Experiences*, ed. M. Ullman and C. Limmer. New York: Continuum.

———. 1987b. The Dream Revisited: Some

Changed Ideas Based on a Group Approach. In *Dreams in New Perspective*, ed. M. Glucksman and S. Warner. New York: Human Sciences Press.

———. 1987c. The Experimental Dream Group. In *The Varieties of Dream Experience*, ed. M. Ullman and C. Limmer. New York: Continuum.

Ullman, M., S. Krippner, and A. Vaughan. 1973. *Dream Telepathy*. New York: Macmillan.

———. 1989. *Dream Telepathy: Explorations in Nocturnal ESP*. 2d ed. Jefferson, N.C.: McFarland.

Ullman, M., and C. Limmer, eds. 1987. *The Variety of Dream Experiences*. New York: Continuum.

Ullman, M., and N. Zimmerman. 1979. *Working With Dreams*. New York: Dellacorte Press/Eleanor Friede.

———. 1985. *Working with Dreams*. Los Angeles: Jeremy Tarcher.

Urbina, S., and A. Grey. 1974. Cultural and Sex Differences in the Sex Distribution of Dream Characters. *Journal of Cross-Cultural Psychology* 6:358–64.

Van de Castle, R. 1968. Dreams and Menstruation. *Psychophysiology* 4:374–75.

———. 1969. Some Problems in Applying the Methodology of Content Analysis to Dreams. In *Dream Psychology and the New Biology of Dreaming*, ed. M. Kramer. Springfield, Ill.: Charles Thomas.

———. 1970. Temporal Patterns of Dreams. In *Sleep and Dreaming*, ed. E. Hartmann. Boston: Little, Brown.

———. 1971. *The Psychology of Dreaming*. Morristown, N.J.: General Learning Press.

———. 1972. Dream Content and Birth Order. *Sleep Research* 1:126.

———. 1974. An Investigation of Psi Abilities Among the Cuna Indians of Panama. In *Parapsychology and Anthropology: Proceedings of an International Conference*, ed. A Angoff and D. Barth, 80–97. New York: Parapsychology Foundation.

———. 1976. Psi Abilities in Primitive Groups. In *Surveys in Parapsychology: Review*

of the Literature With Updated Bibliographies, ed. R. White. Metuchen, N.J.: Scarecrow Press.

———. 1977. Sleep and Dreams. In *Handbook of Parapsychology*, ed. B. Wolman. New York: Van Nostrand Reinhold.

———. 1983. Animal Figures in Fantasy and Dreams. In *New Perspectives on Our Lives With Companion Animals*, ed. A. Kacher and A. Beck, 148–73. Philadelphia: University of Pennsylvania Press.

———. 1986. The D.N.B. Telepathy Project. *Dream Network Bulletin* 5 (1).

———. 1989. ESP in Dreams: Comments on a Replication "Failure" by the Failing Subject. In *Dream Telepathy: Explorations in Nocturnal ESP*, ed. M. Ullman, S. Krippner, and A. Vaughan. 2d ed. Jefferson, N.C.: McFarland.

Van de Castle, R., and P. Hauri. 1970. An Investigation of Psychophysiological Correlates of NREM Mentation. *Psychophysiology* 7:330.

Van de Castle, R., and P. Kinder. 1968. Dream Content During Pregnancy. *Psychophysiology* 4:375.

Van de Castle, R., and T. Smith. 1972. Dream Content and Body Build. *Sleep Research* 1:115.

Vande Kemp, H. 1977. The Dream in Periodical Literature: 1860–1910: From *Oneirocritica* to *Die Traumdeutung* via the Questionnaire. Doctoral dissertation. University of Massachusetts, University Microfilms 77–15, 131.

———. 1981. The Dream in Periodical Literature: 1800–1910. *Journal of the History of the Behavioral Sciences* 17:88–113.

van der Post, L. 1975. *Jung and the Story of Our Time*. New York: Pantheon.

Van Eeden, F. 1913. A Study of Dreams. *Proceedings of the Society for Psychical Research* 26:431–61.

Van Liere, E., and J. Stickney. 1963. *Hypoxia*. Chicago: University of Chicago Press.

Van Vogt, A. 1981. Dreaming and Writing. *Dreamworks* 2:134–38.

Verdone, P. 1965. Temporal Reference of Manifest Dream Content. *Perceptual and Motor Skills* 20:1253–68.

Violani, C., et al. 1983. Dream Recall as a Function of Individual Patterns of Hemispheric Lateralization. *Sleep Research* 12:190.

Voltaire, M. 1947. Somnambulists and Dreamers. In *The World of Dreams*, ed. R. L. Woods. New York: Random House.

von Grunebaum, G. 1966. Introduction: The Cultural Function of the Dream as Illustrated by Classical Islam. In *The Dream and Human Societies*, ed. G. von Grunebaum and R. Caillois. Los Angeles: University of California Press.

von Franz, M.-L. 1986. *On Dreams and Death*. Boston: Shambala.

Wallis-Budge, E. 1899. *Egyptian Magic*. London: Paul, Trench, and Trubner.

Walsh, W. 1920. *The Psychology of Dreams*. New York: Dodd, Mead.

Ward, C., et al. 1973. Birth Order and Dreams. *Journal of Social Psychology* 90:155–56.

Warner, C. 1987. The Positive Animus: Its Evolution in a Woman's Dreams. Paper presented at Meeting of the Association for the Study of Dreams, Marymount College, Virginia.

Warnes, H., and A. Finkelstein. 1971. Dreams That Precede a Psychosomatic Illness. *Canadian Psychiatric Association Journal* 16:317–25.

Warren, H. 1897. Sleep and Dreams. *Psychological Review* 4:549–53.

Warren, R. P. 1981. To the Editor. *Dreamworks* 2:128.

Watson, R., and A. Rechtschaffen. 1969. Auditory Awakening Thresholds and Dream Recall in NREM Sleep. *Perceptual and Motor Skills* 29:635–44.

Weed, S., and F. Hallam. 1896. A Study of Dream Consciousness. *American Journal of Psychology* 7:405–11.

Weisz, R., and D. Foulkes. 1970. Home and Laboratory Dreams Collected Under Uniform Sampling Conditions. *Psychophysiology* 6:588–96.

Welles, O. 1981. Conversations with Filmmakers on Dreams. *Dreamworks* 3 (1):56.

White, T. 1967. The College. In *Such Stuff as Dreams*, ed. B. Hill. London: Rupert Hart-Davis.

Whitman, R., M. Kramer, and B. Baldridge. 1963. Which Dream Does the Patient Tell? *Archives of General Psychiatry* 8:277–82.

Whitman, R., et al. 1962. The Dreams of the Experimental Subject. *Journal of Nervous and Mental Disease* 134:431–39.

Whyte, L. 1960. *The Unconscious Before Freud*. New York: Basic Books.

Wilber, K. 1982. Physics, Mysticism and the New Holographic Paradigm. In *The Holographic Paradigm and Other Paradoxes*, ed. K. Wilber. Boulder: Shambala.

Wilkinson. R. 1991. Anatomy of a Cakewalk. *Newsweek* March 11.

William J. 1967. In *Such Stuff as Dreams*, ed. B. Hill, 21–22. London: Rupert Hart-Davis.

Winget, C., and R. Farrell. 1972. A Comparison of the Dreams of Homosexual and Non-Homosexual Males. *Psychophysiology* 9:119.

Winget, C., and F. Kapp. 1972. The Relationship of the Manifest Content of Dreams to Duration of Childbirth in Primaparae. *Psychosomatic Medicine* 34:313–20.

Winget, C., and M. Kramer. 1979. *Dimensions of Dreams*. Gainesville: University Press of Florida.

Winget, C., M. Kramer, and R. Whitman. 1972. The Relationship of Socio-Economic Status and Race to Dream Content. *Psychophysiology* 7:325–26.

Wiseman, A. 1989. *Nightmare Help: A Guide for Parents and Teachers*. Berkeley, Calif.: Ten Speed Press.

Witkin, H. 1969. Influencing Dream Content. In *Dream Psychology and the New Biology of Dreaming*, ed. M. Kramer. Springfield, Ill.: Charles Thomas.

Witkin, H., and H. Lewis. 1967. Presleep Experiences and Dreams. In *Experimental Studies of Dreaming*, ed. H. Witkin and H. Lewis. New York: Random House.

Wolff, W. 1973. *The Dream: Mirror of Conscience*. Westport, Conn.: Greenwood Press.

Wolpert, E. A. 1960. Studies in Psychophysiology of Dreams. AMA *Archives of General Psychiatry* 2:231–41.

Wood, J., D. Sebba, and R. Griswold. 1989. Stereotyped Masculine Interests as Related to the Sex of Dream Characters. *Sleep Research* 18:133.

Wood, P. 1962. Dreaming and Social Isolation. Doctoral dissertation. University of North Carolina.

Woods, R. L., ed. 1947. *The World of Dreams.* New York: Random House.

Woolger, J., and R. Woolger. 1987. *The Goddess Within: A Guide to the Eternal Myths That Shape Women's Lives.* New York: Ballantine.

Yutang, L. 1948. *The Wisdom of Laotse.* New York: Random House.

Ziegler, A. 1962. A Cardiac Infarction and a Dream as Synchronous Events. *Journal of Analytical Psychology* 7:142–43.

———. 1973. Dream Emotions in Relation to Room Temperature. In *Sleep: Physiology, Bio-Chemistry, Psychology, Pharmacology, Clinical Implications.* Basel: Karger.

Zimmerman, W. 1970. Sleep Mentation and Auditory Awakening Thresholds. *Psychophysiology* 6:540–49.

ILLUSTRATION CREDITS

Page 7. *The Persistence of Memory* [*Persistence de la memoire*], by Salvador Dali, 1931. Oil on canvas, 9½ × 13″. The Museum of Modern Art, New York. Given anonymously.

Page 12. Tate Gallery, London/Art Resource, NY

Page 40. Copyright © The British Museum.

Page 53. Foto Marburg/Art Resource, NY

Page 82. Copyright © The British Museum.

Page 94. Copyright © Cliché Bibliothèque Nationale Paris

Page 110. Copyright © Estate of C.G. Jung. Courtesy of Niedieck Linder AG, Zurich.

Page 118. From *The Psychoanalysis of Dreams* by Angel Garma. Copyright © 1966 by Angel Garma. Reprinted by permission of Times Books, a division of Random House, Inc.

Page 122. *La Trahison des Images (Ceci n'est pas une pipe)*, by Rene Magritte, Belgium (1898–1967). Los Angeles County Museum of Art. Purchased with funds provided by the Mr. and Mrs. William Preston Harrison Collection.

Page 142. Copyright © Karsh.

Page 154. Copyright © Estate of C.G. Jung. Courtesy of Niedieck Linder AG, Zurich.

Page 172. Copyright © Estate of C.G. Jung. Courtesy of Niedieck Linder AG, Zurich.

Page 188. Isidore Ducasse Fine Art.

Page 217. Courtesy of the New York Academy of Medicine

Page 221. Copyright © 1994 M.C. Escher/ Cordon Art–Baarn–Holland. All rights reserved.

Page 248. Copyright © 1994 M.C. Escher/ Cordon Art–Baarn–Holland. All rights reserved.

Page 297. Philadelphia Museum of Art. Louise and Walter Arensberg Collection.

Page 323. Copyright © 1993 C. Herscovici/ Artists Rights Society (ARS), New York. Courtesy of ARS and The Menil Foundation, Houston.

Page 328. Eric Marc Cohen

Page 336. *Phaeton*, by Hendrik Goltzius (The Metropolitan Museum of Art, Harris Brisbane Dick Fund, 1953. [53.601.338(5)]

Page 348. Copyright © 1994 Munch-Museet/ Munch-Ellingsen/Artists Rights Society (ARS), New York. Courtesy of ARS and Nasjonalgalleriet, Oslo.

Page 365. *Anatomical Painting*, by Paul Tchelitchew. 1946. oil on canvas 56 × 46 inches. (142.2 cm × 116.8 cm). Collection of Whitney Museum of American Art. Gift of Lincoln Kirstein 62.26. Copyright © 1995: Whitney Museum of American Art.

Page 380. Davison Art Center, Wesleyen University.

Page 389. *My Room Has Two Doors*, by Kay Sage. Collection of the Mattatuck Museum, Waterbury, Connecticut.

Page 391. Copyright © 1994 M.C. Escher/ Cordon Art–Baarn–Holland. All rights reserved.

Page 401. *Conscious Dreaming* by Fariba Bogzaran. Oil on canvas, 1982. Courtesy of Fariba Bogzaran.

Page 406. *Guardian Spirit of the Waters*, Odilon Redon, French, 1840–1916, charcoal, 46.5 × 37.1 cm, David Adler Collection, 1950. 1428. Photograph 9c) 1993, The Art Institute of Chicago. All Rights Reserved.

Page 421. Victoria & Albert Museum, London/Art Resource, NY.

Page 447. Ethan Speelberg

Page 454. *Queen Katharine's Dream*, by William Blake. Rosenwald Collection. Copyright © 1993 National Gallery of Art, Washington.

INDEX

ABOUT THE AUTHOR

ROBERT VAN DE CASTLE, PH.D., has worked with dreams for more than thirty years. The former director of the Sleep and Dream Laboratory at the University of Virginia Medical School, he recently retired from his post at the same institution as professor in the Department of Behavioral Medicine. Dr. Van de Castle is the coauthor, with Dr. Calvin Hall, of the classic book *The Content Analysis of Dreams*, and he was the senior editor for the *Dream Network Bulletin*. Dr. Van de Castle makes his home in Fork Union, Virginia.